THE FORMATION OF THE MARĀTHĪ LANGUAGE

THE FORMATION
OF
THE MARĀṬHĪ LANGUAGE

BY
JULES BLOCH

TRANSLATED BY
Dr. DEV RAJ CHANANA

MOTILAL BANARSIDASS
DELHI :: PATNA :: VARANASI

Reissued : Delhi, 2010
First English Translation : Delhi, 1970
First Published : Prix Volney, 1914

ISBN: 978-81-208-2322-8

MOTILAL BANARSIDASS
41 U.A. Bungalow Road, Jawahar Nagar, Delhi 110 007
8 Mahalaxmi Chamber, 22 Bhulabhai Desai Road, Mumbai 400 026
236, 9th Main III Block, Jayanagar, Bangalore 560 011
203 Royapettah High Road, Mylapore, Chennai 600 004
Sanas Plaza, 1302 Baji Rao Road, Pune 411 002
8 Camac Street, Kolkata 700 017
Ashok Rajpath, Patna 800 004
Chowk, Varanasi 221 001

Printed in India

BY JAINENDRA PRAKASH JAIN AT SHRI JAINENDRA PRESS,
A-45, NARAINA, PHASE-I, NEW DELHI 110028
AND PUBLISHED BY NARENDRA PRAKASH JAIN FOR
MOTILAL BANARSIDASS PUBLISHERS PRIVATE LIMITED
BUNGALOW ROAD, DELHI 110 007

Foreword

The present work had been published in French, under the title *La formation de la langue marathe,* in 1920, by Jules Bloch. It immediately got a great success and the edition was soon out of print. The Marāṭhī language had since long been described in several grammars. An elaborate dictionary of this language had been published at Bombay as early as in 1831 by J. T. Molesworth assisted by George and Thomas Candy. A second edition of the same, revised and enlarged by J. T. Molesworth, appeared in 1857. This work was very comprehensive and careful and till now remains authoritative. In the *Linguistic Survey of India,* the chapter dealing with the Marāṭhī language, prepared by Sten Konow, had been published in 1905. Much material for a comparative grammar of the Indo-Aryan languages of India had already been collected. But the work of Jules Bloch was the first systematical undertaking to coordinate all the data and to understand the evolution from Sanskrit through Prākrit and Apabhraṁśa to Old-Marāṭhī and from the Old-Marāthī to the modern one.

Jules Bloch had been specially equipped to undertake such a task. After getting a general training in Indo-European linguistics with linguists like Antoine Meillet and indologists like Sylvain Levi, he had been appointed in 1908 as a member of Ecole française d'Extrême-Orient. In this capacity he studied in India both in the field of dravidology and in the field of Marāṭhī. Marāṭhī has been sometimes in the past considered as *drāviḍa.* That was wrong from the linguistic point of view, but, as Marāṭhī has developed in contact with neighbouring Telugu and Kannada, it has been influenced, at least in its vocabulary, by these Dravidian language. Jules Bloch conducted his studies in Tamil and dravidology for a fuller knowledge of Indian linguistics and not only in connexion with his Marāṭhī studies, but his double competence in Indo-Aryan and Dravidian languages, enabled him to properly place the Marāṭhī language in its whole environment.

The special Marāṭhī studies of Jules Bloch had been done at Poona in close contact with scholars like Ramkrishna Gopal Bhandarkar. The fruit has been this book. Later, Jules Bloch produced two other books: *L'Indo-aryen du Veda aux temps moderns* (Paris, 1934) and *Structure grammaticale des langues dravidiennes* (Paris, 1946). Both have been translated into English. The first one, *Indo-Aryan from the Vedas to modern times*, has been largely revised by Jules Bloch himself and translatedby Dr. Alfred Master (Paris, Adrien Maisonneuve, 1965). The other one *The Grammatical Structure of Dravidian languages*, has been translated in English by Dr. Ramkrishna Ganesh Harshe and published by Dr. S. M. Katre for the Deccan College, Poona.

The need for the translation of the oldest-one,i.e. on the formation of Marāṭhī, from French into English, was therefore greatly felt by Indian students who rarely have a proficiency in Western languages other than English. Dr. Dev Raj Chanana undertook the translation with full competence and devotion. He had just completed the task when his premature and sudden death snatched him from his family, his friends and the field of indology itself.

Thanks to our common friend Shambhu Datt Sharma, who kindly took care of the printing, the book is now at the disposal of the scholars.

Copies of the original text were very rare and wanted. Now, in the present English version, this historical work is available again just half a century after its first publication.

College de France, Paris, February 26, 1970.

JEAN FILLIOZAT

Preface

It is my very sad duty to write a few lines by way of a preface to this book. My husband, Dr. Dev Raj Chanana, who most painstakingly translated this book by Mr. Jules Bloch, passed away in May 1968, soon after finishing this work.

I am extremely grateful to Prof Jean Filliozat, Chaire de Langues et Litteratures de l' inde, College de France, Paris, my husband's guide and mentor, for writing the Foreword to the book. I have no words to thank Mr. Shambhu Datt Sharma, a research-student of Dr. Dev Raj Chanana, for his invaluable help in getting the book printed. My thanks are also due to Dr. Romila Thapar, Reader in History, University of Delhi Mrs. R. A. Menon, Reader in Economics, University of Delhi, and Dr. L. Rai for their valuable help at various stages.

My thanks also to Madame Bloch and Madame Caillat of France.

New Delhi, V. Chanana
April 12, 1970.

CONTENTS

Foreword .. .. v-vi
Preface vii
Abbreviations .. .. xiii-xiv
Introduction—The Sanskrit, $ 1-3.—The middle-Indian : Inscriptions, $; Pali, Jaina texts, Northern Buddhist texts, $ 6-8; Classical Prakrits (comparison with the Hindustani), $ 9-11; General characteristics of middle-Indian; 12-17. The modern-Indo-Aryan languages, $ 18-19; Relationship with the middle-Indian group, $ 20-21; The Apabhraṃśa, $ 22. *The Marathi*, $ 23-26 .. 1-38
Bibliography, $ 27 39-43
Phonetics-Generalities, $ 28 44-45
Vowels, $ 29. Treatment of Skr. *ṛ*, $ 30-31 .. 46-50
Alterations depending on the place of vowels in the word. —Accent, $ 32-36.—Final vowels, $ 37-39; As penultimate Syllables, $ 40-42; Before the penultimate Syllable, $ 43; As the initial Syllable, $ 44-49; Inside the word, $ 50-52 .. 51-72
Prakrit Vowels in Contact, $ 53; Insertion of *y* and *v*, $ 54-55; Diphthongs, $ 56-57; Contraction, $ 58-65 72-83
Nasal Vowels, $ 66-72 83-89
Chart of Marathi Vocalism, $ 73-80 .. 89-96
Consonants. Occulsives $ 81; Occulsives following a nasal, $ 82; Aspiration and Deaspiration of occulsives, $ 83-89; Other changes, $ 90. Chart of Marathi occulsives, $ 91 ff. : Gutturals, $ 92-99; Paltatals and *s* arising from *ch*, *kṣ*, $ 100-107; Old cerebrals, $ 108-112; Treatment of *r*+dental, $ 113-116; Spontaneous cerebralisation, $ 117-119; Dentals, $ 120-124; Labials, $ 125-128; Treatment of dental+*v*, $ 129-130 97-141
Nasals, $ 131; *ṇ* and *n*, $ 132-136; *m*, $ 137-138 .. 141-149
Liquids, $ 139-142; *r*, $ 143; *ḷ*, $ 144-147; *l*, $ 148-149 .. 149-159
Aspirate *v*, $ 150-153; Note on *y*, $ 154 .. 159-163

Sifflant, $ 155-157 163-167

Aspirate, $ 158-161 167-171

The word. Phonemes in contact, $ 162-165; Distant action : Vocalic Infection, $ 166; Metathesis, $ 167; anticipation of aspiration, $ 168; dissimilation, $ 169-171; Syllabic superposition, $ 172. End and the beginning of word, $ 173-175. .. 172-182

Morphology. Generilities, $ 176; Loss of dual $ 177 183-184

Declension, $ 178; Stems, $ 179; genders, $ 180; case, $ 181-184 185-192

Group : Direct case, oblique case in nouns terminating in consonants, $ 185-190, in those terminating in a vowel, $ 191 192-198

Traces of other old Terminations : instrumental, locative, ablative, $ 192-196 198-203

Postpositions, $ 197; *s*, *śiṃ*, *sāṭhiṃ*, *stav*, $ 198; *teṃ*, $ 199; *lā*, *lāgiṃ*, $ 200; *neṃ* (*nīṃ*), $ 201; Adjectives of belonging, called "genetive" $ 202 .. 203-216

Relatives, Demonstratives, Interrogatives, etc., $ 203-206; Personal pronouns, $ 207-210 .. 217-222

Numerals, $ 211-226 .. 223-233

Conjugation, $ 227. Strong and weak stems, $ 228-229; Stem of present, $ 230; Stems of Past-participle, $ 231; Causative, Potential, Passive, $ 232. 234-242

Inflexion, $ 233-234. Old Tenses : Past of habitude (old present), $ 235-238; Imperative, $ 239. Modern creations : Future, $ 240-242; Participial tenses, $ 243 : Present-conditional, $ 244-249 ; Past, $ 250-252; Tenses of obligation and Potential, $ 253-254. 242-265

Impersonal Forms of the verb. Present participle, $ 255; Past participle, $ 256; Participle of obligation, $ 257; Future participle, $ 258. Composite tenses, $ 259; Auxiliaries, $ 260; Passive periphrastic, $261. Absolute Forms from Participles, $ 262-264. Verbal noun and Infinitive, $ 265 .. 265-274

The sentence $ 266. Nominal and verbal sentences $267-268. Accord of the Adjective to the enlargement $ 269-272. Order of the words, $ 273-275. Subordination, $ 276-277. 275-286
Conclusion. Place of Marāṭhī in the Indo-Aryan group, $ 278-279 287-289
Appendix. Note on Certain Documents of Old Marāṭhī, $ 280-285 290-293
Etymological Index. 295-416

ABBREVIATIONS

acc. accusative.
Adj. Adjective.
Adv. Adverb.
Amg. Ardha-Māgadhī.
Aor. Aorist.
Apa. Apabhraṃśa.
Ar. Arabic.
Arm. Ro. Armenian Romany.
Ass. Assamese.

B. Bengali.
B.B. Bibliotheca Buddhica, St. Petersburg.
BEFEO. Bulletin de l' ecole Frain,caise d' Extrême Orient.
Bih. Bihari.
Bhojp. Bhojpuri.
Bull. Soc. Ling. Bulletin de la Société de Linguistique de Paris.

Caus. Causative.
Comm. Commentary.
Comp. Compound.

D. Deśī.
dat. dative.
Deśī. Deśīnāmamālā.
Dhatup. Dhātupāṭha.
du. dual.
E.B. Eastern Bengali.
Eur. European.

f. feminine.
Fr. French.

G. Gujarati.
G.G.A. Göttinger gelehrte Anzeigen.
Ger. German.
Gr. Greek.

H. Hindi.
Hem. Hemacandra.

Inscr. Inscriptional.
instr. instrumental.
Ind. Ant. Indian Antiquary.
I.E. Indo-European.
I.F. Indogermanische Forschungen.
J.A. Journal Asiatique.
J.A.S. Journal of the Asiatic Society, Bombay.
J.A.O.S. Journal of the American Oriental Society.
J.BBAS. Journal of the Bombay Branch of the Asiatic Society.
J.R.A.S. Journal of the Royal Asiatic Society.

K. Kashmiri.
Kan. Kannarese.
KZ. Zeitschrift für vergleischende Sprachforschung.

Lat. Latin.
loc. locative.
L.S.I. Linguistic Survey of India.

m. masculine.
M. Maraṭhī.
Māg. Māgadhī..
Mah. Mahārāṣṭrī.
Maith. Maithilī.
Mél. S. Lévi. Mèlanges S. Lévi.
Mod. Modern.
M.S.I. Mèmoires de la Sociéte de Linguistic de Paris.
n. noun.
Nep. Nepalese.
O. Oriya.

P. Pali.

Panj. Panjabi.
pcpl. participle.
Per. Persian.

Pkt. Prakrit.
pl. plural.
poet. poetic.
pron. pronoun.

Raj. Rajasthani.
Ro. Romany.

S. Sindhi.
Śaur. Śaurasenī.
Siṃ. Siṃhalese.

sing. singular.
Skr. Sanskrit.

Tam. Tamil.
tats. Tatsama.

Ved. Vedic.
vulg. vulgar.

W. Panj. Western Panjabi.

Z.D.M.G. *Zeitschrift der Deutschen Morgenlandischen Gessellschaft.*

INTRODUCTION

$ 1. Not one of the Indo-European languages, currently spoken in India, seems to go back to any language greatly different from Sanskrit, made known to us by the Vedic and Classical texts. To write the history of any one of them, Marathi for example, therefore amounts essentially to show as to how the alterations undergone, during the course of history, by the linguistic system of Sanskrit have resulted in the constitution of firstly the various dialects of the Middle Indian, and subsequently of this modern language itself.

In reality this design can be correctly and legitimately carried out only subject to important reservations. In the present state of available documentary evidence, none of the ancient Indo-European languages gives us a sure foot-hold for analysis. Even the most archaic Sanskrit texts have already got the traces of the mixture of important dialectal mixtures and subsequently the different speeches have always been subjected to the influence of Sanskrit, have reacted on one another and have, in their turn, contaminated Sanskrit itself. It is, therefore, but proper to examine first of all each of the known forms of Indo-Aryan and the value of documents representing them, in order to determine the extent to which the sources can be utilised for the study of Marathi.

$ 2. It has been often remarked that the chronological succession of the most ancient texts of Sanskrit corresponds to a progressive geographical extension of this language towards the East. It is but natural that in course of time one notices therein a considerable contribution made by new elements and dialectal mixtures; but the language of the Ṛgveda, so similar to ancient Iranian, and spoken at the borders of the Iranian world, in a domain comparatively so limited, is likely to have represented a definite and pure dialect, capable of serving as a solid base for linguistic comparison. But no such possibility exists.

By isolating the most recent parts such as the tenth Maṇḍala, by taking note of various editings and correcting the various rejuvenations of the text, one does end up with a basically unique language : but this language is traditional and composite (on all these points see Wachernagel, p. X-XXII). Or, to put it in better terms, the editors of the Ṛgveda, as we have it, have partially adapted to their own dialects various religious texts composed in another dialect. Meillet, in his article, 'Les consonnes intervocaliques en védique' (I. F., XXXI, p. 120 ff.) gives the following proofs in support of the above statement :

Firstly, the opening of the intervocalic aspirate sonant, constant in the Ṛgveda for the middle-occlusive **jh*, is also found therein for *bh*, *dh*, notably in grammatical forms (First person plural Middle *-mahe*, Second person singular imperative *-hi*, etc.): but often ancient *-bh* and *-dh* are preserved. This is so because the editors of the actual Ṛgveda have reintroduced in a large number of words the occlusion which had persisted in their dialects. They could not, however, touch the grammatical forms without seriously modifying the- aspect of the religious language borrowed by them.

The distribution of *r* and *l* in Sanskrit is explained by a series of analogous adaptations. The dialect on which rests the Ṛgveda was a Western dialect, where as in Iranian every *l* got mixed up with *r*. Now the presence, in the most ancient parts of the available text, of words where *l* corresponds to an Indo-European *l* proves that the editors of this text have introduced therein several forms of their own dialects. It is in fact known that there has existed an Eastern dialect where *l* represented *r* or *l*. The number of adapations increases in course of time, the vocabulary of Sanskrit and of Middle Indian confronts us on this point with inextricable confusion.

Finally the grammar of the Ṛgveda itself carries the traces of contamination; the arbitrary use of the terminations of instrumental *-ebhiḥ* and *aiḥ* is explained by the conflict of two speeches, one tending to extend *-ebhiḥ* to adjectives, then to nouns, as will be done later by Middle Indian, the other tending to maintain and even extend the termination *-aiḥ*, as will be done by classical Sanskrit.

Vedic Sanskrit is, therefore, in its most authentic and most ancient form, a literary language and ac ommon language. This is all the more reason why classical Sanskrit must show these characteristics and lack the unity.

$ 3. After the Ṛgveda, the other collections and notably the Atharvaveda, then the Brāhmaṇas, the Sūtras, Pāṇini, who opposes the *bhāṣā*, defined by him in an archaic *chandaḥ* (see S. Lévi, J. A., 1891, II, p. 549; M.S. L., XVI, p. 278-79), his commentators, who point out, consciously or otherwise, the progress of the language since Pāṇini, finally the Epics and the classical works mark the successive stages which appear to define the internal evolution of Sanskrit (see Wackernagel, pp. XXII ff, XI-IV ff.). Even by admitting that the ancient sacerdotal literature follows the autonomous development of the language,—and what we know of the Ṛgveda renders this hypothesis improbable—, we quickly reach an epoch where Sanskrit must have come into contact with and been subjected to the influence of other dialects whose existence had been recognised. A century after Pāṇini, Aśoka covers the entire country with inscriptions in Middle Indian. About 150 B. C., Patañjali in a famous passage, (quoted by Bhandarkar, JAS *Bombay*, XVI, p. 335) describes Sanskrit as the language of the cultivated Brahmins of the Āryāvarta : this amounts to saying that in India, it is already an exceptional language and that it would not have survived without the prestige due to its use by religion and by scholarship.

In profane usage,—epigraphy and literature—, Sanskrit appears later than linguistically younger dialects; leaving aside the Epics, whose early editing is not known and which besides in certain aspects, are attached to religious literature, the classical period of Sanskrit begins only in the first century of our era. At that moment Buddhism usurps the language of the Brahmins and employs the same for its propaganda. One of its masters, Aśvaghoṣa "embellishes" with literary forms the pious tales and dogmatic manuals: he writes dramas where Sanskrit has for neighbours the Prākrits already promoted to the rank of cultivated languages (see S. Lévi, JA, 1908, II, p. 57 ff). Several foreign kings having the courage to have their official documents written in Sanskrit (of which Aśoka undoubtedly had no idea : It is a Śaka, the *mahākṣatrapa* Rudradāman who first of all, in 150 A. D., has a long inscription in Sanskrit engraved at Girnar, as evidence of the talent claimed by him "of composing in prose and in verse different works satisfying all the conditions of rhetorics" (see S. Lévi, JA, 1902, I, p. 109, 111, 119). Henceforward completely desecularised, Sanskrit serves, right upto our days, as the literary and scientific language, and as a means of communication between the cultured persons of all the parts of India. Like the usual Latin during the period when Roman languages were already in existence, classical Sanskrit shows two opposite characteristics, which get accentuated in the course of time. Firstly, from the very moment of its fixation it is a fundamentally archaic speech : it has preserved the occlusion of intervocalic consonants and has restored *ḍ* and *ḍh* in place of *ḷ* and *ḷh* of Vedic and Middle Indian, it has preserved several forms already out of common usage, such as the dual number, the middle voice, the Perfect and has inversely eliminated other forms whose survival is attested by the Middle Indian and modern languages (see Wackernagel, p. XXX ff.). But at the same time Sanskrit could not have failed to be subject to influences coming from all sides; the vocabulary in particular, had to be impregnated with borrowed elements, with more or less adaptation, from different Aryan or non-Aryan speeches of India and even from languages foreign to India (see Wackernagel, p. LI ff).

As a consequence during no period can the Sanskrit documents be considered as exactly reflecting the contemporary linguistic state of affairs; and even the difference of aspect presented, periodwise, by Sanskrit, "is not the difference we find between the various phases of a naturally developing popular language"—(Wackernagel, p. XXIII).

$ 4. One can see, therefore, the difficulties and the traps to be encountered in the linguistic interpretation of Sanskrit texts. Will the Middle Indian, which we have seen to appear from a very early date beside these texts, offer us documents, surer and more capable of being put to better use ?—Given their abundance and variety, one could suppose so.

From the middle of the 3rd cent. B. C., Aśoka gets engraved, from the North-West upto Bengal, from the Terai upto Mysore, numerous edicts which are the first known documents of Middle Indian. There is no doubt that the original texts of these edicts had been written in a dialect of Magadha, where the capital of Aśoka had been situated. But the variations presented by these inscriptions are numerous, and if one can not, quite often, attribute them to the errors of the copyists, they can not be easily explained by the existence of clearly separated dialects. We have been led to consider (see O. Franke, *Pali und Sanskrit*, p. 109; T. Michelson, *Am. J. Phil.*, XXX, p. 284; JAOS, XXX, p. 78) that the original text of these edicts, preserved, with a few variants, in the Eastern inscriptions, had been translated by the administrators of the North-West and of the South in local speech, but with a certain number of eastern forms being able to slip into these adaptations. Can these insertions or adaptations be, however, sufficiently explained by the mere presence of the eastern model before the eyes of the translator ? It is not improbable that often the scribes had believed themselves to be able to use the words of the eastern model because such words were not completely alien to their speech, or atleast to the official language of their region. Undoubtedly the religious prestige of Buddhism and the political prestige, already going back to several generations of the Mauryan Dynasty had enabled the language of the Magadha to extend itself over the entire North of India, atleast among the cultured sections of the population and in so far as a part of the vocabulary was concerned (*cf.* Lüders, *Bruchstücke*, p. 40).

But did the original itself not represent the language then current in Magadha ? Here is, on one side, an indisputably Magadhan text, the inscription of Śutanukā at Ramgarh, which palaeographically is contemporary of Aśoka. Found therein is only the palatal sifflant, lacking in the eastern versions of Aśoka (see Lüders, *ibid.*, p. 41). On the other hand the undoubtedly textual citation of Buddhist texts incorporated by Aśoka in the Bhabra edict offers us an example of a Magadhan dialect, already admitting the sonorisation of intervocalic occlusive words (see S. Lèvi, JA, 1912, II, 495 ff., for similar facts in other inscriptions, see Senart, *Inscriptions de Piyadassi*, II, p. 427). What is then the relationship between these three forms of language ?

If only the inscription of Śutanukā were in question, it could be supposed that the language of Aśoka represents a dialect of Magadha, which aleady admitted a dental *s* like the central dialects; that is why Lũders brings it beside the Ardhamāgadhī of the dramas. But the Buddhist citation would seem also to prove that the language of the Imperial chancellory was already tending to be archaic, something which is not surprising, less in India than elsewhere.

Therefore, even when the readings are sure and the meanings well established, none of the inscriptions of Aśoka furnishes us with a direct document concerning some definite dialect of India in the 3rd century B. C. An extremely careful analysis has, however, enabled us to bring out some probable indications concerning the distribution of certain traits. In the eastern group, "there is no cerebral *ṇ* nor a palatal *ñ*, the initial *y* is elided, *l* replaces *r*, the masculine nominative, and ordinarily the neuter is in *-e*, the locative in *-asi*; the other [group] distinguishes the cerebral *ṇ* from the palatal *-ñ*, preserves the initial *y* and *r*, has the nominative singular of masculines in *-a*, the locative in *-amhi* or in *-e*" (Senart, op. cit. II, p. 431). Moreover, the inscriptions of the West preserve the consonantal groups that are assimilated by Gangetic India. Skr. *ṛ* is normally represented in the North-West by *ir*, *ur*, at Girnar by *a*, in the east by *a* or *i*; *r*+dental gives a dental in the west, a cerebral in the east, *kṣ* becomes *ch* in the west and *kh* in the east. Finally the final *-ā* becomes short, *-tiy-*, *-dhiy-*get simplified in *-ty-*, *-dhy-* in the eastern-most inscriptions (see on all these points, T. Michelson, I.F., XXIII, p. 219-71; *Am. J. Phil.*, XXX, p. 284 ff, 416 ff; XXXI, p. 55 ff.; JAOS, XXX, p. 77 ff., XXXI, p. 223 ff.).

These indications are precious and will be utilised further; but it should be, above all, borne in mind that before the Christian era, linguistic influences from Magadha have been active upto the west of India, these being measureable with difficulty but undoubtedly quite profound. It is possible that these influences ceased to be active less than a century after Aśoka : but the long pre-eminence of Magadha is certain; and nothing prevents us from accepting the evidence of the inscriptions of Delhi, which have *l* for *r* and *n* for *ṇ* (see Senart, ibid, II, p. 373, cf. II, p. 434). We know from Patañjali that the forms like *vaṭṭati* and *vaḍḍhati*, which were only Magadhisms during the time of Aśoka, had shortly thereafter penetrated in the usual language of Central India.

$ 5. Right upto the time when Sanskrit becomes the only language for epigraphy, that is to say in Northern and Central India towards 350 A. D. (Fleet, JRAS, 1904, p. 485) there is a large number of inscriptions in Middle Indian, one after the other. New ones are still being found, but the data drawn by linguistics from the same is obscure and fragmentary. As a whole, despite the extremely vast space and the four or five centuries on which they are spread, these inscriptions present a remarkably uniform aspect (see Senart, ibid, II, p. 493); and still, if examined in detail, the phenomena therein are extremely disparate and the dialectal variations appear to be numerous : but for each series of facts the distribution varies (see O. Franke, op. cit., ch. VIII, notably p. 126). It happens often that in entirely neighbouring contemporary inscriptions the phonetic and even morphological characteristics get inextricably mixed up. In certain cases a possible explanation can be found : it is possible that in the Deccan inscriptions the more or less of Sanskrit influence corresponds to the more or less social level of those who had them engraved (see J. Bloch. *Mélanges S. Lévi*, p. 14; cf. Bhandarkar, *JAS Bombay*, XVI, p. 341 and note). But what to say, for example, of the neighbouring donations on the stūpas of Bharhut and Sanchi ? The genitive of the word denoting the Buddhist nun, Skr. *bhikṣuṇī* is at Bharhut (see Hultzsch, ZDMG, XL, p. 60 ff.) sometimes *bhichuniya* (Nos. 27, 31, 101), sometimes *bhikhuniyā* (No. 29, 75, 81), sometimes *bhichuniye* (Nos. 65, 120, 121), and once *bhikhuniyi* (No. 103). At Sanchi (edn. of Bühler, E. I., II, p. 97 ff., p. 370 ff) are found for the same word the forms *bhīkhuniyā* (I, 6, 199, 315, 332), *bhikhuniya* (I, 244, 286, 304, 350; II, 8, 9, 11, 40, 42, 43, 70, 76), *bhikhunaya* (II, 54); *bhichuniyā* (I, 28, 100, 186, 224, 283, 337, 343, 351; II, 29, 47); *bhichuniya* (I, 37, 52, 126, 227, 326, 355; II, 48), *bhichunayā* (I, 119, 353), *bhichuniyā* (I, 253), *bhichanaya* (I, 252); *bhichuniye* (I, 38, 78, 101, 105, 110, 158, 180, 183, 192, 214, 293, 316, 329, 341). Some of these forms are probably mistakes : but nothing permits us to find out the reason for the distribution of *ch* and *kh*, or of the genitive in *-iyá* and in *-iye*; the origin of the donors clarifies nothing: in the inscriptions due to the donors from Besnagar and Nandinagar as in those of the donors from Ujjain, the two terminations are found (however at Kurara-Kuraghara, one does not come across the termination in-*a*,) ; and Skr. *kṣ* is represented in two different forms in two absolutely neighbouring inscriptions and coming in all probability from the same person (*sami-*

kayā bhikhuniya dānaṃ; *sāmikāya bhichuniyā dānaṃ*); Sanchi I, p. 350-51).

The inscriptional documents, therefore, do not yield for linguistics, anything except extremely uncertain informations. In certain cases one could undoubtedly interpret them with the aid of what is known from elsewhere, for example by utilising the Prākrit of the dramas, as has already been attempted by Lüders (*Bruchstücke*, p. 40 ff.); but for the moment one can not go far in this direction.

$ 6. After the inscriptions, now let us examine the texts. The oldest or atleast those whose language is the most archaic, are those of the Buddhist Canon preserved in Ceylon. That the language of these texts—is appropriately called *Pāli*—is of continental origin, something of which no one has any doubt. But to which part of India, to which period of India, does it attach itself? Ignorance on these points is more or less complete. According to the Ceylonese tradition, the definitive editing of the Canon dates from the Council called by the king Duṭṭhagāmanī towards 80 B. C.; this provides the lowest date for the oldest pieces of the Canon. As regards the language, the books themselves call it Māgadhī. Now all that is known to us about Māgadhī through inscriptions or literature goes against this name. Undoubtedly it goes back to the primitive text, which was cited by Aśoka and not to the translation available to us.

We are, therefore, obliged to have recourse to historical induction for determining the place of origin of Pāli : this is a process which rarely leads, atleast in India, to firm and sure conclusions. On one side Oldenberg (*Vinayapiṭakam*, introduction, p. LIV) brings Pāli from Orissa; basing himself for this conclusion on the resemblances shown by this language with the inscription of Khāravela at Udayagiri,—resemblance confirmed by the aspect of certain Ceylonese inscriptions according to E. Müller (*Pāli Grammar*, preface, p. X). But the two dialects are far from being identical ; and the absence of the cerebral nasal, among other traits, clearly separates the dialect of Khāravela from Pāli.

The most generally admitted and the most probable hypothesis locates Pāli more to the west, not far from the large centres of pilgrimage denoted by the most ancient stūpas of Bharhut and Sanchi, more particularly in the Malwa. In the first place, is adduced the argument of the linguistic relationship of the inscriptions of this region with Pāli. We are also reminded of the fact that the capital of Malwa, Ujjain, had been the residence of Aśoka, then of his son, Mahinda, when they had been the Princes. According to tradition the mother of Mahinda had also been born at Ujjain and that Mahinda had passed his childhood there; now we know that the introduction of Buddhism in Ceylon is attributed to the same Mahinda (see notably O. Franke, *Pāli und Sanskrit*, p. 138-9). If the relationship between Ceylonese and the western speeches had been definitively established (see infra, $18) one could very well think of an immigration bringing from the same region a living dialect destined to evolve on the spot and of books written in an already fixed religious language.

In any case, Pāli can not be considered as a purely western dialect; the passage of the occlusive group + *v* or *v* +occlusive to *bb* takes it atleast to the central Plateau (see $ 17). That is not all. Pali is not homogenous; there are atleast seven centuries between the *gāthās* of the Jātakas and their prose-commentry (see Foucher, *Mélanges S. Lévi*, p. 235, 245-47); consequently we need not be surprised to find in Pāli the traces of the most diverse influences from the Magadhisms (see Windisch, *Congrés des Orient a Alger*, I, p. 280 ff.) right upto the loan-words from Ceylonese (see E. Müller, *Pāli Grammar*, p. X-XI).

Of uncertain origin and heterogeneous in essence, Pāli cannot, therefore, but be provisionally considered as a linguistic type representing an ancient form of literary Middle Indian and marking a stage in the general evolution of the Indo-Aryan.

$ 7. If Pāli had been surely a central or western dialect succeeding an eastern dialect in the reduction of the Buddhist Canon, its history in its turn would clear the history of another religious dialect, that of the Jains.

The texts of the Jaina Canon are said to have been edited in Ardha-Māgadhī or "semi-Magadhian." This dialect, also used in the Buddhist and Classical dramas, appears to be more western not only than Māgadhī properly speaking, as it has an *s* and not *ś*, but also more western than the dialect of Aśoka himself, as it has *r* and not *l*; the nominative singular of the masculine nouns is as in Māgadhī, in *-e*. But later on the centre of Jainism, as is known, had been shifted to the Deccan and to

Gujarat; from then on the dialect changes in aspect; the forms in *-o* insinuate themselves in the oldest poetic texts; in course of time the language becomes more and more western and gets increasingly mixed with Māhārāṣṭrī.

$ 8. Pali is, however, not the only Middle Indian dialect of Buddhism. In the neighbourhood of Khotan have been found several fragments of the Dhammapada written before the end of the 2nd century A. D., in a dialect not known before (edn. of Senart J.A, 1898, II, p. 193 ff.). In these dialects the intervocalic consonants had not uniformly lost their occlusion; but the final vowels had been shortened to the point where *-e* and *-o* become most frequently *-i* and *-u*. This last characteristic gives to the dialect a more recent aspect than the classical Prākrits, whereas by the partial preservation of the intervocalic consonants it appears as the most archaic . In any case, on both the points it is in accordance with the general development of the literary Prākrits. But the treatment of consonants following a nasal is altogether unique in this dialect; thereby it separates itself from the remaining varieties of Middle Indian. Thereby also—a unique case in the Buddhist literature—, it enables us to locate it with precision : the speeches of the western Panjab and of the Himalayan North-West even today present the same characteristics (see J. Bloch, JA, 1912, I, p. 331 ff.).

Certain Buddhist texts, notably the *Mahāvastu* and the *Lalitavistara* are written in a strange dialect, or seem to be arbitrarily mixing up Sanskrit, Pali and Prākrit. Are to be found therein, for example side by side forms like *abravi* and *abravīt*, nominative plurals in neuter in *-ā* and *-āni*, etc (see Senart, *Mahāvastu*, I, p. XII-XIII). The study of the syntax has enabled us to recognise therein several strata respectively characterised by the verbal and the nominal phrase (see Oldenberg, GGA, 1912, p. 123 ff.). On the other hand criticism has often enabled us to guess the Middle Indian form of the incorrect forms of Sanskrit in which it abounds (see Wackernagel, p. XXXIX; lastly Kern, IF, XXXI, p. 194 ff.). But to find in their origin only the ignorance of the maladroit adapters is to render more difficult the explanation of the relationship of the different and voluminous texts, and to forget the mastery with which Buddhism had known to handle Sanskrit. Besides, the Middle Indian observed in this incorrect Sankrit is as yet of an un-determined type.

It is, therefore, in every way impossible to recognise the linguistic reality corresponding to these texts. Comparative grammar can help in the philological interpretation of these texts, without however being able to make any use thereof.

These are, therefore, the only documents available to us before the flowering of the classical Prākrit. On a future date one will be, undoubtedly, able to get help from a profane dialect utilised in Central Asia. All that is known, for the moment, amounts to the fact that the language of the tablets brought from Niya by Stein is not related to the group to which belong the leaves of Dutreuil de Rhins (comm. of M. Senart, JA, 1912, I, p. 411).

$ 9. With the drama and lyrical poetry appear in literature new dialects, to which the grammarians have attributed the name of Prākrit . A certain number from among them bear the name of the country. Thus in the enumeration of Bharata (XVII, 48) :

māgadhyavantijā prācyā sūryasenyardhamāgadhī
bāhlīkā dākṣiṇātyā ca sapta bhāṣāḥ prakīrtitāḥ,

six out of seven are geographically determinable and three out of these four (Māgadhi, Śaurasenī, Mahārāṣṭri) are mentioned by Vararuci. Later on Daṇḍin adds to these three Lāṭī "and other similar ones" (*Kāvyādarśa*, I, 35). Should one, therefore, rely on the texts or on grammars as authentic documents concerning the speech of Magadha, Mathura, the Deccan or of Gujarata ?

But we hope in vain. First of all, these geographical names co-exist with names of an altogether different nature. Already that of Ardha-māgadhī, "semi-Magadhan", given by Bharata, is not clear. Later on Vararuci situates the Paiśācī on the same level as the three great Prākrits with a geographical name. Now despite the attempts made in this direction, it is impossible to recognise in this name that of a definite people, and with stronger reason that of a civilised national group as are the three others (see Lacôte, *Essai sur Guṇāḍhya et la Bṛhatkathā*, p. 47 ff.). In reality the names borne by the Prākrits are due to the circumstances of their entry in literature. The names of local appartainance are, atleast in the ancient epoch, those of the groups of actors, of bards or of singers. The name of Paiśācī is to be probably explained by a detail of the Guṇāḍhya legend, or of his work (see S. Lévi, *Théatre indien*, p. 330-32; Lacôte, op. cit.); Ardha-māgadhī, regardless of its origin, looks to be a mixture during a period, when notwithstanding the progress of grammar, we had been far from having discovered that the lines of isoglosses only rarely coincide among themselves (see the quotation of Abhayadeva in Pischel, $ 17). Naturally, the more numerous the Prākrits become, the more acute becomes the confusion of classification. No principle could enable one to clearly demarcate the works of diverse origins, as the traditional method had not been based on any definite principle.

If the grammarians have admitted these incoherences in the denomination of Prākrits,it is because they did not see spoken languages in them. It is not in vain that they find its source *prakṛti* in Sanskrit, that is to say in a literary and traditional language or that they put in opposition to the Prākrit vocabulary, the *deśīs*, that is to say the words used by the writers, but inexplicable according to the rules of Prākrit grammar and unknown to Sanskrit dictionaries (see Bühler, B.B., IV, p. 76 ff.).

$ 10. The real relationship between the Prākrits and the spoken languages gets admirably clarified by a comparison of the modern literary languages of Hindustan. Sometimes they are the speeches fixed during an ancient period and with each of them serving special cycles of legends or of special literary genres. The language of Braj is used for the cycle of Kṛṣṇa, that of Bundelkhand for that of Ālhā-Ūdal, that of Avadha for that of Rāma and generally speaking for the Epic—($ 19). But these languages can not remain pure, when the poets do not belong to the region, whose dialect they borrow or when they sing for people who do not know that dialect. One may expect here borrowings, adaptations and also false adaptations, exaggerating, if one could say so, the traits of the original dialect. The dialect of Braj for example, had invaded Bengal following the renaissance of Vaishavism; the name of *brajaboli* denotes in such cases something new. "It is", says D. C. Sen (*History of Bengali Language and Literature*, p. 387), "a type of Hindi prevalent at Darbhanga. This mixture of Hindi and Bengali is due to the Vaishnava writers' predilection for the dialect of

Vrindāvan [where many of them had lived, see ibid., p. 599]. They adopted it also for imitating Vidyāpati, the great master of lyrical poetry, who wrote in the language of Mithilā." At another place the same author adds that in their efforts for propogating their faith all over India, the Vaishnavas came into contact with the different races of India speaking different languages. Hindi had already become the *lingua franca* of the entire country, united under the sovereign power of the Muslim emperor of Delhi....The Vaishnavas adopted a large number of Hindi words in their works to make them intellegible throughout India." (ibid., p. 599-600). Let us note, finally, without however accepting completely, the affirmation: "The brajaboli is not the spoken dialect of any province and yet it is not an artificial dialect" (ibid., p. 546).

Other types of the formation of literary languages are furnished by Urdu and Hindi, generally known as Hindustani; to bring out this point it will suffice to borrow the terms used by Grierson for describing them in *The Languages of India*, $ 202, 205.

Hindustani, he says, was firstly the speech of the Upper Gangetic Doab; its purest form is that of the neighbourhood of and north of Meerut. This dialect, at the cost of some adaptations of the vocabulary, has become the spoken language of India, chiefly of the entire North India. Even the name oft his language is of European make. As the common language, Hindustani was born in the bazar attached to the Delhi Court (*Urdū*) and was carried all over India by the lieutenants of the Mughal empire. It has been alive since then. It has several recognised varieties, particularly Urdu and Hindi.

Urdu is that form of Hindustani which is written in the Arabic alphabet and which liberally employs Persian and consequently Arabian vocabulary. It is spoken chiefly in the towns of western India, and by the Muslims and Hindus, who have been subjected to Persian influence. Persian words are found everywhere in Hindustani, even in the rustic dialects, but in literary Urdu the use of Persian words is carried to an almost unbelievable degree. In writings of this type are to be found entire phrases where only the grammar is Indian, and where the words are Persian from beginning to end. There is, however, a curious fact, and noted rightly by Charles Lyall, that this Persianisation of Hindustani is not the work of conquerors, ignorant of the popular languages. It has on the contrary, been the result of the efforts of the Hindu, ever busy to assimilate the language of his masters. It is the work of the Persian-knowing Kayasthas and of the Khatris employed by the administration.

Hindi is the language of literary prose for those Hindus who do not use Urdu. It is modern in origin and owes its creation to English influence in the beginning of the last century. Upto that time, when a Hindu wrote prose and did not use Urdu, he wrote in local speech : Avadhī, Bundelī, Braja Bhākhā, etc. Under the inspiration of Gilchrist, Lalluji Lal, by writing his celebrated *Prem Sagar*, changed all this. The prose-parts of this work were in short in Urdu, with Persian words replaced everywhere by Indo-Aryan words. This experiment was a great success : the new dialect gave a "lingua franca" to the Hindus. It enabled peoples of different provinces to talk together without having recourse to the vocabulary, for them imposed, of the Muslims. It was easily intelligible everywhere because its grammar was of the language which every Hindu used in his official relations with administrators, and its vocabulary was the common property of all the Indo-Aryan languages of Northern India. Moreover, except the commentaries and similar works, upto that time very little prose had been written in Indo-Aryan languages. Naturally the language of *Prem Sagar* became the model of Hindu prose throughout Hindustan, from the Bengal to the Panjab. From the time of Lalluji Lal, Hindi has adopted certain rules of style which differentiate it from Urdu. The chief ones concern the order of words which is much more fixed here. Moreover, the vocabulary of Hindi has, since some little while, been under the attack of Sanskrit. In this way Hindi runs the risk of changing as much as Bengali, without having the same excuse. Because the Hindi of the peasant has its own vocabulary,so rich that nine-tenths of the Sanskrit words encountered in modern Hindi are as useless as they are unintelligible; but Sanskrit vocabulary seems to add to the dignity of style.

$ 11. Religious influences, official influences, the prestige of a learned language, the rôle of a literary work serving as the prototype, these are the many traits which might have characterised the birth of ancient literary languages as that of the modern ones. Moreover, let us suppose that the modern dialects fixed or adapted remained tied to the culture of a literary genre, and a moment will come when Brajaboli, Urdu or Hindi will require, for being understood, as much of study as Sanskrit. It will be necessary to prepare their grammars, wherefrom will result, on the other side the biggest normalisation of each of these dialects. That the Prākrits demand in fact some special education, is attested by the passage of the anthology of Hāla, rightly pointed out by Senart (*Inscriptions de Piyadasi*, II, p. 497), where people "not able to read nor listen to the ambrosia of Prākrit poems" are put to shame.

It will, therefore, be in vain to demand from the Prākrits direct documents concerning the spoken languages in the various regions of India in the classical epoch. From the moment they started writing in Prākrit, the authors were prisoners of the literary and grammatical tradition; and during nine or ten centuries Prākrit has undergone only insignificant changes. The vocabulary has been enriched, but we can not rely even on the loan-words. The usage of regular substitutions (see Meillet, *De la méthode dans les Sciences*, II, p. 301), which has increased the Sanskrit vocabulary, enabled in its turn the admission of Sanskrit words as also of vulgar ones. It also undoubtedly hides the frequent mixtures among the Prākrits themselves, so that the evidence of the Prākrits, suspect because of their origin, becomes all the more so with the increase in the number of documents.

$ 12. Can we then say that the written tradition is of no use and should we renounce it to take into account any modern language because we can learn of their ancient forms ? This conclusion would be necessary if Linguistics, above all, were to be the history of vocabulary. To follow the isolated words in their development and in their migration is, in fact, a task possible only in those countries, where the general history of language being known, the study of the minute details of philosophy and dialectology enable us to rigorously delimit the area of use and the epoch of the vitality of different words or of their different forms. But it is a question of, as here, establishing the general history itself of a language, vocabulary is but an instrument; in the words are considered not the words themselves, but the action of the phonetic laws and the use of grammatical forms.

Hereafter, it matters little whether the real aspect of the language has been falsified by the application, in literature, of the principle of regular substitutions. These substitutions reveal to the historian the normal phonetic state of the dialect as imposed on the writers by tradition. This tradition having in short, fixed a real dialect at a given moment of its development, the literature furnishes us with indirect but as a whole certain evidence concerning each of the principal dialects at the moment when it had been fixed. On the other hand, are found several phenomena which go against the general laws determined in this way in each dialect. These divergences are precious and they reveal facts posterior to the fixation of the dialect and which literature has been unable to entirely ignore.

We can, therefore, reconstruct in its totality the history of principal facts making use of the texts available to us. It should, however, be understood that this history will appear to be simpler than it has been in reality. To take an example, the sonorisation of intervocals was not produced everywhere simultaneously. A chance quotation enables us to assure that it was acqired by Māgadhī during Aśoka's time. In Śaurasenī also, the form of the name of the town, *Madhurā* for *Mathurā*, given a century later by Patañjali (*Madhurāpāñcālāḥ*, I, 2, 51, V, 5 quoted by Wackernagel, $ 103) shows that the alteration is old; but in the Deccan it is only in the first century that it is noted by the *Periplus* and the inscriptions. Similarly it has been observed that the dialect of the Dutreuil de Rhins MSS is at some places more archaic and at other more recent than classical Prākrit.

$ 13. Irrespective of these chronological differences we can, therefore, recognise the history of essential phenomena by following them across the different series of texts.

Among the phonemes, the system of vowels has, very early, assumed the aspect it presents till today. Sanskrit had inherited *a*, *i*, *u*, short and long which have subsisted without any change during all the periods of the Indo-Aryan. The Indo-Iranian diphthongs, on the contrary, have been simplified. Those whose first element had been short, * *ai* and * *au*, became long *e* and *o* during the Vedic period; those whose premier element had been long, * *āi* and * *āu*, became, during the same period, *ai* and *au*; but in this new form they were not stable and became in their turn *e* and *o* like the former ones during the most ancient period of Prākrit (see Meillet, *Mélanges S. Lévi*, p. 30). During the same period the groups *-aya*, *-ava* became simplified as *-e* and *-o*.

Moreover Sanskrit possessed two sonant vowels *ḷ* and *ṛ*. The first has never had more than an extremely limited existence even in Sanskrit : long *ṛ* plays therein a purely morphological rôle. As regards *ṛ*, it does not take long to get mixed up with *a*, *i* or *u* (cf. $ 31). The Ṛgveda already presents us with examples of this alteration inside words where *ṛ* was not kept due to the sentiment of morphological gradation (see Meillet, "Sur l'étymologie de l'adjective védique niṇyaḥ', *Mélanges Kern*, p. 121-22) and in certain terminations (see Meillet, "La finale *-uḥ* de Skr. *pituḥ*, *vidhuḥ*, etc.," *Mélanges S. Lévi*, p. 1 ff. chiefly p. 20). The oldest Prākrit, therefore, possessed short **and** long *a*, *i*, *u*, normally long *e* and *o* (shortened before double consonants, like all long vowels, see Müller, *Pali Gram*, p. 13 ff.; Pischel, $ 83-84). It has preserved these elements without any other modification except those depending on their place in the word ; particularly the weakness of final vowels, which has provoked their disappearance in modern times, has already left its traces in the oldest texts of Middle Indian.

$ 14. The history of consonants is more complicated, but the chief traits are equally clear. The articulatory system of the occlusives has remained considerably identical during all the epochs : it has in all its series (labial, dental, cerebral, palatal, guttural) a non-aspirate surd and a sonant and an aspirate surd and a sonant, the only changes that have taken place depend on the place occupied by the occlusives in different words.

Only the initial occlusives have remained. Others have undergone more or less serious changes.

The final consonants have, all of them, disappeared in Middle-Indian. The principle of the loss goes back to the pre-historic epoch (see Meillet, *Introduction*, p. 109-111). In Sanskrit the final consonants had been implosives (see Wackernagel, I, $ 260) and it is known that the occlusion of the sifflants and of final *m* had already become extremely reduced.

From the oldest period of the Middle-Indian all the words, therefore, ended in a vowel, this vowel being nasalised in cases where the lost consonant had been a nasal (see Pischel, $ 348, 350).

All the intervocalic consonants have lost more or less a large part of their occlusion. We have seen in $ 2 that in the case of aspirated sonants, this loss of occlusion was on one hand prehistoric and consequently *h* even in Sanskrit had often to be considered as a phoneme of real Prakritic nature. The intervocalic occlusive surds have resisted longer, undoubtedly because in India they could not be subject to the easier alteration, namely that of the occlusive into a corresponding spirant (see Maillet, 'Des consonnes intervocaliques en védique', I F, XXXI, p. 120-21); but between the 3rd century B. C. and the Ist century A.D., they have, all of them, become sonants. At the end of this period, Middle Indian had at the intervocalic position only the sonant occlusives (except the geminated ones) simualtaneously representing the ancient surds and sonants. It did not take long for these sonants to get transformed into spirants, with the exception of *ḍ* and *ḍh*. Moreover this exception is probably in mere appearance, if one is to judge by the Vedic *ḷ* and *ḷh* (see Meillet, ibid, p. 122) and by the modern pronunciation of intervocalic *ḍ* and *dh*. In the other categories of occlusives, all the aspirates are definitively reduced to *h* (*bh* survives longest, see Vararuci, II, 24-26); *b* becomes *v* (possibly already in old days, see Wackernagel, p. XL VIII, a propos of *kavāṭa-*, found in the *Rāmāyaṇa*), and *d*, *j*, *g* become *y*. Finally *y* thus obtained disappears from the signs of classical Prākrit, save in the Jaina MSS. (see Pischel, $ 187), and in fact gets lost, influencing or not, according to the cases, the timbre of the neighbouring vowels.

The groups of consonants appear, from a very early date, to have been difficult to pronounce. In certain cases, the assimilation is prehistoric and the oldest Sanskrit already offers the geminated consonants (see Wackernagel, $ 97 a *a*). Among the groups maintained in Sanskrit, those having *r* accept the insertion of a vowel from the oldest epoch (see Wackernagel, $ 49-51); and Patañjali, in the 2nd cent. B. C., cites as usual the form *supati-* for *supti-*. The most frequent tendency is that of simplifying the articulation : in the

3rd cent. B. C., Kātyāyana notes the form *āṇapayati* for *ājñā-*, and in the next century Patañjali gives *vaṭṭati, vaḍḍhati* for *vart-, vardh-* as current. In fact in the Aśokan inscriptions all the groups are unified except *st-*, *sṭ* and consonant +*r* which survive at Girnar and in the North-West, that is to say in the regions where these groups have been maintained in the spoken languages upto modern times. In Buddhist Prākrit and in the document of the beginning of the Christian Era (see J. Bloch, *Mél. S. Lévi*, p. 10-15) assimilation is general and the classical Prākrits have in the interior of the word, only the geminated occlusives.

$ 15. Such is, in its totality, the history of the occlusives. That of the continuents is less uniform; yet the sonants have undergone, in the intervocalic position, changes similar to those of the occlusives; *y* has taken in the initial position a particular occlusion and has got mixed with *j* between the Ist cent. (see Lüders, *Bruchstücke*, p. 48, 60), and the classical epoch. Thereby the opposition of the initial and of the intervocalic has been re-established[1]; *m* kept in the initial position, has become the nasal *v* in the intervocalic position (see Pischel, $ 251).

The cerebral nasal and the dental, become cerebral on the one hand and on the other *l*, have remained in classical Prākrit; but the later history of these phenomena reveals similar changes (see infra). Only *r* and *v* remain unaltered during all the periods.

As regards the sifflants, they are everywhere jumbled into a unique one. The ancient inscriptional Prākrit still distinguishes them, but the unification is effected in Pali and in all the extant Prākrits of the Buddhist period, except one, which is the eastern-most of all : it is the Ḍhakkī which still distinguishes *Ś* of Skr. *Ś* from *S* of Skr. *S* and *Ṣ* (Pischel, $ 228). In Prākrit the sifflant is everywhere dental, except in Māgadhī where it is palatal, it will be seen that the aspect of Prākrit is reproduced by modern Indo-Aryan : everywhere, except in the Himalayan North-West and in the Romany

1. In Māgadhī the confusion seems to have occurred in the inverse sense, and *y* represents an old *j* as also *y* (Pischel, $ 252, cf. $ 236) Probably this is but an orthographic tradition.

languages of Europe (where *ś* <Skr. *Ṣ*, *Ś*; *S* <Skr. *S*; see Grierson, *Piśāca Language*, p. 21-22; Miklosich, IX, p. 39); on principle there is only one sifflant and this is *s*, except in Bengali and Oriya where it is *ś* (see Grierson, *Phon.*, p. 18-19).

$ 16. The history of grammatical forms can be reconstructed less easily. However, already the sacerdotal literature of Sanskrit furnishes through its irregularities and incoherences a number of precious documents (see Wackernagel, p. XIV, XXII ff.). Adding classical Sanskrit to the same, one can follow from close enough the progressive dislocation of the hereditary verbal system and the examination of Prākrit only confirms the certitudes already acquired. The declension has been, on the contrary, fixed in Sanskrit in an archaic form. But the inscriptional and literary Prākrits show the evolution whereby the ancient forms disappear and render necessary the creation of new forms (for details of these facts see infra).

$ 17. Such is in its totality the history of Indo-Aryan in the period preceding that of Marathi. But here a difficulty crops up : can we join the history of Marathi to that of the Middle Indian thus defined ? Marathi is far from being the only modern Indo-Aryan language; now to render an account of the formation of Marathi does not mean merely noting from the documents the changes in the hereditary linguistic system which have made possible the constitution of this language. It also amounts to showing and if possible, explaining its relationship with the neighbouring related languages. The question is : since when have come into being the characteristics which differentiate it from those other forms of the same ancient language ? In other terms does the separation, which has given rise to the formation of modern languages, go back to the remote past and is the Middle Indian, with its general curve defined above, a fiction without any relationship with reality, or should we take into consideration the totality of modern languages as being based on a common language attested by Middle Indian ? If the two theses have their part of truth, how should they be combined ? A glance at the distribution and at the most salient characteristics of the modern Indo-Aryan languages will enable us to answer this question.

$ 18. Indo-Aryan covers India in a continuous manner

from the North-Western frontier,[1] where it touches Iranian and Tibetan, upto Assam and Burma, where it again encounters the Tibeto-Burman group; on the other hand it goes as far as the Konkan and the middle basin of Godavari, where it extends its conquests in the Dravidian domain.

Outside this territory, Indo-Aryan occupies the meridinal half of the island of Ceylon, and that for a long time; in fact, Buddhist tradition confirms the fact that the Pali commentary written by Buddhaghoṣa during the 5th cent. is a translation of a Simhalese original. Other pieces of evidence enable us to go higher; besides the first authentic documents of Simhalese appear only in the 10th century (see Geiger, ch. I). This language is grouped with the dialects of Western India (ibid, ch. III); however some of the traits which estabish this relationship, such as the preservation of the initial and geminated *v*, or that of the three types of declension can be considered as archaisms like other traits separating it from the same group, that is the preservation of internal *n* and *l*, of initial and geminated *y*, whereby it evokes Pali and Māgadhī. On the other side the formation of the oblique on the old genitive of Sanskrit, in the singular number as in the plural one, is found only in the Himalayan North-West and in the Romany language. Above all the termination of the masculine plural in *-ahu*, *-o* directly recalls the Māgadhī; and by the simplification of *-ṇṇ-* in *-ṇ-* the Simhalese also separates itself from the western group which has in this case a dental *n*. We may, however, provisionally consider the Simhalese dialect, to the extent that it has not evolved altogether independently of other languages, as belonging more to the western then any other group.

On the continent also the Indo-Aryan has crossed the frontiers of India. Central Asia (see supra $ 8) has yielded to the explorers several ancient documents, of whom atleast one series, analytically examined, reveals to have been really corresponding to a local speech. Even today the Gypsies, from Iran and Armenia upto the western frontiers of Europe speak diaelcts, which are undisputably related to the Indian family. The date of their emigration is not surely known. The

1. Now the frontier of W. Pakistan with Iran, Afghanistan, etc. (Translator).

oldest emigration seems to have taken place in the 5th cent. A. D. (see de Goeje, *Mémoire sur les migrations des Tsiganes à travers l'Asie*); but its origin is surely known : the Romany language is a speech of the North-West. Several traits prove it : the group consonant $+r$ does not survive, the initial vowel of the Skr. word, *ātma-* has not been lost in this language, in Sindhi and in the dialects of the hills. As in the latter (except in Kashmiri), Romany has lost the old relative *ya-*. The Romany of Europe, like these very dialects, still distinguishes the dental sifflant *s* from *ś* issued out of *ṣ*, and *ś* and has preserved the groups *st* and *ṣṭ*; truly speaking the Romany of Armenia is, on these points, in conformity with the Prākrit rule and follows the Indo-Aryan of India (see Finck, 'Die Sprache der Armen. Zigenner', *Mém. de l Académie impériale de St.-Petersbourg*, VIII, 5, $ 57, 72, 73); but the Himalayan dialects and even the Iranian (see Gauthiot, MSL, XVII, p. 157) present several similar variations and show that in the North-Western region the Iso-gloss lines have been able to cross one another in different ways. A fact which isolates Romany from all other Indo-Aryan languages (except the Veron, one of the western most dialects of the Himalayan group, see Grierson, *Piśāca Language*, p. 19), simultaneously localises the same exactly on the Iranian frontier. In the Romany language intervocalic *t* or *d* regularly become *l* (example : *phral*, *phal*—"brother"; see Miklosich, IX, p. 25); in the Armenian dialect the initial *d* also becomes *l* (*lui* "two", *las* "ten", *lel* "to give", see Finck, ibid, $ 73); now the passage of *t* to *l*, in the initial and in the intervocalic position, is a characteristic trait of the north-western Iranian dialects, irrespective of the group to which they may be attached (see Gauthiot, JA, 1910, I, p. 542; MSL, XVII, p, 158).

Quite a large number of small Himalayan dialects are also attached to the speeches of the North-West. Due to their geographical isolation and the absence of literature, these dialects have become different not only from the entire Indo-Aryan group but have also become considerably different from one another. These are the dialects, which are, of course wrongly called "Modern Piśāca" by Grierson (see his *The Piśāca Language*, p. 7 ff.); Z D M G., LXVI, p. 49-86; cf. Meillet, *Bull. Soc. Ling.*, XIV, pl CCXLIX; J. Bloch, B E F E O, 1907, p. 116; Lacôte, *Essai sur Guṇāḍhya et la Bṛahatkathā*, p. 46 ff.,

Sten Konow, Z D M G, LXIV, p. 95-118; J. Charpentier, *Kleine Beitr. Zur indoir. Mythologie*, Uppsala, 1911 p. 1 ff.) Grierson divides these speeches in three groups : in the West, those of Kafiristan; in the centre, the Xowār, spoken in the Valley of Chitral; lastly the Eastern group, spoken lower down on the Indus, in Gilgit, at Chilas and in Kohistan, in Swat and in Kashmir. Kashmiri, which is the better known of these dialects, is also by another side, the least instructive because it has accepted numerous Iranian and Sanskrite lements and has been a literary language.

$ 19. Let us now enter India properly speaking. In the 16th century according to Abul Fazl, the languages, which differ sufficiently so that their speakers do not comprehend one another, are those of Delhi, Bengal, Multan, Marwar, Gujarat, Telingana, Maratha country, Carnatic, Sind, the Afghan lands (between Sind, Kabul and Kandhar), Balochistan and Kashmir (*Ain-i-Akbarī,* transln. of Jarrett, III, p. 119). Eliminating the non-Indo-European languages and arranging others which interest us we see that Abul Fazl finds in the West a Zone rich in individualised speeches, which are, going from North to South : Kashmiri, Panjabi, Sindhi, Gujarati and Marathi. Marwari is the link between these speeches and the language of Delhi, that is to say, Hindustani. The latter covers the entire Gangetic basin upto Bengal, where is localised the dialect mentioned last. Modern linguistics has only comlicated this map; it has not modified the general aspect (for all that follows, see chiefly Grierson, *The Languages of India,* $ 149 ff., and the published volumes of the *Linguistic Survey of India*).

Starting from the western Himalayas, while descending the Indus we meet firstly the domain of Lahnda or western Panjabi. In reality this is a group of numerous dialects without literature and with linguistic characteristics which bring them near both Sindhi and the Himalayan speeches. Nevertheless the vocabulary and grammar are subjected to the influence of Afghani in the West and of Panjabi in the East—and through Panjabi that of Hindi.

Sindhi occupies the lower course of the Indus from its confluence with the Panjab; it is spread, besides, on the western coast of the Runn of Cutch. It comprises three principal dialects ; that of the nomads of the Thar Desert, that of Middle Sindh and that of lower Sindh or Lāru, this last serves as the literary language and this is the one described by grammars as Sindhi.

Following the sea, one comes across Gujarati, then Marathi. The former is spoken around the Runn of Cutch, in the area left free by Sindhi, in Gujarat, at Baroda and Surat and also at Bombay. It has been cultivated from a very early period : a Sanskrit grammar written in Gujarati is dated to the end of 14th century, and from the 15th century poetic works abound. Besides, the region has always been one of the most civilized in India; it is at Girnar that has been found beside an Aśokan inscription, the first inscription in Sanskrit; it is again in this region that flourishing Jainism developed the Prākrit literature and that one of its masters, Hemacandra, in the 12th century, wrote the grammar and collection of *deśī* words, which is the richest document on Prākrit.

To the south of Daman and right up to the meridional limits of Indo-Aryan, Marathi prevails, on which more later. In the east, and going up the Gangetic Basin, are to be found a large number of speeches which are firstly linked with the western group, and then increasingly resemble Hindustani. They are found firstly in the hilly region extending between Ajmer and Nasik on the one hand, Baroda and Indore on the other, the Bhil dialects, the veritable Gujarati *patois* spoken by the tribes of the Munda race. Thereafter follow series of dialects which Grierson arbitrarily groups as Rajasthani; the indigenous people know only the names of isolated speeches, or adopt that of Marwari. This name is properly of that dialect which occupies by the North-West the biggest territory as compared to others. It is spoken by the most numerous population, and particularly by a commercial population whose rôle in the entire country is important, finally this is the dialect which has furnished the oldest and the most abundant literature. Marwari and the group which limits it in the east,whose type is the speech of Jaipur, are clearly linked with Gujarati; in the south-east, Malawi already resembles more the Bundeli and in the north-east Mewati-Ahirwati is quite near western Hindi. These speeches can, therefore, be considered either as the dialects of Gujarati, or as constituting a Zone of transition between Gujarat and Hindustan. Only on the southern side, that is to say on the side of Marathi, the linguistic frontier is quite clear.

Thereafter comes the central group, which occupies the Upper and the middle Gangetic Basin, and even a part of the Himalayas, because the valleys seem to have been colonised by the conquerors coming from Gangetic India and from Rajputana. To the west of the vast region, Panjabi passes, even in popular usage, for a language with its individuality. In fact, its morphology shows us certain traits which isolate it from the speeches of Hindustani properly so called and on the contrary bring it near western Panjabi. The same is true of the vocabulary. But the eastern influences have also been very numerous to the extent that linguistics can not provisionally draw much benefit from this language. Yet, the literature of the Sikhs will probably permit a historical study : because it is known that Panjabi is the language of the Sikh (scriptures) and on this count can extend itself into several regions of India and even outside, upto China.

The name of Hindi is applied, in popular usage, to all the languages spoken from the Panjab upto the Mahananda in the Bengal itself, and from the Himalayas upto the Narmada. We have already separated from this big group the speeches of Rajasthan and those of the Himalayas which are related thereto. The remaining ones are divided into three groups: western Hindi occupies the territory between the frontier of the Panjab and Kanpur; eastern Hindi goes from Kanpur upto almost Banaras; then comes Bihari, which is grouped rather with the far eastern group.

The principal dialect of western Hindi is Hindustani (or better Hindostani) which has been discussed above ($ 10). Also recognised are the Bangru, spoken to the west of Delhi and Braja or antarbedi, occupying the region of Mathura, Agra and Kannauj. This dialect, with an archaic aspect, has literature in abundance, its oldest document is the *Prithviraj Rāsau*, or the ballad of the exploits of Prithviraj Chauhan, the last king of Delhi, killed by the Muslims along with Cand Bardai, the poet in 1193. Later on, the same dialect has been used by Surdas (towards 1550) and Vallabhacharya who sang of Krishna and Rāddhā in the language of the very country, where their legend is situated. Lastly comes Bundeli, the language of

Bundelkhand and Gwalior; it is used by the bards who sing of Ālhā and Ūdal, the two defenders of Parmāl, the king of Mahobā and the adversary of Prithviraj.

Awadhi, spoken chiefly between Lucknow, Allahabad and Awadh is the most important dialect of eastern Hindi. Awadha is the centre of the Rama legend and as a consequence Awadhi is the language of epic poetry celebrating his exploits. It is above all the dialect of Tulsi Das, the greatest modern poet of Hindustan (died in 1624). It is also the dialect in which Muhammad Jayasi sang of the ruin of Chittor under the blows of Alauddin Khilji, during the second half of the 16th century; lastly it is the dialect of the most popular North Indian version of the Mahābhārata.* In Baghelkhand and in Chattisgarh are spoken the dialects belonging to the same group; but less important.

Bihari (called eastern Hindi by Hoernle in conformity with the indigenous classification) is sub-divided into three dialects. Bhojpuri is the westernmost; one of the varieties of Bhojpuri, which is contiguous to Hindi is, by comparison, called *Purbi*, that is to say "eastern". Starting from Patna, the Ganga separates two other domains, in the north, that of Maithili, in the south, that of Magadhi. Of these three dialects, that of Mithila has a literary past; it is notably the dialect in which Vidyāpati Thākur sang of Krishna and Rādhā in the 15th century. His poems have been adapted into Bengali by the Vaishnavas and are at present considered as part of Bengali literature.

There remain three eastern dialects, Bengali, Oriya and Assamese, which are extremely similar, so much so that attempts have been made, undoubtedly wrongly, to regard the two latter ones as the sub-dialects of the former. All the three have an old literature; but the richest, the most beautiful and the most popular of all is, without any doubt, the Bengali literature. The Puranic legends, then the reform of Chaitanya, still later the court-life and the learned culture, both Persian and Sanskrit and lastly the influence of European religion and science have been the sources of this literature. Its influence has, besides, been very strong and the Bengali vocabulary, atleast as revealed to the European student by the dictionaries and the majority of books, is full of Sanskrit and Hindi borrowings to such an

*. A mis-print for *Rāmāyaṇa*—Translator.

extent that for linguistic comparison one can derive little profit therefrom.

$ 20. Such are the modern languages which are related to Marathi. What are their chief characteristics and what is the relationship indicated by these characteristics between these modern languages and Middle Indian ?

It is morphology which chiefly differentiates between these languages. Leaving aside, for certain points, the speeches of the extreme North-West and Simhalese, which diverged in very old times, the forms are everyewhere based on identical types, po terior to Prākrit. The variations of declension in the various dialects depend on the fact whether there are two or three genders, or whether the notion of gender has been lost, or on the fact that an oblique case has been formed on one old case or on another. Thereafter these variations depend on the form of terminations, that it is to say on the formulae concerning the contraction of groups, of final vowels and finally on the word, which used as an oblique postposition constitutes the adjective of appartainance. Now, all these variations go back to a state everywhere similar which, in its turn, is derived from a state common to all the forms of Prākrit. Similarly, the conjugation, in all the dialects, is based upon the forms common to (all the varieties of) Middle Indian. The only old difference which seems to have persisted concerns the distribution of the forms of the absolutive, one proper to Śaurasenī and Māgadhī in *-ia*, and the other, that of Mahāraṣṭrī, in *-tūṇaṁ*, *-ūṇaṁ*. But it should be noted that on the one hand Simhalese, Sindhi and Gujarati accord with the central and eastern group, and that on the other hand, it is not sure whether the Marathi form *-ūn* exactly continues the termination of Māhārāṣṭrī Prākrit. Thus the unique dialectal distribution of modern times, which seems to go back to an old variation, is not clear.

It is equally well known that it is not morphology, but phonetics which separates the Prākrits as they are known to us. What are the main lines of iso-glosses of the modern Indo-Aryan. Here again should be kept aside, firstly, the North Western group, whose characteristic preservation of a hissing sibilant beside a dental sibilant, preservation of *st* and *ṣṭ*, the passage of *sm* to *ss* (in place of *ṁh*), the alteration of occlusives following a nasal have never been noted in classical Prākrit (*sm* >*ss* only in *bhasma* and the termination *-smin*, see Pischel, $ 313; *nt* > *nd* is given as Māgadhī, ibid, $ 275).

Other modern dialects present, in the treatment of Skr.*ṛ*,*kṣ*, *r*+dental, dental+*v*, a confusion which reproduces that already revealed by old documents, and where only a subtle analysis enables us to observe some prehistoric geography. Let us try some other phenomena: the final vowels, everywhere lost, survive in Kashmiri, in Simhalese, in Sindhi, etc. The group of short vowel +double consonant persists as such or in Simhalese, Sindhi, Panjabi, western Hindi, and elsewhere becomes long vowel + simple consonant. In Gujarati, Sindhi and Rajasthani internal *au*, and *ai* get shortened into *o* and *e*; the laws of the contraction of vowels differ according to languages. It is seen that the phonetics of vowels merely shows the variations of recent date. The fate of consonants appears at first more interesting, and the roots of contemporary phenomena seem to be plunged in the past; but only a few cases are decisive. To the initial or geminated *v* in Simhalese, in Armenian Romany, in Panjabi, Sindhi, Gujarati, Rajasthani and Marathi, corresponds *b* in the Romany of Europe, in Hindi and in the entire eastern group (the North-Western Himalayan simultaneously shows *v* and *b*. The presence of *bb* from *vy*, *w*, etc. in Pali seems to prove that this distribution is old in origin; but the rest of Middle Indian has *v* everywhere and it looks as if the passage of *v* to *b* is modern. Besides the distribution of the same phenomenon in Dravidian seems to indicate that the evolution *v*>*b* could have been independent on various dialects. It is known that the initial *v* preserved in Telugu and in Tamil, has become *b* in Kannada : now the Kannada is situated to the west of Telugu. In the entire western group of the continent and in the Hindustani spoken in the upper Gangetic Doab, intervocalic *n* and *l* have been cerebralised, whereas they survived [unchanged] to the east of this Zone; now in Prākrit the cerebralization of *l* is found only in Paiśācī, that is to say in a non-identified dialect; and the same Paiśācī is the only Prākrit which regularly keeps *n*, cerebralised in the initial position everywhere else (save certain recent restorations in Jaina Prākrit). The fate of sibilants is perhaps the only phenomenon regarding which a clear, though partially so, idea had been formed at an early date.

This is so because the preservation of two sibilants, which characterises the North-West, is not to be found anywhere in Middle Indian and the only similar case furnished by Ḍhakkī Prākrit has a different formula (in the North-West *S*>*S*, Ṣ and *Ś*>*Ś*; in Ḍhakkī *S* and Ṣ>Ṣ, *Ś*>*Ś*; see Pischel, $ 228). In a general way, Prākrit has made uniform from a very early date all the sibilants, in the form of *s* in the west and centre, as *ś* in the east (see for Māgadhī, the inscription of Ramgarh cited by Lüders, *Bruchstücke*, p. 41 and Pischel, $ 229). Now it is known that except in the North-West, and leaving out of account certain later variations in Marathi and Gujarati, the entire western and central Indo-Aryan has mixed up the sibilants and has only the dental *s*; whereas in the case of the far eastern group (except in the Bengali of the North-West) the only sibilant is *ś*.

Inversely the dialectal differences noted in the classical Prākrits have almost all of them disappeared from modern languages: thus the intervocalic occlusives remaining as occlusives (sonant) in Śauraśenī and partially in Māgadhī have lost all occlusion (except of course in the *tat-samas* and in the semi-*tat-samas*). The initial and geminated *y* of Māgadhī has become *j* in the ancient domain of Māgadhī as everywhere else. The different terminations while being lost, have generally eliminated the morphological differences, etc. It looks as if therc had been a common Middle Indian, containing at the most like all common languages, the few surviving dialectal variations. Except for certain phonetic changes which can be easily defined and certain indications, besides rare and obscure, concerning special grammatical forms, we may group all the facts in unique historcal series and utilise them for the history of some general Indo-Aryan language, provided that it be located to the east of the Indus.

$ 21. Moreover, it is permissible to think that this uniformisation of the languages of Northern India, as it appears in writing, corresponds to an historically real phenomenon. The social breaking up revealed to us by the Vedic texts and traditions relating to early Buddhism, makes way, early enough, for civilisation, which tends to be unified by the political and religious phenomena. The Mauryas are the first to establish a big empire stretching from the Panjab to the Bengal and as far as Mysore. After them the centre of domination shifts but the

Scythians occupy Rajputana and Hindustan; the coins of Kaniṣka are to be met with as far as Ghazipur, farther than Benaras on the Ganga (see V. Smith *Early History of India* p. 226). In the 4th century Patna becomes once again, under the Guptas, the capital of a big empire spread as far as the Narmada and which (under Samudragupta) covers the entire country. Three centuries later, Harṣa of Kannauja unites, once again under his domination, the same territory. Finally come the Muslims, whose first advances provoke the formation of Hindu federations, while their domination, spreading all over Northern India, ensures the prestige of the "language of Delhi." We should not however, exaggerate the importance of the mixing up of vocabulary, resulting from these successive empires in different provinces. The centres of influence would shift from one end of the country to another. Between the Magadhan of Aśoka and the Urdu of Akbar, have existed other administrative languages. Of these we know only one, the Sanskrit and in fact it has exerted enormous influence. But it is also presumable that documents more ephemeral than inscriptions must have more intimately reflected the real languages of the conquerors, or atleast of the wandering agents and scribes of their administration. This is not all : after Buddhism, renaissant Brahmanism unified the country. It installed Sanskrit everywhere as also the caste-system. As Prākrits in the theatre, similarly in real life the dialects of the different castes rise in tiers in relation to Sanskrit but at the same time they tend to draw near Sanskrit, that is to say to be infiltrated by the same or to imitate it. One may add to all this the recitals of the wandering bards, coming from different points or singing in different dialects, and the voyages, so frequent in India of pilgrims, of traders, of soldiers. This will give some idea of the influences which, in the Middle Ages, have led to the formation of a common language.

$ 22. This common language, whose theoretical necessity and historical possibility we have just now recognised, stops at the Prākrits, properly so called. Certain scholars think that they can date it still later, using for the same purpose other documents notably transmitted by Hemacandra under the name of *apabhraṃśa* (see for ex. Grierson, *Phon.*, p. 393). But the Apabhraṃśa known to us is, in reality, a dialectal document which is not related to a territory as vast as Prākrit and which particularly has nothing in common with Marathi.

In the manuals of Grammar or of Rhetorics the word *apabhraṁśa* denoted an incorrect form from the point of view of the Sanskrit grammar : *Śāstreṣu saṃskṛtād anyat*, says Daṇḍin (*Kāvyādarśa*, I, 36; cf. Pischel $ 4); and it is thus that it was used before Daṇḍin by Patañjali (in the passage cited by Bhandarkar, *JAS*, *Bombay*, XVI, p. 331 and Pischel, $ 8) and after him by Vāmana (in the rule, *pūrva-nipāte 'pabhraṁśo rakṣyaḥ* "a compound where the order of terms is not correct, should, however, be admitted as such", V, 2, 21). In drama and in poetry in general —*kāvyeṣu* says Daṇḍin at that very place— the Apabhraṃśa is a local language admitted for literary usage; but this is allowed only with necessary selections : according to Vāgbhaṭa (cited by Pischel, $ 4) *yat śuddhaṁ tat taddeśeṣu bhāṣitam*; that is to say in short a purified *patois*. This is why not only the forms of Apabhraṃśa show an aspect very recent as compared to the Prakrits, but one often has the impression that they will be better explained more by contemporary rather than old forms. One often asks oneself if they are not a stylised transcription of modern languages rather than an out-come of Prākrit (for ex. in the terminations of the gen-sing-*aha*, gen. pl.-*ahaṁ*, loc.-*ahiṁ*, 3 d pl.-*ahiṁ*).

It results from this second definition of the Apabhraṃśa, that in principle there can be various types of Apabhraṃśa corresponding to various Prākrits. This is, in fact, generally admitted; and it is possible that several among these varieties might have been cultivated : because the literature in Apabhraṃśa is quite old. According to a Tibetan tradition the Buddhist Saṃmitīya school used it (Wassilief, *Buddhismus*, p. 267) and in fact several Buddhist stanzas, late in date, are available (see Bendall, *Muséon*, 1903, p. 376; 1904, p. 245 ff.). Probably Kālidāsa has also used it (see Pischel, $ 29). In any case, at the beginning of the 6th century, the king Guhasena of Valabhī praises himself for his talent of being a writer in three languages, Sanskrit, Prākrit and Apabhraṃśa. But for these different varieties of Apabhraṃśa, we have no document which can be put to use. The only ones of note are related precisely, to that region of India where reigned Guhasena. In fact the names *nāgara* and *vrācaḍa*, given by the Prākrit grammarians take us to Gujarat and to the lower basin of the Indus (see Piśchel, $ 28; Grierson, *L S I. Raj.*, p. 327). On the other hand Bhandarkar links the Apabhraṁśa, known to us, with Gujarati and with the archaic forms of Hindi (*JAS Bombay*, XVI, p. 39); and in truth vaster or narrower, the domain of the phenomena corresponding to the characteristics of Apabhraṃśa always leaves Marathi outside. The preservation of *r* after a consonant, the passage of *s* into *h* is met with only in Gujarati, Sindhi and in the North-West. The unvoicing of *-aṁ* final in *-uṁ* (Piśchel $ 351, 352) explains the termination of the nom. sing. neuter-*uṁ* of Gujarati, but not that of the corresponding *-eṁ* of Marathi (cf. $ 36). The possessive pronouns Apa. *mahāra*, *tuhāra*, *amhāra* or *hamāra*, *tohāra* are used almost everywhere, even in Romany, but are missing in Simhalese, in western Himalayas, in Sindhi and in Marathi. In the verb, the terminations of the second pers. sing. *-ahi* (Pkt. *-asi*), pl. *-ahu* (Pkt. *-aha*) correspond to those of entire Northern India, except Oriya and Marathi. The absolutive goes back everywhere to Apa. *-i* (Śaura-*ia*, Skr. *ya*) except in Marathi. Similarly the so very obscure termination of the third pers. pl. *-ahiṁ* (see J. Bloch, JA, 1912, I, p. 334) covers Gujarat and the entire Hindustan, leaving out once again Oriya and Marathi.

$ 23. As a consequence of what has been seen above, we can study Marathi and utilise under certain conditions all the documents of Middle Indian, with the exception of the Apabhraṃśa which is, at least as known to us, a more recent dialect and has entered into literature after the separation of Marathi and other dialects.

It should be added that one has the greater right to link together Marathi and Middle Indian because the form of the Middle Indian Marathi is the one that has served as the basis for literature during several centuries. In fact the grammarians warn us about the same : from the day of the constitution in Maharashtra of a Prākrit used for lyrical poetry, the old preeminence of Śaurasenī admitted by Bharata tends to disappear. According to Daṇḍin (6th cent.) Māhārāṣtrī is the best Prakrit; and in fact it is this dialect which the grammarians take as the basis for their description. To them Prākrit means the Māhārāṣṭrī Prākrit (see Pischel, $ 2). The continuity between Prākrit and Marathi is noted in a valuable way in the *deśī* collection of Hemacandra. This grammarian was a resident of Gujarat and, therefore a very large number of words noted by him, are to be found in the vocabulary of Gujarati and Marathi.

$ 24. It still remains to define Marathi itself and to rapidly indicate the documents utilised for its study.

Marathi occupies largely the sea-coast and the upper basin of the eastern rivers forming a triangle whose base would be the coast stretching from Daman to Karwar and whose top would be situated in the centre of the region between Nagpur, Jabalpur and Raipur, or at the feet of the hills separating the upper basins of the Waiganga and the Narmada. On the southern side it touches the Dravidian domain—Kannada, Telugu Gond—, on the northern one it meets on the coast, Gujarat, then going up towards the Satpura mountains, the Bhili, Malawi, that is to say Rajasthani, Bundeli, that is to say western Hindi, Chattisgarhi, a dialect of Eastern Hindi and finally Oriya dialects.

This land, which has always been in communication with Northern India has, however, also preserved a certain independence. In the time of the Aitareya Brāhmaṇa, the Andhras are outside the Aryan domain. And in fact we find in Marathi clear traces of a local Dravidian substratum. Independently of the category of cerebrals and of the absence of spirants, which are the common links for the entire country in antiquity, and of the constitution of an oblique case,to which are adjoined simliar postpositions for two numbers, and finally of the fact that the genitive of the noun is a veritable adjective—common traits for the entire modern Indo-Aryan (see *LSI*, *Munda-Dra.*, p. 280, 291), are to be noted in Marathi two phonetic particularities which set it apart from the rest of the Indo-Aryan group and which are found in the contiguous Dravidian languages. The first is the loss of the hissing character of the semi-occlusive palatals before posterior vowels, which draws Marathi near Telugu; the second is the change of initial *e-* and *a-* as diphthongs; which are pronounced as *oye-* and *wo-* (in the case of *e-*, orthography frequently admits *ye-*; the verb *ye-* "to go" is always so written; cf. Molesworth, preface, p. XIV). This is a common trait of all the Dravidian languages. In truth the change of *e* and *o* into diphthongs is to be found even inside the word, in certain dialects of the Konkan (see *LSI*, *Mar.*, p. 65, 157); the two phenomena seem to be independent of each other.

Situated on the frontier of the Aryan world, the Deccan does not tarry long to get included therein. Aśoka enumerates the Andhras among his Buddhist vassals; and a hundred years later, the king of Kaliṅga, Khāravela, refers to the military powers of Śātakarṇi, his neighbour to the west. Besides, Pliny mentions in a good rank the Andarae, as whose power he mentions thirty fortified towns, numerous villages, an army comprising of a hundred thousand foot-soldiers, two thousand horses and a thousand elephants. The Śātakarṇi dynasty ruled for several centuries at Paiṭhan. The pious endowments multiplied by this dynasty are a sign of its power and its wealth. Shaken for a moment by the Kṣatrapas, it comes into its own again with Gotamiputa, who rules over the Konkan, the Deccan and Malwa. It is under this dynasty that the local Prākrit becomes the literary language. To one of its kings, Hāla, is ascribed the famous anthology of seven hundred stanzas in Māhārāṣṭrī, the *Sattasaī*. With the same king is linked the legend of Guṇāḍhya, the creator of Paiśāci Prākrit (see *Lacôte*, op. cit., p. 27 ff.). Naturally, where Prākrit is cultivated Sanskrit also flourishes. Śarvavarman, the presumed author of the *Kātantra*, is a minister of a Śātakarṇi; and it is a king of the same dynasty, to whom is addressed the *Suhṛllekhā* of Nāgārjuna, the famous scholar of Mahāyāna. After the ruin of Śātakarṇi, the history of the Deccan remains obscure for more than three centuries. At the end of this period the Cālūkyas installed at Badami dominate the country as far as the sea. One of them, *Pulikesi* II, stops at the Narmada (towards 620) the arms of Harṣa, the emperor of Northern India, which had been victorious everywhere else. Hsuan-Tsang, who visited the country during this period noted the power of the kingdom of Mahārāṣṭra (Mo-ho-la-tch'a) and the war-like zeal of its inhabitants. But shortly thereafter Pulikesi himself became the victim of the conquerors of the South and after him there followed a number of dynasties—the last Cālūkyas of Badami, the Rāṣṭrakūṭas of Nasik and of Malkhed, the Cālūkyas of Kalyan and the Yādavas of Devagiri—perpetually at war, where the frontiers get narrowed and extended in turn : but all, in short, maintain in the North the limit fixed by Pulikesi.

The dialects spoken to the south of this constantly defended frontier had, therefore, some chance of experiencing, less than others, the infiltrations from the languages of Hindustan. It has been noted later on that the resistance of the Marathas to the influence of Delhi had been strong enough to make the contribution of Hindi and chiefly of Persian comparatively weak in their language (see Ranade, *Rise of the Maratha Power*, p. 27 ff.). On the other hand inside the Deccan itself, the instability of the dynasties and the continuous shift of the centres of influence must have contributed, early enough, to the formation of a composite common language. As a consequence, despite the administrative unification realised later by Shivaji and his successors and which had imposed the dialect of Poona particularly, it is explained that the Marathi vocabulary and phonetics betray the mixture, renovated during all the periods and do not offer the relatively coherent aspect of a language based on a predominant dialect.

It need not be observed that in Marathi as elsewhere, the influence of Sanskrit, strong in all the periods, has only increased during the course of time. Bhandarkar observes that the chief reason for the obscurity of the old poets is due to the substitution of Sanskrit loan-words for words having had a natural evolution, thus *gambhir*, "deep", *nāth* "master", *prasād* "favour" have replaced *gahiru*, *nāh*, *pasāy* (JAS *Bombay*, XVI, p. 259). The pronunciation itself has been adapted to Sanskrit phonetics and the Marathas are capable of correctly articulating the phonemes which Marathi, properly called, has lost, such as *ṛ*, *kṣ* and other groups of consonants (except *jñ* become *dñ*). Naturally the Sanskrit element will be passed over in silence in this work designed not to be the description of a language, but to be the history of its formation.

$ 25. The Marathi dialect which is used as a common language is that of *deś*, that is to say of the region situated between the Ghats and the frontier of Berar. It has been the political centre of Maharashtra during all the periods and most of the Marathi poets have come from this region. Citing only those whose texts have been used, we have first, Dñānadev, born at Aḷandi, near Poona. He is the author of *Jñāneśvarī*, a versified commentary on the Bhagavadgītā. This poem, written in 1290, is the first literary text in Marathi, whose date is sure. Namdev, probably as old as Dñānadev, wrote in a less archaic language. He lived at Pandharpur, near the shrine of Viṭhobā, who inspired his hymns. Similarly Eknath, who revised the text of *Jñāneśvarī* in 1584, was a Brahmin of Paithan. Tukaram, 1608-1649, the greatest and the most popular of all, hailed from Dehu, near Poona.

The dialect of *Deś* is, therefore, spoken by the cultivated classes all over the Maratha territory and represents Marathi in the rest of India, for example at Bijapur, in Kannada territory, and even at Tanjore, in an entirely Tamil domain, or again in the courts of princes of Baroda and Indore. Beside this dialect, there are a number of *patois* whose individuality is marked by the names received by them in indigenous usage. It is no use enumerating them and giving their detailed descriptions here. This has been done, as is known, with abundant information in the volume of the *Linguistic Survey of India* devoted to Marathi. Most of the information given here is drawn therefrom.

Moreover, all these speeches are close neighbours of one another and the only ones that are clearly distinct from the common language are those of Konkan, or at least of a part of Konkan. Grierson distinguishes to the west of the Ghats two groups of speeches, in the north and in the centre, the Marathi of Konkan. Its dominant forms are the Parbhi or the dialect of Prabhu spoken from Daman to Bombay and the Saṅgameśwarī or the language of Saṅgameśwar (near Ratnagiri), spoken from Bombay to Rajapur. The second group comprises Konkani proper : its most common varieties are the speeches of Goa, of Malwan and that of the Chitpawan Brahmins of Ratnagiri. Due to its geographical characteristics and because of its population (the Prabhus, the Kolis and the Thakurs are found in Gujarat), Konkan is linked with the region of Surat and Gujarat. The same is true for the language also. The common traits are more striking and numerous in the south. Let us point out here the nominative sing. masc in *-o* (common Marathi *-ā*), the plural neuter in *-āṁ* (common Marathi *-eṃ*), the pronoun of the First person sing. *hāṃv* (common Marathi *mī*) and the infinitive in *uṃ* (com. Mar. *-ṇeṃ*). The "Konkan Marathi" ignores these shades, but it has, however, in common with Konkani and Gujarati a large share of vocabulary and an exceptional construction for the past tense of the verb. It seems, therefore, that in principle Konkan was an intermediary region between Gujarat and the Deccan. The influence of the speech of *Deś*, particularly strong in the northern and central region, covers this old relationship between Konkani and Gujarati.

$ 26. The direct heir of Prākrit, remaining relatively free from foreign influences, represented by an abundant literature and partially near enough the spoken language, Marathi moreover presents, for study, the practical advantage of being well known. The dictionary of Molesworth, in reality the work of a group of local scholars, is the best available dictionary of any modern Indo-Aryan language. Its vocabulary is very rich, and moreover contains, besides an etymological part though incomplete and naturally inadequate, precious indications concerning the dialectal or social origin of the cited words, or concerning their particular sense in the [various] dialects. Adding the grammars of Joshi and Nawalkar to the same, which are atleast as good as any of the grammars written in any native language and the abundant documentation of the Linguistic Survey, we possess a totality of sufficient and easily verifiable data for European reader. The descriptive part of this work has thereby been rendered light to that extent.

In these conditions, it appears that without waiting for the dialectological or philological studies made by local scholarship and whose results will bring more certainty in many questions, an European reader could usefully benefit from the progress realised by Indology since the times when Beames did the inaugural work for the comparative grammar of modern Indo-Aryan and when Bhandarkar in his *Wilson Lectures* tried to make the first effort for englobing the entire history of Indo-Aryan. Speaking only of the language, enough is known and it will be seen later on each page, how the documentation has become richer and how research has been made easy by the appearance of Pischel's *Prakrit grammar* and by the several works fromthe pen of or due to the inspiration of Grierson. General Linguistics has also progressed during this period and the new points of view enable us to see a bit more clearly the history of the Indo-Aryan languages or at leas to pose the problems regarding the same in a more precise manner.

Lower down will be seen the list of major works or documents used in this work, but this is the place to point out that

I have not limited myself to a study of the books alone. R. G. Bhandarkar has added to his encouragement, the loan of the *MSS* of his last *Wilson Lectures*, unhappily still unpublished. If I have not generally cited the same, it is because the major argument has already appeared in the grammar by Joshi, who has also been able to consult the same. Besides Bhandarkar, V. B. Patwardhan, V. K. Rajvade, P. R. Bhandarkar and T. K. Laddu, other Maratha scholars have also helped me in various ways. By thanking them here by a brief mention, I do not forget that I have been able to benefit from their learning, thanks to the two successive missions of the *Ecole Française d' Extrême Orient*.

In Europe also I am under obligation to more than one. But I do not wish to name other than my teachers, Sylvain Lévi and A. Meillet. This work is based on their teaching and its appearance is due to their encouragement and their advice.

BIBLIOGRAPHY

$ 27. The books or texts most frequently used or cited in an abbreviated form in this study are given below:—

For Indo-European :

Meillet, *Introduction á l'étude comparative des langues indo-européennes*, 3rd edn., Paris, 1912 (Meillet, *Introduction*).

For Sanskrit :

J. Wackernagel, *Altindische Grammatik*, I and II, I, Göttingen. 1896-1905 (Wackernagel denotes the first volume).

W. D. Whitney, *A Sanskrit Grammar*, 3rd edn., Leipzig-London, 1896 (Whitney)

J. S. Speyer, *Vedische und Sanskrit Syntax* (Grundriss der indo-arischen Philologie), Strassburg, 1896.

Uhlenbeck, *Kurzgefasstes Etymologisches Wörterbuch der Altindischen Sprache*, Amsterdam, 1898-1899.

A. Walde, *Lateinisches etymologisches Wörterbuch*, 2. Aufl. Heidelberg, 1910.

For Middle Indian :

E. Senart, *Les inscriptions de Piyadasi*, 2 vols, Paris, 1881-1886 (Senart).

O. Franke, *Pali und Sanskrit*, Strassburg, 1902.

E. Müller, *Pali Grammar, London*, 1884.

H. Lüders, *Bruchstücke buddhistischer Dramen*, Berlin, 1911, (Lüders, *Bruchstücke*).

R. Pischel, *Grammatik der Prakrit-Sprachen* (Grundriss der indo-ar. Phil.), Strassburg, 1900 (Pischel).

The research in this work has been largely facilitated thanks to the work of Don M. de Zilva Wickremasinghe, "Index of all the Prakrit words occurring in Pischel's *Grammatik der Prakrit-Sprachen*", reprinted from the *Indian Antiquary*, Bombay, 1909.

" " *Materialien Zur Kenntuiss der Apabhraṁśa* (Abh. der Kgl. Ges. Wiss. Göttingen, Phil.-Hist. Kl., Neue Folge, V, 4), Berlin 1902 (Pischel, *Materialien*).

„ „ *The Deśīnāmamāla of Hemacandra*, pt. I, Text and critical notes, Bombay, 1800. For convenience the commentary has been cited, the figures relate to the page and the line of Pischel's edn.

H. Jacobi, *Ausgewählte Erzählungen in Māhārāṣṭrī*, Leipzig, 1886 (Jacobi, *Ausgew. Erz.*, the paragraphs refer to the grammatical introduction).

For Modern Languages :

General works or articles :—

J. Beames, *A Comparative Grammar of the Modern Aryan Languages of India* ; to wit, Hindi, Panjabi, Sindhi, Gujarati, Marathi, Oriya and Bengali, 3 Vols., London, 1872, 1875, 1879 (Beames).

R. Hoernle, *A Comparative Grammar of the Gaudian Languages*, with special reference to the Eastern Hindi, London, 1880 (Hoernle).

R. G. Bhandarkar, *Wilson Lectureship* : Development of Language and of Sanskrit, Pali and other dialects of the Period; Relations between Sanskrit, Pali, the Prakrits and the Modern Vernaculars (*Journal of the Bombay Branch of the Royal Asiatic Society*, Vol. XVI, p. 245-345); —The Prakrits and the Apabhraṃśa (ibid., Vol. XVII, p. 1-48). Cf. Introd., $ 26.

G. A. Grierson, "On the Phonology of the Modern Indo-Aryan Vernaculars", ZDMG., XLIX, p. 393-421; L. p. 1-42 (Grierson, *Phon.*).

„ „ "On Certain Suffixes in the Mod. Indo-Aryan Vernaculars", KZ., XXXVIII, p. 473-491 (Grierson, *Suffixes*).

„ „ "On the Radical and Participial Tenses of the Modern I.A. Language" *JAS. Beng.*, LXIV, 1895, p. 352-375.

„ „ *The Languages of India*, being a reprint of the chapter on languages contributed...to the Report on the Census of India, 1901. Calcutta, 1903.

For languages other than Marathi :

G. A. Grierson, *Linguistic Survey of India*, being published. As regards the Indo-Aryan languages, besides the volume on Marathi, have already appeared, the volumes noted below :—

Vol. V, Eastern Group, pt. I, *Bengali and Assamese*

Languages,
pt. II, *Bihari and Oriya Languages*,
Vol. VI, Mediate Group, *Eastern Hindi Language*,
Vol. IX, Central Group, pt. II, *Rajasthani and Gujarati Languages*,
pt. III, *Bhil Languages, including Khandesi, Banjari or Labhaṇi, Bahurupia, etc.*

Rasamay Mitra and B. N. Ghosal, *A Dictionary of Bengali Language*, Vol. I, Bengali and English, abridged from Dr. Carey's *Quarto Dictionary*, 12th edn. Calcutta, 1906.

Rāmakamala Vidyālankāra, *The Prakritibada* or an illustrated etymological dictionary of the Sanskrit and Bengali languages, 5th edn., revised...by S. C. Karmakāra, Calcutta, 1901.

G. A. Grierson, "An Introduction to the Maithili Dialect of the Bihari Language", pt. I, grammar, *J. and Proc. of the As. Soc. Bengal*, Vol. V, ext No. 2, 1909..., Calcutta 1910, (Grierson, *Maithili Gram.*).

S. H. Kellogg, *A Grammar of the Hindi Language*, in which are treated the High Hindi, Braj, and the Eastern Hindi of the *Ramayan* of Tulsi Das as also the colloquial dialects of Rajputana, Kumaon etc., 2nd edn., London, 1893 (Kellogg, *Hindi Gram.*).

E. Greaves, *A Grammar of Modern Hindi*, Banaras, 1896 (Greaves, *Hindi Gram.*).

J. T. Platts, *A Dictionary of Urdu, Classical Hindi and English*, London 1884.

S. W. Fallon, *A New Hindustani-English Dictionary*, Banaras, 1879.

W. St. Clair Tisdall, *A Simplified Grammar and Reading Book of the Panjabi Language*, London, 1889 (Tisdall, *Panj. Gram.*).

" " *A Simplified Grammar of the Gujarati Language*, London, 1892, (Tisdall, *Guj. Gram.*).

J. Wilson, *Grammar and Dictionary of Western Panjabi*, as spoken in the Shahpur Distt., Lahore, 1899.

O. Brien, J. Wilson and Pandit H. K. Kaul, *Glossary of the Multani Language, or S-W. Panjabi*, Lahore, 1903.

E. Trumpp, *Grammar of the Sindhi Language*, London- Leipzig,

1872 (Trumpp).

G. Shirt, Udharam Thakurdas, S. F. Mirza, *A Sindhi-Gujarati Dictionary*, Karachi, 1879.

M. B. Belsare, *An Etymological Gujarati-English Dictionary*, Ahmedabad, 1904.

G. A. Grierson, *The Piśāca Langs. of N-W. India*, London, 1906 (Grierson, Piś. Lang.).

„ „ *A Manual of the Kāśmiri Language*, 2 Vols., Oxford, 1911 (Grierson, *Man. Kaś.*).

F. Miklosich, *Ueber die Mundarten und die Wondernngen der Zigeuner Europa's*, VII-XII Extr. des Vols. XXVI-XXXI des Denkshr. der Phil.-Hist. Kl. der Kais. Ak Wiss. Wien, 1877-1880 (Miklosich) The fasc. VII and VIII contain a comp. vocabulary, IX phonetics, X theme-formation, XI declension and conjugation, XII syntax.

F. N. Finck, *Die Sprache der Armenischen Zigeuner*, Mêm de l'Acad. des Sc. de St.-Petersburg, VIIIth ser., Vol. VIII, 5, St. Petesburg, 1907.

W. Geiger, *Etymologie des Singhalesischen*, Grund. der indo-ar. Phil., Ch., XXI, 2, Munich, 1897.

„ „ *Litteratur und Sprache der Singhalesen*, Grund der indo-ar. Phil., Strassburg, 1900, The abbreviation, Geiger, refers to the second part devoted to grammar, p. 26 ff.

For Marathi :—

G. A. Grierson, *Linguistic Survey of India*..., *Specimens of the Marathi Language* (this Vol. has been prepared by Mr. Sten Konow), Calcutta, 1905 (*LSI*, *Mar.*). Contains besides the specimens and their translation, a linguistic map of Marathi, an important introduction as also a bibliography.

J. T. Molesworth, *A Dictionary of Marathi and English*, 2nd edn., Bombay, 1857 (Molesworth). With an important preface and notes by John Wilson comprising among other things a short summary of the literary history of Marathi.

Reo. Ganpatrao R. Navalkar, *The Student's Marathi Grammar*, 3rd edn., Bombay, 1894 (Navalkar).

K.S. Godbole, *A New Grammar of the Marathi Language*, 3rd edn., Bombay, 1895 (in Marathi only the title and notices are translated into English).

R. B. Joshi, *A Comprehensive Marathi Grammar*, 3rd or English edn., Poona, 1900 (Joshi).

V. K. Rajwade, *Śrī Jñāśvarāṃīl Marathi bhāṣa ceṁ vyākaraṇ* (Grammar of the Marathi of *Jñāneśwari*), Dhulia, Śaka 1831; Essay of the historical grammar of Marathi-insufficient. The same author has published several articles on the history of Marathi declension in the *Śri Sarasvati Mandir* of Bombay, Śaka 1830; on the etymology of a certain number of words in the same periodical, Śaka 1826 and 1829 and in the *Granthamālā*, Bombay, February, 1906 and lastly in these very reviews and in *Viśva-vṛtta*, Kolhapur, several articles concerning chiefly the un-published documents of old dates : some of these will be reproduced later. The grammar of the language of *Jñāneśwarī* was published in an edn., of this poem, reviewed in JA, 1909, I, p. 564 ff.

The citations of *Jñāneśwarī* have been taken from the edition of R. V. Madgamkar, *Śrī Jñānadevakṛtā Bhāvārthadīpikā Jñānadevī* (*Jñāneśwarī*), Bombay, 1907. This edition contains a useful critical apparatus, although the MSS cited are neither described nor classified. Pages 11 to 16 contain a list of archaic forms which have been used for the history of declension. At the end is to be found a vocabulary of over two hundred pages giving the sense of certain difficult or old words, with exact references.

For other poets, it has been sufficient to consult the extracts given in a school anthology, the *Navnīt athavā Marathi kavitāṁ ce vece* of Paraśuram Pant Tātya Godbole, 5th edn., revised by N. B. Godbole, Bombay, 1907.

We have, lastly, utilised the old prose-texts, almost all epigraphical. We have thought it useful to collect all of them at the end of the work.

PHONETICS

Generalities

$ 28. The Indo-Aryan languages current to the east of the Indus can be distinguished from one another chiefly by their grammatical forms. Their phonetic system is, on the contrary, considerably identical, at least as long as one limits oneself to observing the essential characteristics which faithfully reproduce those of Middle Indian. However, on examining the phonetics of any one of these languages separately, we find it to have contradictions and irregularities without number. This is due to the fact that in all of them the vocabulary has been subject to multiple infiltrations. During all the periods, Gangetic India and the Deccan have had a common civilization and all its regions have been united by constant relationships. But this unity came from the uniformity of the social system and not because of the durable pre-eminence of a centre of expansion. No region of India has imposed its language on the entire country, no province has imposed its dialect on the entire Maharashtra. Since then there was nothing to stop a dialect from the tendency of borrowing; this tendency could work all the more easily because each of the castes could independently enrich its vocabulary with elements, which it would, in its turn, contribute to the common language.

We thus find that within each dialect there is a large quantity of words or series of words which have had a history independent of the dialects where they have been found in use. This history, which can be established with some difficulty even in the case of well-known languages as those of Europe, is altogether impossible, atleast provisionally, in India. We should be content to observe and if possible, to classify the irregularities caused by these borrowings in each of these speeches without explaining them.

In Marathi, the proportion of these mixtures seems to be less than elsewhere, at least in so far as it concerns the modern period. But it will be sufficient to recall what is said below regarding numeration to see how even a series of generally ancient and homogenous vocabularies presents difficulties and contradictions from the point of view of phonetics. We should, therefore, be ready to find in Marathi, on the one hand simple and general rules, which are common to this language and to the majority of the Indo-Aryan languages. On the other hand there is a large number of generally inexplicable peculiarities, which gives a confused and complicated aspect to the phonetics of Marathi.

VOWELS

Elements of Marathi Vocalism

$ 29. We have seen, in $ 3, that Middle Indian possessed the vowels *a*, *i*, *u*, short and long and *e*, *o*, normally long. The timbre of these vowels has remained unchanged in Marathi. Examples are: *āg* (*agni-*), *tin* (*trīṇi*), *pūt* (*putra-*) *yeneṃ* (*eti*), *tel* (*taila-*), *jot* (*yoktra-*), *cor* (*caura-*). The old diphthongs having been eliminated in Middle Indian, all the Marathi diphthongs are recent in origin and are due either to the contact of two vowels formerly separete as in *pri-* (*prati-*), *cauthā* (*caturtha-*), or are due to savant borrowings as in tatsama *gaurav* or *gair* (A. *gair*).

Treatment of the Vowel Ṛ

$ 30. In Middle Indian *a*, *i*, *u* correspond not only to the corresponding Sanskrit vowels, but are also the development of *ṛ*. Three treatments are found in Middle Indian, without the principle of distribution being left to be clearly determined and without the treatment being unique in each of the words (see Pischel, $ 49-53). In Marathi also are found the three treatments and numerous doublets. The examination of words which had a *ṛ* in Sanskrit will furnish a good example of the contradictions presented by Marathi phonetics and the difficulties inherent in explaining the same. —In the list given below can be distinguished the examples attested in Prakrit, more recent examples and the Marathi doublets which will be pointed out therein.

1. Treatment *a* :—found in Prakrit : *aswal* beside *rīs* (*ṛkṣa*; cf. *acchabhalla-*), *kānhā* with reference to tatsama *kiseṇ* (*kṛṣṇa-*), *taṇ* (*tṛṇa-*), *tanh* (*tṛṣṇā*), *dāḍhā* (*dṛḍha-*), *dāvṇeṃ* (if it is from a root *dṛp-*), *pāṭh* (*pṛṣṭha-*), *mau* (*mṛdu-*), *maḍeṃ*, *melā* (*mṛta-*), *māṭhṇeṃ* beside *miṭṇeṃ* (*mṛṣṭa-*), *māṭī* (*mṛttikā*), *sāṃkhal* (*śṛṅkhalā*). Both *dākhirṇem* and *dekhṇeṃ* should be left aside : the former goes back, undoubtedly, not to *dṛś-* but to *drākṣ-* and the second results from the analogy of the Pkt *pekh-*, Skr. *prekṣ-*

(see Pischel, $ 554 and note 10),—The words *kac* (*kṛtyā*) and *paḍkay* (*-kṛti*) go back to *deśī* origins.

The following are found only from a recent date : *kātyā* (*kṛttikā-*, could have been influenced by *kārtika-*), *ghāṭṇeṃ* beside *ghusaḷṇeṃ* (*ghṛṣṭa*), *tāṭh* (*tṛṣṭa-*) and probably *bāhṇeṃ* (*bṛh-*). The word *saḍhal* is opposed to Skr *śithila-*, Pkt *siḍhla-* (see Wackernagel, $ 16).

2. Treatment *i* :—found in Prakrit : *riṇ* (*ṛṇa-*), *rīs* beside *aswal* (*ṛkṣa-*), *iṭī* (*ṛṣṭi-*), *kivaṇ* (*kṛpaṇa*), *kisāṇ* (*kṛṣāṇa-*), *ghī* (*ghṛta-*), *gheṇeṃ* (*gṛh-*., possibly *grahi-*), *tīj*, cf. *aḍīc* (*tṛtīya-*), *disṇeṃ* (*dṛśya-*), *dīṭh* (*dṛṣṭi-*), *bhiṃgruṭī* (*bhṛṅga-*), *śiṃg* (*śṛṅga-*), *śīṭ* (*sṛṣṭi-*, the *a* of *nisaṭṇeṃ*, cf. Skr *niḥsṛṣṭi*-is undoubtedly due to its position inside the word, see $ 43), *hiyyā* (*hṛdaya-*).

Recent :—*taisā* (*tādṛśa-*), *miṭṇeṃ* with reference to *māṭhṇeṃ* (*mṛṣṭa-*), probably also *piṭṇeṃ* (*pṛṣṭa*). The root *khiṃḍ-* is probably a doublet of the Skr. and M. root *khamḍ-*. This can also be possibly a contamination of this latter with *khid-*. The word *viṃcū* (*vṛccikā*, Pkt. *viṃchua-*) has betrayed its nature of a loan because of its *c* which can not come into Marathi from Pkt. *ch*.

3. Treatment *u* :—are found in Pkt.; *ujū* (*ṛju-*), (re. a special treatment in the initial position, which possibly explains the reduplication of *j* in Pkt *ujja-*, see $ 106), *opṇeṃ* (cf. Skr. *arp-*), *guṃthṇeṃ* (cf. Skr. *granth-* and M. *gāṃṭhṇeṃ*), *ghusalṇeṃ* with reference to *ghāṭ* (*ghṛṣ-*), *pāūs* (*prāvṛṣa-*), *pusṇeṃ* (*pṛcch-*).

Modern examples are doubtful : *komṇeṃ* resembles several *Deśī* words where *r* appears, but the exact form of the prototype can not be reconstructed; *nijhūr* is related to *nijharṇeṃ* (Pkt. *nijjharai*, Skr. root *kṣar-*), and *Deśī* has two words *nijjhūra-* and *nijjhara-*, but the preservation of the consonant *r* makes the word a case of suspected contamination, either with other forms of the same root, or even with other words; finally *pohā* (*pṛthuka-*) can be explained both by Pkt. * *pahna-* and *puhna-*.

$ 31. Which is the principle of differentiation among these various treatments ? Firstly it seems that one could appeal to purely phonetic influences. In all the old examples of *ṛ*>*a* except in *mṛdu-*, the vowel of the syllable following *ṛ* is *a*. In the majority of those where *ṛ* is represented by *u*, the following vowel is *u*, or *ṛ* is in contact with a labial consonant (since then the Pkt. *mau-* can be conceived as the result of dissimilation). Finally in several cases where *ṛ* has become *i*, can be observed the presence of an *i* in the neighbouring syllable, or the contact of a sibilant. Similar or analogous principles take into account the Pkt. treatments noted by Pischel, $ 49-51 and also certain Pkt. forms which have penetrated into Sanskrit. Thus are explained the oppositions of *púṇyaḥ* : *niṇyáḥ*, of *kaṅkaṇaḥ* : *kiṅkiṇi* (see Meillet, *Album Kern*, p. 121).

But neither in Sanskrit, nor in Prakrit and not even in Marathi, does phonetics suffice to explain all the cases. It seems that we have also to consider the dialectal mixings and ascribe a partly geographical base to the distribution of certain treatments.

If we go upto the Veda, it will be observed that the most frequent treatment in the Prakritisms which have penetrated therein is *a* : thus *avaṭa-*, *kaṭuka-*, *vikaṭa-*; *aṇu-*, *kaṇa-*, *gaṇa-*, *phaṇ-*, *kaṣati*, *paṣṭha-*, *bhaṣa-*, *iraj-* (see Wackernagel, $ 9, 146, 172, 208). *u* and *i* (*púṇya-*; *niṇyá-*, *śithirá-*, *krìmi-* beside *kṛmi-*, see Wackernagel, $ 16, 19) are rare and are always explained by special phonetic reasons. But the moment we arrive in the *Sūtra* period, the confusion between the different treatments is complete. Similar is the case for Pali, which like Sanskrit, is a mixed literary language.

On the contrary, on examining the various recensions of the inscriptions of Aśoka, despite the mixture which obscures them, a curious distribution is to be found. The version of Girnar ignores the treatment *i* (in *tārisa-* etc. there is probably no *ṛ*, see Wackernagel, Preface, p. XXI, which, however, is contradicted by Brugmann, *Grundriss*, II, 1, p. 496, note). *u* is found only twice and in regard to *paripuchā*, *vuta* are to be found, despite the labial *vaḍhi*, *maga*, *magavya*. Moreover a small group of words shows a significant variation : to *kata*, *daḍha*, *maga*, *magavya*, *vaḍhi* of Girnar corrsepond, at Shahbazgarhi *kiṭ(r)a* beside *kata*, *diḍha*, *mrugo* beside *magavya*, *vuḍhi* beside *vaḍhi* and *vaḍhanaṃ*, at Kalsi *kitaṃñata* with regard to *kata*, *diḍha*, *mige*, *migavya*, *vuḍhānam* beside *vuḍhi* (Senart, *Inscr. de Piyadasi*), II, 330, 348, 369, 370; cf. the observations of T. Michelson, *Am. J. Phil.*, XXX, 428, XXXI, 56, 58;

JAOS, XXXI, 231, 249). This distribution seems to render legitimate the hypothesis that *a* is the dominant treatment in the South-West. The treatment *i* on the contrary seems to belong to the dialects of the north and the east, cf. at Bhabra, *adhigicya* (Skt. *adhikṛtya*) whose eastern character is manifest (see S. Lévi, JA, 1912, II, p. 512.).

The examination of literary languages leads to the same hypothesis. The Middle Indian speeches of the north did not have the fortune of becoming the literary languages. But if the Prakrits of the fragments of Buddhist dramas edited by Lüders know solely the treatment *i*, is it not because they belong to the central and eastern regions. During the classical epoch, if the words, for which several treatments are represented, are examined, it is found that Māhārāṣṭrī has most normally *a*, *i* being in Śaurasenī or Māgadhī (one should leave out the Jaina Prakrits, which are mixed). Thus *kida-*, *ghida-*, are the Śaura. and Māga. forms; cf Mg. *pisṭa*, Śaur. *tiṇa*, *miu-*, *miccu-*, *puṭṭha-*, *vusaka-*, *diḍha-* beside *daḍha-* (Pischel, $ 49, 52, 53).

If we now return to Marathi, it is found firstly that the forms, where Skt. *ṛ* is represented by *i* or *u*, are found in the cognate languages of the continent, except, naturally, when the words themselves are missing in these languages. Moreover the form containing *a* : dāḍhā, *mau*, *maḍeṃ*, *melā*, *saḍhaḷ*, (*ghi*, *taisā*, which are exceptions, are the universal words in India). And when there is hesitation in modern languages, Marathi prefers the forms in *a* : *taṇ*, *tānh*, *pāṭh* *mātī*, *sāṃkhal*. Now, for example, Hindi has for these words *tin*, *tis* (*tṛṣā*), *pīṭh*, *miṭṭī* (beside *maṭṭī*), *sīkaḍ* (beside *sāṃkal*, cf. Bgl. *Śikhal*). On the other hand Gujarati and Simhalese are the only languages having *a* in the corresponding position of Skr. *tṛṇa*. Simhalese alone with Marathi continues the Pkt. *accha-* simultaneously with *riccha* (*ṛkṣa-*). Of the M. group *māṭhṇeṃ* : *mitṇeṃ*, Simhalese only knows the former. On certain points Gujarati and Simhalese go farther than Marathi : they are the only ones having an *a* for the *ṛ* of Skr. *hṛdaya-*, M. *hiyyā* (a word of literary language, undoubtedly borrowed from some other dialect). Simhalese has only an *a* in the words corresponding to M. *gheṇeṃ*, *Śiṃg*, *Śīṭ*.

We are, therefore, led to suppose that the variations of treatment of *ṛ* in Marathi are explained, not only by phonetic influences, but also by the mixing due to borrowing from the dialects of Central India, undoubtedly going back to an extremely early period and renewed since then. Leaving aside these borrowings, Marathi belongs in so far as the treatment of *ṛ* is concerned, to a south-western dialectal group, to which also belong Gujarati and Simhalese.

CHANGES DEPENDING ON THE PLACE OF VOWELS IN THE WORD

Preliminaries : *Accent*

$ 32. Although Marathi vocalism has been constituted with the same elements as that of Middle Indian, the Marathi vowels in certain cases do not always agree with the corresponding Prakrit vowels. The latter have, in effect, been subjected to a variable evolution depending on their place in the word.

1. The final syllables of polysyllabic words have all dropped out. Therefore, save certain archaic forms, all final Marathi vowels have resulted from the contraction of the old final vowel with the old penaltimate vowel.

2. The penultimate vowels have survived; they have preserved their timbre and, when short, have become long. The old penultimate syllable has become, in Marathi, the final syllable and the rhythmic summit of the word : thence the use of rhyme in Marathi poetry.

3. The elements preceding the penultimate have lost their quantity and even if, they had been in an interior syllable, they have lost their own timbre.

The analogy shown by these alterations with those undergone by Latin words in Roman languages has often been noted, and it has been generally inferred that they were also due to the action of the accent of penultimate intensity, combined with an initial counter-accent, as given in the Darmesteter formula (see for ex. Beames, I, p. 17 ff., cf. Brandreth, 'The Gaurian compared with the Romance languages,' JRAS, 1879, p. 287 ff., 1880, p. 334 ff.). As a consequence the phonetic history of modern Indo-Aryan is prefaced by an account of accent and its history (see Grierson, *Phon.*, p. 395 ff.; Geiger $ 4 ff.). This method would be necessary, if the existence and the laws of the accent had been established for each period. But the history of the accent and as a consequence the effect of its action are more difficult to determine than it appears at first sight.

$ 33. As regards the old period, there is an absolute

lack of positive data. Neither the literature nor the grammatical texts furnish us with any clear indication. It can, however, be presumed that if the accent of intensity had been noticeable in the classical period, the teaching relating to the Vedic tone would have had its equivalent in the study of the *bhāṣā*, at the cost of certain corrections or even of misunderstandings. This would have been almost certainly the case if the accent of intensity had taken the place of the old tone, as suggested by Pischel (see $46). Jacobi has justly dealt with this view; in his opinion the accent would have been placed on the first long vowel beginning from the end of the word. Moreover, a secondary accent would have struck the initial. This is not the place to discuss this theory in detail, which besides admits serious exceptions (see Jacobi I.F., XXXI, p. 219); but on reading the article of Jacobi (ZDMG, XLVII, p. 574 ff.), it will be seen that the weakness of the finals, all that is known of the Indo-European rhythm and the ordinary laws of Prakrit contraction suffices to explain the majority of cited examples, especially if note is taken of the presence of numerous tatsamas in Prakrit. One should, however, note the curious rules of the *phiṭsūtras* of Śāntanava cited by Jacobi (KZ, XXXV, p. 586) and which are said to yield traces of a tone placed according to a rhythmic rule beside a traditional one. Is this second tone in reality an accent of intensity ? In all, the presence of an accent is not proved for the ancient period. It should even be recalled that the theories on this subject start from the observations of scholars of German origin (Haug, Bühler) on the modern pronunciation of Sanskrit—observations likely to have been falsified by a prejudice natural to these scholars, and which are, besides, contradicted by not only my personal experience, but also by phonographic recordings (see Felber, "die indische musik der Ved. u der klass. zeit," *Sitzsher, kais. Akad. Wiss. Wien, phil.-hist. kl, CLXX*, VII, 1912, p. 77 ff.).

$ 34. A description of the modern accent is, also, difficult and not certain. Beames admits his incapability of advancing a satisfactory theory. He alleges that the subject, obscure in all the cases, is particularly so in the languages that have passed a long period of their existence without any literature (I, p. 17,21). Evidently this reason is false but an author with such a clear and penetrating mind would have undoubtedly determined the laws of accent in the Indo-Aryan languages, if observation had been even a little easier. One fact is certain, it is that where others point out the accent, they present it as very rarely marked and as getting mixed up with quantity. This, for example, is the case in Bihar (see Grierson, *Maith. Gram.*, $ 28). In Hindi, Greaves says that accent does not exist (*Hindi Gram.*), $ 26). With less firmness, Kellogg says practically the same thing ("...although unquestionably existing (accent) is much less marked than in English and is quite subordinate in importance to quantity..." $ 35). Almost everywhere else, the grammarians agree in not mentioning the accent. In Bengali Anderson notes the existence of a phrase which, as for example in French, renders the accent of the word insignificant (see JRAS, 1912, p. 1074-5). In Marathi, Joshi admits its existence and "generally" puts it on the penultimate, or on the final if it is long ($ 176). Navalkar expresses himself as follows ($ 39), "In Marathi, each word is pronounced by an equal tone, the initial syllable alone being, during the effort of pronunciation, lightly raised above others. But accent, in the sense of *increased intensity* as in English, is unknown to Marathi, except in the three cases given below. "The cases cited by him are those of a vowel followed by two consonants (*ghaṭṭ*, *pakkā*; *Śabda*, *bakka*, etc.), of a short one followed by an anusvāra (*baṇḍ*, etc.) and of a vowel followed by a visarga (*duḥkha*, etc.). It can be easily seen that all these are consonantal groups, and result from borrowed words, either from Sanskrit or from other modern languages. Finally, and this is a particularly characteristic fact, the grammars written in indigenous languages (Goḍbole, Ciplūṇkar) totally omit the question of accent. Besides, recently collected evidence shows that the indigenous people have neither any idea of the accent nor a word for designating the same.

$ 35. Moreover, by accepting the current descriptions of Sanskrit and modern accent, one could not surely establish a link between the two periods. The abbreviation and the discolouration of interior vowels have been produced at different times and they do not have the character of necessity and consistence which would be expected if they had been solely due to intensity. The lengthening of the penultimate vowels become finals can also be explained in another way. Cases have been found where the dropping of the final vowels alone determines the lengthening of the preceding vowel (see Streitberg, IF, III, p. 310-11). Moreover, the Marathi lengthening is recent in origin. This difficulty is found not only in Marathi. In the course of constructing a theory of accent for other languages, scholars have encountered a number of contradictions. Geiger ($ 4) is forced to suppose two different periods in the history of intensity in Simhalese and two different strata in the languages. In his general explanation of Indo-Aryan phonetics (*Phon.*, p. 398-99), Grierson has had to admit the attractions of the accent of one syllable on the other and the absorptions of the principal accent by the counter-accent. What else can then be said except that the history of accent can not be construed in a continuous manner.

$ 36. It will also be useful to recall that all the facts of dissimilation pointed out below depend on laws which, according to the researches of Grammont, do not pre-suppose the accent of intensity.

Therefore it is useful to take into consideration the regular variations of quantity and even the timbre of vowels as depending on a purely quantitative rhythm. This will be done in what follows.

A. *Final Vowels*

$ 37. Following the loss of the final consonants in Sanskrit, Middle Indian had only known words ending in vowels. The characteristic weakness of the final element of the word, then, affected these vowels. It seems that the first trace of this phenomenon can already be found in the inscriptions of Aśoka : in the eastern versions of the Pillar-edicts, the final *ā* is written short (see T. Michelson, IF, XXXIII, p. 228-39; cf. Meillet, JA, 1908, II, p. 312). But undoubtedly because the abbreviated final long vowel had, however, remained longer than the non-final short vowels, all the literary Prakrits have preserved the traditional spelling upto a late date. In classical Prakrit, sometimes final -*ā* is found abbreviated : but this happens under morphologically determined conditions. Thus *jaha*=Skr. *yathā*, *va* =Skr *vā*, etc. can be explained according to the interpretation of T. Michelson, as doublets of Indo-European origin. The terminations of the third sing.

of the aorist in *-tthā* : *ttha* are in any case obscure (Pischel, $ 547, c.f $ 520). As regards the absolutives in *-ua* (*kadua, gadua,* etc., Pischel, $ 581) of the eastern dialects, which seem to recall the spelling of the eastern edicts of Aśoka, one may at least see therein a contmination of *tvā* with *ya*. There remain two facts of abbreviation which are sure and are common to all the classical Prakrits. 1. All nasalised long vowels become short in the final position (Pischel, $ 83). 2 *-e* and *-o* also become short and are written as *-i* and *-u* from the time of the fragments found by Dutreuil de Rhins and in Prakrit texts in verse (Pischel, $ 85). Probably the abbreviation and the closing of the final *-o* have, to some extent, contributed to the disappearance, general in Prakrit, of the middle conjugation to the benefit of the active conjugation (see Pischel, $ 452).

In almost all the modern Indo-Aryan speeches, the final vowels have dropped out. The only exceptions are Bihari (see Grierson, *Maith. Gram.*, $ 8-10), Kashmiri, Sindhi (see Grierson, *Phon*, $ 400) and Simhalese (see Geiger, $ 28, 2c, $ 30). In Marathi final vowels survive only in the middle part of the Konkan, where all of them are short. This survival is undoubtedly due to the influence of Dravidian habits (see LSI, *Mar.*, p. 167, 188, 189). This exception apart, there are no final vowels in Marathi which are not archaisms or are the product of contractions, or finally the result of similar innovations.

$ 38. The dropping of *-a*, short or long, pure or nasal, is anterior to the constitution of Marathi and its traces can be detected only in poetic scansion. On the contrary, *-i* and *-u* have continued longer. The manuscript tradition of ancient poets is not fixed; but it constantly gives the termination of the dative singular and of the second pers. sing. in *-sī* (mod. *-s*), the termination of the third pers. pl. in *tī* (mod. *-t*), the nom. sing. masc. normal in *-u* and even in *-o* after a vowel, after *v*, *y* and *h*. Thus we read in the *Abhilaṣitārtha-cintāmaṇi* the forms *rāvo nārāyaṇu*. Same is the case in the old inscriptions : at Pandharpur, *phāgani-pur, devarāyāsi, vivaru* (l. 3), *paṇḍitū* (l. 28). Are also to be found in the texts of the 16th century (*Granthamālā*, March, 1902 p. 31-3), *paṭailu* and *pāṭelu, sāvantu, sāmantaḥ*). During the later period at least these spellings are very probably archaic,

It will not be possible to explain without this the incoherence of the tradition. If one finds final *-i* written indifferently short or long in *Hemāḍī*, short in *māli*, *joisi* (Pandharpur, l. 4, 17), it is undoubtedly because during this period final *i* is already common. Therefrom are derived the spellings *jarī*, *tarī* (mod. *jar*, *tar*, Skr. *yarhi*, *tarhi*), *-asī*, *-atī* (mod. *-as*, *at*, Skr *-asi*, *-anti*) etc. of the old literary texts, in forms where it concerns the short *i* in Sanskrit.

Simultaneously along with quantity, the timbre of *-i* and *-u* has changed. Both the phonemes have got mixed up with *-a*. Its proof is to be had in the pronunciation of the enclitic *-c*, which is a dental affricate, whereas the form of this enclitic in old Marathi and in Konkani is *-ci*. Now, it is known that the palatals preserve the old pronunciation before *i* (see infra). A similar example is probably furnished by *-s*, which is added to the nouns of relationships (*ājā-s*, *ājī-s*, etc.) and to the names of divinities (*lāṃv* : *lāṃs* = *Deśī lāmā*). This *s* undoubtedly represents the Skr *-Śrī*. Now the pronunciation of this phoneme is *s* and not *ś*, which proves that *-ī* got mixed up with *a* before disappearing.

The treatment of certain diphthongs in the final position will be examined from $ 60 onwards. Here are given examples of the loss of simple vowels :

$ 39. Pkt. *-a* and *-aṃ* have been dropped in: *āj* (*adya*), *āṭh* (*aṣṭa*), *pāṃc* (*pañca*); nom., acc., neut. *nāṃv* (*nāma*), *jal* (*jalaṃ*), *pān* (*parṇaṃ*); the termination of the inst. sing. in *-eṃ* (*-ena*).

Pkt. *-ā* and *-āṃ* have been lost in nom., -acc., sing. fem. as *āt* (*Deśī attā*), *ās* (*āśā*, *āśāṃ*), *kaḷ* (*kalā*, *kalāṃ*) *vel* (*velā*), *velāṃ*), *vāṭ* (*vartman*), Pkt. fem. *vaṭṭā*, *vaṭṭāṃ*), in the nom. -acc., pl. masc. Skr. *-āḥ*, *-ān*, in the termination of the oblique pl. masc., neut. *-āṃ* developed out of the Skr. *-āṇāṃ* and fem. *-īṃ*, developed out of Skr. *-īnāṃ*. The adverb *haṭh* is obscure; it can not be determined whether it represents the Pkt. *heṭṭhā* or a case (acc. neut. or loc.) of the Pkt. adj. *heṭṭha* (Pischel, $ 107). In Marathi, final *-ā* or *-āṃ* is the result of a contraction : this is the case in the oblique pl. masc. neut. cited above or in the termination of the second pl., where it goes back to Pkt. *-aha*, Skr. *-atha*. Similarly the nom. masc. sing. in *-ā* goes back to the Pkt. *-ao* As regards *sahā* "*six*". *dahā* "ten", their final vowel has been added afterwards.

It should be remarked in passing that final *-āṃ* has been lost in Marathi without having changed its timbre as a preliminary. In the Middle Indian dialects, which are at the origin of certain other languages, the nasality had rendered this vowel into a surd. From there comes the opposition between the termination of the nom. -acc. neut. sing., which in Gujarati is *-uṃ* and the corresponding form of Marathi *-eṃ* (*-akaṃ*). Similarly the word for "hundred", Skr. *śatāṃ*, has become in the languages of the centre and of west, other than Marathi, S. *sau*, G. *śo*, H. Pj. *sau* beside *sai*, whereas we have on the other hand M. *Śeṃ*, H. Pj. *sai*, O. *Śae*, B. *Śaye*, Simh. *Siya*. This is how we can undoubtedly explain the termination of the oblique pl. in Hindi *-oṃ* (*-ānāṃ*) corresponding to the *-āṃ* of Marathi, Rajasthani, Panjabi, Sindhi (and possibly Gujarati). It is not impossible that the enigmatic termination of the first pers. sing. *-ūṃ* of Hindi (*-āmi*) had the same origin. Apabhraṃśa is included among the dialects which have thus unvoiced the final *-aṃ*. It is known that *-aṃ* becomes therein *-u* and that *-akam* becomes *-auṃ* (Pischel, $ 351-52). Similarly the termination of the first pers. sing. there is *-auṃ*. Therefore irrespective of the value of the evidence furnished by the same (cf. $ 22), Apabhraṃśa parts company with Marathi on this important point and is put in the group of the Central dialects. Probably the preservation of the original timbre of the final *-aṃ* in the Middle Indian dialect preceding Marathi has something to do in the preservation of the neuter gender in the nominal declension. In fact,*-aṃ* remained distinct from *-o*, in termination of masculines (*devo*, etc.) On the contrary in those languages where Pkt. *-aṃ* became *-u*, this termination got mixed up with *u* developing out of the Pkt. *-o*.

Pkt. *i* and *iṃ* have been dropped in the nom.-acc. of the nouns in *-i* : *āg* (*agniḥ*, *agniṃ*), *āṃc* (*arciḥ*, *arciṃ*), etc, in the termination of the second pers. sing. present *-s* (*-si*), in that of the third pl. of the same tense *-t* (*-nti*), in the prefix *paḍ-* (*prati-*, Pkt. *paḍi-*) and in the conjunction *paṇ*, anciently *paṇi*.

Pkt. *-ī* and *-īṃ* have been lost in the nom. -acc. sing. and pl. of the fem. nouns of Skr : *-ī*, *-īṃ*, *-in*, as shown in the chapter on declension. *ārāt* (* *ārātri*), *kel* (*kadalī*), *dāvaṃ* (*dāmanī*), etc.; adj. fem. in *-īṇ*, Skr. *-inī* : *dudhīṇ* etc.—The

Marathi nouns in *-ī* go back to Pkt. *-io*, *iā*, *-iaṁ*, for which see the same chapter. The verbal forms—*āthī*, *nāthī* (*asti*, *nāsti*), the pronouns *ahmī*, *tumhī* "us, you" are the forms fixed during their evolution; *jarī*, *tarī* for *jar*, *tar* (*yarhi*, *tarhi*) belong to the poetic language.

Pkt. *u* and *-uṃ* have been dropped in the nom. -acc. sing. of the nouns in *-u* : *taṃt* (*tantu-*), *kāṃg* (*kaṅgu-*), *khāj* (*kharju-*), *jāṃbh* (*jāmbū-*), *pāṃg* (*paṅhu-*), *phāg* (*phalgu-*), *buṃd* (*biṅdu*), *vīj* (*vidyut-*, Pkt. *vijju-*), *hiṃg* (*hiṅgu*); cf. the derivative *Śegaṭ* (*śigru-*).

Examples are lacking for the final *-ū*. It is a morpheme already rare in Sanskrit (Whitney, *Skrt. Gram.*, $ 1179); *-ū* and *-ūṃ* of Marathi go back to Pkt. *-uo*, *-uā*, *-uaṃ*. They frequently answer for the Skr. *-u*, because the Sanskrit stems have been most often enlarged; this is why there are forms like *pāṃgū*, *vijū* beside *pāṃg*, *vīj*, etc.

Skr. *-e* and *-o* got at first reduced to *-i* and *-u* and then were lost; *-e* is attested indirectly in the pronouns *ahmī*, *tumhī*; of it nothing remains in the adverbial forms *ās*, *āspās* which are the old locatives (*aśre*, *pārśve*). Similarly *-o* has been lost in the adverb *āgas* (*agraśaḥ*) and in the nom. sing. masc. It survives only in the pronouns (*jo*, *to*), in the participles used as indicative present (*uṭh-to*, etc, see infra), in *rāo* (*rājan-*) and the nouns whose last consonant is *h* : *kaḷho* (*kalaha-*), *māho* (*māgha-*), *lāho* (*lābha*) *loho* (*loha-*). Moreover Navalkar ($ 104) prefers *ḍoh*, *moh* to *ḍoho*, *moho* and finally in proper nouns like *kanho-bā* (*kṛṣṇa-*), *viṭho-bā* (*viṣṇu-*). The reduced form of the same case will also be found in *kāū* (*kāka-*), *pihū* (*priya-*), in the hypocristics like *Rāmū*, etc. (see Joshi, $ 206a)and in a derivative of the type *mehu-ḍā* (*megha-*).

B. *As Penultimate Syllables*

$ 40. As a general rule, the timbre of the penultimate vowel has been preserved without any change since Prakrit and if it had been short, it had been lengthened.

For *-i* and *-u*, the fact is noted in the script. Example : the termination of feminine in *-īṇ* (Skr. *-inī*) as *pattīṇ*, *rajputīṇ*, etc., *kaṇīs* (kanis; oblique sing. *kaṇsā*), *halīs* (*halīṣā*), tats. *kaṭhīṇ* and *kaḍhīṇ*, *kuṭi*, the termination of the second and third sing.

of the future in -*śīl*, -*īl* (see infra), *gugūl* (*guggulu*), *niṭhūr* (*niṣṭhuṛa-*), *māṇus* (in compositio *māṇas-* : Skr. *mānuṣ*(*y*)*a-*), *lākūḍ* beside *lakḍā* (Skr. *lakuṭa-*), *lasūṇ* beside *lasaṇ* (*laśuna-*), *hiṃgūl* (*hiṅgula-*), tats. *ākūl* (*ākula-*).

For *a* the notation is more hesitating. In a general way, the etymological quantity is preserved. We have, thus, on one side : *kavāḍ* (*kapāṭa*), *kiṣāṇ* (*kṛṣāṇa-*) and on the other *kaval* (*kavala-*), *kāpaḍ* (*karpaṭa-*), *pākhar* (Desī *pakkharā*), *pātaḷ* (Deśī *pattala-*); but *a* is found most often in the case where this vowel precedes an ancient geminated consonant : *āḷas* (*ālasya-*), *karavat* (*karapatra-*), *savat* (*sapatni-*), as regards *umās* (Deśī *ummacchia-*). On the other hand we have *kirāṇ* (*kiraṇa-*) in a tatsama. The treatment of *pahār* (*prahara-*), *vahāṇ* (*upānah-*) on the one hand and of *rahāṭ* (*araghaṭṭa-*) on the other is special and is explained by the presence of the aspiration between two *a*s (see infra). The incertitudes of symbols should create no illusions as regards the quantity of the vowel : in reality the vowel noted as *a* in Devanagari is always long in the final syllable (see Joshi, $ 170).

$ 41. The penultimate syllable of Prakrit has become the final in Marathi, In fact either it had been separated from the final vowel by a geminated consonant and in this case the final vowel of Prakrit has fallen, or the fall of an old intervocalic consonant has put the penultimate and the final vowels in contact and in this case these two vowels have become short. We may, therefore, formulate the rule concerning the lengthening of the Prakrit vowel as follows: *in Marathi the last vowel of of the word is always long.*

As a result of this law all the vowels of the mono-syllabic words are long. Examples : 1. Penultimate : *kac* (*kṛtya-*) also written *kāc*; *kaḷ* (*kalā*), *jaḷ* (*jala-*), pronounced *koec*, *koeḷ*, etc.; *āt* (Deśī *attā*), *ār* (*ajagara-* cf. *arā*), *āg* (*agni-*), *khāj* (*kharju-*), *īṭ* (*iṣṭā*), *gidh* (*gṛdhra-*), *kīr* (*kīla*), *ūs* (*ikṣu-*), *kās* (*kakṣa-*), *pūl* (Pers. *pul*); 2. Finals : *thā* (Deśī *thāha-*), *bīṃ* (*bīja-*), *gahūṃ* (*godhūma-*), etc. —This rule does not apply to accessory words, as *cir* "fast !" (*ciram*), *paṇ* "but" (*punaḥ* Pkt. *pana*), or to pronouns like *to* "he."

The lengthening is of recent date. The old texts do not note it with regularity and a word like *udīd* is still in Deśī *udiḍo*.

$ 42. Exceptions. 1.—The vowels followed by a nasal

and occlusive are long or short, according as they are nasalised or not nasalised and as the nasal has lost or kept its articulation (see $ 68). 2. In a certain number of words, the penultimate vowel of the polysyllabic words has been weakened, in accordance with the rule concerning the interior vowels. We have thus *kilac* beside *kilic* (Deśī *kiliñca-*), *nāraḷ* beside *nārel* (*nārikela-*), *nisān* and *niśīn* (*niḥśreṇi-*), *pares*, *pāras*, and *parīs* (*parīkṣā*), *paral*, *parāḷ* and *pareḷ* (Deśī *pariatī*); *phāṇas* and *phāṇus* (Arab., Pers. *fānūs*), *lasan* and *lasūṇ* (*laśuna-*), *sābaṇ* and *sābūṇ* (Arab. *sābūn*). The form with *ī* or *ū* is missing for *āṃvas* (*amisa-*), *avaḷ* (Deśī *avila-*), *kavaṭh* (*kapittha-*), *puḷaṇ* (*pulina-*), *vaṇaj* (*vāṇijyā-*), *saḍhal* (*Śithila-*), *Śiras* (*śirīṣa-*), *haraṇ* (*hariṇa-*); *kukar-* (*kukkura-*). Similarly is found the shortened *ā*, atleast in appearance, in *iṅgaḷ* (*aṅgāra-*, Pkt. *iṅgāla-*), *paḍkhar* (Deśī *padhikhāro*), *paḷas* (*palāśa-*), *paiṭhaṇ* (*Pratiṣṭhāṇa-*), *māvlaṇ* (*mātulāṇi*), *mhasaṇ* (*Śmaśāna-*) and probably in *āḷas* (*ālasya-*).

All these variants are difficult to explain. No doubt that some words must be put aside, as *pāras* where could be seen a contamination of *parīkṣā* and of *sparśa-*; *kukar*, suspected to be borrowed, the usual word for "dog" being *kutrā*, *kutreṃ*; the short of *kuṃvar* masc. beside *kuṃvār* fem., (*kumāra-*, *kumārī*) is found since Prakrit. The *a* of *hāḷad* (*haridrā*) is also given by Prakrit grammarians (see, however, Pischel, $ 115). But the totality of facts is interpreted with difficulty. Should one see therein the trace of the borrowings of Marathi from the neighbouring dialects ? In fact it is known that Gujarati often reduces *i* and *u* to *a* in all positions (see Grierson, *Phon.*, $ 20, 23) and *avaḷ*, *kukar*, *phaṇas*, *lasaṇ*, *haraṇ*, *haḷas* are actually to be found in this language. In the dictionaries of Hindustani are to be found doublets similar to those of Marathi. If the hypothesis enunciated above were exact, it will be necessary to consider that in the case of Hindustani one of the series would come from a dialect of Rajsthan. But this explanation does not take into account the shortening of *a* : except *kuṃvar*, all the forms cited above belong to Marathi.

It is no less difficult to determine the date of these changes. Prakrit has already got *hāḷadda-*, *kumara-*, *sirisa-*. The Sanskrit of the later period possesses *kurala-* beside *kuruḷa-* : cf. Marathi *kural* and *kurūḷ*. In Desī *ṇīsaṇī* is found by the side of *avila-*, *kilimci*, but the *Jñāneśvari* also writes *āṃvis*, which in the modern language is *āṃvas*, and it is quite possible that *phāṇas* may be a very modern loan.

C. *Before the Penultimate Syllable* :—

$ 43. In the entire part of the word preceding the penultimate syllable of Prakrit, that is to say the final syllable of Marathi, the quantity is uncertain and tends to be short. This law is common to Marathi and to the Panjabi-Hindi-Bihari group, and probably to other languages also (see Grierson, *Phon.*, $ 34, 2, p. 414; *Maithili Gram.* $ 32 ff; Hoernle, $ 25, 146; Beames, I, $ 40). In Marathi, it applies more rigorously to *i* and *u* and more to *e* and *o* than to *a*. For this last phoneme, the shortening appears to be less frequent, and it seems that contradictory actions are produced. But the question is obscured by the fact that the indigenous notation of quantity can also denote the timbre (cf. $ 15). If it is a question of noting open short *ä*, the writing will fatally hesitate between the signs representing *a* and *ā*, which are both of them false, the first in regard to timbre and the second in regard to quantity. However, it is not impossible that the biggest regularity of writing concerning *i* and *u* expresses a real phenomenon. It is known in fact that, all else being equal the closed vowels tend to be pronounced as short as they are more closed (see Meillet, MSL, XV, p. 265-67).

In the initial syllable, only the quantity is effected. As the non-initial syllable, the brevity is pushed to the point where *i*, *u* and even *e*, *o* lose their own timbre and get mixed with *a*. This is why the *e* of *vimcṇī*, for example, is a dental affricate, although the old form was *vimciṇī*. In fact, it will be seen below that the old palatals have lost their hushing character only before *a*, *u* and *o* and have preserved it before *i* and generally before *e*.

1. *As the Initial Syllable* :

$ 44. As the initial syllable, *i* and *u* are always short. Thus beside *gilṇeṃ* (*gil-*), *civaḍṇeṃ* (*cipiṭa-*), *tivaṇ* (*triparṇa-*); *tusār* (*tuṣāra-*), *tuḷas* (*tulasī*), *tulṇeṃ* (*tūl-*), where these vowels are short because of their origin, one also finds, corresponding to old *ī* and *ū* :

jiṇeṃ (*jīv-*), *jirṇeṃ* (*jīrya-*) *pivḷā* (*pītala-*), *piṣṇeṃ* (*piṃs-*, Pkt. *pīs-*), *pīḷṇeṃ* (*pīḍ-*), *kudṇeṃ* (*kūrd-*), *dhutārā* (*dhūrta-*), *purā* (*pūrita-*), *suār* (*sūpakāra-*), *suī* beside *sū* (*sūcī*), where *i* and *u* had been long by nature. They had been so because of position in the old forms of *khijṇeṃ* (*khidya-*), *citā*, *citārī* (*citra-*), *nikāmī* (*niḥkarma-*), *nisaṇ* (*niḥśreṇī*), *bhitar* (*abhyantara-*), *riṭhā* (*ariṣṭaka-*), *ritā*, cf. *rikāmā* (*rikta-*); *kudāla* (*kuddāla-*), *cukṭī* (Deśī *cukka-*), *cukṇeṃ* (Deśī *cukk-*), *duhal* (*duḥkāla-*), *putḷā* (*putra-*), *punav* (*puṃnāga-*), *pusṇeṃ* (*proñch-*), *bujhṇeṃ* (*budhya-*), *bhukuṇeṃ* (*bhukk-*), *rusṇeṃ* (*ruṣya-*).

This law has been generally noted. Firstly a propos of the dissylables terminated by a long vowel as *isāḍ*, derived from *is* (*īṣā*), *kiḍā* (*kīṭaka-*), *gidhāḍ* (*gṛdhra-*), *citā* (*citra-*), *ritā* (*rikta-*); *khujā* (*kubja-*), *cukā* (*cukra-*), *cuḍā* (*cūḍā*), *cunā* (*cūrṇa-*), *jui* (*yūtikā*), *junā* (*jīrṇa*), *juvā*, (*dyūta*), *purā* (*pūrita-*), *pulā* (*pūla-*), *puvā* (*pūpa-*), *mudī* (*mudrikā*), *rui* (Deśī *rūvī*), *sukā* (*śuṣka-*), *sugī* (Pkt. *sugga-*), *śunā* (*śūnya-*); cf. Grierson, *Phon.*, $ 13. Secondly, as regards the compounds like *dhūpāṃgrā* (*dhūp*+*aṃgārā*), *phulel* (*phul*+*tel*), see Grierson, ibid, $ 34. In this case orthography often dissimulates the abbreviation, but we should not be misled by the same. On the word *kūlkarṇī*, Molesworth, has this to say, "This form of spelling is desirable, for system is desirable; but the People favour it not"; and he refers back to *kulkarṇi*, which is the form in vogue.

As has been seen, the abbreviation is not limited to these two cases and occurs in all types of words. Thereby Marathi is the opposite—at least if we trust the writing—to languages bordering it in the east. In the North, Gujarati does not distinguish between the quantity of *i* and *u* in writing (see Beames, I, 151) and often transforms *i* and even *u* into *a* (see LSI, *Rajasth.*, p. 329). Marathi is, therefore, possibly not isolated and is a part of, from the view-point of initial vowels, of a western group.

As a consequence of the observation made above, a word like *pīḍṇeṃ* is borrowed or re-made on *piḍ-*. Similarly a word like *jīvā* "bow-string" (*jyā*) is betrayed by its form like a tatsama.

$ 45. As regards *e* and *o*, orthography does not generally enable us to observe the same phenomenon. But the

Kannada script, which notes short *ĕ* and *ŏ*, enables us to recognise in the central dialects a gradation *ek* : *ekā*, *lok*: *lôkā* similar to that of *kīḍ*: *kiḍā*, etc. (see LSI, *Mar.*, p. 168, 194). The closing consecutive upon abbreviation has been noted more than once in the script : thus *dikīl* "will see", from *dekh*, *hutā* "was" from *ho* (ibid., p. 122). The same abbreviation is indirectly revealed in the equivalences *a* and *o* in *cotkar*, *catkar* for *catkor* (*cauth*+*kor*) , *gamūtra* for the tatsama *gomūtra*, etc., cf. also the form *kupīṇ* for Skr. *kaupīna-*, *gurūṃ* (*gorūpa-*), and *gahūṃ* (*godhūma-*).

If we judge by the form *akrā* (*ekādaśa*, Pkt. *ekkaraha*) whose initial vowel has, besides, an enigmatic timbre, this phenomenon must go back far in to the past.

One should not, however, consider all initial *es* or *os* as short on the same count as the short *i*, for example. Radical *e* or *o* notably tend to remain long. Beside *ĕkā-lā*, dative of *ek*, we have *ěklā* "alone", derived from the same word. Similar is the case with the verbs *ṭhepṇeṃ*, etc. On the other hand, we pronounce *mī tyālā bheṭlom hôtôṃ*. "I have called on him", but under the influence of the rhetorical accent, the *e* of *tethwar* "upto that' (*tatropari*) will be pronounced clearly long. The question is all the more complicated by the frequent exchange of *e* and *i*, of *o* and *u*, which goes back to Prakrit and which will be discussed later.

$ 46. As in the case of *e* and *o*, the quantity of *a* as the initial syllable is not constantly determined. When the vowel is preceded by a consonant, its etymological quantity is generally preserved. Examples :

a> a : *kaḍem* (*kaṭaka-*), *kaḍtar* (D. *kaḍantara-*), *kaḍap* D. *kaḍappa-*), *kaḍhṇeṃ* (*kvath-*), *kavḍā* (*kaparda-*), *kavaḷ* (*kavala-*) (*kavala-*), *kasṇeṃ* (*kaṣ-*), *kaḷṇeṃ* (*kaḷ-*), *kalaṃb* (*kadamba-*), *kaḷvā* (*kalāpa-*), *kaḷas* (*kalaśa-*), *kaḷī* (*kalikā*), *kharaḍ* (*khara-*), *kharṇeṃ* (*kṣar-*), *khavaṃ* (*kṣapaṇika-*), *khavā* (D. *khavaa-*), *khaḷṇeṃ* (*skhal-*), *gaṇṇeṃ* (*gaṇaya-*), *gavaṣṇeṃ* (*gaveṣa-*)), *gaḷā* (*gala-*), *ghaḍṇeṃ* (*ghaṭ-*), *ghaḍā* (*ghaṭa-*), *caḍhṇeṃ* (Pkt. *caḍ-*), *caṇā* (*caṇaka-*), *cavṇeṃ* (*cyav-*), *jaḍṇeṃ* (root *jaṭ-*), *jaḷū* (*jalaukā*), *jhaḍṇeṃ* (Pkt. *jhaḍ-*), *jhaṃvṇeṃ* (*yabh-*), *tarṇā* (*taruṇa-*), *tarṇeṃ* (*tar-*), *taraṃs* (*tarakṣa-*), *taroḍ* (D. *taravaṭṭa-*), *tavā* (*tap-*, D. *tavaa-*), *taḷṇeṃ* (D. *tal-*), *taḷāv* (*taḍāga-*), *tharū* (*tsaru-*), *thavā* (*stabaka-*), *dahīṃ* (*dadhi-*), *dharṇeṃ* (*dhar-*), *naī* (*nadī*), *navā*, *navrā* (*nava-*, *navavara-*), *navas* (*nam-*), *paḍṇeṃ* (*pad-*), *paḍhṇeṃ* (*paṭh-*), *paṇat* (*pranaptṛ-*), *pahilā* (cf. *prathama-*), *paḷṇeṃ* (*palāy-*), *paḷas* (*palāśa-*), *paḷheṃ* (D. *palahī*), *phaḷā* (*phalaka:*), *baisṇeṃ* (*upaviś-*), *barū* (D. *barua-*), *balūṇ* (*bhaginī*), *mau* (*mṛdu*), *maḍhṇeṃ* (*mṛṣ-*, Pkt. *maḍh-*), *maḍhū* (*madhu-*), *marṇeṃ* (*mar-*), *maśī* (*masī*), *mhasaṇ* (*śmaśāna-*), *mahāg* *mahārgha-*), *mahāḷ* (*mahālaya-*), *maḷṇeṃ* (*mala-*), *mhais* (*mahiṣī*), *raḍṇeṃ* (*raṭ-*), *rasāḷ* (*rasāla-*), *rahaṃvar* (*ratha-*), *rahas* (*rahasya-*), *rahāṭ* (*araghaṭṭa-*), *lavaṇg* (*lavaṅga-*), *lasūṇ* (*laśuna-*), *lahar* (*laharī*), *lahu* (*laghu-*), *vaṇvā* (D. *vaṇava-*), *varaī* (*varāha-*), *varaṃḍā* (D. *veraṇḍa-*) *varāt* (*varayātrā*), *vasṇeṃ* (*vas-*), *vahū* (*vadhū-*), *vaḷṇeṃ* (*val-*), *valeṃ* (*valaya-*), *saī* (*sakhī*), *saḍṇeṃ* (*śaṭ-*), *sarṇeṃ* (*sar-*), *sarvā* (D. *sarivāa-*), *saru* (*tsaru-*) *savaṃg* (*samargha-*), *savaḍ* (D. *savaḍa-*), *savat* (*sapatni-*), *saṃothal* (*sama-*), *savā* (*sapāda-*),, *savaṃ* (*samaya-*), *sasā* (*śaśa-*), *haḍakṇeṃ* (root *haṭh-*, *haḍḍi-*), *haṇṇeṃ* (*han-*), *haraṇ* (*hariṇa-*), *harṇeṃ* (*har-*), *haryāl* (*haritāla-*), *hasṇeṃ* (*has-*), *haḷad* (*haridrā*), *haḷīs* (*haḷīṣā*), *halū* (Pkt. *halu-*).

ā>*ā* : *kāṇā* (*kāṇa-*), *kārṇeṃ* (*kāraṇa-*), *kāḷā* (*kāla-*), *khāṇeṃ* (*khād-*), *gāū* (*gāv-*) ,*gāḍhā* (*gāḍha-*), *jāi* (*jāti-*), *jāū* (*yātṛ-*), *jaṇṇeṃ* (*jānāāti*)), *jāṇeṃ* (*yā-*), *jāṃvaī* (*jāmātṛ*), *jāḷem* (*jālaka-*), *tāvṇeṃ* (*tāpaya-*), *tāḷū* (*tālu-*), *thāvarṇeṃ* (*sthā*), *thāḷā* (*sthāla-*) *dāvaṇ* (*dāmanī*), *nhāvī* (*nāpita-*), *nāṇeṃ* (*nāṇaka-*), *nāreḷ* (*nārikela-*), *nāṣṇeṃ* (*nāśaya-*), *pāū* (*padona-*), *pāūs* (*pravṛṣa-*), *pāṇī* (*pānīya-*), *pāradh* (D. *pāraddha-*), *pārvā* (*pārāvāta-*), *pāravḍā* (*prākāra-*), *pārā* (*pārāta-*), *pāvṇeṃ* (*prāp-*), *pāḷṇeṃ* (*pālana-*), *phāṇūs* (Ar. *fānūs*), *bāvlā* (D. *bāullī*), *bāher* (*bāhira-*), *māḍī* (D. *maḍia-*) *māṇas* (*māṇuṣa-*), *māho* (*māgha-*), *māḷā* (D. *mālā-*), *rāī* (*rājikā*), *rāūt* (*rājaputra-*), *rāuḷ* (*rājakula-*), *rāhī* (*rādhā*), *vāḍhā* (*vāṭa-*), *vāṇī* (*vāṇija-*), *vārṇeṃ* (*vyāhar-*), *vārā* (*vāta-*), *vārik* (D. *vāria-*), *vārū* (*vāru-*), *vāvar* (*vyāpara-*), *vāḷā* (*vāḷa-*), *vāḷū* (*vālukā*), *sāū* (*sādhu-*), *sāy* (D. *sāha-*), *sāyar* (*sāgara-*), *sārī* *sārikā*), *sāḍe* (*sārdha-*), *sāvantu* (*sāmanta-*), *sāṃvar* (D., (*sāmarī*), *śāvaḷ* (D. *sāhuli-*), *sāvlī* (*chāyā*), *sāṃvā* (*śyāmāka-*) *sāṃvlā* (*śyāmala-*), *śalā* (*śyāla-*).

$ 47. Similarly the lengthening of *a* as a compensation for the simplification of a geminated consonant is generally maintained. *ākhā* (*akṣata-*), *āthi* (*asti*), *ādhā* (*ardha-*), *āpaṇ* (*ātman-*), *kāṃkaḍi* (*karkaṭikā*) *kājaḷ* (*kajjala-*), *kātar* (*kartarī-*) *kāṇaḍā* (*karṇāṭaka-*), *kāpaḍ* (*karpaṭa-*), *kāpūr* (*karpūra-*), *kāpūs* (cf. *karpāsa-*), *kāṃsav* (*kacchapa-*), *khājuṃ* (*khādya-*), *khāpar* (*kharpara-*), *gājṇeṃ* (*garj-*), *gāḍhav* (*gardabha-*), *gātădī* (D. *gaṭṭāḍī*), *cākhṇeṃ* (*cakṣ-*), *Śāṭṇeṃ* (cf. Pkt. *caḍḍai*), *cāṭū* (D. *caṭṭu*), *jāmpṇeṃ* (*jalp-*), *jhālar* (*jhallarī*), *thāḍā* (Pkt. *thaḍḍha-*) *dājṇeṃ* (*dahya-*), *ḍāvā* (D. *ḍavva-*), *tatāvṇeṃ* (*tapta-*), *tāpṇeṃ* (*tapya-*), *tāṣṇeṃ* (*takṣa-*), *nāgā* (*naga*), *nācṇeṃ* (*nṛtya-*), *nāṭhā* (*naṣṭa-*), *nātū* (*naptṛ-*), *pāṃklī* (*pakṣmala-*), *pākhar* (*upaskara-*), *pākhrūṃ* (*pakṣi-*), *pāṭhaviṇeṃ* (*prasthāpya-*), *pāḍā* (cf. D. *paḍḍī*), *pāṭaḷ* (D. *pattala-*), *pāḍṇeṃ* (*pard-*), *pālā* (*pallava-*), *bābar* (*barbara-*), *bhājṇeṃ* (*bhrajj-*), *bhādarṇeṃ* (*bhādra-*), *bhādvā* (*bhādrapada-*), *mākhaṇ* (*mrakṣaṇa-*), *māgṇeṃ* (*mārg-*), *māṃjar* (*mārjāra-*) *māṃjṇeṃ* (*marj-*), *mātī* (*mṛttikā*), *māthā* (*mastaka-*), *māṃdṇeṃ* (*mard-*), *mānṇeṃ* (*manya-*), *māśī makṣikā*), *rākhṇeṃ* (*rakṣ*), *rāṇī* (*rājñī*), *rātā* (*raktā-*), *rābṇeṃ* (cf. *rambh-*, *larb-*), *lāgṇeṃ* (*lagna-*), *lāḍṇeṃ* (*lard-*), *lādhṇeṃ* (*labdha-*), *vākhāṇ* (*vyākhyāna-*), *vāguḷ* (D. *vaggolai*), *vājṇeṃ* (*vādya-*), *vāṭṇeṃ* *vāṭḷā* (*vart-*), *vāḍhṇeṃ* (*vardh-*), *vāḍhāyā* (*vardhaka-*), *vāṇṇeṃ* (*varṇ-*), *vādal* (*vardalikā*), *vādhī* (*vardhra-*), *vāsrūṃ* (*vatsa-*), *sākhar* (Pkt. *sakkarā*, *Gk.* *sakkhari*) *kājṇeṃ* (*sajj-*), *sāṃḍṇeṃ* (*chard-*), *sātvaṇ* (*sapta-*), *sātū* (*saktu-*), *sādaḷṇeṃ* (*śādvala-*), *sāsū* (*śvaśrū-*), *hāṭṇeṃ* (Pkt.*haṭṭ-*), *hālṇeṃ* (D. *hall-*).

But we also find numerous examples of the abbreviation of *ā* and some cases of the lengthening of *a* :

$ 48. In a general way, when a play of morphological gradation emphasises the rhythmic importance of the end of the word, the *a* of the beginning tends to be short, like other vowels. To Skr. *carpaṭa* corresponds Marathi *cāpaṭ* which has thes ame sense of "below, level." But the expansion provokes the abbreviation of the initial syllable in *capḍā*. Similarly *tāṭī* has as its derivative *taṭyā*. As regards *cāḷṇeṃ* "to go", we have the imp. second pl. *calā*. Similarly *vatīṃ* is the locative of a word* *vāt*, lost, derived from the Skr. *vaktra-*. Thus is explained the opposition of *paṭhār*, *pathārī* on the one hand and *pāthar* (*prastāra*) on the other. From there comes the abbreviation of the initial syllable in the derivative and compound words; which give rise to the following oppositions :

khāṭ (*khaṭvā*) : *khaṭaṃg* (*khaṭvāṅga-*), *gāḍhav* : *gadhḍā* (*gardabha-*), *cāk* (*cakra-*); *cakvī* (*cakravāka-*), *nāṭ*, *nāṭhā* : *nathārā* (*naṣṭa*:), *nāk*: *naktā-* (Pkt. *nakka-*), *phāṭṇeṃ* :

phaṭakṇeṃ (*sphat-*), *māvḷā* (*mātalaka-*): *māvḷaṇ* (*mātulānī*); *lākh* : *lakārī* (*lākṣā*), *vākhāṇ* : *vakhāṇṇeṃ* (*vyākhyāna-*), *vāṇī* (*vāṇija-*); *vaṇaj*, *vaṇjār* (*vāṇijya-*); infin. *vāḍhṇeṃ* : part *vaḍhinnalā* (*vardh-*) Similarly the reduplicatives *haḷhāḷ*, *halahvāl* beside *hāl-ahvāl*, the only one conforming to its original in Arabic. Similar also are the causatives : *maṭhāviṇeṃ*, *maṇā-viṇeṃ* with reference to *māṭhṇeṃ* (*mṛṣṭa-*), *mānṇeṃ* (*manya-*).— The rule, moreover, is not absolute; cf. for ex. *māṭkulā* beside *maṭgā* (D. *maṭṭa-*).

But all the cases of abbreviation are not equally clear. One can at best attribute to the same tendency the enlarged or derived form of certain words whose simple (form) is missing in Marathi: thus *lavḍā* with reference to Pkt. *lāū* (Skr. *alābu-*), *kabrā* which for ex. in Hindi is grouped with *kābar* (*karbura-*); cf. *bhaṭakṇeṃ* (*bhraṣṭa-*), *kacrā* (*kaccara-*). But how to explain the short *a* of Pkt. *pall*, Skr. *pary-* in *palāṭan*, *palaṃg*, *palāṇ*, in comparison with *pālaṭ*, *pālthā* formed from the same (the doublet *pālāṇ* is less correct than *palāṇ*), or in comparison with *pālā*, Skr. *pallava-* ? How to explain at the same time *maṭhā* (*mastu-*) and *māthā* (*mastaka-*), of *vaṭhāṇ* (*upasthāna-*) and of *pāṭhaviṇeṃ* (*prasthāpaya-*), of *ratī* (*raktikā*) and of *rātā* (*raktaka-*), of *bhalā* "good" (*bhadra-*, *bhalla-*) and *bhālā* "pike" (*bhalla-*) ? A good part of the words with short *a* are found in other languages : does the recourse to the hypothesis of borrowing suffice for explaining these anomalies ?

Quite a large number of monosyllables have short *a* before an old geminated consonant. A word like *nakh* can be considered as a tatsama, and the Pkt. *ṇakkha-* is only the notation of this fact. But this explanation is not valid for *khaj* (*kharju-*), *nath* (D. *ṇatthā*), *laṭṭh*; *laṭ* (Pkt. *laṭṭhi*), *sak* (*ṣaṭka-*) and *haṭ* beside *hāṭ* (*haṭṭa-*).

In the verbs it seems that an other action may have taken place; namely the sentiment of opposition between the stems of active-causative and of passive-neuter. We had the model *mārṇeṃ* "to kill, to beat" : *marṇeṃ* "to die"; *pāḍṇeṃ* "to cause to fall" : *paḍṇeṃ* "to fall"; *gāḍṇeṃ* "to bury : *gaḍṇeṃ* "to be buried". Hence, contrary to phonetics, comes the opposition of *kāṭṇeṃ* "to cut" and its passive *kaṭṇeṃ* (*kart-*); of *ghāṭṇeṃ* "to crush" and *ghaṭṇeṃ* "to shrink" ((*ghṛṣṭa-*). From them one would expect all verbs with a short *a* to express the state : such as *macṇeṃ* "to inflate oneself" (Pkt. *maccai*), *khapṇeṃ* (*kṣapya-*), "to sell oneself, to finish oneself", or even *sakṇeṃ* (*śakya*) "to be able to."

But *khacṇeṃ* "to set in a bezel" is an active verb : will it be called a tatsama ? In a word like *vaṭṇeṃ* "to crush the cotton", which has no known etymology, this explanation is not possible.

The question is, therefore, totally impossible. To judge from a number of double examples—*tāpṇeṃ* (*tapyate*), *hākṇeṃ* (Pkt. *hakkai*) more usual than *tapṇeṃ*, *hakṇeṃ*; *thākṇeṃ* in poetry beside *thakṇeṃ* which has both the neuter and active sense (Pkt. *thakkai*); *khasṇeṃ* and *khāsṇeṃ* "to cough" (*kāsate*)—it would seem proper to take into consideration the dialectal mixtures. Moreover, it should never be forgotten that the phonemes noted by ă and *ā* in the alphabet have a difference of timbre. Therefore the differences in writing can, in a large number of cases, correspond to the variations of timbre and not of quantity.

$ 49. Inversely, *a* of the initial syllable is lengthened. This case is more rare. It is present :

1. in the compounds with prefixes : thus *pāḍśī* (D. *paḍicchiā*) with reference to *paḍsād* (*pratiśabda-*), *paḍs* (*prativāsa-*) etc., *pārakhṇeṃ*, *pāras* (*parīkṣ*), *pārusṇeṃ*, *pārosā* (*paryuṣ-*), with reference to *paraṇṇeṃ* (*pariṇayana-*), *parvat* (*parivarta-*), *parasṇeṃ* (*paryeṣ-*), *parīs* (*parīkṣā*). This is due to a morphological action, a trace whereof is found from Prakrit onwards and as far as Sanskrit (see Pischel, $ 77-78).

2. in the verbs, where undoubtedly the extension of the stem of the causative has been able to play a rôle : but there is no difference of meaning between *khaṇṇeṃ* and *khāṇṇeṃ* "to *dig*", between *harṇeṃ* and *hārṇeṃ* "to carry"; *cārṇeṃ* denotes to make graze" but also "to graze" as *carṇeṃ*; hence the hesitation between the compounds *saṃcarṇeṃ*, *visăvṇeṃ* (*viśram-*), etc; cf. the cases of the internal *ā* cited in $ 52. In certain cases the stems of the passive have been able to exert their influence : thus *ḍāgṇeṃ* (*dah-*); *lāhṇeṃ* makes a pair with *lādhṇeṃ*, *lābhṇeṃ* (*labh-*).

3. in the words where the interpretation is difficult or impossible. Is *kārandā*, the doublet of *karandeṇ* (*karamandikā*)

a case comparable to the Pkt. *kāḷasutta* (Skr. *kalā-*) or of Pkt. *gāhāvai-* (*gṛhapati-*) ? But in Middle-Indian the explanation of the phenomenon is not easy; see Pischel, $ 78, Jacobi, ZDMG, XLVII, p. 580 ff. Elsewhere a borrowing can be suspected; *pāvṇā* is a frankly dialectal word, but it can be correct : cf. Skr. *plāvayitṛ-* with reference to *plavika-*; *kāvaḍ* (*kamaṭha-*) is found in Gujarati; but the lengthening of the initial is not the rule in this language. Elsewhere the analogy of some other word has exerted its influence; thus *sāsrā* (*śvaśura-*) has taken the long vowel from *sāsū* (*śvaśrū-*). Beside *kavāḍ* (*kapāṭa*) are found *lākaḍ*, *lākūḍ* (*lakuta-*). The list of examples easily grows longer but is of no use for interpretation.

When *a* is in the initial position, the hesitation is, so to speak, the rule. The lengthening is licit in *āvas* (*amāvāsyā*), *ālśī* (*aṭasi-*); the privative *a* is even noted as long in *ārogṇ*(*eṃ*). But these are also the examples of shortening which predominate : *arsā* (semi-tatsama *ādarśa-*), *alaṃbeṃ* (*ā-lamb-*) *avatṇeṃ*, poet. *āvatṇeṃ* (*āmantraṇa-*), *avḷā* (*āmalaka-*), etc. Similarly, before consonant, which had earlier been geminated; *āḍ* with reference to *ādhā* (*ardha-*), *akhitīj* (*akṣaya-*) *ākhā* (*akṣata-*), *āglā* (*agra-*), *agyā* (*agrega-*), *ăgaḷ* (*argala-*) *āphalṇeṃ* (*āsphal-*), etc.

In these doublets, Molesworth always prefers the form with short *a* (see Preface, p. XIV), but without saying if it is due to theoretical reasons or due to the observation of the usage. As regards *aḍ*(*h*)- (*ardha-*), however, he gives an interesting indication : after having established a nuance of meaning between *aḍ-* and *āḍ*, he agrees that the usage is against his definitions : in reality *aḍ*—is the form of the Deśī, *āḍ-* of Konkan. Is that the key to all the hesitations of the sign of *a* in the initial syllable ? Moreover, does this refer to a difference of timbre or of quantity or concurrently to both ? These are the questions to which direct experience alone will be able to provide an answer. It is, however, true that if one relies on the sign, then the cases of abbreviation of *ā* in the initial syllable are more numerous than the lengthening of *a*—a fact which accords with the constant shortening of *i* and *u* and the general tendency of the abbreviation of the first part of the word.

2. *As the non-initial Syllable* :—

$ 50. Inside the word, *i* and *u*, short and long, lose their own articulation and get mixed up with *a* (cf. Beames, I, $ 37, 39). Examples :—

i :—*āgṭī* (*agni-*), *umalṇeṃ* (Pkt. *ummilla-*), *kiṃkaṇī* (*kiṃkiṇī*) seems to be borrowed from Sanskrit or from a language in the neighbourhood of Marathi), probably *ciraknem* (D. *cirikkā*), *paḍos* (for * *paḍavas-*, Skr. *prativas-*), *paraṇṇeṃ* (*pariṇaya-*) and other compounds of *pari* and * *paḍi- pākhrūṃ* (*pakṣi-rūpa-*), *vikharṇeṃ* (*viṣkir-*), *viṃcṇī* (Pkt. *vimcinī*; see $ 40), *sarvā* D. *sarivāa-*); one should undoubtedly join *avakṇeṃ*, probably derived from *aviknem* for *avaviknem* by syllabic superposition. It is difficult to say if *aḷtā* is or is not independent of *aḷitā* (*ālakta-*,*ālipta-*). The words, where internal *i* subsists, are therefore borrowed : *mahinā* is Persian, *bahirā* (*badhira-*) is undoubtedly Hindi, *vahilā* (Pkt. *vahilla-*) belongs to the poetic language.

ī at first became short; when internal *i* subsists, it is preferably short : thus *gahirā* (*gabhīra-*), which is besides a dialectal word; *alikaḍe* "on that side" is more usual than *alīkaḍe* (*-kaṭa-*). The short vowel has been generally reduced; hence the opposition of *joskī*, *jospaṇā* and of *jośī*, see M. *joisī* (*Jyotiṣ*); of *kaṇsā*, a form of the oblique sing. and of the nom. *kaṇīs* (*kaniśa*), This opposition is also found in all the nouns with penultimate *-ī* (see Joshi, $ 173).

u : *aṃgṭhā* (*aṁguṣṭha-*) with reference to *aṃgūṭhā* the normal form in other Indo-Aryan languages (Grierson, *Phon.*, p. 27) but in Marathi reserved for the poetic language, *aṃgḷī* beside *aṃgulī* (*aṅgulī-*), *uphalṇeṁ* (*utphulla-*), probably *ulaṭṇeṃ* (Pkt. *ulluṭ-*), *kabrā* (*karbura-*), *tarṇā* (*taruṇa*) *sāsrā*, *sāsreṃ* with reference to *sāsū* (*śvaśrū-*, *śvaśura-*); in *khajurī* *u* is undoubtedly maintained by the influence of *khajūr* (*kharjūra-*), but one also finds *māṇas-* in a compound as against the simple *māṇūs* (*mānuṣa-* or *mānuṣya-*), *lakḍā* with reference to *lākūḍ* (*lakuṭa-*), *hiṅgḷūk* with reference to *hiṃgūḷ* (*hiṅgula-*). The same opposition is found in the declension of names with a penultimate *u* (see Joshi, $ 173). The word *nirutā* (*nirukta-*) belongs to the poetic language; in *purusṇeṃ*, *u* subsists because it is in reality initial, the word being a compound (*pary-uṣ-*). As regards *bāhulā*, it is a word without real existence, the current form being *bāvlā* (D. *bāullī*).

ū got mixed with *ā* in *udhalṇeṃ* (*uddhūlaya-*), it has disappeared in *upṇeṃ* (*ut-pū-*), *aḷkuḍī*, a compound of *alū* (*alu*) and in the tatsama *unmalṇeṃ* (*unmūlana-*).

$ 51. *e* and *o* tend to become short by closing themselves and by being, as a consequence, subjected to the same alterations as *i* and *u*. Examples :—

e : *uḍṇeṃ* (*uḍḍayana-*), *gavasṇeṃ* (*gaveṣa-*), *parasṇeṃ* beside the poetic forms *parisṇeṃ* and *parieṣṇeṃ* (*paryeṣ-*), *paraṇṇeṃ* (*pariṇayana-*), *pālaṭ*, *palāṭaṇ* with reference to the poetic *paleṭṇeṃ* (*paryaṭ-*), *māvṇeṃ* (*māpaya-*), *vāṇṇeṃ*, poetic *vāṇiṇeṃ* (*varṇaya-*), *vikṇeṃ* (*vikraya-*) with reference to *keṇeṃ* (*kraya-*). We should probably also add *gaṇḍrī* (D. *gaṇḍīrī*, Guj. *gaṇḍerī*). The words *akhjā* as *akhitīj* (*akṣaya-*) belong to the religious language. In the causatives in *-v-* (*-paya-*), *i* survives facultatively : we have, for example, *karaviṇeṃ* and *karavṇeṃ*; the first syllable of *neḍṇeṃ* (for *na deṇeṃ*) "not to give" shows that this word should not be listed here; it has been re-made on the model of *neṇṇeṃ* "to ignore" (*na jānāti*).

o : *aḷaṇī*, a compound of *loṇ* (*lavaṇa-*), *ucaṃdalṇeṃ* a compound of *aṃdoḷṇeṃ* (*amdole-*), *kartī* tatsama (*karoti-*); but *kaḍmoḍa* survives beside *kaḍmaḍ*, *pārosā* beside *pārsā* (*paryuṣita-*); *paḍosī* has been subjected to the influence of *paḍos* (*prativāsa-*); *aṃgocha* (*aṅguccha-*) is borrowed, as proved by the presence of *ch*. On *mehuḍā* (*megha-*) see $ 39. Here should be recalled the cases where *-ava-* has been reduced to *a*, certainly passing through *o*, and *u*, as is attested by the equivalent forms such as *pāravasā* : *pārosā*, cf. *paruṣṇeṃ* : *pārsā* (*paryuṣ*). Beside the family names like *rājvaḍe*, *kaḷvaḍe* are found *khoparḍe*, *pimparḍe*, *boparḍe*, *bhambharḍe*, *ramḍe*. All these are the compounds with *vāḍā* (*vāṭa-*) which denotes a locality : cf. *āitvāḍeṃ*, *vilvavāḍeṃ* attested in the 8th century. Similarly are found, *kāraṃḍā*, *kāraṃḍeṃ* beside *karavaṃd*, *karavaṃḍī* (*karamadikā*); *paraṭṇeṃ* beside *paravaṭṇeṃ*; *karat* is the popular form corresponding to the popular form *karvaṭ*; *uṭṇeṃ* (if its etymology by the Skr. *udvart-* is exact) is the only form attested.—There are, however, certain cases wherein the loss, indeed the re-establishment, of *-va-* has been aided by the sentiment of the gradation of the simple and of the causative.

$ 52.—Similarly *ā* tends to become short within a word :

āv (a)sā, aṃs (a) ḍī (Pkt. *āsaṭikā*), *ubhal (a)ṇeṃ* (D. *ubbhālaṇa-*), *ujav (a)ṇeṃ* (*udyāpana-*), *oṃbal (a)ṇeṃ* (D. *ombālai*), *oṃv (a)sā* (*upavāsa-*), *kaḍhaī* (*kaṭāha-*), *kaḷ (a)vā* (*kalāpa-*), *gav(a) ḷī* (*gopāla-*), *jāniv (a)sā* (*janyavāsa-*), *nivaṇeṃ* with reference to *vāṭṇeṃ* (*vart-*), *nis (a)ṇā* (*niśāna-*), *pal (a)ṇeṃ* (*palāyana-*), *pār (a)vā* (*pārāvata-*), *bhiṃg (a)ruṭī* (D. *bhiṃgārī*). Similarly before a double consonant, we have : *āvagṇeṃ* (*āvalg-*), *ār (a)tī* (*ārātrika-*), *upajṇeṃ* (*utpadya-*), etc. and following a contraction as in *das-(a)rā* (*daśaharā*).

The long has, however, been preserved :

1. in certain cases where *ā* is the result of a contraction : *taṇārā* (*tṛṇāgāra-*), *divāḷī* (*dīpāvalī*), *marāṭhā* (Pkt. *marahaṭṭha*);
2. in the cases where two *a*s follow each other with an *h* in between we have, in such cases indifferently *-ahā-*,*-āha-* and even, less correctly *-āhā-* (see Molesworth, *Preface*, *Orthography*, $ 8, p. XIV) : beside ǎ*hṇā*, *dāhṇeṃ*, *pāhṇeṃ*, *bāhṇeṃ*, *rāhṇeṃ*, *vāhṇeṃ* and *sāhṇeṃ* are found *āhāṇā* and *āhāṇā*, *dahāṇeṃ* and *dāhāṇeṃ*, etc. Beside *sāy*, we have *sahā* (D. *Sāha-*). In none of these words, except *ahāṇā*, the second *ā* is not etymologically long. The long quantity is, therefore, recent and is due to the presence of *h*. This is confirmed on the one hand by words like *kolhāḷ* (Skr. *·kolāhala-*), *vahāṇ* and *vāhāṇ* (*upānah-*, Pkt. *vāhaṇa-*), where the long vowel of Marathi, which is invariable, corresponds to an old short vowel and on the other by the case of the disjunction of the group *hn* : *tahān* (*tṛṣṇā*), *nahān* (*snāna-*), *lahān* (Pkt. *laṇha-*), cf. *sahāṇ* for *sāṇ* (Skr. *śāṇa--*).
3. in certain morphemes : the participle of obligation in *-āvā-* (*-avya-*) : *dyāvā*, *karāvā*, etc., the suffixes of enlarged adjectives : *-ārā* (*-akāra-*), ex. : *kārṇarā*, *marṃārā* serving as fut. part.; *naṭhārā*, *dhutārā*; *āḷu-*, etc, as in *jhoṃpaḷū* ("one who sleeps"; from *jhumpṇeṃ* to sleep), *pisālvṃ* (D. *pisalla-*), etc. and the stem of the cauative in *āvirṇeṃ* or *-av (i) ṇeṃ* (*manāvirṇem*), etc).
4. in certain compound verbs or nouns where *ā* belongs to the first syllable of the principal term : with reference to *ujavṇeṃ*, *ubhalṇeṃ*, etc. we find two quantities, for ex. in *visāvṇeṃ* (*viśrama*), *upahāṇṇeṃ* (*utphaṇ-*) and only the long one in

nihālṇeṃ (*nibhal-*). Similarly *vaḷṇeṃ*, *uvalṇeṃ* but *omvālṇeṃ* (*val-*). It seems that the verbal substantives preferably preserve the long vowel : *pasārā* is the participle of the causative of *pasarṇeṃ* (*prasar-*) and felt as such. But we also have the substantive *nivāṇeṃ* with regard to the verb *nivṇeṃ* (*nirvāṇa-*). The same holds true for *ukhāṇā* (*upakhyāna-*), *utāṇā* (*uttāna-*) and *ubhārā* (*udbhāra-*). The form *pathārī* seems to be borrowed : *pāthar* is the normal form (*pra/tara-*);

5. in the semi-tatsama words, as in *ujagar* (*ujjāgara-*), *kaḍāsaṇ* (*kaṭāsana-*) and in other obscure words like *kaṃḍārṇeṃ* (Pkt. *keṇḍārei*).

It is difficult to specify the date of these changes. In Prakrit and in later Sanskrit are found a certain number of cases of the abbreviation of internal vowels (see Jacobi, ZDMG, XLXII, p. 574-581). The loss of the characteristic timbre of *i*, *u*, *e* and *o* seems, on the contrary and at first view to be altogether modern, if we have to judge by the comparison of forms like *joisī* and *jośī* or *āṃguṭhā* and *āṃgṭhā*. However, the inscription of Pandharpur gives the name of the town *Phāganipur* (*Phālguṇī-*) an example of the decoloration of *ū*; *ī* subsists (as short) because it is final. Chiefly the *Periplus of the Erythrean Sea* gives, from the first century, the form *dikhanos* with regard to the name of the country *Dakhinabadis* (*dakṣiṇāpatha-*) : is this not a first index of the loss of the timbre of the internal *i* ? If the antiquity of this tendency were admitted, one could render an explanation of the co-existence in Sanskrit of the doublets like *kaphoṇi* and *kaphaṇi* "elbow", and above all of the Prakrit forms, *haladdā* (*haridrā-*), *nīsaṇī* (*nihśreṇī*) attested much earlier than M. *haḷad* and *nisaṇ*. Regardless of the rareness of these examples (most of them cited by Pischel for *i* in $ 115 and for *u* in $ 123 are doubtful. Pischel had, moreover, recognised this for a number of these words), possibly they are, however, the only remnants of the phonetic notation of a reality in the Prakrit, generally tending to be archaic.

III. *Prakrit Vowels in Contact* :—

$ 53. Following the dropping of the intervocalic consonants of Sanskrit, several vowels have normally come into contact inside a word. In Prakrit, the hiatus is avoided only exceptionally : at a relatively late time and according only to the Jaina tradition, *y* is inserted between any two vowels (Pischel, $ 187); *v* is also found in certain cases where it replaces *g*, *y* and may be *t*, *d* of Sanskrit (Pischel, $ 231, 246, 254 and note 1; cf. also the forms cited by Sachau, *Alberuni*, p. 46, following Weber). As against Prakrit, the modern languages tend to eliminate the hiatus as much as possible (see Grierson, *Phon.*, $ 37, Hoernle, $ 68-98).

Marathi, like other cognate languages, treats the vowels in contact, in three ways : it preserves their individuality by the insertion of *y* or *v*; it changes them into diphthongs and lastly it makes them short.

I. *Insertion of y and v* :—

$ 54. In other languages, *y* and *v* seem to be indiscriminately used; in Marathi the insertion of *y* and *v* is rare.

There are certain cases in the old language, where *y* replaces a Sanskrit dental, and notably in the participles : the oldest monument of Marathi gives a specific example thereof : *Śrī-cāvuṇḍārājeṃ karaviyaleṃ* "made on the order of Cāvuṇḍa"; later on in the *Abhilaṣitārtha-cintāmaṇi* are found the forms *āṇiyale*, *vāṇiyale*, but the *Jñāneśvarī* is already writing *Śikavileṃ*, *karavileṃ* (XI, 28, etc.).

In the modern period only sporadic traces of this usage survive and possibly they are dialectal. Are pointed out *tuyeṃ* beside *tuveṃ* "by you" (LSI, *Mar.*, p. 173); *sāyar* (*Sāgara*--), found in the *Abhilaṣitārtha-cintāmaṇi*, has completely disappeared; even there where it had been in the midst of a compound (*saṃsāra-sāyara-tāraṇa*) and gives the impression of a quasi-tatsama; *soyara* (*sahodara*-) has been preserved in its purely Prakrit form, certainly because it is a term of relationship; *oyarā* is an obscure word; its sense of "daily nourishment" leads us to suppose for the same a prototype like * *avahāra* : but the sense of "kitchen" or of "the internal part of the house" enables us to see therein a doublet, undoubtedly dialectal, of *ovarā* (*apavaraka*-). Similarly, as against *parāvā* (*parāgata*-) is found *parāyā*, thence onwards suspected to be borrowed.

$ 55. It is the insertion of *v* which is normal in Marathi. It is produced irrespective of the origin of the hiatus. Thus *v* replaces one by one :

Skr. *k* in *nāgvā*, beside *nāgā* (*nagnaka-*), *suvā* beside *suā* (*śuka-*);

Skr. *g* in *taḷāv* (*taḍāga-*), *nivḷī* (*nigaḍa-*), *parāvā* (*parāgata-*), *punav* (*puṃnāga-*);

Skr. *j* in *tavṇeṃ* (*teja-*), *rāv* and *rao* (*rāja-*);

Skr. *t* in *kaṃgavā* (*kaṅkata-*), *kevḍā* (*ketaka-*), *ghāv* beside *ghāy* (*ghāta-*), *cavṇeṃ* (*cetana-*; *caiṇeṃ* is found the *Jñāneśvarī*), *jov* (*dyota-*, Pkt. *joī*), *juvā* (*dyūta-*), *vāv* (if it refers to *vāta* and not to *vāyu*:-);

Skr. *d* in *osavā* (*avacchada-*), *pāv* (*pāda-*), *śev* (*cheda-*); possibly the same phenomenon also explains the form *bor* (*badara-*) found in Deśī, in Gujarati and in Dravidian languages, whereas Sindhi and the central and eastern languages have *ber*;

Skr. *y* in *māv* (*māyā*),*sāṃv* (*snāyu-*), *sāvlī* (*chāyā*), in *māvṇeṃ* if this word goes back to Skr. *mayate* and *vāv*, if it represents the Skr. *vāyu-*;

lastly different aspirates in Sanskrit represented by *h* in Pkt., in *asval* (*acchabhalla-*), *ugavṇeṃ* (*udgrahaṇa-* and * *udagrathana*), *mevūṇ* (*maithuna-*), *rov* (*roha-*; possibly influenced by the Marathi root *rov-*, Skr. *rop-*), *sāvaḷ* (D. *sāhulī*, derived from Skr. *śākhā* ?). In the tatsama *saṃdhevīṃ* (*saṃdeha-*) and in *mhoṃv* (*moha-*), the rôle of *v* is all the more clear as the aspiration has been preserved and displaced. Its Skr. prototype is unknown, but the insertion of *v* is sure in *govaṃḍ* (D. *goaṇṭa-*), *Śivrā* (D. (*sīhara-*).

Should be distinguished therefrom those cases where *v* represents an old *u* or *o*, as in *sāv* which is equal to *sāū* (*sādhu-*). One will be possibly tempted to put in this last category masc. substantives such as *pāv* (*pāda-*), *śev* (*cheda-*) and to consider the last *v* of these words as corresponding to the old *-o* of the nominative. But the feminine form *māv* (*māyā*) decides the issue. Doubt can, however, persist regarding words like *rāo*, *ghāo*, written as *rāvo*, etc. in old texts, cf. $ 57.

II. *Diphthongs* :—

$ 56. The Marathi alphabet has two diphthongs, *ai* and *au*, which are used to denote the grouping of *a*+*i* or *e* on one side and *u* or *o* on the other :

ai<*a*+*i*; archaic termination of fut., third sing. *-ailu*, etc. ; *pai* (Skr. *prati-*; *paikhṇem*, *paij*, *paithaṇ*, *paiṇ*, *pailā*), *paiṭhā* (*praviṣṭa-*), *baisṇem* (*upaviś-*), *mhais* (*mahiṣī*).—*kaivāḍ* (*kaitava-*), *dain* (*dainya-*), *vair* (*vaira-*), *sair* (*svaira-*) are the old semi-tatsamas, found in later Prakrit (see Pischel, $ 61);

ai <*a* + *e* : *kaik* (*eka-eka-*), *pais* (*praveśa-*).

au <*a* + *u* : *cau-* (*catuḥ-*) in *cank cauth*, *caudā*, *causār*, *mau* (*mṛdu*), *vauṃl* (*vakula-*).

au <*a* + *o* : *pauḷ* (*pratoli:-*).

Are also found, though rarely, *au* < *oa*: *auṭh-* beside *ohaṭ-* (D. *ohaṭṭa-*) ; *jauḷ* beside *jov* (*dyota-*).

$ 57. When one of the vowels *a*, *i*, *u* is long, the hiatus generally persists; ex. *ghaīvaṭā* (*ghāṭa-*); *mauśi* (*matṛ-*), *rāuḷ* (*rājakula-*), *naī* (*nadī*), *varai* (*varāha-*); *gāī* (Pali *gāvī*), *rāī* (*rājikā*), *gāū* (*gātu-*, *gau-*), *jāū* (*yātu-*), *rāūt* (*rājaputra-*).

Moreover, these groups are not stable. Beside *vaī* (*vṛti-*) is found on one side *vahī* and *vai*; *pāūṇ* has a doublet *pauṇ* (*pādoṇa-*); *aitvār* a semi-tatsama, represents the Skr. *āditya-*; in *paiṃ* (*prāyeṇa*), in *taisā*, *kaisā*, etc. (*tādṛśa-*, etc.) originally the *a* had been long.

By the side of pure and simple diphthongisation are found (chiefly in the final position) the signs *āy*, *āv* or *ay*, *av* : *kāy* si more usual than *kāī* "what ?", *bāy* is the popular form of *bāī* "woman", similarly we have *gāy*, *ghāy* (cf. *ghāivaṭā*; *ekāghāīṃ*), *sāy* (cf. *sāī*, *sahā*); *say* beside *saī* (*sakhī*, *smṛti-*), dial. *paḍkay* (*prati-kṛti-*), *naohe* (=*na-hoe*, Skr. *na bhavati*), *cāvdas* the vulgar form of *caudas* (*caturdaśa*), *bāvḷā* beside *bāhuḷā* (D. *bāullī*), *māvḷā* (*mātula-*), *māvśī* (beside *māuśī*, Pkt. *māussiā*), *lavḍā* (*alābu-*), *sāv* for *sāū* (*sādhu-*). This is due to the ease with which *i*, *u* and *y*, *v* can be interchanged constantly in writing : thus *v* denotes *u* in *mevṇā* for *mehuṇā* (*maithuna-*); inversely we have *naurā* beside *navarā* (*nava-*), *dauḍ* beside *davaḍṇeṃ* (*drav-*); similarly the tatsamas *udaik* and *aitā* represent Skr. *udaya-* (cf. M. *udyāṃ*) and *āyatta-*. Cf. also the doublets difficult to interpret; *rāv*: *rāo*, *pāo* : *pay*, the tatsamas *nyāv*, *upāv*, see M. *nyāvo*, etc. (*nyāya*, *upāya*).

III. *Contraction*

(a) The first vowel is *a*.

a+*i*, *e*, *u*, *o*.

$ 58. Thus, as we have seen, the recent diphthongs *ai* and *au* tend to be reduced.

ai is one of those which has subsisted longest ; however, *heṭ* (* *adhiṣṭāt* for *adhastāt*) goes back to Prakrit; beside *paiṭhan* (*pratiṣṭhāna-*) we have *peṭh* (*pratiṣṭhā*), which is old enough to have passed into the Dravidian languages under the Prakrit form * *peṭṭhā* (cf. Tam. *peṭṭei*); if *bail* has subsisted, *khair* (*khadira-*) has *kher* as its doublet, which brings Marathi near Gujarat; we have *saveṃ* (*samavāya*) as against *paiṃ* (*prāyena*). It is chiefly at the end of the word that the reduction has taken place : see M. *daḷvaī* >mod. *dalvī* (*dalapati-*); cf. *śeṇvī* (*senāpati-*); the termination of the 3rd person sing. *ai-* (*-atī*) has become (except probably in the exclamation *sai*) *-e* in the present from the oldest period, and in the future during the modern period. The same is the case with the termination of the 1st pers. sing. present *-eṃ*, future *-en* (earlier *-ain*), that of the oblique sing. of feminine nouns of Pkt. *āe*>* *ai* >M. *-e*, of the nom. -acc. pl. of neuter nouns of Skr. *-āni* >Pkt. *-āiṃ* >M. *-eṃ*, the imp. sing. in poetry *-eṃ*=Pkt *āhi*. The reduction here is, undoubtedly, due to the diphthong being at the end of the word.

A curious transformation of *ai* consists in making it turn up, in certain cases, as *-a-*; beside *taisā*, *kaisā*, etc. and of *baisṇeṃ*, are concurrently employed and even quite usually, the forms *tasā*, etc., and *basṇeṃ*. It is not possible to suppose in the case of pronominal adjectives a similar action, tending to unify the stems, because such action is, so to say non-existent in Marathi; cf. *jo* "who", *to* "that", *hā* "this"; *koṇ* "who ?", *kāy* "what ?". On the other hand, one could, at first sight, imagine for *ba*(*i*)*sṇeṃ* 'to seat oneself" a contamination of the root *vas* "to reside, to be established" : but in this case it will be necessary to admit the influence of a Hindi form with *b* in the initial position. Now this form in the sense of "to seat oneself" does not exist; Hindi has formed its verb on the past participle : *beṭhanā* (cf. *upaviśati* : *upaviṣṭa-*).—The reason for the reduction of the diphthong must have had its origin in phonetics and be due to the presence of *s*. Curiously before *s*, even now an example of inverse action is found: to Pkt. *asīī* "80" corresponds M. *aiśīṃ*, Guj. *aisī*; other languages have *asī*. Marathi also has *eṃśī* and in compound-*yaśīṃ*, which probably gives the etymological form, if *y* could be considered as a phoneme of insertion. It is difficult to explain all these facts in the same manner. But their *rapprochement* enables us to suspect a mixture of dialects, of whom some would admit a depalatalising action of *s*. The case of *maind* (*manda-*) is altogether obscure.

$ 59. The reduction of *au* is still more general . It is reduced to *o* in *co-* (*covīs* beside *cavvīs*, *cohīṃkaḍeṃ*, *cotkor*; Skr. *catuḥ-*), *poḷ* (beside *pauḷ*; Skr. *pratoli-*), *bhorūp* (*bahu-*), *moh-* (*madhu-*), *u* in *māgutā*, cf. *māgauteṃ*; in the ablative-absolutive -*ūn*(*i*), earlier -*auni*; *deuḷ* (*devakula-*) goes back to Prakrit. Moreover circumstances there had been more favourable : a sort of haplology could have been produced here : **deva-*(*v*)-*ula-* >*de*(*v*)*ula-* (cf. *rāuḷ*, Skr. *rājakula-*). Inside the word, an old *au* has completely dropped out in *gāvḍā* (*grāma-kūṭā-*), undoubtedly passing through *o*, then *u*.

$ 60. In the final position, -*au* is reduced in two ways, according as it represents the Pkt. -*au* or Pkt. -*ao*. In the first case it becomes -*o*, then in certain cases -*ū* : this is the case with the third pers. sing. imp. in -o, Skr. -*atu* (cf. *jāṇo*, *jāṇū* "as if", fixed imperative; poetic form : *jāṇau* which is trisyllabic). In the second case on the contrary, it is reduced to -*ā*, whether the original *a* had been long or short :

Skr. -*ako* : the nom. sing. masc. with lengthening *āmbā* (*āmra-*), *avḷā* (*āmalaka-*), *caṇā* (*caṇaka-*), etc.
Skr. -*ato* : *ākhā* (*akṣata-*);
Skr. -*ado* : *paḍvā* (*pratipada-*), *bhadvā* (*bhādrapada-*);
Skr. -*ajo* : *kuḍā* (*kuṭaja-*);
Skr. -*ayo* : tatsama *āsrā* (*āśraya-*), *saṃcā* (*saṃcaya-*), *oṃcā* (*uccaya-*);
Skr. -*avo* : *pānhā* (*prasnava-*), *pālā* (*pallava-*);
Skr. -*āko* : *cakvā* (*cakravāka-*);
Skr. -*āco* : *pisā* (*piśāca-*);
Skr. -*āto* : *cultā* (*culla-tāta-*);
Skr. -*ādo* : *pārā* (*pārāda-*),*savā* (*sapāda-*);
Skr. -*āyo* : *pāṃ* (*prāyaḥ*);
Pkt. -*āo* : nom. fem. pl. -*ā* : *iḷā*, *ghāḍiā*, etc.; see infra.

The intermediary between -*āo* and -*ā* has surely been -*au*. This is evident from a comparison of the terminations of the nom. sing. masc. in the different languages : Hindi poetry has kept the nom. in *-au*, and the group Sindhi-Gujarati-Rajasthani-Nepali constitutes the same case in *-o*.

The only means of taking note of this double evolution in Marathi seems to lie in supposing that the passage of Pkt. *-as* to *au* is later to that of Pkt. *-au* to *-o*. This hypothesis is, moreover, not verifiable, the two evolutions being anterior to the oldest documents and there being nothing similar even in Marathi.

When nasalised, the Pkt. group *-āo* has evolved as *-au* : first pers. pl. verbal in *-oṃ*, *ūṃ* (Skr., Pkt. *-āmo*).

a+a.

$ 61. —When one of the vowels is long, the resultant of the contraction is *ā*.

I. The first *a* is long.

Skr. *-āja* : *rāūt* (*rājaputra-*), *rāuḷ* (*rājakula-*);

Skr. *-āta* : *māṃg* (*mātaṅga-*), *vāv* (*vāta-*);

Skr. *-āda* : tatsama *ārsa* (*ādarśa-*), *sāṇ* (*chādana-*), *savā* (*sapāda-*), probably *pavādā* (*prāvāda-*);

Skr. *āya* : *vāṇ* (*vāyana-*); tatsama *kāst* (*kāyastha-*), *-nāk* (*nāyaka-*), old. sing. masc. *-ā* (*-āya*);

Skr. *āva* : *divālī* (*dīpāvalī*);

Skr. *-ākā-* : *pāravḍā* (*prākāra-*);

Skr. *āgā* : *ār* (in *gābhār*, *taṇārā*, *dhavḷār*, *bhāṃḍār*, *etc.*, Skr. *āgāra-*);

Pkt. *-āya*: : *vār* (D. *vāyāra-*); cf. already in Deśī *bhāujjā*; M. *bhāvjai* is re-made (*bhrātṛ-jāyā*);

Pkt. *-āha-* : *thā* (*thāha-*);

Pkt. *-āa*, the termination of the instrumental fem. (Pischel, $ 375) : *heḷā* (*helayā*). It is, since then, difficult to admit that *piseṃ* is derived directly from * *piśācaṃ*, it is the neuter of *pisā*, cf. for the sense, Pkt. *pisallo*: M. *pisāleṃ*.

II. The second *a* is long.

-akā has changed, quite early, to *-ā*; *vaṇjār* (*vāṇijyakāra-*; cf. *vaṇijāraka* in a Nasik inscription), similarly *andhār*, *kumbhār*, *cāmhār*, *citārī*, *dhutārā*, *suār* etc.; the participles in *-ṇār* (cf.

$ 52, 3rd section); *bhādarṇeṃ* (*bhadrakāraṇaṃ*);

Similarly :

-ayā in *varāt* (*varayātrā*);

-avā in tatsama *upās* (*upavāsa-*);

probably-*atā-* in *cār* (* *catāro* for *cattāro* after *caturo-*).

One should not include here the word *pāīk*, which does not go back to Skr. *padātika-*; it is borrowed from Persian and rather early (Pkt. *pāikka-*).

The nom. pl. of masc. nouns with lengthening ends in *-e*. This is due to the fact that *-ā* final has become short. It is connected, therefore, not with *a*(*k*)*ā*, Skr. *akāḥ*, but with *-a*(*k*)*a*.

On this point Marathi is in agreement with the languages of the centre (Hindi and Panjabi) and seems to be opposed to Gujarati (*-ā -o*) and to Sindhi (*-ā*), but it is, at best, possible that another terminal ending may be the origin of these forms (cf. Simhalese *-āhu*, *-o*; see Geiger, $ 34, III and infra, the chapter on declension).

$ 62. The two vowels are short.

When separated by *y* in Sanskrit, the contraction has been effective since the times of the Middle-Indian; for ex. the term ending of third pers. sing. pres. in Pali is *-eti*, in Pkt. *-ei* (Skr. *-ayati*); in this way are explained in Marathi the forms *neṇeṃ* (*neyana-*), *bheṃ* (*bhaya-*) etc. Moreover, we have seen in $ 14 that certain unaspirated occlusives had become intervocalic having passed by *y*. This phoneme has reacted on the Prakrit group *-aya-* as in *-aya-* coming from Sanskrit. That is why the Marathi *-e-* represents :

Skr. *-aka-* in the nom. -acc. neut. sing. in *-eṃ* (*-akaṃ*) and the nom. masc. pl. in *-e* (*-akāḥ*);

Skr. *-aga-* in *śelḍūṃ*, *śeḷī* (*chagala-*), in the name of the town *Ter* (*Tagara-*), and in *ṇer* (*nagara-*) the second term of the compound forming town-names;

Skr. *-aja-* in *neṇṇeṃ* (*na-jan*, of *jñā*);

Skr. *-ata-* in *gelā* (*gata-*), *sāmpeṃ* (*sāmprataṃ*), *śeṃ* cf. *ś*(*y*)*aṃbhar* (*śataṃ*);

Skr. *-ada-* in *keḷ* (*kadalī*) and probably *per*(*pradara-*).

As a result of these examples we can not decide if *kelā*, Skr. *kṛta-*, goes back to Pkt. * *ka*(*y*)*a-* or to **kia*; on the contrary, for *melā* (*mṛta-*) *a* is more or less sure, *i* having been found nowhere (see $ 30).

During the recent period, *aa* has combined in the semi-tatsama *asand* (*aśvagandha-*) and in the reduplicated forms : *gaḍāḍṇeṃ* (cf. *gaḍagaḍṇeṃ, kaḍāḍ* (from *kaḍakaḍa-*); *h* between two *a* has been dropped, which comes to the same thing in *gāṇ* (*gahana-*), *āṇā* (*ābhāṇaka-*), *marāṭhā* (Pkt. *marahaṭṭha-*, Skr. *mahārāṣṭra-*), in the tatsama *agrār* (*agrahāra*) and finally in the term. ending of the second pl. indic. *-ā(ṃ)* <*-atha*; the *a* resulting from this contraction is, in its turn, shortened in *dasrā* (*daśaharā*), cf. $ 52.

(b) The first vowel is *i* or *e*.

$ 63. Before *ā*, the phonemes *i* and *e* are generally preserved as *y* : *pyār* (*priya-kāra-*), *pyās* (*pipāsā*), *vyāhī* (*vivāha-*), *haryāl* (*haritāla-*), *agyā* (*agreya-*) and the participles of obligation such *dyāvā* (root *de-*), *calaviṇyā*, etc. (we find *cālāveā* in the Pandharpur inscr. of 1195 Śaka; in 1289 Śaka it is *calaviā* and in 1494 Śaka *sāgaṃvyā*). But *maṇer* is found beside *maṇyār* (*maṇi-kāra*) and the Persian word *myān* has as its doublet *meṇ, menā*.

When *i* or *e* are followed by short *a*, contraction, most often, is the result.

e + *a* <*e* : *kedhavaḷ* (for *kevadha-*), *kevḍā* (*ketaka-*), *tevṇeṃ* (*teja-*), *der* (*devara-*), *veṇ* (*vedanā*), *śev* (*cheda-*).

i+*a* gives either *e* or *i* inside the word and *ī* at the end of the word except where *a* is nasal.

e : *neḷ* (*nikaṭa-*) *śeṃḍā* (*śikhaṃḍa-*), *śerā* (*śikhara-*), (*y*)er (*itara-*), *ahev* (*avidhavā*), *nesṇeṃ* (Gujarati distinguishes *nes-*< *nivas-* from *nās* < *nivās-*). —Similarly *pareḷ* (D. *pariali*) for ex. *māher*, (*mātṛ*+*ghara-*) etc., and in the final syllable the neuters : *jānaveṃ* (*yajñopavītaṃ*), *koḍeṃ* (D. *koḍiyaṃ*), etc, and some fem.: the pronouns *te, he* (mod. *tī, hī*) etc, *vhaṇse* (Pkt. *-ssiā*).

i : *tideṃ* (*trika-*), *viṇeṃ* (*vijan-*), *vīth* (*vitasti, śilā* (*śitala-*), *dī* (*divaḥ*), *dīs* (*divasa-*), *parīṭ* (D. *pariaṭṭa-*), *dīḍh* (Pkt. *divaḍḍaa-*), the causative participle in *-ileṃ* (*-ita-* + *-l-*), see M. *-iyaleṃ* (*kāravyaleṃ* in the Cāmuṇḍa inscr.). Similarly *piṇeṃ* (*piba-*), *jiṇeṃ* (*jīva-*) which go back to Prakrit.—At the end of the word *ī* is the normal characteristic of the fem. sing., Skr. *-ikā*, therefore Pkt. *-iā* > *ia* : *āgśī* (*agniśikhā*), *kaḷī* (*kalikā*), *pī* (*plīhā*), *māvśī* (Pkt. *māussiā*), etc.; similarly the neuters *ghī*, *dahīṃ*, *pāṇī*, *jāhnavī* beside *jānhaveṃ* (*yajñopavīta-*).

i+i>i : *tīj*, *aḍic* (*tṛtīya-*, *ardhatṛtīya-*).

When *e* and *i* meet, no matter in what order, *e* carries the day inside the word and *i* at the end.

Inside the word : *nārel* (*nārikela-*), *veḍhḷā* (D. *veiddha-*). However, we have *parisṇeṃ* for *pariesṇeṃ* (*paryeṣ-*); but this can also be the first degree of the weakening leading towards the form *parasṇeṃ*.

In the final position : terminal endings : of the oblique fem. sing. of Pkt. *-ie*, M. *-ī* (*bhiṃti*), of the third pers. sing. caus. of Pkt. *-ei*, M. *ī* (*karī*); the poetic imp. of the same Pkt. conjugation *-ehi*, M. *-ī*(*ṃ*); similarly, with nasalisation, the 1st sing. of Skr. *-ayāmi*, M. *-īṃ* (*karīṃ*) and the nom. acc. pl. neuter with lengthening in Skr.*-akāni*, Pkt.*-a*(*y*)*āim*,M. *īṃ*.

Before *u*, *i* disappears in *duṇā* (noted as *duuṇa* in Pkt, Skr. *dviguṇa-*), in the infinitive as *-ūṃ* >Skr. *-ituṃ* (see LSI, *Mar*, p. 9), in *pārusṇeṃ* (*paryuṣ-*). On the contrary at the end of the word, *-i* predominates over *-u* resulting from *-o* Hence the nom. masc. sing. in *-ī* as *nhāvī* (*nāpita-*), *vāṇī* (*vaṇija-*), etc. This confirms what has been said above regarding the relatively late passage of *-ao* to *-au*.

(c) The first vowel is *u* or *o*.

$ 64. When there is contraction, the timbre *u* or *o* always predominates.

u+a>o : *ohmāy* (*vadhū-*), *pophal* (*pūga-*), *mohaḷ*, *samor* (*-mukha-*);

u+a>u : *jūḷ* (*yugala-*; cf. *juṃval*), *dhuṇeṃ* (*dhunoti*; M. *dhuvaṇeṃ* is poetic), *lulā* (*lūna*), *jūṃ* (*yugaṃ*), *tūṃ* (Pkt. *tumaṃ*), *gahūṃ* (*godhūma-*) and all the fem. in *-ū*, Skr. *-ukā* and the neut. in *-ūṃ*, Skr. *-ukaṃ* cf. also *uṭṇeṃ* if it refers to *udvart-*. The hiatus of *suār* (*sūpakāra*) is only apparent; it supposes an intercalated *v*, representing Skr. *p*, exactly as in *kuvā* (*kūpa-*), *puvā* (*pūpa-*), etc.

u+o>u : *nirū* (*niruja-*), *pū* (*pūya-*) and the other nom. sing. in *ū-*, Pkt. *-ūo*. In reality it refers to :

u+u which has given *u* from the Prakrit period in *ukhaḷ* (*udūkhala-*), *uṃbar* (*udumbara-*); we also find *o* denoting the long of *u* in the semi-tatsamas *garodar* (*guru-udara-*), *koykamal* (*kumuda-*).

u+i When the hiatus does not subsist as in *juī* (*vūtikā*), *dhuī* (*dhūmikā*), *bhuī* (*bhūmi-*), *ruī* (D. *rūvī*), the resultant is *u*. We have *sū* beside *suī* (*sūcī*), whereas other languages do not have *sūī* as in Prakrit. Similarly, for *kuruṃd* (*kuruvinda-*) and chiefly for *dhūv* (*duhitṛ*), a form which accords with that of Simhalese and which is already noted in Deśī (*dhūā*), whereas other languages of the continent have *dhī* or variants of the same form.

o+a>o : *thoḍā* (*stoka-*), *poḷ* (Pkt. *puala-*). In *jaḷū* (*jalaukā*), assimilation has possibly taken place among nouns in *-ū*, Skr. *-ukā* (In Marathi there is only one feminine in *-o* : *bāy-ko* "woman", besides not explained). A reduction of the same type must have been the cause of the doublet *janūṃ* (* *jaṇṇovaṃ* ? for *jaṇṇovaviaṃ*) of *jānhavem*. The group *ova-* has been reduced to *u-* from Deśī in Skr. *opaśa-*, D. *usaa-*, M. *useṃ*, but generally the hiatus persists : juvārī <D. *jovarī*.

o+i is reduced to *o* inside the word; thence *ḍokeṃ*, *ḍokī* with reference to *ḍoī*, *josī*, earlier *jõisī*; *oi* is only the vulgar pronunciation of *ovī* (D. *ovia-*); but in *koil* (*kokila-*; cf. the doublet *koyal*), the hiatus persists.

Contraction of Three Vovels.

$ 65. It is rare that these vowels could have been abbreviated in Marathi. Generally the vowels have been so grouped as to become a diphthong. Such is the termination of the oblique sing. of the nouns masc. -neuter with lengthening, Skr. *-akāya*> M. *eā*, *-yā*, or that of the nom. -acc. fem. pl. of the nouns in *-i* : Pkt. *-iāo* > M. *eā*, *-yā*. The contraction of three *a*s in *ār* (*ajagara-*), *ā-lā* (*āgata-*) is not at all certain. In appearance are found *i-a-o* < *ā* in *pasārā* (*prasārita-*) *pārosā* (*paryuṣita-*), *purā* (*pūrita-*), *vipārā* (*viparīta-*). But it is equally possible to see in the last case the consequence of a morphological action bringing these participles back to the normal type of adjectives (*-itaka-* > *-aka-*). The regular form is preserved in the proper noun *pāṃḍyā* (*paṇḍita-ka-*), *pāṃḍe* being only its dialectal doublet. The final diphthongs with the first element *i* get contracted into *ī* in the terminations of the nom. pl. fem. (Pkt. *-iae*> *ī*) and of the neut. pl. (*-iāiṃ* >*īṃ*). The intermediary is undoubtedly *ie*, as in the accessory word *śīṃ* (if it represents the Skr. word *sahitena*).

The Nasalisation of Vowels.

$ 66. In principle the long vowels, resulting from the contraction of two vowels, the latter of whom had been nasal, are nasal in the final position. Ex. : *śeṃ* (*śataṃ*), *śiṃ* (*sahitaṃ* or *sahitena*), the diminutives in *-rūṃ* as *vas-rūṃ* (*vatsa-rūpaṃ*), etc., the nom. sing. neuter in *-eṃ*, *-īṃ*, *-ūṃ* (Pkt. *-aaṃ*, *-iam*, *-uaṃ*). Among these last ones, the nasality of the final vowel is not noted in writing when it is preceded by a nasal consonant. Thus we write *pāṇī* (*pānīyaṃ*), *loṇī* (*navanītaṃ*). This exception is only apparent, see Joshi, $ 167. As regards *ghī* (Skr. *ghṛtaṃ*), it is probably a borrowed word, as is particularly shown by the *i* treatment of the vowel *ṛ*.

In the termination of the genitive plural *-ānāṃ*, become in Marathi the termination of the oblique pl. *-āṃ*, *n* coming in contact with the final nasal vowel has lost, early enough, its own articulation. Its sign has preserved its memory in classical Prakrit under the form *-āṇa* (see Pischel, $ 370) which, if it had been real, would render impossible the explanation of M. *-āṃ*. Moreover, later on Apabhraṃśa notes the modern phenomenon under the form *-āhaṃ* or *-ahaṃ*, where it is useless to seek explaining the aspiration (besides this sign is ascribed by Hemacandra to Māgadhī, contrary to the manuscript tradition, see Pischel, $ 370). In the instr. sing., the final vowel had been nasalised in Prakrit and the termination, which is *-ena* in Sanskrit, had become *-eṇaṃ* (Pischel, $ 182). Here again the intervocalic *n* has lost its articulation and the resultant in Marathi, as in Apabhraṃśa, is *-eṃ*. The terminations of the neuter pl. also present the same nasalisation of the final vowel, followed by the loss of the intervocalic *n* : Skr. *-āni* is noted in Prakrit *-āiṃ*, *-āmiṃ* or even *-āi* (see Pischel, $ 182, 367). To these forms correspond the Marathi terminations *-eṃ* (Skr. *-āni*), *-īṃ* (Skr. *-ikāni*).

$ 67. We will see later on that the old intervocalic *m* has become a spirant and has ended up as a nasal *v*. The nasality of this essentially unstable phoneme is, in principle, carried back to the preceding vowel; moreover, it has altogether disappeared, at least in its sign in a large number of words. But in certain terminations, the nasality had subsisted, whereas the labial articulation, on the other hand, had been lost. Thence the fact that the first person of the verbs in the singular terminates in *-eṃ* (Pkt. *-āmi*, *-ami*), *-īṃ* (from *-ayāmi*, Pkt. *-emi*), in the plural in *-oṃ* (*ūṃ* -Pkt. *-āmo*, *-amo*) concerning the pronoun *tūṃ* (*tvaṃ*, Pkt. *tumaṃ*, see $ 208.

$ 68. Inside the word, the group : short vowel+nasal+ occlusive, is susceptible of several treatments (cf. Navalkar, $ 38.).

When the occlusive is a surd, the result is indifferently one of the two stated below :—

1. short vowel+nasal+occlusive surd.
2. long nasal vowel+occlusive surd.

Thus we have on one side *nimb* (Skr. *nimba-*), *paryant-* (ts.) and on the other *āt* (*auta-*), *cāpā* (*campaka-*), *cōc* (*cañcu-*), *vāṭā* (root *vaṇṭ-*). In principle the two treatments are licit and hence the doublets *tant—tāt* (*tantu*)-, *khuṇṭ-khāṭ*, etc. The regularity of this gradation is responsible for the fact that the only sign of *anusvāra* suffices to note the two cases : in the case where the vowel is short, it represents the nasal of the same order as is the following consonant. If the vowel is long, the *anusvāra* has the same value as the *anunāsika*. When the occlusive is a sonant the result is :

3. nasal vowel+nasal+occlusive sonant.

The quantitative relationship is not the same as in the first case : the vowel is a bit longer than the normal short vowel, and the occlusion of the nasal is shorter than that of an intervocalic nasal (letter of P.R. Bhandarkar). Examples : *bhāṇḍ* (*bhāṇḍa-*), *jheṇḍā* (*dhvaja-*), *māṇḍaṇem*, *tōṃḍ* (*tuṇḍa-*), *khāṇḍ* (*khaṇḍa-*), *cānd* (*candra-*), *vāñjh* (*vandhyā*), *āmb* (*āmra-*), *khāmb* (Pkt. *khaṃbh-*), *būnd* (*bindu-*), *pāṅg* (*paṅgu-*), etc.

In this case, which is intermediary between the former two, is still to be observed the trace of the tendency to eliminate the occlusion of the nasal in favour of the preceding vowel. This tendency is found in all the cognate languages, with the exception of the North-Western group. In Sindhi and Panjabi (examples in Beames, I, p. 296-9) and also in Simhalese

Geiger, $ 17), the vowel remains pure and short even in the case of the assimilation of the consonants. In fact these languages do not allow the lengthening of the vowels before a reduced consonantal group. Everywhere else, the two former treatments co-exist and in the case of the sonant, a third one is juxtaposed, in which the vowel is denasalised but is lengthened, while the consonantal group is reduced by being made, not an occlusive, but a nasal (see Grierson, *Phon.*, p. 34; *Maith. Gram.*, $ 27; Hoernle, $ 23). The treatment of Marathi is, therefore, parallel to that of other continental languages, without however being completely identical.

$ 69. The long vowels preceding a reduced old consonantal group tend to be noticeably nasalised, as in Prakrit, when the first of the old consonants had been an *r*, and when the group contained a sifflant or an aspirated palatal (see Pischel, $ 74). Thus beside *āg* (*agni-*), *āthi* (*asti-*), *āp* (*ātmá-*), *āsare* (*apsaras-*), and above all *māg* (*mārga-*), *sāp* (*sarpa-*), etc., we come across, on the one hand, *āṃc* (*arci-*), *kaṃvaṃtal* (Pkt. *kavaṭṭia-*), *kāṃkaḍī* and *kākḍī* (*karkaṭikā*), *koṃpar* and *kopar* (*kūrpāra-*), *jhāṃjrī* (*jharjharī*), *bhāṃbhaḷ* (*bharbh-*), *māṃjar* and *mājar* (*mārjāra-*), *māṃjṇeṃ* (*mārjaya-*), *vāṃk* (*vakra-*), *savaṃg* (*samargha-*) with reference to *mahāg* (*mahārgha-*), *sāṃḍṇeṃ* and *sāḍṇeṃ* (*chard-*). On the other hand we have *āṃkh* and *āṃs* beside *ās* (*akṣa-*), *āṃtharṇeṃ* and *ātharṇeṃ* (*āstar-*), *oṃṭh* beside *oṭh* which is more correct (*oṣṭha*), *kavaṃṭh* and *kavaṭh* (**kapiṣṭha-*, cf. Skr. *kapittha-*), *kāṃkh* and *khāṃk* beside *kākh* and *khāk* (*kakṣa-*), *kāṃsav* beside *kāsav* (*kaśyapa*, *kacchapa-*), *taraṃs* beside *taras* which is more usual (*tarakṣa-*), *rīṃs* and *rīs* (*ṛkṣa-*), *pāṃkḷī* (*pakṣma-*); *umśīt* (*utsikta-*), *vāṃsrūṃ* and *vāsrūṃ* (*vatsa-*), *kāṃcyā* and *kācyā* (*kaccha-*), *viṃcū* (*vṛccikā-*) : These two last words are, besides, probably borrowed; *āṃsū* and *āsū* (*aśru-*), *pāṃsolī* (*pārśva-*). We also find before other articulations : *phāṃkī* (*phakkikā*), *hāṃkṇeṃ* (*hakk-*); *sāṃcā* beside *sāc* (*satya-*), *uṃc* and *oṃcā* beside *ocā* which is less frequent (*ucca-*), *jhuṃjhṇeṃ* beside *jhujhṇeṃ* (*yudhya-*); *kuṃṭaṇ* beside *kuṭan* and *kuṭṭin* (*kuṭṭanī*), *bhīṃt* and *bhint* (*bhitti-*), *piṃpal* (*pippala-*) etc.

How should we explain this contradiction ? The examination of the cognate languages brings no clarity. There also we find the nasal of *āṃc*, *āṃsū*, *jhāṃjrī*, *bhāṃbal*, *māṃjar*, *vāṃk*, *hāṃkṇeṃ*; but the nasal of *sā*(*ṃ*)*ḍṇeṃ* is found only in Gujarati and that of *kāṃkh* only in Hindi. Hindi, Panjabi and Gujarati have, like Marathi, *māṃj* = Skr. *marj-*, but Sindhi, Bengali and Oriya have merely *māj*. Except Marathi, everywhere else the forms for *kāṃkḍī*, *kāṃcyā*, *koṃpar*, *sāṃcā*, *vāṃs-* (but here it may be due to abbreviations as in 'Hindi *bacchā*) are without the nasal. The form *piṃpal* is also the only one and Oriya has the nasal only where the word is borrowed from Marathi (see Beames, II, p. 24, note 2).—On the other hand with regard to Marathi and Gujarati *māg* (*mārga-* and root *mārgaya-*), all the other languages from the N-W to the east (except Oriya and Assamese) have *māṅg-* or *maṅg-*. With regard to Marathi *māj*(*h*), Guj. *maj-* (*madhya-*), Sindhi and Kashmiri have the nasal, and Hindi and Panjabi have both the forms, but the treatments of the Sanskrit word *mudga-* are distributed otherwise : *mūg*, Panj. *mugg*, old Beng. *mug*, H. and Bih. *mūṃg*, Sindhi *mūṅu*.

$ 70. Every long vowel tends to develop a nasal resonance. This fact is undoubtedly at the root of the preceding phenomenon, and is probably more frequent than is revealed in writing. It is shown as being optional before *y*, *r*, *l*, *v*, *ḷ* (see Molesworth, *Preface*, $ 6). But one cannot explain otherwise *ā*(*ṃ*)*sḍī* (Pali *āsaṭikā*), *aṃcavṇeṃ* (tatsama * *ācamana*), *kā*(*ṃ*)*c* (tatsama *kāca-*), *keṃs* and *keṃsar*, popular and archaic for *kes*, *kesar* (*keśa-*); *boṃḍ* (goes back to Deśī, Dravidian *buḍboḍ-*), *he*(*ṃ*)*sṇeṃ*, *hi*(*ṃ*)*sṇeṃ* (root *heṣ-hreṣ-*). The final vowels offer more than one example of this spontaneous nasalisation. Thus we have *nāhiṃ* "no" with reference to *āhe* "he is"; the termination of the second pl. *-āṃ* (Skr. *-atha*); the adverbs *tar*(*h*)*īṃ* (*tarhi*) and its opposite *nātarīṃ*, *ekadāṃ*, *evhāṃ*, *etheṃ*, etc. One can suspect that the same fact is at the origin of certain obscure terminations (instr. *tvāṃ* "by you"; the locative terminations in *-āṃ*, *-īṃ*, cf. infra) and it has been seen in $ 66 that this is certain for the terminations of the instrumental sing. and oblique plural. We should, undoubtedly, separate, on the one hand, the case of *jiṃkaṇeṃ*, *liṃpaṇeṃ* (root *ji-*, *lip-*) where morphological influences have been able to come into play and that of *paṃvleṃ*, *paṃvāḍā* (*pravāla*, * *pravāda-*), where the anusvāra has to note, chiefly, the unvoicing of *a*, which yields forms like *povleṃ*, *povāḍā*. In *uleṃḍhāleṃ* (D. *ull-ehaḍo*), the internal *e* can be nasalised under the influence of some sort of reduplication : cf. the form *ulaḍhāl*. Lastly are to be noted certain obscure cases where the vowel is short : thus the first syllable of *ka(ṃ)vaṃṭāl* cited above and the curious tatsama *vinanti* beside *vinati*.

Here also Marathi has parallels with other languages. If *kāc* and *kes* are the only forms noted in Hindi, one also finds there the form *aṃcavan* (Tulsī Dās) and the spontaneous nasalisation is found sporadically elsewhere; thus H. *bāṃh*, S. *bāṃhan* (Skr. *bāhu-*), M. *bāhī*; Guj. *bheṃs* (Skr. *mahiṣī*), M. *mhais*.

$ 71. Inversely, Marathi presents numerous traces of denasalisation. In a number of words, where the nasal is etymological, the nasality is optional. Thus *mā(ṃ)s* (*mās* is the popular form; Skr. *māṃsa-*), *vā(ṃ)sa* (*vaṃśa-*), *ha(ṃ)sṇeṃ* (*haṃs-*), *cā(ṃ)pā* (*campaka-*), *sā(ṃ)peṃ* (*sāmpratam*), *sā(ṃ)-khal* (*śṛṅkhalā*); *āvatṇeṃ* is the current form corresponding to the poetic *āvaṃtaṇeṃ* (*āmantraṇa-*), *guphā* is the popular form of *guṃphā*; *kothrib* that of *kothambīr* (*kustumbarī*); to Skr. *māñca* correspond the two forms *maṃcī* and *mācā*; to *saṃlagna-* corresponds *salag*; the words given below have lost their nasality since the period of the Deśī : *kilac* or *kilīc* (D. *kiliñci-*), *khājaṇ* (*khaṃjana-*), *micakṇeṃ* (*miṃc-*), *umaḍ-* (*ummaṇḍa-*), *orapṇeṃ* (root *ramp-*). There is no trace of the nasal in *kohleṃ* (*kuṣmāṇḍa-*), *bhijṇeṃ* (*abhyañjana-*), *vijṇā* (*vyañjana-*), in *bhuī* (*bhūmi*) and other words with an old intervocalic *m*, nor in *pusṇeṃ* (Skr. *proñch-* : Deśī has both the forms).

The denasalisation is more or less constant for a short vowel preceding *nt*: to *avatṇeṃ* (*āmantra-*) cited supra, should be joined *kaḍtar* (Pkt. *kaḍantara-*), *bhitar* (*abhyantara-*), *śeṃvtī* (*sīmantikā*) and above all the terminations of the third pl. present in *-ati*, *-at* (*-anti*) and of the pres. part. in *-at* (Pkt. *-anta-*). In the former the nasal has disappeared since the earliest texts, but its traces are still found in the latter. The inscription of Pātan, beside *vikateyā* the oblique sing. of *vikat*, the pres. part. of *vikṇeṃ* (*vikrī-*) offers the form *hoṃtā*, the nom. sing. of the pres. part. of *hoṇeṃ* (mod. *hotā*). Similarly the editions of the *Jñaneśvari* often preserve the nasality in the pres. participle of the verb "to be" *sāṃt-* (for ex. IV, 117, 154). But during the modern epoch nasalisation has generally disappeared and forms like *cintaṇeṃ*, *nicint*, *manthaṇeṃ* (cf. *mathṇeṃ*, *mathṇī*) are rare and in all probability are tatsamas.

In all these respects Marathi behaves like other Indo-Aryan dialects. The majority of examples is found to be identical in the cognate languages. The nasal preceding *t* is missing particularly in all the speeches from Gujarat to Bengal, it subsists only in Oriya and Assamese on the one hand and on he other in those western languages where *nt* becomes *nd* (cf. J. Bloch, JA, 1912, I, p. 333).

But the nasality of the intervocalic *m* in the words of the type *bhūmi* is preserved in the group formed by Gujarati, Sindhi, Panjabi and Hindi and these very languages still make a distinction betweeen the roots *proñch-* and *pṛcch-*, whereas Marathi has *pus-* in both the cases.

$ 72. In the existing state of our knowledge, it is impossible to explain all the details of these contradictory facts. Most probably the reason lies in their dependence on the general character of the articulation in Marathi and in the cognate idioms. All these languages are pronounced with the soft-palate hardly raised. Thence one can say that all the vowels are more or less nasal and that their nasality is noted somewhat accidentally, but still more constantly in the cases where, the vowel being long, the nasal resonance has more chances of being noted. The variations in the notation are, therefore, largely a matter of spelling.

Besides, the nasalisation can be more or less strong and consequently can appear more or less worthy of being noted, depending upon the dialects. In Marathi, it is notorious that it is particularly developed in Konkan (see LSI, *mar.*, p. 78, 167, 189). It is weaker and can, as a consequence, seem to be absent in the northern and eastern speeches (ibid, p. 22, 24). But these differences do not present a clear-cut characteristic : at Thana have been noted, beside *rānāt* (for *rānāṃt*) "in the forest", not only *tāntlā* 'among them", where the nasal is etymological, but also *mānjā* for *mājā* (Pkt. *majjha-*) and *kanthā*, tats., for *kathā* (ibid, p. 65). Even in the *deś*, nasality remains notable in the terminations and it is known that the presence of a nasal vowel changes into *nl* following the first pers. sing. of the future (*-n* for *-ṃ-l*) and in the dative plural (*-āṃnā*) for *-āṃ lā*), cf. the demonstrative *tyānlā* '"to them".

The tendency to nasalise the vowels must have started from a very early epoch. Pāṇini notes that in Sanskrit *a*, *i* and *u*, short and long, take at the pause a nasal resonance; the same fact is met with in Pali (see Pāṇini, VIII, 4, 57; Wackernagel, $ 259). On the other hand, for the scribes who have inscribed the rock edicts of Aśoka, the nasal and the long vowels are always equivalent terms (see Senart, *Inscr. de Piyadasi*, I, 16; this remark does not apply to the pillar-edicts, see T. Michelson, IF, XXIII, 257). Lastly in the Buddhist Sanskrit texts, certain variants seem to be due to the same phenomenon. We come across *jantu* in the leaves of Pelliot (*Dharmapada*, II, 20) and also *jantu* in the corresponding Pali text (*Saṃyutta-nikāya*, I, 117) with reference to *jātu* in the *Divyāvadāna* (p. 224); *Samācaret* of *Divyāvadāna* (p. 224) is similarly opposed to *samaṃ caret* (*Saṃyutta-nikāya* I, 117).

Marathi Vowels :

$ 73. It remains to prepare the chart of Marathi vocalism by taking it back to its origins. The rules enunciated below generally suffice for the explanation and some difficulties of detail will be examined when required.

a

$ 74. As the initial syllable, *a* represents Pkt. *a* arisen out of Skr. *a* or *ṛ*, see $ 33, 46 ff. It results from a contraction, see $ 61, 62, 65. It can also be the substitute of *u*, either by dissimulation (*gamūt*, *garū*, *garodar*, *gahūṃ*, *ravaṃṭh* for *rovaṃth*, possibly *sarū*, Arabic *surū*), or due to obscure influences (*maft* is probably borrowed from Gujarati; *sar* looks like a contamination of Skr. *surā* and *sāra*-).

In the final position -*ā* results from a contraction, see $ 39, 60 ff, 65, 70. Inside the word, *a* can represent any vowel, $ 40, 42, 52 ff. It can form the diphthongs *ai*, *au* with *i*, *u* representing *i*, *e*, *u*, *o*, $ 56 ff. Exceptionally it represents *e* in *akrā* (*ekādaśa*).

i

$ 75. *i* = Pkt. Skr. *i* or *ṛ*, see $ 30, 39, 40 ff. 50, 55 ff. *i* = Pkt. *e* in the initial position, for ex. in *itukā*, in the internal syllable, $ 51, 63 and in the final syllable in *ahmī*, *tumhī*, $ 39. In certain cases, it goes back to Pkt *ai* ($ 58) and to all the diphthongs whose first element is *i* or *e* (see $ 63, 65).

It represents Skr. *ya* after a consonant in certain words which are, without doubt, all of them, semi-tatsamas : *bhijṇeṃ* (*abhyañjana-*), *bhītar* (*abhyantara-*), go back to Prakrit. *vijṇā* (*vyañjana-*), *jānivasā* (*janya-vāsa-* are found to be made on the same model; in this latter word one can also admit the influence of a sort of syllabic super-position, real or felt of *nivāsa-*). In *udīm* (*udyama-*) and *nīm* (*niyama-*) beside *nem*, the *m* proves that we have to deal with veritable tatsamas : it is the same influence which has re-established *vivsāv* beside *vāvsāv* (*vyavasāya-*). Is also found *i* in a certain number of cases where *a* was expected : *iṃgal* (*aṅgāra-*), *pīkā* (beside *pāk*, Skr. *pakva-*) go back to the oldest Prakrit. The *i* of *hirvā*, *hirḍā* (beside *haryāḷ*, *haḷad*) is found since the Veda (*harita-*, *hiri-*, *hiraṇya-*, see Wackernagel $21 c).It is remarkable that Marathi is the only one to have kept these forms.—Equally old, but common to Marathi and other languages is the *i* of *mirā* (*merica-*), *niḍ*(*h*)*al* (*lalāṭa-*, Pkt. *ṇiḍāla-*), *ukiḍavā* (cf. *ukuḍavā*, *ukaḍ*), *ukirḍa* (*ukarḍā*). The two last examples are evidently the doublets due to the multiplicity of the treatment of *ṛ*. This is, undoubtedly, the way in which can be explained also *khiṇḍ*, *khiḍkī* (with reference to *khaṃḍṇeṃ*, *khaṃḍā*, *khāḍā*, etc.). Beside *paṃjar* (*pañjara-*) is found *piṃjrā* as also *mañjirī* (*mañjarī*), *khirṇeṃ*, along with *kharṇeṃ*, *jharṇeṃ* (*kṣar-*). Should all these examples be explained as the more or less old loans ? This hypothesis, though in accordance with the general tendencies of Marathi, lacks proofs. Moreover one must also take into consideration the dialectal influences or recent evolutions. Molesworth has noted that *cirhāṭ*, *girhā* for *carhāṭ*, *graha* are popular forms and besides it is possible that a large number of examples escape observation, given the disappearance of the internal *i*, cf. $ 50.

i is often written *y*, see $ 57, 63.

u

$ 76. *u*=Pkt *u*, Skr. *u* and *ṛ*, etc., $ 30, 44, 50, 57.
u is the result of diverse contractions. It represents *au*,

$ 60, *iu* $ 63 and those groups whose first vowel had been *u* or *o*, see $ 64. Moreover, *u* frequently represents Pkt. *o*-, Skr. *ava-*, *apa-*, see $ 51, 64, 67. In the initial position this phenomenon, besides very old, probably presupposed a confusion with the pre-verb *ud-* : cf. the observation of Wackernagel, $ 141, regarding *ujjhāyati*, Skr. *ujjihi*.

Just as *i* represents *ya* after a consonant in certain semi-tatsamas, similarly Prakrit admits *u* for *va*, as in the gerundive in -*ūṇa*, if it be really the successor of the Vedic-*tvāna* (see Pischel, $ 584) and in *turiaṃ*, unless it is not a contamination of *tvaritam* and *tūrtam*, etc. In Marathi, the traces of their gradation are extremely rare : in *kuṭheṃ*, we are not sure if it is *kva* + a word of the Sanskrit family *sthā* (cf. $ 110) ? As long as the etymology of *koṃ* "who" (cf. *kāy* "what") is not sure, nothing definite can be said on this point. The words *sūr* (*svara-*), *dhūn* (*dhvani-*) are probably borrowed. The dental of *dhūn* renders this word specially suspect; the Prakrit had the cerebral (Pischel, $ 561). As regards *tūṃ*, it represents Pkt. *tumaṃ* and not Skr. *tvaṃ* and *suṇeṃ*=Skr. *śunaka-*.

-*u* is the vowel of support near a labial consonant; ex. : *sugūṃ*, *hukūm*, words borrowed from Skr. *sugama-* and Arabic *hukm*.

u alternates with *a*, notably in the imitative or expressive words, in the neighbourhood of *r* or of a cerebral consonant. Thus *taḍ-* : *tuḍ-*, *phaṭakṇeṃ* : *phuṭṇeṃ*, *ghaḍghaḍṇeṃ* : *ghurghur* or *gurgur-*; cf. *ghoṭṇeṃ* and *guhṭghuṭ* with reference to H. *ghaṭaknā* "to swallow". This relates, evidently to the different treatments of *ṛ*, the indifference regarding the vowel being greater because in this type of words, it is the consonants which predominate. —The root *kṣar-*: *jhar-* which gave the doublets in *i*, also furnishes us with forms in *u* : *vikhurṇeṃ*, *nijhūr* beside *vikharṇeṃ*, *nijharṇeṃ*. Prakrit does not know of forms except in *a* and *i*, but Deśī has *ṇijjhūra-* beside *ṇijjhara-*. Moreover the forms in *u* seem to be exclusive to Marathi. The Sanskrit *kisalaya-*, Pkt. *kisala-* is represented by *kisūḷ* in Marathi, without doubt under the influence of the cerebral *ḷ* (see $ 79). Finally are also met with *kulolī*, *kululī* beside *kalolī* "the rut of horses"; cf. the doublet in Hindi *kalol-kilol*. Is there here some trace of the influence of *kulā* "buttock" ?

u is found for *i* in *bund* "drop", Skr. *bindu-*. It seems that there has been a metathesis of *i* and *u*, if we were to judge by the opposition of *undar* "rat", the form in Marathi, Gujarati and Simhalese and *indūr*, the form in eastern languages. In Sanskrit we already find beside *puñjīla-* and *piñjūla-* "tuft" (see Wackernagel, p. XXXIII, 277). It is remarkable that *bind* and *bindeṃ* are alive in Marathi, with a slightly specialised sense: "drop of the sperm, sperm",—*cuṇṇem* goes back to Prakrit and differs from *ciṇṇeṃ*; the *u* of *susar* (*śiśumāra-*) is also found in Prakrit and is due to assimilation.

u is often written *v*, See $ 55 and 57.

e

$ 77. *e*+Pkt. *e* coming from

Skr. *e* : *ek* (*eka-*), *eṇeṃ* (*eti*), *kevḍā* (*ketaka-*), *kes* (*keśa-*), *khevā* (*kṣep-*), *cevaviṇeṃ* (*cetana-*), *dev* (*deva-*), *des* (*deśa-*), *deh* (*deha-*), *deuḷ* (*devakula-*), *pej* (*peyya-*), *pekhṇeṃ* (*prekṣ-*), *pesṇeṃ* (*preṣ-*), *mehuḍā* (*megha-*), *set* (*śreṣṭha-*), *śeṇvī* (*sena-*), *veśvā* (*veśyā*), *vet* (*vetra-*), *śet* (*kṣetra-*), *śev* (*cheda-*), etc., and the instrumental in *-eṃ* (Skr. *-ena*).

Skr. *ai* : *gerū* (*gairika*), *tel* (*taila-*), *mehuṇā* (*maithuna-*).

Skr. *aya* : *keṇeṃ* (*kreyaṇa-*), *vaḷeṃ* (*valaya-*), *je* (*jaya-*); *deṇeṃ*, whence *leṇeṃ* (Pischel, $ 474), see $ 62.

Skr. *i* : *peṃḍ* (*piṇḍa-*), *bel* (*bilva-*), *veṭh* (*viṣṭi*); cf. infra.

e results from contractions, see $ 62, 63.

Exceptionally, *e* represents *a* under the influence of the neighbouring *i* : *śej* (*śayyā*) goes back to Prakrit, *mer* (*maryā-*) and *vel* (*vallī*) as in Deśī. This is frequent in Konkani (LSI, *Mar.*, p. 171). It is in fact in Konkan that we get *verīṃ* "upto": M. *var*(*ī*). In any case in *uver*, *ḍher*, possibly *eṃḍ* and the extraordinary form *aiśīṃ* "80" (see $ 58), the alteration is surely modern.

Some obscure examples of *e* for *a* are : *śeṃvrī* with regard to *śāṃvar* (*śālmalī*) goes back to Prakrit, *ḍheṃkūṇ* (daṃ- ?) as in Deśī; *āgheḍā* beside *āghāḍā* is probably borrowed from Gujarati and *kheṃkaḍ* (*karkaṭa-*) probably form Hindi. The word *hiseb* is a Persian form of Ar. *ḥisāb*, *kherīj* is undoubtedly a pronunciation borrowed from Urdu (where it is written *kharīj* for *khārij*). But one could not explain *uleṃḍhāleṃ* beside *ulāḍhāl*, *paletaṇ* beside *palātaṇ* (etymological form, confirmed by Deśī), neither *be-* with regard to *bā-* "two" (*dvā-*), nor *cave-* with regard to *cāv-* "four" (*catuḥ*) in the compound nouns of numerals.

ṭhevṇeṃ is not the direct successor of Pkt. *ṭhāai*, *ṭhāi* (*sthā-*): it develops from a Pkt. * *ṭhei* extracted from *uṭṭhei*, etc.

o

$ 78. Pkt. *o*=*o*, Skr. *o* : *oṃṭh* (*oṣṭha-*), *koṇ* (*koṇa-*), *koṭhā* (*koṣṭha-*), *kor* (*kora-*, *kola-*), *kolhāl* (*kolāhala-*), *koṃval* (*komala-*), *kos* (*krośa-*), *goṭhā* (*goṣṭha-*), *goṇ* (*goṇī*), *got* (*gotra-*), *jogā* (*yogya-*), *jot* (*yoktra-*), *jośī* (*jyotiṣ-*), *ḍolā* (*dola-*), *loṃ* (*loma-*), *lohār* (*lohakāra-*), *sos* (*śoṣa*), *solā* (*ṣoḍaśa-*), etc. The final *o* of the nominative after *h* : *kalho* (*kalaha-*), *ghoho* (D. *goha-*), *māho* (*māgha-*), *moho* (*moha-*), *loho* (*lobha-*); cf. $ 39. Skr *-au* : *koslā* (*kauśa-*), *kolī* (*kaula-*), *goḍ* (*gauḍa-*), *gorā* (*gaura-*), *cor* (*caura-*), *tol* (*taulya-*), *motīṃ* (*mauktika*), *mol* (*maulya-*).

Skr *apa* in *ovarī*, *osarṇeṃ*, *osar*, *osrī*.

Skr. *ava* : *hoṇeṃ* (*bhava-*), *loṇ* (*lavaṇa-*), *loṇī* (*navanīta-*). In the initial position : *oṇavṇeṃ*, *oṃvālṇeṃ*, *oṃvaḷā*, *orapṇeṃ*.

Skr. *uva* : *soṇeṃ* (*suvarṇa-*).

Pkt. *uva*, Skr. *upa*: *oṃvas* (*upavāsa-*), *oḷakhṇeṃ* (*avalakṣ-*), etc.

N.B.—Given the frequent exchanges between *o-* and *u-*, we cannot, in principle, determine in a compound word beginning with *o-*, if that prefix represents Skr. *apa-*, *ava-* or *upa-*, nor often *ut-*, see $81.

ava- tends to be reduced to *o* not only in Prakrit, but since then, and during all the periods: that is how are explained *loṇī* (*navanīta-*), *paḍosā* (*prativāsa-*), *koṇ* (if *kavaṇa-* "who ?" is not merely an etymological type carried into literature), *daroḍā* (D. *ḍaḍavaḍa-*). During the recent period numerous doublets have been found : *keḍhol* beside *keḍhaval*, *ekosā* the popular form of the tatsama *ekavasā*; similarly *amos*, *amūs* with regard to *avas* (Skr. *amāvāsyā*). *angochā* (*aṅgavastra-*) is probably a loan. The intermediary is evidently *au* : cf. *dauḍ* (*drava-*).

In the initial position, *va-* and *o-* get mixed up: For example *vaṭṇeṃ* (*vat-*, *vart-*), *vatīṃ* (*vaktra-*), *vaḷṇeṃ* (*valana-*) are the only forms found, but we have *oḍhṇeṃ* beside *vaḍhṇeṃ* (*vardh-*), *ovar* beside *va(u)/var* (*vadhuvara-*), *ohmāy* beside *vahmāy* (*vadhu-mātṛ-*), *oḍhaṇ, ohaṇ, ohaḷ* beside *vāhaṇ, vāhṇeṃ, vāhḷī* (root *vah-*). It is true that in *ohaṇ* for example, which is a dialectal word, one can suppose the influence of a word like Skr. *ogha-*; cf. also *ojhṃ*. As a consequence we do not often know if we have to do with a direct reduction of *ava* to *o*, or should we suppose the apocope of the initial *a*, apocope whose traces, besides, are found in Sanskrit texts (Wackernagel, II, $ 29 b *a*, *d*; Whitney, $ 1087). The two processes must have co-existed : thus are explained the doublets *oṇavṇeṃ* : *vaṇavṇeṃ* (*avanam-*), *ohaḷ* : *vahaḷ* and *oghaḷ* : *vaghaḷ* (*avagal-*, *avaghṛ-*), *omj(h)aḷ* : *vaṃjaḷ* (obscure etymology : *añjali-* or *avāñjali-* ?), *osvā* : *vasvā* (*avacchada-*), *oḷaṃg(h)ṇeṃ* : *valaṃgṇeṃ* and probably *vapṇeṃ* : *opṇeṃ* "to sell". Similarly *oṃgal* : *vaṃgaḷ* (*amaṅgala-*), *oḷ*; *vaḷī* (*āvalī-*), *ouṃl* : *vauṃl* (*vakula-*) : cf. *vovā* as against *vāṃv* (*vyāma-*).

$ 79. These exchanges are rendered easier by the fact that the short *a* has a posterior pronunciation. In Mahari this tendency is pushed to the extreme and results in the pronunciation of *o* : *ānond* (*ānanda-*), *haros* (*harṣa-*), *duckol* (*duṣkāla-*), see LSI, *Mar*, p. 157. In a general way, in the Konkan, *o* tends to replace *a* :

1. Under the influence of a labial, giving rise to examples cited above, LSI, *Mar.*, p. 167 : *boreṃ* "well" (M. *bareṃ*), *boiṇ* "sister" (M. *bahīṇ*), *mhuṇ-* and *moṇ* "to say" (M. *mhaṇ-*), *poḍ-* "to fall" (M. *paḍ-*). This also happens in the normal speech, chiefly when this *a* is nasalised, that is to say when it has already spontaneously the tendency to be unvoiced, cf. *kauṃs-*, the popular pronunciation of tatsama *kaṃsa*, and inversely *kaṃśā*, the pronunciation proper to women for *kovasā* "one who takes revenge". Thence, on the side of forms with *a*, *povḷeṃ* (*prabāla-*), *povāḍā* (*pravāda-*), *bhoṃvṇeṃ*, *bhoṃva-ḍṇeṃ* (*bhram-*), *bhoṃvar* (*bhramara-*), *bhoṃs* (D. *bhamāsa-*), *loṃbṇeṃ* (*lambana-*), *ṭhoṃb* with reference to *thāṃb-* (*stambha-*). Inversely we find *laṃv* for *loṃ* (*loma*). Where there is no nasality, the phenomenon is much less frequent : cf. *mahāg* with regard to Gujarati *moghuṃ* (*mahārgha-*).

2. Under the influence of the cerebral *ḷ* : Thence *visul-ṇeṃ* beside *visaḷṇeṃ* (*vikṣal-*), *saṃgulṇeṃ* the Konkani form of

saṃgaḍṇeṃ (*saṃghaṭ-*), *iṃgoḷ* (rare) and *kiḷos* (given as dialectal) beside *iṃgaḷ* (*aṅgāra-*) and *kiḷas* (*kilāsa-*), *kisūl* (where there is probably a substitution of the suffix, either * *kisaula-* <*kisalaa-* following the doublet *devālaya-* : *devakula-*, Pkt. *devaula-*, *deula-*), *pākoḷī* beside *pīṃkḷī* (*pakṣma-*).

3. Under the influence of *u* in a neighbouring syllable : *korn*=*karūn* "having done". This is almost unknown to the normal language.

4. By the assimilation of *o* of the preceding syllable if the intermediary consonant is *h* : *loho*, *moho*, the nom. sing.; cf. *mohorā*, *ḍoholā* for *mohrā* (*mukhara-*), *dohḷā* (*dohada-*) in the poetic language (see Joshi, $ 175, 3).

Observations common to *e* and *o*

$ 80. *e* and *o* replace *i* and *u* under ill-defined conditions. In Prakrit, just as *i*, *u* used to denote short *e*, *o*, notably before a geminated consonant (Pischel, $ 79-84), *e* and *o* replace *i* and *u* in this position (ibid, $ 119, 122, 125, 127). Its reasons are visible : on the one hand the absence of any symbol for short *e* and *o* (see Jacobi, KZ, XXV, 29) and on the other the closing of the phonemes *e* and *o*. But if it had been a case of pure graphic notation, one would expect in the modern languages, either the general re-establishment of *i* and *o*, or their total disappearance. Now, such is not the case; with reference to the normal examples of *i* and *u*, we find *e* and *o*.

1. In certain words specifically found in Prakrit with *e* and *o* : *etheṃ* (*itthaṃ*), *peḍhī* beside *piḍheṃ* (*pīṭha-*), *bel* (*bilva-*), *veṭh* (*viṣṭi-*), *śendūr* (*sindūra-*); possibly *gheṇeṃ* (Pkt. *geṇh-*, Skr. *gṛh-*) and *kheḷṇeṃ* (Pkt. *khel-*, Skr. *krīḍ-*); *ol* (*udra-*), *kohḷeṃ* (*kuṣmāṇḍa-*), *koḍh* (*kuṣṭa-*), *toṃḍ* (*tuṇḍa-*), *thor* (*sthūra-*), *pokhar* (*puṣkara-*), *pothī* (*pustaka-*), *polā* (*pūla-*), *mogar* (*mudgara-*), *moth* (*mustā-*), *mol* (*mūlya-*, but probably also * *maulya-*; cf. *tol*=* *taulya-*); *soṇḍ* (*śuṇḍā*) corresponds to the Pali form (*soṇḍā*); to Deśī go back *koḍ* "*love*", *koḷeṃ* "hump of the buffalo", *coj* "marvel", *bokaḍ* "billy-goat" (*bukka-*), *mocā* "slipper" (which is borrowed from Persian *mūcah*).

2. In other words it, undoubtedly, refers to a gradation of Indo-European origin, notably in verbal stems of the type : *pheḍṇeṃ* : *phiṭṇeṃ* (Pkt. *phiḍ-*); thus *cepṇeṃ* : *cipṇeṃ* (this latter is popular ; cf. Skr. *cipiṭa-*), *bhokṇeṃ* : *bhukṇeṃ* (Pkt. *bhukk-*), *ghoṭṇeṃ* : *ghuṭghuṭṇeṃ* (Pkt. *ghuṭṭ*, *ghoṭṭ-*) and by analogy pos-

sibly the creation of *śendanem̩* (*chid-*), *leṭṇem̩* (root *lī-*), *kopṇem̩* (*kupya-*; unless it be a verb re-made on the tatsama *kopa*), *lehṇem̩* (popular) : *lihiṇem̩* (*likh-*); cf. *him̩ṣṇem̩* whose *i* found in Deśī corresponds to *e* of Skr. *heṣ-* (*hreṣ-*) and of M. *he*(*m̩*)*sṇem̩*. Similarly for the gradation of the verbal substantive and of the verb; *tilā* (cf. *toḍī* and *toḍṇem̩*) with regard to *tuṭṇem̩* (*truṭ-*), *khoḍā* of *akhuḍṇem̩* (*khoḍa-*, *kuṇṭha-*). Lastly it is the transfer of the verbal stem in the participle which explains the vocalism of the compound expression *denlen* (Pkt. *diṇṇa-*).

3. In the obscure cases: in *vehiā*, one could admit, either a differentiation of two *i*s of Skr. *vibhītikā*, or a Pkt. intermediary **vehiḍiā*. But it should not be forgotten that it is the name of a plant and, moreover, that there are in Sanskrit similar names of plants, such as *vihvala-* and *vedhaka-*. The plant-name *terḍā*, whose doublet is the dialectal *tirḍā*, seems to be older. But as in the case of examples going back to Prakrit, it is not possible to provisionally put forward a satisfactory explanation for the vocalism of *aherā* (cf. *ahirā*), *śegaṭ* (*śigru-*), *ocā* (*uccaya-*), *osam̩gā* (*utsaṅga-*, with the substitution of the preverb *ava-* for *ut* ?), *koḍem̩* (D. *kūḍa-*), *kom̩ḍāḷem̩* (*kuṇḍala-*), *gophā* (*gulpha-*), *tondel* (cf. *tund*), *tor* (beside *tūr*, Skr. *turī*), *com̩c* (*cañcu-*) *coclā* (D. *cum̩culia-*), *nikhorḍā* (D. *nikhuria-*) *pom̩kh* (*puṅkha-*), *bhoj* (*bhūrja-*), *mos* (Dialec. beside *mūs*, Skr. *mūṣa-*), *moḷi* (*mūlikā*), possibly *oj* (*ūrjas-*), *kor* (*krūra-*), *kolī* (*kulyā-*), *poṭ* (*puṣṭa-*).—Inversely *tūṇ* is in agreement with Sanskrit and differs from Pkt. *toṇa-*; *sum̩ṭh* has been kept whereas Hindi and Kashmiri have *som̩ṭh*, *śom̩ṭ*, and *kudāl* (Skr. *kuddāla-*) survives only in Marathi and Hindi, other languages have *o*.

It is possible that these are the traces of doublets going back deep in the past : cf. in the *Divyāvadāna* the co-existing forms *mūṭa* (*mūḍha-*) and *moṭa-*, whose equivalents are found in Marathi as *muḍī*, *moṭ*. For the time being it is not possible to attempt a deeper explanation.

In *bāher*, with regard to Pkt. *bāhim̩* (*bāhira-*), see M. *bāhirilā* (Inscrip. of 1206) *e* is certainly short.

The *i* of Persian seems to be represented by *e* in *mehtar*, *pehran* but this is because Persian *i* before *h* opens in Persian itself, see Hoern., "Neupers. Schriftspr.", *Grundriss d. Iran. Phil.*, I, 2, $ 4). To the *u* of Arabic corresponds *o* in *morāmbā*, possibly for some similar reason (ibid., $ 6). Besides, popular etymology seems to have intervened here.

CONSONANTS

Occlusives

$ 81. We have seen in $ 14 that following the alterations effected in the Middle Indian by older inter-vocalic consonants, there were, no longer, any occlusives inside Prakrit words, except when they were geminated. Later on, by one of the last consequences of the weakness of the intervocalic (consonants), the geminated became, most often, simplified at least in the Western languages except Panjaḅi (see Grierson, *Phon.*, p. 21 ff.) and notably in Marathi, where the exceptions seem generally to be due to borrowing.

In this way, we arrive in Marathi at a system where there is opposition between the initial occlusives or those developing from old geminated ones and the remnants of old intervocalic consonants or their substitutes. This opposition has been extended, since Prakrit, to *y* (the initial *y* and *-yy-* give in Prakrit and M. *j*; the intervocalic *y* disappears; M. *y* does not have a real existence, see $ 54, 56 and infra) and to *m* (Pkt. *m* and *-mm-*>M. *m* are opposed to Pkt. M. *-m̃v-* issued out of the Sanskrit intervocalic *m*). It is found also in the case of *n* and *l*. In fact, *n* and *l* are the initial and geminated forms corresponding to *ṇ* and *ḷ*, forms reserved for the intervocalic position. Here, curiously, the difference concerns the point of articulation and not the manner of articulation. Everything happens as if *ṇ*, *ḷ* had been in relation to *n*, *l* as *y* in relation to *j*, or *h* in relation to *kh*, that is to say as if the cerebral had been an intervocalic, therefore weak, dental form.

Only one series of occlusives seems to contradict the rule of opposition between the old intervocalic and the old initial or geminated consonants. They are the cerebral sonants *ḍ* and *ḍh* which, if one were to trust the sign, would indifferently represent initial and geminated Skr. *ḍ* and *ḍh* on the one hand and the intervocalic ones on the other. Now the uniformity of the sign hides a real phonetic difference : P. R. Bhandarkar has informed me that the consonants in question were articulated at the same point as *ṭ* and *ṇ*, that is to say on the anterior part of the palate (*g* of the figure given by Jesperson, at the end of his *Lehrbuch der Phonetik*) when they are in the initial position or are in group. But in the intervocalic position, *ḍ* and *ḍh* are articulated at the same point as *ḷ*, that is to say on the soft palate (just before the point *i* of the same figure). The articulation, therefore, takes place in *ḍāg*, *ḍhag*, *kaḍhṇeṃ* for ex. further ahead than in *kāḍhā*. It will be observed that this opposition (which is found probably in the central languages, where the intervocalic *ḍ* is noted *ṛ*, see Grierson, *Phon.*, $ 52), occurs in the same direction as that of *n* and *l* on one side and of *ṇ* and *ḷ* on the other. The strongest articulation is, at the same time, anterior.

The table, given below, summarises the oppositions characteristic of the system of Marathi occlusives.

	Initial or developed out of Prakrit geminated ones		Developed out of old intervocalics	
	Non-aspirates	Aspirates	Non-aspirates	Aspirates
Gutturals	*k, g*	*kh, gh*	*nil*	*h*
Palatals	*c, j*	*s*,[1] *jh*	*nil*	
Cerebrals	*ṭ, ḍ*	*ṭh, ḍh*	*ḍ*(*ḷ*)see supra,	*ḍh*
Dentals	*t, d*	*th, dh*	*nil*	*h*
Labials	*p, b*	*ph, bh*	*v*	*h*

The occlusives thus defined have, in principle, subsisted in Marathi without any change. However, the method of articulation of the occlusives has undergone a number of irregular changes affecting mainly the consonants following a nasal and the aspiration.

Occlusives following a nasal

$ 82. In the group, nasal +occlusive, it is the occlusive which is, in Marathi, the resisting part. The nasal is susceptible to different treatments, wherein its fate is linked with that of the preceding vowel (see $ 69). The consonant, on the contrary, remains in principle, unchanged. On this point Marathi agrees with Gujarati and both of them are opposed to the north-western group on one hand, where a nasal changes

1. *s* developed out of Pkt. *ch* is mixed with Skr. *s*, *ṣ*, *ś* and like all palatals is susceptible to two pronunciations in accordance with the timbre of the following vowel.

the following occlusive surd into a sonant and on the other to all the central languages, where the nasal tends to dominate over the sonant occlusive (see J. Bloch, JA, 1912, I, p. 332 ff, and the examples given by Grierson, *Phonol.*, p. 34 to 38; cf. infra, $ 124). Of these two last types of change, only exceptional cases are found in Marathi.

The words *kuṃjī* (*kuñcikā*) and *palaṃga* (*paryaṅka*—: cf. M. *pālak*, *pālakh* are found in almost all the dialects and are probably borrowed, largely from one another among them. One need not be surprised that the word for "key" and for a type of "bed" has travelled. As regards *kaṃgaṇī* (*kaṅkaṇa-*) and *kaṃgavā* (*kaṅkata-*) which co-exist with *kaṃkaṇ* and *kaṃkavā*, it is possible that the sonorisation therein has some phonetic principle. In fact, they are the only ones among the words beginning with *k*, where the group *ṅk* goes back to Sanskrit. Now in these words there must have been hesitation in Sanskrit itself and it shows, for example, the doublet *kaṅku-*: *kaṅgu-* (m. *kāṃg*). On the contrary where Marathi has preserved the internal *k*, it is because of its being an old *kk* (*kaṃkoḷ*=Skr. *kakkola-*, *kaṅkola-*) itself developed generally out of *rk* (*kāṃkḍī* <*karkaṭikā*, *kaṃkar* <*karkara-*, *kukar* <*kukkura*, *kurkura-*); *kuṃkūṃ* seems, therefore, to go back not to Skr. *kuṅkuma-* (cf. Sindhi *kuṅgū*), but to the form found in Tokharian, *kurkama-* and Sogdian *kurkumba-* (forms communicated to me by Sylvain Lévi and Gauthiot).

The second type of change is found only in the recent doublets of the type *vindhṇeṃ* : *vinhṇeṃ* (*vyadh-*, Pkt. *vindh-*) and the aberrant forms of the word for the number "five", which are, on the contrary, quite old and which have been studied in the chapter on the words for numbers.

Aspiration

$ 83. The aspiration of the occlusive gives rise in Marathi as in the related languages to frequent variations, which remain, nevertheless too sporadic and too irregular to enable us to discern any law therein. Everywhere are found cases of the aspiration of the non-aspirated occlusives and of the loss of aspiration of the aspirated occlusives. Only Simhalese like its neighbours, the Dravidian languages of the South, is ignorant of all aspiration (Geiger, $ 14, 3 and $ 27).

$ 84. Among the phenomena of aspiration two cases should be distinguished. In the initial position of words, the aspiration often goes back to Prakrit and is also often found in the cognate languages. Such is the case in *khasṇeṃ* (*kas-*), *khāpar* (*karpara-*), *khīḷ* (*kīla-*; *khīla* is found in later Vedic and in Pali), *khujā-* (*kubja-*).

kheṃkaḍ (cf. *kāṃkḍī*; Skr. *karkaṭa-*), *kheḷṇeṃ* (if it is related to Skr. *krīḍ-*; *khel-* is found from the *Rāmāyaṇa* onwards), *phaṇas* (dialectally *paṇas*, *panasa-*), *pharas* (*paraśu*), *phāsā* (*pāśa-*, cf. *sphāṃcī*), *phāsolī* besides *pāsolī* (*pārśva-* ? cf. Pali *phāsulikā*), *bhiseṃ* (*bisa-*), *bhīṃs* (*bṛsī*), *bhukṇeṃ* (*bukk-*), *bhūṃs* (*busa-*). The explanations given so far for the Prakrit forms of these examples are insufficient. The prosthetic *s-*, alternating in Indo-European under unknown conditions with the initial consonant *k-* or isolated *p-*, which is probable in a case like *khāpar*, and is possible elsewhere (see Wackernagel, I, 230 b, Pischel, $ 205, 206, n. 2), does not allow us to render account of the aspiration of the sonants. The influence of neighbouring *r* or *s*, admitted by Jacobi (*Ausgew. Erz.*, $ 21), seems to be better applicable to this case (cf. the very old Skr. example of *jaṣa-*: *jhaṣa-* cited by Wackernagel in $ 141) and to render account, for example, of *ghoṃs* (*gucchā*). Besides, it is possible that the modern forms with initial *bh-* be in reality more authentic than the corresponding Sanskrit forms with *b-*; and in that case *b-* itself would then be the result of a dissimulation by the sifflant. It is known, in fact, that the Indo-European *b-* is very rare and that the Sanskrit *b-* represents more than once *bh* (see Wackernagel, $ 105; cf. the observation of Pischel on *ghep-* cited in $ 106). In this case, the modern forms would be due to the maintenance of the old *bh-* in the presence of *s* or *r*. Thus may perhaps be explained *bher* (H. *ber*, M. *bor*, Skr. *badara-*), *bhukṇeṃ* "to bark" is the only example without a sifflant; but the word can admit as an expressive word special treatment of the same type as in *kās-*> *khas-* "to cough".

In short, except in the case of *b-*: *bh-* one can admit it is a case of assimilation—moreover abnormal—of the aspirated initial implicit in the sifflant or *r*: this hypothesis seems to get confirmation by the examination of different forms corresponding to Skr. *kubja-*, *kubhra-*, cf. *khujā*, *khubā* besides *kubḍā* and by *jhuṃjhṇeṃ* (*yudhya-*).

An example similar to the preceding one is found in *bhāph* beside *bāph* (*vāṣpa*), but it does not, certainly, belong to Marathi. The existence of *vāph* in this language makes us suspect that the form with *b-* is a loan. The same can be said with regard to *phattar* because of its duplication (cf. *pāthar*) and of *themb* (Skr. *tip-*: *step-*) because of the sonorisation of *p* after the nasal.

Certain examples can again be explained by contamination. Thus *ghāgar* (*gar-gara-*) "water-pot" can have been subjected to the influence of its homonym *ghāgrā* "chatter" (*gharghara-*), which also expressed the babbling of water. The name of the 'net" *phāṃs* or of the 'dice" *phāsā* (*pāśa-*, *pāsaka-*) can have been under the influence of the root *sparś-*. This had, in addition, the advantage of disencumbering the radical **pās-* already representing *pārśva* and *pāścāt*, indeed *pakṣa-* (inversely the deaspiration of the initial in the semi-tatsamas done after *sparś-*: *paras* is observed; see Grierson, *Phon.*, $ 60 and cf. Pkt. *apuṭṭha*=*aspṛṣṭa-*, M. *apūṭ*). But certain forms remain outside the domain of all explanations, as *phol* with reference to *pol* (Pkt. *polla-*) and as, chiefly the words with initial *jh-*. Herein the aspiration is posterior to Deśī in *jhāḍ* and *jhoṭiṃg*; cf. *jhompṇeṃ*" to sleep" with reference to Kanarese *jomp-*. The exclamation *jheṃ* beside *jeṃ* "what" (*yat*); *jhaṇi* "even if" which seems to be related to "*jāṇū*" as if, as "of the root *jaṇ* (Skr. *jñā*), chiefly *jhālā*, the past participle of the verbe "to be", which replaces sometimes the old *jālā* (*jāta-*). The words with the initial *jh-* are, moreover, generally obscure; cf. $ 107.

$ 85. At the end and inside a word, the examples of aspiration are still more sporadic and obscure.

The tatsamas *kaṃp*(*h*), *aṃk*(*h*) furnish sure examples for the final. The doublet *kap*: *kaph* denoting "cotton" is difficult to interpret in the absence of etymology for the forms *kāpūs* and *kapās*. It is possible that *kap* represents the oldest form, *kaph* being since that time its alternative form. It is equally possible that *kaph* had been borrowed from some dialect where *s* became *h* (cf. Sindhi, Panjabi *kapāh*, or *kapā*) and then lost its aspiration. The words *jāmb*(*h*) (*jambu-*), *vāk*(*h-*) (*valka-*) are not isolated: cf. *jāmb*(*h*)*ūḷ* and *vāk*(*h*)*al* cited below.

$ 86. The examples of aspiration inside the word are somewhat more numerous.

Some are probably purely apparent. The word *voghal-oghaḷ* (*avagal-*) has been subjected to the influence of the tat-sama *ogha-* or of *ojhar* (*avakṣar-*); *muṃḍ(h)ā* "bald" (*nuṇḍa-*) has been subjected to that of *muṃḍhī* "head" (*mūrdhan-*), which by a return action has become *muṃḍī*; *olaṃghṇeṃ* possibly carries the trace of a contamination with the roots *lag-* "to hold" and *laṅgh-* "to jump", or *lambh-* "to hang" ; *buj(h)ṇeṃ* (Pkt. *bojja-*) can have been influenced by its homonym *bujhṇeṃ* (*budhy-*); *guṃphā* "sylvestrian retreat, cradle, cavern" seems, despite the authority of Hemacandra, to be nearer Skr. *guṣp-*, *guph-*, *gumph-* "to weave" than the root *gup-* "to hide, to protect."

A separate group is formed by the words with *-mb(h)-*, where the gradation is old : the Vedic has *ramb-*: *rambh-*, Sanskrit opposes *ambu-* to *ambhas-* and *abhra-*, later still *jambīra*, to *jambha-* and *jambhīra-* (Wackernagel, $ 109). Undoubtedly thus can be explained the forms *āḷamb(h)eṃ*, *jāmb(h)ūḷ*, *bāb(h)ūḷ*, perhaps even *cumb(h)āḷ* (Pali *cumbaṭa-*). But there still remain several examples which are altogether obscure : thus *niḍ(h)aḷ* (*lalāṭa-*, Pkt. *nidāla-*), *pāṃḍhar* (*pāṇḍara-*), *pārak(h)ā* (*pārakya-*), *pālkhī* more frequent than *pālkī* (*paryaṅka-*), *peṃḍ(h)ī* (*piṇḍa-*), *vāphā*, *vāphṇeṃ* (tats. *vap-*).

$ 87. The deaspiration of the aspirated occlusives is exclusively met with inside and at the end of the word. Cases, where an initial non-aspirated consonant seems to correspond to an old aspirate, are found under special conditions. Thus *garat* for *gharat* (*gṛhasthā*) can come from dissimulation provoked by the old final *-th* of **gharatt(h)ā*. As regards *dāī* "*nurse*", it is not the Pkt. *dhāī*; it is an Iranian loan.

$ 88. The final position is particularly favourable to deaspiration; its examples are also numerous at this place. Besides, to judge from the hesitations of signs, not only in Marathi but also in the parent languages and from one language to another, the deaspiration must be more general than is shown by spelling. Are noted in Marathi :

Gutturals : *bhīk*(*bhikṣā*), *bhūk* (*bubhukṣā*); *cauk* (*catuṣka-*); *jāṃg (h)* (*jaṅghā*), *mahāg* (*mahārghya*), *savaṃg* (*samargha-*);

Palatals : *gūj* (*guhya-*), *māj*(*madhya-*), *vāṃj* and *sāṃj*, less used than *vāṃjh* and *sāṃjh* (*vandhyā, sandhyā*);

Cerebrals: *īṭ* (*iṣṭā*) and *ūṃṭ* (*uṣṭra-*) had already lost their aspiration during the Prakrit era (*iṭṭā, uṭṭa-*, Pischel, $ 304). We have similarly got *apūṭ* (*aspṛṣṭa-*, Pkt. *apuṭṭha-*), *kaṭ* (*kaṣṭa-*), *kaṃṭ* (in relation to *kaṃṭhā, kāṃṭhem*, etc., Skr. *kaṇṭha-*), *nāṭ* (in relation to *nāṭhā*, Sk. *naṣṭa-*), *pālaṭ* (wherefrom *pālaṭṇeṃ*; cf. *pālthā*; Skr. *paryasta-*); *laṭ* (Pkt. *laṭṭhi-*), *lāṭ* (Pkt. *laṭṭha*), *saṭ*(*h*) (*ṣaṣṭi-*), *śīṭ* (*sṛṣṭi-*), *heṭ* (Pkt. (*heṭṭha*); *ākhāḍ* (*āṣāḍha-*; but it is certainly a loan-word; cf. the Gujarati and Sindhi forms), *koḍ*(*h*) (Skr. *kuṣṭha-, koṭha-*) *dīḍ*(*h*) (Pkt. *divaḍḍha-*), *meḍ*(*h*) (Pkt. *meḍhī*);

Dentals : *garat* (*gṛhasthā*), *rohaṃt* beside *rovaṃth*, *roṃt*(*h*) (*romantha-*), *vīt* (dial. *vīth*, Skr. *vitasti-*), *śīt* (1. Skr. *siktha-*; 2. Deśī *sitthā*), *hāt* (*hasta-*); *ansūd* (*anna-śuddhi-*), *āsand* (*aśvagandha-*), *khād* (Pkt. *khaddha-*), *gīd*(*h*) (*gṛdhra-*), *pārad*(*h*) (Pkt. *pāraddhi-*), *saband*(*h*) tats. *sabandha-*; *band* on the contrary has nothing in common with Skr. *bandha-*, it is loan from Persian), *sāṃḍ*(*h*) (*samdhi-*);

Labials : *julūp* (Pers. *zulf*), *śem*(*b*) (*śleṣma*).

$ 89. Inside the word, examples of de-aspiration are equally quite numerous. It is often difficult to say if the change does not have its origin in a shorter word where the aspirate had been in the final position. Thus it is not known as to which is the original form, *bhūk* or *bhukṇeṃ*, *samṭ*(*h*) or *sāṃṭ*(*h*)*ṇeṃ*, *-sūd* or *sud*(*h*)*ā*, nor whether the verbs with the radical in *-ṭ*, the termination of an old participle, have received their radical without aspiration or have lost the same later on. Inversely, the forms of Pkt. *iṭṭā, uṭṭa-*, if they are not of archaic re-making, seem to indicate that the change of consonants considered above as finals has been produced at the moment when they had not been in that position. Finally, it is such a case where the hesitation between an aspirated consonant and the non-aspirated one is old. This happens in the word for "sugar", formed on the one hand in the Sanskrit form *śarkarā*, Pkt. *sakkara-*, and on the other in the Pali form *sakkharā*, cf. *Sakkhari*, a transcription coming uṇdoubtedly from Western India.

Even while taking note of these observations, it is impossible to explain phonetically all the facts. In the lists that follow, it is not possible to note the frequency of words containing a sifflant or an aspirate. The dissimulation due to the presence of these phonemes undoubtedly explains for a large part the loss of aspiration. This remark, besides, is applicable to a good number of examples of de-aspiration which are in the final position. But the divergent cases are too numerous to enable one to be satisfied with this explanation. It is better to group, here, the examples without seeking to explain all of them.

Surd Gutturals : Skr. *ṣk* is represented by *kh* in *pokhar* (*puṣkara-*) *vikharṇeṃ* (*viṣkar-*), but by *k* not only in *dukaḷ* (*duṣkāla-*; cf. (Pkt. *dukkara-* < *duṣkara-*), *nīkāmī* (*niṣkarma-*) where the composition, being felt, has been able to preserve in the main word its initial *k* (cf. Deśī *nikhaḍo* < (*niṣkaṭa-*, and probably *nikāl-* borrowed by Marathi from Hindi), but also in *sukā* (besides *sukhā*, rare and undoubtedly a stranger; Skr. *śuṣka-*). Similarly Skr. *ks*, normally represented by *kh* (see $ 104); is shown as *k* in *śikṇeṃ* (*śikṣ-*), *bhukṇeṃ* (*bubhukṣ-*; cf. *bhūk* < *bubhukṣā* above), probably also in *pek*(*h*)*ṇeṃ* (*prekṣ-*) and two other verbs, also undoubtedly, derived from the root *īkṣ-*, *paikṇeṃ* "to wait" and *aikṇeṃ* "to listen." There is also no trace of the aspirate in *pākḷi* (*paksma-*). Leaving aside the doublet *sākhar*: *sākar*, Marathi has two co-existing forms in *sāṁk*(*h*)*ṇeṃ*, *sāṃk*(*h*)-*aḷṇeṃ* (Pkt. *saṃkhāi*), *sāṃk*(*h*)*aḷ* (*śṛṅkhalā*, the form without aspiration is found in Jaina Prakrit).— The same holds true for the sonant : *saṃgad*, *sāṃgaḍṇeṃ*, *sāṃguḷnem* (*saṃghat-*), *sāṃgṇeṃ* (Pkt. *saṃ*(*g*)*h*, *saṃgneṃ* (cf. Deśī *suṃghia-*).

Sonant Palatals : the passives *ḍājṇeṃ* (*dahya-*), *ruj*(*h*)*ṇeṃ* (*ruhya-*; but there is perhaps in existence an Indo-Iranian doublet without aspiration, see the Lexicon), *reṃjṇeṃ* (*rih-* ?), *śijṇeṃ* (*sidhya-*; *śijhṇeṃ* also exists, but is less authentic); similarly *samajṇem* (*-dhyā-* ?; cf. H. S. *samajh-*), *mājīṃ*, *mājārīṃ* (*madhya*; cf. *māj* cited supra). On *niśc-* > *nic* see $ 101.

Cerebral Surds : *agṭ*(*h*)*ī* (*agnistha-*), *āṭkeṃ*, *aḍṭīs*, *aḍsaṣṭ* (*aṣṭa-*), *bhaṭakṇeṃ* (*bhraṣṭa-*), *sāṃṭ*(*h*)*ṇeṃ* (*saṃsthā-*), *śeṭ*(*h*)*ī* (*śreṣṭhin-*). One should add here verbs made on the stems of the participle in *-ṭṭha* : *umaṭṇeṃ* (*unmṛṣṭa-*?), *ghāṭṇeṃ* (*ghṛṣṭa-*), *nīsaṭṇeṃ* (*nis-ṛṣṭa-*), *piṭṇeṃ* (**pṛṣṭa-*), *miṭṇeṃ* (*mṛṣṭa-*; cf. *māṭhṇeṃ*). The etymology of *sāṭ*(*h*)*iṃ* "for" is not certain. It seems, at first view, that it has something to do with *artha-* : but the Sindhi form *sāṭo* (exchange", Guj. "*sāṭa*" "in exchange for" lead us to suspect the confusion of two words neighbouring in meaning and similar except in aspiration : moreover, *sāṭ-* has no known etymology.

Sonant Cerebrals : *aḍīc*, *aḍkā*. *sāḍe* (*ardha-*; cf. *dīḍ*(*h*), *oḍ*(*h*)*aṇ*, *oḍ*(*h*)*aṇī* (D *oḍḍhaṇaṃ*, *ohāḍaṇi*), *sāḍ*(*h*)*ū* (*śyālivoḍha-*); *gāḍṇeṃ* is not sure, it may represent *gart-* as well as *gāḍh*-as regards *muṃḍhī* (*mūrdhan-*) this word can have been influenced by *muṇḍa-*, on which, it has in its turn, reacted. (see $ 85).

Dental Surds : *ut*(*h*)*al* (Pkt. *utthal-*), *kot*(*h*)*rīb* for *kothimbīr* (*kustumbarī-*).—

Dental sonants: *udav* (*uddhav*), *sud*(*h*)*ā* (*śuddha-*; cf. *ansūd* cited supra); *vindrūṃ*, doublet of *vindhrūṃ* perhaps contains, not the root *vindh-*, but Skr. *vidra-*.

Labial Surds : *apūṭ* (*aspṛṣṭa-*, Pkt. *apuṭṭha-*) can go back to a certain doublet, without *s*, of the root *sparś-*, or can be the result of dissimilation (Pkt. **phuṭṭha-*) >*puṭṭha-*). The etymology of *pāpṇī* (*pakṣma-* ?) is doubtful : cf. *pākḷī*. The form *vāphā* is more usual than *vāpā* (*vāpya-*) : the homony m*vāph* (Skr. *vāṣpa-*) could have influenced it ?—

Labial Sonants : *kubḍā* (Skr. *kubhra-*) goes back to a radical earlier containing two aspirates, or the dissimilation has been effected in both the directions; cf. *khubā* and *khujā* (Skr. *kubja-*); *hambā*, *hambar-* result from a similar dissimilation (Skr. *hambhā*, *hambhāra-*). As regards *jābāḍ*, beside *jābhaḍ*, it is all the more strange that if it is definitely a compound of *jāmbh*+*hāḍ*, then the aspiration would have had double reason for subsisting.

$ 90. The changes concerning the mode of articulation

set out above and that of *ch* into *s* (see $ 102) are the only ones undergone by Marathi consonants in a regular manner. The exchange between the surd and the sonant (except when this exchange is determined by the contact of two consonants, see supra, $ 82 and farther down) is almost unknown. The verb *macṇeṃ* seems to be related to *madya-*: Prakrit has already got *maccai*, so the difficulty goes back to an epoch anterior to that of Marathi. Moreover, it is not sure if there had been some contamination (cf. the observation of Pischel on the subject of Pkt. *vaccai*, root *vraj-*, $ 202, note 3). In the final position of certain loan words a trace of hesitation is found : thus *jāp* beside *jāb* (Per. *jawāb*); tats. *akāṃt* (Skr. *ākranda-* "lamentation" possibly influenced by *ākrānta-* "tormented by passion"). Dialectally *s* is pronounced *j* (that is to say *z*) *zakalā*, *zhavlī* for *sakalā*, *sāvlī* in the Konkan (cf. Molesworth, *sāvlī* and LSI, *Mar.*, p. 6). A curious and inexplicable evolution, but found from Prakrit onwards, concerns the development, in certain cases, of Skr. *ṣṭ* and *ṣṭh* not only upto *ṭṭh* and *ṭh*, but upto *ḍh* in the intervocalic position, see $ 112.

Marathi Occlusives and their Point of Articulation

$ 91. The point of articulation of the Marathi consonants is, in principle, the same as that of the Sanskrit ones. Certain partial modifications, not based on any general principles, will be set out apropos of each of the category of the occlusives.

Gutturals.

k

$ 92. In the initial position, *k* succeeds the Pkt. *k* which is :

Skr. *k* in *karṇeṃ* (*karaṇa-*), *kām* (*karma*), *kīḍ* (*kīṭa-*), *kuvā* (*kūpa-*), *keḷ* (*kadalī-*) *koḍ*(*h*) (*kuṣṭha-*) and numerous other words which are found in the Lexicon;

Skr. *kr* in *keṇeṃ* (*krayaṇa-*), *kos* (*krośa-*), *kolhā* (*kroṣṭhuka-*);

Skr. *kv* in *kadhṇeṃ* (*kvath-*); *kaḍhaī* (*kaṭāha-*) is perhaps of the same family; for *kāīl* "kettle", it is more doubtful.

$ 93. In the interior or final position, *k* goes back to :
Skr. *k* after the nasal : *sāmkaḍ*, etc., cf. $ 82;
Pkt. *kk* developed out of :
Skr. *kk* in *cikaṇ* (*cikkaṇa-*), in the expressive words *śīṃk* (*chikkā*) and *hakārṇeṃ* (*hakkhāra-*), perhaps in *cukṇeṃ* (*cukk-?*);
ky in *pārkā* (*pārakya-*), *sakṇeṃ* (*śakya-*), *śīkem* (*śikya-*);
kv in *pikā* (Pkt. *pikka.*=*pakka-*, Skr. *pakva-*);
kr in *cāk*, (*cakra-*), *cukā-* (*cukra-*), *tāk* (*takra-*), *vāṃk* (*vakra-*), *sūk* (*śukra*);
ṭk in *sak* (*ṣaṭka-*);
tk in *ukḍā* (*utkaṭuka-*), *ukar* (*utkara-*); *ukaṭṇeṃ* (*ut-kṛt-*) *ukaḍṇeṃ* (*ut-kvath-*, Pkt. **uk-kaḍh-*), *ukaḷṇeṃ* (*ut-kalaṇa* certainly do not go back to Sanskrit. They can have been the Prakrit compounds with *u-*(<*ut-*, *upa-*, *apa-*, *ava-*, cf. $ 78);
kr in *kaṃkar* (*karkara-*), *kāṃkḍī* (*karkaṭikā*), *kuṃkūṃ* (* *kurkuma-*), see $ 82; *bakrā* (*barkara-*), *mākaḍ* (*markaṭa-*), *sākar* (*śarkarā-*);
ṣk in *cauk* (*catuṣka-*), *dukāḷ* (*duṣkāla-*), *sukā* (*śuṣka-*), etc., see $ 89.

$ 94. According to Pischel, the *k* of *mukṇeṃ*, *mokaḷ*, *moklā* would go back to Skr. *kn*. It is certain, in fact, that the Prakrit participle *mukka-* can not go back to *mukta-*, which normally gives *multa-* (cf. Simhalese *mut* and the examples of M. *t* —Skr. *kt* given below); Not one of the examples of the participles collected by Pischel in $ 566 of his grammar can be surely explained by the morpheme *-na-*. Perhaps it will be better to recognise therein simply a direct action of the Sanskrit radical. This influence is particularly probable in the case of *mukṇeṃ*, etc., whose relationship with the tatsamas of current usage, *mukta-*, *mukti-*, *mokṣa-* could not fail to be recognised.

In this hypothesis, the *kk* of Pkt. *mukka* is not to be phonetically interpreted. It will be simply a sign of the Skr. *k* rendered necessary by the Prakrit rule that in the intervocalic position there can only be geminated consonants. This is how are similarly explained *lākaḍ* (Pkt. *lakkuṭa-*, Skr. *lakuṭa-*), *mukā* (Pkt. *mukka-* beside *mūa-*, Skr. *mūka-*), and above all *ek* (Pkt. *ekka-*, Skr. *eka-*), a word particularly indispensable,—this can be maintained only at the cost of an artifice.

The Pkt. *-kk-* is inexplicable in *ṇakka-*, M. *nāk* (cf. Skr. *nāsā*, *nāsikā*). It is frequently used in classical Prakrit as a morpheme: see Lūders, *Bruchstcüke*, p. 38, 41; Pischel, $ 194, 598. This morpheme is, undoubtely, already noted in some of the Aśokan inscriptions (see Fleet, JRAS, 1906, p. 407-410; T. Michelson, *J. Phil.*, XXXI, p. 59). In Marathi, its clear examples are rare. It is found in *ṭhākṇeṃ* (*sthā-*: cf. Apabh. *thakkei*), in expressive words like *khuḍakṇeṃ*, *caḍak-micakṇeṃ*, *phaṭak-*, in several words with unknown etymology: *ḍokī* (cf. the doublet *ḍoī*, *ḍhakkā ḍhāṃkṇeṃ* (root *dhā-* ?), *ucak-ṇeṃ*, (*ucca-* ?). This morpheme goes undoubtedly back in part to Skr. *-kya-*. The word *pārkā* clearly proves the same, but other influences could have been active. The notation *pāikka-* of Prakrit is in reality merely a transcription of the modern form *pāīk*, which is a loan from Iranian, and not the successor of Skr. *padātika-*. On the other hand, it is known that *-kk-* is a current morpheme in the Dravidian languages (see Caldwell, *Comp. Gram. of the Drav. Languages*, 2nd edn., p. 97), Now the existence of words like *cikkā* in Deśī (M. *cikkar*, *cike*) proves that the Dravidian loans are old in Marathi, and it is permissible to put near each other the gradation, Mar. *caḍ*, *caḍak* "smack slap" and that of Kanarese *caḷa* "noise of a bubble that bursts": *caḷaka* "dexterity, speed", *caḷaken* "cramp, sposmodically contracting oneself."

kh

$ 95. In the initial position *kh-* represents :

Skr. *kh* in *khacṇeṃ* (*khacya-*), *khaj* (*kharju-*), *khaju* (*khar-jūra-*), *khaḍī* (*khaṭī*), *khaṇṇeṃ* (*khan-*), *khaṇṭeṃ* (*khani-traka-*), *khar*, *kharaḍ* (*khara-*), *khaḷa* (*khala*-subst. and adj.), *khāṭ*, *khaṭa* (*khaṭvā*, *khaṭvāṅga-*), *khāṇḍṇeṃ*, *khāṃḍ*, *khāṃḍā*, *khaḍā* (*khaṇḍa-* cf. *khiḍ*, *khiṇḍ* etc., see $ 75), *khāṇ* (*khāni-*), *khāt* (*khātra-*), cf. of the same root *khāī* (Pkt. *khāiā*), *khāṇeṃ*, cf. *khāū* (*khādana-*), *khād* (Pkt. *khaddha-*), and *khājeṃ* (*khādya-*), *khijṇeṃ* (*khidya-*), *khuḍṇeṃ*, *khuḷṇeṃ*, *khuḍā*, *khuḷā*, *khoḍ*, *khoḍā* (root *khuṇḍ-*, *khuḍ-*), *khūr* (*khura-*), *kheḍeṃ* (*kheṭaka-*), *kher* (*khadira*);

Skr. *sk* in *khāṃd* (*skandha-*), *khāṃb* (*skambha-*) and undoubtedly in *khavā* (cf. Lat. *scapula*);

Skr. *skh* in *khaḷṇeṃ*, *khaḷbaḷṇem* (*skhalana-*);

Skr. *kṣ* in *khapṇeṃ* (*kṣapya-*), *kharṇeṃ* cf. *khirṇeṃ* (*kṣar*), *khavaṃ* (*kṣapaṇika-*), *khār* (*kṣāra-*), *khirṇi* (*kṣīriṇī*), *khūr* (*kṣīrikā*), *khubalṇeṃ* (*kṣubh-*), *khevā* (*kṣepa-*), *khoḍ* (*kṣoḍa*), *khoḍṇeṃ* (*kṣuḍ-*)

Skr. *k* in *khāpar* and the words studied in $ 84; by the metathesis of aspiration in *khāṃk* (*kakṣa-*), *khāḍīṇ*, *khaḍaṇ* for *kadhīn* (*kaṭhina*), etc.;

Skr. *ṣ* in the words borrowed from languages where Skr. *ṣ* gets mixed in the tatsamas with *kh*: *vikh* (*viṣa-*), which besides in Hindi itself co-exists with *bis*, as *ākhāḍ*, the name of the month of *āsāḍha-* co-exists there with *aṣahr*.

$ 96. Inside the word, *kh* goes directly to Skr. *kh* in the tatsamas *nakh* (written in Prakrit *ṇakkha-*), *mukh*, etc., and in the compounds whose second member begins with *kh* : *pakhāl* (*pra-kṣal-*), *ākhuḍṇeṃ* (*ākhuṭ-*); the reason why *kh* has been preserved in *udūkhala-* >Pkt. *ukkhala-* > M. *ukhaḷ* is not clear. For *ukhaḍṇeṃ*, it is difficult to choose between a prototype* *ut-khuṭ*-and a prototype *utkṛṣ-*, Pkt. *ukhaḍh-*, where a metathesis of aspiration had to be supposed.

kh represents in addition :

Skr. *kh* after a nasal in *sāṃkhaḷ* (*śṛṅkkhalā*), cf. $ 89;

Skr. *khy* in *vākhāṇ* (*vyākhyāna-*) and perhaps in *ukhāṇā* (* *upa-khyāna* ?);

Skr. *ṣk* in *pokhar* (*puṣkara-*), *vikharṇeṃ* (*viṣkir-*); cf. $ 89 and 92;

Skr. *kṣ* in *āṃkh* (*akṣa-*), *ākhā* (*akṣata-*), *kākh* (*kakṣa*), *kukhāvart* (*kukṣi-*), *cokh* (*cokṣa-*), *pākh*, *pākhrūṃ* (*pakṣa-*, *pakṣi-*), *pekhṇeṃ* (*prekṣaṇa-*), *mākhṇeṃ* (*mrakṣaṇa-*), *rākh* (*rākṣā*), *rākhṇeṃ* (*rakṣaṇa-*), *rākhīsmukh* (*rākṣasa-*), *rukhā* (*rūkṣa-*), *rūkh* (*rukṣa-*), *lākh* (*lakṣa-* and *lākṣā*), *lākhṇeṃ*, *olākhṇeṃ* (*lakṣaṇa-*, *avalakṣ-*), *līkh* (*likṣā*). Add here *śikṇeṃ*, etc., see $ 89;

Skr. *kṣṇ* in *tīkh* (*tīkṣṇa-*) and Skr. *kṣm* in *pākḷī* (*pakṣma-*).

g

$ 97. In the initial position, *g* represents Pkt. *-g* developed out of :

Skr. *g* in *gaṃḍ* (*gaṇḍa*-, cf. (*gāṃḍ*), *gaṇṇeṃ* (*gaṇaya*-), *gadhḍā* and *gādhav* (*gardhabha*-), *gaṃdh*, *gaṃdhā* (*gandha*-), *garaḷ* (*garala*-), *gar*(*h*)*āṇeṃ* (*garh*-), *gavasṇeṃ* (*gaveṣaṇa*-), *gavā*, *gavlī* (*gāv*-), cf. *gāī*, *gāulī*, *gavlī* (*gopāla*-), *gahirā* (*gabhīra*-), *gahūṃ* (*godhūma*-), *gaḷṇeṃ* (*gal*-), *gaḷā* (*gala*-), *gāū* (*gātu*), *gājṇeṃ* (*garjana*-), *gāṃjā* (*gañjā*) *gāṃjṇeṃ* (*gañjana*-), *gāḍhā* (*gādha*-), *gāṇ* (*gahana*-), *gāṇeṃ* (*gā*-), *gāt* (*gātra*-), *gābh*- (*garbha*-), *gāl* (*galla*-), *gāḷ* (*gālī*), *gilṇeṃ* (*gil*-), *gīdh* (*gṛdhra*-), *gugūḷ* (*guggulu*-) *guṇ* (*guṇa*-), *guṇṇeṃ* (*guṇana*), *gurūṃ* (**go-rūpaṃ*), *gū* (*gūtha*-), *gūj* (*guhya*-), *gūḷ*, *guḍ* (*guḍa*-) *gelā* (*gata*), *gerū* (*gairika*-), *goṭh* (*goṣṭha*-), *goṭhī* (*goṣṭhī*-), *goḍ* (*gauḍa*-) *uḍ* (*guḍa*-*goṇ* (*goṇī*), *got* (*gotra*-), *gophā* (*gulpha*-), *gorā* (*gaura*-), *govar*, *gosavī* (*govaraṃ*, *gosvāmin*), *golā* (*golaka*-), perhaps *gadaḷ* (cf. Pers. *gil*), *gāṃjṇeṃ* (Pkt. *gañj*-);

Skr. *gr* in *gāṃṭhṇeṃ*, *gaṃṭh* (*grantha*-); cf. *gumṭh*-; *gāṃv* (*grāma*-) *gīm* (*grīṣma*-); perhaps *gyāj* (*grīvā*-).

$ 98. Inside the word, *g*, obscure in certain cases as in *vāguḷ*, *pāgṇeṃ* goes back to :

Skr. and Pkt. *g* after a nasal : *aṃg*(*u*)*ṭha* (*aṅguṣṭha*-), *nāṃgar* (cf. *laṅgala*-), *nāṃgḷī* (*lāṅgalikā*-), *pāṃg* (*paṅgu*-), *maṃgaḷ* (*maṅgala*-), cf. *oṃgal* (*amaṅgala*-), *raṃg* (*raṅga*-), *laṃgḍā* (*laṅga*-), *saṃgeṃ* (*saṃgata*-), *hiṃg* (*hiṅgu*-), etc., or in the semi-tatsamas *jag* (*iagat*-), *jūg* (*yuga*-);

Pkt. *gg* developed out of :

Skr. *gy* in *jogā* (*yogya*-);

Skr. *gr* in *agyā* (*agrega*-), *agḷā* (*agra*-), *āgas* (*agraśaḥ*);

Skr. *gn* in *āg* (*agni*-), *nāgvā* (*nagna*-), *salag* (*saṃlagna*-);

Skr. *dg* in *mogar* (*mudgara*-), probably also *uga*(*va*)*ṇ* (*udgamana*-);

Skr. *rg* in *āgaḷ* (*argalā*), *māg* (*mārga*-), *māgṇeṃ* (*mārgaya*-); cf. *sugī* (Pkt. *sugga*- as in *dugga*-, Skr. *durga*-);

Skr. *lg* in *āvagṇeṃ* (*āvalg*-);

Skr. *k* in a certain number of semi-tatsamas as has been the case during all the periods (cf. for Prakrit Pischel, $ 202, for Apabhraṃśa, $ 192) ; *asog*, *osag* (*aśoka*-), *kāg*, *kāgdā* (*kāka*-; cf. the doublet *kāu*;

Kannada has *kāgi*, *kūgi*), *pragaṭ* (*prakaṭa-*) *bagḷā* (*baka-*), *mugūṭ*, *mugṭā* beside *mukṭā* (*mukuṭa-*), *sagā* (*svaka-*) *sagḷā* (*sakala-*), *sāg* co-exists with *sāy* (*śāka-*). To the sentiment of this gradation, rather than to the phonetic assimilation, is due the form *askānd* re-made on the semi-tatsama *asgandha* (*aśvagandha-*)

gh

$ 99. In the initial position, *gh-* represents Skr. *gh-* in *ghaḍṇeṃ* (*ghaṭ-*), *ghaḍā* (*ghaṭa-*), *ghaḍī* (*ghaṭikā*), *ghaṇ* (*ghaṇa-*), *ghāṃṭ* (*ghaṇṭā*), *ghāṭ* (*ghaṭṭa-*), *ghāṭṇeṃ* (*ghṛṣṭa-*), *gham* (*gharma-*), *ghāy*, *ghāv* (*ghāta-*), probably *ghāḷṇeṃ* (cf. *jigharti*), *ghāsṇeṃ* (*gharṣaṇa-*), *ghās* (*ghāsa-*), *ghī* (ghṛta-) *ghoḍā* (*ghoṭaka-*). Similarly in the initial position of the first member of compounds, as in *vighadṇeṃ*, perhaps *āghād.*

In the initial position and inside the word, *gh-* comes from Skr. *ghr-* Pkt. (*g*)*gh-* in *ghāṇ* (*ghrāṇa-*; cf. *ghāṇa*), *vāgh* (*vyāghra*).

The old *gh* after a nasal has subsisted : *laṃghṇeṃ* (*laṅgh-*), etc.

In the initial position *gh-* comes from the recent *rapprochement* of *gh-* belonging, earlier, to two different syllables : *ghov* < D. *goho.* Perhaps the same holds true for the Prakrit forms corresponding to M. *ghā*, *gheṇeṃ* *ghepṇeṃ* (*graha-*, *grahi-*) . On the contrary the initial aspirate can, however, go back to Indo-European, cf. Pkt. *ghara-*, M. *ghar* with reference to Skr. *gṛha-*.

The origin of the initial *gh-*, in a certain number of words, which are not found before Deśī, remains obscure : *ghaḍakṇeṃ*, *ghusalṇeṃ*, *ghumṇeṃ-*, *ghulṇeṃ-*, *ghoṭṇeṃ*, *ghoḷṇeṃ* (see the Lexicon).

-gh- represents Skr. *kh-* in the semi-tatsama *regh* (*rekhā*).

Palatals.

$ 100. The mi-occlusive palatals of Sanskrit have not preserved a uniform pronunciation in Marathi. In fact, before the vowels, *a*, *u*, and *o*, they have lost their hushing character. The old articulation is constantly preserved only before *i*. Before *e* it is not uniform. In the initial position, it is normally palatal (*śeḷā*). Inside the word, it is variable; thus we say *coi*, loc. *cośet*, but "oblique of the genitive" *tyā-ce* as *tyācā* and *vācen* first sing. future as in the infinitive *vācṇeṃ*. It seems that morphological influences have been active here. There must have been several dialectal variations here : thus the *Survey* gives the dental pronunciation of *c* before *e* as being normal in Konkan (LSI, *Mar.*, p. 22, 66). The hushing pronunciation before *a* reveals the recent fall of an *i*. Thus the oblique of *rāzā* (*rājā*) is *rājā*, which is for **rājeā* > *rājya*. The same pronunciation is also often the sign of a loan : in this case, sometimes one writes *cy* for noting the alien pronunciation (*kāṃcyā*, for ex. *cyār* for *cār* "four").

In the Skr. group *jñ*, *j-* could not keep its palatal pronunciation. This impossibility has facilitated the differentiation of two continuant consonants and the group has ended up as *dñ*.

Marathi is the only Indo-Aryan language, having these peculiarities of pronunciation. But it shares them with languages belonging to other families, which are contiguous to it in the East, namely, Telugu and the Dravidian languages; probably Kurku, Muṇḍa dialect (see LSI, *Muṇḍā and Drav. Langs.* , p. 169, 479, 586).

Elsewhere they have no influence on the ancient history of the language, and in this work we can consider the group of palatals as unique.

c

$ 101. In the initial position, *c* represents Skr. *c* in *cakvā* (*cakravāka-*), *citā* (*citraka-*), and in a large number of other words to be seen in the Lexicon; Skr. *cy-* in *cavṇeṃ* (*cyav-*).—The enclitic *-c*, see M. *-ci*, has been treated as an independent word. In Gujarati and Sindhi, on the contrary, the same particle has evolved upto the sonant stage *-j* (see LSI, *Rāj.*, p. 59).

Inside the word or at the end of the word, *c* represents Skr. *c* after a nasal : *caṃcarṇeṃ* (cf. *cañcarin-*), *caṃcaḷ* (*cañcala-*), *coṃc* (*cañcu-*), *pāṃc* (*pañca-*), *lāṃc* (*lañca*), *saṃcarṇeṃ* (*saṃcaraṇa-*), *sāṃc*(*ā*) (*saṃcaya-*), *siṃcṇeṃ* (*siñc-*), cf. *kilac*, *kilīc* (D. *kiliñcī-*). The word *māc* : *maṃcī* is obscure and can as well go back to Kannada *maccu* as to Skr. *mañca-*.

In the same position, *c* goes back to Pkt. *cc*, that is to say to:

Skr. *cc* in *uṃc* (*ucca-*), *ucāṭ* (*uccāṭana-*), *oṃcā* (*uccaya-*), *kacrā* (*kaccara-*) *cūṃc* (*cuccu-*);

Skr. *cy* in *khacṇeṃ* (*khacya*), *rucṇeṃ* (*rucya-*), perhaps in *micakṇeṃ*;

Skr. *ty* in *kāc* (*kṛtyā*), *nācṇeṃ* (*nṛtya-*), *sāc* (*satya-*) probably *aḍīc* (*ardha-*, **tṛtya-*); perhaps Skr. *ṭy* in *roṃcṇeṃ* (root *ruṭ-*);

Skr. *rc* in *āṃc* (*arci-*), *kuṃcā* (*kūrca-*).

In the compounds with *niḥ-*, whose second member begins with *c*, the result is not *ch*, but *c* : thus *nicarṇeṃ*, *ṇicaḷ*, *nicint*. Perhaps there has occurred here a substitution of the prefix *ni-* for *niś-*; perhaps the meaning has helped preserve the simple word (cf. *niṣka->nik.*, $ 89; see also the observation of Pischel regarding Pkt. *ṇahaara* and *harianda* in $ 301).

Elsewhere *c* is recent as in *maccā* (*madh-cā*) or belongs to a borrowed word, either from Sanskrit (*aṃcavṇeṃ kā*(*ṃ*)c *vācṇeṃ*) or to other languages (for ex. *upakharc* compound of a Sanskrit preposition and an Arabic word). In this last case *c* often transcribes *ch* of the congeneric languages. This is due to the fact that *ch* does not normally exist in Marathi. The fact is evident in *kā*(*ṃ*)*cyā* where *y*, destined to note a palatal pronunciation, unusual in Marathi, betrays the loan; *kā*(*ṃ*)-*cyā* (*kaccha-*), *kaḍcī* (D. *kaḍacchū*) are the loans which should be interpreted exactly as *aṃgochā*, *ucchāv*, *guch*, *chabilā*, *chāvḍā*, *chāvā*, *chāvṇī*, *paṃchī*, etc. Only *viṃcī*, *viṃcṇī* (*vṛścikā*) is old: The form without aspiration, already noted by Hemacandra, is natural to Marathi; it is, besides, inexplicable.

As regards *cultā* and other words of the same family where an aspirate should be expected, (Skt. *kṣudra-*), they form a group where the hesitation is old and is to be explained outside Marathi; see Wackernagel, $ 116 and Pischel $ 325.

s (Pkt. *ch*)

$ 102. In Sanskrit *ch* is not, from its origin, the aspirate corresponding to *c*. It is in reality the substitute of old consonantal groups simplified according to the formula generalised in Middle-Indian (see Wackernagel, $ 131 ff.). Thence the fact that in Sanskrit *ch* had already been geminated in the intervocalic position, and that this phoneme has not undergone either in Prakrit or in Marathi any change depending on its place in the word. Marathi has only one treatment of *ch*, which is that of the initials and of the geminated ones.

In Marathi, Pkt. *ch* has got mixed with the sifflant *s* (*ś* before the palatal vowel). The same evolution has been independently produced in various dialects. The best-known case is that of popular Bengali (see Beames, I, 218-219; cf. Ch. Eliot, JRAS, 1910, p. 1171, note and LSI, *Bengali*, p. 28). Its traces are found in western Hindi, in Rajasthani and in Gujarati (see LSI, *Rājasth.*, p. 20, 330). In As samese the evolution is surely not identical : there *s* represents all the surd palatals (Grierson, *Phon.*, p. 3-4). The same is also true of a number of dialects inside Marathi itself (see *Survey*, p. 147, 151-52; cf. 161). The same confusion is produced in Simhalese, but that is due to the fact that this language has lost all its aspirates (see Geiger, $ 23, 1.).

The hesitation regarding pronunciation goes back far enough in the past. The N. W. inscriptions of Aśoka have *cikisā* in place of Girnar *cikīchā*, the word corresponding to Skr. *cikitsā* (see O. Franke, BB, XXIII, 177-78). The Buddha, who is called *Krakuchanda* in Sanskrit, becomes *Kakusandha* in Pali. Pali also transcribes Skr. *kṛcchra-* as *kasira-*. Later Hāla writes indifferently *māussiā* (*mātṛ* (*sva*) *sṛkā*) and *māucchiā* (Pischel, $ 148). Hemacandra admits the equivalence of the forms, *puṃchai*, *puṃsai*, *pusai* (Skr. *proñch-*, *poñch-*) and for Deśī that of *kasso* and *kaccharo* (Skr. *kaccara-* ?). Lastly should be noted the equivalence *kaśyapa-*, *kacchapa-* (M. *kāṃsav* is equally well explained by either of the forms). These facts must be distinguished from those that are explained by the Indo-European gradation *k-*: *sk-* (Wackernagel, $ 230), that is, the cases where Pali and Prakrit have *ch* for Skr. *ś* (Pischel, $ 211). Thus Skr. *śakṛt-*, *śava-*, *śāpa-* : Pali *chaka-*, *chava-*, Pkt. *chāba-*, Ved. Skr. *śepa-*: Taitt. Saṃh. *parucchepa-*, Pali Pkt. *cheppa-*; Skr. *śāna-*: D. *chāṇa*).

$ 103. Marathi *s*, coming from Pkt. (*c*)*ch* corresponds to :

Skr. *ch*, initial, in *saḷ* (*chala-*) *sāṃḍṇeṃ* (*chard-*), *sāvḷi* (*chāyā*), cf. *osvā* (*avacchada-*), *śiṃk* (*chikkā*), *suṭṇeṃ*, *soḍṇeṃ* (root *chuṭ*) cf. *solṇeṃ*; *śeṃdaṇeṃ* (*chind-*; cf. *śiṃdal*), *śeṇ* (*chagaṇa-*), *śev* (*cheda-*), *śeḷdūṃ* (*chagala-*).

Skr. *cch*, inside, in *usaḷṇeṃ* (*ucchal-*), *kās* (*kaccha-*), *kāṃsav* (*kaccapa-*), *tuśī* (*tuccha-*), *pusṇeṃ* (*pṛcch-*), *puṣṇeṃ* (*proñch-*); add here *asṇeṃ* (Pkt. *acchai*, Skr. root *as-*);

Skr. *chr* in *usāṇ* (*ucchrayaṇa-*);

Skr. *chv* in *usāsā* (*ucchvāsa-*);

Skr. *thy* in *umās* (*unmathya-*);

Skr. *ts* in *sarū* (*tsaru-*), *vāṃsrūṃ* (*vatsa*);

Skr. *tsya* in *māsā*, *māsḷī* (*matsya*);

Skr. *ps* in *āsare* (*apsaras-*);

$ 104. Skr. *kṣ*.—This case requires a special study. In fact, Skr. *kṣ* is represented in Prakrit not only by *kh* (see $ 95, 96), but also by *ch* and *jh*. This latter treatment, which corresponds to a particular origin of Skr. *kṣ*, will be examined later ($ 107). As regards the former two, they seem to be equivalent, and from Pali upto the modern languages, there is no dialect where they are not concurrently represented, often in the same words. The treatment *ch* goes back far enough in the past to have been noted in certain signs of the Atharvaveda (Wackernagel, $ 135 b), and on the other hand we already find in the Mahābhārata *kheṭa-* "village", the probable doublet of *kṣetra*—. Since then all hypotheses tending to explain the distribution of the treatments *kh* and *ch* by etymology seem distined to be weak. Such is particularly the case with the explanation proposed by Pischel in his grammar and which is confronted by too many contrary examples and too numerous doublets to be admitted as valid (Pischel, $ 318-321; cf. Geiger, $ 16). There are, on the contrary, certain indices which would tend to make one suspect a dialectal distribution at the origin.

It has been noted since long that in epigraphic Prakrit *kh* was the constant representative of Skr. *kṣ* in the Eastern inscriptions while *ch*, on the contrary, dominated the northwest and the west (O. Franke, *Pali und Sanskrit*, p. 118; T. Michelson, JAOS, 1910, p. 88; regarding a special sign for *ch* in the Kharosthi texts, see A. M. Boyer, JA, 1911, I, p. 423-30). On the other hand the unique treatment in the fragments of the Buddhist dramas published by Lūders is *kh*. These fragments have been written in the eastern or central dialects. Lastly it is known that latter-day grammarians ascribe to Magadhi the sign *sh* or *ḥk* in the intervocalic position (Pischel, $ 324). Irrespective of the opinion one may form concerning the real value and the date of this sign (see Lüders, *Bruchstücke*, p. 37; cf. Meillet, *Bull. Soc. Ling.*, 1911, p. XLIV), it confirms the eastern character of the guttural treatment. Inversely the modern languages of the extreme north-west agree till today with the Kharosthi texts : the almost unique correspondent of Skr. *kṣ* therein is *ch* (see Grierson, *Piś. Lang.*, p. 94; Beames, I, p. 312).

We are, therefore, led to suppose the existence, at an early date, of a dialectal distribution of the treatments *ch* and *kh* of Skr. *kṣ*. The question then arises as to which of the old groups is Marathi to be attached ? It is difficult to answer this question, because in Marathi, as in other Prakritic languages, intermixing and doublets are abundant (cf. Beames, I, 309-310; Grierson, *Phon.*, $ 77, 81). While waiting for a detailed analysis concerning each of the other languages, we have to be content with indices.

It is known that Simhalese is often in agreement with Marathi. Now in this language, where the treatments are as mixed as elsewhere, the only example, cited by Geiger, which goes away from both Prakrit and Pali is an example of *s* < *ch* (*Lit. u. Spr. der Simghal.*, $ 16, 3). On the other hand, classical Mahārāṣṭrī also had, in many cases, *ch* for the *kh* of other dialects (Pischel, *Hemacandra*, II, p. 60, cited—by Geiger, $ 16, note 3). Similarly the analysis of the examples of Marathi and Gujarati yields a minimum residue of words where Skr. *kṣ* is represented by *s* (in Gujarati *ch* or *s*). We have to distinguish in fact :

1. words where *kh* is common to Marathi and other Prakritic languages. They form the major part of the examples given in $ 95 and 96.

2. words where *s* of Marathi corresponds to *s* or *ch* of other languages. These latter are rare : *rīṃs* (*ṛkṣa-*), *surā* (*kṣura-*), *tāsṇeṃ* (*takṣ-*; this word exists only in the western dialects); *sahā* (*ṣaṭ-*) has its place here, because it goes back through the Middle Indian *cha-* to an Indo-Iranian **ksakṣ*, cf. ZD. *xśvaś* (see Meillet, *Revue slavistique*, V, p. 160). Here should be added *māśī* (*makṣikā*) whose *ch* is found in other languages besides *kh* and *saṇ* (*kṣaṇa-*) which in the sense of

"festival", preserved in Marathi has *ch-* since Prakrit and in all the dialects, the type of Prakrit *khaṇa-* being reserved in the sense of "moment". In this latter sense, the word is missing in Marathi.—The word *khār* (*kṣāra-*) formed part of an old group of the same type; *khār* is found everywhere in the specialised sense of "alkaline salt;" *chār* in that of "ash". This latter word is missing in Marathi and has been replaced therein by *rākh.*

3. Marathi doublets whose two terms are found in other dialects. Skr. *akṣa-*; *āṃkh* beside *āṃs* (the word is rare and is found only in Gujarati; for Skr. *akṣi-*, Simhalese has the two forms; everywhere else it is *kh*).

Skr. *kakṣa-*: *kākh* (=G., H., B., O.) and *kāṃs* (=S. Panj. Siṃh., H.).

Skr. *kukṣi-*: *kukhāvart* (a semi-learned word; *kh* in G. S. Panj., H.) and *kūs* (=S., Simh.).

The doublet *khāl* (=G., S., Rom., H.) : *sāl* (G., S., H.), whose Sanskrit prototype is missing, is of another group. The Prakrit words *challī*, *khallā* seem to be juxtaposed to Skr. *carma*, *kṛttiḥ* as Lat. *scortum* in relation to *corium*, *cortex.*

4. Lastly, words where Marathi, generally in agreement with Gujarati, has the treatment *ch*>*s* as against other dialects :

ūs (Skr. *ikṣu-*; *s* in Guj. and Maldiv.; *kh* in Panj.).

tarams (Skr. *tarakṣa-*; *s* in Guj., *kh* in Panj.).

śet (Skr. *kṣetra-*; all the other languages have *kh*).

In reality *kūs* (*kukṣi-*) cited above should be listed here because *kukh-* exists only in an isolated and semi-learned word. Perhaps we should also have added *visaḷṇeṃ* (*vi-kṣal-*) and *suṃḍṇeṃ* (Pkt. *chund-*, undoubtedly related to Skr. *kṣudh-*), but we have found these words only in Gujarati, where they have *ch.*

Despite the exiguity of this residue, the data, it furnishes, are so precise and accord so well with those drawn, on the one hand from Prakrit and on the other from languages closely neighbouring Marathi as Simhalese and Gujarati, that we have every right in joining Marathi to the western group where Skr. *kṣ* normally gave *ch* (save naturally those cases where it corresponded to Pkt. *jh*, see $ 107).

j

$ 105. In the initial position, *j* goes back to Pkt. *j* developed out of :

Skr. *j* in *jaḍ* (and *jaṭ*; Skr. *jaṭā*), *jaḍ* (*jaḍa-*), *jaṇ* (*jana-*) *jaḷ* (*jala-*), *jaḷū* (*jalaukā*), *jāī* (*jāti-*), *jāgṇeṃ* (*jāgrat-*), *jāṃgh* (*jāṅghā*), *jāṇṇeṃ* (*jānāti*, root *jñā-*), *jān* (*i*) *vāsā* (*janya-*), *jā* (*ṃ*)*pṇeṃ* (*jalp.*), *jāṃb* (*jambu-*), *jāṃbhāḍ* (*jambha-*), *jā* (*ṃ*)*vāī* (*jāmātṛ-*), *jāḷ* (*jāla-*) *jiṇeṃ* (*jīv-*), cf. *jī* and *jīv* (*jīva-*), *jirṇeṃ* (*jīrya-*) *jireṃ* (*jīraka-*), *jībh* (*jihvā*), *juṇā* (*iīrṇa-*), *je* (*jaya*);

Skr. *jy* in *jeṭh*, *jeṭhā* (*jyeṣṭha-*), *jośī* (*jyotiṣika-*);

Skr. *jv* in *jar* (*jvara-*), *jāḷ*, *jāḷṇeṃ* (*jvāla-jvalana-*);

Skr. *dy* in *juvā* (*dyūta-*), *jov*, *jopāvṇeṃ* (*dyota-*);

Skr. *y* in *jamṇeṃ* (*yaṃ*), *jar* (*yarhi-*), *jav* (*yava-*), *jaṃv* (*yāvat*), *jas* (*yaśas-*), *jāū* (*yātṛ-*), *jāṇeṃ* (*yā-*), *jāṇhveṃ* (*yajñopavīta-*), *juī* (*yūtika-*), *juṃpaṇeṃ* (root *yu-*), *juṃvaḷ*, *jūḷ* (*yugala-*), *jū* (*yūta-*), *jūṃ*, *juṃv* (*yuga-*), *jogā* (*yugya-*), *jot* (*yoktra-*), *joḍ* (root *yut-*) and the semi-tatsamas *jatan* (*yatna-*), *jūg* (*yuga-*).—Excepting only the word *ūṃ*: in regard to Skr. *yūka-*, Deśī has already *ūā*; all the other dialects have the expected initial *j*.

$ 106. Inside the word, *j* represents Skr. *j* after a nasal : *gāṃjā* (*gañja*), *pāṃjar* (*pañjara-*), *bhāṃjṇeṃ* (*bhañj-*), *bhijṇeṃ abhyañjana-*), *vijṇā* (*vyañjana-*); exceptionally Skr. *ñc* in *kuñji* (*kuñcikā*), see $ 82.

It goes back to Pkt. *jj* arising out of :

Skr. *jj* in *kājaḷ* (*kajjala-*), *bhājṇeṃ* (*bhrajja-*), *lāj* (*lajjā*), *sajṇeṃ* (*sajja-*); cf. *ujāgar* (*ujjāgara*);

Skr. *jñ* in *sāṃjeṃ* (*saṃjñā*), *paij* (*pratijñā*), with reference to the treatment *ṇ* of *pain*, *āṇ* (*ājñā*); Prakrit already admitted *ṇṇ* beside *jj* (Pischel, $ 276). Similarly Hindi has *sān* and *an* beside *paij*.

Skr. *jv* in *ujal* (*ujjvala-*);

Skr. *jy* in *vaṇjār* (*vāṇijya-*);

Skr. *rj* in *khaj* (*kharju-*), *khajurī* (*kharjūra-*), *gājṇeṃ* (*garjana-*), *bhoj* (*bhūrja* *māṃjar* (*mārjāra-*), *mājṇeṃ* (*mārjana-*) perhaps *oj* (*ūrjas:*).

Skr. *bj* in *khujā* (*kubja-*);

Skr. *dy* in *āj* (*adya*), *ujaviṇeṃ* (*udyāpana-*), *khājeṃ* (*khādya-*) *khijṇeṃ* (*khidya-*), *nipajṇeṃ* (*niṣpadya-*), *pāj* (*padyā*), *māj* (*madya-*), *vājṇeṃ* (*vādya-*), *vijū* (*vidyut-*);

Skr. *ry* in *ājā* (*ārya-*), *kāj* (*kārya-*) *bhāj* (*bhārya*);

Skr. *yy* in *śej* (*śayyā*);

Skr. *y* in the passives ending in -(*i*)*ji* (Skr. *-yate*); in *dej* (*deya-*), *pej* (*peya-*) and perhaps *bheṃj*(*h*)*ūḍ* (*bheya-*); in *dujā, tīj* (*dvitīya-, tṛtīya-*). This takes us back really to the preceding cases. In the passives and in the formations attached thereto, Pkt. *jj*, which replaces Skr. *-y-* (Pischel, $ 535, 571, 572) is certainly not explained by the influence of the accent as proposed by Pischel ($ 91), but by the analogical extension of cases where *jj* was regular as in *chijjai, bhajjai, bhijjai, bhujjai* (see Pischel, $ 546). In the case of *dvitīya-, tṛtīya-*, one is tempted to suppose the substitution of the suffix *-yya* for *-ya-*. This suffix, very rare in classical Sanskrit (for example, *śayyā* in relation to *śaya-*), is on the contrary quite alive in Vedic (see Whitney, *Sanskrit Grammar*, $ 1216, 1218). Should we then admit that here also Prakrit is nearer Vedic, being separate from classical Sanskrit ?

In *ujū* (Pkt. *ṛju-*), the intervocalic *j* has been kept instead of being dropped. Prakrit already wrote *ujju*, which does not look to be a tatsama. The reduplication of the intervocalic *j* perhaps comes, according to an explanation suggested to me by Meillet, from the fact that *ṛ* had, in the initial position, a special treatment of the type *ur-*. Since then Skr. *ṛju-* regularly led to Pkt. *ujju-* through *urju-.

The dental pronunciation of *j* partially explains the confusions of the type *māṃdūs* for Skr. *mañjūṣā*; *khād* "itch" for *khāj* (Skr. *kharju-*) has been probably influenced by the words of the family of *khad-* "to eat". The group *gāṃḍṇeṃ*: *gāṃjṇeṃ* "to torment", is obscure. The sense of Skr. *gañjana-* "contempt" is too far removed to have any value for the *rapprocehment*. Maybe it is a phonetic doublet but from two different formations of the Skr. family *gada-* "disease". In that case, Pkt. *gajja-, gāgejja-* will have to be separated from this family.

jh

$ 107. This phoneme is rare in Sanskrit. It appears here in the words without any etymology or in those with a clearly Prakritic nature (Wackernagel, $ 141). It is thus separate from *j* as *ch* is from *c*. In Prakrit *jh* represents Skr. *hy* and *dhy*. Moreover, it corresponds to Skr. *kṣ* and seems to belong to a dialect, independent of Sanskrit, which would have preserved the sonority of an aspirated guttural+spirant group of the Indo-European. Besides the majority of words cited by Pischel in $ 326 have no sure etymology. Whatever be the case, the *jh* of Marathi continues the Pkt. *jh*. Moreover, it appears in a certain number of words found at a later date in Deśī, in Apabhraṃśa, and besides of unknown origin, perhaps purely local (see examples of initial *jh-* in the Lexicon). Where its value is clear, there *jh* represents :

Skr. *hy* in *ojheṃ* (*vahya-*), *mājhā*, *tujhā* (cf. *mahyam,tubhyam*), *rujhṇeṃ* (*ruhya-*); cf. *gūj* (*guhya-*);

Skr. *dhy* in *jhuṃjhṇeṃ* (for **juṃjh-*, Skr. *yuddhya-*), *bujhṇeṃ* (*budhya-*), *mājhārīm* *māj* (*madhya-*) *vāṃjh* (*vandhyā*), *sāṃjh* (*sandhyā*); perhaps *samajṇeṃ* (root *dhyā* ? cf. $ 88);

Skr. *kṣ* in *jharṇeṃ*, *ojhar*, *nijharṇeṃ* beside *khirṇeṃ*, *vik harṇeṃ* (root *kṣar-*), *jhiṇā*, *jhijṇeṃ*, *vijhṇeṃ* (root *kṣi-*) perhaps in *jhoḍ* beside *khaḍṇeṃ*, *khoṭ*, etc. (root *kṣuṭ*); perhaps Skr. *dhv* in *jheṃḍ* (*dhvaja-*);

Lastly Pkt. *j*+*h* earlier separated by a vowel in *jhaṃvṇeṃ* (*yabh-*); the form *jhavije* is found already in an inscription of the year 1109.

In the initial position, Mar. *jh-* seems, often, to be a pure and simple doublet of *j*: see $ 84.

Cerebrals

$ 108. It is known that the cerebralisation of old dental occlusives is an innovation peculiar to India (see Wackernagel, $ 144). This cerebralisation has not occurred atonce and depends upon various conditions. In Sanskrit it has taken place in two cases :

1. In contact with a cerebral sifflant. The assimilation

is constant and is kept up in Middle-Indian as also in the modern languages. This is the case with *ḍ* in *nīḍ* (*nīḍa-*, i.e. **ni-zdo-*), with *ṭh* in *āṭh* (*aṣṭa-*), etc.

2. In contact with *r* (vowel or consonant) dropped while cerebralising the dental. As against the preceding one this change seems to have a dialectal origin. In fact, on the one hand, it does not reach all the words placed in similar phonetic conditions and on the other, it becomes more frequent with the passage of time in Sanskrit (see Wackernagel, $ 146-7) and in Prakrit (see Pischel, $ 289-294). Basing himself on the study of the Aśokan inscriptions, T. Michelson considers the cerebralisation of the Middle-Indian as an eastern phenomenon (see *Am. J. Phil.*, XXX , p. 240, 294, 416, 418). The evidence of Vararuci corroborates on one point the evidence of inscriptions. According to this grammarian, the participles in *-ḍa-* of the roots in *-ṛ* (*kaṭa-*, *maḍa-*) belong to *Māgadhi* (X, 15) and whereas Pali has *kaṭa-*, and Simhalese, following Pali, has *kaḷa*; *maḷa* (in relation to *giya*<*gata-*), the majority of western Prakrits has *kaa-*, *maa-* as *gaa-* (Pischel, $ 219, 12; cf. M. *ke-lā*, *me-lā* as *ge-lā*); *maḍa-* is found only later and as a provincialism (*Deśīnāmamālā*, p. 233-9, *maḍo kaṇṭho mṛtaś ca*; cf. perhaps 226, 5 and 223, 9) and Marathi keeps it only with special meanings (*maḍ* "man to be hated, pest, bother", *maḍeṃ* "corpse"). As against the same, Bengali and Oriya are the only ones having a cerebral in *cauṭh* <Skr. *caturtha-*: all the other dialects have *cauth* (Beames, I, 333).

For determining the position befitting Marathi among other dialects, we have to eliminate first of all cases where Marathi cerebrals have been inherited from Sanskrit or from Middle-Indian. This manner of proceding has the handicap of hiding the real continuity of phenomena and also of mixing up phenomena of various types, because this will group together cerebrals due to the neighbourhood of a cerebral sifflant and those due to the neighbourhood of *r*. But, besides the fact that in a very large number of cases the real origin of cerebrals is not discernible, this method is suitable only when we do not have to render account of all the Marathi cerebrals, but only to see how it deals with dentals, which have been cerebralised by it at a recent date.

I. *Old Cerebrals*

ṭ

$ 109. Inside the word, *ṭ* goes back to :

Skr. *ṭ* after a nasal, in *kāṃṭā* (*kaṇṭaka-*), *ghāṃṭ* (*ghaṇṭā*); *vāṃṭṇeṃ* (*vaṇṭ-*);

Skr. *ṭṭ* in *aṭaḷī* (*aṭṭālikā*), *kaṭār* (*kaṭṭāra-*), *kuṭaṇ*, *kuṭṇeṃ* (*kuṭṭana-*), *kuṭīṇ* (*kuṭṭinī*), *koṭ* (*koṭṭa-*), *ghāṭ* (*ghaṭṭa-*); *pāṭ* (*paṭṭa-* for *patra-*; cf. on the other side *karvat* <*karpattra-*).

Skr. *ṭv* in *khāṭ*, *khaṭaṃg* (*khaṭvā*, cf. Skr. *khaṭṭi-* "bed", "bier").

Skr. *ṭ* in *karṭī* (*karoṭī*), *kuṭiḷ* (*kuṭila-*), *kuṭumb* (*kuṭumba-*), *koṭ* (*koṭa-*), *peṭī* (cf. *piṭaka-*), *moṭ* (*moṭa-*); these words are, in reality, tatsamas. In fact, Prakrit or other languages often have *ḍ* with reference to Marathi *ṭ*. Perhaps we should list here *khāṭ*, *khaṭṭā* (cf. Skr. *śaṭa-*). Beside *cāpḍā* is found *cāpaṭ* (*carpaṭa-*); this shows the existence of two suffixes, one in *-ṭ-* and the other in *-ḍ-*.

There also exist a certain number of verbal stems where *ṭ* corresponds to Skr. *ṭ*; thus *aṭṇeṃ*, cf. *palāṭaṇ* (*aṭati*), *ucaṭṇeṃ*, cf. *ucāṭ* (*uccāṭana-*), *cāṭṇeṃ* (Skr. *cāṭu-*, Pkt. *caḍḍ-*). Here the surd is explained by the constant opposition of the doublets to the sonant and to the surd, respectively representing the occlusive and the occlusive + *y* of Sanskrit . They are reintegrated into the series : *jaṭṇeṃ* : *jaḍṇeṃ*, *juṭṇeṃ* : *joḍṇeṃ*, *tuṭṇeṃ*:, *toḍṇeṃ* (cf. *toṭā* and *toḍī*), *nivaṭṇeṃ*: *nivaḍṇeṃ*. Thus we have on the one hand *khuṭ-*, *khuṃṭ-* and even *khoṭ-*, and on the other *khuḍ-*, *khoḍ-* (Skr. *khuṇḍati*, *khoḍayati*), etc.

There remain a number of obscure words like the names of plants, *taroḍ* and *taroṭā*, which, truly speaking, denote two different plants; and above all *neṭ* (Skr. *nikaṭa-*), where the vowel proves the link with a tadbhava. The corresponding words in other languages have *ḍ* or its equivalents. We should admit here a return action of the Sanskrit original.

Words like *ghoṭṇeṃ*, (*ghoṭṭai*), *cāṭū* (*caṭṭū*), *dāṭ* (*daṭṭa*), *viṭāl* (*viṭṭāla-*) are not found in Sanskrit but are common to Prakrit and to the totality of languages. We may consider as going back to the common language words like *āṭ* (H. B. *āṭā*, etc., Iran. **ārta-*), *maṭ-ga* (root **mort-*) *ulaṭṇeṃ* (*ulluṭ-*).

ṭh

$ 110. Inside the word, *ṭh* goes back to :

Skr. *ṭh* after a nasal in *kāṃṭhṇeṃ* (*kaṇṭha-*), *sūṃṭh* (*śuṇṭhi*), etc.—We may add here *gāṃṭh* (*grantha-*) where the cerebralisation is old: cf. Skr. *nighaṇṭu-*, Pkt. *guṇṭhai* whose participle *guttha-* has led in Marathi to *gūth*, wherefrom *guṃthṇeṃ*);

Skr. *ṣṭ* in *āṭh* (*aṣṭa*), *tāṭh* (*tṛṣṭa-*), *dīṭh* (*dṛṣṭi*), *māṭhṇeṃ* (*mṛṣṭa-*), *miṭhā* (*miṣṭa-*), *mūṭh* (*muṣṭi*), *riṭhā* (*ariṣṭaka-*), *sāṭh* (*saṣṭi-*). Add here *aṭhī* (later Skr. *aṣṭi-*, see infra), *ghāṭṇeṃ*, etc., see $ 89.

Skr. *ṣṭh* in *aṃgṭhā* (*aṅguṣṭha-*), *oṃṭh* (*oṣṭha-*), *kāṭhī* (*kāṣṭha-*), *kaṭha* (*koṣ ṭhaka-*), *goṭhā* (*goṣṭha-*), *goṭhī* (*goṣṭhī-*), *jeṭh*, *jeṭhā* (*jyeṣṭha-*), *niṭhūr* (*niṣṭhura-*) *pāṭh* (*pṛṣṭha-*), *sāṭh* (*ṣaṣṭhī*), *śeṭhī* (*śreṣṭhin-*).

Skr. *st*, *sth*, irregularly because the normal representative of Skr. *st*(*h*) is Pkt. *tth*, M. *th*. The principle of the extensio n of the cerebral at the cost of the dental goes back to Sanskrit (Wackernagel, $ 205, 206). In the family of *sthā*, the two sounds have been neigh bours since the ancient-most period of Prakrit. Besides the words with dentals, which will be cited in their place, we find in Marathi : *thāṇ* (*vaṭhāṇ*), *ṭhār*, *ṭhāy*, *ṭhāv*, *gāvṭhā*, *gāvṭhaḷ*, *ku-ṭhem*, *ṭhākṇeṃ*, *ṭhepṇeṃ*, *ṭhevṇeṃ*, *uṭhṇeṃ*, *saṁṭhṇeṃ*; *kavaṃṭh* is joined or has been joined in course of time to the same family. It goes back to **kapiṭṭha-* for the Skr. *kapiṭṭha-*. In *pāṭhaviṇeṃ* (*prasthāpaya-*), perhaps has been joined the action of the *r* of *pra-* as in Pkt. *paḍi-* <Skr. *prati-*, *paḍhama-* < Skr. *prathama-*; cf. *pālaṭ* beside *pālthā* (*paryasta-*) and *paṭhār* beside *pathārī* and *pāthar* (*prastāra-*). Similarly *ṭhāḍā* (*stabdha-*), where the initial cerebral has brought in the cerebralisation of the internal group since Prakrit (*ṭhaḍḍha-*); *ṭhoṃb*, the doublet of *ṭhāmb* (*stambha-*), where in addition the unvoicing of the vowel is irregular (see $ 79); *ṭhag* (root *sthag-*), *ṭhulī* beside *thulī* (*sthūla-*), *ṭhī* (*strī*), a rare form besides, can come from a dialect where *tr* becomes *ṭ*. It is also possible that *aṭhī* and *hāḍ* go back to a prototype forming with Skr. *asthi-* and old doublet of the Greek type, *òsteon*: *ostrakhon*. As regards *heṭ*, Pkt. *heṭṭhā*, it has been explained by Wackernagel as the result of the contamination of Skr. *adhastāt*+*upariṣṭhāt*; but *māṭhā* (*mastu-*) resists all efforts of interpretation.

ṭh represents Skr. *ṭh* in the tatsamas of the type *kaṭhīn* and Skr. *ṣṇ* in *viṭhobā*, *viṭhaḷ* < Skr. *viṣṇu*. The normal treatment of Skr. *ṣṇ* being Pkt. *ṇh*>M. *n*, one has to recognise here a recent semi-tatsama, probably borrowed. Finally *ṭh* comes from *ṭ*+*h* belonging to two different syllables in *auṭhṇeṃ* for *ohaṭṇeṃ*.

ḍ

$ 111. Inside the word, *ḍ* goes back to

Skr. and Pkt. *ḍ* following a nasal : *aṃḍ* (*aṇḍa-*), *kaṃḍ* (*kaṇḍu-*), *karaṃḍā* (*karaṇḍa-*), *kuṃḍ* (*kuṇḍa-*), *koṃḍāḷeṃ* (*kuṇḍala-*), *khāṃḍ* (*khaṇḍa-*), *gaṃḍ* (*gaṇḍa-*), *daṃḍ* (*daṇḍa-*), *pāṃḍyā* (*paṇḍita-*), *piṃḍī* (*piṇḍa-*) *bhāṃḍ* (*bhāṇḍa-*), *bhāṃḍār* (*bhāṇḍāgāra-*), *maṃḍ* (*maṇḍa-*), *maṃḍaḷ* (*maṇḍala-*), *māṃḍav* (*maṇḍapa-*), *muṃḍā muṃḍṇeṃ* (*muṇḍa-*), *rāṃḍ* (*raṇḍā*), *leṃḍūk* (*leṃḍa-*), *sāṃḍ* (*ṣaṇḍa-*), *śeṃḍā* (*śikhaṇḍa-*), *soṃḍ* (*śuṇḍā*); *govaṃḍ* corresponds exceptionally to D. *goaṇṭa-*, see $ 82;

Pkt. *ḍ* arising out of Skt. *ṭ* in *aghāḍā* (*āghāṭa-*), *aḍaṇ* (*aṭani-*), *aḍulsā* (*aṭarusā*) *āḍ* (*avaṭa-*), *āḍī* (*āṭī-*), *kaḍ* (*kaṭi-*), *kaḍāḍ* (*kaṭakaṭā*), *kaḍāsen* (*kuṭāsana-*), *kaḍu* (*kaṭuka-*), *kaḍeṃ* (*kaṭaka-*) *kavāḍ* (*kapāṭa-*), *kāṃkḍī* (*karkaṭikā*), *kānḍā* (*karaṇāṭaka-*), *kāpaḍ* (*karpaṭa-*), *kudapṇeṃ* (root *kuṭ-*), *kuḍav* (*kuṭapa-*), *kuḍā* (*kuṭaja-*), *kuḍi* (*kuṭī*) *ghaḍṇeṃ* (*ghaṭ-*), *ghaḍā* (*ghaṭa-*), *ghaḍī* (*ghaṭikā*), *ghoḍā* (*ghoṭaka-*), *capḍā* (*carpaṭa-*), *cāḍ* (*cāṭu-*), *jaḍ* (*jaṭā* ?), *jaḍṇeṃ* (root *jaṭ-*), *joḍṇeṃ* (root *yuṭ-*), *toḍṇeṃ* (*truṭ-*, cf. *tuṭṇeṃ*), *toḍī* (*troṭakī*), *dhāḍ* (*dhāṭi-*), *paḍaḷ* (*paṭala-*), *puḍā* (*puṭā-*) , *phaḍā* (*phaṭā*), *bhāḍ* (*bhāṭi-*), *mākaḍ* (*markaṭa-*), *raḍṇeṃ* (*raṭ-*), *vāḍā* (*vāṭa-*), *viḍī* (*vīṭikā*), *saḍṇeṃ* (*śaṭ-*), *saraḍ* (*saraṭa*), *sāṃkaḍ* (*saṃkaṭa-*);

Pkt. *ḍ* going back to Skr. *t* cerebralised under the influence of a neighbouring *r* in *paḍ* and its derivatives (Skr. *prati-*);

Pkt. *ḍ* <Skr. *ḍ* in *khoḍ* (*kṣoḍa-*), *goḍ* (*gauḍa-*), *tāḍṇeṃ* (*tāḍ-*) *nāḍ* (*nāḍī*), *nīḍ* (*nīḍa-*), *pīḍṇeṃ* (*pīḍā*), *haḍḍā* (*haḍī*);

Pkt *ḍ* <Skr. *ḍḍ* in *uḍṇeṃ* (*uḍḍī-*);

Pkt. *ḍ* < Skr. *ḍr* in *vāḍ* (*vaḍra-*);

ḍ for *ḍh*, see $ 89.

ḍh

$ 112. *ḍh* comes from :

Skr. *ṭh* in *paḍhṇeṃ* (*paṭh-*), *piḍheṃ* (*pīṭha-*), *maḍh* (*maṭha-*), cf. *kurhāḍ* (*kuṭhara-*);

Skr. *ḍh* in *gāḍhā* (*gāḍha-*), *dāḍhā* (*dṛḍha-*), probably in *oḍhaṇ* (cf. Vedic *voḷhave*);

Skr. *ḍhr* in *maṃḍhā* (*meḍhra-*);

Skr. *th* cerebralised under the influence of prehistoric **r* in *saḍhaḷ* (*śithila*);

The recent *ḍh* represents *ḍ+h* in *ḍher* (D. *ḍaharī*), *h+ḍ* in *ulemḍhāleṃ* (D. *ullehaḍa*), *l+ḍh* in *sāḍhū* (*śyālīvoḍha-*).

A curious evolution is that which has led in certain cases to (*ṭ*)*ṭh* arisen out of Skr. *ṣṭ* or *ṣṭh* to *ḍh*, contrary to the normal phonetics of Prakrit. This is the case with *aḍ*(*h*)- in the compound words for numbers (*aṣṭa-*), *kāḍhṇeṃ* (*kṛṣṭa-*; cf. *ukhaḍṇeṃ* *koḍh* (*kuṣṭha-*) *dāḍh*, *dāḍhī* (*daṃṣṭrā*), *maḍhṇeṃ* (*mṛṣṭa-*), *veḍhṇeṃ* (*veṣṭ-*), *hāḍ* (*asthi-*, *aṣṭi-*). This evolution is ancient, Sanskrit having already incorporated forms like *dāḍhikā* (Manu), *koṭha* (Suśruta), *kaḍḍhaya* (in Buddhist formulae). Pali has *veṭhati*; *aḍha* (*aṣṭa-*) is found in the Jaina texts and attempts have been made to recognise it even in the Aśokan inscriptions (Fleet, JARS, 1906, p. 401 ff, see notably p. 413ff). On the other hand *maḍhai* is found only in later Prakrit and *hāḍ* has its antecedents only in Deśī. But both are common to the chief Indo-Aryan languages.—On Skr. *ṣṭ* represented by M. *lh*, see $ 148.

II. *The treatment of r+dental in Marathi.*

$ 113. The treatment of this group shows no uniformity in Marathi. Contradictions are found, even inside certain word-families and are undoubtedly explained by the frequency of borrowings.

rt

$ 114. In the family of the root *vart-* are to be found, on the one hand, *vāṭṇeṃ*, *nivaṭṇeṃ* (*vartana-*) *vāṭṭā* (*vṛtta-*), *vāṭ* (*vartman-*), cf. *vāṭī* "bowl"; on the other we have *vāt* (*vartikā*) and *parvat*, *paratṇeṃ* (*parivarta-*). It is impossible to render a phonetical account of this opposition, but it gets clarified if it is observed that all the words, having a cerebral are found with the same cerebral in Prakrit and in all the modern languages. Simhalese is the only exception with its dental in the only word *vat* (*vartman-*). On the contrary the dental of (*vartikā*) found in Māhārāṣṭrī Prakrit is found in the dialects of the centre and of the east, whereas Sindhi, Gujarati and and Simhalese agree in showing a cerebral.

Similarly in the family of *kart-*, cerebrals are found everywhere in the words corresponding to *kāṭṇeṃ* "to cut". Dentals are also found in those corresponding to *kātṇeṃ* "to spin", *kātar* (*kartarikā*), *kattī* (*kartṛkā*), *kātḍeṃ* (*kṛtti-*), *kātyā* (*kṛttikā* or *kārtika-*); but to *kāṃt* "shaving", *kāṃtaṇ* "cut, harmful insect", correspond in Sindhi and in Hindi, words with cerebrals, either because it relates to a phonetic treatment, or because these words have been joined to the root of *kāṭṇeṃ*, etc. But Gujarati has *kātaro* in the sense of "harmful insect;" which relates it to Marathi.

The dental of *dhutārā* (*dhūrta-*), found in Prakrit is found everywhere. On the contrary that of *mātī* (*mṛttikā*) is unique. All the other languages, Simhalese included, have *ṭ*. The proper Marathi treatment consists, therefore, probably in the dental. Words like *kavaṃṭāl*, *ohaṭ*, found only in this language, are not in agreement with this probability, but the etymology is far from being sure. As regards the cerebral of *gaḍṇeṃ* (active re-made on a root **gaṭ-*, cf. Skr. *garta-*), it is found everywhere.

rth

Examples are rare. On the one hand are found *cauth, cauthā* (*caturtha-*) and on the other *sāth, sāthī* (*sārtha-*), whose dental is found everywhere, except the first word in the far-eastern group and Kashmir.

In Marathi even the proposition *sāṭhīṃ sāṭīṃ* "in view of, for" seems, at first view to contain *artha-*. However Gujarati and Sindhi give evidence of a word *sāṭ* denoting "exchange" coexisting in the first of these languages with *sāthī* "why? because." The form with an aspirated cerebral of Marathi seems to give evidence of the contamination of these two words, where the second alone appears to be derived from *sārtha-* (cf. $ 89).

rd

$ 115. Words containing a cerebral are rare and are not original. They are *kavḍā* (*kaparda-*), *maḍ, maḍeṃ* (*mṛta-*) and *saṃḍṇeṃ* (*chard-*). The eastern character of the word *maḍ* has already been noted. The dental is also found everywhere in*v ādaḷ* (*vardalikā*) and *caudā* (*caturdaśa-*; the *ḍ* of S. *cauḍahaṃ* and of Raj., West. Panj. *coḍā* proves nothing, because it is found in S. *ḍaha,* West. Panj. *ḍāh* < Skr. *daśa-*). Gujarati, Bengali and Hindi agree with Marathi and show a dental not only in *kudāl* which goes back to Sanskrit (*kuddāla-*) but also in *kudṇeṃ* (*kūrdana-*), *pāḍṇeṃ* (*pard-*), *lāḍṇeṃ* (*lard-*). Sindhi has a cerebral in all these words and Simhalese agrees with this language in regard to *pard-*. Oriya like Sindhi has *koḍ-* with reference to *kuddāla-*, but perhaps this is a direct derivative or a word under the influence of the root *kuṭ-*.

rdh

The treatment of this group is perhaps the most confused.

The cerebral of *mumḍhi* (*mūrdhan-*), of *vāḍhayā* (*vardhaka-*) is universal. The same is true of *vāḍhṇem* (*vardh-*), except a particularly strange exception : Sindhi here has a dental, although ordinarily it prefers a cerebral. As against the Skr. *gardabha-*, Marathi has both *gāḍhav* and *gadhḍā*, Sindhi having the form with the cerebral and Gujarati, Hindi having only the form with the dental. Simhalese, like Marathi, has both the forms. The most obscure case is that of the representatives of Skr. *ardha-*: in face of *ādhā*, *ad-*, *adhāv* (*ardha-*) are found *sāḍe* (*sārdha-*) *dīḍ* (*h*) (*dvi-ardha-*), *aḍīc* (*ardha-tṛtīya-*) and *aḍ*(*h*) (*ardha-*) used as a pejorative prefix. This opposition is found as such in all the dialects, except in Simhalese which seems to recognise only the cerebral. This opposition goes back to the Prakrit epoch.

$ 116. It is impossible to draw any sure conclusion from such confused lists. Exchanges and contominations go back too far in the past to enable us to distinguish in each case the phonetic treatment of the borrowing. All that we can say amounts to the fact that the examples of *r* + surd dental provisionally give the impression that the phonetic treatment of Marathi is the dental. This will be in agreement with the data available regarding the ancient period.

III. *Spontaneous Cerebralisation.*

$ 117. Altogether different from the preceding one is the case where an old dental has spontaneously become a cerebral, or has been so changed without any recognisable influence. Its examples are extremely rare in Sanskrit, the Vedic root *dī-* "to fly" has become in classical Sanskrit *ḍī-*. This is the only word with an initial cerebral whose origin is known. The cerebral is found again inside certain words collected in the grammar of Wackernagel ($ 148 b, p. 173) and of whom none goes back to the Veda. The list starts getting longer the moment we reach the ancient-most period of classical Prakrit. Whereas Vararuci considers *maḍa-* and the other participles of the roots in *-ṛ-* as belonging to Māgadhī, he ascribes to common Prakrit, not only *paḍisara-* (*prati-*) *paḍhama-* (*prathama-*), *siḍhila-* (*śithila-*, for **śṛ-*) where the influence of *r* has been felt again, but *paḍāā*, *veḍisa-* (II, 8) *ḍola-*, *ḍaṇḍa-*, *ḍasaṇa-* (II, 24) and the roots *paḍ* (*pat-*), *saḍ* (*sad-*), *kaḍh-* (*kvath-*) (VIII, 39, 51; Beames, I, 219 ff). During the latest periods of Prakrit the phenomenon becomes extremely widespread, without our being able to determine its conditions any further. It is then that the dental nasal in particular becomes a cerebral in all positions (*no ṇah sarvatra,* Vararuci, II, 42; cf. Pischel, $ 224). Last of all, during the modern epoch the word having a cerebral occlusive and found in Sanskrit or in Prakrit preserves this cerebral and the intervocalic nasal has remained a cerebral in the group Marathi-Gujarati-Sindhi-Panjabi. Moreover the intervocalic *l* has become a cerebral as the nasal in three of the dialects.

Here also it seems that it is a case of a dialectal phenomenon, but distributed entirely otherwise than in the case of the influence of *r*. It is remarkable that during the ancient period neither the Aśokan inscriptions nor the known fragments of Buddhist dramas contain any examples of spontaneous cerebralisation, other than those of Sanskrit. On the contrary, spontaneous cerebralisation is particularly frequent in classical Māhārāṣṭrī and in the Jaina Prakrits. During the modern period, the three western dialects alone know of the cerebral *ḷ*. They are the same dialects, with Sindhi and perhaps some of the speeches of the North-West Himalayas (see Grierson, *Piśāca Lang.*, p. 19), which have preserved the intervocalic *ṇ*. Lastly it is the western group, and in this group Sindhi, which is known for paticularly affecting the cerebral occlusives, there where one would expect dentals (Beames, I, 236; Grierson, *Phon.*, $ 55, 57, 91).

In Marathi, the examples of spontaneous cerebralisation are to be found in the initial position and inside the word.

$ 118. Inside the word, classical Sanskrit already presents us with some cases of cerebralisation : thus *aṭati, uḍumbara-* in relation to Vedic forms *atati, udumbara-*. The list gets a little longer in Marathi, but it is remarkable that the examples go back to old Prakrit : *joḍṇeṃ* has already got its equivalent in the Dhātupāṭha; *kaḍhṇeṃ* (*kvath-*) and *paḍṇeṃ* (*pat-*), found in Vararuci, are also found in all the Prakrits; *meḍh* (*methi-*) is to be read in the Jaina Aṅgas. Only *maḍhū* (*madhu-*) seems to be recent. Here analogies have played their part. It is by the influence of *paḍi-* = Skr. *prati-* and *paḍhama-* =

Skr. *prathama-* that Wackernagel tries to explain the cerebralisation of Pkt. *paḍai* ($ 133, rem.). Similarly *mathi-* has taken the cerebral of *meḍhra-* and *madhu-* has been subjected to the analogy of the lost doublet of *mau-*, where the *d* of Skr. *mṛdu-* had been cerebralised. Whatever these attempts at explanation may amount to, it seems clear that these words are not, properly speaking, Marathi words. It is also significant that in the word *umbar* Marathi is in agreement, like Pali and Prakrit, with Vedic (*udambara-*) and is different from classical Sanskrit, which admits the cerebral (*uḍumbara-*).

With stronger reason, we may consider as strangers to Marathi words where an old intervocalic dental has been replaced by *l* or *r*. Representing the adaptation of *l* to Marathi phonetics, is found *ḷ*, in the names of plants *alśi* (*atasī*), *kaḷamb* (*kadamba-*), *vehḷā* (*vibhītika-*) : the *l* of the first is confirmed by all the languages, that of the second goes back to old Prakrit; the third is not easily found and perhaps carries the trace of a contamination. We also still find *ḍohḷā* (*dohada-*), but here it concerns, in reality, a *ḍ* obtained under the influence of *r* (**dauhṛda-*; see Wackernagel, $ 194 b). In *ukhaḷ* Marathi, as other dialects, has opted for *udūkhala-* against the Vedic *ulūkhala-*. On the other hand *r*, which is exactly speaking, a treatment of the far north-west and of east (see Grierson, *Phon.*, $ 52, p. 52), is found in the word for the number "ten" in compounds *akrā*, *bārā*, *terā*, *pandhrā*, *satrā*, *aṭhrā*, (*ekādaśa*, *dvādaśa*, etc.) and that of "seventy" *sattar* (*saptati-*); on these words see $ 143.

$ 119. More frequent and more characteristic is the cerebralisation of the initial. It is almost unknown in Sanskrit : *ḍī-* is the only clear example (it has survived in modern dialects as *uḍḍī-*, M. *uḍṇeṃ*). Later on words corresponding to Marathi *ḍiṃb*, *ḍhāḷ* are found, but it is chiefly in Deśī, the western dialect, that such examples are numerous. In the collection of Hemacandra are found *ṭār*, *ṭirṭir*, *ṭol*, *ḍamb*, *dhāṃkan*, *ḍhekā*, *ḍhekūn*. Other languages have in common with Marathi and Deśi the words *ṭāṃk*, *ṭīp*, *ḍāvā*, *ḍāl*, *ḍoī*, *ḍokī*, *ḍoṃgar*, *ḍoḷā*, *ḍoḷī*, *ḍheṃk* (Sindhi has the dental *dh*), *ḍher*. Although not found in the lexicon of Hemacandra, still other dialects confirm *ṭaḷṇeṃ*, *ṭikṇeṃ*, *ṭikā*, *tekāḍ*, *dāṃg*, *ḍabṇeṃ*, *ḍoṃb*.

The explanation of these cases is particularly difficult.

In certain words it concerns cerebralisation under the influence of *r* in a group; thence *ḍoṇ* "boat" beside *doṇ* "boat" (*droṇi-*) and perhaps *dāṃg* (cf. also *ḍoṃgar* ? Skr. *draṅga-*). This treatment is not indigenous in Marathi where *dr*>*d*. These words are then suspected of being borrowed from another dialect, perhaps Sindhi (see Beames, I, p. 336-7).

Elsewhere it looks as if it were a case of assimilation to a cerebral of the same word, but not in contact with an initial. Thus *ḍākhūṇ* (*dakṣiṇā-*; the cerebral is found in Sindhi, Multani and in the Eastern group); *ḍar* (*dara-*), *ḍav*, c.f *ḍabbā*, a form evidently borrowed from an eastern dialect as also the eastern form with the dental *dabḍa* (*darvī*); *ṭāḷī* (*tālikā*), *ṭāṭū*, *ṭāḷem* (*tāla-*) *ṭilā* (*tilaka-*) *ḍohḷā* (**dohada-*), *ḍoḷā*, *ḍoḷī* (*dol-*).

This cerebralisation at a distance is, in any case, contrary to the habitudes of Marathi. This dialect, as also its neighbour, Gujarati, preserves the initial dental of *taṃṭā*, *ṭāṭī*, *tāṭh*, *thaṃḍā*, *thoṃt*, *dāṭ*, *dāḍh*, *dāḍhī*. The cerebralisation in these words is found only in Sindhi, Hindi and Begali (see Beames, I, 237); also in Romany, for ex. *ran*=Skr. *daṇḍa-*.

It is remarkable that in the words, to whom this explanation does not apply, the cerebral is found, since the oldest period of classical Prakrit, for two families : that of Sanskrit *daṃś* (*daśṇeṃ*, *ḍaṃkhṇeṃ*, *sāṃḍas*) and of Skr. *dah-* (*ḍājṇeṃ*, *ḍāhṇī*, *ḍāgṇeṃ*). Others, *ḍhaṃkṇeṃ*, *ḍhakkā*, *ḍhuṃḍāl-ṇeṃ* (and *dhāṃḍulṇeṃ*), *ḍhusṇeṃ* have an obscure origin, but are also found in most of the dialects. It is thus legitimate to admit here several borrowings direct or otherwise from a western language. In addition to the facts cited above, we may recall that Aśoka writes at Girnar *osūḍhāni* whereas the eastern inscriptions have *osadhāni* (*auṣadhāni*).

This hypothesis is, however not absolutely necessary or at least not necessarily unique. The dictionary of Molesworth gives as belonging to Konkan the word *ṭāṇ* (*tāṇa*) corresponding to *tāṇ* of the normal language. It will be useful to verify if Marathi does not combine two series of dialects, of whom one, that of the Deccan, had preserved the old dentals and the other, that of the coast, in agreement with a group, whose most characteristic group is Sindhi, had admitted various types of cerebralisations unknown to the normal language. In this case the existence of doublets like *ṭāḷū*: *tāḷū*, *ṭilā*: *tiḷ*, *ḍāhṇī*: *ḍāhṇeṃ*, *ḍamb* (*hī*): *damb* (*hi*), *doṃgar*- *ḍoṃgar*- : *duṃg*, *ḍhakkā*: *dhakkā* would be easily explained.

Dentals

$ 120. Except in the cases of cerebralisation examined above and the case of the old group : dental +*v* which will be found in $ 129, the treatment of the old dentals presents no difficulty. It will be remarked that, except in the words where the cerebralisation is very old and found in Sanskrit, the group dental +*r* ends normally in a dental : this is, besides, the general treatment in the Indo-Aryan, except in Sindhi (see Beames, I, p. 337).

t

$ 121. In the initial position, *t* goes back to :

Skr. *t*: *taḍ* (*taṭī*), *taṇ* (*tṛṇa*-), *tahān* (*tṛṣṇā*), *tāv* (*tāpa*-), *tīkh* (*tīkṣṇa*-), *tīḷ* (*tila*-), etc;

Skr. *tr* : *tīn* (*trīṇi*) cf. *tīj*, *tiḍeṃ*, *tivaṇ*, *tisaḷ* (*tri*-); *tuṭṇeṃ* (*truṭya*-) *toḍṇeṃ* (*troṭaya*-) cf. *toṭā*; *toḍī* (*troṭakī*);

Inside the word, *t* represents :

1. Pkt. *t* after a nasal : *āṃt* (*anta*-), *kaḍtar* (*kaḍantara*-), *bhitar* (*abhyantaraṃ*), *saṃt* (*śānta*-), *sāvantu* (*sāmanta*-), *śeṃvtī* (*sīmantikā*), 3rd. pers. pl. indic. -*at*(*i*) (-*anti*), pres. partic. in -t (-*nta*-);

2. Pkt. *tt* arisen out of

Skt. *tt* in *utaṇṇeṃ* (*uttṛṇa*-) *utarṇeṃ* (*uttaraṇa*), *utrāṇ* (*uttara*-), *utāṇā* (*uttāna*-), *utāvaḷ* (*uttāpa*-), *saṃpat* (*saṃpatti*-); cf. the childish word *āt* (D. *attā*);

Skr. *kt* in *aḷṭā* (*alakta*-), *nirutā* (*nirukta*-), *pāṃt* (*paṅkti*-), *bhāṭ* (*bhakta*-), *ratī* (*raktikā*), *rāt* (*ā*) (*rakta*-), *ritā* (*rikta*-), *sātū and sattū* (*saktu*-);

Skr. *pt* in *tātavṇeṃ* (*tapta*-), *nāt*, *nātū* (*naptṛ*-), cf. *paṇat* (*pranaptṛ*-), *Sāt* (*Sapta*-), cf. *satrā* (*saptadaśa*), *sattar* (*saptati*-), *sātvaṇ* (*scptaparṇa*-); perhaps in *alitā* (*ālipta*- ? cf. *aḷṭā*), and in *uṃśīt* (*utkṣipta*- ?);

Skr. *tn* in *savat* (*śapatnī*);

Skr. *tr* in *āṃt* (*antra-*), *ārat* (*ārātrika-*), *karvat* (*karapatra-*), *got* (*gotra-*), *carit* (*caritra-*; the short *i* gives the word an air of a tatsama-), *cāt* (*cattra-*), *citā* (*citraka-*), cf. *citaḷ* (*citrāṅga-* for the sense) and *citārī* (*citra-kāra-*), *pāt* (*patra-*), *pūt* (*putra*), cf. *rāūt* (*rājaputra-*), *mahāvat* (*mahāmātra-*), *mūt* (*mūtra-*), *rāt* (*rātrī*), *varāt* (*varatrā* and *varayātrā*), *vet* (*vetra-*), *sūt* (*sūtra-*); cf. *atāṃ* (*atra*) ?

Skr. *ktr* in *jot* (*yoktra-*).

Remark :—*t* has been lost in recent compounds of *teḷ* "oil", *araḍel*, *āvel*, *tiḷel*, etc.

th

$ 122. In Sanskrit this consonant has no real existence in the initial position. Thence it is that M. *th* does not go back to Skr. *th* except inside the word and following a nasal, as in *paṃth* (*panthan-*) *ma*(*m*)*thṇeṃ*, *māthṇī* (*manth-*). Everywhere else M *th* represents an old group containing a sifflant, that is :

Skr. *ts* in *tharū* (*tsaru-*);

Skr. *st*, initial, in *thanā* (*stana-*), *thavā* (*stabaka-*), *thā*, *thāṃg* (*sthāgha-*), *thāṃbṇeṃ* (*stambha-*), *them* (*stip-*), *thoḍā* (*stoka-*);—inside the word, in *āthi* (*asti*), cf. *nāthi* (*nāsti*), *kothambir* (*kustumbarī*), *pāthar* (*prastara-*; *cf. pāṭhār*), *pathārī* (*prastara-*), *pālthā* (*paryasta-*; cf. *pālaṭ*), *pothī* (*pustaka-*), *māthā* (*mastaka-*), *vithar* (*vistara-*), *vīth* (*vitasti-*); probably *vaṃth* (*vastu-*); also *thoṃṭ*; on *hāt*, *hattī* for * *hāth* (*hasta-*) see $ 88;

Skr. *sth*, always initiably, in *thaḷ* and its compound *saṃvthal* (*sthala-*) *thāvar* (*sthāvara-*) and the other derivatives of the root *sthā-*: *thāpṇeṃ*, *thār*, with reference to which, forms with cerebrals are found : *ṭhār*, etc., see $ 110; *thāḷa* (*sthāla-*), *thīr* (*sthira-*), *ther* (*sthavira-*), *thor* (*sthūra-*), *thulī* beside *ṭhulī* (*sthūla-*).

d

$ 123. In the initial position *d* goes back to Pkt *d* arisen from :

Skr. *d* in *dāṃt* (*danta-*), *dahīṃ* (*dadhi-*), etc.; see the Lexicon;

Skr. *dr* in *doṇ* beside *ḍeṇ* (*droṇi-*);

Inside the word, *d* goes back to Skr.-Pkt. *d* after a nasal, in *kuruṃd* (*kuruvinda*), *maṃd*, (*manda-*); the development of a *d* in *śiṃdal*, product of the differentiation of *nn* in *śin*(*n*)*aḷ* (*chinna-*) is contrary to the normal phonetics of Marathi. It must be a loan on the same lines as *vāndar*, the vulgar form of the tatsama *vānar*, influenced by H. *bandar*;

d, internally, also represents Pkt. *dd* arisen from :

Skr. *dd* in *kuḍāḷ* (*kuddāla-*);

Skr. *bd* in *sād* and its compound *paḍsāḍ* (*śabda-*, *pratiśabda-*);

Skr. *rd* in *kudṇeṃ* (*kūrdana-*) *candā* (*caturdaśa-*), *pādṇeṃ* (*pard-*), *lādṇeṃ* (*lard-*), *vādaḷ* (*vardalikā*)), perhaps in *gadaḷ* (root **grd-* ?);

Skr. *dr* in *dād* beside the semi-tatsama *dādar* (*dadru-*), *nīd* (*nidrā-*), *bhādvā* (*bhādrapada-*), *bhādarṇeṃ* (*bhadrakāraṇa-*), *mudī* (*mudrikā*), *viṃdrūṃ* (*vidra-*), *haḷad* (*haridrā*). Beside this treatment is also found for Sanskrit *dr* the corresponding ones *ḍ* (see $ 119) and *l* (see $ 141). The former appears to have a dialectal origin and the second goes as far back as Sanskrit: it is the dental treatment which looks to be normal in Marathi.

dh

$ 124. In the initial position, *dh* represents Skr. *dh* in *dhaṇ* (*dhana-*) *dharṇeṃ* (*dhar-*), etc.; see the Lexicon.

Inside the word *dh* goes back to Skr. *dh* after a nasal in *aṃdhārā* (*andhakāra-*) *bāṇdhṇeṃ* (*bandhana-*), *viṃdhṇeṃ* (root *vyadh-*), *sāṃdh* (*sandhi-*). The occlusive has been exceptionally lost in *vinhṇeṃ*, the doublet of *vindhṇeṃ* . This then is a totally abnormal treatment in Marathi, and which is regular in Bihari, Panjabi and certain dialect of the extreme North-West (see $ 82);

dh, inside the word, also goes back to Pkt. *ddh* arisen from :

Skr. *ddh* in *budh* (*buddhi-*) and the compounds *udharṇeṃ* (*uddhar-*), *udhaḷṇeṃ* (*uddhūl-*), probably *uddhav*

(*ud-dhava*);
Skr. *gdh* in *dūdh* (*dugdha-*);
Skr. *bdh* in *lādhṇeṃ* (*labdha-*);
Skr. *dhr* in *gīdh* (*gṛdhra-*).

The treatment *dh*< Skr. *dhy* in *madh* is totally irregular (cf. $ 107) and betrays a tatsama.

We find *dh* resulting from a *rapprochement* of *d* and *h* originally belonging to different syllables in *dhūv* (*duhitṛ*) which goes back to Prakrit, and in *edhavāṃ* (Pkt. *eddaha-*), and *saṃdhevīṃ*, corruption of *saṃdehīṃ*; to this *rapprochement* is due the form, *pandhrā* (*pañcadaśa*, Pkt. *paṇṇarasa*, *paṇṇaraha*) where the *d* inserted between *n* and *r* has taken the aspiration of the final *h* (cf. H. *pandarah*).

Labials

Except for the treatment of dental +*v*; which will be examined separately, the history of labials offers no difficulty.

p

$ 125. In the initial position *p* represents :

Skr. *p*. in *paḍṇeṃ* (*pat-*), *pāv* (*pāda-*), *pyās* (*pipāsā*), *pūt* (*putra-*), *pej* (*peya-*), *pothī* (*pustaka-*) and numerous other words which will be found in the lexicon; *puvā* goes back to *pūpa-*, the elided form of *apūpa-*, which is found since Sanskrit : in *pākhar* (*upaskara-*) and the tatsama *pekṣāṃ* (*apekṣā*), the elision is or looks to be more recent;

Skr. *pr* in the compounds of *pa*<*pra-*: *paṇat* (*pranaptṛ-*), *pasar* (*prasara-*), *pahār*, *pār* (*prahara-*), *pahilā* (*prathama-*), *pāṃ*, *paiṃ* (*prāyaḥ*, *prāyeṇa*), *pāūs* (*prāvṛṣa-*), *pākhaḷṇeṃ* (*prakṣālaya-*), *pājharṇeṃ* (*prakṣar-*), *pāṭhaviṇeṃ* (*prasthāpana-*), *pāthar*, *pathāri* (*prastára-*), *pānhā* (*prasnava-*), *pāphuḍṇeṃ* (*prasphuṭ-*), *pāvṇeṃ* (*prāpaṇa-*), *pāhuṇā* (*prāghuṇa-*), *pusṇeṃ* (*proñch-*), *pekhṇeṃ* (*prekṣaṇa-*), *pesṇeṃ* (*preṣaṇa-*), *povāḍā* (*pravāda-*), *povḷeṃ* (*pravāḍa-*), *poḷ*, *pauḷ* (*pratolī*), *paiṭhā* (*praviṣṭa-*), *pais* (*pradeśa-*), compound words with *paḍ-* and *pai-* (*prati-*); cf. also perhaps *peṃṭh* (*pratiṣṭhā*); the word *piyo*, *pihū* (*priya-*);

Skr. *pl* in *pāvṇā* (*plava-*), *pī* (*plīhā-*);

Skr. *py* in *pohā* (*apyūha-*).

Inside the word *p* represents Skr. and Pkt. *p* after a nasal in *kāmpṇeṃ*, *cāṃpā*, *limpṇeṃ*; it goes back above all to Pkt. *pp* arisen out of :

Skr. *pp* in *piṃpaḷ* (*pippala-*); cf. *āpā*, a childish word (*appa-*);

Skr. *py* in *rupeṃ* (*rūpya-*);

Skr. *tp* in the compounds of *ut* :- *upaj* (*utpadya-*), *upaṭṇeṃ* (*utpāṭana-*), *upaḍṇeṃ* (*utpat-*), perhaps *upaṇṇeṃ* (*utpavana-*) and *upeḍ* (*utpraidh-*); the same prefix *u-* is found in *upalāṇā*, cf. *palāṇ* (*paryāṇa-*);

Skr. *tm* in *āpaṇ*, *āp* (*ātma-*);

Skr. *rp* in *kāpaḍ* (*karpaṭa-*), *kāpūr* (*karpūra-*), *kāpūs* (*karpāsa*), *cāpaṭ* (*carpaṭa-*), *sāp* (*sarpa-*), *sūp* (*śūrpa-*). probably also in *sopṇeṃ* (*samarp-*),*opṇeṃ* (*arp-* or *ṛpy-*) and in *kāpṇeṃ* (* *karp-*);

Skr. *lp* in *śiṃpī* (*śilpin:*), perhaps in *aprā*, if this word contains Skr. *alpa-*.

ph

$ 126. The initial *ph* goes back to Pkt. *ph* arisen out of :

Skr. *ph* in *phal* (*phala-*) and its compounds *phaṭār* (*phalāhāra-*), *pophāḷ* (*pūgaphala-*), cf. *phaḷā* and *pharā* (*phalaka-*), *phāg* (*phalgu-*), *phāḷ* (*phāla-*), *phūl* (*phulla-*), *pheṇ* (*pheṇa-*);

Skr. *sp* in *phāṃḍṇeṃ*, *phaṃd* (*spanda-*); cf. *phirṇeṃ* (i. e. **spir-*);

Skr. *sph* in *phāṭṇeṃ*, *phāḍṇeṃ*, *phāḷṇeṃ* (*sphaṭ-*), *phār* (*sphāra-*); *phuṭṇeṃ*, *phoḍ* (*sphuṭ-*, *sphoḍa-*), *phurṇeṃ* (*sphur-*), cf. *phiṭṇeṃ*, *pheḍṇeṃ*;

Skr. *sphy* in *phāvḍā* (*sphya-*).

Inside the word, *ph* represents Pkt. *pph* arisen from :

Skr. *ṣp* in *vāph* (*vāṣpa-*), probably *guṃphā* and *gophaṇ* (*guṣpa-*).

Skr. *ṣph* in *niphaḷ* (*niṣphala-*);

Skr. *tph* in *uphāṇṇeṃ* (*ut-phaṇ-*), *uphaḷṇeṃ* (*utphulla-*), *uphāḷṇeṃ* (*utphal-*);

Skr. *lph* in *gophā* (*gulpha-*);
Skr. *sph* in *aphaḷṇeṃ* (*āsphālana-*), *pāphuḍṇeṃ* (*prasphuṭ-*).
For exchange of *p* and *ph*, see $ 84 ff.

b

$ 127. In the initial position *b* represents Pkt. and Skr. *b* in *bak*, *bagḷā* (*baka-*), *bakrā* (*barkara-*), *bīṃ* (*bīja-*), *bujhṇeṃ* (*budhya-*), *bel* (*bilva*), *bokaḍ* (*bukka-*), and other words to be found in the Lexicon. Marathi has kept up in the initial position the distinction between old *b-* and *v-*, see infra.

b, initial, also goes back to Skr. *br* in *bāmaṃ* and *bāṃbhurḍa* (*brāhmaṇa-*);

Lastly it represents Skr. *p*, become initial, as a consequence of an apocope during the period when surds had been made into sonants in the word *baisṇeṃ* (*upaviśa-*). Pali already has *uviṭṭha-*, which supposes a haplology of **uvaviṭṭha-*, and is consequently dated from an epoch when the intervocalic *b* had already become *v*. Here Gujarati and Sindhi are in agreement with Marathi; Kashmiri has *v*. As regards Romany, it is divided : that of Europe has *bes-*, that of Armenia *ves-*. The accessory word *bī* (*api*) carries the trace of the same accident : here the Romany of Europe also has the treatment of the intervocalic (*vi*).

Inside the word, *b* goes back to Pkt. *b* after a nasal, firstly there where Sanskrit had already *mb* : *uṃbar* (*udumbara-*), *kāṃbḷā* (*kambala-*), *kusuṃb* (*kusumbha-*), *lāṃb* (*lamba-*), *niṃb*, *liṃb* (*niṃba-*), *sāṃbar* (*śambara-*), etc. and secondly there where Pkt. *mb* goes back to *ml* : *āṃb* (*āmla-*) or to *mr*: *āṃb* (*āmra-*), *tāṃbeṃ* (*tāṃra-*). It is known that in similar cases cognate languages simplify *mb* into *m*: Marathi ignores this evolution. It is strange that a final occlusive has been re-established where it was opposed by etymology, in *śeṃb* beside *śem* (*śleṣma*), a form which is given as less suitable and which is, however, the only regular one. Similarly we have *theṃb* beside *them* (*stim-*).

Moreover, internal *b* represents Pkt. *bb* arisen from Skr. *lb* in *suṃb* (*śulba-*), and of Skr. *rb* in *kabrā* (*karbura-*), *dubḷā* (*durbala-*), *bābar* (*barbara*). Here also Marathi makes a distinction between Pkt. *vv* and Pkt. *bb*, contrary to the opinion of Grierson (*Phon.*, 11, 33). The opposition of *ḍabbā, dabḍā* and of *ḍāv* (*darvī*) suffices to prove that the first two forms are borrowed. Moreover, the reduplication of the consonant is not normal in Marathi and adds to the alien character of *ḍabbā*. If, therefore, *ūb* represents D. *uvvā*, it cannot be a purely Marathi form; and the *rapprochement* of *dābṇeṃ* with Pkt. *dāvai* (Pischel, $ 261) is suspect.

b is the product of de-aspiration in *khāṃb* (*skambha-*), *thāṃbṇeṃ* (*stambha-*), *kubḍā* (*kubhra-*).

bh

$ 128. In the initial position, *bh* represents Pkt. *bh* arisen out of :

Skr. *bh* in *bhāt* (*bhakta-*), *bheṃ* (*bhaya-*), etc.; see the Lexicon;

Skr. *bhr* in *bhaṭṭā* (*bhrāṣṭra-*; a word suspected to be borrowed), *bhaṃvāi* (*bhrū-*), *bhāū* (*bhrātṛ-*), *bhājṇeṃ* (*bhrajj-*), *bhoṃvṇeṃ*, *bhoṃvaḍṇeṃ* (*bhrama-*), *bhoṇvar*, *bhoṇvrā* (*bhramaraka-*).

Skr. *b*, see $ 84.

Inside the word, *bh* represents Pkt. *bh* after a nasal, in *āraṃbhaṇeṃ*, *kumbh*, *kuṃbhār* (*kumbhakāra-*), *jāṃbhāḍ* (*jambha-*); *baṃbhurḍā* goes back to *bambhaṇa-*, the doublet of *baṃbhaṇa-* (M. *bāmaṇ*) found since the oldest Prakrit.

It goes back to Pkt. *bbh* arisen out of :

Skr. *rbh* in *gābh* (*garbha-*), *dābh* (*darbha-*), *nibhagṇeṃ* (*nirbhagna-*), perhaps *bhāṃbhaḷ* (*bharbh-*);

Skr. *bhr* in *ābh* (*abhra-*);

Skr. *bhy* in *lābhṇeṃ* (*labhya-*) after whom has been formed *dubhṇeṃ* (*duhya-*); *bhya* has become *bhi* in *bhitar* (*abhyantara-*), *bhijṇeṃ* (*abhyañjana-*);

Skr. *hv* in *jībh* (*jihvā*).

Lastly *bh*, is found as a result of the *rapprochement* of *b* and *h* originally belonging to different syllables, in *bhūk* (*bubhukṣā*), *bharā*, the dialectal form of *bahirā* (*badhira-*), the recent tatsama *bhorūp*; in *bhiṇeṃ* there is perhaps not only the spontaneous reduction of *bihiṇeṃ*, but also the influence of *bheṇeṃ* (*bhaya-*, *bibheti*); the co-existence of H. *nibāhnā* and *nibhnā* proves that the aspirate has the same origin in *nibhṇeṃ* (*nirbādh-*).

The Sanskrit Group : dental+v.

$ 129. This group has two treatments equally well attested in Marathi : one consists in a dental consonant, and the other in a labial. Both go back to Prakrit. During the oldest period, they seem to have been distributed according to geographical regions and not in accordance with the phonetic principles.

In fact, among the inscriptions of Aśoka, those of Girnar are the only ones which have protected and even reinforced the labial articulation. They show the absolutive in *-tpā* in relation to *-tu* (*-tvā*) or *-tī* (Vedic-*tvi* ?) of other inscriptions; are also found therein the forms *catpāro* (*catvāro*), *hitatpā* (*hitat-vāt*), *dhādasa* (*dvādaśa*); in relation to *tadattaye-* (*tadatva-*) which is found at Shahbazgarhi and Mansehra (*tādatvāye* at Kalsi and Dhauli; *tadātvane* at Girnar and of *mahatatā* (*mahatva-*) of the inscriptions of Sahasram and Rupnath. The inscription of Girnar does not show any examples of the group : dental +*v* before *i*, so that we cannot say if inside the dialect of this region, there had been a diffference of treatment according to the vowel. It could be suspected, if we compare the place-names, *Barakhi* (*Dvārakā*) and *Diu* (*dvīpa-*), both of whom belong to the same region. Unfortunately if *Barakhi* is found in the first century of the Christian era, the second is modern and belongs to a period when the name of the "island" could have been very well made uniform in the different dia-lects. In any case, since Ptolemy, it is the form with the dental which is found in the word of *Iavadion* (*yavadvīpa*). This very form is shown in the name of Ceylon given by Cosmas and his successors, *Selediba* (*Śiṃhaladvīpa-*). Nothing prevents us from supposing that even from the time of Aśoka, the name of *Jambudīpa-* had already become fixed. This hypothesis is based on the fact that at Mysore, we read, beside forms like *mahatpā* which has the same relationship to Skr. *mahātmā* as *ātpā* of Girnar to Skt. *ātmā*. Now the tratment of *tm* and *tv* seems to be near each other (we also read at Brahmagiri *garut-*; but it is impossible to guess the end of the word). What-ever be the treatment before *i*, there remains a clear opposition between the dental group + *v* before *a* between the dialect of Girnar and those of other inscriptions.

To judge from current readings, there would have been a serious exception in the form of the word for the number "twelve" at Shahbazgarhi. We generally read *baraya* or *badaya*, but the end of the word is in any case incorrect. Moreover, the parallel inscription of Mansehra shows the form *duvadaśa*. Finally and above all, Bühler admits that the first two syllables of the word are badly read (Z D M G, 1889, p. 138; on the totality of facts, cf. Senart, *Inscr. de Piyadasi*, II, p. 353 ff., p. 379 ff. T. Michelson, JAOS, XXX, 79-80, XXXI, 235, 244).

As soon as we reach Pali and literary Prakrits, we find that the two treatments are found, in parallel, in the same texts. It seems, however, that the more frequent of the two in normal classical Prakrit, that is to say in Māhārāṣṭri, is the dental treatment. We find, from Hāla onwards, *dāra* and *bāra* (*dvāra-*) side by side. Hāla has similarly *biuṇa* whereas the old Jaina Aṅgas have *duguṇa* (*dviguṇa-*); but *ubha-* has entered literature after *uddha-* or *uḍḍha-* (*ūrdhva-*) and the replacement of the suffixes *-tta*, *-ttaṇa* (*-tva*, *-tvana*) by *-ppaṇa* starts only with the Apabhraṃśa (see Pischel, $ 298-300; cf. 436).

$ 130. Despite the confusion presented by modern languages, we see therein a distribution similar to the one shown by Aśokan inscriptions. Kashmiri, beside *bar* "door", which can be a loan like *darwaza*, has *zah* "two", *dòyum*" "second', *ödil* "right, just"; the suffix of the gerundive *-ith* recalls the *-ti* of Aśokan inscriptions. Similarly Baśgali has as the suffix of the gerundive *-ti* and *dū* for denoting "two" and "door"(Sten Konow, JRAS, 1911, p. 20.) In the far South, Simhalese has *uḍha* "right", *dora-* "two", *diuṇu* "double" and even, contrary to the generality of the languages of the continent, *ḍolos* "twelve" (beside the Elu *bara*). On the other hand it is remarkable that the only two dialects, where the word for the number "two" begins with a labial, are Sindhi (*ba*)and Gujarati (*be*), that is to say precisely the dialects of the region where Girnar is located.

The distribution of the two treatments in Marathi seems to clearly indicate that, there also, the dental is normal.

To Skr. *tv* correspond on the one hand, M. *t* in *nāteṃ* (*jñātvā-*), *sat* (*satva-*) and the probably borrowed word *sattā* (*satva-*); on the other hand M. *p* in the suffix *-paṇā* (*-tvana-*) whose labial contradicts Prakrit as seen above, and which consequently could very well have come as a loan from some Central language.

To Skr. *dv* corresponds M *d* in *daṃd* (*dvandva-*), *dār* (*dvāra-*), *sādaḷṇeṃ* (*śādvala-*). As against the same *bārī* "window", probably derived from *dvāra-*, is found in Gujarati beside *bār* "door". It is, thus surely, not a word which is indigenous to Marathi. As regards the forms of the word for the number "two", their history is too obscure and extension too general and too old to enable us to draw any conclusions therefrom. We have, on the one hand, *don* "two", *duṇā* "double", *dujā* "second", and on the other *bīj* "second day of the Moon", *be* "two" (in multiplication), *bārā* "twelve", etc.; see the chapter on the words for numerals.

To Skr. *dhv* correspond on the one hand *dh* in *dhāṃsaḷṇeṃ* (*dhvaṃs*) and in the semi-tatsama *dhajā* (*dhvaja-*), and on the other *bh* in *ubha*, *ubhṇeṃ* (*ūrdhva-*), which, as has been seen, have later on replaced in classical Prakit, the word with dental *uddha-*.

In addition to these two treatments, Prakrit seems to furnish several cases, where the old group dental+*v* ends up in a palatal. All the examples, given by Pischel in $ 299 in this connection, are not equally sure : *kiccā* for example is probably the result of the contamination of **kittā* < *kṛtvā* by **kicca-* <*kṛtya-* . They are, in general, late except one *jhaya-*(*dhvaja-*), found quite early in the Jaina texts and which has, continued upto the epoch of Marathi, where it is become *jheṃḍ*.

Lastly *v* has been vocalised in the sami-tatsamas *turūt* (*tvarita-*; *tūrta-* ?), *dhūn* (*dhvani-*). The absolutive in *ūn*, as will be seen, does not undoubtedly correspond to Pkt. -(*d*)*ūṇa*<Ved. *-tvāna*, see Pischel $ 586. Regarding *cār* (*catvāraḥ*), see the chapter on words for numerals.

Nasals

$ 131. Neither in Marathi nor in Sanskrit do the guttwral and palatal nasals have any independent existence. The only nasals found elsewhere than in contact with the occlusives of their group and notably in the intervocalic position, are the cerebral, dental and labial nasals. In Pali and in Buddhist Prakrits the geminated palatal nasal *ññ* representing Skr. *ny* and *jñ* is found (see Lüders, *Bruchstücke*, p. 48-9). But this has been an unstable phoneme and it has ended in classical Prakrit as *ṇṇ* in all the dialects except Māgadhī and Paiśācī (Pischel, $ 276, 282; cf. $ 243). Today, except in certain sporadic cases of recent origin, of the type noted by Hoernle in Bihari (*Comp. Gram.*, $ 13), all the dialects including Simhalese preserve, as Marathi, the aspect of the normal Prakrit. The western group consisting of Sindhi (see Beames, I, 78; Trumpp, *Sindhi Grammar*, $ 9, 14) and Panjabi, at least of its western dialects (O'Brien and Wilson, *Glossary of the Multani Lang.*, p. 1-2; J. Wilson, *Grammar...of Western Panjabi*, p. 1-2), seems to be separate from the Prakritic languages. It admits *ṅ* arisen out of Skr. *ṅg*; is also found there *ñ* for Skr. *ny*; but the absence of this phoneme in the case where it would represent Skr. *jñ* and the co-existence of *n* or *nn* with *ñ*, where it refers to Skr. *ny* proves that it relates to a recent phenomenon, here as elsewhere. The same phenomena are still found in the dialects of the N.W. Himalayas: Kashmiri *beña* (*bhaginī*) is evidently recent. Nothing can be deduced from the examples of *ṅ* < *ṅg* in Bengali cited by Sten Konow (JRAS, 1911, p. 23).

On the loss of *n* and *m* as penultimates in certain terminations, see $ 66, 67.

ṇ and *n*.

$ 132. In Sanskrit the dental nasal and the cerebral nasal had been clearly distinct. In literary Middle-Indian, *n* has been cerebralised in all positions. At least such is the case in classical Prakrit (see Pischel, $ 224.), but if the change is not found in Buddhist Sanskrit, its debuts must, however, go back farther. Pāṇini, for example, knows a word *māṇava-* "young Brahmin", the doublet in a specialised sense of the Vedic word *mānava-* "man" (see Wackernagel, $ 173; for a different explanation of the word, ibid., 172 b), and the intervocalic *ṇ* is found several times for *n* in Pali, notably after *u* or *o* (see Kern, *Festschrift Thomsen*, p.73).

In such a case one would expect a category of nasals in

the Indo-Aryan languages. This is true only in Hindi and in the Central dialects, where, moreover, this nasal is generally a dental (see Grierson, *Phon.*, $ 54; for the trace of *ṇ* in vulgar Bihari, see Hoernle, $ 13; on Simhelese, Geiger, $ 25). The western dialects have re-established the distinction of *n* and *ṇ* according to the place occupied by the nasal in the word. In Marathi the intervocalic *ṇ* of Prakrit has subsisted; but the initial or geminated *ṇ* has become a dental (see Sten Konow, JARS, 1902, p. 419) : so much so that the cerebral nasal behaves in relation to the dental nasal as a spirant with reference to an occlusive, for example as Pkt. nasal *v* in relation to *m*. The rule of Marathi applies also to Gujarati, Rajasthani, Sindhi where **ṇṇ* arisen out of *ṇḍ* has, in its turn, become *nn*, see J. Bloch, JA, 1912, I, p. 335), to Panjabi and perhaps to certain dialects of the W. Himalayas, in any case to Baśgali (see Sten Konow, JRAS, 1911, p. 23-4; Grierson, *Piśāca Lang*, p. 19, 112). The same sign is found in Prakrit but at a later date. The Jaina manuscripts on paper are the only ones which show it and except Hemacandra, the earliest grammarian who allows it is Kramadīśvara, whose date, besides uncertain, can not be anterior to the IXth century (Pischel, $ 224, 37; cf. Bhandarkar, JBBAS, 1887, p. 5, note). Given the date and the nature of the texts where it is noted, we may consider the dentalisation of the initial *ṇ* and of internal *ṇṇ* as a recent and western phenomenon. It is to be noted that this latter characteristic is in accordance with the distribution of the modern dialects.

$ 133. Besides, the opposition of the intervocalic *ṇ* coming from *ṇ* and *n*, and of the initial or internal *n* arisen from *ṇṇ* has been disturbed in Marathi by special changes occurring in different speeches. Observers agree in noting the uncertainties of pronunciation, but the details given by them are insufficient or contradictory. According to Navalkar *ṇ* becomes a dental in the Deccan (p. 8). According to the informations of the Linguistic Survey this change is found in the popular languages of the Konkan (LSI, *Mar.*, p. 66, cf. 109, 161, 173, 198) and in Vidarbha and in the Central Provinces (ibid., p. 225), that is to say, in the dialects where in addition *ḷ* becomes *l* or *r*. The spread of this phonetic phenomenon, combined on the other hand with the influence of

Sanskrit, explains the frequency of the mix-up of the dental *n* and of the cerebral *ṇ* in the common language. A few examples of this confusion will be given below.

$ 134. *ṇ* is found only inside or at the end of the word. It comes from Pkt. *ṇ* arisen out of :

Skr. *ṇ*, in *kaṇ* (*kaṇa-*), *kāṇā* (*kāṇa-*), *kāraṇ* (*kāraṇa-*), *kivaṇ* (*kṛpaṇa-*), *keṇeṃ* (*krayaṇa*), *gaṇṇeṃ* (*gaṇaya-*), *goṇ* (*goṇī*), *ghaṇ* (*ghaṇa-*), *caṇā* (*caṇaka-*), *tāṇ* (*tṛṇa*), *tarṇā* (*taruṇa-*), *doṇ* (*droṇi-*), *phaṇ* (*phaṇa-*), *pheṇ* (*pheṇa-*), *maṇī* (*maṇi-*), *loṇ* (*lavaṇa-*), *vaṇ* (*vraṇa-*), *saṇ* (*śaṇa-*), *saṇ* (*kṣaṇa-*). Some of these words are probably tatsamas. The fact is clear for words like *kirāṇ-*, *koṇ* or *rīṇ* (*ṛṇa*). It is made probable for words like *kiṇ*, *köṇ* by the co-existence of forms with the dental due to more recent changes: *kinā*, *konā*, *konyā*; see below :

Skr. *n*, in *aṃgaṇ* (*aṅgana-*), *āṇṇeṃ* (*ānayana-*; cf. *paraṇṇeṃ* of *pariṇayana-*) *uṇā* (*ūna-*), *oṇavṇeṃ* (*avanam-*), *kuṃṭaṇ*, *kuṭīṇ* (*kuṭṭaṇī*, *kuṭṭinī*), *jaṇ* (*jana-*), *jāṇṇeṃ* (cf. *jānāti*), *tāṇ*, *tāṇṇeṃ* (root *tan-*), *dhaṇ* (*dhana-*), *dhaṇī* (*dhanikā*), *pāṇī* (*pānīya-*), *puḷaṇ* (*pulina-*), *bahīṇ* (*bhaginī*), *māṇas* (*mānuṣa-*), *loṇī* (*navanīta-*), *vīṇ*, *viṇeṃ* (*vinā*), *hāṇ* (*hāni-*); all the infinitives in *-ṇeṃ* (*-nakaṃ*) and the feminine adjectives in *īṇ-* (*-inī*); as also the negative prefix *aṇ-* (*an-*).

The sentiment of gradation : Skr. *n*, M. *ṇ* has remained so alive that it has resulted not only in the adaptation of the tatsamas like *kaṭhīṇ* (*kaṭhina-*) but also in the cerebralisation of *n* in certain words borrowed recently, such as *phaṇūs*, *phāṇas* (Ar. -Pers. *fanūs*), *maṇ* (Arab. *man*), *meṇ* (Pers. *myān*), *sābūṇ*, *sābaṇ* (Ar.- Pers. *ṣābūn*). Inversely the co-existence of the tatsamas like *tān* and of the tadbhavas like *tāṇ* (*tāna-*) could have led to the restitution of the false tatsamas. In this manner will be explained, for example, *kinā* beside *kiṇ* (Skr. *kiṇa-*), *konā*, *konyā* beside *koṇ* (*koṇa-*), forms moreover in use since a period probably old, as is shown for example by the Deśī transcription *koṇṇa-*. The case of *kisān*, in relation to Skr. *kṛṣāṇa-*, is undoubtedly different. It relates probably to a loan from Hindi.

$ 135. The initial *n* goes back either to Skr. *n* in *na*, *nako*, *nāthi* (*na*), *nai* (*nadī*) and the majority of words with initial *n*, which are found in the Lexicon, or to Skr. *jñ*, in *nāteṃ* (*jñātvā-*).

Inside the word, *n* comes from Pkt. *n* before a dental occlusive. Thus we have *daṃt* (*danta-*), *daṃd* (*dvandva-*), *rāṃhṇeṃ* (*rāndhana-*), etc. It also goes back to Pkt. *ṇṇ* arisen out of :

Skr. *ṇṇ*, in *punav* (*puṃnāga-*);

Skr. *nn*, in *ansūd* (*anna-*), *śinā* (*chinna-*);

Skr. *ny*, in *ān*, *ānsā*, *ān*(*i*) *khī* (*anya-*; to the same word is undoubtedly joined the conjunction *āṇi*, *āṇ*, pronounced *āni* in the Konkan, see LSI, *Mar.*, p. 173. Like Marathi, Gujarati possesses beside the dental form another with the cerebral. This latter is probably of Indo-European origin), *jānivasa* (*janyā-*), *dhān* (*dhanya-*), *mān* (*manyā*) *mānṇeṃ*, *manāviṇeṃ* (*manya-*), *sunā* (*śūnya-*);

Skr. *ṇy* in *rān* (*araṇya-*) beside which is found the form with the cerebral *rāṇ*. This latter is the only one found in the compound *usrāṇ* (D. *ucchuraṇaṃ*).

Skr. *jñ* in *vīnavṇeṃ* (*vijñāpaya-*), *jānaveṃ* (*yajñopavīta-*). Beside the *n* treatment two more are also found : 1. *ṇ* in *āṇ* (*ājñā*), *paiṃ* (*pratijñā*) a poetic form and *rāṇī* (*rājñī*) which could at best be considered as a loan; 2. *j* in *paij* (*pratijñā*). the doublet of *paiṇ*, and *sāṃjeṃ* (*saṃjñitaṃ*). The three treatments go back to Prakrit (see Pischel, $ 276); and neither in ancient history nor in the distribution of modern dialects is found any indication enabling us to render account of this diversity;

Skr. *rṇ* in *kān* (*karṇa-*), *kāṇaḍā* (*karṇāṭaka-*), *cūn* (*cūrṇa-*), *junā* (cf. *jīrṇa-*), *pān* (*parṇa-*), *vān* (*varṇa-*), *soṇeṃ*, *sonār* (*suvarṇa-*). But *śīṇ* (Skr. *śīrṇa-*), *vāṇ* and *vāṇṇeṃ* are found beside *vān*, *sātvaṇ* (*saptaparṇa-*) beside *pān* and *cuṇī* beside *cūn* and *cunā*. In this last case the two forms go back to Deśi. A case of old simplification of Pkt. *ṇṇ* is that of Pkt. *kaṇiyāra-* (*karṇikāra-*) found in the oldest texts of the Jaina Canon (Pischel, $ 287, cf. 258).

$ 136. Pkr. *ṇ* forming a group with *h* has become a dental like the geminated *ṇ*. As a consequence, it is the Marathi *nh* which corresponds to Skr. *sn*, *ṣṇ* in *kānhū* (*kṛṣṇa-*), *tānh* (*tṛṣṇā*), *pānhā* (*prasnava-*). Most often, when the vowel preceding or following the group is *a*, another *a* is inserted inside the group : thence *tahān* beside *tānh* (*tṛṣṇā*), *nahāṇ* beside *nhāṇ* (*snāna*) *nāhāvī* beside *nhāvī* (**snāpita-*). Similarly in *sāhan* (*ślakṣṇa-*), where *kṣṇ* is moreover irregularly treated as *ṣṇ*, cf. $ 96. Sometimes the aspiration also disappears : thence *ūn* beside *ūnh* (*uṣṇa-*), *upas-tān* besides *tānh* and *tahān* (*tṛṣṇā*), *sān* beside *sāhan* (*ślakṣṇa-*), *sūn* (*snuṣā*, Pkt. *suṇhā*).

There is probably a relationship between this instability of aspiration in the group *nh* and its appearance in certain words where it is not rendered legitimate by etymology. Such words are *dinhalā* (Pkt. *diṇṇa-*), whose stem, moreever, is found in other languages; *jānhaveṃ* beside *jānaveṃ* (*yajñopavīta-*) which on the contrary seems to belong to Marathi, as also *joṃdhḷā*, if it refers to Deśī *joṇṇaliaṃ*.

In this last word, the differentiation has led to the development of a dental occlusive. The same fact is found in *śindaḷ*, the doublet of *śinnaḷ*, *śinal* (*chinna-*). In these two cases, the development of *d* is recent. The doublet *vānar* : *vāndar* (*vānara-*), on the contrary, should go back far in the past as its equivalents are found not only in Hindi, but in Kashmiri and even in Simhalese . In Marathi the word is suspected to be simply borrowed from Hindi *bǎndar*, whose spread is well-known (cf. Wackernagel, $ 157).

m

$ 137. This labial nasal exists in the tadbhavas of Marathi only where it goes back to initial *m* or to internal *mm*, *mh* (see Beames, I, 342, 345, 347; Grierson, *Phon.*, $ 96, 102). The old intervocalic *m* has become a spirant and has ended as a nasal *v*, an unstable phoneme whose nasality has generally been carried to the neighbouring vowel or has even totally disappeared. This spirantisation of the intervocalic *m*, universal in Aryan India, except in Simhalese and in the mountain dialects of the North-West (see Grierson, *Piśāca Lang.*, p. 118; Beames, I, p. 254 ff; Grierson, *Phon.*, p. 16) seems to be quite late. Its traces in Sanskrit are rare and suspect (Wackernagel, I, $ 177, note, 196 note). Classical

Prakrit admits it only in a number of particularly favourable positions : in the root *nem-* and in a few analogous cases it has been brought in by the dissimilation of nasals. Examples collected by Pischel in the first part of $ 251 of his grammar relate, on the contrary, to the assimilation of an *u* in touch with *m*. An example of the same type is found in the oldest known Marathi inscription : *Cāvuṃḍarājeṃ* (*Cāmuṇḍarājñā*); but judging by the transcriptions *Śimulla* and *Komarśi* of the *Periplus of the Erythrean Sea*, this change itself seems, in Western India, to be posterior to the first century A. D. (see *Mél. Sylvain Lévi*, p. 9.) In any case, the rule of spirantisation of the intervocalic *m* is admitted for the Apabhraṃśa in its generality by Hemacandra. The same author also admits the intervocalic *m* in his notation of Deśī. This is how we find in his collection the forms *gāmauḍa*, *bhūmi-pisāa*, *sāmara*, *somala*, etc., the equivalents of the Marathi words *gāvḍā*, *bhuiṃ*, *sāṃvar*, *soṃvaḷ* , etc. But this notation is perhaps conventional. In fact, *v* is found not only in the Marathi texts posterior by a few years (for example, *gāṃvu* in the Paithan inscription of 1273) but in the *Deśīnāmamālā* itself. Is found therein *karavandī* as the equivalent of *karamandikā*. Above all words like *tamo* and *tamaṇaṃ*, respectively translated by *śoka-* and *cullī*, seem clearly to go back to the Skr. root *tap-*, Pkt. *tav-* (cf. Mar. *tāv*) and should, therefore, be read as **taṃvo*; **taṃvaṇaṃ*. Similarly, *vimalia-* is found evidently going back to the root *val-*. It is true that here, at best, a dissimilation is admissible. In short, it seems that *m* became a spirant in all positions, either after the epoch of Hemacandra, or earlier, but at a date which was late enough to enable this author to preserve the graphic tradition of the intervocalic *m*.

The sentiment of the gradation *m* : *v* has led to the re-establishment, in certain words, of *m* in place of *v* itself, whereas *v* went back to a non-nasal labial. This fact is noticeably met with in Gujarati and in the eastern dialects. (see Hoernle, *Comp. Gram.*, p. 74; Grierson, *Phon.*, p. 17). Marathi does not seem to have any examples of the same.

$ 138. In the initial position, *m* goes back to :

Skr. *m* in *mau* (*mṛdu-*), *māg* (*mārga-*) and in a large number of other examples to be found in the Lexicon;

Skr. *mr* in *mākhṇeṃ* (*mrakśaṇa-*);

Skr. *śm* in *masaṇ* (*śmaśāna-*), beside which is also found the form with a tendency to archaism, even from the view-point of Prakrit, *mhasaṇ* (cf. Pischel, $ 104).— A distinction should be made between this case and the one where a recent *mh* goes back to *m*+*h* earlier separated by a vowel, as in the words *mhais* (*mahiṣī*), *mhātārā* (*mahattara-*), *mhetar* (for *mehetar*, *mehtar*; Pers. *mihtar*), *mhoṃv* (*moha-*), etc. In this group also the aspiration is unstable : that is why we have *māūt* beside *mahāvat* (*mahāmātra-*), *motsāv*, *motsāh* (*mahot-*), *moḷeṃ* beside *mohaḷ* (cf. Skr. *mukha-*). Inside the word, *m* goes back to :

Skr. *m* in contact with a labial consonant, in *uṃbar* (*udumbara-*), *kuṃbh* (*kumbha-*), *kusuṃb*) *kusumbha-*), *kothambīr* (*kustumbarī*), *cuṃbaṇeṃ* (*cumb-*), *cuṃbaḷ* (Pali *cumbaṭa-*), *niṃb* and *liṃb* (*nimba-*), *liṃpṇeṃ* (root *lip-*), *haṃbā* (*hambhā*).

Pkt. *n̠m*, itself arisen out of :

Skr. *nm* in the compounds of *un* + a word beginning with *m* : *umagṇeṃ* (*unmagna-*), *umajṇeṃ* (*unmajjana-*), *umaḷṇeṃ* (*unmil-*), *umaḷṇeṃ* (*-mala-*), *umāṇṇeṃ* (*unmāna-*), *umās* (*unmathya-*); *unmaḷṇeṃ* (*unmūlana-*) on the contrary is a *semi-tatsama*; as regards the word *sāmāśī* one should see therein a recent compound of *sā*, that is to say, *sahā-* "six"+*mās-* (*māsa-*) rather than a representative of Skr. *ṣaṇmāsa-*;

Skr. *mm* perhaps in *samor* (cf. *sammukha-*)?

Skr. *rm* in *kām*, cf. *nikāmī*, *rikāmā* (*karma-*), *ghām* (*gharma-*), *cām* (*carma-*), *dhāmā* (*dhārmika-*); undoubtedly also *ghumṇeṃ* (**ghūr-m-*; Skr. *ghūrṇ-*);

Lastly, *m* goes back to Pkt. *mh*, representing either Skr. *mh* as in *bāmaṇ* (*brāhmaṇa-*; the form *bāṃbhurḍā* goes back to Pkt. *baṃbhaṇa-*), or Skr. sifflant + *m* as in *amhī* (*asme*; cf. *tumhī*), *gīm* (*grīṣma-*; cf. *śiṃgā*). It will be noted that aspiration has dropped everywhere except in personal pronouns, normally of archaic form. In *cāmhār* the aspiration is adventitious and has been correctly explained by Beames (I, 346) as being due to the analogy of *kvm*(*b*)*hār*.

In view of the principles enunciated above, the intervocalic *m* represents Skr. *m* only in the tatsamas or semi-tatsamas; such is the case in *udīm* (*udyama-*), *koykamaḷ* (*kamala-*), *gosāmī* beside *gosāvī* (*gosvāmin-*), *namṇeṃ* in relation to *onavṇeṃ* (*nam-*), *nem* or *nīm* (*niyama-*), *vamṇeṃ* (*vam-*) and *vām* (*vāma-*) in relation to *vāṃv* (*vyāma-*), *somaḷ* beside *soṃvaḷ* (D. *somāla-*, cf. Skr. *sukumāra-*) etc.

r and *l* (*ḷ*)

$ 139. These two phonemes can, at no moment of the linguistic history of Aryan India, be independently considered. The oldest Vedic texts already show a disturbed linguistic aspect, supposing the introduction in a dialect where *r* had been the normal representation of both the Indo-European *r* and *l*, atleast in certain positions (see $ 2). Later on the mixtures become more numerous and the spread, due to religious and political circumstances, of a dialect where *l* represented both the Indo-European *l* and *r* must have been responsible for the increasingly frequent substitution of *r* by *l* in the vocabulary of classical Sanskrit and Prakrit (see Wackernagel, $ 191-193, Pischel, $ 256, 257, 259). Modern idioms, heirs of Sanskrit and Prakrit, show the same mixtures as these languages; and there is no more any dialect having generalised either *r* or *l* in all positions. Besides, the detail of the vocabulary is never more identical from one dialect to another; so much so that we must admit that the loans and adaptations have continued to be effected during all the periods and undoubtedly in all directions. In addition, evolutions particular to certain speeches have occurred. Thus in Sindhi the intervocalic *l* has become *r* (Beames, I, 247); in Bihari and often in Bengali the same alteration has taken place, not only between vowels (Hoernle, *Comp. Gram.*, $ 30, 110; Grierson, *Phon.*, 66) but also in the initial position, as is shown, for example by the name of the village of *Rummindeī*, whose old name is *Lumbinī* or *Lumminī-* (Windisch, *Actes du XIV Cong. des Orient.*, Algiers, I, 280 note; Fleet, JRAS, 1906, p. 177). In this latter case the passage of *l* into *r* looks all the more remarkable because of its occurrence in the domain of old Māgadhi, where all *r*s became *l*. It is true that in the Eastern dialects *r* is dental (Grierson, *Phon.*, $ 65), so that the transformation of *l* into *r* is similar only in appearance to the one found in Sindhi. It represents one of the consequences of the instability of *l* in these speeches, verified besides by the frequent change in Bengali and in Oriya of *l* into *n* (Beames, I, 248; Grierson, *Phon.*, $ 66, p. 15).

$ 140. Marathi offers, like other dialects, a large majority of cases where *r* and *l* (*ḷ*) respectively respond to *r* and *l* of classical Sanskrit. This is how M. *piṃpḷī* agrees with Skr. *pippalī* as the forms of Hindi and Bengali, whereas the words of Gujarati and Sindhi go back to the form noted by Greek *péperi*. Similarly, M. *sārī* reproduces Skr. *sārikā* (cf. Hindi *sār*) whereas Pali had an *l*, which is found in Simhalese. When the Sanskrit tradition admitted two forms, Marathi has opted for different meanings according to the words. Thus we have on the one hand *loṃv* (*loma-*, *l* is found in Simhalese and in Sindhi; *l* in Gujarati, Panjabi, Hindi, Bengali,) *soṃvaḷ* (=**sukomala-* rather than *sukumāra-*; cf. M. *koṃvaḷ* <*komala-*; see Pischel, $ 123), *gaḷṇeṃ*, *ugaḷṇeṃ*, *gaḷā*, *gilṇeṃ* (*gal-*, *gala-*, *gil-*; *l* everywhere except Sindhi, where *r*=*ḷ*), On the other hand *thor* (*sthūra-*; *r* in Gujarati, *l* in Simhalese, *rohī* (*rohita-*, *r* everywhere). Sometimes Marathi opposes Sanskrit also.

$ 141. In a sufficiently large number of words Marathi shows *l*, whereas Sanskrit has *r*. Most of these forms are found since the ancient-most period of classical Prakrit. Such is the case with *iṃgaḷ* (*aṅgāra-*), *haḷad* (*haridrā*) in relation to *har-yāḷ*, *hirḍā*, *hirvā* (*harita-*) which are noted in Vararuci (II, 30); of *cāḷīs* (*catvāriṃśat*) whose *l* is current in Pali. Of certain words where *ry* preceding *a* 'has been noted since Prakrit as *ll* : *palaṃg*, *pālakh* (*paryaṅka-*), *palāṭan*, *pālaṭ*, *paletṇeṃ* (*paryaṭ-*), *palāṇ* (*paryāṇa-*), *pālthā* (*paryasta-*), *pelṇeṃ* (*prerya-*); and finally of the words where Skr. *dr* has become *ll* : *āleṃ* (*ārdraka-*), *ol* (*udra-*), found in old Prakrit, *cultā*, whose prototype *culla-* is current in Pali (cf. *kṣulla-*, the other form of *kṣudra-* in the Atharva-veda), *bhalā* (*bhadra-*). The form *bhalla-* has been introduced in classical Sanskrit), *śīl* (*chidra-*, in the Konkan *śil*) which goes back to Deśī. We should probably add here on the one hand the adjectives in *-r* (Pkt. *-lla-*, Pischel, $ 595) and on the other the name of the ogress *lāṃv* (*rāmā* : the form with *l* of *rāma-* is already found in the old word *lamaka-* and its patronym *lāmakāyana-*, without counting the perfect *lalāma* of the root *ram-*, found in the *Harivaṃśa*), the word *malāī* derived from the caste-name, *malla-*, which itself is only the name of the eastern branch of a people known in ancient Panjab as *madra-*; finally the word *las* "pus", as the Skr. *laśa-* "resin" of the later texts is, without any doubt, an adaptation of a modern word, the doublet of the Skr. *rasa-* "juice". Of similar type are *aḍuḷsā* (*aṭaruṣa-*), *ghoḷṇeṃ* (*ghūrṇ-*), *coḷṇeṃ cūrṇ-*), *nihāḷṇeṃ*, *saṃbhāḷṇeṃ* (root *bhar-* ?) which are recent but are found with *l* in other languages (with the exception of the first) as the names of isolated plants. As regards *nikāl* (*niṣkar-*) the fact that *l* herein is a dental leads us to suspect that it is a word borrowed from Hindi.

$ 142. Marathi has *r* where Sanskrit has *l*. Thus *kir* (*kila-*), the only one found in old Prakrit; *sāṃvar* (*śālmalī*; cf. M. *śeṃorī* and Pali *simbalī*) and *pharā*, the doublet of *phaḷā* (*phalaka-*) are noted in Deśī. Most of the examples are recent: *avher* in relation to *heḷṇeṃ* (*helana-*), *ujrī* in relation to *ujaḷ* (*ujjvala-*), *kusri* in relation to *kusaḷ* (*kuśala-*), *nāṃgar* (*lāṅgala-*), probably *saver* in regard to *veḷ* (*velā*). These words, doubling other words of identical meaning, are suspected to be borrowed either from some eastern dialect, or from a Marathi speech where the intervocalic *l* had become *r*. It is known in fact that in the speeches of Konkan, Vidarbha and Central Provinces, this change is normal (see $ 144). The dictionary of Molesworth gives *ohar* as a form of the Konkan, opposed to normal Marathi *ohaḷ*. As regards *nāṃgar* (*lāṅgala-*) which contrasts with *nāṃgḷī* (*lāṅgalikā*), it is probably also a provincial word. In fact the current term for the "plough" in the Deśī is *aūt* (see Molesworth, s. v.).

The Marathi words in which *l* or *ḷ* correspond to *r* of Sanskrit are, thus, numerous and old, chiefly if we take into account the rarity and the recent character of the inverse cases. This fact is particularly in accordance with the hypothesis that Marathi is derived from a common language whose vocabulary would have contained a sufficiently strong eastern element.

We have now to examine cases where *r* and *l* of Sanskrit have been preserved right upto Marathi.

r

$ 143. In the initial position, *r* goes back to Skr. *r*; examples are : *raṃg-*(*raṅga-*), *raḍṇeṃ* (*raṭ-*), *ratī* (*raktikā*) and all the words with the initial *r* to be found in the Lexicon.

Inside the word, *r* represents :

Skr. *r* in *aṃtar* (*antara-*), *ār* (*ajagara-*), *ārat* (*ārātrikā*), *ukar* (*utkara-*), *utarṇeṃ* (*uttar-*), *utrāṇ* (*uttara-*) *uṃdar* (*undura-*), *uṃbar* (*udumbara-*), *er* (*itara-*) *eraṃḍ* (*eraṇḍa-*), *ovrī* (*apavaraka-*), *kaṃkar* (*karkara-*), *kacrā* (*kaccara-*), *kabrā* (*karbura-*) *kar* (*kara-*), *karṇeṃ* (*kar-*), *karvat* (*karapattra-*), *kāvrā* (*kātara-*), *kāṃsār* (*kāṃsyakāra-*) and the other nouns for agent in *-ār* <*-kāra-* as *kumbhār*, *cāmhār*, *maṇyār*, *lohār*, etc., *khar* (*khara-*), *kher* (*khadira-*), *garodar* (*guru-*), *gahirā* (*gabhīra-*), *gābhār* (*garbhāgāra*) and other nouns composed with *-ār* <*-āgāra-*, such as *kaulār*, *dhavlār* and *bhāṇḍār* (this last one already found in Sanskrit), *gerū* (*gairika-*), *gorā* (*gaura-*), *carṇeṃ* (*car-*), *cār* (*catvāri*), *ciṃvar* (*cikura*), *cor* (*caula-*), etc.;—*ghar* corresponds not to Skr. *gṛha-* but to Pkt. *ghara-*;

Skr. *rh* in *jar*, *tar* (*yarhi*, *tarhi*), *gārāṇeṃ*, the doublet of *gắrhāṇeṃ* (*garbha-*);

Skr. *d* or *t*, contrary to the general law of the disappearance of intervocalics, in certain nouns of numerals composed with Skr. *daśa* and in *sattar* (*saptati-*), see $ 118, 221 and 223. The pronominal adjectives *sarisā* or *sarsā* and *sārikhā* should not be cited here. These words are not based on *sādṛśa-*, **sādṛkṣa-*, cf. *taisā* (*tādṛśa-*), *jaisā* (*yādṛśa-*), etc., which give the normal phonetic treatment; see Wackernagel, p. XXI.

Skr. *ry* : the normal treatment of this group is *j* (see $ 106); under special circumstances it also allows the treatment *l* (see $ 141). As regards *r*, according to Pischel, it appears in Prakrit only after *ī* and *ū*, and besides in the words where one may suspect the substitution of a morpheme (see Pischel, $ 284). The examples of Marathi can be explained in this manner only in the case of *vīr* (*vīrya-*) and of the word, undoubtedly remade on this model, *dhīr* (*dhairya-*); *vipārā* is a tatsama, where *viparyaya-* seems to have been influenced by *viparīta-* and can be interpreted as a compound of *vi-* and *pār* "the other bank, on the other side;" *parisṇeṃ* or *pares-*

ṇeṃ (*paryeṣaṇa-*) seems to be a recently adopted tatsama, the poetic language having preserved *pari-yeṣaṇeṃ*; such is also the case of *vyarā* (*abhyavahāra-*, cf. *abhyavahṛta-*) and undoubtedly even of *pāruṣṇeṃ*, *pārosā* (*paryuṣ-*). But forms like *tirkā*, *tirsā* (*tiryak-*) or *mer* (*maryādā*), whereof one, moreover goes back to classical Prakrit and the other to Deśī are, for the time being, inexplicable.

ḷ

$ 144. This phoneme is found in Marathi only inside or at the end of the word. It comes firstly in place of Skr. the intervocalic *l*. This treatment is comparable to that of *n*. Like *n* also, the initial or geminated *l* has remained a dental (see Sten Konow, JRAS, 1902, p. 417-8). The same law applies in Rajasthani (see LSI, *Rājasth.*, p. 20), in Panjabi, Gujarati, and Oriya Beames, I, 244). At first view, the domain of *ḷ* appears to be cut up into a number of groups of isolated speeches. This would be astonishing, if this were not a case of pure apparence. In fact, on the one hand, Sindhi, which occupies the region lying between Gujarat and Panjab, converts intervocalic *l* into *r*. Whatever be the history of this change, it offers along with that of the neighbouring speeches, the common character of representing a passage of dental articulation to the cerebral. This interpretation applies, without doubt, also to those cases, where intervocalic *l* is represented by *r* in the dialects of the N. W. mountains, which seem then, to be attached to the same group (see Grierson, ZDMG, 1912, p. 82, 83). On the other hand, Oriya is not as isolated from the western group as it seems. In fact, the Dravidian languages, all of them contiguous on the meridional frontier, have the cerebral *ḷ*, as has been remarked by Beames (I, 245). The same is true of Simhalese where *ḷ* also represents the cerebral occlusives of Sanskrit, and not *l* which is preserved (Geiger, $ 14, 6; $ 25). India considered as a whole is, thus, divided into two groups : the first, which includes the Indus valley, the entire Deccan and Ceylon, has *l* and *ḷ*; the second, which includes the dialects of the N. W. mountains (see Grierson, *Piśāca Lang.*, p. 124) and the speeches of the valley of the

Ganges, has only the dental *l*, this *l* being susceptible, in its turn as we have seen, of being transformed into *r*, equally a dental.

But since which period has *l* been cerebralised in the Marathi areas ? The Prakrit sources are obscure : Paiśācī is the only dialect which is shown as normally converting the intervocalic Skr. *l* into *ḷ*. But it should also be noted that the rules concerning the same date from Hemacandra, that is to say from a very late epoch (Pischel, $ 260). The texts, written in other dialects, do not have a uniform sign. Thus, as could be expected, the meridional manuscripts have *ḷ*, while those of the North keep *l*, but the grammarians know only *l*, even where it represents *ḍ*, that is to say, where the Vedic had already *ḷ* (Pischel, $ 226). In old Marathi, only *l* is found in the inscriptions of Patan (1206 A.D., see note 9 of Rajwade), of Pandharpur (1273, 1276), in a mss. of the *Jñāneśvarī* (1290 A. D. ?—see JA, 1909, II, p. 565); but it is noted in the verse of the *Yogaratnamālā* in 1400 (see *Granthamālā*, March, 1903, p. 33).

It is impossible to determine if the script has been adapted to the pronunciation almost along with its evolution, or if the signs of the grammarians of Prakrit of the lower period had not, already, been late as regards the real pronunciation.

The rule of the cerebralisation of *l* admits, in the local speeches, a number of exceptions. The dental articulation is maintained on the coast, from Thana to Rajapur; *ḷ* is replaced by *r* (and even by *y*) in the Central provinces and Vidarbha (LSI, *Mar.*, p. 23, 220). We have seen above that in the Konkan *r* had also been a possible substitute of *ḷ*.

$ 145. However *ḷ* is the normal development of the intervocalic *l* as is shown by examples given below.

agaḷ (*argala-*), *aṃgḷī* (*aṅguli-*), *aṭāḷā* (*attālikā-*). *avḷā* (*āmalaka-*), *aḷṭā* (*ālakta-*), *aḷaṃbem* (*ālamb-*), *aḷī* (*alin-*), *aḷeṃ* (*ālavāla-*), *āṃduḷṇeṃ* (*āndolana-*; cf. *ucaṃdaḷṇeṃ*, *hiṃduḷā*), *āḷ* (*alaya-*, *āli-*), *āḷas* (*ālasya-*), *isāḷā* (*īrṣyāla-*), *īḷā* (*īlī*), *ukhaḷ* (*udūkhala-*), *udhaḷṇeṃ* (*uddhūlaya-*), *eḷā* (*elā*), *oṃgaḷ* (*amaṅgala-*), *olaṃgṇeṃ* (*avalagaya-*), *olambṇeṃ* (*avalamb-*), *ouṃḷ* (*vakula-*), *oḷ* (*valī*), *kaḷ* (*kalā*), *kaḷṇeṃ* (*kalana-*), *kaḷvā* (*kalāpa-*) *kaḷas* (*kalaśa-*), *kaḷho* (*kalaha-*), *kaḷī* (*kalikā*), *kāvḷā* (*kāka-*; D. *kāyala-*), *kāḷ* (*kāla-*, subst., cf. *dukaḷ*), *kāḷā* (*kāla-* adj.), *kīḷ* (*kīla-*), *kudāḷ* (*kuddāla-*), *kusaḷ* (*kuśala-*), *kūḷ* (*kula-*), *keḷ* (*kadalī*), *koil* (*kokila-*), *koykamaḷ* (*kamala-*), *kolhāḷ* (*kolāhala-*), *koṃvḷā* (*komala-*), *koḷī* (*kaulika-*), *koḷeṃ* (*kavala-* and D. *kola-*), *khaḷ* (*khala-* subst. and adj.), *khaḷṇeṃ* (*skhal-*), *khīl* (*kīla-*), *gaḷṇeṃ*, *gaḷā* (*gala-*), *giḷṇeṃ* (*gil-*), *garaḷ* (*garala-*), *goḷā* (*golaka-*), *cāḷṇeṃ*, cf. *nicaḷ* (*cālana-*), *jaḷ* (*jala-*), *jaḷṇeṃ* (*jvalana-*; cf. *ujaḷṇeṃ*), *jaḷū* (*jalankā*), *jaḷ* (*jāla-*) *jhoḷī* (*jhaulikā*), *tāḷī* (*tālikā*), *ṭāḷū* (*tālu-*) *ṭāḷeṃ* (*tāla-*), *ṭiḷā* (*tilaka-*) *ḍoḷā* (*dola-*) *taraḷṇeṃ* (*tarala-*), *tisaḷ* (*triśūla-* ?) , *tīḷ* (*tila-*), *tuḷ*, *tuḷṇeṃ* (*tulā*, *tulana-*), *tulśī* (*tulasī-*), *thaḷ* (*sthala-*), *thāḷā* (*sthāla-*), *daḷ* (*dala-*), *dubḷā* (*durbala-*), *deuḷ* (*devakula-*), *dhavaḷ* (*dhavala-*), *naḷ* (*nala-*), *nāṃglī* (*lāṅgalikā*) ,*nāreḷ* (*nārikela-*); *nāḷ*(*nāla-*), *paḍaḷ* (*paṭala-*), *paḷṇeṃ* (*palāyana-*), *paḷas* (*palāśa-*), *pākhaḷṇeṃ* (*prakṣālana-*), *pāḷ* (*pālī*), *pāḷṇeṃ* (*pālana-*), *piṃpaḷ* (*pippala-*), *pivḷā* (*pītala-*), *puḷaṇ* (*pulina:*), *paul* (*pratoli-*), *phaḷ* (*phala-*; cf. *uphāḷ*, *jaiphaḷ*, *niphaḷ*, *pophaḷ*, *phaḷār*, etc.), *phaḷā* (*phalaka-*), *phāḷa* (*phāla*) *baḷ* (*bala-*, *bali*), *baḷ* (*bāla-*), *bīḷ* (*bila-*), *bhāḷ* (*bhāla-*), *maṃgaḷ* (*maṅgala-*), *marāḷ* (*marāla-*), *mahāḷ* (*mahālaya-*), *maḷ* (*mala-*, cf. *oṃvlā*, *umaḷṇeṃ*), *māvḷā* (*mātula-*), *māḷ* (*mālā-*), *miḷṇeṃ* (*milana-*), *mūḷ* (*mūla-*) *meḷ* (*mela-*), *moḷī* (*mūlikā-*), *rasāḷ* (*rasāla-*), *rāuḷ* (*rājakula-*), *rāḷ* (*rāla-*), *lāḷ* (*lālā*), *loḷ-* (*lul-*), *vaḷṇeṃ* (*valana-*; cf. *oṃvaḷṇeṃ*) *vaḷeṃ* (*valaya-*), *vāḍaḷ* (*varadalikā*), *vāḷā* (*vāla-*), *vāḷū* (*vālukā-*), *visaḷṇeṃ* (*vikṣal-*), *viḷavṇeṃ* (*vilapana-*), *veḷ* (*velā*), *saraḷ* (*sarala-*), *saḷ* (*chala-*), *sādaḷṇeṃ* (*śādvala-*), *sāḷ* (*śālā*, *śālī*) *sāḷā* (*śyāla-*), *saḷī* (cf. *śala-*), *śiḷā* (*śītala-*), *śiḷ* (*śila-*), *sūḷ* (*śūla-*), *seḷ* (*chagala-*), *soṃvaḷ* (D. *somāla-*), *haryāḷ* (*haritāla-*), *haḷ* (*hala-*) *haḷīs* (*halīṣā*), *haḷu* (*laghu-*), *heḷṇeṃ* (*helana-*); and all the adjectives with the suffix *-aḷ* (*misaḷ*, *mokaḷ*, *mohaḷ*, *śīnḍaḷ*, cf. *pivḷā*, *poḷ*, etc.) or *-āḷ* (Skr. *-āla-*, *-ālu-*), of whom the majority is recent or found at the most in Deśī.

$ 146. Secondly *ḷ* comes from the intervocalic Skr. *ḍ*.— The passage of *ḍ*, *ḍh* to *ḷ*, *ḷh* is one of the oldest cases, found in Sanskrit, concerning the opening of the intervocalic occlusives. It is, in fact, constant since the *Ṛgveda*, but classical Sanskrit has restored the archaic pronunciation and reintroduced *ḍ* and *ḍh* everywhere (Wackernagel, p. XXIII; Meillet, IF, XXXI, p. 123). The aspirated sonant, as it has been reestablished by classical Sanskrit has been kept without apparent change in Prakrit and Marathi (cf. $ 112). On the contrary, *ḷh* is a group of consonants in Prakrit as in Vedic and ends, as a consequence, in *lh*, *l* in Marathi; cf. Pischel, $ 247 and infra $148. As regards *ḍ*, it is represented in Marathi both by *ḍ* and *ḷ*.

We find *ḍ* in a small number of words where Skr. *ḍ* seems to have been artificially preserved both in Prakrit and in the modern languages. Many of these words have, beside them, the forms in *ḷ*, which confirms this interpretation . Its examples are given above in $ 111. The treatment *ḷ*, on the contrary confirmed by Guj. *ḷ*, H. *l*, S. *r*), is more frequent and seems to correspond to a real phonetic evolution. Does it go back directly to the Vedic language ? We dare not affirm it. It is, nevertheless, true that the tendency to open *ḍ* is found during all the epochs. Its traces are found in classical Sanskrit since the *Atharva-veda* (Wackernagel, $ 194a) The change of *ḍ* into *ḷ* is normal in a series of Pali texts and in many dialects of Buddhist Prakrit (see Lūders *Bruchstücke*...,, p. 44 and 55). It is equally shown as being the rule in classical Prakrit. Besides this rule is at first optional (see Vararuci, II, 3 and the commentary), and suffers from sufficiently numerous exceptions confirmed by the state of modern vocabulary (Pischel, $ 240). But as a whole, the tendency is clear and it is this tendency which explains the Marathi examples given below.

In the case of *kheḷṇeṃ* (*krīḍ-*: *khel-*), of *gūḷ*, *goḷā* (*guḍa-*, *gauḍa-*: *gola-*; cf. M. *goḍ* adj.), of *nāḷ* (*nāḍi-*: *nāla-*; cf. M. *nāḍī*), the form with *l* is noted since classical Sanskrit, but the etymology and history agree in showing its secondary character. For *taḷāv* (*taḍāga-*), *piḷṇeṃ* (*pīḍ-*; cf. M. *pīḍṇeṃ* with a moral sense), *soḷā* (*soḍaśa*), words that are etymologically clear, *ḷ* is found in Prakrit Similar is the case for *nivḷī* (*nigaḍa-*), whose *ḍ* is not explained. Later still, or even recent, are the forms *taḷapṇeṃ* in relation to *taḍphaḍ*, *taṭtaṭ* (cf. *tāḍ-*), *kolapṇeṃ* (D. *kuḍ-*), *māḷ* in relation to *māḍī* (D. *māḍia-* and perhaps *māla-*) *ukhaḷṇeṃ* coexisting with *ukhaḍṇeṃ* (root *kaḍh-*), finally *sāṃguḷṇeṃ* the Konkani form of *sāṃgaḍṇeṃ* (*saṃghaṭ-*). We should also add here *cumbaḷ* (Pali *cumbata-*). Other cases which one will be tempted to cite also are of little help : *khuḷā* and *khoḍā* (*khoḍa-*: *khola-*) can be different words; *phāḷṇeṃ* and *phāṭṇeṃ* (*phal-*; *sphaṭ-*) are the forms drawn from different stems, although from the same root.

One should consider *paṃvḷeṃ* as being regularly attached to Skr. *pravāla-*, whose doublet *pravāḍa-* is less definitely attested. As regards *kohḷeṃ* (*kuṣmāṇḍa-*), it is a completely obscure word (cf. $ 170). It seems that in certain cases a return action had been caused : thus beside *nāṃgḷī* (*lāṅgalikā*) are found *naṃgoḍā*, *nāṃgḍā* (*laṅgūla-*?) but nothing is known regarding the origin of this group of words.

$ 147. To the preceding cases should be added those where *ḷ* represents Skr. *r* or *t* or *d* and which have been described above ($ 118, 141) and the only word of its type *veḷū* (Skr. *veṇu-*), where *l* is found very early in Pali and in Prakrit and is perhaps etymologically primitive.

l

$ 148. In the initial position, M. *l* represents Skr. *l* in *lasaṇ* (*laśuna-*), *lahu-* (*laghu-*), *lāj* (*lajjā*), *lohār* (*lohakāra-*) and a large number of words with *l* as initial given in the Lexicon. In Prakrit and as a consequence in Marathi, the initial *l* sometimes represents dissimilated Skr. *n* : *limb* (*limba-*); *loṇī* (*navanīta-*); it corresponds, in appearance atleast, to *y* in the word *laṭh*, which is joined to Skr. *yaṣṭi-*. Lastly Pkt. *ḍ* > *l* in *lekruṃ* (*ḍekka-*).

Inside the word, *l* goes back to Pkt. *ll* arisen from :

Skr. *l* after a nasal, in *salag* (*saṃlagna-*);

Skr. *ll* in *asval* (*acchabhalla-*), *gāl* (*galla-*), *cūl* (*cullī*), *jhālar* (*jhallari*), *pakhāl* (*-khalla-*), *pālav* (*pallava*), *phūl* (*phulla-*). There is hardly any need for showing how recent and of Prakritic aspect, all these words are and even in Sanskrit (cf. Wackernagel, $ 195). There is no serious reason for separating therefrom the cases where Pkt. *ll* represents either Skr. *ry*, or Skr. *dr*, cf. $ 141, nor the words only in Prakrit or even in Deśī, such as *kol* (*kulla-*), *khāl* and *sāl* (*challī*, *kholī* (*khulla-*), *celā* (*cilla-*), *vel* (*vellā*), *velhāl* (*vellahala-*).

Skr. *ly* in *kāl* (*kalya-*), *kolī* (*kulyā*), *tol* (*taulya-*), *mol* (*maulya-*) *sal* (*śalya-*; cf. M. *sāḷī*);

Skr. *lv* in *bel* (*bilva-*): this case is doubtful, as *rv* gives *v*, cf. $ 152.

Combined with aspiration, *l* is found in *kolhā* (become in its turn *kolā*), which goes back to Pkt. *koḷhna, kuḷha-* (*kroṣṭu-*). Here the Prakrit sign, no matter how badly explicable, is in short more correct than *ḍh*, because *ḷh* in Prakrit represents, as is correct, an old group of consonants (see Pischel, $ 242, cf. $ 304). This character is confirmed by the dental articulation of the Marathi phoneme. The word *kolhāḷ* (*kolāhala-*) is a semi-tatsama, because it is difficult to accept the theory that the fall of the internal *ā* has been even during the recent period, so complete as to allow the agglutination of *ḷ* + *h* and the dentalisation of the group. A curious result of the equivalence of *l* arisen from *ll* and of *lh* is the existence of the doublets with *l* or *ll* and *lh*, where etymology does not authorise the aspiration : thence *ulhāḷā* besides *ullāḷā* and *ulāḷa* (*ullāla-*), *kulhā* beside *kullā* and *kulā* (D. *kulla-*), *malhār* for Skr. *mallārī*. In Deśī is found *palhaṭṭai* beside *palaṭṭai* (cf. M. *pālaṭ*, *pālthā*), but here it can be a case of the aspiration brought out by the old sifflant of Skr. *paryasta-*. Regarding *lh*: *ll* in Sanskrit, see Wackeragel, $ 212 a.

$ 149. By means of preceding examples, we have already seen that contrary to the general rule of the simplification of the intervocalic consonants ($ 81), *ll* has often been preserved. Similarly are found *pillūṃ* (P. *pillaka-*), *ullū* (*ulūka-*), *killī* (*kīla-*). It is true that the first is a childish word and the second the name of a bird, used also as a term of abuse. As regards the last one, it co-exists with *khīḷ* and could, therefore, come in through borrowing.

The form *kilac* which goes back to D. *kitiñca-* is curious. Should we take it that in Deśī *l* between two palatal vowels could not become cerebral ? In that case the word *killḷī* would rightly be opposed to *khīḷ* whose prototype would be **k*(*h*)*ilā*, But *iḷī* (*ilī*) for example has a cerebral and moreover *kilac* can belong to the family of *killī*. It is impossible for the time being to push the question any farther.

In the alien words *l* has not undergone a uniform treatment. We have, on the one hand, *pūl*, *alaṃg* (see Printz,

KZ, XI-IV, p. 18) and on the other *javaḷ* It is impossible to say if this difference of treatment is due to the greater or lesser antiquity of the borrowed words or to other circumstances.

The same difference is found in the compounds whose second term began with an *l* : in relation to *alaṇī* (*a*+*lavana-*), *hilagṇeṃ* (*alhilagna-*), we find not only *aḷambeṃ* (*ālamba-*), which is a common noun since the Deśī, and *viḷavṇeṃ* (*vilapana-*) whose simple stem has disappeared, but *oḷakhṇeṃ* (*avalakṣ-*), *olaṃgṇeṃ* (*avalaṅgh-*), *olaṃbṇeṃ* (*avalamb-*), which co-exist with the simple verbs or other compounds of the same verbs, and where the sentiment of the composition is, without doubt, not lost.

v

$ 150. In the initial position of a word, M. *v* represents Skr. *v*. Marathi is a member of the group of western languages —Gujarati, Sindhi, Panjabi, to whom is joined on the one hand Simhalese and Kashmiri on the other—, they having preserved the initial Skr. *v* The central and the eastern languages have, on the contrary, mixed up *v* and *b*. Classical Prakrit does not take note of this innovation in any of its dialects, but it is known that since the Veda, sporadic exchanges of *b* and *v* have occurred (Wackernagel, $ 161); and it is possible that that the abundance itself of *b* in classical Sanskrit is due to some local influence, because it is a phoneme, almost unknown in Indo-European (ibid., $ 158, 162). In the Nāgarī Script, *b* is merely a *v* provided with a diacritical sign. Whatever be the origin of the Sanskrit phonetic system, it is this system which is faithfully reproduced in Marathi, at least in the initial position of the word. Marathi, therefore, enables us to recognise, when the orthography of Sanskrit texts is hesitant, as to which of the forms is authentic. Thus *oṃuḷ* can not but go back to *vakula-* but *bīṃ* and *bīḷ* guarantee Skr. *bīja-* and *bila-* Similarly the *b* of *buḍṇeṃ*, confirmed by Gujarati and already by Prakrit, contradicts the *v* of *voḍita-* of the *Divyāvadāna*. The case of *bāph* : *vāph* (*bāṣpa-*, *vāspa-*) is obscure; the word appears only in classical Sanskrit and possesses no known etymology. Pāli and Prakrit, like all the modern languages, have *b*. There is also in Marathi a form *bhāph*, which seems to be borrowed (see Beames, I, 191). Therefore it is legitimate that *bāph* be considered as a compromise between *vāph* and *bhāph*, or as an equally borrowed form. In fact, Marathi has had to borrow forms from the eastern dialects. This is proved by the example of the co-existence of *bijlī* and *vijū* (*vidyut*). Similarly the comparison of Gujarati *vāo* and Simhalese *voeva* shows that *bāvḍī* (*vāpī*) is a Hindi word.

These considerations enable us to leave aside certain *rapprochements*. Thus it has been wrong to explain *bāp* by Skr. *vaptṛ*. Moreover *pt* develops normally as *tt* and not *pp* and moreover the nominal stems in *-ṛ-* give the nouns in *-ī* or *-ū*. This etymology cannot be depended upon in any case. Similarly *biṭī* should, undoubtedly, be separated from Skr. *viṣṭhā*, which is represented in Marathi by *viṭ-*, *viṭāl*: in fact Simhalese has *b* in the corresponding word and *biṭī* is missing in the Hindi dictionary, which seems to exclude the hypothesis of a loan.

A curious case, and explicable with difficulty, is that of certain words found in Deśī with two pronunciations, and where Marathi has uniquely *b* (*barū*, *bāhulā*, *beḍā*, *beḷkeṃ*), and the words *bāj* and *bujṇeṃ* ("to frighten)" found in Prakrit, seemingly, with *b*, but in Deśī with *v-*. Prakrit has a *u* and Deśī *b* in the word to which seem to correspond the Marathi forms, *vaṭvaṭṇeṃ* and *baḍbaḍṇeṃ*, but it is equally possible that these two be two words of different origin, which had got near each other due to meaning.

The Arabo-Persian *baghair* "except, without" is represented in Marathi and Gujarati by *vager*; however *bagar* is more usual in Marathi as in Hindi. No doubt *bagar* has been influenced by *vagaire* "et cetera", a word equally borrowed from Arabic.

$ 151. The initial *v*, representing Skr *v*, is found in *vaṭṇeṃ* (*vart-*), *vaḍ* (*vaṭa-*), *varth* (*vastu-*), *var* (*vara-*) and in most of the words with *v* as initial gathered in the Lexicon.

Initial *v* can also go back to Pkt. *v* arisen from, either Skr. *vr* in *vaṇ* (*vraṇa-*) and the semi-tatsama *vaḍvat* (*-vrata-*), or from Skr *vy* in *vākhāṇ* (*vyākhyāna-*), *vāṃg* (*vyaṅga-*), *vāgh* (*vyāghra-*), *vārṇeṃ* (*vyāhar-*), *vāṃv* (*vyāma-*), *vāvar* (*vyāpāra-*), *vāvsā* (*vyavasāya-*), *vecṇeṃ* (*vyaya-*) and the semi-tatsama *vagra* (*vyagra-*); *vihū*, as against Pkt. *vūha-*, is a tatsama (*vyūha-*).

In *vakhār* (*avaskara-*), *vaṭhāṇ* (*upasthāna-*), *var* (*upari*), etc., *v* has become initial only as a consequence of a relatively recent apocope.

$ 152. Inside the word, *v* goes back to :

1. Pkt. *v* arisen from :

Skr. *v* in *ahev* (*avidhavā*), *avsā* (*āvāsa-*) *oṃvra* (*apavaraka-*) *oṃvsā* (*upavāsa-*), *gavasṇeṃ* (*gaveṣaṇa-*), *cavṇeṃ* (*cyavana-*), *jav* (*yava-*), *dāv* (*dāva-*), *dev*, *devaḷ* (*deva-*, *devālaya-*), *dhāṃvṇeṃ* (*dhāva-*), *nav* (*nava-*), *navā* (*nava-*), *nāv* (*nāvā*), *nīv* (*nīva-*), *nīvī* (*nīvi-*), *pārvā* (*pārāvāta-*), *pāvṇā* (*plav-*), *pālav* (*pallava-*), *paisāv* (*-srav-*), *bhāv*, cf., *mānbhāv* (*bhāva-*), *marvā* (*maruvaka-*), *lavaṃg* (*lavaṅga-*); *vakhār* (*avaskara-*), *vasvā* (*avacchada-*) and the words, where the initial *va-*, alternating with *o* represents Skr. *ava-*. In the verbal compounds whose second term has *v* as the initial, such as *avaḷṇeṃ*, *oṃvāḷṇeṃ* (*val-*), *āvagṇeṃ* (*valg-*), *nivaṭṇeṃ* (*vart-*), etc., it is most often impossible to decide if it is the internal *v* or the initial one. We find *vh* corresponding to Skr. *śv* in *parv(h)āṃ* (*para-śvaḥ*), cf. $ 157.

Skr. *p* in *utavṇeṃ* (*uttapana-*), *karvat* (*karapattra-*), *kavḍā* (*kaparda-*), *kavāḍ* (*kapāṭa-*, cf. Wackernagel, p. XLVIII), *kāṃsav* (*kacchapa-*), *kivaṇ* (*kṛpaṇa-*), *kīṃv* (*kṛpā-*), *kuvā* (*kūpa-*), *khavaṇ* (*kṣapaṇika-*), *civaḍ* (*cipiṭa-*), *tāv* (*tāpa-*), *tivaṇ* (*triparṇa-*), *daḷvī* (*dalapati-*) and other proper nouns formed with—*pati-*, *divā* (*dīpa-*), *nhāvī* (*nāpita-*), *pāḍvā* (*pratipad-*), *pāvṇeṃ* (*prāpaṇa-*), *bhādvā* (*bhādrapad-*), *mahāvat* (if it refers to *mahāputra-*), *mānḍav* (*maṇḍapa-*), *rovṇeṃ* (*ropaṇa-*), *vaṭhāṇ* (*upasthāna-*) *var* (*upari-*), *vāvar* (*vyāpāra-*), *viḷavṇeṃ* (*vilapana-*), *savat* (*sapatnī-*), *savā* (*sapāda-*), *sātvaṇ* (*saptaparṇa-*), *śiṃsav* (*śiṃśipa-*); add here *firstly* perhaps *dāvṇeṃ* if it refers, as suggested by Pischel, to Skr. *dṛp-* and *khavā*, whose corresponding term is missing in Sanskrit (Lat. *scapula*); *secondly* the recent compounds of *pāṇī* (*pānīya-*), where this word appears under the form *-vaṇī*, as *aṃbavaṇī*; smilarly *aviknem* (*ava+piknem* with syllabic superposition), *ahāroḷī* (*āhāra+poḷī*), *bāroḷī* (*bārā+pāyālī*) and *thirdly* all the causatives, where *-va-* or *-vi-* goes back to Skr. *-paya-*. Thus we have *vimaviṇeṃ* (*vijñāpaya-*), *karavṇeṃ* (*kar-*) and the analgous formations like *kamaviṇeṃ* (*karma-*);

Skr. *b* in *thavā* (*stabaka-*), *lavḍā* (*alābu-*), *lavā* (*lāba-*)

2. Pkt. *vv* : here the eastern languages have regularly *b*. From the correspondences noted in the Lexicon, it will be seen that the languages of the Centre and of the North-West have often a *v*. The rule, postulated by Grierson, (*Phon.*, p. 11), and following which rule, Pkt. *vv* always becomes *b* in the modern Indo-Aryan languages, is not exact. At least for Marathi, the examples given below are telling :

Skr. *vy* : *sav* (*savya-*), *śivṇeṃ* (*sīvya-*); the termination *-āvā* of the participle of obligation (*-tavya-*), ex. : *dyāvā* "which should be given";

Skr. *rv* : *cāvṇeṃ* (*carv-*), *ḍav* (*darvī*; M. *ḍabhā* is evidently a loan of eastern origin), *nivṇeṃ*, *nivāṇeṃ* (*nirvāṇa-*);

Skr. *vr* : *nīv* (*nīvra-*).

3. Pkt. intervocalic *m* (see $ 137 and 138) in *avaṃtṇeṃ* (*āmantraṇa-*), *avḷā* (*āmalaka-*), *avas* beside *amos* (*amāvāsyā*), *āṃv* ((*āma-*), *āṃvas* (*āmiṣa-*) *ugavaṇ* (*udgama-*), *oṇavṇeṃ* (*avanamana-*), *oṃvḷā* (Pkt. *avamalia-*), *kuṃvar* (*kumāra-*), *gāṃv* (*grāma*), *gosāvī* (*gosvāmin-*), *jevṇeṃ* (*jim-*), *ṭhāv* (*sthāma-*), *tāṃv* (*tamas-*), *tevṇeṃ* (*tim-*), *dāvaṇ* (*dāmanī*), *nāṃv* (*nāma-*), *bhoṃvṇeṃ* , *bhoṃvar*, etc. (*bhrama-*), *revṇeṃ* (D. *rem-*), *rovaṃth* (*romantha-*), *lāṃv* (D. *lāmā*), *vāṃv* (*vyāma-*), *visavṇeṃ* (*viśrama-*), *savaṃg* (*samargha-*), *saveṃ* (*samaya-*), *saṃvthaḷ* (*sama-*), *sāvaṃtu* (*sāmanta-*), *sāṃvḷā* (*śyāmala-*), *sāṃvar* (D. *sāmarī*), *sāṃvā* (*śyāmāka-*), *śeṃvti* (*semantikā*), *soṃvaḷ* (D. *somāla-*), *hiṃv* (*hima-*), finally the suffix of the ordinal starting from *pāṃcvā* (*pañcama-*).

$ 153. The articulation of *v* in Marathi is relatively weak and it is known that for representing English *v*, the Marathas use the group *vh*.

It is this indistinct character of articulation which has made *v* to be inserted between the vowels forming a hiatus or being exchanged with *u* ($ 55, 57). Hence also the frequent reduction of *ava-*), even recent, into *o* (see $ 78) or into *a* as in *ugaṇ* (cf. *ugavṇeṃ*) or *kārand* (*karamandi-*), *bhoṃr* for *bhoṃvar* (*bhramara-*), *soṃpṇeṃ* (*samarpaya-*). It still happens that *v* is dropped between vowels of different quantity or timbre, above all when it refers to the nasal *v* arisen from the intervocalic *m*; 1. before *i* : *koykamaḷ* (*kumada-*), *dhuī* (*dhūmikā*), *bhuīṃ* (*bhūmi-*), *sāī* (*svāmin-*; cf. *gosāvī*); 2. in the penultimate position, notably after the labial vowel, *loṃ* for *loṃv* (*loma-*), *jaṇū* (**jaṇṇovaṃ*), *kuṃkūṃ* (*kuṅkuma-*) *gahūṃ* (*godhūma-*) and in certain termination like *-eṃ*, *-iṃ* (*-āmi*, *ayāmi*) see $ 66, 67.

The loss of *v* before *i* is extremely frequent in the initial position of the word; see LSI, *Mar.* , pages 23, 66, 83, 161, 169, 195, 225 : for example we say *īs* for *vīs* (*viṃśat*) or *īgār* for Pkt. *vicar*; similarly before *e* : *yeḷ* (that is to say *eḷ*) for *veḷ*; inversely *v* is abusively re-established, for example in *vīṭ*, the form more common than *īṭ* which is however justified by etymology (*iṣṭā*), or in *viṭā* which co-exists with *iṭā* (*ṛṣṭi-*), in *visāḍ* in relation to *īs* (*īṣā*).

Note on y

$ 154. This sonant has no real existence in Marathi, leaving aside the tatsamas, it is found :

1. as the resultant of the differentiation of the initial *y* : examples, *yeṇeṃ* for *eṇeṃ* (*eti*), *yer* for *er* (*itara-*), *yeḷ* for * *eḷ* the substitute of *veḷ* (*velā*), etc., this is, no doubt, the same differentiation which is found in *-yāśīṃ*, a form of *eṃśīṃ*, *aiśīṃ* "80" in compounds.

2. in certain cases where *y* replaces in old intervocalic consonant, see $ 54;

3. as the symbolic equivalent of *i* or *e* in a diphthong : *i*+vowel : *pāṃḍyā* (*paṇḍita-*), *pyār* (*priyakāra-*), *pyās* (*pipāsā*), *pyāhā* (*plīhā*), *maṇyār* (*maṇikāra-*); *e*+vowel : *āgyā* (*agrega-*), *dyāvā* (cf. *deya-*); the obliques in *-yā*, earlier *-eā* : see $ 191; vowel+*i* : *paḍkay* (*pratikṛti-*), *vay* beside *vai* (*vṛti-*); the two signs frequently co-exist chiefly in the final position; here in relation to *i*, *y* plays a rôle similar to that of *v* in relation to *u*; cf. $ 57.

Sifflant

$ 155. There is only one sifflant in Marathi (see $ 15), which is susceptible of two pronunciations, according to the timbre of the following vowel : it is a dental before *a*, *u* and *o* and palatal before *i* and undoubtedly before *e*. The sifflant of Marathi, irrespective of its origin, thus belongs to the same phonetic category to which belong the occlusives derived from ancient Prakrit palatals (see $ 100). The words borrowed from other languages have been adapted to the tendencies of Marathi. This is how the Persian words *śarm*, *śuman*, *śīśā*, *gumaśt* have become *saram* (*śaram* also exists), *sumar*, *śīsā*, *gumastā*. As regards *śāi*, it clearly represents *śyāhī* rather than *śāī*. The loss of old *y* explains here the palatal pronunciation of *s*, as that of *j* in *rājā* in the oblique cases. Therein lies, probably, the origin of the palatal sifflant of *bhoṃśā-ūs* where *bhoṃśā* is the oblique case of *bhoṃs*. In *śaṃ-bhar* or *savā-śā*, the palatal sifflant can have come either from the ancient *ya-śruti*, or from the direct analogy of *śeṃ* (*śataṃ*). In favour of this last hypothesis, cf. the dialectal form *śeṃbhar* cited in the LSI, *Mar.*, p. 22-23.

The history of the sifflant is the same, whether it is simple or geminated, initial or internal.

$ 156. We have already seen, $ 102 ff., the cases where *s* (*ś*) comes from Pkt. *ch-*. Through Pkt. *s* it goes back to :

Skr. *s* (1) initial in *saī* (*smṛti-*), *saī* (*sakhī*), *sakār* (*satkār*), *sagaḷā* (*sakala-*), *saṃgeṃ* (*saṅga-*) *saṃcarṇeṃ* and the other verbal compounds of *sām* (*saṃ-*), cf. *salag* (*saṃlagna-*), *sat* (*sattva*), *sarṇeṃ*, *sār* and their compounds *osarṇreṃ*, *osrī*, *osār*, *nisarṇeṃ*, *saṃsār*, etc. (*sar-*, *sāra-*), *sav* (*sap-*), *sav* (*savya-*), *savat* (*sapatnī-*) and the other compounds of *sa-* as *savā* (*sapāda-*), *sāḍe* (*sārdha-*), etc., *saṃvthaḷ* (*sama-*), *saveṃ* (*samaya-*), *sāū* (*sādhu-*), *sāk* (*sākṣī-*), *sāc* (*satya-*), *sājṇeṃ* (*sajj-*), *sāṃjh* (*sandhyā-*), *sāt* (*sapta-*), *sāṃtā* (*sant-*), *sātu* (*saktu-*), *sāth* (*sārtha-*), *sāṃdh* (*sandhi-*), *sāp* (*sarpa-*), *sāṃpeṃ* (*sāmpratam*), *sāvantu* (*sāmanta-*), *sāyar* (*sāgara-*), *sāhṇeṃ* (*sah-*), *śijṇeṃ* (*sidhya-*), *sivṇeṃ* (*sevana-*), *śiseṃ* (*sisā*), *śīṃ* (*sahita-*), *śīṭ* (*sṛṣṭi-*), *śīt*, cf. *uśīt* (*siktha-*), *śīv* (*sīmā*), *suār* (*sūpakāra-*), *suī* (*sūcī-*), *sugī* (*su-*; cf. *sureṃg*, *soṃvaḷ*), *sūraṇ* (*suraṇa-*), *sūt* (*sūtra-*), *sūr* (*surā*), *śeṇvī* (*senā-pati-*), *śeṃdūr* (*sindūra-*), *śeṃvtī* (*semantikā-*), *soneṃ* *suvarṇa-*), *sopṇeṃ* (*samarp-*, *soyrā* (*sodara-*), *soṃvaḷ* (*somala-*); —(2) internal in *usāsā*, *nisās* (*ucchvāsa-*, *nihśvāsa-*), *dās* (*dāsa-*), *dīs* (*divasa-*), *pyās* (*pipāsā-*), *māṃs* (*māṃsa-*), *mās* (*māsa-*), *ras* (*rasa-*), *vesṇeṃ*, *vās* (*vāsa-*) and its compounds, cf. *oṃvsā* (*upavāsa-*) *vevsā* (*vyavasāya-*), *hasṇeṃ* (*haṃs-*);

Skr. *ś*, (1) initial in *sakṇeṃ* (*śakya-*), *saḍṇeṃ* (*śaṭ-*), *saḍhaḷ* (*śithila-*) *saṇ* (*śaṇa-*), *saṃt* (*śānta-*), cf. *sāṃt* (*śānti-*), *sasā* (*śaśa-*), *sāṃkū* (*śaṅku-*), *sāṃkaḷ* (*śṛṅkhalā*), *sāṃgṇeṃ* (*śaṃs-*?), *sāḍī* (*śaṭa-*), *sāṇ* (*śāṇa-*), *sād*, cf. *paḍsād* (*śabda-*), *sādalṇeṃ* (*śādvala-*), *sāṃbar* (*śaṃbara-*), *sāy* (*śāka-*), *sāḷ* (*śālā* and *śāli-*), *śāḷī* (*śalya-*), *śikṇeṃ* (*śikṣ-*), *śīkeṃ* (*śikhya-*), *śiṃg* (*śṛṅga-*), *śiṃpī* (*śilpin-*), *śiras* (*śiriṣa-*), *śiṃsav* (*śiṃśipa-*), *śilā* (*śītala-*), *-śī* in *āgśī* (*śikhā*), *śīṇ* (*śīrṇa-*), *śīr* (*śiras-*), *śīs* (*śīrṣa-*), *śīḷ* (*śīla-*), *śiḷ* (*śilā-*), *suā* (*śuka-*), *sukā* *śuṣka-*), *śuṃth* (*śuṇṭhi-*), *suṇeṃ* (*śunaka-*), *śudhā* (*śuddha-*), cf. *ansūd* (*śuddhi-*), *sunā* (*śūnya-*), *suṃb* (*śulba-*), *susar* (*śiśumāra-*), *sūk* (*śukra-*), *sūp* (*śūrpa-*), *sūḷ* (*śūla-*; cf. *tisaḷ*), *śeṃ*, cf. *savāśā*, *śaṃbhar* (*śataṃ*), *śegaṭ* (*śigru-*), *śej* (*śayyā-*) *śeṃḍā* (*śikhaṇḍa-*), *śerā* (*śikhara-*), *soṃḍ* (*śuṇḍā*), *sos* (*śoṣa-*); (2) internally in *asog* (*aśoka-*), *āgas*, cf. *māgas* (*agraśaḥ*), *ās* (*āśā*), *useṃ* (*opaśa-*), *kasā* (*kaśa-*), *kusaḷ* (*kuśala-*) *kes* (*keśa-*), *kesar* (*kesara-*), *taisā* (*tādṛśa-*), *das* , cf. *dasrā*, *candas* (*daśa*), *des* (*deśa-*), *nās* (*nāśā-*), *nisṇa* (*niśāna-*), *pisā* (*piśāca-*), *pais* (*pradeśa-*), *phāsā* (*pāśaka-*), *masaṇ* (*śmaśāna-*), *rās* (*rāśī*), *lac* (*laśa-*), *lasaṇ* (*laśuna-*), *vasne* (*vaśa-*), *vāṃsā* (*vaṃśa-*), *vīs* (*viṃśat-*), *śiṃsva* (*śiṃśipa-*);

Skr. *ṣ* (1) in the initial position in *ṣahā* (*ṣaṭ-*), cf. *sak* (*ṣaṭka-*), *soḷā* (*ṣoḍaśa-*), *sāṃḍ* (*ṣaṇḍa-*); (2) internally in *āṃvas* (*āmiṣa-*), *kas* (*kaṣa-*), *gavasṇeṃ* (*gaveṣaṇa-*), *joṣī* (*jyotiṣika-*), *tusār* (*tuṣara-*), *tūs* (*tuṣa-*), *mīs* (*miṣa-*), *mhais* (*mahiṣī*), *rīs* (*riṣ-*), *rusṇeṃ* (*ruṣya-*), *so* (*śoṣa-*).

§ 157. Through Pkt. *s* or *ss*, Marathi sifflant goes back to the groups :

Skr. *sy*, in the initial position, without doubt, in *sāḷā* and perhaps *sāḍhū*, (*śyāla-*); Sanskrit also has *śyāla-*, which seems more recent);—(2) internally in *avas* (*amāvāsyā*), *āḷas* (*ālasya-*), *kāṃseṇ*, *kāṃsār* (*kāṃsya-*), *rahas* (*rahasya-*) ;

Skr. *śy* (1) as initial in *sāṃvḷā* (*śyāmala-*), *sāṃvā* (*śyāmāka-*); —(2) internally in *disṇeṃ* (*dṛśya--*), *vesvā* (*veśyā-*), and perhaps *kāṃsav* (*kaśyapa-*) ;

Skr. *ṣy* in *pūs* (*puṣya-*);

Skr. *sr* in *usteṃ* (*usrā*), *paisāv* (*pratisrava-*); *āsrā* (*āśraya-*) is thus a tatsama;

Skr. *śr*, as initial, in *śeṭ* (*śreṣṭhin-*) internally in *āṃsū aśru-*), *misaḷ* (*miśra-*), *viśāvṇeṃ* (*viśrama-*), *sāsū* (*śvaśrū-*) and in *-s* as a suffix to the nouns of relationship (*śrī*); cf. *nisaṇ*, *niśīṇ* (*niḥśreṇi-*);

Skr. *śl* in *sān* (*ślakṣṇa-*), *śeṃbā* (*śleṣma-*);

Skr. *sv* in *sāī*, *gosāvī* (*svāmin-*) and the semi-tatsamas *sair* (*svaira-*) and *sagā* (*svaka-*); *sūr* (*svara-*) is thus a learned word;

Skr. *śv*, as initial in *sāsū*, *sāsrā* (*śvaśrū-*, *śvaśura-*), internally in *āsand*, *āsupaṭhi* (*aśva-*), *pās*, cf. *pasoḷī* (*pārśva-*); it is the passage of *śv* to *ss* which has favoured the abridgement of Skr. *mātṛśvāsṛkā* into Prakrit *māussiā*, Marathi *māvśī*. Similarly when the group *śv* is preceded by an aspirate in Sanskrit : *niśās* (*niḥśvāsa-*); *parhvāṃ*, if it is indigenous, does not therefore represent Skr. *paraśvaḥ*;

Skr. *rṣ* in *śīs* (*śīrṣa-*) and undoubtedly *kasṇeṃ* (*karṣa-*); *varasṇeṃ* (*varṣa-*) and also *ārsā* (*ādarśa-*) are therefore tatsamas, besides old (see Pischel, $ 135);

Skr. *s*, as initial followed by a nasal. The examples *sāṃv* (*snāyu-*) and *visarṇeṃ* (*vismar-*) are sure and are opposed to the treatment *nh*, *mh* whose examples are given in $ 136 and 138; *sūn* (*sunṣā*) is explained otherwise : this is a case of an old metathesis, shown by Pkt. *suṇhā*. The case of *śm* is obscure. We have on the one hand *rassī* (*raśmi-*), which is suspected to be borrowed due to the gemination of the sifflant, and which, besides, is the only form in Prakrit, and *āsand* which is explained equally well by both *aśvagandha-* and *aśmagandha-*, and on the other hand *m*(*h*)*asaṇ* where the alternation of the initial sifflant can have been favoured by dissimilation (such is also the case in Prakrit of *maṃsu-*

— Skr. *śmaśru-*; see Pischel, $ 312). It is difficult to settle the problem : all that is known is that the change of the internal *śm* into *ss* is normal in the dialects of the North-West, like that of internal *sm* (Grierson, ZDMG, 1912 p. 77) and therein it goes back pretty far into the past. Pliny had already noted the form *casiri*, which corresponds to Kashmiri *kāśiru* (*kaśmīra-*); Arrian writes '*Assaikhinoi*=Aśmaka and the fragments of Dutreuil de Rhins, where the group *sm* is generally preserved, perhaps offer, in declension, a trace of the same evolution : if the form of the genitive *-sa* (*-sya*) can be used as a locative, we can think that it is due to evolution of the locative in *-smin* into *-si* (cf. Senart, J A, 1898, II, p. 214 etc.).

The Aspirate

$ 158. In Sanskrit *h* is already the resultant of achange undergone by old aspirated sonants, notably in the intervocalic position (see $ 2). In the Middle-Indian all the intervocalic aspirated consonants have lost their occlusion, continuing in this way the evolution which had begun since Vedic Sanskrit. There is, therefore, no essential difference between *h* of Sanskrit, Prakrit and of the modern languages; and the distinctions established below have only the value of classification.

$ 159. In the initial position, Marathi *h* succeeds Prakrit *h* arisen out of :

Skr. *h* in *haṇṇeṃ* (*han-*), *haraṇ* (*hariṇa-*) and the majority of words with *h* as initial, that are to be found in the Lexicon;

Skr. *bh* in *hoṇeṃ* (*bhū-*) : the passage of *bh-* into *h-* is due to the frequent use of this word as an accessory one in the sentence. It is found since the oldest Prakrit (Lūders, *Bruchstücke*, p. 60-61). The case of M. *haṃḍī*, if it refers, as it looks, to a doublet of *bhāṃḍ* (*bhāṇḍa-*), is more obscure. The simple aspiration is found Since VII century, but in a compound, where *bh* would be inside the word; on the other hand, *haṇḍika* is found only in an anthology of the

XVth century.

Inside the word, *h* represents Pkt *h* arisen out of :

Skr. *h* in *ahār* (*āhara-*), *kolhāḷ* (*kolāhala-*), *geh* (*geha*), *bāher* (*bahir*), *bāhi* (*bāhū-*), *moho* (*moha-*), *rahas* (*rahasya-*), *roh* (*roha-*), *rohī-* (*rohi-*, *rohita-*), *lahar* (*lahari-*), *lohār* (*loha-*), *vahāṇ* (*upānah-*), *vāhaṇ* (*vahana-*), *vivāh* (*vivāha-*), *sāhṇeṃ* (*sah-*);

Skr. *kh* in *duhī* (**dukha-* for *duḥkha-*);

Skr. *gh* in *pāhuṇā* (*prāghuṇa-*), *māho* (*māgha-*), *mehuḍā* (*megha-*), *rahāṭ* (*araghaṭṭa-*), *lahu* (*laghu-*); cf. *māher* (*mātṛgṛha-*);

Skr. *th* in *pohā* (*pṛthuka-*), *mahuṇ* (*maithuna-*) *rahaṃvar* (*ratha-*);

Skr. *dh* in *ahev* (*avidhavā*), *gahūṃ* (*godhūma-*), *dahīṃ* (*dadhi-*), *bahirā* (*badhira-*), *moh* (*madhu-*), *rāhī* (*rādhā*), *vahū* (*vadhū-*);

Skr. *bh* in *ahāṇā* (*ābhāṇaka-*), *gahirā* (*gabhīra-*), *nihāḷṇeṃ* (*nibhal-*, *lāhṇeṃ* (*labh-*), *loho* (*lobha-*), *hilagṇeṃ* (*abhilagna-*); for the surd examples are lacking, cf. Pischel, $ 200 and Beames, I, 271. Moreover in Sanskrit, even *ph* is relatively rare and often obscure in origin, see Wackernagel, $ 158;

Skr. *s* or *ṣ* in a group with *n* or *ṇ*, whence Pkt. *ṇh*; where the aspiration is not lost, it subsists by admitting insertion of a vowel, see $ 136; on Pkt. *mh*, see $ 138.

$ 160. It is generally admitted that in certain cases *h* goes back to an old sifflant. It is true that in the north-western group (Sindhi, Panjabi, Kashmiri) the opening of the intervocalic *s* is frequent (see Beames, I, 259 ff., Grierson, *Phon.*, $ 68). This change is also found in common Gujarati and in Western Rajputana (LSI, *Bhili*, p, 2, 11, 27; *Raj.*, p. 4, 330). But in Marathi it has been noted only at two points located at the frontier of Gujarati and in the speeches which are morphologically near this language (LSI, *Mar.*, p. 144, 148).

In Marathi, all the Sanskrit sifflants, initial or intervocalic, are normally preserved. All the divergent examples are to be left aside or cxamined.

The most important ones are drawn from numeration Beside *das*, the normal representative of Skr. *daśa*, is found *daha* which is the most used form as also the nouns for the units of the 'second ten', from "11" to "18", *akrā, bārā, terā, caudā, pandharā, soḷā, satrā, aṭhrā,* These forms are not found in Aśoka, but are already authorised by Vararuci (Pischel, $ 263, cf. 443 and 446). The word for "seventy" *sattar* (*saptati-*), combined with the units, becomes *-hattar.* This form goes back to a relatively lower period of Prakrit (Pischel, $ 264).

This change of the intervocalic sifflant is only one of the numerous phonetic irregularities shown by the nouns of number, if they are considered from the purely Marathi point of view. This is because numeration must provide for the greatest part of the common languages, anterior to the fixation of modern speeches. Hence the fact that the irregularities, shown here, are found in all the cognate languages (Beames II, 134 ff; cf. I, 288).

By the side of *divasa* Prakrit has *diaha-* (Pischel, $ 264), which seems to be present in M. *dī,* the popular doublet of *dīs.* But it is probably simpler to recall à propos of M. *dī* that in Deśī the form *dio* is found, which is evidently based on Skr. *diva-,* passed from neuter into masculine under the influence of *divasa-.*

It is, then, illusory to explain the termination of the oblique singular of the nouns by the Skr. genitive in *-asya* (cf. $ 183), and efforts to directly link *āhṇeṃ* to the root *as-*, *pāhṇeṃ* to Skr. *paś-*, *or bāhṇeṃ* to the Skr. *bhāṣ-*, should be given up (see these words in the Lexicon). The demonstrative pronoun *hā, hī, heṃ* is not explained by the unique form of the nom. sing. masc. of Apabhraṃśa *ehu,* which is derived from Skr. *eṣa* (Pischel, $ 263). Prakrit *aha, aho* (Pischel, $ 432) are enigmatic, but do not necessarily go back to *asau.* Should we recognise herein the prothesis of a particle *ha,* that had been earlier an eclitic (cf. Brugmann, *Demonstrative-pronomina,* p. 69)? In this case, the word itself would not be surely indigenous to Marathi, because if *hevam* is found in the *Divyāvadāna,* it appears only in the eastern versions of the inscriptions of Aśoka (T. Michelson, *Am. J. Phil.,* 1909, p. 291, note 1).

$ 161. As has been seen ($ 81 ff.), the aspiration is unstable in the occlusive aspirates. There is all the more the reason for the same when it is a simple sonant breath intercalated between two vowels, or preceding a vowel in the initial position (examples in LSI, *Mar.,* p. 144, 169, 332). This is not, moreover, a fact exclusive to Marathi. It is, on the contrary, very frequent everywhere. We will limit ourselves to the languages neighbouring Marathi, cf. LSI, *Rajasthani*, p. 20, *Gujarati*, p. 330, 347, etc.

The instability of aspiration is the cause of a sufficiently large number of cases of anticipation, pointed out in $ 168.

The common language often admits the fall of the intervocalic *h* and consequently the contraction of the surrounding vowels :

aha->*ā* : *akrā* and the nouns of the units of the second ten, cited in $ 160 (Pkt. *daha*); *agrār* (*agrahāra-*), *aṇā* beside *ahāṇā* (*ābhāṇaka-*), *thā* (*stāgha-*), *pār* beside *pahār* (*prahāra-*), *phaḷār* (*phalāhāra*) *marāṭhā* (*mahārāṣṭra-*), *mānbhāv* (*mahānubhāva-*), *lāṇī* beside *lāhṇī* (*lābh-*), *vārṇeṃ* (*vyāhar-*), *sāmāśī* in relation to *sahā* (*ṣaṭ*), *sutār* (*sūtra-dhara-*);

ahi>*ai*, and even *e*, *ī* : *varaī* (*varāha-*), *sai* (*sakhī*), *sāy* beside *sahā* (Pkt. *sāha-*); *eḍ* (*aṃhrī-* ? see Grierson, *Phon.*, p. 403); *śīṃ* (*sahita-*);

iha>*e*, *i* : *āgśī* (*śikhā*), *pī* beside *pihā* (*plīhan-*), *śeṃḍ* (*śikhaṇḍa-*), *śerā* (*śikhara-*);

eha>*e* : *upeḍ* (D. *uppehaḍa-*);

ahu>*au*, *o* : *vomāī*, *ovar* and *vavar* beside *vahū* (*vadhū*), *sāū* (*sādhu-*);

aho>*o* : tatsama *motsāv*, *motsāh* for *mahot*;

uha>*u* : *amū* (*amukha-*), *gū* (*gūtha-*);

oha>*o* : *oyrā* (*avahar*), *moḷeṃ* beside *mohaḷ* (*mukha-*), *lokhaṇḍ* beside *loh*, *lohār* (*loha-*), *samor* in relation with *mohrā* (*mukhar-*);

uhi—*ui* : *duī* beside *duhī* (*duḥkha-*);

ehu—*eu* : *mevuṇ*, *mevṇā* beside *mehuṇ*, *mehuṇā* (*maithuna-*).

Inversely, *h* simply marks the hiatus in *bāhulā*, the doublet of *bāvlā* (D. *bāulla-*); *pihū*, the doublet of *piyo* (*priya-*); *nahī* for *naī* (*nadī*); *vahī* for *vai* (*vṛti-*).

Lastly, *h* seems to be altogether adventitions in *kohḍeṃ* beside *koḍeṃ* (*kūṭa-*), *jahālā*, *jhālā*, see M. *jālā* (*jāta-*), *dāhaḷ* (cf. Skr. *dala-*), cf. $ 136 and LSI, *Mar.*, p. 66, 157, 169; *sāhāṇ* for *sāṇ*, which is found only dialectally (*śāna-*), could have been influenced by *sahān* : *śān* (*ślakṣṇa-*). The aspiration of *kaṇher*, the doublet of *kaṇer* (*karavira-*), is already noted by Hemacandra; that of *cāmhār* (*carmakāra-*) comes from the analogy of *kuṃbhār* (*kumbhakāra-*).

THE WORD

I. *Phonemes in Contact*

$ 162. Indigenous Marathi words are, in principle, composed of regularly alternating consonants and vowels, and do not seem to compulsorily include vowels in hiatus or groups of consonants. We see frequently recently borrowed words undergoing changes tending to make them conform to the system. Thus : apenthesis in *taras-* (*tras-*), *sapan* (*svapna-*), *kiristāṃv* (Europ. Christ), *hukūm* (Arab. *hukm*); metathesis in *girhā* (*graha-*), *gokraṇ* (*gokarṇa-*), and the reduction of groups in *cikśā* (*cikitsā*), *pant* (for *paṇḍit*), *maśīd* (Arab. *masjid*).

Recent Consonantal Groups

$ 163. However, even in the words cited above, the existence of consonantal groups is observed. It is because the extreme reduction of the median vowels, referred to in $ 50 ff. has brought near one another consonants belonging to different syllables. The contact is immediate in numerous cases. This seems to occur notably when one of the consonants is a continuant. Thus for the sifflants (*ispiṭal*,. Europ. *hospital*; *mhotsav*, Skr. *mahotsava-*; *cikśā*, Skr. *cikitsā*), for *r* (*girhā*, *gokraṇ* cited above; *catrā* —Skr. *catura-*, *cirhāṭ* —D. *cirihiṭṭi*, *circir* —D. *ciricirā*, *bakrā* —Skr. *barkara-*), *h* (cf. *vahvar*, *vavar* <*vadhuvara-* and various aspirated consonants duẹ to the *rapprochement* of *h* with an occlusive, see $ 99, 107, 110, 112, 124, 128). When the consonants with neighbouring articulations, such as the cerebrals and the dentals, are thus brought together, the narrowness of contact seems to depend, on the one hand, on the sonority of the occlusives. According to the evidence of P. R. Bhandarkar, two surds (cerebr. +dent. : *taṭṭaṭṇeṃ* "to be drawn to breaking point", *vāṭto*, 3 sing. pres. of *vāṭṇeṃ* "it seems"; the examples of dental + cerebral are lacking) or two sonants (cereb. + dental : *haḍdeṃ* "obstacle", *uḍdā-* obl. of *uḍīd* "phaseolus radiatus"; dent. + cereb. :

gadhdā "ass") constitute real groups; on the other hand; if *poṭdukhī* "stomach-ache" sounds tri-syllabic, a vocalic group is quite clearly distinguished in the group dent. + sonant cereb. : *kātḍeṃ* "leather", *cuṭḍā* "vagina."

$ 164. Consonants once in contact have reacted on one another. This is, undoubtedly, the origin of a number of metatheses or dissimilations cited above. A number of assimilations are thus produced. They can affect :

1. Sonority—In this case the assimilation is generally regressive; sonant+ sud : *adhikārī* — *ātkārī* "functionary"; *adh-pāv*>*ātpāv* " 1/8th of a seer", **adh-śer* >*accher* "½ a seer" (but *aḍ-śerī*, "2-½ seers" subsists), *madh-cā* >*maccā* "*Median*", but in the inverse sense *gartā* >*gardā* "hole";

surd+*sonant* : *dhukdhukṇeṃ*—*dhugdhugṇeṃ* "to palpitate" : *roṭgā*>*roḍgā*".

2. Articulation—the assimilation is regressive in *pastīs* for *paṃc-tīs* "35", *paṃsaṣṭ* for *paṃc-saṣṭ* "65" progressive in *sāḍhū* (*śyālīvoḍhṛ-*), *śemī* for *śeṃdṇī* (name of a plant); P. R. Bhandarkar observes that the group *ḷl* is pronounced in a manner, which is almost similar to that of *ḷḷ*.

There is no need for citing, among the consequences of the contact of consonants in Marathi, the insertion of *d* between *n* and *r* in contact in *vāndar* (*vānara-*) and *pandhrā* (Pkt. *paṇṇaraha-*, Skr. *pañcadaśa*); because the concordance with other languages shows that these forms are anterior to Marathi.

Vowels and Consonants in Contact

$ 165. In Marathi, as in all the Indo-Aryan languages (except Kashmiri, see Grierson, *Man. Kaśm.*, $ 8) vowels and consonants very rarely react upon one another. The most interesting case of this type is that of the palatals and the sifflant, whose pronunciation is dental before *a*, *u*, *o*, palatal before *i* and partially *e*. Dialectally the gutturals are susceptible of being palatalised before *ye* (=Common Mar. *e*). Thus we find in the Konkan *jelā* beside *gyelā*, *gelā* "he is gone", *jheūn* beside *gheūn* "having taken", *celāṃ* beside *kelāṃ* "done" (see LSI, *Mar.*, p. 65). On this point, as on many others, Konkani is in agreement with Gujarati (LSI, *Rāj.*, p. 330). The nasalisation of *l* following a nasal vowel in the termination *-nā* of the dative plural and *-n* of the 1st sing. fut. has already been noted.

We also find traces, chiefly in the dialects, of the coloration of a vowel by the neighbouring consonant : *a* becomes a surd when in contact with a labial or the cerebral *l* ($ 79). In the poetic language, the timbre of the vowel inserted between two consonants depends on the articulation of these consonants. In a word whose last consonant is *r*, *l*, *ḷ* or a cerebral occlusive, the penultimate inserted vowel is *i*, if the preceding consonant is a palatal and *u* after all the other consonants, (*āpula*, *baguḷā*, *bāpuḍā*, *mehuḍā* but *sājirā*, etc.). The vowel to be inserted after *r* is always *u* (*daruśan*, *mārūg*, for *darśan*, *mārg*); see Joshi, $ 175. On the gradation of *u* with *a* before a cerebral, see $ 76.

II. *Distant Action*

Vocalic Infection

$ 166. In certain words are found traces of the changes in the articulation of vowels under the influence of elements belonging to the syllable that follows. These cases have already been pointed out : *a* becomes *i* in *maṃjirī* (*mañjarī*), *mirī* (*marīca-*), *vel* (*vallī*); *ai* in *aiśīṃ* (*aśīti*); *e* before a consonant followed by *y* : *mer* (*maryā-dā*), *śej* (*śayyā*) *uver*, conc. *verīṃ* "upto", for *var*, *varī* (*upari*); *i* is assimilated to *u* in *susar* (*śiśumāra-*), *bund* beside *bind* (*bindu-*), etc., see $ 75 ff. These cases are isolated and seem, in their majority, to be anterior to Marathi. However, in the Konkan, the phenomena of the same type seem to be quite frequent : *korn*, Common Mar. *karūn* "having done", *ger* for *gari* "in the house" (LSI, *Mar.*, p. 167). Outside Marathi, also, these facts are rare. The best known case of this type is of the word *kerā* which is used to form the relative adjective in the central languages and seems to go back to Skr. *kārya-* (Beames, II, p. 281 ff). But this word is already noted in the Sanskrit period (see Pischel, $ 176; cf. Grammont, *Mél. S. Lévi*, p. 76) and contradicts the totality of the phonetics of the Indo-Aryan languages (see Beames, I, p. 134 ff.). The only exception seems to be Kashmiri which has developed a system of vocalic harmony, altogether abnormal in India (Grierson, *Man. Kaśm.*, $ 6).

Metathesis

$ 167. Cases of metathesis are particularly frequent in Gujarati, if we have to judge by the documents of the *Linguistic Survey* (*Raj.*, p. 331). But according to Beames (I, p. 271) they are current throughout India, atleast among the lower classes and they are not generally speaking taken into consideration because they are thought to be the "result of ignorance or caprice." However, the examination of the dictionary of Marathi leads us to isolate a certain number among them, which are admitted in the common language. Some of them even go quite far back, as far example, the word *haḷū* (Skt. *laghu-*), given as *halua*, by Hemacandra (Pischel, $ 354). Also found in Prakrit are *bahīṇ* (*bhaginī*), *marāṭhā* (Skr. *mahārāṣṭra-*); *niḍāḷ* goes back to the oldest periods of Prakrit (Skr. *lalāṭa-*, Pali *nalāṭa-*, Pkt. *niḍāla-*). Similarly, *vahāṇ* (Skr. *upānah-*, Pali *upāhanā*) and *kurhāḍ* (*kuṭhāra*) is anterior to the dissimilated form of Prakrit , *kuhāḍa-*. Pischel is certainly not right in equating with the preceding examples Pkt. **dīraha-*, which he supposes to be found nowhere. But the Marathi word *der* "delay" goes to an old form **derī* attested by Sindhi *deri* and derived from the word borrowed from Pehlavi or Persian *der* "a long time". The Pkt. form *dīhara-* is only an interpretation of this Iranian word. On the other hand, *sūn* (*snuṣā*) is based on an equally old metathesis (*snuṣā* > **hnuṣā* > *suṇha*: the interpretation of Pischel, $ 139, should be rejected).

Metathesis is found at a recent date only in certain words. We can cite with certainty : *kothrīb*, the doublet of *kothambīr* (*kustumbarī*), *pharaḷ*, the doublet of *phaḷār* (*phalāhāra-*), *khaṭraḍ* beside *khaḍtar*, the form in other languages. As regards *pehraṇ*, it seems to clearly join, through D. *parihaṇa-*, Skr. *paridhāna-*. But this could also be a Persian word, which could have been merely interpreted by Hemacandra in Sanskrit. Outside the aspiration and the continuants, metathesis seems to be altogether rare : *kekat* for *ketak*, though current (cf. *kekatpan* "ornament of gold for the hair") is only a learned word, that is badly pronounced : it is the corresponding *tad-bhava kevḍā*. The word *nuskan* (Arab *nuqṣān*) is a tentative adaptation to the ordinary system of Sanskrit (cf. *skandha-*, etc.). Extremely rare are also cases of vocalic metathesis : *osag* for (*aśoka-*), *aḍulsā* (Skr. *ataruṣa-*) are the names of plants; *nedṇeṃ* for *na deṇeṃ* "not to give" is not to be cited here : in reality it is made after the model of *neṇṇeṃ* (*na jānāti*) which is regular.

A curious case is that of the name of the festival, *śiṃgā* : it seems to be derived from Deśī *sugimhao* (*sugrīṣmaka-*). Therefore, it all seems as if the elements *-ug-* and *-imh-* had been entirely interverted and the the exchange of consonants is particularly strange.

$ 168. We should distinguish from metathesis the frequent anticipation of aspiration, undoubtedly due to the sentiment of its instability (see $ 161, 169; cf. Grammont, *l. l.*, p. 66).

In the final position, *h* is incorporated into the word for subsisting : this appears in loan-words like *rāhā* for Pers. *rāh*, *tarhā* for P. *tarah* (Molesworth, *Pref.*, obs. 8). Thence also partially the fact that the old final vowel has been preserved in the nominatives of nouns with *h* as *lāho*, *moho*, see $ 78. It is undoubtedly again for the same reason that aspiration has not been shifted during the metathesis of *kuḍhāra-* into *kurhāḍ*.

As has been seen, this metathesis is old and in fact a certain number of cases regarding the shifting of aspiration are anterior to Marathi. Among the monosyllables, this is the case with *hāḍ* (*asthi-*; cf. *aṭhī*), found in Deśī and in several Indo-Aryan languages; certainly also that of *hoṃṭ*, the doublet of *oṃṭh* (*oṣṭha-*). The Marathi form is common to all the western languages. Besides, Beng. *ṭhoṃṭ* seems to indicate that the phenomenon has not, surely, been simple in this word. Similarly *khāṃk* (*kakṣa-*) can surely result from the shifting of aspiration of *kāṃkh*, as a result of the dissimilation of aspiration following an assimilation. The intermediary degree **khāṃkh* will have been obtained like *jhuṃ-jhṇeṃ* (*yudhya-*), where assimilation is evident. Moreover, the form *jhuṃṇeṃ* of the latter word enables us to suspect that probably assimilation has been the normal stage of the anticipation of aspiration.

Inside the polysyllables, the tendency of aspiration to be grouped with a preceding occlusive has been noted several times here ($ 163). Moreover, it is frequent in other languages (Beames I, p. 191-192). In *gheṇeṃ* (*grahi-*). the fact goes back to Prakrit. It is found again in *jhaṇeṃ* (*yabh-*) *mhais* (*mahiṣī*), *mhātārā* (*mahattara-* and in a general way in all these words where *mha-* comes from Skr. *mahā*), *mhetar* (Pers. *mihtar*) : *phattar* seems to be altogether recent, because *patthar*, wherefrom it is derived, is a loan, this being the result of a geminated consonant. To the same tendency is due the form *kaḍhaī* (*kaṭāha-*) which can have been influeneed by the root of *kaḍhṇeṃ* (*kvath-*). We should also recall here the inversion of the groups of the continuant $+h$, mentioned by Molesworth (type *vivhal*; see observation 14, Preface. p. XV).

Dissimilation

1. *Dissimilation affecting aspiration*

$ 169. The examples are quite numerous : *khād* (Pkt. *khaddha-*), *khāṃd* (*skandha-*), *khubaḷṇeṃ* (*kṣubh-*), *jhāṃkar* (D. *jhaṃkara-*), *jhāṃj*, *jhaṃjrī* (*jhañjhā*, *jharjharī*), *jhaṃjṇeṃ* (cf. *jhuṃjhṇeṃ*, Skr. *yudhy-*), *ṭhāḍā* (Pkt. *ṭhaḍḍha*:), Skr. *stabdha-*,) *thāṃg* (D. *thagga-*; cf. *thā* : Skr. *sthāgha-*) *thāṃbṇeṃ* (*stambha*,) *dhīṭ*, *dhāṭ* (*dhṛṣṭa-*), *bhaṭṭā* (no doubt borrowed in the form *bhaṭṭhā*' cf. however *bhaṭakṇeṃ*; Skr. *bhraṣta-*), *bhik* (*bhikṣā*), *bhūk* (*bubhukṣā*, D. *bhukkha*), *haḍakṇeṃ* (*haṭh-*), *hambā*, *hambarṇeṃ* (*hambhā*), *hāt*, *hattī* (*hasta-*, *hastin-*). In all these cases, the dissimilation is progressive contrary to the three firstly laws proposed by Grammont in his *Dissimilation consonantique* (p. 103); cf. the Skr. examples given by him on p. 106. In all these words, or in the stems on which they are based, the second aspirate had been final. Now it is in the final position that aspiration is most easily lost (cf. $ 88). In a true dissylable as in *lokhaṇḍ* (*loha-khaṇḍa*), dissimilation is regressive according to rule and similarly in *garat* which goes back to **garath* arisen out of **garhath* (*gṛhastha-*). The form *gharat* has, no doubt, been contaminated by *ghar* "house". The case of *paḷheṃ* "cotton-plant" is obscure : Deśī has both the forms, *palahī* and *phalahī*; the second is perhaps primitive, but can equally be derived from the first by the contamination of *phaḷa-*.

2. *Dissimilation affecting the mode of articulation*

$ 170. A certain number of cases are found since Prakrit. Thus for *liṃb* (cf. tats. *nimb-*, see Grammont., op. cit., law VIII, p. 44); of *nāṃgar*, *nāṃgḷī* and perhaps *nāṃgoḍā* (*lāṅgala-*, etc.; Grammont, ibid., law XVII, p. 84), *kaṇer* (*karavīra-*), *niḍāḷ* (*lalāṭa-*), perhaps also *bail* (Pkt. *bailla-* for *bal- illa-* ?). Under the same conditions the cerebral of Pkt. *paḍi* (*prati-*) is lost quite early before a cerebral, and in Marathi, whereas we find *paḍ-* and *pai-* in competition before other consonants, *pai-* is found alone before the cerebrals (J. Bloch, *Mél. S. Lévi*, p. 9). The Prakrit prototype of *kohleṃ* seems also to come from dissimilation (*kuṣmāṇḍa*— * *kumhāṃḍa*— *kūhaṃḍa*, Grammont, op. cit. law XVIII, *l. l.*, p. 86).

Under the action of the law XVIII of Grammont, more recent changes have occurred : *daroḍā* (D. *daḍavaḍa-*), *lavṇeṃ*, the vulgar doublet of *navṇeṃ* (*nam-*); *luksān* (Arab. *nuqsān*), *loṇī* (*navanīta-*); perhaps also *ṭoṃc* for *coṃc* (*cañcu-*). But the form of eastern dialects *coṃṭ* contradicts this explanation and makes one suspect reciprocal influences between the word for 'beck" and that of the "tip", *oṃṭh*, *hoṃṭ*, Beng. *ṭhoṃṭ* (*oṣṭha-*).

The consonant of the word for the number "eight", which preserves the form *aṭh-* (*aṣṭa-*) before seven of the words for the tens (*aṭhrā*, *aṭṭhāvis*, etc.) has become a sonant where it had been in immediate contact with a surd : thence *aḍtīs* "38", *aḍsaṣ* "68" (law XI of Grammont). This relates not to dissimilation but to the differentiation of phonemes in contact.

The popular form *khaḍṇeṃ* "to dig" should not be regarded as being due to the dissimilation of the nasals of *khaṇṇeṃ* (*khan-*) . This is a word of the same family to which belongs *khāḍā* (D. *khaḍḍa-*) "hole" The word *gadhḍā* is regularly derived from Skr. *gardabha-* and is independent of *gāḍhav*. Dissimila ion is equ: lly improbable in *kuṃḍal* for *kuṃḍaḷ* (form found in Gujarati and Panjabi), where it is legitimate (law XIV) : *kuṃḍal* is, no doubt, a simple tatsama.

On certain dissimilations anterior to Marathi, attested by the words for number, see $ 217, 221, 223.

3. *Dissimilation of Vowels*

$ 171. When two *us* or *os* are successively found in the same word, the first generally is open : *kamod* tats. (*kumuda-*), *gamūtr* tats. (*gomūtra-*), *gahūṃ* (*godhūma-*); *catkor* or *cotkar* for *cotkor* (*cautha+kor*); *kapūt* (*kuputra-*) seems to be similarly made, although one may suspect here the pejorative Skr. prefix *kā-*; *garodar* (*guru-udara-*) probably contains the representative of Pkt. *garu-*. We may include here the probable case of the differentiation in *gavḷi* (*gopāla-*). Two *is* seem to be dissimilated in *vejit* tats. for *vijit*, *vehḷā* (*vibhītaka-*). In *niḍāḷ*, Pkt. *ṇiḍāla* for *naḍāla-*, one should, no doubt, see therein an abusive insertion, besides old, of the preverb *ni-*.

Syllabic Superposition.

$ 172. The cases arising in the wake of the definition given by Grammont (ibid., p. 147), at the contact of two morphologically different elements, of whom the latter recovers the former:

- *avakṇeṃ*, *avikṇeṃ* for *ava-vikṇeṃ* (of *pikṇeṃ* "to mature");
- *ekāmīṃ* "in one turn", of *ek-kām-*, cf. *du-kām-* "in two turns";
- *káṃphaḷ* "fruit of *kuṃbhā*", therefore : **kumbha-phala-*;
- *ketāḍ* "a type of palm" for *kekat-tāḍ* (according to Navalkar, p. 256).
- *gurākhyā* "shepherd" from *gureṃ* "cattle" + *rākhyā* guardian" (ibid.);
- *jānivasā* "sojourn" (or "habitation") in the betrothed's house (or "the betrothed") : *janya-nivāsa*;
- *divāḷī* "festival of lamps", from *divā* (Skr. *dīpa*) + *āvaḷī*;
- *dhuvaṇ* "dirty water left after washing " beside *dhuvavaṇī* (*dhuva+pāṇī*);
- *navrā* "betrothed", from *nava+vara*;

nākāṭī, *nākāṭṇī* "action of lengthening (litt. cutting) the nose out of spite"; from *nāk+kāṭ-*;
nāteṃ "relationship" from *jñāti-tva-*; anterior to Marathi;
pathvar "betrothed for the first time", popular for *prathama-var-* tats.;
rikāmā "empty, vain" from *rikā + kām* (*rikta-karma-*);
lakārī "polisher" from *lākh* (Skr. *lākṣā*)+*kār-*;

The abnormal instr. sing. of the pronominal Mar. word, *eṇeṃ* "by him", arisen from *etena+anena* should, no doubt, be similarly interpreted.

III. *The End and the Initial of the Word*

$ 173. During the period of the formation of Marathi, the place of phonemes in the word has had a major influence on their evolution. As regards notably the end of the word, the fact has been noted à propos of the loss of old finals ($ 37 and ff.), of the quantity of the penultimate vowel ($ 40 ff.), of the formulae of contraction particular to the final consonants ($ 14), of the fate of the penultimate nasals ($ 66) and of the deaspiration of the finals ($ 88). But except in the case of adaptations of loan words to the system of the language (for ex. *rahā* <Pers. *rāh*; *ṭikīṭ* beside *ṭikaṭ* < Eng. *ticket*, see Navalkar, p. 59), in modern Marathi no phonetic change exclusive to the final is noticed. Similarly, the loss of aspiration, which is particularly frequent therein, does not uniquely depend on this place.

$ 174. The consonantal initial has remained free from change during all the periods (concerning the general history of *n* and *l* in the initial position, see $ 132, 144).

The vocalic initial, on the contrary, has undergone a number of changes :

1. *e* and *o*, in the initial position, become diphthongs : *yeṇeṃ* (*eti*), *yer* (*itara*) are generally written in this manner due to an orthographic caprice, but ordinarily the writing does not betray the dipthongisation, though recognised as being general (Molesworth, see under *yek* and *vo-*; cf. LSI, *Mar.*, p. 21, 168). According to a remark generally made, this is one of the traits by which Marathi recalls the Dravidian languages (Caldwell, *Comp. Gramm. of the Dravidian Langs.*, 2nd edn., p. 4).

2. During different periods, a brief initial vowel gets elided (cf. Beames, I, p. 176-180). In Sanskrit *pi-* beside *api* is an Indo-European doublet, on which is modelled *va* for *ava-* (Wackernagel, II $ 29, *y*, *d*). It is possible that in Marathi the equivalence *o-* : *va*: in the initial position had something to do with the phenomenon in Sanskrit. Elsewhere the vocalic initial has dropped in Sanskrit in very few words (ibid, I, $ 53, c, d). The origin of the word *apūpa*:- *pūpa* is not known. It should be noted that Marathi *puvā* and the corresponding words of other languages are derived from the shortest form. But the existence of the *saṃdhi* in Sanskrit and the change of initial vowels resulting therefrom show that the vocalic attack of the words does not show especial resistance in India. Thus the frequence of elision in Prakrit is explained without having recourse, with Wackernagel (*l. l.* and $ 254), to the accent of intensity. The same frequency is found in the modern languages. Thus 1, *a* is missing before a liquid in : *rahāṭ* (*araghaṭṭa*), *rān-* (*araṇya-*), *riṭhā* (*ariṣṭaka-*), *lavḍā* (*alābu-*); 2, *u* has been lost during different periods in the prefix *upa-* : *pākhar* (*upaskara-*) is common to all the languages and attested since Deśī; but *baisṇem* (*upaviś-*) is a word fixed earlier to *vaṭhāṇ* (*upasthāna-* or *avasthāna-* ?) in, any case to *vahāṇ* (*upānah-*), *var* (*upari*). These words have, moreover, different aspects according to languages; 3, more recent are *bhitar* (*abhyantara-*), *hīlagṇeṃ* (*abhi-lag-*); but these words are found in Hindi, and the dental *l* of the second is not regular. We have, thus, to do with loan words; but does *ṭhī*, attested in the *Jñāneśvarī*, come directly from *strī* (cf. Pkt. *thī*) or from Pkt. *iṭṭhī* ? In any case a popular form like *mop* for *amop* "much" (*māp-*) is certainly recent. Recent also are the tatsamas *nantar* "after" for *anantar*, *peksāṃ* "in comparison with" for *apekṣāṃ* : but it is, probably, not a true case of an apocope. These words have in reality, postpositions and *tyānantar*, *tyāpekṣāṃ*, the inevitable pronunciation of *tyāanantar*, *tyā-apekṣāṃ* are naturally cut into *tyā*+*pekṣāṃ*, *tya*+*nantar*.

There remain a number of changes, altogether isolated, like the loss of *y-* of the Skr. *yūkā*, M. *ū*, which is proper to Marathi today, but is found as far as Pali (Pischel, $ 335) and the unexpected abbreviation and the decoloration of *ek* "one" in the compound *akrā* "eleven", which is found under variable fcrms in other languages of the family.

$ 175. Except for some irregularities, for which Marathi seems only exceptionally responsible, the Marathi word remains intact, at its two ends. It is, therefore, as a whole, independent in the sentence. Thereby is undoubtedly explained in part the relative archaism of its morphology and even the constitution of its sentence.

MORPHOLOGY

Generalities

$ 176. India has been a terrain particularly favourable for the general tendencies which have, in the majority of the Indo-European languages, led to the reduction and the normalisation of the grammatical forms (cf. Meillet, *Introduction*, p. 410 ff.).

The prehistoric system of sonants, already altered a great deal during the Vedic epoch, is completely ruined the day when *ṛ* is lost. Later, the quantity and even the timbre of the vowels depend on their place in the word and lose all grammatical value. Since then the play of ancient vocalic gradations has become impossible. Nothing comes to replace it. Because if, during any period, some accent of intensity has existed, in no case has it provoked in the stems new gradations of the French type *sire* : *sieur*, *seigneur* or *meurs* : *mourons*. As regards inflexion, the loss of final consonants, then the effacement of final vowels and the disappearance of intervocalic consonants ruin the opposition between the stem and the termination, and necessitate the establishment of a new inflexional system, with single stems and relatively much less numerous types of terminations (cf. Meillet, ibid., p. 413-419).

$ 177. The grammatical category common to the noun and the verb, that of the number, has been affected, besides in conformity with the general march of the Indo-European dialects (Meillet, ibid, p. 412). The dual disappeared quite early. Undoubtedly classical Sanskrit preserves this number as it had been received from the Vedic and seems to even develop its use (Cuny, *Le nombre duel en grec*, p. 68). But all the texts written in the dialects near the real speeches ignore this number. Since the epoch of Aśoka, the wordm for the number "two" has a form of the dual fixed in the nominative, but in the oblique cases it has the terminations of the plural (for ex. instr. *duvehi*) and the noun to which it relates is in the plural (for ex. *duve morā* "two peacocks", Girnar, I,

4). The same is exactly the case in Palī (Müller, *Pali Gram.*, 61-2) and in Prakrit (Pischel, $ 360). It is, therefore, certain that since the 3rd century B.C. Indo-Aryan had lost the dual number in current usage.

On the contrary, the two subsisting numbers, singular and plural, are still clearly distinguished in Marathi. In one single case, that of the nominative masculine of the type *dev*, the singular is similar to the plural : M. *dev* represents simultaneously Skr. *devaḥ* and *devāḥ*. All the other nominal or verbal forms have remained distinct in the singular and in the plural.

DECLENSION

$ 178. Marathi has preserved, but by reducing and simplifying them to the utmost, the inflexional system of the Prakrit, Moreover, whether it is a question of the formation of the stems or of the grammatical categories, the old system had already been strongly reduced in the Middle-Indian.

Stems

$ 179. Sanskrit had preserved the gradations of the old sonants *y, v, r* : *i* : *u* : *ṛ*; but the day *ṛ* got mixed with *a, i* or *u* the declension of the old stems in *-r-* must have been brought to that of the subsisting vocalic stems. This is the state shown by all the inscriptions of Aśoka, except that of Girnar (Senart, *Inscrip. de Piyadasi,* II, p. 338, 358, 389) and which is noted, including some archaisms, by the Prakrit literature (Pischel, $ 389 ff.). As regards the declension of the stems in *-i-* and *-u-* which has continued longer (ibid, $ 377 ff.), it has been, as will be seen, brought to that of the stems in *-ī* and *-ū* and brought to that of the feminines in *-ā*.

On the other hand, the loss of final consonants, combined with the opening of the intervocalic ones, has provoked in Prakrit the almost total disappearance of consonantal stems. Undoubtedly, in the declension of nouns in *-t*, *-n* and *-s*, Prakrit texts still preserve, probably under the influence of the literary traditions, a large number of old forms, but the adaptations to the vocalic declension is, since Aśoka, the most frequent thing (Senart, op. cit., Müller, op. cit., p. 64-65, Pischel, $ 355, 395 404-406, 409).

It is, therefore, the vocalic declension of Prakrit that is found to be the cause of the Marathi declension of all the nouns and adjectives and of all the pronouns other than the personal pronouns. In fact, Marathi knows of only two types of inflexion : 1, that of the nouns ending in a consonant, which go back to old stems in *-a-* (fem. *-ā*), *-i-* and *-ī-*, *-u-* and *-ū-*; 2, that of the nouns ending in a long vowel resulting from a contraction, notably in the enlarged stems where the vowels *-a-*, *-i-* *-u-* had been followed by the suffix *-ka-* (on this suffix, see Pischel, $ 598; Beames, II, p. 29 ff.; Grierson, *Phon.*, $ 13, 30, 37; Joshi, p. 17 ff.).

In all the cases, the radical is fixed and admits of only those gradations consisting of quantitative variations depending on the place of the vowels in the word, and bereft of grammatical value. It is only the terminations which express the categories, characteristic of declension.

Gender

$ 180. Prakrit has preserved, and Marathi has preserved in its turn, the distinction of three genders, which has been obliterated in most of the modern languages. Moreover, Marathi is not the only one to still possess the three genders; the same is true of Gujarati (and the dialects joined thereto, see LSI, *Bhil Lang.*, p. 12; *Raj.*, p. 5, 331) and Simhalese. Except in these three languages, which constitute a continuous group in the south-west, the neuoer gender has disappeared everywhere in Aryan India, even in a speech with as archaic in aspect as Sindhi. Elsewhere only isolated traces of this gender remain : such as, in Hindi and no doubt in Panjabi, the termination of the nom.—acc. pl., which has been utilised in the declension of feminine nouns (Beames, II, p. 206 and infra, $ 187). Even at the eastern end of the domain, an entire group of dialects totally ignores the grammatical gender : it has disappeared from Bengali and Oriya since the oldest texts (Beames, II, p. 178, cf. p. 147); it is unknown to Assamese; its usage is restricted in Nepali and in the largest part of Bihar (LSI, *Bihari*, p. 38, 50) where the adjective is invariable. We should, no doubt, see therein an inheritance of the languages spoken by the populations of these regions before their apprenticeship of the Indo-European. In fact, it is known that the Tibeto-Burmese does not have the grammatical gender (LSI, *Tibeto-Burman*, vol. I, p. 6; cf. the observations of Meillet concerning Armenian and Iranian, *Gram. Comp. de l'arm. class.*, $ 60). In any case the tendency to reduce the number of genders must have made itself felt very early in the eastern speeches. Pischel notes that the passage of the neuter nouns in *-a-* to masculine declension is very frequent in Māgadhī and altogether rare in other dialects ($ 357) : the nominative singular neuters in *-e* of the Aśokan inscriptions are witness to the passage to masculine declension (Senart, *Inscrip de Piyadasi*, II, p. 339).

Moreover, if Marathi preserves unchanged in its terminations the Indo-European distinction of genders, the use of forms therein also shows another influence. The distinction into animate and inanimate ones, appears at two points of Marathi syntax (LSI, *Munda and Drav. Lang.*, p. 280, 289). Firstly, the direct complementary noun of a verb is in the direct case, if it denotes a thing and in the oblique one followed by *s* or *lā* if it denotes a person. The animate beings other than men are included in either of these two categories (Joshi, $ 458; Navalkar, $ 490, 491). Secondly, the accord of the verb or of the predicative adjective, as will be seen, varies according to the nature of the beings designated by the substantives. Whatever be, besides, the origin of this distinction, Marathi is not the only language to apply it. We will see that in Sindhi the accord of the predicate is done more or less like Marathi. The rule regarding postpositions is found in other languages also : in Gujarati, (Tisdall, p. 33), Sindhi (Trumpp, p. 455 ff.) and Hindi (Kellogg, $ 678), etc.

Cases

$ 181. The same languages, that have lost the category of the gender, have also, more or less, lost all causative terminations (Beames, II, p. 227 ff). Marathi, on the contrary, like the majority of the languages of the family, has preserved a part of the old inflexion and has used it for constructing a new system.

From the moment when the final vowels lost their quantity and then their characteristic timbre a progressive confusion of the monosyllabic finals was bound to follow. The fact is chiefly apparent in the declension of masc.-neutre nouns in *-a-* and fem. in *-ā*, that is precisely in the type of declension which has, little by little, supplanted all other types. Hence the need felt by Prakrit for new differentiations : the abl. sing. *-āt*, which disappeared quite early, is enlarged to *-ādo*, *āo* by the use of the old adverbial Skr. termination *-taḥ*; the accusative plural in *-ān* is replaced by the pronominal accusative in *-e* (Pkt. *te*; cf. the acc. in *-āni*, Asokan East., etc.) and the nominative-accusative plural of feminine nouns in *-āḥ*, which became similar to the nominative singular when the final aspiration was lost, is enlarged to *-āo* by the cumulation or assimilation of the terminations. Imitating the same the nominative masc. plural undergoes similar changes, etc. Of all these adaptations tried by literary Prakrit, very few have survived, but they show a moving state of the language, where with the old terminations getting disintegrated, it became necessary to reduce their number or to make them more consistent. This second tendency is that of literature, which is naturally conservative. It is the first one that has prevailed in the real speeches, which have developed into modern languages.

$ 182. First of all, the nominative, the vocative and the accusative have got mixed in one single case, the direct one. The vocative singular subsists in the nouns in *-a-* only with an artificial lengthening of the final vowel or gets mixed with the nominative (Pischel, $ 366 b). In the feminines in *-ā*, the vocative in *-e*, the only one known to Vararuci, also quickly enough cedes the place to the nominative (Pischel, $ 375). As regards the nominative-accusative group, there subsists almost no distinction the moment the vowels are so abridged that nasality is no longer marked therein; only in the masculine singular *devu* has, perhaps, been distinct from *deva*(*ṃ*) for the longest period. But whether this nasality had brought in a slight closing of the vowel (this fact is surely known only for the languages of the type of Apabhraṃśa see $ 39) or whether the group has undergone the effect of the analogy of others, the general result is a unique form of the nom.-acc.-voc. for each number :

	sing.	pl.
masc.	*devo- devaṃ*	*devāḥ-devān*
neut.	*sūtraṃ*	*sūtrāṇi*
fem.	*mālā-mālāṃ*	*mālāḥ* (*mālāo*)

These considerations, which would find their counterparts, if the stems in *-i* and *-u* were to be examined, explain the formation in Marathi and in a general manner in the modern languages of a direct case, which at least in the nouns ending in a consonant, is finally felt as the form itself of the word (cf. Meillet, *Introduction*, p. 413).

This case designates the subject and the object of the verb, irrespective of the nature of this object (Laddu, JRAS, 1910, p. 871).

$ 183. Among other cases, those expressing concrete relationships have, in conformity with a general tendency common to the Indo-European languages, progressively disappeared from usage (Meillet, ibid., p. 425). Since Sanskrit, are established various equivalences in the use of different cases (Speyer, *Ved. u. Sanskr. Syntax*, $ 53-5, 73-4, 82, 84). This is the first stage in the history of the mixing of the indirect cases, for which so very frequent examples are offered by a text like the *Mahāvastu* (see the notes of the Senart edn., passim). In Marathi, remain only traces of the old instrumental, of the locative and of the ablative. The real relationships are expressed during the modern period by the postpositions fixed to an unique oblique case, the substitute of the old genitive and dative cases.

These two cases were frequently used with the same value in Sanskrit (Speyer, ibid., $ 43, 71, 72). Even in the language of the Brahmins, the termination of the genitive-ablative fem. sing. (class. Skr. *-āḥ*) got mixed up in all the cases with the termination of the dative in *-ai* (Whitney, $ 365 d). In Buddhist Sanskrit, we find in a text as old as the *Divyāvadāna* constructions as given below : *tasya tatrāropayiṣyāmi* "I will put this *on* him" (p. 510) and *bahir vihārasya* "out side the monastery" (p. 490). Confusions of the same type are, for still stronger reasons, more numerous in the *Mahāvastu* (see the notes to I, 123, 130; 309, 10, etc.). In Pali and in Prakrit the unification is almost complete and the genitive generally replaces the dative (Müller, *Pali Gram.*, p. 67, Pischel, $ 361). It is, therefore, the genitive alone or joined to a word determining the special shade of the meaning to be expressed, which we expect at the base of the modern oblique case.

The same is definitely the case, atleast in the plural. All the Indo-Aryan languages, not only of Gangetic India or of the Indus (Beames, II, p. 218 ff.), but also the speeches of the N.W. mountains (Grierson, *Piś. Lang.*, p. 33) and Romany (the hypothesis of Miklosisch, XI, p. 4 does not take into account the parallelism with the singular, nor the uniformity of the termination across different types of inflexion), as also Simhalese (Geiger, $ 34, IV, $ 36, IV) present an oblique plural going back to the old genitive.

In the singular, the accord is far from being the same. No doubt, it is still the genitive which is found in the oblique of certain speeches of the far N.W., notably Kashmiri (see Grierson, *l. l.*) and probably Romany, if we have to decide from the opposition of the masc. *rakles* : fem. *rakl'a,* which recalls, very closely, the Sanskrit *-asya*:*-yāḥ* (Miklosich puts forward this interpretation very timidly in so far as it concerns the masculine and leaves the termination of the feminine completely unexplained, ibid., p. 3, 12). It is not impossible that the same may be the case in Simhalese although Geiger explains in this manner only the masculine ($ 34, II) and for the feminine appeals to the termination of the accusative ($ 36, II; however, it is, at best, possible that *-a* goes back to Skr. *-āyāḥ*; cf. *kā* < *kāya-*, $ 3, 1). But in the central languages, the explanation meets with serious difficulties. The passage of *-s-* to *-h-* which is to be invoked for explaining the termination of the oblique masculine, is in-admissible in the majority of cases. Among modern languages, Simhalese —where moreover the form *-asa* is preserved in the old inscriptions—and on the continent Sindhi and Panjabi alone admit this change. Prakrit also does not allow it : the *-aha*, *-āho* of Apabhraṃśa could only be the transcription of a modern form, probably western. In the ancient period, the termination *-aha* is exclusive to Māgadhī and besides obscure (Pischel, $ 366, cf. $ 264). Moreover, the survival of the old *s* in the pronominal oblique cases of Hindi *kis*, *tis*, cf. Pkt. *kissa,* does not allow us to admit its disappearance in other cases.—One may be even led to suppose a number of abnormal phonetic developments in the terminations of the feminine gender.

Only the old terminations of the dative enable us to render account of the forms of the oblique singular in Marathi and in the Gangetic group, without making an appeal to accessory hypotheses. Despite the general tendency of Prākrit to help the genitive triumph over the dative, the survival of this case in the singular is not impossible to admit. First of all, normal Prākrit itself offers a striking example of the opposition of the *dative sing.*; *genitive pl.* in the pronominal declension : with regard to the plural *amhāṇaṃ*, it preserves in the singular, beside *mama*, the form *majjhaṃ*, arisen from the old dative *mahyam*. Now it is this last form which has proved to be imbued with the greatest amount of vitality, because it furnishes the oblique of the personal pronouns in a large number of modern central languages (M. *majh-*, H. *mujh*, etc., see Beames, II, 304 ff.; in the group of the North-West,—see Grierson, op. cit., p. 45; Miklosich, op. cit., p. 22—and in Simhalese,—see Geiger, $ 47, 1—the pronominal declension is formed according to other principles. On the other hand, the fact that Vararuci, in agreement in this matter with the oldest Prakrit texts, completely prohibits the usage of the dative, whereas Hemacandra admits the same precisely in the singular (III, 132), as was the case with Pali for expressing the intention, seems to prove that there had existed in real usage, a tradition which had been, at first, resisted by literature but to which it had finally to adapt itself. Since then the replacement, pointed out above, of the termination of the fem. gen.—abl. by that of the dative in the language of the Brahmins seems to be the first manifestation of a more general evolution, dissimulated by mediaeval literary tradition.

This origin of the oblique case explains its use : in the oldest texts, it acts, simultaneously, as the genitive (examples in the preface of Māḍgāṃvkar in the edition of the *Jñāneśvarī*, p. 14-15) and as the dative (ibid., p. 11; cf. *Jñān.*, III, 67; X, 91, 106; XIII 453, 505; XIV, 44; XV, 193; XVI, 471-72-3; XVIII, 1289, 1327, 1331, etc.; the Patan inscription, : *maḍhā dinhalā* "given to the temple". The oblique has taken the value of the universal indirect case only later on, when the usage of the postposition had spread and when the old indirect cases had totally disappeared. During the old period it is the direct case, the veritable accusative, which accompanies *vāṃcūṇī*" except" (*heṃ-iśvaru*, etc., *Jñān.*, edn. of *Māḍgāṃvkar*, p. 15-16), and the instrumental which is formed with *sīṃ* "with", p. 14) and *vīṇa* "without" (ibid., p. 16).

$ 184. The group of two cases, direct and oblique, thus

constitutes the essential of Marathi inflexion. We have still to study, however, its different types.

1. *The Group : direct case, oblique case*

I

$ 185. The declension of Marathi nouns ending in a consonant goes back to that of the masc. and neuter nouns in *-a-*, and that of the feminines in *-ā* and *-ī* of Sanskrit.

$ 186. The prototype of the declension of the masculines in *-a-* is constituted in Sanskrit as given below :

	Sing.		Pl.
nom.	*devaḥ* (*devo*)	nom.	*devāḥ*
dat.	*devāya*	gen.	*devānām*

from there in Prākrit :

	deva	*devā*
	devāa	*devāṇaṃ*

The development in Marathi :

Direct case	*dev*	*dev*
Oblique case	*devā*	*devāṃ*

The old nominative singular in *-o* is preserved in the pronominal adjectives *jo, to* : these are then the archaisms common to all the cognate languages (Beames, II, p. 315) and are due to the monosyllabic character of these words. The same nominative is found, no doubt under the influence of pronouns, in the present participles adapted to conjugation and finally in the words wherein the last consonant is *h*. This final *-o* has been preserved for protecting the aspiration (*loho, lāho*, etc.). The intermediary stage of *devu* type is noted in the Apbhraṃśa and is in current use in old Marathi, as in the majority of related languages during the old epoch. This is the form noted by Al-biruni towards 1000 A. D. (cf. Al-biruni, *India*, transln. of Sachau, II, p. 258-59). Today it is preserved only in Sindhi : in this language where the final vowels are still showing resistance, the distinction of the nominative sing. and plural is still clear (*devu* : *deva*). Similarly Romany has lost the final in the singular but has preserved it in the plural (*cor* : *cora*). Western Panjabi has preserved a trace of the old opposition in the gradation of the type *kukkuṛ* - *kukkaṛ* (Pkt. *kukkuḍo* : *kukkuḍā*). Except these languages, the differentiation between the singular and plural has been everywhere effaced as in Marathi.

The contraction of the group *-āya* of the oblique singular has resulted in *-ā* as in Marathi, Sindhi, Western Panjabi (where is found the form *kukkuṛ* <**kukkuṛā*) and Maithili, Except in these dialects, the oblique is similar to the direct case in all the languages which have not preserved the old genitive.

$ 187. The declension of neuter nouns in *-a-* is in Sanskrit identical to that of the masculines, except in nom.-acc., which have the forms given below :

singular	Skr.	*sūtram*	>	Pkt.	*suttam*
plural.	Skr.	*sūtrāṇi*	>	Pkt.	*suttāiṃ*

From where in Marathi we have,

singular	*sūt*
plural	*suteṃ*

In Gujarati, as in Marathi, the form of neuter nouns is similar to that of the masculines (this explains the confusion of *devo* and *devam*, cf. $ 182). Simhalese, on the contrary, opposes the masc. *-ā* to neut. *-a* (the termination of the masc. is obscure; see Geiger, $ 33, I, $ 36).

In the plural contraction has occurred differently at Goa, where the termination of the neut. pl. is *-āṃ*. The termination of common Marathi is found in that of Hindi fem. pl. *-eṃ*; that of Goanese in the same termination of the Panjabi fem. pl. *-āṃ*. Gujarati has no trace of the old termination of the neut. plural. It is replaced by the termination *-o*, which is found in this language, optionally, in all the genders. It should be understood that Gujarati has enlarged a zero termination found for example in the *Mugdhāvabodha-mauktika* (written in 1394, see LSI, *Guj.*, 4 .354). Like Gujarati, Simhalese has eliminated the old termination of the plural and has had to take recourse to new methods (Geiger, $ 38, II).

$ 188. Most of the masc. and neut. nouns in *-i* and *-u* have been enlarged into *-ika-*, *-uka-* . Among those that have subsisted, those in *-u-* are declined like the ones in *-a-* : *ūs* (*ikṣu-*) and *bund* (*bindu-*), *moh* (*madhu-*) are declined as *dev*, *cor* or *sūt*. Those in *-i* have had a different fate (we can not identify M. *hāḍ*, neut. and Skr. *asthi-*; neither M. *laṭh* masc. and Skr. *yaṣṭi-*). They have been assimilated with the feminines in *-i*; thus we have M. *āg* fem. < Skr. *agni-* masc.

$ 189. The prototype of the declension of the fem. nouns in *-ā* is constituted by the following forms of Sanskrit :

	Singular	Plural
nom.	*iṣṭā*	*iṣṭāḥ*
dat.	*iṣṭāyai*	gen. *iṣṭāṇam*

On examining this table it becomes immediately clear that at the loss of final aspiration, there remained nothing to distinguish the nominative plural from the nominative singular. This led in Prākrit to the development of a declension where the totality of the nominatives of the three genders appeared as follows :

	Singular	Plural
masc.	*devo*	*devā*
fem.	*iṭṭā*	*iṭṭā*
neut.	*suttaṃ*	*suttāiṃ*

Thus the feminine nominative plural no longer remained distinct, neither from the nominative singular of the same gender, nor from the masculine nominative plural. This was a paradoxical state which could not have endured. Therefore, when the reduction of the genders in the dialects of the Māgadhī type took place, the termination of the nominative plural neuter was adapted for the paradigm of the feminine nouns, to which even today Hindi and Panjabi bear witness.[1] From there also we have the enlargements in *-āyo* and *-āo*. The former, exceptional in Aśoka and usual in Pali, seems to have been formed in imitation of the feminine nominatives in *-īyo* (this was the only form which was not the same in the two inflexions; cf. Johansson, *Der Dial. der Shāhbazgarhi-redaktion*, II, p. 55; V. Henry, *Gram. pālie*, $ 160). The second, common in Prākrit, is the culmination of the former, rather than the result of a cumulation of the terminations as is suggested by Pischel ($ 367, 376; cf. *-āyai*> *-āe*). We have, therefore, to propose as the origin of the Marathi inflexion the following forms of Prākrit :

1. In these languages, substitution could have been favoured by the honorific use of the neuter in place of the feminine, as is found in Marathi and Gujarati; cf. infra.

	Singular	Plural
	iṭṭā	*iṭṭāo*
	iṭṭāe	*iṭṭāṇaṃ*

Thence in Marathi :

	Singular	Plural
Direct case	*īṭ*	*iṭā*
Oblique case	*iṭe*	*iṭāṃ*

The plural of Kashmiri *māla* (Siṃ. *māl*) and that of Romany (*-ya*, that is to say, *-i -a*) agrees with the Marathi form.

Here again we find in Goanese and in Gujarati another culmination of the contraction : the nom. pl. herein is in *-o*; in Sindhi both the forms are found : *ā* and *ū* according to the dialects (Trumpp., p. 109). Nowhere except in Marathi has been preserved the form of the oblique sing. distinctly from that of the direct case in the central languages. Kashm. *māli* (Pkt. *mālāe* ?) seems to be related to the Marathi form ; cf. Romany *-ya*.

$ 190. The prototype of the declension of the feminine nouns in *-ī* is constituted by the following forms of Sanskrit :

	Singular		Plural
nom.	*rātrī*	nom.	*rātryo*
dat.	*rātryai*	gen.	*rātrīṇāṃ*

When *y* in a group with an occlusive lost its articulation, in place of the old *y*, *ī* was established everywhere. This gave the Prākrit forms :

rattī	*rattīo*
rattīe	*rattīṇaṃ*

These forms culminate in Marathi in the paradigm given below :

rāt	*rattīo*
rattīe	*rattīṇaṃ*

Sindhi presents a comparable declension: the nom.sing. *bhitĕ*, pl. *bhiteū*; obl. sing. *bhitĕ*, pl. *bhit* (*i*)*ĕ* (Trumpp. ibid., p. 110, 128). Cf. the plural of West. Panjabi in *-īṃ* (*akkhī*, etc.). Kashmiri offers a striking parallelism with Marathi, that is the nom. sing. *rāth*, dative sing. and nom. pl. *rōtˢü*, dat. pl. *rotˢün* (Grierson, *Manual of the Kashmiri Lang.*, p. 32).

II

$ 191. The declension of Marathi nouns in *-ā, ī, -ū, o* is based on the same principles as the consonantal declension. These nouns come from Sanskrit nouns where the penultimate vowel being *a, i, u,* the last consonant of the stem is lost. The final vowels then get contracted according to the rules set out in $ 60. To this declension belong in particular the nouns and adjectives with enlargement of the types *-a-ka-, -i-ka-, -u-ka-,* which are extremely frequent and always have a living formation.

The terminations then take on the following aspect :

1. Nouns in *-a.*

Masculines in Prākrit : *-ayo* *ayā*> *-aya*
-ayāya *-ayāṇaṃ*

From where, in Marathi, the terminations :

-ā *-e*
-eā, yā *eāṃ, yāṃ*

Neuters : only the nominatives differ. In Prākrit they are :

-ayaṃ *-ayāiṃ*

whence in Marathi :

-eṃ *iṃ.*

The feminine nouns in *-ā* are all borrowed. They are declined as the nouns ending in a consonant, derived from old nouns in *-ā.*

2. Nouns in *-i-.* Masculines :

In Prākrit : *iyo* *-iyā*
-iyāya *-iyāṇaṃ*

whence in Marathi :

-ī *-ī*
yā *yāṃ*

The nominative neuters are :

Pkt. *-iyaṃ*>Mar. *-īṃ*
Pkt. *-iyāiṃ*> Mar. *-yeṃ.*

Feminines.—The final feminine in Skt. *-ikā,* rare in Vedic (F. Edgerton, *The k-Suffixes of Indo-Iranian,* I, p. 58, cited by Meillet, *Bul. Soc. Ling.*, 59, p. LIV), has had in Sanskrit (specially in western Sanskrit, see S. Lévi, *Vartakā* "La Caille", JA 1912, p. 513) as in Iranian a greater development in course of time and is used as the normal termination of the feminine gender in the enlarged nouns and adjectives of modern Indo-Aryan. Its forms in Prākrit are :

iyā	*-iyāo*
iyāe	*-iyāṇaṃ*

Whence in Marathi :

-ī	*-yā*
-ie, -ī	*-yāṃ*

The nom. sing. in *-e* has been preserved in the pronouns of poetic language : *te* or *tī* "she".

The oblique sing. *-ie,* common also in the poetic language, is preserved only for the words, *strī* (tats.) and *bī* (*bīja-*).

3. The etymologically regular paradigms of the nouns in *-u-*, obtained according to the same principles as those of the nouns in *-i-*, are as given below :

Singular	Plural
m. *-ū,* n. *-ūṃ,* f. *-ū*	m. *-ū,* n. *-veṃ,* f. *-vā*
m. n. *-vā,* f. *-ve*	m.f.n. *-vāṃ.*

These forms are all partially preserved, but several analogies have disturbed the regularity of the system. Firstly, the oblique sing. fem. has as the oblique sing. of the feminines in *-ī,* become similar to the direct case. On the other hand, the plural direct case of the feminines is reduced to *-ū,* no doubt in imitation of the masculines, whereas the oblique case sing. masc. became, in its turn, similar to the direct case as that of the feminines. Thence as inflexion of the masc.—fem. constituted as follows : direct case sing. and plural *-ū*; oblique case, sing. *-ū,* pl. *-vāṃ.* It can be easily explained that the last stage of levelling, marked by the oblique pl. *-ūṃ* (obtained according to the types in masc. neut. sing. *-ā,* pl. *-āṃ,* fem. sing. *-ī,* pl. *-īm* or sing. *-yā,* pl. *-yāṃ*) be affected in a large number of cases.

The old declension in masculine is preserved only in a small number of cases (whose list, besides, differs according to the grammarians; see for ex. Joshi, p. 98-77; Navalkar, p. 65). In the feminines, the old inflexion is legitimate only in the Konkan. Finally in the neuters is observed a growing interference of the terminations coming from the terminations in *-a-* : the commonest result is as given below :

-ūṃ	*-eṃ*
-ū or *-ā*	*-yāṃ*

In the present state of research, it is impossible to follow the detailed history of these changes.

2. *Traces of other old terminations*

$ 192. In addition to the terminations preserved in living inflexion, and examined upto here, Marathi has preserved certain traces of old indirect cases, beside the genitive and the dative.

Instrumental

$ 193. In various languages, there seem to exist certain forms of the instrumental, whose origin is doubtful (Beames, II, p. 224, Grierson, *Intr. to Maith. Lang.*, p. 44-45). Only in the group of the South-West, there remain certain surely old traces thereof. In Simhalese only the termination --*ena* has remained, which under the form -*en*, -*in* is found in the sing. neut. of the nouns and in the word *visin* (*vaśena*) used as a post-position. It is this very termination which one is tempted to recognise in old Gujarati sing. -*iṃ*, *üṃ*, and in modern forms like *śeṃ* "by whom ?". Lastly, in Marathi the instrumental has been a living case in the old period of the language, and there remain certain fixed forms during the modern period. The terminations of old Marathi also belong to the declension of the nouns in -*a*; but they include those of the singular and plural masc.-neut. and of singular feminine.

1. The termination of the instr. sing. masc.-neut. is -*eṃ* <Skr. -*ena*. In the *Jñāneśvarī*, its examples are numerous. In the old inscriptions are found *Cāvuṇḍarājeṃ* "by the king Cāvuṇḍa" (Śravaṇa Belgola), *gādhveṃ* "by an ass" (Parel), *bāyakeṃ* "by a woman", *senavaieṃ* "by the general", *deveṃ* "by the *god*", *rāeṃ* "by the king', etc. (Pandharpur); *māpeṃ* "according to (with ?) the measure" (Patan).

This termination, in Marathi as everywhere, is almost the only one whose notable traces have survived in the modern period. It is found in the words used as postpositions like *pramāṇeṃ* "the manner of", *mūḷeṃ* "because of", *saṃgeṃ* "in the company of, with", probably *neṃ* "by means of" (*naya*- ?), *saveṃ* and *śīṃ* "with" (Skr. *samam*, *sahitam* with the termination of the instrumental, due to the influence of meaning) and in the forms joined to the post-position *karūṇ* "thanks to that", for ex. *teṇeṃ karūṇ* "thanks to that" (the termination *-eṃ* has been extended to other types of inflexion; *aplyā kṛpeṃ karūṇ* "by your favour" (see Navalkar, $ 353, note).

2. In the plural, the termination is *-īṃ* (Pkt. *-ehiṃ*, Skr. *-ebhiḥ*). Its examples are rare since the oldest texts : *Jñāneśvarī* : *donhīm* "by both" (XVIII, 245, cited by Māḍgāṃvkar), *cinhīṃ* "by the signs" (XVI, 14); inscrip of Pandharpur: *bhaṭīṃ*, *paṇḍitīṃ*. In the modern language *nīṃ*, postposition of the instrumental plural, is the plural form of *neṃ*.

3. In the feminine singular, the termination is *-ā*. Māḍgāṃvkar has given numerous examples thereof in his edition of the *Jñāneśvarī*, p. 12-13. It will suffice to cite here *voja* "by honour", *ātmasukhāciyā goḍiyā* "due to the taste of the egoist pleasure"; similarly, in the inscription of Pandharpur, *deviā* "by the goddess'. Probably it is this termination, which is found again in the adverb *heḷā* (Skr. *helayā*) "easily".

The origin of this form is less clear than that of the masculine terminations. There is in Prākrit, beside the oblique in *-ae*, a termination of the instr.-gen.-loc. in *-āa*, which Vararuci does not accept, but which is preserved in the texts and to which Hemacandra is finally led to lend his authority (Pischel, $ 375). It is probably the same termination as the Pali *-āya*, which has the values of instrumental, genitive, ablative and dative. This termination has most probably its origin in the contamination of gen. -abl. *-ayāḥ*, loc. *-āyām* and instr. *-ayā*, where the first vowel has been lengthened by analogy with other cases, as has been lengthened the *-i* of the fem. pl. Pkt. termination *-īo*. It is this Pali termination *-āya*, Pkt. *-āa*, which we should undoubtedly recognise in the instr. fem. in *-ā*.

Since the oldest period, the instrumental plural is missing for the feminine. It is the oblique which replaces the same (*vividhāṃ pūjāṃ* "by different homages"). It is again the oblique which is used in the plural for the enlarged masculine and neuter nouns and adjectives in *-ā*: *-eṃ* (*śrotāṃ* "by the listeners"; *aisāṃ cinhīṃ* "by such signs").

In the masc. neut. nouns and adjectives in *-ā* : *-eṃ*, the instrumental singular in old Marathi takes a particular form, which at first view looks to be a tatsama. Thus in the

Pāṭan inscription we have : *mādhīcena māpeṃ* "according to the measure used in the temple" and in the Jñāneśvarī *vārena* (=*vāryā neṃ* "by wind", XIII, 24). But in reality the termination is *-nī*. The form *-na* is only a variant, though a rare one thereof. Besides the constancy of the groups of the type of *moheṃ mājireni* ("due to bewilderment and folly", XIV, 253), *taisenī jñāṇeṃ* ("by this knowledge", XVIII, 1100) does not lend much of probability to the á priori restitution of the Sanskrit termination in cases, that are so clearly defined. We have to recognise here the oblique in *-e*, constant in the old texts, followed by a postposition with *n* as initial, no doubt precisely the one that has taken the extension, known to us, in the modern language under the form *neṃ* : *nīṃ*. Thence the confusion that has occurred in certain editions : thus in place of *jānateni* "by one who knows", I, 25, the popular editions have *jānate neṃ*. It is the same postposition which is used, since the oldest texts, with the nouns in *-u*, that is to say, with the enlarged nouns in *-ū*, ex. *vāyūni*.

Locative

$ 194. There are in old Marathi two terminations for the locative, both in the singular : one is *īṃ* and is used with nouns ending in consonants, ex. *pāsīṃ*, masc. "on the coast, near", *veḷīṃ*, fem. "at the time of, in time", *gharīṃ*, neuter "in the house". The other is used with the masc.-neut. in *-ā*, *-eṃ* : ex. *gaḷāṃ*, masc. "in the throat", *cāndināṃ* "in the moonlight", and for adjectives of the same type; ex. *āṃgīṃ mājhyāṃ* "in my body" (*Jñān.*, VI, 139), *prathamīṃ*, *dujāṃ*, *cauthīṃ* (ib., X, 24; cf. the examples cited by Māḍgāṃvkar, p. 15), *īyāṃ pāṭaṇīṃ* "in this town of Patan" (inscrip. of 1128 śaka). It will suffice to recall here the principles for the declension of nouns ending in a consonant and those ending in a long vowel for putting aside the hypothesis of the identity of the two terminations : the two have different origins and have been adapted to two types of inflexion.

Simhalese also has two terminations for the locative, both used with neuter nouns and arbitrarily distributed. According to Geiger, one goes back to Skr. *-e* and the other to Pali *-amhi* (Geiger, $ 38, I, 3). And in fact, in the Prākrit usage the two terminations in *-e* and *-mmi* co-exist in the texts without any possibility of any principle of distribution being recognised therein (Pischel, $ 366a). If these are the terminations that are found in Marathi, it should be admitted that as regards the former, during the period when final *-e* became *-i* (cf. Pkt. *ahme*, M. *āhmī*), this *i* has, probably, been nasalised under the influence of other terminations, like that of the instrumental in *-eṃ* or of the neighbouring locative in *-āṃ*, which has enabled it to subsist.

On the other hand, the identification of the termination *-āṃ* with Pkt. *-ammi* creates phonetic difficulties. The reduction of *-mm-* to *-m-*, itself declining, is altogether abnormal. Should we see herein a special treatment for the end of the word ? Even in this case, it is difficult to understand as to why the final *-i* has not tinged the preceding vowel as in *-eṃ*, the termination of the neut. pl. (Skr. *-āmi*) or of the first pers. sing. (Skr. *-āni*).

Other languages do not present any element for solving this problem. In Panjabi, we find a sing. term. *-oṃ* and pl. *-īṃ*. Beames sees in the form of the singular an ablative. In this case the nasality herein would have come from the plural termination which would have been, not the equivalent of the Marathi locative singular, but an instrumental (Pkt. *-ehiṃ*, *M*. *-īṃ*; in the text of Beames, II, p. 223, line 6 from below, read *is now*... in place of *is not restricted.*)

The locative singular in *-i*, on the contrary, is found in many places. Sindhi has preserved it in the masculine nouns in *-u* (Trumpp, p. 120) and the same is the case in Gujarati (LSI, *Guj*., p. 354). This *-i* had normally been destined to be everywhere dropped. This is why the poems of Tulsi Das abound in locatives without terminations. In the nouns enlarged into *-au* (Pkt. *ao*, M. *-ā*), the locative regularly takes in old Gujarati the form *-ai* (LSI, *Guj*., p. 356). The form in *-e*, which in modern Gujarati has the value of the instrumental and of the locative (*ghoḍe* beside *ghoḍā-e*) undoubtedly represents this termination contaminated with that of the Pkt. ablative in *-āhi*. It is legitimate to suppose that this very confusion explains the Apabhraṃśa termination in *-ahiṃ* like the terminations of old Maithilī in *ahi*, *-ahiṃ* (> *e*, *eṃ*; Grierson, *Introduction to the Maithilī Dial*., $ 78). Or. and Beng. *-e* go go back to this termination and not to the Skr. *-e* (Beames, II, p. 223). The Marathi form in *-īṃ* is independent thereof.

The terminations of the locative as such are dead in modern Marathi. The termination *-īm* is, however, retained in a fixed form in words like *gharīṃ*, *pāśīṃ*, *veḷīṃ*. The form in *-āṃ* furnishes the forms derived from present participles of the type *pāhtāṃ* "on seeing", *kāritāṃ* "for". The distinction of stems is not clearly felt in the Konkan, where one says *śetāṃ* (from *śet*, Skr. *kṣetra-*), *garāṃ* (M. *gharīṃ*), see LSI, *Marathi*, p. 174.

Ablative

$ 195. The ablative masc.-neut. singular in *-āt* has disappeared from India and Ceylon. It seems to subsist only in Romany *-al* (Miklosich, XI, p. 5). The Prakrit *-āo*, which has replaced it, is the base of Sindhi *-āu* (Trumpp., p. 118; according to Beames II, p. 225, the modern termination *-āṃ* is identical to the same. In the case, it would have been felt like a postposition as it is added to the oblique plural), probably also of Panjabi loc. sing. *-oṃ* cited above and postpositions of the type, Hindi *ko*, Sindhi *khauṃ*, *khāṃ*, etc. (Grierson, KZ, XXXVIII, p. 476).

It seems clear that it is the same termination, Pkt. *-āo*, combined with the affix-word *-ni*, *-n*, (p. 204, 261) in the ablative singular of old Marathi in *-auni*, *-onī*, (*meghauni* "of the cloud", *divūni* "since the day", etc.), which subsist uniquely in the words of grammatical function like *kaḍūn*, *pāsūn* (see M. *pāsauni*) "on the side (of)", *āṃtūn* "from within" (cf. Beng. abl. in *-tun* ?) or the adverbs like *māgūn* "after". The poetry and the texts of the Mānbhāv sect have preserved, for marking the ablative with the value of *pāsūn*, a form *pāsāv* which clearly seems to be the ablative of the word *pās* in the pure state. The absence of all aspiration in these old forms and the rarity in the old texts of the juxtaposition, oblique+gerundive of the verb, "to be" *hoūn* (mod. *hūn*), renders improbable the current explanation whereby old M. *-ūn* would be a form derived from the modern one in *-hūn* (cf. Beames, II, p. 234). As will be seen, on the contrary the inverse is more probable. Old M. *-āo* normally culminates in modern M. *-ā*. This renders possible the explanation of the postposition *lā* "for" by a word in the ablative; see infra. $ 200.

$ 196. Thus, except the gen. -dative, old Marathi preserved only some old terminations of indirect cases. Even the little thus left has been reduced to almost nothing during the modern period. The concrete relationships and some of the grammatical relationships must have been then accompanied by affix-words, which we have still to examine.

3. *Postpositions*

$ 197. The reduction in the number of cases, in conformity with a law, observed more than once (cf. Bréal, *Sémantique*, 3rd edn., p. 14 cited in Meillet, *De quelques innovations...* p. 28), has coincided with an increasingly constant usage of accessory words destined to specify the shades of meaning left in obscurity by the use of an unique indirect case. In classical Sanskrit, the number of old indeclinable prepositions gets restricted, but on the other hand, an ever increasing number of nouns fixed in one of their cases and the gerundives shed off, little by little, their original meaning and are used to explain periphrastically the usual relationships (Speyer, *Ved. u. Sanskr. Syntax*, $ 89, 91, 93). This then is the origin of the words or particles fixed to Marathi nouns, which give to modern declension what is incorrectly known as its terminations.

Some of these affixes are clear, such as the word *var* "on", Skr. *upari* : this is the only old indeclinable preserved by the popular language. Similar again are the various forms of the words *-āṃt* "inside" (loc. *āṃt*, abl. *āṃtūṇ*, Skr. *antaḥ*), *kaḍ* "side" obl. *kaḍe*, abl. *kaḍūni*, Skr. *kaṭi-*), *ghar* "house" (loc. *ger* "with" in Konkanī, LSI, *Mar.*, p. 174), *pās* "side" (loc. *pāśīṃ*, abl. *pāsūn*, Skr. *pārśva-*), *māg* "route" (instr. *māgeṃ*, abl. *māgūn*, Skr. mārga-), or the gerundives like *vāṃcun* "except", *hoūn*, *hūn* "from (abl.)". Others like *-si*, *-teṃ*, *lā* "to, towards", *neṃ*, pl. *nīṃ* "by" are obscure. That is why grammarians are in the habit of classifying them differently : "What distinguishes a termination from a postposition, says Joshi, is that the former is not a word, as it has no meaning by itself. It acquires a meaning only in conjunction with the word to which it is affixed" (*Compreh. Gram.* $ 209). He also recognises that some of the postpositions, such as *lāgiṃ*, *sāṭhiṃ*, have no independent existence during the modern period and have the role of true terminations.

Such is, for example, the case of *-ṃt* "termination" of the modern "locative". In reality, this is the word *-āṃt* "interior", which comes either from Skr. *antram*, which is known in Sanskrit only in the sense of "entrails", cf. *antara-* "interior" or from Skr. *antaḥ* (Pali and Prākrit *anto*) "inside". In old Marathi this word is still independent. We find in the Jñāneśvarī, *gāṃvā āṃtu*, VI, 311; *sarpakuḷā āṃt*, X, 242; *akṣarāṃ āṃt*, X, 269; *guḍhāṃ āṃt*, X, 298 (here the words are separated by the rhythm : *guḍhāṃ* rhymes with *puḍhāṃ*) and even with the intercalation of a particle, *tayā āghaveyāṃ ci āṃt*, XI, 586 (in *varṣāṃtīṃ*, XV, 285, it is the locative of *-anta-* : "at the end of the rains"). Are found in Tukaram and Eknath, *sabhe āṃt* and even in Moropant *tumhāṃ āṃt* (examples cited by Godbole, *A New Gram.*, 3rd edn., p. 131). But since Namdev the affixation is produced in favourable cases : *kṣīrasāgarāṃt* (*Navanīt*, p. 16), similarly in Tukaram: (ibid., p. 48) or Vāman : *toṃḍāṃt*, *divasāṃt* (ibid., p. 129). It is generalised in the modern language : thence, for ex., the forms *nadīṃt*, *katheṃt*.

There is no prohibition against supposing that other postpositions might have had a similar evolution; but notably those which express grammatical relationships are often so changed that it becomes almost impossible to reconstruct their history.

In fact, this interpretation encounters two types of difficulties :

1. The words that are so affixed have, by becoming grammatical tools, possibly undergone a considerable change of meaning beyond the realm of conjecture. Such is the word *mārga-* "path", which has taken on the sense of "behind, after" in Mar. *māgeṃ māgūn*. The same evolution of sense is, no doubt, to be seen in Kash. *path*, *pata*, if this word goes back to Skr. *panthan* (the word denoting "*path*" in Kashmiri is *wath*, that is to say, Skr. *vartman-*, M. *vāṭ*). Similarly in Pali,

piṭṭhe, whose original sense is "on the back", comes to denote not only "on" (*sayanpiṭṭhe* "on the bed", *vālukāpiṭṭhe* "on the sand") but "in" (*samugggapiṭṭhesu*, lit. "on the backs of boxes", "in the boxes"; examples taken from the note to *Mahāvastu*, edn., of Senart, I, p. 624). This very word in the form *peṭh*, *peṭhi* in Kashmiri denotes "on" and "in", and in another case, undoubtedly the ablative, *peṭha* signifies "from above, since, during" (Grierson, *Man. Kashm.*, II, p. 123-4; Grierson gives this etymology only as a possibility in his *Piśāca Lang.*, p. 35).

2. Because of its accessory position and because of their semantic weakness, these words are often subjected to an irregular phonetic evolution. We have seen the loss of the vowel in *āṃt*. One of the better-known examples of the same fact is that of Skr. *madhya-*. This word is correctly preserved in Marathi in the form, *māj* "belt" and it is the tatsama *madhyeṃ* (with spontaneous or analogical nasalisation of the postpositions in the instrumental, *māgeṃ mūleṃ*, *kāraṇeṃ*, *neṃ*, etc.) which is used for constructing the periphrastic locative. But in other languages, where besides, the phonetically correct form often exists in the sense of "circle, belt, etc." the word has undergone changes, that can not be explained by ordinary phonetic rules. In Sindhi, beside *maṃjhāṃ* "out of", we find *me* "in", *māṃ*, *moṃ* and above all, *meṃ* "in". This example will suffice to show the imprevisible accidents undergone by these accessory words, that mislead the historian. One is thus left, for postpositions whose sense is not immediately apparent, to hypotheses chiefly destined to render, as far as possible, account of the forms assumed by the same word in various languages. Because it is perhaps more urgent to classify the forms than to explain them. The remarks that follow should be read taking these reservations into account.

The postpositions are of two types : the indeclinables are nouns fixed to certain cases or the words originally indeclinable. The most important ones, which are at the same time the most obscure, are those that express, during the various periods of the language, the relations of "dative" and of "instrumental." Only one postposition is declinable : it is an adjective of belonging, generally designated as a "genitive."

1. *Postpositions of the Dative*

-si, -s

$ 198. This is the only postposition, among others, of the dative which has remained alive during all the periods of the language. If it is missing in the inscription of Patan (it is the oblique above which has the sense of the dative : *maḍhā dinhalā* "given to the temple"), it is found in that of Pandharpur (*viṭṭhala-deva-rāyāsi*, *teyāsi* "to him"). In Jñāneśvar and later poets despite the competition of the independent oblique case and other postpositions, it is frequent. In the form *-s*, it is current in the Bakhars and even today it is in frequent use in the Deś and in constant use in the Konkan.

Generally this postposition in *-s* is related to the Skr. genitive in *-sya* (cf. Grierson, KZ, XXXVIII, p. 981; the latest to write is Lesny, JRAS, 1911, p. 179). If it is admitted that the oblique sing. in *-ā* is an old dative, then we are no longer obliged to suppose two developments of the same termination in the same language—an improbability that has not stopped any of the learned so far—and the current hypothesis becomes *à* priori, plausible. But then it meets with other difficulties. Without talking of the meaning, which is always that of the direct or indirect object, and never the possessive or partitive one, the form itself interdicts this explanation. On the one hand, as has been remarked by Rajvade (*Śrī Jñāneśvarīṃṭīl maraṭhī bhāṣeceṃ vyākaraṇ*, p. 11), this explanation does not specifically take into account the old form, *-si* of whom *-s* is only a normal alteration; because Skr. *-sya*>Pkt. *-ssa*. On the other hand, it will apply, if it must be admitted, only to the gen. sing. of consonantal masc.-neuters. Not only the plural of the same nouns (*meghāṃsi*, II, 14), but the forms of other types of inlexion (*dṛṣṭisi*, *rucisi* I, 23, 35); *tuṃhāṃsi*, IV, 42) would remain unexplained, except by an improbable analogical extension. In reality, everything happens as if *-si*, *-s* had been added to the various forms of the oblique[1]—of the substantives and the pronouns.

1. Rajvade (ibid., p. 10) has recognised in *-ā* of the type *putās*, old termination of the dative *-āya*. It is curious that it has not led him to similarly explain the genitive in *-ā*, i. e., the oblique itself (cf., ibid., p. 13.)

This is what has led Rajvade to the ingenious idea of putting together the adverb, *āspās* "all around", composed of two words in the locative (cf. S. *āsipāsi*, W. Panj. *āsepāse*). The second is *pās* = Skr. *pārśve*, the former, for which Rajvade constructs an etymology that is not acceptable, is probably the locative of the Pkt. word, *assa-*, Skr. *aśra-* "side", still found in independent form in Deśī (*asayaṃ nikaṭaṃ*) and in Simhalese (*as* "side", corner", no. 993 in Geiger, *Etym. wōrt.*). If the proposed etymology is exact, we should admit that the initial *ā-* has been reduced in the same way as that of *āṃt* later on (cf. $ 197).

Whatever be the etymological interpretation of this affix, it should, in any case, be clearly distinguished from another affix with *s-*, that is *śīṃ* "with". This word is undoubtedly related to *sahita-*, of which it is a locative or an instrumental. Whereas *-si* "to" is known only to Marathi, probably also to Bhili, the obl. pl. in *-es*, LSI, *Bhil. Lang.*, p. 3), its role elsewhere being played, above all, by the words in *k-* (exceptional in the Marathi area, traces being found in the coastal dialects, see Joshi, *Comp. Gram.*, p. 142), or in *-r*, the word *śīṃ* "with" is found in almost all the suffixes in *-s* of other dialects : Simhal. *hā ihi* "with", Rom. *sa* "with", Kashm. *sütin* "by", Sindhi *sā, sāu, sẽ, senu* "with", Guj. *suṃ* "with", Konkani *sū* "of (abl.)", *sī* among", Braj. *so*, Raj. *saī, sū* "of", Hindi *se* "with" (cf. the use with the verbs *milnā* "to meet each other ", *bolnā* "to talk" or the expressions like *bahut sāmān se ānā* "coming with a lot of luggage"), "of, by", Nep. *sita* "of", Bhojp. and Magahi *se*, Maith. *sā, sāu* "by". The concordance of meanings and forms shows that this is clearly some other word, common to Marathi and to almost all other related languages (Panjabi in the west and the far eastern group, Oriya, Bengali, Assamese seem to ignore this word. Panjabi *sī* "upto" as Sindhi *sīa*, of the same sense, are taken to, and in all probability Skr. *sīmā* by Trumpp, *Sindhi Gram.*, p. 401). This word seems to be found in another case (the instrumental) and with a special use in the dialects of Berar, Konkan and at Bijapur in the forms *-śeni, -śyāni, -sanyā*, with the termination of the gerundive (LSI, *Mar.*, 50, 67, 92, 222).

The question now arises, whether the word *sāṭhīṃ* (*sāṭīṃ* ?)

should be attached to the suffix *s* indicating direction. According to an hypothesis of Hoernle (*Comp. Gram.*, $ 365), this word is composed of *-s* + a case of the word derived from Skr. *artha-*. This explanation, acceptable if *-s* had been the termination of the genitive, becomes more difficult with the interpretation proposed above or some similar one. The word *sāṭhīṃ* is probably an independent one, related to Gujarati *saṭ* "exchange"; cf. $ 89, 114.

The postposition *stav* "for" is also perhaps an independent word. It has been proposed with some degree of probability to recognise therein the tatsama *prastava*, "occasion, circumstance", shortened because of its accessory role. A difficulty, provisionally insoluble, arises, however, from the fact that texts of the *Mānbhāv* sect show a suffix of the ablative *-tav* beside *-stav*. Can we then say that *stav* is a compound of *s-* + *tav* ? In that case *tav* would be, either the Skt. word *tāvat*, moreover preserved in Marathi (cf. *ājtaṃv* vulg. "uptill today"), or the ablative of the word whose postposition *teṃ*, which we will now examine would be the instrumental.

teṃ

$ 199. This postposition, very liberally used in the oldest literary texts, disappears from usage very early, even in poetry, except with the pronouns of the first and second persons singular, where the monosyllabic forms were avoided (cf. infra, $ 200). Rajvade (ibid., p. 12) remarks that the *Christian Purāṇ* writes *theṃ*; similar is the case with his manuscript of the *Jñāneśvarī*. He brings in, a phonetically correct and semantically probable manner, this *theṃ* to Skr. *arthena*. In fact, the Pandharpur inscription has it with the tatsama as *Śrīviṭṭhalarāyā arthe*. This is, then, the *theṃ* from which, according to Rajvade ,*-teṃ* would have developed. But the aspirate-less form is found earlier than the other one and it is known that the *Christian Purāṇ* is written in the Konkani dialect. It seems that we have to distinguish here two series :

1. *theṃ*, probably dialectal and related to the forms of the ablative in Bhili, *tho*, *ho-*, Panj. *tho*, Guj. *thī* "of, with".

In dialectal Gujarati there is even a declinable adjective *tho* "coming from" (Grierson, KZ, XXXVIII p. 476). Despite the deviation in meaning, we can accept that it is the Skr. *artha-* : cf. with the cerebral, the Oriya *ṭhū* "from (abl.)" in relation to Simhalese *aṭ* "for".—Beames, (II, p. 218), would propose for H. *taim* an etymology by Skr. *sthāne*. There is, in fact, a family of postpositions surely linked with the root *sthā* : Beng. *thakeyā*, the gerundive used as the termination for the oblique, *thāne* of ablative or *ṭhāre* "in", *ṭhārū* "of". These words seems to be peculiar to the eastern group.

2. *teṃ*, belonging to a series found everywhere except in Simhalese, Gujarati and in the western part of Rajasthan : *te* "towards, in" (preposition and postposition), Panj. *te* "from (abl.)", western Panj. *to*, *tõ*, *tū* "of", *te* "to, in", Sindhi *te* "on", *tõ*, *to* "from above", *te*, *tāī*, *toī* "upto", Raj. of the north-east *taī* "of", Braja *te* "of", Hindi *tāi* "upto"; to, Bih. *te* 'by", Beng. *te* "by" (rare; cf. *hoite*) Or. *te* "in, of" (cf. Beames, II, 222, 273). But how to render account of this particle ? None of the proposed explanations seems to prevail. Bhandarkar sees therein the pronominal for *ehiṃ*, given by Hemacandra as being equivalent in the Apabhraṃśa to Skr. *arthe* (IV, 425). It remains, however, to be known if the Apabhraṃśa forms *tehiṃ* and *kehiṃ* themselves are not transcriptions of **ke*(*ṃ*) and *te*(*ṃ*). Moreover, *-ehiṃ* should yield in Marathi *-īṃ* (cf. $ 63) and neither the forms of other languages nor the evolution of meaning is explained thereby. The only thing to remain is the hypothesis of a substantive, besides rendered probable by constructions like Hindi *is ke taiṃ* "to him", *śahr ke taiṃ gayā* "gone to the town", but nothing allows us to decide as to which substantive can this be. Is it the Skr. *nimitta--* "motive, reason", or a word of the *tan-* family (cf. Lat. *tenus* "upto", Avadhi *tan tanā* "towards, to, like", Grierson, KZ, op. cit., p. 484) ? In any case, it is probably not related to *ante*, *antike*, because if the Marathi form would be squarely in accord with this explanation, the languages of the north-west would not have contradicted it, which they do. The consonant therein is a surd and we know that *nt* herein normally becomes *nd* (cf. $ 82).

lā

$ 200. This affiix is missing in the oldest texts and appears only in Namdev, where it is used only with monosyllabic personal pronouns, that is to say, with those in the singular. Thus we have beside *tya*, *maja* and *tutem̟*, etc., *majlā*, *tylā* and *malā*, *tulā* in relation to *amhām̟si*, *tyāsi*, *koṇāsi*, *sarvāṇgāsi*. In Tukaram its use spreads and here also it is mostly used with the pronouns. In the one hundred and ninety-four abhangs given in the *Navnīt*, are found *tulā* twice, *malā* once, *tyālā* five times, *kaśālā* and *jyālā* once but a form like *vāthyālā* "in the stomach" is unique.

In the historical texts of the 18th century, its usage seems to be more restricted and the only usual forms are those in *-s*. The Bakhars present more or less the same aspect as the poems of Tukaram. Lastly in the ballads and in the recent texts, *-lā* is constant and almost unique. It is by basing himself on the recent character of the usage of this affix that Rajvade (*l. l.*, p.12; cf. *Marāṭhyām̟cyā itihāsācīm̟ sādhaṇem̟*, VIII, *upaprastavanā*, p. 57 ff.) has had the idea of seeing therein a loan and specifically that of the Persian *rā*. In addition to the phonetic absurdity of this *rapprochement*, it should be noted that for Rajvade, *lā* appears only during the time of Shivaji and of Tukaram. In reality it is older, as it is found in Namdev (Rajvade recognises this fact, *l. l.*, p. 57). Moreover, nothing prevents us from supposing that it is still older : because if *lā* appears only in Namdev, the same is the case with *ām̟t* and *nem̟*, one surely and the other almost surely old. Their appearance in Namdev and Tukaram is due to the popular character of these poets and probably these postpositions are missing in Jñānadev, exactly as they are missing three centuries later in Eknath or later still in Mahīpati, because they are the learned poets. Undoubtedly for the same reason, the official texts of the 18th century are more reserved in the use of *lā* than the popular ballads. Nothing, therefore, prevents, as á priori, from seeking an etymology for this word in Marathi itself.

The word *lā* dialectally takes the forms *lī*, *le* (LSI, *Mar.* p. 81, 220ff). Similar is the case with the Bhil dialects (ibid., *Bhil Lang.*, p. 95, 158, 205). It is found also, undoubtedly, in Sindhi *lāe* "because of, for", West. Panj. *lā* "from (abl.), Panj. and Hindi *lo* "upto", Hindi *le* "with", Nep. *lāi* "to", *le* "by", Bih. *lā* "for."

In the same usage there exists a word which seems to be related to the former and which is found, on the one hand in Gujarati-Rajasthani and in Bengali on the other, where *lā* does not seem to have an equivalent : it is Mar. *lāgīṃ* "near, towards", Simhalese *laṅga* "near", Guj. *lāgu* "near", Nep. *lāgi* "for, on account of", beside *laī* "to, for", Sindhi *lāge* "in view of", H. and Bih., old Beng. *lāgi* "for". This word is surely a locative of the past participle in Prākrit *lagga-* from the root *lag-* "to fall", cf. Mar. *lāgṇoṃ* and related words; *lāgīṃ* denotes, therefore, "touching" (Beames, II, 26., Hoernle, p. 222).

It is tempting to put together these two words. Bhandarkar also proposes to see in Mar. *lā*, the gerundive of *lāgayati*, Pkt. *lāivi*. The relationship between *lā* and *lāgīṃ* in that case would be more or less that between *lāiṇeṃ* and *lāgṇeṃ* , atleast concerning their formation. Truly speaking this hypothesis can clearly explain the forms like Nep. *lāi*, H. *le* and by a deviation (by appealing to the infinitive *lāiuṃ*) Panj. *lo* for example. But specifically in Marathi, the gerundive in -*i* has never existed and moreover -*ai* should have been shortened to -*e* and if it concerned **lāiuṃ*, the resultant would, undoubtedly, have been similar to the form in Panjabi. The same objections would apply to an interpretation by the root *lā-* "to take" (Pkt. ger. *laï*, Pischel, $ 594) which would suggest the form of Simhalese *lāva* "by, with", the ger. of *lanu* "to take", Moreover, the root *lā-* has been replaced in Prākrit and in the modern languages by *le-*: Mar. *leṇeṃ*, Hindi *lenā*, whose oblique participle *liye* has, in fact, taken the sense of "in view of, for", etc.

A more satisfactory interpretation has been proposed by by Hoernle (*Comp. Gram.*, p. 225), who sees in Mar. *lā*, Sindhi *lāi*, Nep. *lāi*, the Skr. locative *lābhe* "to the profit of." To make this etymology phonetically correct, we have to see in the forms in -*ā* and -*ŏ* other cases of the same word; Mar. *lā* will be sufficiently well explained by the ablative in Pkt. **lāhā* or **lāhāo*.

In this case we will have to separate the indeclinable *lā*

from the adjective called "genitive" of Konkani *lo, li lem̥* (Beames, II, p. 276), which seems to be only an abbreviation of the more current form *gelo*. This *gelo* is the past part. of the verb "to go" (Mar. *gelā*) which has taken the sense "belonging to". And in fact all the postposition of the dative in Marathi seem to be the fixed forms of substantives and to no one of them seems to correspond the adjective of belonging. It is known that many other languages have an entirely different aspect (Grierson, KZ, XXXVIII, p. 476).

2. *Postposition of the Instrumental*

sing. *nem̥*, pl. *nīm̥*

$ 201. This affix, absent from the oldest literary texts, is found in an inscription of 1397 (*daḷavaiyā nem̥*; see Rajavade, *Marāṭhayām̥cyā itihāsācīm̥ sādhanem̥* part 8, Preface, p. 33) and is found in literature among the popular poets, (for ex. Namdev : *tayā nem̥*, *Navanīt*, p. 18, 21, *vālmīkā nem̥ evaḍhyānem̥*, ibid., p. 19, *Harīnem̥*, *āvaḍīnem̥*, p. 22, *pakṣiśvāpadām̥ nīm̥*, p. 23, *viyogā nem̥*, *cinte nem̥*, p. 24).

In the Konkan, it takes the forms of *n*, *na*, *nī* (LSI, *Mar.*, p. 66, and is dialectally found with the sense of "to" : *manā* "to me", ibid., p. 161).In old Marathi its forms in- *ni* form the termination of the instrumental in the enlarged nouns and adjectives (cf. $ 193), and *-ni* or *-niyām̥* are added to the ablative of the nouns (cf. $ 195) and probably to the gerundive of the verbs (infra). In Mavchī *ne* expresses the relationship of the ablative, in Dehvalī that of the dative (LSI, *Bhil Lang.*, p. 95, 158). These two values of the word are found in other central languages, atleast during modern times: Guj. *ne* "for", Raj. *ne, nai* "for" and "by" (LSI, *Raj.*, p. 7), Panj. *nai* "by", *nū* "to", Braj *n*, Hindi *ne* "by". The same word appears in a declined form, in the use of the adjective of belonging in certain dialects of the Konkan (LSI, *Mar.*, p. 132), in Gujarati (*no, nī, nūm̥*) and dialectally in west. Panjabi (*nām̥, nīm̥*; see Wilson, *Gram. of Western Panj.*, p. 30). It is missing at the extreme points of the Indo-Aryan domain. It is not found either in the eastern group or in Simhalese and (in the N-W., Kashm. *nu* is put by Grierson in the same series, ibid., p. 477; but the form given by him in his *Manual of Kashm. Lang.*, I, p. 34, that is *unu*-, does not agree with this interpretation).

Several hypotheses, of whom not one is definitive, have been or can be proposed for rendering account of this affix.— 1. The identification of the suffixes with *l*- and with *n*-, the phoneme *l*- being considered as the original, is admitted by Hoernle (*Comp. Gram.*, $ 375, 2), but the passage of *l* to *n*, normal in the eastern dialects, which are cited by him, can not be admitted elsewhere; 2. the Skr. suffix -*lāna*- reported by Beames (II, p. 287 ff.) and Grierson (KZ, XXXVIII, p. 473, 477, 489) should also be probably rejected. In fact the intervocalic *n* is everywhere cerebralised in Prakrit and the Apabhraṃśa texts give the form in *tāṇa*. For explaining the dental of Marathi and probably even of Gujarati, regardless of what Beames may think thereof (II, p. 288), it will have to be supposed that the suffix is borrowed from an eastern dialect. This hypothesis, however, is supplementary and can not be verified, all the more so as the word appears late in other dialects like Marathi (Beames, II, p. 267 ff.), 3. a word related to the root *tan*- (wherefrom, besides, is derived the Skr. suffix -*tana*-, originally having a purely temporal sense, see Brugmann, *Grundriss*, 2nd edn., II, 1, $ 197) is found in certain modern speeches (Beames II, p. 289; Grierson, ibid., p. 484). Probably this is precisely the word, and not the old Sanskrit suffix, which is transcribed by the Apabhr. *taṇa*- "relative to", but its initial *t* is kept intact and if it has an equivalent in Marathi, it is improbable that it be *neṃ* : *nīṃ*; 4. The gradation, sing. *neṃ*, pl. *nīṃ*, leads us to look for a substantive as the origin of the affix, cf. Pali *piṭṭhe* : *piṭṭhesu*. The question then arises if it is the Skr. *naya* "reason, method, means" (*cf. mahīṃ dharmanayena pālaya*, *Jātakamālā*, Kern edn., p. 17, l. 2) or *nyāya*- "rule, manner" (cf. H. *nāīṃ* "in the manner of...") ? The difficulty crops up due to the use of the word as an adjective. It is moreover possible that this usage be due to an extension of analogy; 5. we could think, for explaining this use, of a participle like the Skr. *nī*-, Pkt. *ne*; the word would then signify "led by, resulting from". In this hypothesis, the difficulty arises due to the use of the indirect cases of the word, the locative, instrumental sing. and plural. For the time being we should not draw any conclusion : probably the truth lies in a combination of the two last hypotheses set out above.*

3. *Adjectives of Belonging, called "genitive"*

cā, cī, ceṃ, etc.

$ 202. This adjective is normally constructed with the oblique of nouns and pronouns; it is also affixed to certain indirect cases (*gharīṃ-cā* "from inside the house"; cf. *gharīṃ-hūn*, *gharāṃtūn* "outside the house") and in the direct cases of consonantal nouns (*gharcā* "of the house, familiar", *sakāḷcā* "of yesterday", *Gujrāth cā* "of Gujarat").—Its use is as old as the Marathi language itself; it seems to be already announced in the form of possessive adjectives *amheccaya-*, *tumheccaya-* "ours, yours" noted by Hemacandra in his grammar (II, 149; cited by Hoernle, p. 238).

One or several adjectival affixes of the same type or playing the same role are found in all the languages of the continent. Simhalese is the only one which differs from the rest on this point; the relation of the genitive herein is expressed by an indeclinable word *ge* (Skr. *gṛhe*) which originally denotes "at the house of". The eastern group also seems to be an exception; but this exception is only apparent, because the affixes in *-r* are really the adjectives that are normally invariable in the languages wherefrom the inflexion has disappeared (cf. Grierson, KZ, 38, p. 487).

But if the adjectives in use like *cā* are common, the Marathi word itself remains remarkably isolated and that in two ways. Firstly, it will suffice to refer to the tables given by Grierson in his article on case-suffixes (ibid., p. 474-5) to observe that no other language has a declinable affix with a palatal surd as initial, playing the role of the adjective of belonging. Moreover, there is nowhere in Marathi, a fixed form of the same word used as a postposition. Now these forms coexist with all the other adjectives, either in the same language or in another. Grierson has given numerous examples thereof in the article cited above (p. 476 ff). To the examples of words with *k-* as initial cited by him, we can also add *kā*,

* The most convincing etymology is traced by Tessitori (1913), according to whom *nain, naï, nî, ni, ne* is a shortening of *kanhaïṃ* found in Old Rajasthani texts. *Kanhaïṃ* (< Apabhramsha *kaṇṇahî*) comes from the reconstructed * *karṇasmin* (< Sanskrit *karṇe*), a locative form meaning "aside, near".

the suffix of the dative in Konkani (LSI, *Mar.*, p. 172) and *kerehi* which is used for forming the locative in Simhalese (Geiger, $ 30, A b, 7). Similarly with reference to Panj. *dā* : *dī* are found *de*, *do* used along with *te* and *lā* to express the relations of the instrumental and of dative in Sāmvedī (LSI, *Mar.*, p. 148). We can also compare the instr. in *he*, *e* of the same dialect and the declinable suffix in *tho*, *ho* of Gujarati and of the neighbouring dialects (LSI, *Bhil Lang.*, p. 3), of whom one case-form *thī* is used as the termination of the ablative in Gujarati. The Sindhi form *jo* alone seems to be isolated as the Marathi one. There is also in the same language a termination of the gerundive *-ije* which Grierson reports (ibid., p. 483). In any case the Konkani form *jūn*, the termination of the ablative should be separated therefrom (LSI, *Mar.*, p. 66), as it is in reality the gerundive of *jā-* 'to be'' (past part. of M. word *jālā*, mod. M, *jhālā*) and thus exactly corresponds to the Marathi termination *hūn*, *ūn*, which is the gerundive of *ho-* "to become', to be". The absence of the fixed case-form of *cā* in Marathi seems to be the correlative of the isolation of the suffixes of the dative, which in Marathi have no longer any declinable equivalent (on the possible relationship, but with little probability, of *lā* with Konkani *lo* (*gelo*), see $ 200).

This isolation of the Marathi word makes it difficult to find out its origin. The most satisfying explanation has been proposed by Grierson, on the suggestion of Sten Konow (ibid., p. 490). A large number of similar suffixes can be explained as being the participles, drawn notably from the verbs "to make", "to be", "to give" (the etymology of Panj. *dā* : *dī* given by Hoernle, refuted by Grierson, is more acceptable than the altogether abnormal archaism proposed by the latter. In view of the geographical prioximity of Kashm. *handu* on the one hand and Sindhi and Marwari *hando* on the other, one could also think of the present part. of the verb "to be"); cf. the interpretations pointed out above of Mar. *neṃ* and *lā*. That would be the participle of obligation *kṛtya-* found in the *Mahāvastu* in a role already near that of the modern adjectival affixes (see the examples cited, ibid., p. 486) to be derived by Mar. *cā*. In that case, the word would not be completely isolated. Kashmiri possesses an adjective *kyutu* (fem. *kits-ü*) which is constructed witht he dative of the nouns and takes the sense of "for" : now *kyut-* comes from Skr, *kṛtya-* as the suffix of the gerundive *-ith* comes from *-tya* (Grierson, ibid., p. 480).

Grierson seems to personally prefer another explanation to this one, which he has borrowed from Beames, and which is also supported by Bhandarkar (see Joshi, p. 144). According to these authors, M. *cā* would go back to a suffix of the Skr. adjective *-tya-*. Grierson even believes himself to be able to recognise the distribution of the uses of *-tya-* on the one hand with an indeclinable of the type of *ihatya*, *tatratya* and on the other with a word fixed in an oblique case of the of *dakṣiṇātya*, *pāścātya*, *dūretya* in the two uses of M. *cā* on the one hand with the stem (*gharcā*) and on the other with the oblique (*gharācā*). It is no use showing as to how much this interpretation is forced. But the Skr. suffix *-tya-* can be usefully invoked to explain the type *gharcā*. On the model of *dūretya*, etc., it has been possible to form a series of the type * *gṛhetya*, **araṇyetya*, of whom the Marathi *gharcā*, *rāncā* would be the normal development, not only from the point of view of phonetics, but also from the point of view of sense, because this derivation also takes into account the difference existing between *gharā cā* "of the house", cf. Eng. *of the house*, and *gharcā* "relating to the house, familiar", Eng. *household* (cf. Navalkar, $ 104 note).

Relatives, Demonstratives, Interrogatives, etc.

$ 203. The relative pronoun *jo* (Skr. *ya-*) has only one stem, and is declined as an adjective with a normal enlargement.

		Masc.	Fem.	Neut.
Sing.	dir.	*jo*	*jī* (M. verb *je*)	*jeṃ*
	obl.	*jyā*	*ji* („ „ *jiye*)	*jyā-*
Pl.	dir.	*je*	*jyā*	*jīṃ*
	obl.	*jyāṃ*	*jyāṃ*	*jyāṃ*

Its correlative *to*, *tī* (*te*), *teṃ*, which is also used as the demonstrative of the distant object, is similarly declined.

The demonstrative of the near-by objects is *hā*, *hī*, *heṃ*, obl. sing. *hyā* (*yā*), *hī* (*ī*), obl. pl. *hyāṃ* (*yāṃ*), etc.

In the demonstratives, *j* is frequently inserted in the wake of the oblique ex. *tyājlā*. This morpheme has no etymological value and is derived from personal pronouns like *maj-lā*, *tuj-lā* "to me, to you."

The characteristic principle of these forms is to have pushed as far as possible the tendency, already notable in Prākrit (Pischel, $ 524) of identification with the nominal inflection. Without talking about the demonstrative *hā*, which betrays itself as being recent because of the absence of a sure etymology and because of its absolutely identical form with that of any adjective (cf. $ 160), the demonstrative *to* has the trace of an extension of the oblique stem, of whom another example is furnished by Gujarati *te* alone. The Romany, Kashmiri, Sindhi and the central and eastern languages have preserved the gradation of the type *sa*: *sā*, *tad*: *tasya*, etc. (Beames, II, p. 315; Miklosich, XI, p. 16; Grierson, *Kashm. Lang.*, $ 32, p. 40; Simhalese has lost this pronoun, see Geiger, $ 47, II, $ 48).

Like the stems, the terminations have been assimilated to those of the nominal declension. Marathi, like Jaipuri and Marwari have preserved, in the correlatives, the distinction of the masculine and feminine, lost elsewhere (Grierson, *Ind. Ant.*, XXX, p. 554). Among these terminations, only the pronominal termination, in masc. sing. in *-o* remains; this is archaic.

If the form of the pronouns has been modified, its usage has remained unchanged. On the one hand, the stem of Skr. *ya-* still retains in Marathi and in all the Indian languages, its value of a relative. It is known that this fact is unique in the entire Indo-European group (Meillet, MSL, XVIII, p. 242). On the other hand, the demonstratives have preserved their full meaning and Marathi does not possess the definite article. Here again Marathi is in agreement with the cognate languages. The only exception is Romany and that too on two points. One of its demonstratives has the value of the article, a fact which Miklosich considers as a loan from Greek. On the other, it is the interrogative pronoun, which has replaced the old relative. It is probable that the migrations of the Gypsies have something to do with this innovation (Miklosich, XII, p. 10, 11).

$ 204. Different from the demonstratives, the interrogative pronoun still has a stem for neuter, different from that of the masc.-fem. The forms of masc.-fem. are common :—

	Sing.	Pl.
Dir.	*koṇ*	*koṇ*
Obl.	*koṇā*	*koṇāṃ*

The origin of these forms is doubtful. According to Beames, all of them come from the Pkt. masc. nom. *ko uṇa*, Skr. *kaḥ punaḥ*; cf. Apabh. *kavaṇa-*; see H. *kaun* (and the correl. H. verb *taun*), Panj. *kauṇ*, Guj. *koṇ* (beside *kao*, fem. *kaī*, N. *kauṃ*) are in fact the forms proper to the nominative (Beames, II, p. 323; cf. 314, 326).

In the neuter, the nominative is *kāy* (*kādṛk*), the oblique sing. *kasā* or better *kaśā*, Mar. word *kāsayā* (etymological type **kādṛksāya* or *kādrśkāya* or *kasya*+the termination of the oblique of enlarged nouns ?). The old Skr. nom.-acc. *kim* seems to have been preserved with the value of conjunction : *kīm* "that" (but probably it is a locative; cf. the enlarged locative *kāṃ* "why ?"); *kiṃ* is clearly found only in Simhalese (*kimda*, cf. *kisi*=Skr. *kiṃcit*; Geiger, $ 49, 51); it is undoubtedly Beng., Or. *ki*, Panj. *kī*, perhaps H. *kyā*, obl. *kis* (Pkt. *kissa*); Guj. and Sindhi are aberrant (Beames, III, p. 324).

$ 205. The reflexive (cf. Beames, II, p. 328 ff.) is *āpaṇ*, which goes to the stem of the Skr. oblique *ātman-*. The same is the case with Bengali (*āpni*) and Oriya (*āpaṇ* beside *āpe*) on the one hand and in the entire N.W. on the other,: S. *pānu*, Kashm. *pāna*, etc. (Grierson, *Piś. Lang.*, p. 76, see the word *self*). Elsewhere the form is that of the nominative *ātmā* : H., Panj., Guj. *āp*, Nep. *āphu*, etc. The stem of other cases has been used to form the possessive adjective : H. *āpnā*, Panj. *āpṇā*, Guj. *āpṇo*, Nep. *āphnu*. The distribution has been disturbed in Rajasthani because there *āp* often takes the sense "ourselves" inclusive (cf. LSI, *Raj.*, p. 9, 23, 38, 46, 56). Similarly in Simahlese, *api* is used as a personal pronoun of the first pers. plural, *tamā* of the reflexive (Geiger, $ 37, 51). In Marathi and Sindhi, the distribution is inversely to other central languages : it is *āp-* which has provided the possessive : S. *pāhaṃ jo*, *jī*, etc., *Māplā* (later Pkt. *appulla-*).

$ 206. Marathi possesses a sufficiently large number of adjectives and adverbs drawn from pronominal stems. Some are old, as *jaisā* "such as (*yādṛśa-*), *jai*, *jaiṃ* "if, when "(*yadi*) *jauṃ* "till", (*yāvat*). Most of them go back at the most to Prākrit, as the Mar. word *jetī* "as much as", *itkā*, *titkā* "as much" (Pkt. *ettia-*, *tettia-*, see Pischel, $ 153), *etheṃ*, see M. *eth* (Pkt. *ettha*, arisen according to Pischel, $ 107, from Vedic *itthá*), *edhvāṃ* "then", (Pkt. *eddaha-*) and are no less obscure. Lastly, certain adverbs or conjnnctions are the fixed pronominal forms like *kāṃ* (loc.) "why", *jeṃ* (nom. -acc. neut., like Skr. *yat*) "that". It need not be pointed out that here analogy has multiplied and normalised the forms and this since a very old period; thence probably their etymological obscurity.

Personal Pronouns

$ 207. The pronouns of the first and second persons present a large variety of aspects in the Prakrit texts and a still larger variety among the grammarians (Pischel, $ 416). However, the modern forms, despite the obscurity of some among them, can be brought to forms that are easy to analyse and neighbour the nominal declension. It is difficult to decide if the complication of Prakrit is due to a disequilibrium, real and prolonged in usage, or whether on the contrary the new forms having been established sufficiently early, and having appeared since thento be out of harmony with the literary tradition, learned reconstructions could be made in diverse arbitrary ways.

1. *Direct and Oblique Cases*

$ 208. The clearest forms are those of the plural. Those of the nominative *āhmī, tuhmī* go back to Pkt. *amhe, tumhe* which are, by their origin, forms of the indirect case (Ved. *asmé, yuṣmé,* cf. Skr. Ved. and class. *asmā́n, asmā́bhiḥ,* etc.). The stem of the nominatives has thus disappeared, here as in the case of the pronominal adjectives, before those of other cases.—The forms of the oblique *āhmāṃ, tuhmāṃ* represent Pkt. *amhāṇaṃ, tuṃhāṇaṃ,* whose termination is borrowed from the nominal declension. Besides all the languages are here in agreement with Marathi, with slight variations (Beames, II, p. 307-8, 310-11).

In the singular, only the oblique is fully clear. From the Skr. dative, Ved. *máhya,* classical *mahyaṃ,* become in Prākrit gen. *majjhaṃ,* comes the stem of the first person *majh-, maj-,* which is found only in Marathi, Gujarati and Hindi (in Hindi and in Mevati —the dialect of Rajasthan that is contiguous to Hindi—the vowel has become *u* under the influence of *tujh-*). Similarly Skr. *tubhyam,* adapted to the form of the first person. becomes Pkt. *tujjhaṃ,* from where comes the Marathi, Gujarati and Hindi forms *tujh, tuj.* The oblique forms *mā, tu-* (for ex. *mā teṃ, Jñāneś.,* XII, 233=mod. *malā* "to me") are still found, of whom atleast the first is more difficult to explain. It is not possible to agree with Pischel and take Pkt. *maha* back to *máhya* or *máhyam,* like the Pkt. *majjha* (see $ 418). Perhaps *maha* comes from a contamination of the stem of the indirect cases *ma-* with the nominative *aham.*

In the nominative, the pronoun of the second person, *tūṃ,* goes back to Pkt. *tumaṃ.* The Prākrit form is, besides, quite obscure and seems difficult to explain except as a transcription of the modern form, which then would be the Vedic *t(u)vám,* whose nasality would have reached the first vowel. In fact it is known that the penultimate *m* before a nasal vowel has lost its own articulation in the terminations like *-āmi* (see $ 67). For all the more reason, should it not represent some articulation defined between a labial vowel and a nasalised one. The nasalisation is missing in this pronoun in Romany, and in a group including Hindi, Nepali and the languages situated to the east of these three.

The form of the first person, *mī* is much more obscure. It has a recent doublet *mīṃ*, which is used simultaneously as a subject and the instrumental. The nasalisation therein is perhaps similar to that of *tūṃ*. Perhaps it also comes from the form of the instrumental. To M. *mī*, undoubtedly corresponds the form *mmi*, *mi* being found only in Hemacandra, but this is a form, which given its late appearance in Prakrit, itself requires to be specially explained. For Pischel, it is the first person sing. of the verb "to be", *asmi* ($ 417). It is more probable that we should see a pronominal form herein. We have seen that Skr. *asme*, *mama* had been able to take on the value of the subject case. This authorises us undoubtedly to see in *mī* (dialectally *me*, LSI, *Mar.*, p. 211) either Skr. Pkt. *me* or Pkt. *mai* (found only in Śauraseni) coming from Skr. *mayi*. The evidence of other languages is of no help here. An important group consisting of principal western languages (Kashmiri, Sindhi, Gujarati, Goanese Konkani, Marwari and Braj.) has pre- served the representatives of *aham* uptill today.. In Panjabi, Rajasthani, Hindi the instrumental *maiṃ* has taken the place of the nominative. The Romany *me*, Nepalese *ma* are obscure and the Simhalese aberrant.

In the eastern group, Beng. *mui*, *tui*, Or. *mu*, *tu* seem definitely to go back to the locatives of the type *mayi*, *tvayi* (Ved. *tve*) and yield singulars corresponding to Skr. *asme*, *yaṣme* and of whom the Mar. *mī* could be an isolated representative.

2. *Instrumental*

$ 209. This case has several forms still living today and the postosition *neṃ* : *nīṃ* does not apply to the personal pronouns.

Here again the plural alone is clear. From the Pkt. *aṃhehiṃ*, *tumhehiṃ*, where the old oblique arisen from the

Vedic *asmé*, *yuṣmé* serves as the stem and has got co-agulated with the traditional termination, are regularly derived *āhmīṃ*, *tumhīṃ*.* * t- is an import from the singular, replacing original y-.

In the singular, the old and always alive forms are *miyāṃ*, *myāṃ*; *tāṃ*, *tuvāṃ*, *tvāṃ*. Skr. *mayā*, *tvayā* have furnished the forms of the oblique case in Simhalese (Geiger, $ 47, I, 1), but *mae*, *tae*, which represent in classical Prākrit Skr. *mayā*, *tvayā* could not be at the origin of the Marathi forms. It should be supposed that the Sanskrit pronouns have been enlarged in very old times with the termination of the instrumental case of the nouns : **mayāṇa* or **māyāṇaṃ*, **tvayāṇa* or **tvayāṇaṃ* ($ 66) are the probable prototypes of M. *myāṃ*, *tāṃ* or *tvāṃ* in the Middle-Indian.

3. *Possessive Adjective*

$ 210. In the plural of the pronouns, the relation of the genitive is noted as in the nouns by *cā*, which is added, not to the oblique, but to the stem of the oblique : *āum*, *tum-*, that is to say Pkt. *amha-*, *tumha-*. The adjectives *āṃcā* (*āmucā*), *tumcā* are found from the oldest texts upto our time.

In the singular, Marathi has formed an adjective on the oblique; *mājhā*, *tujhā* are, therefore, like the Skr. *māmaka-*, *tāvaka-*. This creation isolates Marathi from all the related languages. Simhalese has no possessive, Sindhi forms its possessive like that of the nouns in the singular as also in the plural number and the group of the N.W seems to do the same where it shows an adjective (Grierson, *Piś. Lang.*, p. 45, 47; *Manual of Kashm. Lang...*, $ 30). Everywhere else, there exists in the singular as also in the plural an adjective of the Apabh. type *mahāra*, *tuhāra*, *amhāra* *tumhāra* (Pischel, $ 434; to the examples given by Beames, II, p. 312, should be added the forms of Rajasthani given by in LSI, *Raj.*, p. 8, the Armenian Romany *merav*, *terav* and European Romany *minro*, *timro*, pl. *amaro*, *tumaro*).

APPENDIX

Numerals

$ 211. The series of numerals shows particularly the disparate origin of the elements of Marathi vocabulary. It also enables us to observe us to how a good number of its elements had already been juxtaposed in the vocabulary of common Prakrit. In fact, it will be observed that the majority of the numerals have undergone a similar evolution in all the different dialects. Where the Marathi word seems to go back directly to Sanskrit, the regular form is also found in Prakrit and in almost all other modern Indo-Aryan languages. Where, however, on the contrary the Marathi form is irregular, the irregularity besides explicable by the character of the accessory words of the numerals is found since the Middle-Indian itself and is verified in other related languages. This concordance of aspect is so frequent, that one asks oneself if the direct *rapprochement* between a Marathi form and a Sanskrit one is not a trap, and if Marathi has not taken her entire numeration from an indeterminate Prākrit where already the correct and incorrect forms had been neighbours. What renders the verification of this hypothesis more difficult is the fact that the numeration is not, so to say, found in the Middle-Indian since Pali upto the more recent texts of Jainism (see the examples in Pischel, $ 435 ff; Beames has studied the modern forms, II, p. 130 ff.).

$ 212. The numerals for "one" to "four" are the adjectives; those of "five" and above are constructed either as indeclinable adjectives, or as the substantives in masc.-neut. whose oblique is in *-ā* (Navalkar, $ 128). Except the possible reproduces a difference of the Indo-European period (Meillet, *Intro.*, p. 399 ff.).

$ 213. *Ek* "one" is a tatsama preserved in Prākrit (Skr. *eka-*, Pkt. *ekka-*) and in all the Indo-Aryan languages. This tatsama has undergone a slight change due to the brevity of the initial vowel (see $ 174) in *akrā* "eleven". But in this word as in *ekuṇīs* "nineteen", the surd consonant is maintained. These are, however, the forms reconstituted at a recent date, because except in Simhalese (*ekolasa*, *ekunvisi*) and in Kashmiri (*kah*, *kunanwah*; the forms of other Himalayan dialects are missing in the table given by Grierson, *Piś Lang.*, p. 37), the old *k* has, in all these words, everywhere evolved upto *g*, the stage where it has been fixed (for ex. H. *igārah*, *agunīs*).

$ 214. *Don* "two" is a form exclusive to Marathi only, while the Pkt. pl. neut. *doṇi*, whence it is derived, is common to Māhārāṣṭrī and Śaurasenī. But the word, whose analogy has influenced *don*, that is to say Pkt. *tiṇṇi*, M. *tīn* has been preserved in all the Indo-Aryan languages.

The eastern Prakrits equally use for "two (in all the genders, like the forms to be discussed later) the form *do*, derived from Skr. *dvau*. Preserved unchanged in Hindi and Panjabi, it is also preserved in Marathi, on the one hand in the oblique *dohiṃ* or *dohoṃ* (obtained by the assimilation of vowels, like *cohoṃ*, on the model of *tihiṃ*), and on the other in the compound adjective masc. *doghe*, fem. *doghī*, neut. *dogheṃ* "the two (together)", of when the second element is moreover obscure.

The eastern Prakrit have generalised *duve*, to which is joined the Apabh. *duvi*. This form is represented today on the one hand in the eastern group (Maith, Or., Beng. *dui*, Avadhi *dvi*, *dūi*) and in the N-W (Rom. *dui*, *lui*; in the Himalayas *u* has been palatalised as a consequence of contact with *i*, and in its turn the initial consonant has been diversely changed, see Grierson, *Piś. Lang.*, p. 30-39).

Skr. *dve* subsists also in the Simhalese form *de* and in the Pkt. form still current in Gujarati *be*. As ergards Sindhi *bā*, does it go back to Ved. masc. *d*(*u*)*vā́* or does it come from the compound forms of the type of masc. M. bārā "twelve", *bāvīs*" twentytwo" ? Nothing can be said about it.

The initial labial, normal in Gujarati and Sindhi, is found in Marathi, by the side of the dental found in Simhalese and which is undoubtedly phonetic in Marathi (see $ 130).

This is how we have on the one hand *dīḍh* "one and a half" (*dvi*+*ardha*-), *dujā* "second", other "(*dvitīya*-), *duṇā* "double" (*dviguṇa*-) and on the other, *be* "two" in the multiplication tables and in the compounds (*dve* and *dvaya*- have, no doubt, been mixed therein), *bīj* "second day of the Moon" (*dvitīyā*). *bārā* "tweilve", *bāvīs* "twentytwo."

$ 215. *Tīn* "three". Except in the Himalayan N-W (see Grierson, ibid.), all the modern forms go back to Pkt. *tiṇṇi* (*tiṇṇaṃ* in Simhalese, Geiger, $ 45). What is then, the relationship between Pkt. *tiṇṇi* and Skr. *trīṇi* ? The explanation offered by Pischel on this point is manifestly insufficient (see $ 438). Perhaps *tiṇṇi* is simply the sign for a quasi-tatsama, restored during an epoch when the intervocalic penultimate *ṇ* tended to disappear, or as a consequence the Pkt. **tīṇi* (*tīṇiṃ* ? see $ 66) became **tīṃ*, that is to say that the numeral for "three" had a consonant only as initial. It is undoubtedly to avoid this lack of consistency that *ṇṇ* has been maintained in *tiṇṇi* and added in *doṇṇi*.

The oblique is *tihiṃ* which has served as the model for *dohoṃ* and *cohoṃ*. This form is undoubtedly an adaptation of the Pkt. instrumental *tīhiṃ* (Skr. masc. neut. *tribhiḥ*) which has taken the value of the genitive because of the nasalisation which brought it near the genitive plural bcome oblique in the nouns.

By the side of the stem *ti-*, Skt. *tri-*, we have in Marathi *tī-* arisen from *tṛti-* in *tīj* "3rd day of the Moon" (*tṛtīyā* and *te-* arisen from *traya-* in *terā* "thirteen" (Pkt. *teraha*) *tevīs* "23", *tetis* or *tehtīs* "33"; but the group *tr-* is restored in *trecāḷīs* "43", *trepann* "53", etc.

$ 216. *Cār* "four" is irregular in two ways. Firstly, the palatal pronunciation of *c* before *a* is against Marathi phonetics. Now it is often pronounced and even written *cyār* and the same thing occurs in the compounds *cyauvis* "24", *cyopaun* "54" (*catur-*). Therefore, even if the word is old in Marathi, it has been subjected to foreign phonetic influences.

Secondly, the word *cār* goes back to *cāri* which is preserved, till today in Sindhi and in the eastern group after having been noted in the Apabhraṃśa. But *cāri* does not correspond to any Sanskrit form. It is evidently an abbreviation of *cattāri* (*catvāri.*) Of course, we find in Prākrit a certain number of words where geminated *tt* arisen out of an old group seems to have been simplified and made *y* like an old intervocalic *t*. Thus we have *āyā* (and *ādā*) for Skr. *ātmā*, found in some of the oldest Jaina texts whereas others have *appā* as the *Māhārāṣṭrī* (Pischel, $ 401). In the same works are also found *goya* (*gotra-*), *pāya* (*pptra-*). Moreover a form of this type, *rāī* (*rātrī*) is found in *Māhārāṣṭrī* since the anthology of Hāla and the equivalent *rādī* is equally found in Śaurasenī (Pischel, $ 87; the form *dhāī* drawn by Pischel from Skr. *dhātrī* is in reality a loan from Persian). It seems, therefore, that there had been, in some part of Hindustan, a dialect wherein geminated *tt* rejoined quite early the intervocalic *t* and, like the latter, become *d*, then *y*. The numeral *cār*, which is pan-Indian, perhaps, comes from this dialect. We can also explain the irregularity of this form as being due to analogical changes frequent in the numerals.

In this hypothesis, which can moreover be combined with that of a loan, *cattāri* would have been abridged under the influence of *cauro* and other forms of the stem, Skr. *catu-*, Pkt. *cau-*, M. *cau-*, *co* (*caughe* "the four", *cauth* "4th day of the Moon", *cauthā* "fourth", *caudā* "fourteen", *cauvīs* "twentyfour", etc.; *cohoṃ*, oblique of *cār*). The intervocalic *t* arisen from the geminated *t* in *cattāri* would have disappeared as that of *catur-*, because it became necessary to render all the first numerals equally disyllabic in the modern languages. Probably this evolution has been aided by the existence of a form *cauri* found in the dialects of the scripts of Dutreuil de Rhins and confirmed by the actual forms of the Himalayan N-W. (Kashm. *cor*, G. *cūr*, etc.). The relatively artificial character of the loss of *t* in *cār* is rendered probable by the co-existence of *cāḷīs* and *tāḷīs* (in compounds) for "forty".

$ 217. *Pāṇc* "five" is regularly derived from Skr. *pañca*. Moreover, this form is universal in India, except the normal phonetic changes mentioned in $ 82.—In the numeral for "fifteen" *pandhrā* for **panrāh*, *pañc-* has been subjected to an abnormal alteration, found in *pannās* "fifty". According to an explanation of E. Kuhn cited by Pischel in $ 274 of his grammar, these forms come from the dissimilation of the supported palatal of *pañca* by the intervocalic palatal sifflant in *pañcadaśa* and *pañcāśat*. This dissimilation, in conformity with the law XVII of Grammont, supposes a stage where the vowel *a* of the first syllable of *pañca-* had already become a nasal and long, but where *ś* had not, as yet, been identified with *s*.

$ 218. *Sahā* "six" does not exactly correspond to Skr.

ṣaṭ, Pkt. *cha*. This form, special in Marathi, seems to result from the same need of providing consistency to the end of the word, as already shown by *don* and *tīn*. Here no occlusive was available; it became necessary, therefore, to reserve a part of the aspiration contained in the initial and prolong the vocalic emission. The existence of *dahā* "ten", Pkt. *daha* has also favoured this change. It is found in S. *chah* (cf. Apabh. *chaha*, which Pischel tries to explain by the adaptation to Skr. *ṣaṭ* of the morpheme *-a-* of the nominal declension, see $ 441), which co-exists in Sindhi with *cha*, the normal form in Hindi and Gujarati. The Marathi *sahā* in compound again becomes *sā-* (*sā- saṣṭ* "66", etc.).

Elsewhere Pkt. *cha* seems to have been lengthened in another way either with *i* (H., Panj. *che*, Beng. *chay*, Simh. *saya* beside *sa*, Kashm. *śih* and probably even M. *śe-* in *śaltāḷis* "46", *śahattar* "76", or with *u* (Maith. *chau*, Rom. *śov*). All these forms, equally obscure, start from the same single principle.

In M. *sahā*, the initial *s* can equally represent both Skr. *s* and Pkt. *ch*. In *sak* (*ṣaṭka-*) *soḷā* (*soḍaśa*), *saṭh* (*ṣaṣṭhi-*), the same doubt can persist. But the loans of Marathi from other languages are made evident by the fact that beside *savvīs* "26", *sāsaṣṭ* "66" on the one hand, and *śetāḷīs* "46", *śehattar* and *śāhattar* "76", *śāṃyaśī* "86", *śaṇṇav* "96" on the other, we find *ch* in *chattīs* "36" and *chappann* "56" whose geminated consonants moreover show its foreign character.

$ 219. *Sāt* "seven", *āṭh* "eight" (on *aḍ*, in the compounds, see $ 170), *nav* and *nau* "nine" are derived or seem to be directly derived from the Skr. *sapta*, *aṣṭau*, *nava*. The same is the case with other Indo-Aryan languages.

$ 220. *Dahā* "ten", in reference to Pkt. *daha*, shows a regular lengthening of the final vowel, which is explained by the tendency described á propos of *don*, *tīn* and *sahā*, and which has been favoured by the fact that of the two *a*s encircling the aspiration, the second is generally long (see $ 52).

But the aspiration itself of M. *dahā* is altogether disconcerting. It is known that normally the sifflant is preserved in Marathi and before Marathi (see $ 160) in Prakrit. Now *daha* is found quite early in Prakrit. According to Vararuci, *dasa* subsists in numeration and becomes *daha-* in the proper nouns, whose current form is to be respected by the literary texts, whereas the isolated word is subjected to the influence of Skr. *daśa.* The form *daha* does not take long in being imposed even in numeration. The texts accept it and Hemacandra had to authorise it, at least in Māhārāṣṭrī, because the eastern Prakrit preserves the sifflant (Pischel, $ 262).

In modern Indo-Aryan, the forms are distributed as in Prakrit. Along with Romany and the majority of the speeches of the Himalayan West, the dialects of Hindustani, central and eastern, exclusively preserve the sifflant. In Simhalese and in Panjabi the two types co-exist, as also in Marathi, but *das* is rare and is found only in certain words belonging to the religious language and where it is a true tatsama (*dasvandan, dasuhāṇeṃ, dasrā*). The aspirate alone is found only in Kashmiri, Sindhi and in certain Gujarati dialects : there it is phonetic. It is known that in Sindhi the passage of *s* to *h* is normal and the dialects of Gujarati, which have *dah* for "ten" also have *hāt* for "seven."

Therefore, it seems that *dahā* goes back to some western or central form, but this form must have been borrowed very early, because it is already imposed on the literature of classical Prakrit.

$ 221. We have seen the forms of the numerals from "eleven" to "eighteen". The numeral "ten" has been changed throughout therein where *d* had been earlier intervocalic. In Marathi and in other languages only *caudā* (*caturdaśa*) and *soḷā* (*ṣoḍaśa*) are phonetically treated. In the former, *d* had been geminated; in the second it had been, since its origin, replaced by a cerebral.

The agreement between Marathi and the rest of Indo-Aryan (except the far N-W. : in Kashm. *kah* "eleven", *bah* "twelve", etc., the intervocalic *d* is regularly lost) is quite constant in so far as the phonetic irregularity shown by the numerals *akrā* "11", *bārā* "12", *terā* "13", *pandhrā* "15", *satrā* "17", *aṭhrā* "18" is concerned. In all these words, the intervocalic *d* had been replaced by *r*. The fact is already noted in the oldest Jaina texts and is also found in Vararuci (Pischel, $ 443). It is explained that the need to protect the initial of the numeral for "ten" in these words must have been felt very early, but the passage of *d* to *r* is not normal (cf. $ 143). According to Pischel, here *r* comes from *ḍ*, found in fact in the eastern inscriptions of Aśoka (Michelson, I F, XXIII, p. 247, note 3). In this case the analogy of *ṣoḍaśa* immediately comes to mind, but *ḍ* normally ends in *ḷ*, that is why we have in M. *soḷā*. Undoubtedly the explanation is valid for Simhalese, which has in fact generalised *ḷ* (*koḷaha*, *doḷasa* like *soḷosa*), but not for the forms whith *r* of the Middle-Indian and modern languages. Here probbably we should admit a very early dissimilation of the intervocalic *d* by the initial *d* of *dvādaśa*, indeed by the initial *t* of *trayodaśa* (law XIV of Grammont) and the supported *t* of *saptadaśa* (law VIII of Grammont. These nouns would have acted as a model for others (explanation suggested by Meillet).

$ 222. *Ekuṇīs* "19" is formed according to the formula of Prakrit, which leaves intact the initial vowels of the second members of compounds. Even the languages, where *ek-* has generally become *-eg-* or *g-*, have preserved the *u* of Skr. *ūna-* changed into *o* in *ekonaviṃśati-*. The prototype of Marathi is, therefore, **ek-ūna-vīs*, where the median *ū* has naturally been abridged, and where the intervocalic *v* has disappeared, not being protected by the sentiment of the series as in the numerals above "twenty", such as *bāvīs* "22", *tevīs* "23", *cauvīs* "24", etc.

Tens

$ 223. The numerals for tens show forms that are still more obscure than those discussed above.

Vīs "twenty", *tīs* "thirty". In Prakrit, there is no longer any trace of the Sanskrit nasal *viṃśati-*, *triṃśat*, that are besides altogether abnormal and obscure from the Indo-European point of view (Brugmann, *Grundriss*, 2nd edn., II, 2, p. 31). In Prakrit *vīsai* and even *vīsaī*, the form of the substantive, normally corresponding to Skr. *viṃśati-* have been noted. But the more usual forms are *vīsaṃ* (neut.) and *vīsā* (fem.), which are both of them, the adaptations of Skr. *viṃśat* formed on the type of *triṃśat*. In Marathi *vīs* and *tīs* are, like all the numerals above "four", declined on the type of masc.-neut. *dev* or *ghar*. Other languages possess the same words with normal phonetic variants; for ex. Guj. *vīs*,

H. *bīs*, S. Panj. *vīh*, Kashm. *vuh*; Guj., Hindi, Beng. *tīs*, Panj. *tīh*, S. *ṭīh*, Kashm. *trah*.

Cāḷīs "forty", in relation to *catvāriṃśat*, appears as a Māgadhism : in Pali, *cattārisaṃ* and *cattāḷisaṃ* co-exist but Prakrit has only the forms in *ḷ*. The first part of the word has not the same fate as *cār* for *cattāri*, but here *t* has been optionally preserved in compounds. Thus we say *ekcāḷīs*, *ekecāḷīs* and *ektāḷīs*, *eketāḷīs* "41", *cavvecāḷīs* and *cavvetāḷīs* "44", etc. The form with *t* does not seem to be usual in Marathi (Molesworth gives it regularly, but Beames denies its existence), but it is current in other western and central languages (Beames, I, 215).

Pannās "fifty", Skr. *pañcāśat* is a very old form, provided the explanation given in $ 217 be correct. But in its isolated state it is present only in Marathi and Simhalese (*peṇas*). Everywhere else the word for "five" has been re-introduced in that of "fifty".

Moreover, the fact, that the form *pannās* is not indigenous to Marathi, comes out from the gemination of the nasal.

In a compound with the units, Pkt. *paṇṇāsaṃ* has been, in its turn, abbreviated : thus we have *ekkā-vaṇṇaṃ*, *bā-vaṇṇaṃ*, etc. and *ekāvann*, *bāvann*, etc. in Marathi. These forms are found all over central and eastern India.

Sāṭh "sixty" is normally derived from Skr. *ṣaṣṭi-*, Pkt. *saṭṭhi-* Here again the forms of other languages are in agreement with Marathi and seem to correspond to the same Sanskrit prototype: Kashm. *śaith*, Panj. *saṭṭh*, S. *saṭhi*, H., Guj. *sāṭh*, etc.

Sattar "seventy" corresponds to Skr. *saptati-*. Here the intervocalic *r*, found in the Middle-Indian and preserved everywhere except in Kashmiri and Simhalese, should go far back in the past. It is undoubtedly explained by the dissimilation of the intervocalic *t* by the stressed *t* (law VIII of Grammont) as in *satrā* "seventeen" (*saptadaśa*), see $ 221.—In the compounds *s* is changed into *h* : *ekāhattar* "71" etc. We have seen in $ 160 that this alteration is foreign to Marathi. This series of numerals is, therefore, perhaps entirely borrowed from a western or central dialect.

Eṃśīṃ, *aiśīṃ* "eighty" coincides with G. *eṃśi*, *heṃśī* but not with Panj., H. *assī*, etc., which normally represent Skr.

aśītī, Pkt. *asīṃ, asīī*. Regarding this vocalic infection rare in Marathi, see $ 166.

Navvad "ninety", like the languages of Hindustani, has a geminated, cf. Panj. *navve*, Beng. *nabbai*. But the end of the word is peculiar to Marathi. That of Skr. *navati-* is correctly found in Panj., H. *navve*, S. *nave*, Beng. *nabbai*, Or. *nabe* and even Kashm. *namăth*. Marathi seems to have fixed this word during the course of evolution and represents a Middle-Indian **navadi*. It has also shortened the same into *-ṇṇav* in the compounds *ekyāṇṇav, byāṇṇav*, etc. Gujarati has subjected the same word to more obscure transformations (*nevuṃ*). None of these forms corresponds to Pkt. *nauiṃ, nauī*, itself irregular, This word is thus entirely disconcerting.

Hundred and above

$ 224. *Śambhar* "hundred" is obscure. We recognise therein *śatam* to which seems to be joined a word denoting "charge, weight" or "capacity" (*bhar-* or *bhār-*). The word *śambhar* is employed in absolute. It has for its equivalent the indeclinable neuter substantive *śeṃ*, always preceded by *ek* and which is used for forming the numerals above hundred : *ek śeṃ* "hundred", *ek śeṃ ek* "one hundred one", *don śeṃ* "two hundred", etc. The word *śeṃ* phonetically corresponds to Skr. *śataṃ*, which is also the case with all the corresponding forms of Indo-Aryan (except in certain Himalayan speeches where "hundred" is "five twenties", Grierson, *Piś. Lang.*, p. 37, 39). The end of the caste-name *savāśā* has another form of the same word, declined on the model of masculine adjectives. It refers to a caste of "hundred twentyfive", Skr. *sapāda-śataka*.

Hajār "1000" is borrowed from Persian as almost everywhere else in India. Sanskrit *sahasram* seems to be preserved only in Kashm. *sās* and in Simh. *dahas* (if it does refer to *sahasram* having borrowed the initial of *daha* "ten", as is suggested by Geiger, $ 45,). One could also simply see in this word a compound of *daha* and *siya*, that is "ten hundreds").

Lākh "100,000" corresponds to Skr. *lakṣa-* as is the casex with all the corresponding forms of the same number in Indo-Aryan; *koṭ* "10 million" is a tatsama from Skr. *koṭi*.

the Hindi form *karoḍ*, which is general in India (cf. Anglo-Indian+*crore*) has not been explained so far.

Fractions of Unity

$ 225. We have already explained the forms denoting fractions of units, which are : *ādhā. adh-*, *aḍ-* (*dīḍ* "one and a half"; *aḍīc* "two and a half"; *sāḍe-* "and a half", from three onwards), Skr. *ardha-*; *pāv* "a quarter-, Skr. *pāda-*, and its compounds *pāūṇ* "three quarters", exactly "minus a quarter", Skr. *pādona* (*pāuṇedon*" 1¾", *pāuṇetīn* "2¾", etc.), *savā* or *savvā* "one and a quarter" Skr. *sapāda* (cf. *savvādon* "2¼ etc.).

Ordinals :—

$ 226. Beginning from "fifth", the ordinal adjectives have all been formed with the suffix *-vā* (*-āvā* from "nine-tenth" onwards) : *pāṃcvā* "fifth", *sātvā* "seventh", *dahāvā* "tenth", *śambharāvā* "hundredth", etc. This suffix corresponds to Skr. *-ma-* extended by analogy to all the numbers at an early date, except in the case of *sahāvā* "sixth", (Skr. *ṣaṣṭha-*, Pkt. *chaṭṭha-*) where the analogy starts in Marathi. Hindi (*chaṭṭhā*) and Gujarati (*chaṭo*) still preserve the traditional form which, like Marathi, has disappeared from everywhere (Beames, II, p. 143).

Pahilā "first" results from the adaptation to Skr. *prathama* of the Pkt. suffix *-illa-*. Wherever the tatsama is not used in India itself, we find the forms of the same word (in Simhalese and in the N-W., the systems are different; see Geiger, $ 44, 3; Grierson, *Man. Kashm.*, $ 28). Its extension, however, seems to be recent. It is missing in Prakrit (the usual form is *paḍhama-*) and it should be noted that the Marathi form is identically that of Hindi and Panjabi, which has spread on the other hand in the languages of the eastern group (Beames, II, p. 142).

Dusrā "second", *tīsrā* "third" are also common to Marathi and central languages. Marathi also possesses *dujā* "other', *bīj* and *tij* fem. "second" and "third day of the Moon" which correctly go back to Skr. *dvitīya-*, *tṛtīya-* and are found in Panjabi, Sindhi, Gujarati. The words *dusrā* and *tisrā* are still not explained.

Cauthā "fourth" develops normally from Skr. *caturtha-* as in all the languages of India properly so called (see Beames, I, 144).

Conjugation

$ 227. The verbal system of Marathi is based on a simplification similar to the one which is the basis of declension. But this simplification seems to have commenced earlier in the verbs than nouns. In fact, if the disappearance of the dual becomes a *fait accompli* only at the beginning of the Prakrit period, and if the absorption of the middle conjugation in the active conjugation is still more recent, because the middle one is partially preserved in the inscriptions of Aśoka and in Pali (for Prakrit, cf. Pischel, $ 452, 457), then it is possible to follow, in the Sanskrit literature itself and that from its ancient period, the progressive impoverishment of the old inflexion. During the interval that separates the editing of the Ṛgveda from that of the Brāhmaṇas, words other than the indicative have undergone considerable losses. The subjunctive exists only in the present and in the aorist, and there also its use has become less frequent; the optative and the imperative are also limited to the present (J. Bloch, 'La phrase nominale en Sanskrit', MSL, XIV p. 31). In the *Mahāhārata* all the verbs tend to be reduced to the indicative and the imperative; of the subjective and the injunctive only skeletons remain and the optative is in decay (ibid., pl 37-9). In the indicative itself, the tenses of the past lose most of their characteristic forms and their meanings (ibid., p. 46). On the conditional, almost non-existent, see Whitney, $ 941. On the contrary regarding the future, which has had a recent extension, it continues to develop, and the present, preserved intact in its form, sees its usage being extended (ibid., p. 64.).

The results of this evolution are noted in Prakrit, where the only usual forms are those of the indicative present and futures and those of the imperative. Only, or almost only the Jaina dialects have preserved other old forms : the imperfect (Pischel, $ 515) and exceptionally the perfect (ibid., $ 518; cf. Bloch, *l. l.* p. 73 and note 2), the aorist normally as also the optative (Pischel, $ 516-7, 459). It is remarkable that the optative and above all the aorist be also so very frequent in Pali. This coincidence shows the archaic or archaising character of the Jaina dialects, notably that of Ardhamāgadhī (cf. Pischel, $ 18).

The Sanskrit of late period confirms the data furnished by Prakrit literature. In the *Vetālapañcaviṃśātikā* the only vivacious verbal forms are those of the indicative present (with varied meanings, see Bloch, *l. l.*, p. 67 ff.), future and the imperative present. It is the nominal sentence which fills up the lacunae resulting from the reduction of the conjugable forms (ibid, p. 94).

Stems.

$ 228. In the nominal sentence, can be introduced various participles, that is to say, declinable words but joined by their stems to the conjugation. Now among these participles, only the adjective in *-ta-* (with its derivatives in *-tavant-* and *-tavya*)- preserves a verbal stem other than that of the present, to which all the conjugable forms are joined. The mediaeval verbal system is thus based on two stems : 1. that of the present, on which are formed, on the one hand, the indicative present and future and imperative and on the other, the present participle and the infinitive; 2. that of the past, preserved in the participle in *-ta-*. Thus the Sanskrit verb has evolved in parallel with the rest of the Indo-European languages, that have been constituted in course of time of the conjugative with two stems (see Meillet, *Introduction*, p. 418; cf. MSL, XIII, p. 350 ff). In detail, its history recalls especially that of the majority of the Iranian dialects, where also the verb has been reconstituted around the old present and of the verbal in *-ta-* (Re. Persian, see Sulemann, *Grundriss der Iran. phil.*, I, 1, p. 295, Horn., ibid., I, 2, p. 148; on the Afghan, and Balochi, Geiger, ibid., I, 2, p. 218 and 242; Re. the Kurd, Socin, ibid., I, 2, p. 280-81; re. the dialects of the Pamirs, of the Caspian and of the centre, Geiger, ibid., p. 321, 362, 394; cf. p. 416).

But the two stems have not taken long to react on each other in India and the majority of the modern languages preserve the old opposition only in a restricted number of cases (Beames, III, p. 136-147). It is in Sindhi that the old participles have preserved most of this independence with regard to the stem of the present. In Panjabi, in Hindi the list of these participles has become very short. Marathi is, with the languages of the east, the one where the levelling has been the most complete.

$ 229. Only two verbs therein have preserved the trace of the old gradation of stems, the strong and the weak one suppletory nature infinitive *marṇeṃ* (*mārṇaṃ*), *karṇeṃ* (*karaṇaṃ*) part. *me-lā* (*mṛta-*), *kelā* (*kṛta-*). These are the two very usual verbs, whose radica ends in *r* and which constitute a group. In Oriya the only strong participles are also *malā*, *kalā*.

Elsewhere the opposition of the two stems has been maintained when facts of suppletory nature have occurred :

Infin.	*jāṇeṃ* (*yāti*) "to go" :	part. *ge-lā* (*gata-*)
	yeṇeṃ (*eti*) "to come"	*ā-lā* (*āgata*)
	hoṇeṃ (*bhavati*) "to be"	*jā-lā*, *jhālā* (*jāta-*)

The archaic language has also preserved a certain number of old forms. Such are the forms *pātlā* (*prāpta-*), *pāvṇeṃ* "to attain", since replaced by *pāvlā*; *bhinnalā*, pure tatsama replaced by *bhinlā*, cf. *bhinṇeṃ*, *bhiṃdṇeṃ* "to penetrate"; *dinnalā* (*dinhalā*), which preserves the Pkt. form *diṇṇa*, has been replaced by *dilā*, nearer *deṇeṃ* "to give"; *minlā*, made after a type **mil-na-* (cf. Pkt. *ummilla-*) is less authorised than *millā* from *miḷṇeṃ* "to join."

A certain number of irregular past participles have remained in use. Their origin is more recent and their form is obscure :

1. Those characterised by *-t* : *ghātlā* "posed", from *ghālṇeṃ* is easily explained, as has been rightly seen by Sten Konow, JRAS, 1902, p. 421, by the opposition of a verbal **ghal-ta-* and of a present **ghal-ya-ti*, Pkt. *gallai*. Such words and those like *pātlā* cited above, as also the tradition of the Skt. verbal in *-ta-*, *-ita-* must have had been the starting point for the analogies which have determined the formation of *ghetlā* "taken" (*gheṇeṃ*), *dhūtlā* "washed" (*dhuṇeṃ*), *baghitlā* "seen" (*baghṇeṃ*), *māgitlā* "demanded". (*māgṇeṃ*) *mhaṇitla* "said" (*mhaṇṇeṃ*, *sāṃgṇeṃ*), etc.

2. The verbs with a radical in *ṇ* optionally change this *ṇ* into *ṭ* in the past : *khaṭlā* from *khaṇṇeṃ* "to dig", *mhaṭlā* from *mhaṇṇeṃ* "to say", *hāṭlā* from *haṇṇeṃ* "to strike".

The origin of this gradation is not known (cf. Sten Konow, *l. l.*).

3. The monosyllables in *ī* form the stem of the past by adding *-ā* : *pyālā* (*piṇeṃ*) "drunk", *bhyālā* (*bhiṇeṃ*) "fear", *vyālā* (*viṇeṃ*) "engendered", etc. It seems that here the old stems *bhīta*, etc. have been preserved, though enlarged by the suffix of the Pkt. adjective *-alla-*. Moreover, quite a large number of verbs form the past participle in *-ālā-* rather than in *-lā* (cf. Navalkar, p. 130).

4. The monosyllables in *ā* can add *i* in the past : *gāilā* "sung" (*gāṇeṃ*), *dhyāilā* "reflected" (*dhyāṇeṃ*) : this can go back to Prakrit : cf. Māg. *gāida-* in the *Mṛcchakaṭikā* (Pischel, $ 565).

But *khāṇeṃ* "to eat" (*khād-*) has in the past, beside *khadilā*, which is a tatsama, the *khālā*, which is altogether obscure : cf. however, Pkt. *solla-* for Skr. *sūnita* "cooked" (Pischel, $ 566).

5. The verbs in *-e* diverge : *neṇeṃ* "to lead" (*nī-*) keeps the *e* in *nelā* but *leṇeṃ* "to take" (Skr. *lā-*, Pkt. *le-*) is treated like a stem in *i* : part. *lyālā* and on the other hand *deṇeṃ* (*dā*, Pkt. *de-*) has replaced its old participles, moreover irregular, *dinnalā* and *didhalā* (cf. Guj. *didhlo*) by *dilā*.

A large number of these forms are optional : we may as well say that the system of strong forms of Marathi does not appear to have a definitive solidity. Besides the largest part of these forms are in reality relatively recent and in fact they are exclusive to Marathi.

It is suspected that they date from a period when the language tended to maintain the opposition of two stems despite the confusion provoked by phonetic evolution (cf. Pkt. *khāi*, *khāa*; *bihai*, **bhīa-*, etc.). But it is difficult to discover the original types that were the points of departure for similar forms.

Except the cases enumerated above the Marathi verb, as also the verb of other related languages, normally has only one stem (Beames, III, p. 28).

$ 230. When the modern conjugation is based on an old verbal stem, this stem is most often that of the present. Thus are found in Marathi vocabulary, traces of different formations which have lost their old morphological signification.

The athematic stem could not be extended to the tenses of the past in any case : only the stems of *yeṇeṃ* (*eti*) and *jāṇeṃ* (*yāti*) subsist thereof and they belong, as we have seen, to defective verbs as also the archaic third person *āthi* (*asti*), which already in old Marathi, is altogether isolated (except the participle *āthilā* "summer"). But those enumerated below are found in all the tenses :

Stems with the suffix *-a-*, like those of *utavṇeṃ* (*uttapati*), *khāṇeṃ* (*khādati*), *neṇeṃ* (*nayati*), *paḍhṇeṃ* (*paṭhati*), *pekhṇeṃ* (*prekṣate*), *baisṇeṃ* (*upaviśati*), *hoṇeṃ* (*bhavati*); is found exceptionally the reduplication preserved in *bihiṇeṃ* (*bibheti*), (*piṇeṃ* (*pibati*). Its trace can still be felt in the cerebral of *ṭheṇeṃ* and other words derived from the root *sthā-*; the stems with the suffix *-aya-*, like *uḍṇeṃ* (*uḍḍayati*), *kāpṇeṃ* (*kalpayati*), *cāvṇeṃ* (*carvayati*), *mākhṇeṃ* (*mrakṣayati*), *māgṇeṃ* (*mārgayati*), *sāṃdṇeṃ* (*chardryati*) and in a general way all the causatives of the type *tāvṇeṃ* (*tāpayati*), *toḍṇeṃ* (*troṭayati*), etc.;

Stems with weak vocalism and the suffix *-ya-*, as *upajṇeṃ*, *nipajṇeṃ* (*utpadyate*, *niṣpadyate*), *junjhṇeṃ* (*yudhyate*), *nācṇeṃ* (*nṛtyati*) *bujhṇeṃ* (*budhyate*), *mānṇeṃ* (*manyate*) and particularly the stems of the passive like *tapṇeṃ* (*tapyate*), *tuṭṇeṃ* (*truṭyate*) opposed to the causatives cited above (cf. Beames, III, 47 ff), *dājṇeṃ* (*dahyate*), *disṇeṃ* (*dṛśyate*), *pelṇeṃ* (*preryate* in the transitive sense), *lābhṇeṃ* (*labhyate*, cf. M. *lāhṇeṃ*); cf. *rujhṇeṃ* **ruhyate*), *dubhṇeṃ* made on the model of *lābhṇeṃ* (*duh*), *sakṇeṃ* (*śakyate*) where the verbal *śakya-* and even the present *śaknotī* have collaborated with the stem of the present passive.

Rare stems with nasals : one very old and the only one of its type, *jāṇṇeṃ* (*jānāti*); others with a nasal inserted in the stem and replacing the stems of the more archaic type, either since Sanskrit (cf. Meillet, MSL, XVII, p. 194) as in *bandhṇeṃ* (*bandhati-*), *bhaṃjṇeṃ* (*bhañjayati*), *rundhṇeṃ* (*rundhati*), or in Prakrit as in *viṃdhṇeṃ* (Pkt. *vindhai*, root *vyadh-*), *suṃdṇeṃ* (Pkt. *chundai*, root *kṣud-*), *seṃdṇeṃ* (Pkt. *chindai*, root *chid-*). Prakrit has in one way or in another eliminated the majority of stems with the nasal : cf. *joḍṇeṃ*, *thāṃbṇeṃ*, *dhuṇeṃ*, *pāvṇeṃ*, *phetṇeṃ*, *saṃcṇeṃ*, *sakṇeṃ*; and

two stems in *-ccha-*, one old, *pusṇeṃ* (*pṛcchati*), the other found only in the Middle-Indian, *asṇeṃ* (Pali *acchati*, Pkt. *acchai*).

To the stems of the present are joined a number of much more rare forms, based on the infinitive like *bhetṇeṃ* (*bhettuṃ*), or on the present participle, as *jāgṇeṃ* (*jāgrat-*; Prakrit already has in the present *jaggai*).

$ 231. In addition are found a certain number of verbs formed on the stem of the old past participle. These are the only vestiges of the old second stem of the mediaeval verb. The explanation proposed by Beames (III, p. 38) does not clarify the process whereby the participle lost its value of the past. Besides, if it had been a case of only this participle, it would be difficult to understand as to why all the verbs derived therefrom have not been intransitives. Now this is, undoubtedly, the case with the largest number : thus we have *umagṇeṃ* (*unmagna-*), *uphalṇeṃ* (*utphulla-*, cf. Whitney, $ 958), *umalṇeṃ* (Pkt. *ummilla*, Skt. *unmīlita-*), *bhāgṇeṃ* (*bhagna-*; cf. *bhāṃgṇeṃ* made after Skt. *bhaṅga-*), *mukṇeṃ* (Pkt. *mukha-*), *lādhṇeṃ* (*labdha-*; cf. *lābhṇeṃ* <*labhyate* and *lāhṇeṃ* drawn from *lābha-*), *rudhṇeṃ* (*ruddha-*); cf. *rujhṇeṃ* <*ruhyate*), *lagṇeṃ* (*lagna-*), *sutṇeṃ* (*śuṣka-*; cf. Whitney, $ 958), *suḍāvṇeṃ* (Pkt. *chūḍha-*, Skt. *kṣubdha-*). But right from the period of Prakrit we find the root of *kāḍhṇeṃ* "to draw" (*kṛṣṭa-*) with the transitive sense. Are used in the same way, *ghāṭṇeṃ* "to crush" (*ghṛṣṭa-*; cf. *ghaṭṇeṃ* "to be crushed"), in relation to *ghāsṇeṃ* "to rub", *ghusṇeṃ* "penetrate by force", *gheṇeṃ* "to take, receive" (*gṛhīta-*, Pkt. *gahia-*), *dinhṇeṃ* "to give" (Pkt. *dinna-*), *māthṇeṃ* "to polish", *madhṇeṃ* "to cover", *miṭṇeṃ* "to efface", drawn from *mṛṣṭa-* (cf. *māṃjṇeṃ* "to oil, to wipe off"; coming from the Skt. present *mārjati*); *piṭṇeṃ* "to beat", drawn from (the not found) participle of the root *pṛṣ-* "to do harm". In order to be able to understand the change of meaning, it should, undoubtedly, be recalled that in Sanskrit, the participle in *-ta-* is normally accompanied by a feminine substantive in -ti-. This is specifically how we have beside *kṛṣṭa-*, *ghṛṣṭa-*, *mṛṣṭa-*, *kṛṣṭī* (found only with other meanings), *ghṛṣṭi-*, *mṛṣṭi-*. The verbs formed on the stem of the past participle must have, therefore, passed for denominatives.

Moreover, it is not always clear as to which of the two stems, the modern verbs is joined. Thus *umalṇeṃ*, *pelṇeṃ* can go back to the passives **unmīlyate*, *preryate* (in the latter case it would be essential to admit the formation by analogy of an active **preryati*) as to the Pkt. participles *ummilla-*, *pellia-*, all the more so because the Prakrit participles go back to the stems of the passive (re. *ummilla-*, see however Pischel, $ 566). Similarly *lagṇeṃ* can indifferently be derived from *lagna-* or *lagya-*; *khāṇeṃ*, *piṇeṃ* are equally easily explained by both the present and the participle (cf. $ 229). The verbs like *umagṇeṃ*, *bhagṇeṃ*, *mukṇeṃ* can be based as much on the participles as on the presents like **magnāti*, **bhagnāti*, **muknāti*, etc.

$ 232. From the point of view of Marathi, all the stems mentioned above, constitute a single category, wherein are also included those formed during the modern period, for example denominatives like *utaṇṇeṃ* (*u *ut-tṛṇa-*), *uphalṇeṃ* (*utphulla-*) or *vācṇeṃ* (*vācya-*), *vājṇeṃ* (*vādya-*), (cf. Joshi, $ 334 ff.). On the stems of this category, that can be called the primary stems, are formed by derivation, the secondary stems, those of the causative, the potential and of the passive.

I. The causative is formed in Marathi in two ways :—

1. by the *guṇa* of the radical vowel : ex. *paḍṇeṃ* "to fall", *pāḍṇeṃ* "to cause to fall'; in this case the verb directly goes back to the Skt. causative (Navalkar, $ 392, p. 232). This form has been pointed out above and does not interest us here, because it does not constitute a special category neither from the stems nor from that of inflexion;

2. by the addition of the morpheme *-ava-* or *-avi-* : ex. *basṇeṃ* "to sit" : *basav(i)ṇeṃ* "to seat". This morpheme derived from Skr. *-paya-*, Pkt. *-ve-*, reserved at first for the roots in *-ā-*, was then extended to other vocalic or consonantal roots (Whitney, $ 1042, Pischel, 551-552). The Prakrit *-ve-* normally culminates in M. *-vi-* whose vowel, being interior, is unstable. The *Apabhraṃśa* texts often note this decoloration of the characteristic vowel, which results in a confusion of the primary and causatiue conjugations (Pischel, $ 553). The vowel preceding *v* is in principle *-a-*. Comparison with other languages shows that originally it had been the long *ā* (Guj. *-āva-*, Panj., Hindi *-āu ā-* , Sindhi, Beng., Oriya *-āi-* cf. Beames, III, p. 76). This vowel being interior, has been abridged. Marathi, the only one among the cognate dialects, shows another form of the same morpheme wherein the first vowel is *-i-* or *-ī-*. Thus we have *karīv(i)ṇeṃ* beside *karav(i)ṇeṃ* "to get done." The question is whether here it is

the phonetic action of the following vowel. We are allowed to think that it is the trace of an old causative; the co-existence of Pkt. *kārei* on the one hand and of *kārvei* and *kāravai* on the other could have provoked the formation of a type **kārevai*, *-*kārevei*.

The inflexion of the causatives is that of all the transitive verbs of Marathi.

II. A deceiving analogy of form has led certain grammarians to mix up with the morpheme of the causative that of the verb expressing possibility. In reality, the latter is *-va-* and never *-vi-* and moreover the construction of the verb is intransitive, therefore essentially different from that of the causative : *mājhyā-neṃ karavateṃ* "I can do". Taking into consideration this peculiarity of the syntax, Navalkar identifies the potential with the passive of Sanskrit ($ 400), forgetting that this form has been maintained by being transformed in Prākrit and right upto Marathi. It is Beames who has given the true explanation of this morpheme of the potential, by recognising therein the suffix of the participle of obligation in *-tavya-* (III, p. 157). In Marathi has been constituted, on the participle in *-v-*, a conjugation of the same type as the one constituted on the present participles in *-t-* and the past part. in *-l-* (cf. $ 243 ff.).

III. Different from the causative and potential, the passive is a form in complete decay. In reality, modern Marathi no longer has a passive verb; the passive sense being expressed by a periphrase similar to that of French, composed of the past participle joined to the verb *ho-* "to be" or *jā-* "to go". The old passive is represented only by a fixed form become the conjunction *mhaṇije* "that is to say", literally "is said" and by an abnormal verb *pāhije* "is necessary", literally "is seen" (Navalkar, $ 259 ff.). But in old Marathi the morpheme *-ij-* was normally used to form the passive verbs (ibid., $ 718; Joshi, $ 292; cf. in the inscriptions : *jhavije* "is seized, should be seized", Parel; *māvije* "is contained", Patan). This morpheme which is also found in Sindhi, Rajasthani (Beames, III, 72; LSI, *Raj.*, p. 10), in one of the speeches of the far N-W (Grierson, ZDMG, 1912, p. 12) and probably, with a little change of meaning, in the radical of the "respectful imperatives" of Hindi and Gujarati (cf.

Hoernle, p. 340; Beames, III, 110-113, Grierson, JRAS, 1910, p. 162-3 give a different explanation of these forms), goes back to Pkt. *-ijja-* which in the western dialects is the normal morpheme of the passive. Curiously, Panjabi alone still has clearly the form *-īa-* of the Śaurasenī and Māgadhī Prākrits or *-iyya-* of Paiśācī (Pischel, $ 535; Grierson, ZDMG, 1912, p. 85; cf. concerning Hindi *cāhiye,* etc., Grierson, JRAS, 1910, p. 163). The middle terminations having as we have seen, disappeared since the Prākrit period, the passive is, in old Marathi as in Prakrit, not a voice, but a secondary stem, whose inflexion is identical to that of all the intransitive verbs.

These are then the only secondary verbal suffixes of Marathi which have a definite morphological value.

Inflexion

$ 233. Verbal stems so constituted always remain distinct from terminations. The latter are distributed in two groups, according to whether the verbs are transitive or intransitive. In other words, Marathi has preserved in its inflexion, the distinction between verbs with stems in *-ati,* Pkt. *-ai* and causatives in *-ayati,* Pkt. *-ei.* This, then, is an archaism which is found again only in Sindhi (Trumpp, p. 284-5, 313 ff, 322 ff; Beames , III, p. 115) and moreover which tends to disappear in Marathi itself. The morpheme of the transitive *-i-*, developed out of the morpheme of the Pkt. causative *-e-* is found in the participial tenses between consonants inside the word. It thus becomes unstable therein and in fact grammars prescribe it as optional (Joshi, p. 204, 208). Even in the present and future, where dipthongisation gives to the transitive conjugation an aspect different from that of the intransitive conjugation, the first and second persons of plural are normally unified on the intransitive type, and there is wavering in respect of usage in other persons as well (Joshi, p. 198-9, 214; LSI, *Mar.*, p. 26).

$ 234. The conjugable forms of the Marathi verb are distributed as given below :

1. Old present indicative (become the past of habitude);
2. Future, formed on the old present;

3. Imperative;
4. Tenses remade, during the modern epoch, on participles and inflected according to the type of the present.

Past of habitude (*old present*)

$ 235. The terminations of the Skt. present have persisted upto Marathi without almost any other change than normal phonetic changes.

The table given below will suffice to bring out this regularity :—

	Intransitive			*Transitive*	
Skr.	Pkt.	Mar.	Skr.	Pkt.	Mar.
-āmi	*-āmi*	*-eṃ*	*-āyāmi*	*-emi*	*-īṃ*
-asi	*-asi*	*-asi, -as* or *-es*	*-ayasi*	*-esi*	*-īs*
-ati	*-ai*	*-e*	*-ayate*	*-ei*	*-ī*
-āmaḥ (*-āmo*)	*-āmo*	*-oṃ* ,*-ūṃ*	*-ayāmaḥ* (*ayāmo*)	*-emo*	....
-atta	*-aha*	*-ā* (*-āṃ*)	*-ayatha*	*-eha*	
-anti	*-anti*	*-at* (*i*), *at*	*-ayanti*	*-enti*	*-itī, -īt*

In the first and the third person of the singular, the forms **-aiṃ*, **-ai* which are at the origin of modern terminations (cf. $ 58) have not been preserved; but in the future the contraction has occcurred later, and the texts preserve *-ain*, *-ail* beside *-en*, *-el*; cf. $ 240. Regarding *-īṃ*, *-ī*, see $ 236 and for the first person pl. *-oṃ*, *-ūṃ*, $ 67.

The final vowel of the old terminations of the second sing. and third pl. is of same quantity ; cf. $ 38. The modern forms of the same terminations pose a delicate problem : should we consider—*as* in the second sing. as developed out of *-es* and this form as being phonetically regular, ? This is not impossible, see $ 58; but it is equally possible that *-as* be only phonetic and that in consequence *-es*, a form moreover more nasal, be due to the analogy of other persons of singular. The same explanation would fit the corresponding termination of the transitive, *-īs*. As regards the third pl. *-iti*, *it*, the preservation of *a* in *-ati*, *-at* shows that it is the same analogy which affects the timbre of the vowel.

The nasalisation of the second pl. *-āṃ* is spontaneous (cf. $ 70); it is missing in the imperative and future. Moreover even in the present its usage is far from being constant (Joshi, $ 299, 14, p. 200).

$ 236. The regularity of Marathi forms is all the more striking when we see that except Simhalese (Geiger, $ 58) all other languages have disagreements and obscurities, both of them more or less serious and numerous.[1] Only the termination of the third person sing. is everywhere identical (Beames, III, 102; Romany has *-el,* which is derived in regular manner from Skr. *-ati*).

In the second person plural, *-a* is found in a clear way only in Nepalese. In view of the relationship between this dialect and the Rajput dialects, Raj. *-āṃ* can be considered as being identical also with the Marathi form. The languages of the centre have *-o* (Apabh. *-ahu*) where one can see the result of a normal unvoicing of the final *-a.* Being. and Or. *-o* go back either to *-a* or to *-ahu.*

Phonetics already has more difficulty in explaining the forms of the first person. In the singular, only the eastern dialects agree with Marathi (Or. *-eṃ,* Beng. *-i,* Meith. *-ī*) ; everywhere else the vowel is *-ā* or *-o* (Panj., Sing., *-āṃ,* Guj. Him. Raj. Nep. *-oṃ* , Av. *-auṃ*; cf. Apa. *-auṃ*). Should we admit here a particular evolution due, or the one hand, to the premature loss of final *-ī* which is found in European Romany *-āv.* and on the other, the vocalic unvoicing provoked by nasalisation in the central dialects (cf. $ 39) ? What complicates the question is the fact that the palatal timbre, which is missing in the singular, is found again in the same languages (except in Sindhi) in the plural. One would say, observes Beames (III, p. 105), that an exchange has taken place between the two forms. This is not place to discuss the explanation proposed by him. It is more important to note that the agreement of Marathi with the eastern dialects and its disagreement with those of the central region is found elsewhere.

1. It will be seen from the table given in Grierson, *Piś. Lang.*, p. 57 and the observations that follow, as to how divergent and obscure are the forms in the mountainons group of the N-W, except in first person sing. We will also not take into account these speeches here.

In the second person sing., *-s* is found only in Bengali, Avadhi, Nepalese and Romany (the *-u* of Oriya is totally aberrant, see Beames, III, p. 104). Elsewhere are found the terminations of the Apabhraṃśa type *-ahi.* Can we say that in all these cases it is the phonetically regular passage of the intervocalic *s* into *h*, as is the case in Simhalese ? This is improbable (cf. $ 160). Perhaps Apabh. *-ahi* is, in part, the notation of *-ai,* coming from the assimilation of the second person to the third, for which more than one example is given by the present-day dialects (in Marathi of the Vidarbha region, *tu āhe* "you are", LSI, *Mar.*, p. 27; moreover the cases of analogy are more frequent in the plural, ibid., p. 43, 44, 45, 173, 195). Perhaps again this form and that of the first person in the same dialects come from the imperative (see $ 239).

Finally the *t* of the third pl. Skt. *-nti* has been preserved, in addition to Marathi and Simhalese, only in Oriya. We find in the other languages, on the one hand, the terminations in *n* (Beng. *-en*, *-an*, Nep. *-un*, *-an*, Sin. *ani*, Panj. *-an*, *-aṇ*, West. Panj. *-in*, Rom. *-en*) and on the other, the terminations of the Apabh. type *-ahiṃ* (Av., Maith. *-aiṃ*, Mag. *-īṃ*, Him. *-eṃ*, Raj. *-aiṃ*, *-ai*, Guj. *-e*). Neither one nor the other seems likely to be explained by normal phonetics (cf. Beames), III, 103, J. Bloch, JA, 1912, I, p. 333-4).

The opposition of the phonetically regular forms of Marathi with that of the languages of Apabhraṃśa type is a point of reference that is extremely important for the general history of the Indo-Aryan languages.

$ 237. This tense is used in Marathi chiefly for denoting an action repeated in the past, but it is the iterative sense which is the main thing here, because the same forms are used with the sense of the present, not only in archaic verbs like *hoy*, *āhe* "he is", *pāhije* "it should be", but also in proverbs (Joshi, $ 603 c). In other words, they mark the eventuality, which moreover, is, noticed when they are used in negation (Navalkar, $ 611, Joshi, $ 603 *e*; cf. the fixed locutions *nalage* "is not necessary", *naye* "does not work, should not have been"; see Navalkar, p. 151-2), with an interrogative pronoun (Joshi, $ 603 *d*), in the propositions of subordinate sense (Navalkar, $ 611, 3-4) and in a general way wherever it is a question of indicating the possibility (ex. *heṃ kām nū-c karūṃ jāṇeṃ* "I know that I will know how to do this job well", cited by Joshi, *l. l.*) In old Marathi, they also have the sense of the present, future or past according to the context. Thus we have in the same passage of *Jñāneśvarī* (=*Gītā*, III, X-11) :

Pārthā, āṇika hī eka
neṇasī tū heṃ kavatika... "You do not know of this marvel." (III-79)

dekheṃ : anukramādhāreṃ
svādharma jo ācare
to mokṣa teṇeṃ vyāpāreṃ
niścita pāve.

"See, the one who according to the order practises his dharma, certainly attains salvation by such conduct" (III, 80).

taiṃ nityayāgasahiteṃ
sṛjitīṃ bhūteṃ samasteṃ
pari neṇātī ci...

"Then all the beings were created with the eternal sacrifice; but they did not know." (III, 86).

teveḷī prajīṃ vinavilā brahmā
devā, āśrayo kāi etha āhmā
taṃu hmaṇe to kamaḷajanmā.

"Then the creatures asked Brahmā : O God, who is our support ? Whereupon the Lotus-Born talked to the beings" (III, 87

je yeṇeṃkarāni samastāṃ
paritoṣa hoila devatāṃ
maga te tuṃhāṃ īpsitā
ārthā teṃ deti
...yogakṣema niścitā
karitī tumcā.

"If the gods are satisfied, they will then bestow on you the object you desire; ...they will give you property complete and sure" (III, 95-96).

Cf. also the examples cited by Joshi, p. 399 and 191. The sense of eventuality is particularly clear in the inscription of Parel : *jo koṇhi e śasan lopī...* "whosoever will destroy this edict...."

$ 238. It can be seen that the sense, properly speaking

temporal, is extremely secondary in Marathi. What characterises the form is precisely the temporal indetermination. The same trait is found in other languages. In Simhalese, in Romany (Miklosich, XII, p. 48), in Oriya (LSI, *Or.*, p. 381) and besides in the majority of the non-literary dialects (Beames, III, p. 102) the sense of the present is normal, but in Bengali the same tense is used as historical present (Beames, III, p. 107) and almost everywhere in India, it takes up the function of the eventual future, of the subjunctive (Beames, III, p. 102, 107; Grierson, JAS *Beng.*, 1895, p. 353 ff.; cf. Grierson, *Maithili Gram.*, $ 196 ff.; Greaves, *A Gram. of Mod. Hindi*, $ 191 ff., etc.).

The origin of this indetermination of sense goes back very far in the past. The stem of the Skt. present denotes the notion of duration and, as is observed by Speyer, the absence of a tense expressing duration in the past must have been for quite something in extending the present to the past (*Ved. und Sanskr. Synt.*, $ 172). In the prose of the *Mahābhārata* are found several verbs in the present intercalated in a series of the forms of past tense : the former by their sense of duration are clearly opposed to the latter. (J. Bloch, MSL, XIV, p. 35). In any case, already for Pāṇini the present with *sma* denotes the past in its generality and the usage is constant in classical literature (J. Bloch, ibid., p. 67-8; Speyer, op. cit.).—But at the same time, it seems that due to the competition of the forms of the future, present also more slowly takes on the sense of the near or eventual future, preferably under certain conditions—in the first person, in answers, with *nanu* or *purā*, above all in the interrogative and relative sentences, that is to say, those corresponding to the subordinates in Marathi (Speyer, op. cit, $ 173; J. Bloch, op. cit., p. 36, 68-70).

The past of habitude of Marathi is thus the true successor of the Sanskrit "present", not only in its form, but also in its use. For expressing with precision the moments of duration, Marathi must have been obliged, by combining the elements it had received from Sanskrit, to constitute new forms.—Before reviewing them it will be useful to examine the imperative which is, with the present, the only group of conjugable forms of old origin in Marathi.

Imperative

$ 239. The terminations are as follows :—

	Sing.	Pl.
1.	*-ūṃ*	*-ūṃ*
2.	(*-a*)	*-ā*
3.	*-o*, *-ū*	*-ot*, *-ūt*

Those of the second and third sing. are the only ones whose transmission has been regular since Sanstkrit: Skr. Pkt., M. *-a*; Skr. *-atu*, Pkt. *-au*, M. *-o*.

In the second and third person plural, Prakrit had replaced the terminations of Sanskrit imperative by those of the present indicative (Pischel, $ 470, 471). Given the indeterminate value of the present, the decision or order are easily expressed by this form. Moreover, the loss of the past tense in Sanskrit must have, quite early, resulted in a serious weakness of the secondary terminations. In fact, everywhere the second plural of the imperative is similar to that of the indicative (Beames III, p. 108; on Simhalese, see Geiger, $ 62; on Romany, see Miklosich, XI, p. 43). However, as regards the first person plural, the history of the replacement of *-āma* by *-āmo* is probably not as simple as it looks. It is known that Pali had generalised the secondary termination *-ma*, and that it is found also in the future in archaic Prakrit (Lūders, *Bruchstücke*, p. 51). In any case, it is true that the termination of the present indicative has finally prevailed over that of imperative, as everywhere else.

The terminations of the first singular and third plural are clearly similar. The former is constructed on the type *-ati* : *-atu*, *-āmi* : **-āmu*. In fact Prakrit grammarians give the form *-āmu*. Bhāmaha (before 800 A. D.) even gives *-amu* (Pischel, $ 467). As regards *-ot*, it seems to have been re-made on the sing. *-o*, as the third pl. indic. active *-īt* has been on that of the sing. *-ī*, unless it be that the form *-untu* found in Oriya beside *-antu* (cf. also Beng. *-un*; see Beames, III, p. 108-9) is also the cause of the origin of the Marathi termination.

Oriya and Bengali with Marathi are the only languages having special forms of the imperative in the third person (Or. *-u*, *-untu*; Beng. *-uk*, *-un*). Everywhere else it is the old present which is used to express the order or the decision to be taken in all persons except in the second sing. This latter has its termination *-u* in Sindhi and *-a*, that is to say zero, in other languages. The form of second sing. imperative is, thus, everywhere, except in Sindhi, identical to the stem of the verb itself.

Old Marathi still has in this person a termination, that has now disappeared from usage : *-eṃ* in the verbs of intransitive type, *-īṃ* in the transitive ones; ex. *sāṃgeṃ* "say", *karīṃ* "do" (Joshi, p. 215). Should we then put this form in relationship with the corresponding termination *-hi* preserved in old Hindi poets and with the final *-ya* of the Kathiawar-dialects (Beames, III, 109; cf. LSI, *Guj.*, p. 427) ? The *rapprochement* is not sure, because we know that *-ahi* in these languages is the termination of the second sing. of the indicative, unless it be that we admit that only the forms of the first and second sing. of indicative are in reality borrowed from the imperative. Whatever be the case, the Marathi form seems directly to go back to the Prakrit form in *-hi* coming from the Skt. *-dhi* and extended to all the stems. Prakrit seems to have avoided the use of the stem *nu*: thence forms like *karetu*, *karehi*; *ruasu*, *ruehi* and those, notably frequent in Ardhamāgadhi, like *harāhi*, *vandāhi* (Pischel, $ 467-468). The form in *-su* has disappeared, undoubtedly because at the moment of the fall of the finals there was nothing to distinguish between *-su* and *-si*. But *-āhi*, *-ehī* have been partially maintained and undoubtedly Mar. *-eṃ*, *-īṃ* (with spontaneous nasalisation ? cf. $ 70) go back to these forms.

Future

$ 240. The future, tense of modern creation, but found in the oldest texts, is formed from the present, to which is added the indeclinable suffix *l*. The only exception is the first person plural, which is not distinguished from that of the old present nor that of the imperative. This confusion is surely due, on the hand, to the fundamental identity of the sense in the three cases and on the other hand, to the existence of an inconjugable form in *-ūn*, the gerundive. The terminations of the future are as follows :

Intransitive	Transitive
-ain, -en	*-īn*
-aśīl	*iśīl*
-ail, -el	*-īl*
(*-ūṃ*)	(*-ūṃ*)
-āl	*-āl*
-atīl	*-itīl*

These terminations do not raise any difficulty of a phonetic nature (re. the final *n* resulting from *l* after a nasal vowel, see $ 72), but even their formation is obscure. Only the comparison with other languages enables us to see as to what is *l*, the characteristic of future.

$ 241. The sigmatic future of Sanskrit seems to have existed everywhere. It exists without competition in Gujarati, West. Panjabi, and with a deviation in sense, in Kashmiri (Grierson, *JAS Beng.*, 1895., p. 356, 375; cf. Beames, III, p. 112), but it is found co-existing, the most often, with more recent forms, in various dialects, which are as follows : Marwari which is situated between Gujarati and West. Panjabi (suffix in *-h-*; LSI, *Raj.*, p.12), Bhili, contiguous to Gujarati (suffix in *-s-* and *-h-*, LSI, *Bhil Lang.*, p. 4), to the east of the preceding ones Jaipuri (suffix in -s-), Braj and Bundeli (suffix in *-h-*, LSI, *Raj.*, p. 12), and even in the eastern group, the dialects of eastern Hindi and Bhojpuri, where the suffix *-b-* has entrenched itself only in the two first persons (suffix in *-h-*, LSI, *East. Hindi*, p. 7). No trace of this future is to be found during any period of Marāṭhi.

Almost everywhere it has ceded the place, or is progressively ceding the same to other forms. In Sindhi and in Simhalese, the future is constituted by the present participle to which are added the personal terminations (Beames, III, p. 126; Geiger, $ 61). A variant of the same formation is found in Konkani (present part., fixed at masc. + *l* + personal suffixes; ex. *nidtoloṃ* "I will sleep", LSI, *Mar.*, p. 170, 173). "The third variety " of the future in Maithili is equally made on the present participle (Grierson, *Maith. Gram.*, $ 204). It will be noted that this formation is that of the present n Marathi (see infra, $ 244). On still another participle, but this time on the future participle, is formed the future of all the eastern dialects (*-ba-* <Skr. *-tavya*, LSI, *East. Hindi*, p. 6-7). The same holds true, with a different participle, in certain mountainous dialects of the N-W. (Grierson, *Piś. Lang.*, p. 61-2).

As a result of the preceding observations it is clear that all the languages situated on the borders of the Indo-Aryan domain have preserved the old sigmatic future or have replaced the same by using a participle. The only exception is the language that occupies our attention. In fact on this point Marathi is joined to the group of central languages, whose future is constituted by the old present followed by a single suffix (the dialects of the far N-W. seem to utilise the present alone, as in Iranian , see Grierson, *l. l.* Romany does the same or makes use of the periphrase, for ex. with the verbs denoting "to desire", according to a formula found also in Iran, see Miklosich, XI, p. 48 ff; cf. Hoernle, *Grundriss der Iran. Phil.*, I, 2nd edn., p. 155; Geiger, ibid., p. 327, 370-1).

The suffix of the future is not identical everywhere; *l* is found, in addition to Konkani already cited, in the suffixes *lo* or *lā* of Bhili (LSI, *Bhil Lang.*, p. 3) and Marwari (LSI, *Raj.*, p. 13). To the east of this last-named dialect, in Jaipuri *lo* is added to the present, but this suffix therein is declinable like an adjective. The same gradation is found between the most meridional dialect of Rajasthan, the Malvi, where the suffix for future is *gā* (which is found in Marwari and Bhili) and in its eastern neighbour, Bundeli, where this suffix is an adjective, masc. sing. *go* (LSI, *Raj.*, *l. l.*). It seems, therefore, that a dialectal line separates the dialects of the S-W. (Marwari, Malvi, Bhilī, Marathi), wherein the suffixes of the future are indeclinable, from the dialects that are properly speaking central, where they are declinable adjectives. And in fact if we continue more to the east and north, we will find *gā* declined in Panjabi, in Braj and in all the dialects of Hindi and *lā* declined in Nepali (in Garhwal and Kumaun *lo*, declined, see Beames, III, p. 162, LSI, *Pahari*, 141, 292) and in Bhojpuri (declined, LSI, *Bihari*, p. 48-9, 52).

$ 242. Marathi is thus quite in its place in the group with indeclinable suffixes. We are, moreover, authorised to think that the indeclinable suffix *l* is only a reduced form, a stem that has not undergone or preserved the enlargement of the adjectives, of the adjective *lo* or *lā* of the eastern group. Which is this adjective? The competing word *gā* is the Pkt. part. *gaa-*, Skr. *gata-*; Hindi *karūṃ gā* thus definitely denotes exactly "I am going to do—(I have) departed" that is to say "I have departed for doing" (see among others Beames, III, p. 161). From this, we are led to think that the adjective *lā* is also a participle, for ex. that of the Skt. root *lā-* "to take" or of the root which has generally supplanted it in Prakrit *le-* (cf. Mar. *lāvṇeṃ*, *leṇeṃ*). This is how in Russian Romany the verb *la-* "to take" is used in the periphrase denoting the future, as in Greek Romany the verb *kam-* "to desire" (Miklosich, XII, p. 49). If Marathi had been the only one in question, we could at best consider *l* as the residue of the participle **gel-* **gelā* equivalent to Hindi *gā*, Skt. *gata-*. In fact we have seen that in Konkani the suffix of the dative could have been *gelo* or *lo* (cf. $ 200), but the existence of *lo* or *lā* in the dialects as in those of Rajasthani or of Nepal, where the past participle is formed without the suffix *l*, and where the participle of the verb "to go" in particular is *gayo* (LSI, *Raj.*, p. 27, 29, etc.; Grierson, ZDMG, LXI, p. 664) is an obstacle in the way of this hypothesis.

That it concerns a participle is in any case made extremely probable, besides the future in *gā* of the central dialects, by the existence in Sindhi of a tense formed in an identical manner. The present indefinite (durative and inchoative) consists therein of the potential, that is to say of the old present, plus the participle *tho* (Skr. *sthita-*), ex. *āūṃ halāṃ tho* "I go, I am going" (Trumpp, p. 293).

Participial Tenses

$ 243. The nominal phrase of Sanskrit led to the increasingly frequent use of participles, the nominal element for the form, but with an all the more characteristic verbal value as they replaced verbal forms fallen in dis-use (see J. Bloch, MSL, XIV, p. 56 ff., 84 ff). These participles had been those in *-ta-*, *tavya-*, *-tavant-* The last one among these, which has had a relatively recent extension, howeve, quickly goes out of usage, its convenience notwithstanding (ibid.,

p. 58, 85). The two others, on the contrary, have subsisted upto a point where numerous formations, expressing, in the modern languages, the past and the obligation (or the future) are based on the verbals in *-ta-* and *-tavya.*

This is not all : the present participle, which in classical Sanskrit was used only in opposition to a complement or a subject of another verb, has taken in the modern epoch, a usage similar to that of other participles. Sometimes, it is found, especially in Vedic prose, in juxtaposition to a verb expressing the state and thus taking the value of a verb durative in time or of the mode determined by the form of the verb expressing the state. But this construction, whose examples will be found in Whitney ($ 1075) and Speyer (*Ved und Skr. Synt.*, $ 205), becomes exceptional during the classical period. However the temporal value of the old present gets weakened and the participle is used to form a new periphrase expressing the duration in the present. Several periphrases playing the same role are found in different languages (Meillet, *Scientia*, 1912, p. 399), but in the modern period, a type comparable to the Indo-Aryan exists only in English (in the type *I am going, he is reading the Bible*) and in Greek, on the one hand during the period of *koine* and on the other in certain modern isolated dialects, notably the Tsaconian (Moulton, *Einleitung in die Spr. des Neutest.*, p. 357-60; similar examples of the classical period are contested by Alexander, *Am. J. Phil.*, 1883, p. 291 ff). Moreover neither in English nor in Greek is found the intimate union of the elements, which characterises the Indo-Aryan.

In fact, without there being anything in the history of Sanskrit to let us foresee it, new tenses have been constructed on the participle in *-ant-* like the verbal adjetives in *-ta-* and *tavya-*. These recent creations are found in almost all the languages of continental India (Grierson, *JAS Beng.*, 1895, p. 367 ff. Beames, III, p. 126 ff.). Among the causes that could have favoured the new extension of the present participle, we can count, on the one hand, on the vaccum resulting in the conjugation due to the love of the temporal value itself of the present indicative, and on the other, to the disappearance of the participle in *-tavant,* practically a homonym and synonym of the participle in *-ant-*. It is probably useful to recall also that the Dravidian verb is essentially a participle with a pronominal suffix, alike the pronouns varying in gender in the third person (LSI, *Munda and Dran. Lang.*, p. 295 and passion; cf. Vinson, *Man. de langue tamoule*, fl $ 46-48) and that at present the thematic characteristic of this participle is *t* in the northernmost Dravidian languages, except Brahui (LSI, *ibid.*, p. 296).

Definitively it can be said that the present participle furnishes, in the same way as the past and future participles, several new formations to the modern Indo-Aryan languages. Moreover, irrespective of their age, all these participial formations are modern and have been independently developed in various dialects. In fact if the principle is common to all of them, the methods have not been the same.

The formation of the participial tenses continues even today. Thus we can observe in the eastern dialects a progressive replacement of the sigmatic future by the future in *-b-* (Skr. *-tavya-*). From speech to speech we can notice hesitations in the distribution of forms, that show an unstable state LSI, *East. Hindi*, p. 7). Similarly in Marathi, the various forms drawn from the past participle are in competition, where logic or scholarly authorities can do nothing. One can see herein the beginning of the changes in the conjugated verb of the participle in *-vā* (*-tavya-*). From there one can conceive that in the absence of philological statistics or of minute dialectal descriptions, history of all the forms often remains obscure, even when its origin and principles are clear.

Tenses formed on the present participle in -t

Present, Conditional

$ 244. The nominal origin of these comes out in the terminations of the singular, which vary according to genders. Those of the plural, on the contrary, are almost completely assimilated with the verb.

The terminations of the present are as follows :

Sing. 1. m. *-toṃ*, f. *-teṃ* (*-tyeṃ*), n. *-teṃ*
2. m. *-tos*, f. *-tes* (*-tyes*, *-tīs*), n. *-teṃs*
3. m. *-to*, f. *-te* (*-tye*, *-tī*), n. *-teṃ*.
Pl 1. *-toṃ*
2. *-tāṃ*
3. *-tāt* (fem. dial. *-tyāt*).

The termination of the conditional (irreal, see Navalkar, $ 622, 675) are :

Sing. 1. M. *-toṃ*, f. *-tīṃ*, n. *-teṃ*
2. m. *-tās*, f. *-tīs*, n. *-teṃs*
3. m. *-tā*, f. *-tī*, n. *-teṃ*

Pl. 1. *toṃ*
2. *tāṃ*
3. m. *te*, f. *-tyā*, n. *-tīṃ*.

$245. The differentiation between these two forms seems to be recent in date. In the *Jñāneśvarī*, the nominal forms of the first type are absolutely missing, those of the second have the sense of the present and moreover they are not found in the first person. Are found for the sigular.

second person : *dāvitāsi* (var. *dāvisi*) "you show" *pāḷitāsi* (var. *pāḷisi*, *pāḷitosi*) "you protect" (XI 311), *bujhtāsi* "you understand" (XVIII, 1340), *hotāsi* "you have been" (XI, 274), *dekhtāsi* "you see' (XVIII, 1545).

third person : *puravitā* "he fills" (I, 27), *hotī* "she is" (V, 15), *positā* "he supports" (XVIII, 1650). Is also encountered the same form used in conditional propositions, XVIII, 1702, 1704, but no conclusions need be drawn, as the same passage has on old present, made in the same way.

In the third person plural, the modern form is frequently found : *dumdumitāti* (var. *dumdumitī*) "resound" (or "resounded"; the entire passage is a description of past facts, I, 130), *hiṃvatāti* "shiver, shivered" (I, 135), *varṣatāti* "rain, rained" (I, 166), *giṃvasitāti* (? var. *giṃvasīt āhāti*) "purify, search" (XI, 307), *śinatāti* "tire themselves" (XI, 677), *dekhatāti* "see" (XIII, 59), *mānitāti* 'consider" (XIII, 1133), *pusatāti* "demand" (XV, 1158), *nāṃdatāti* "enjoy themselves" (XVIII, 1594), etc.

Besides the forms with verbal terminations, is also found with the same meaning, the form of the modern "conditional" : *ja hote* "those that are" or "had been" (I, 164), *juṃjhate je* "those who fight" (I, 170), *he marte* "they die" (II, 137).

$ 246. The forms of the modern "conditional", to the extent that they do not recover those of the "present", are in reality participles with the normal enlargement of the adjectives in *-ā* (Pkt. *ao*).

The participle in *-t* alone has survived in the modern language, with the exception of *hotā*, which has taken the sense of past, and perhaps of several adverbial forms in *-tāṃ*. (see $ 194). But in the *Jñāneśvarī*, the participle in *-tā* is as normal as the other one. It is found in the juxtaposed ones like *boltā jāltā* "said", literally "had (been) saying" (XII, 20, XV, 48), *kartā hoil* "will do", literally, "will be doing" (IV, 21). It is used alone with the value of a verb in the third of the present, by the application of the old rules of the nominal sentence. Joined to a personal pronoun, it has, following the same rules (cf. J. Bloch, MSL, XIV, p. 54, 76, 90), the value of a present in the person expressing that pronoun. We find, for example, in the first singular *mī māritā he marte* "I strike, they die" (II, 1377), *mi kartā* "I do" (XVIII, 515), *tarī mī na mhaṇatā, jari...nadekhatā* "I would not say that, if I had not been seeing..." (VI, 122).

Finally, as had been the case with the Sanskrit verbal in *-ta* (J. Bloch, ibid., p. 91-2), the present participles of Marathi can be accompanied by a verb expressing existence.

Sometimes the elements of the group are disjoined, as in *karit ci ase* "he does" (XVIII, 1177); the most often they are juxtaposed. Thus we have in the *Jñāneśvarī*; *mī arcit aseṃ* "I adore" (IX, 14), *mī...bolat āhe* "I say" (IX, 144); *tūṃ... karitu āhāsi* "you do" (II, 6, 12) *tūṃ...mhaṇat āhāsi* "you say" (II, 137), *karavīt āhāsi* "you make do" (III, 5), *parisat āhāsi* you listen" (VIII, 54); *kāṃpat ase* "he trembles" (I, 129), *mhaṇat ase* "he says" (I, 169), *karīt ase* "he does" (II, 1), *det āhe* "he gives" (VII, 61), *vicarijat ase* "is demanded", *galatī āhe* "is drained" (the subject is in feminine, XV, 287);

āhmī sāṃgat asoṃ "we say" (VI, 162), *pāhat āhoṃ* "we look" (X, 182);

bolat asāṃ "you say" (IV, 184);

pāhat āhātī "they look" (XIII, 642), *pāvate hotī* "they acquire" (subject in the masculine, III, 44), *kāriteṃ āhāti* "do" (subject in neuter, XIII, 306), *vartateṃ* (var. *vartat*, *vartatīṃ*; the subject is in neuter) *āhāti* "they meet" (VII, 37).

$ 247. It will suffice to compare those of the groups consisting of the not-enlarged participle and the verb *āhṇeṃ* with the forms cited in $ 245 for finding out their identity. The aspiration, unstable between vowels, is particularly so between two as : *dejhtāsi* and *dekhat āhāsi*, *pāhatāsi* and *pāhat āhāsi* are thus not only equivalent but identical. Moreover, that these juxtaposed ones be formed exclusively with the non-enlarged participle, is neither certain nor universal. The dialects of the Konkan preserve, in the third person plural, a feminine termination *-tyāt* which goes back to *-tyā āhāt*. It is, therefore, possible that, at a relatively recent date, various unifications of forms, with the masculine always prevailing over others have occurred (cf. infra).

In the third person plural, the juxtaposed one has preserved in the normal language the sense of the present; the nominal forms are reserved for the conditional. But the three forms of the singular have taken the value of the conditional. The question is : to what is this change due ? This evolution has nothing so very abnormal in itself and similar facts are to be met with in Hindi, Bengali and Oriya (Beames, III, p. 129, 132). But it is impossible to trace its history in Marathi. In any case it is met with in the *Deś* proper, because the dialects have generally preserved the present, which is found in the *Jñāneśvarī*. Thus the present of *nid-* "to sleep" is in the Konkan : sing. 1. *nidtāṃ*, 2. *nidtāy* (cf. *asāy* "you are"; in Goa one would say *nidtās*, see Joshi, p. 188), 3. *nidtā*; pl. 1. *nidtāv*, 2. *nidtāt* (the second pl. is always assimilated to the third), 3. *nidtāt* (LSI, *Mar.*, p. 173). We see that the nominal value of these forms has entirely ceased to be felt. This is all the more noticeable in the fact that only the masculine form subsists in the singular. Moreover it is not impossible that this form may have been derived, in these dialects, through borrowing from the common language, because the enlargement therein is *-ā*, whereas the normal enlargement in these dialects is *-o*.

$ 248. Inversely, the *Deś* normally ignores the enlargement in *-o-*. Now the actual present is based on a participle with the masc. termination *-to*, whose extension seems to be linked with the change of meanings of the participles in *-tā*. The Jñāneśvari does not know of these forms: in this text *pāḷitosī* is merely an incorrect variant of *pāḷitāsi* (XI, 311) and similarly *stavito* "he praises" (XVIII, 1137), *bhogito* "he enjoys" (XVIII, 1154), which are given in certain texts, should be read as *stavī to*, *bhogī to*. They are the forms of third person present followed by the pronoun which serves for their subject, like *anubhavī to* "he experiences" (V 57) for which no variant has been found. But Namdev already knows the new forms *yetoṃ* "I come", *pāhtosi* "you see", *karito* "he does". Whence come these forms ? A loan can not be admitted because the dialects, with the nornal enlargement in *-o* have precisely adopted the form in *-ā*. The verb *hoṇeṃ* is equally not in question, because *o* is not found in all the genders. Most probably we have to recognise the pronominal terminations in the actual present. In fact the feminine of these forms does not have an *i* but on *e* as in the pronouns (cf. Navalkar, p. 94). We can moreover conceive the thing in two different ways. Either it is an extension of the pronominal termination, due to the frequent place of the pronoun after the verb or the participle to which it is joined. Besides forms like *anubhavī to* cited above, we find for example *puravitā to* "he fills up " (I, 27). An easy haplology (*purvitā to* >*purvito*) would have fixed the pronominal termination to the participle. Or the form is not more recent, but is older, despite appearance than the form in *-tā*. We have already seen that the popular poets present forms which, though missing in the Jñāneśvarī and learned poetry in general, had been old in date. We should also not forget that we have in the Jñāneśvarī itself the terminations of the first person sing. of the past in *-loṃ* beside the terminations of the second person in *-lāsi*.

It is, thus, not impossible that the type *pāhtosi* of Namdev be as old, indeed older than the type *dekhtāsi* of Jñāneśvar and that the participial terminations, on which is based the modern present, be contemporary of the pronominal forms and not re-made after them. In other terms, it is not impossible that both of them be equally the remains of the archaic declension.

$ 249. Leaving aside the terminational variations, the present-conditional, is thus, a juxtaposed one of the present participle and of the verb *āh-* "to be", where the welding of the two words is more complete than in the periphrases consisting for example of the same participle and of *as-* or *ho-*. The history of Marathi is found again in the largest part of the Indo-Aryan languages.

In the central and western languages, the participle

alone is equivalent to a personal verb (Beames, III, p. 131-2; Grierson, *JAS Beng.*, 1895, p. 367-8). In Sindhi this usage is reserved for poetry. In current language, the participle is followed by oblique pronominal forms (Grierson, ibid., Trumpp, p. 289-91, 294). The affixing of the oblique pronouns is also found in certain speeches of the Himalayan N-W. (Grierson, *Piś. Lang.*, p. 57). However, almost everywhere, the participle is commonly found as juxtaposed to a verb denoting "to be". Most often the two words remain independent in form. Such is the case in Sindhi, Panjabi, Braj., Hindi, Bundeli Bengali, in the dialects of Central Himalayas (Beames, III. p. 179 ff., 192 ff., 203 ff., Grierson, LSI, *Raj.*, p. 13; cf. *Bhil Lang.*, p. 4), in Kashmiri (Grierson, *Man. Kash. Lang.*, $ 60 ff.). But in Western Panjabi the welding is frequent with the verb *hā-* (Wilson, *Gram. of West. Panj.*, *Glossary of Multani Lang.*, p. 52). Despite certain difficulties of detail, it is probable that the present (with the conditional in Bengali, Bihari and Baiswari) of all the languages of the eastern group is explained by a welding similar to that of Marathi. In fact, whereas in the third person the participle remains without addition, in other persons terminations similar to those of the old present are added thereto (Beames, III, p. 129-30, and compare the tables given by Grierson in the article cited above, p. 368, 354). Lastly, the speeches of the far N-W., despite their obscurity, enable us to observe similar facts (Grierson, *Piś. Lang.*, p. 58).

Marathi is, thus, in agreement with the majority of the related languages. At the same time, it clearly differs from the dialectal group, which is contiguous in the North. In Gujarati the participle subsists in isolation with the value of the conditional or of the indefinite past according as it has or lacks an enlargement (Tisdall, *Simpl. Gram.*, p. 48-9). But it is not found in any juxtaposition used to denote the present. Modern Gujarati (in old times it had only the archaic present, LSI, *Raj.*, p. 360), Northern Bhili and the dialects of Rajasthan (LSI *Raj.*, p. 13, *Bhil Lang.*, p. 4) agree in that they form the present by juxtaposing two conjugated forms, that is the archaic present and the present of the verb "to be". This type is unknown elsewhere.

Past

$ 250. The terminations of the past are as follows :

		masc.	fem.	neut.
Sing.	1.	*-loṃ*	*-lyeṃ, -leṃ*	*-leṃ*
	2.	*-lās*	*-līs*	*-leṃs*
	3.	*-lā*	*-lī*	*-leṃ*
Pl.	1.	*-loṃ*	)	
	2.	*-lāṃ*	) in three genders	
	3.	*-le*	*-lyā*	*-līṃ*

These terminations are based on the past participle in *-lā* as was the case with the present with regard to the present participle in *-tā*. But its fixation seems to be older. In the Jñāneśvarī, the provisionally inexplicable opposition of the pronominal masc.- fem. terminations in first person singular and of the nominal terminations in the second person is already normal therein (curious variants are, however found. *mī bolilāṃ* or *boliloṃ* "I have said", *mī...pātlāṃ* or *pātloṃ* "I have fallen", XVIII, 1767, 1774).

In the second person plural we find beside *-lāṃ*, either *-lāṃt*, or a variable termination in masc. *-let*, fem. *-lyāt*, neut. *-līṃt*. These forms, frequent in poetry, are given nowadays as provincialisms (Joshi, p. 208, cf. LSI, *Mar.*, 0. 43). They come from the frequent assimilation in the dialects, as we have already seen, of the second person plural with the third person. Moreover they pre-suppose the existence of the third person of the juxtaposed ones with *āhāti* of the same type, as those that have furnished the termination of the present. The *Jñāneśvari*, in fact, offers several examples of these juxtaposed ones (*ghātale āhātī* "are taken", XVIII, 1064, cf. *gele asati* "are gone", I, 86).

$ 251. The use of these forms requires certain observations. The Marathi participle in *-lā*, like the Sanskrit participle in *-ta-*, which it has succeeded, takes according to the sense of the root, the intransitive or the passive value. The former requires no explanation. *jhāḍ paḍleṃ* "the tree has fallen", *mī paḍloṃ* "I have fallen " are the nominal sentences of normal type. In the second case, the original construction has undergone various secondary changes, among whom a few have reacted on the form itself.

In principle, the logical object of the action is in the nominative and the logical subject in the instrumental. Examples are :

Cāvuṇḍarājeṃ karaviyaleṃ "made on the orders of (*Cāvuṇḍarāja*" (Inscrip. of Śravaṇa Belgola);

myāṃ abhivandila śrīguru ci "I have offered my adorations to the guru" (*Jñāneśvarī*, I, 27); *aiseṃ pāhileṃ myāṃ* "this is what I have seen" (ibid., XI, 275), *jeṃ tuṃhī vākya bolileṃ* "the words that you have uttered" (ibid., III, 1); *kṛpā kelī tumhīṃ* "you have had pity" (ibid., XI, 255); *tumhīṃ mī aṅgīkārilā* "you have accepted me" (ibid., I, 65).

A particular case of this construction concerns the one where the participle in the neuter singular is not accompanied by any opposition expressing the logical complement. This type of sentence, extremely frequent in Sanskrit and Prakrit (J Bloch, MSL, XIV p. 58 ff. 89 ff; Jacobi *Ausgew. Erzāhl., Gramm.*, $ 82), persists in Marathi as everywhere else; example: *arjuneṃ mhaṇitaleṃ* "Arjuna said *Jñān.*, III, 1).

But the rôle of this turn in a large number of modern Indo-Aryan languages does not stop here. To the originally selfsufficient group, which is composed of the neuter participle accompanied by its logical subject in the instrumental, has been added a logical complement in an oblique case. This explains the use of pronominal suffixes juxtaposed to the participle in such a way as to constitute a new conjugation in the groups of the N-W. and the east (Grierson *JAS Beng.*, 1895, p. 363 ff.) as also, for example in Hindi, the existence of sentences like *tab rājā ne is bāt ko batāyā* (masc. in the sense of the neuter), beside the logically constructed sentence : *tab rājā ne yih bāt batāī* "then the king explained the affair" (example taken from Greaves, *Gramm. of Mod. Hindi*, $ 153; cf. Grierson, ibid., p. 361 ff.), The same turn is found in Marathi : thus we say *tyā neṃ Rāmās mārileṃ* in place of *Rām mārilā* "he has struck Rām." Moreover, it has been recently introduced therein and is used only when the logical complement is the name of a person or of an animated being and in this case it is but optional (Joshi, $ 462, 468 *d*).

$ 252. As against the foregoing, several innovations have been introduced in Marathi whose principle is the tendency to maintain the logical subject in the nominative.

The simplest consists in the mixing of two nominal constructions set out below : Instead of saying : *tyāṇeṃ āplā mulgā śāḷemt pāthavilā* or *tyāṇeṃ āplya mūlās śālemt pāṭhavileṃ* "he has sent his son to school", one would say, *tyāṇeṃ āplyā mulās śālemt pāṭhavilā* (Joshi, $ 466 *b*). This turn, incorrect from the point of view of the grammarian, is quite frequent and is to be found in poetry. According to the investigators of the Linguistic Survey, it belongs to Konkan (LSI, *Mar.*, p. 67, 170). In addition it is found in Gujarati normally and in Rajasthani a number of times (LSI, *Raj.*, p. 332).

Another mixing is produced in a certain number of verbs. Instead of saying *tvāṃ* (*tumhīṃ*) *kām keleṃ* "you (both sing. and pl.) have done the work", we re-establish the personal pronoun in the nominative and add to the declined participle the normal termination of the intransitive verbs. Thus we get : *tūṃ kām keleṃs* "you have done the work", *tūṃ pothi lihilīs* "you have written the book.', *tūṃ pothyā lihilyās* "you have written the books" and *tumhī kāṃ keleṃt* "you have done the work, etc.

Its apparent complication notwithstanding and despite the authorities incharge of Public Instruction, this turn is in constant use and modern poets do not hesitate to use the same. In the Konkan, it is extended even to the third person. But here, as the termination added to the participle can not be verbal, it is borrowed from the nominal declension: it is the termination of the instrumental. Thus we say *yā saheban* (*sahebanīṃ*) *malā dile-n* (*dilenīṃ*) "the sahab has (the sahabs have) given me a tip" (exemples drawn from the notes of Bhandarkar; cf. Joshi, $ 466 and LSI, *Mar.*, p. 67, 221).

The last consequence of this tendency to keep the logical subject in the nominative and of keeping it in accord with the past participle has led to the constitution of a veritable past participle with active value An entire series of verbs, classified by grammarians in the *umajgaṇ,* have thus transformed the traditional construction. We do not say, *myāṃ teṃ umajleṃ myāṃ goṣṭ visarlī* but *mī teṃ umajloṃ* "I have understood that", *mī tujhī goṣṭ visarloṃ* "I have forgotten your story" and similarly *tī aseṃ mhaṇālī* "he has said that", etc. (Joshi, $ 468 *b*).

The class of verbs under question is constituted by the

following verbs as given by Joshi ($ 299, 4) : *umaj-* "to understand", *āṃcav-* "to rinse the mouth", *ok-* "to vomit", *utar-* "to cross", *kheḷ-* "to play", *caḍh-* "to climb", *cuk-* "to miss", *tar-* "to pass", *pasav-* "to deliver (mare, she-ass) to burst (ear of grain)" *pāv* "to obtain", *pohaṃc-* "to arrive at, to obtain", *poh-* "to swim across", *prasav-* "to give birth", *baḍbaḍ* "to gossip", *bol-* "to say", *bhaj-* "to adore", *bhul-* "to forget", *muk-* "to lose", *laḍh-* "to combat", *lābh-*, *lāh-* "to obtain, to gain", *vad-* "to say", *visar-* "to forget", *visamb-* "to neglect", *śik-* "to learn", *samaj-* "to understand", *smar-* "to recall to oneself", *hag-* "to excrete", *huk-* "to miss", *mhaṇ-* "to say" (*mhaṇālom*, etc., the form *mhaṭlem* keeps the passive sense). The list, whose order itself reveals recent reshuffling (*āṃcav-* should have been the first) is not complete. The verbs *gā-* "to sing", *pī-* "to drink", *le-* "to take", *kar-* "to do", (in certain expressions *snān karnem-* to take a bath", etc.), *ghaḍ-* "to touch", *ācar-* "to practice, to do", and still many more can be constructed in the same way (Joshi, $ 468, *c*, *e*, *f*; cf. $ 299, 6; cf. Molesworth, *Preface, gener. intim.*, $ 13, p. VIII).

The innovation, referred to here, is not recent in Marathi. We find, for example, already in the *Jñāneśvarī*: *hem bolilom* "I have said that" (XVIII, 1131), *mī granthalom* "I have composed" (XVIII, 1770), *leilāsī* "you have taken" (XI, 294), etc. (On the other hand, *jeṇem tārilom hā saṃsāra-puru* "(the guru), thanks to whom I have traversed the high waves of transmigration" (I, 22) seems incorrect in any case, as the noun is in the nominative. The variant *tārilā* should have been introduced in the text.).

Found since the days of origin, dominating by becoming increasingly frequent, it seems that the active construction of the past with intransitive verbs has, from now on, acquired enough vitality in the first two persons for eliminating the traditional passive construction. In fact the sentences, as those given below and taken from the Jñāneśvarī are, because of their origin (cf. J. Bloch, MSL XIV, p. 58), 60, 86, 90), absolutely correct ;—

mi...kavaḷilom mohem "I have been a prey to bewilderment" (III, 10);

hem paḍhavilom Jī-svāmi-Nivṛttidevīm "this is what

I have learnt from N." (XII, 247);

and *myāṃ dekhilāsi* "you have been seen by me" (XI, 306, cf. 258, 282), are because of their origin (cf. J. Bloch, MSL, XIV, p. 58, 60, 86,90) absolutely correct and yet they have gone out of use (Joshi, $ 302, *i*; cf. $ 465).

The actual tendency of Marathi is thus to establish in the past a unique conjugation constituted in two first persons by the forms with verbal termination, in accord with the logical subject in the nominative. In the third person, the two constructions still co-exist but the trouble found therein already points to a state of provisional disequilibrium, which will perhaps also lead to unification.

Tenses formed on the participle of obligation

$ 253. The participle in *-āvā* (Skr. *-tavyaḥ*) can be constructed in a purely nominal manner in all the persons except the second singular, where the characteristic *-s* has prevailed in usage. In the plural, beside the nominal forms, are also found the same verbal terminations as in the past tense. The tense under discussion is, therefore, still in the process of formation, and when grammarians list it as being equal to other tenses, that is not correct. Their forms are as given below :

		masc.	fem.	neut.
Sing.	1.	*-āvā*	*-āvī*	*-āveṃ*
	2.	*-āvās*	*-āvīs*	*-āveṃs*
	3.	*āvā*	*-āvī*	*-āveṃ*
Pl.	1.	*-āve*	*-āvyā*	*-āviṃ* or *-āveṃ* (indecl.)
	2 and 3.	*-āve* or *-āvet*	*-āvyā* or *āvyāt*	*-āviṃ* or *āviṃt.*

The use of these forms is similar to that of the forms of the past. In the case of intransitive verbs, the participle is in accord with the subject if it denotes an inanimate being. It can also be construed in the neuter, the logical subject being in the instrumental, if it is an animated being. Examples are : *ātāṃ pāūs paḍāvā* "now the rains should come." *to gharīṃ yāvā* or *tyāneṃ yāveṃ* "he should come to the house" (ex. of Joshi, $ 468 *i*). In the case of roots with transitive sense, the passive construction is the rule; ex. *ahmī kāy karāveṃ* "what should we do ?" (*Jñān.*, III, 6), *tumhī...voḷagaveti ahmīṃ* "we should attach ourselves to you" (ibid., XII, 247). But an entire series of verbs, i.e. *aikṇeṃ, pariṣṇeṃ* "to hear", *dekhṇeṃ* "to see" *baghṇeṃ* "to regard", *pusṇeṃ* "to demand", *sāṃgṇeṃ*, *mhaṇṇeṃ* "to say", *bhajṇeṃ* "to adore", *ḍasṇeṃ* "to bite", *cāvṇeṃ* "to masticate", *śivṇeṃ, ghaḍṇeṃ* "to touch", *jhagaḍṇeṃ, jhomṃbṇeṃ, lagatṇeṃ* "to get hold of", are constructed in the neuter, the logical subject being in the instrumental (Joshi, $ 468, *g, h*). Moreover, the future participle is changed into active verb like the participle in *-lā* by the addition of *-s* in the singular, and of *-t* in the plural, into the regularly declined form. An example given by Bhandarkar is as follows : *tūṃ granth lihāvās, pothi vācavīs āṇi dusreṃ kām karāveṃs* "you should write a book, read another and do something else."

$ 254. The entire conjugation of the potential should probably be taken back to the same participle, although several grammarians abusively link it with the causative, whose construction as well as sense are entirely different. In fact, the logical subject of the potential is always an indirect case, ordinarily in the instrumental : *mājhyāṇeṃ* or *malā cālavleṃ, cālavleṃ* "I can walk, I have been able to walk"; *mājhyāṇeṃ* or *malā dhaḍā śikavlā* "I have been able to learn the lesson", *mājhāpṇeṃ* or *malā tyālā śikavaleṃ* "I have been able to teach him", cf. *āhmīṃ śaktihiṇeṃ kaiseṃ karavel teṃ neṇeṃ* "deprived of force, what I can do, I do not know" (Tukārām); (see Navalkar 233 ff.; Joshi, $ 329 ff., $ 468 *j*; examples from texts in Godbole, $ 293).

Impersonal Forms

Participles

$ 255. The present participle is in *-t* and therefore goes back to the active participle of Sanskrit, *-ant-*, Pkt. *-anta-* (Pischel, $ 560). The same form is found in Gujarati, Rajasthani and Hindi. It is found indirectly by the infinitive *-ite* of Bengali. In the languages where a surd becomes a sonant after a nasal, i. e., in Romany, Sindhi Panjabi and Nepali, the corresponding participle is *-nd* or *-d* (Beames,

III, p. 123 ff., cf. LSI, *Raj.*, p. 14; Miklosich, X, p. 44). In the mountain dialects of the N-W., some have preserved *-ānt* or *-t*, others have *-an* or *-ān* which probably go back to the same form. This, at least is the explanation proposed by Grierson in his phonetics (*Piśāca Lang.*, *Phonol. Det.*, $ 182, p. 144), but in his morphology, he seems to prefer to see therein the middle participle of Iranian Zend *-āna*, Peh. *-ān*. Truly speaking if it refers to a middle form, it would probably be better to have recourse to the Skr. participle *-āna-*, common in Pali and found exceptionally in Prakrit also (Pischel, $ 562). The vitality of this form is guaranteed by its Simhalese derivative in *-na* (Geiger, $ 55). The fact, in any case, remains that with the exception of the isolated dialects of the far-off frontiers,—Simhalese, Oriya (extremely obscure, Beames, III, p. 125) and probably the N-W. Himalayan—the universally used form is the one, which is also preserved in Marathi.

The participle in *-t* has been enlarged in two ways : 1. the form in *-to* is reserved for conjugation; 2. the form in *-tā*, to the extent that it forms a part thereof, takes on the value of the past (Joshi, $ 341, 8) and as a consequence of the conditional (see $ 244 ff.), but it is also normally used as an adjective (Joshi, $ 617, *c*).

$ 256. The past participle is formed by the declinable suffix *-lā* being added to the stem of the past, whether this stem be the old stem of the Skr. participle *-ta* or the only stem of the verb, (cf. supra, $ 229). Because of its origin, this suffix is nothing but, as has been shown by Sten Konow (JRAS, 1902, p. 417, 420) the suffix of the Pkt. adjective *-alla-*, a variant of the more frequent one *-illa-* The Marathi participle is thus merely an enlarged form of the Skr. verbal *-ta-*. This is apparent in the irregular participles like *kelā* (*kṛta-*), *gelā* (*gata-*), *pātlā* (*prāpta-*), etc. Prakrit did not have this development of the suffix *-illa-*, *-alla-*. The case of *āṇilliya-* (*ānīta-*) herein is an isolated one and is explained by particular reasons (Pischel, $ 595, p. 403). However, several dialects have enlarged their participle by *-l*. They are, on the one hand, of the eastern group, Bihari, Oriya, Bengali, Assamese and on the other Gujarati the neighbour of Marathi (where the participle in *-lo* replaces one in archaic *-o*, see LSI, *Raj.*,

p. 342) and lastly perhaps certain speeches of the Himalayan N-W. (Grierson, *Piś. Lang.*, p. 55). The isolation of these dialects, when joined with the recent character of the suffix which can be verified in many among them, proves that the morphological value of the suffix in *-l-* has been independently developed among each of them. It is all the more remarkable that it has failed to join the Indian speeches to the group of Indo-European languages where the adjectives in * *-l-* (undoubtedly here * *-l-ya-* > Pkt. *-lla-*) have been joined to the verbal stems. As is known, this group consists of the Slav, Armenian and Tokharian (S. Lèvi and Meillet, MSL, XVIII, p. 22).

Elsewhere the suffix in *-l-* has, in Marathi, maintained its adjectival value : cf. for ex. *pahilā* "first". (cf. *prathama-*), *āglā* "who is in the lead", (*agra-*), *aṇḍīl* "male" (*aṇḍa-*). The participle in *-lā-* can, therefore, have a purely adjectival value. It is to avoid the confusion resulting from its use, that there has been constituted recently the form in *-lelā* which has only an adjectival function (Joshi, $ 619).

$ 257. The participle of obligation in Sanskrit in *-tavya-* has given in Marathi the participle in *-āvā* having the same sense. The same adjective exists in Sindhi and Gujarati in the sense of the present passive participle. It is found again, fixed as one of these forms with the value of the infinitive, first in Gujarati and the contiguous group of Rajasthan (LSI, *Raj.*, p. 14) and then in the eastern group, Bihari-Bengali-Oriya-Assamese (Beames, III, p. 153-5; LSI, *Beng.*, p. 8, 403). In the last-named languages, the participle must have existed with its original value, as they possess a future in *-b-* which is derived therefrom (Beames, III, p. 158).

$ 258. The participle in *-āvā* having kept its passive value in Marathi (save some recent exceptions) and in any case its sense of obligation, Marathi was deprived of its future participle. This need is sought to be provided for by the adjective in *-ṇār*. This form, however, is not of Marathi itself and is found with the value of the noun of agent in Gujarati. But here the old form is provided with an aspiration : *karaṇahāra* "one who does" (LSI, *Raj.*, p. 362). The same form and the same sense is found in Sindhi, for ex., *sirjaṇahāra* "creator", *likhaṇahāru* "writer, one who is going to write" (Trumpp, p. 75) as also Hindi : *dekhnehārā* "one who sees". The sense of future, which has come into Sindhi, seems to be recent in Marathi. In the following example of Namdev (*Navnīt*, p. 18, abh. 18, 3) we have to deal only with an agent-noun :

dharma artha kāma mokṣa cārī stana l
dohoṇār dhanya Puṇḍalīka ll

"The law, the interest, the desire and the deliverance are four breasts, one who milks them is the lucky Puṇḍalīk."

This adjective is evidently drawn from the agent-noun in *-na-* which has elsewhere given the infinitive in *-ṇeṃ*. Which then is this suffix ? Is it similar to that of the nouns like *andhār* "obscurity" (*andhakāra-*), *kumbhār* "potter" (*kumbhakāra-*), *suār* "cook" (*sūpakāra-*) ? or should we recognise herein that of *sutār* "carpenter" (*sūtradhāra-*). The aspirate of other languages would seem to make us lean towards this last explanation, without taking into account the fact that we are tempted, in so far as the meaning is concerned, to put *-dhāra-* "support" near *-pāla-* "protector, guardian", a word which is at the origin of the well-known Hindi suffix in *-vālā*, having a similar usage. It is true that often *h* is only a sign for hiatus, notably in the languages of the Apabhraṃśa type (cf. supra $ 22, 66, 161, 210 and Trumpp, *l. l.*) and that the origins of this use of *-dhāra-* are much less clear than those of *-pāla-*. Making an avowal of his preference for the first hypothesis (III, p. 238), Beames hesitates and in the absence of decisive arguments, we have only to follow him.

Like the participle in *-t*, this one, taking an enlargement in *-ā*, becomes an adjective, keeps the use as the agent-noun and loses the value of the future participle. Examples are : *yeṇāre lok* "the persons who have to come", *bolṇāre puṣkal, karṇāre thoḍe* "many who speak, few who act" (Navalkar, $641-2), or also *pohṇārā buḍto, lihṇārā cukto...* "the swimmer (alone) is drowned, the scribe (alone) commits mistakes..." (cited by Molesworth, s. v. *pohṇeṃ*).

Use of Participles; Auxiliary Verbs.

$ 259. The use of all these forms is not identical. The

participle of obligation has maintained, as a whole, its original value and right upto the potential conjugation its construction has remained indirect. On the contrary, the other participles, having been isolated from the enlarged forms with adjectival values, have taken on, in course of time, an increasingly clear verbal value and a uniform construction. Its characteristic trait is their juxtaposition with the verbs denoting "to be." We have already seen that the "participial tenses" are in reality nothing more than groups so constituted. From the same though isolated elements, are constituted the "composite tenses." As a reaction against the habitude, in fact due to more than one reason, of modelling the descriptive grammars of Marathi on those of English, Joshi condemns ($ 595, cf. on the contrary Navalkar, $ 313 ff.) the notion of composite tenses and gives a list thereof only as a practical concession. In fact the composite tenses do not constitute a definite system. But as certain simple tenses are already in reality, composed of a participle and an auxiliary, the separation of *mī caltoṃ* "I walk" from *mī calat āheṃ* "I walk", *mī calat hotoṃ* "I had been walking" would not give a faithful image of the verbal system. Moreover, the principle of these formations is common to the majority of Indo-Aryan languages (Beames, III, chap. IV, p. 170 ff. ; cf. Grierson, *Man. Kaśm.*, $ 45, 60 ff; Geiger, $ 63).

$ 260. The auxiliaries used in Marathi are *as-* and *āh-* "to be" (the former has the durative sense, Joshi, $ 315). The former is found everywhere except in Panjabi and Sindhi and the latter seems to be natural to Oriya and the western group : Marathi , Gujarati (in the negative verb), Sindhi, Panjabi and Hindi. The verb *ho-* , currently used all over central India, in Panjabi and Gujarati, is used in Marathi only in the participial tenses and with the value of the past tense.

$ 261. The verb *jāṇeṃ* "to go" (Skr. *yā-*) is used to form the periphrastic tense with the passive sense : *to mārilā jāīl* "he will be beaten", *to mārilā gelā* "he has been beaten". This construction is recent in Marathi and also little used (see Navalkar, who gives in $ 305 the various more usual equivalents; cf. Joshi, $ 593, 5, p. 391). It is also found in Gujarati where it has started competing with the normal passive in *-ā-* (Tisdall, p. 67-9, LSI, *Raj.*, p. 343). Marwari and Sindhi, like old Marathi, only have the old passive in *-ij-* (Beames, III, p. 71 ff.). The periphrastic passive in Marathi and Gujarati clearly seems to be borrowed from the central languages, notably from Hindi, where this turn is current (Beames, III, p. 213-4). Whatever be the case, the origin of this construction remains obscure. The verb meaning "to come", combined with an oblique case of the infinitive, is equal to a passive in Kashmiri : *gupana yima* "I will be hidden" (Grierson, *Man. Kashm.* $ 91), cf. the Hindi construction *dekhne meṃ ātā* "it is seen." For the verb meaning "to go" the same type is made use of. Thus in Marathi *teṃ jalūn jaīl*, lit. "that will pass being burnt" is equal to "that will be burnt." It is possible that the homonymy of the Skr. verbal adjective *jāta-*, Pkt. *jāa-* "become", which is readily joined to a verbal adjective in *-ta-* expressing the state in Sanskrit (chiefly in the form of the compound *saṃjāta-*: for ex. *sā virahapīḍitā saṃjātā*, *Vetāla.*, edn. of Uhle, 14, 5) and in Prakrit (see Jacobi, *Ausgew. Erz. Gram.*, $ 113; cf. *muttāṇaṃ ghaṇareṇuna vva churio jāo mhi etthantare* "here I am (become) covered as if with pearl-dust", *Karpūramañjarī*, I, 29 *d*), be for something in the new use of the verb, *jā-* "to go" (and in fact it is so found in a verse of the *Jñāneśvarī*, XVIII, 783), *jāti* denoting "they become, they produce themselves", without our being able to clearly see if it is a verb re-made on the participial stem *jālā* "been" or of the verb meaning "to go". That the verb meaning "to go" could take the sense of "being" and be used in that case for forming the passives, is proved not only by the Dravidian, where it is rare (Beames is, therefore, wrong in citing the same, III, p. 74) but also Iranian. We know that in Persian *śudan* "to become", earlier "to go " (cf. Skr. *cyu-*) has succeeded the Pehlavi *estātan* "to hold oneself" (cf. Skr. *sthā-*) in the function that now concerns us, and the Afghan has done the same (Geiger, *Grundriss der Iran. Phil.*, I, 2nd edn., p. 155, 222). Moreover, the native opinion attributes the construction with *jāṇeṃ* to a loan from Persian (Joshi, p. 391). We can only point out this hypothesis, which is not absurd but which is not necessary also.

Absolute Forms from Participles

$ 262. The present participle, fixed in one of its cases, supplies us with a form which is construed in an absolute form : *to caltāṃ caltāṃ khālīṃ paḍlā* "while walking, he has fallen", *bārā bājtāṃ yā* "come (when) midday is struck", *tyālā kheḷtāṃ myāṃ pāhileṃ* "I have seen him play (playing)" *āhmī kheḷat astāṃ to ālā* "he came when we were busy playing". Beside the form in *-tāṃ* , there exists a form in *tāṃnā,* having the same sense: *myāṃ jevitāṃnā tujhī ciṭī vācūṃ ṭākilī-* "I have finished your letter while taking my food", *myāṃ tyālā ghoḍyālā mārtāṃnā pāhileṃ* "I have seen him beat the horse."

There is a general agreement to see in this form the locative of the participle enlarged in *-tā*. For the meaning, this would very well correspond with the forms in *-te* of Gujarati and Bengali, whose use is similar (Beames, III, p. 124-5). But this explanation does not help us understand the affix *-nā* (Beames, *l. l.* and Joshi, p. 237, content themselves by characterising the same as "emphatic"). Moreover, Gujarati possesses, beside the forms in *-te*, the form in *-tāṃ* of Marathi. If it is a declined form of the participle, a single hypothesis can render account of all these forms : that it is a case of oblique plural, i. e., the old genitive and in the case of the form in *-tāṃnā* of the dative plural—it is known in fact that the affix *lā* takes after the nasal vowel of the oblique of the form *nā* (see $ 72). In Gujarati, the termination *-āṃ* is that of the neuter plural, Skr. *āni.* It can more reasonably represent Skr. *-ānām.* Here it would refer to a genitive *commodi* (cf. Speyer, *Ved. u Skr. Syntax,* $ 72). This hypothesis is, moreover, not verifiable, because since the oldest texts the form is already used with the freedom, shown by examples cited above (and borrowed from Navalkar, $ 640, 1).

We should not, however, omit to recall the absolute of Pali in *-tvānaṃ* and that of Ardhamāgadhī in *-ttāṇāṃ* (Pischel, $ 585). The origin of these forms is obscure (Wackernagel, p. XXIV, note 3). It is not impossible that this be the origin of the Marathi and Gujarati absolutive in *-tāṃ* (cf. Rajvade, *Vyākaraṇ,* p. 109). In this case the addition of the affix *nā,* i. e., *lā* would be similar and would be due to the confusion with the form of the oblique plural.

$ 263. The past participle and the participle of obligation are often used as verbal nouns. The former, while keeping its subject in the nominative, is put in the oblique case and is accompanied by a postposition : *tujhī āī vārlyāpāsūn* "since your mother died, since the death of your mother." The latter is construed in the oblique case of the singular as the verbal noun in *-ṇeṃ* : *āmcā bāg pāhvayās calā* "please go to see my garden", *āpṇāśīṃ malā kāmhīṃ bolayāceṃ āhe* "I have something to tell you" (Navalkar, p. 345, 348-9; cf. LSI, *Mar.*, p. 27). The neuter noun, to which these forms are attached, is the exact equivalent of the Gujarati infinitive in *-uṃ* with the only difference that it is precisely the nominative corresponding to the form of Gujarati which does not have the value of the infinitive in Marathi.

$ 264. The absolutive in *-ūn* should certainly be joined to this very verbal noun, which in meaning corresponds to Skr. *-tvā* : *māmāpuḍheṃ jāūn mī pāyāṃ paḍeṃ* "I will go to find my maternal uncle (and having come before him), I will throw myself at his feet." It is the similarity of meaning which has led most of the scholars to explain Mar. *-ūn* by the Pkt. form *-ttūṇa, -ūṇa* (Navalkar, p. 107, Joshi, p. 239, Beames, III, p. 233, etc.)

The absolutive in *-ūṇa* is in fact normal in Mahārāṣṭrī Prakrit and in Jaina Prakrits in the form *-dūṇa, -ūṇa* (Pischel, $ 586), but the final dental *n* causes some difficulty, as has rightly been noticed by Sten Konow (JRAS, 1902 p. 419). The intervocalic nasal, far from subsisting in the form of a dental, had to fall (see $ 66) and as a consequence the form must have got confused with the infinitive arisen from Skr. *-ituṃ*. In this embarassment, the examination of other languages is useless; everywhere the absolutive seems to go back to Skr. *-ya*, preserved in the eastern Prakrits (Pischel, $ 589 ff.) and whose culmination *-i*, noted in Apabhraṃśa (Pischel, $ 594) is found in a more or less clear manner in Simhalese (Geiger, $ 56, 2), in Guj., Sindhi, *-ī*, Panj., Hindi *-i* (>zero), *-e* Beng. *-iyā* (Beames, III, p. 230 ff.).

The key of the Marathi form is precisely the final nasal which creates the difficulty in the hypothesis mentioned above. This nasal appears in the old language in the from *-nī* or *niyāṃ*. Now this is a well-known post-position and it is improbable to suppose it as being affixed to an isolated form of declension, as the infinitive in *-tum* or the absolutive in *-tvā*. Moreover, the preceding vowel had been earlier not *-ū* but *-o* and even *-au*. This, excluding any recourse to a stem in *-u-*, leads us to consider the form as the ablative of a stem in *-a-*, of the same type as *meghauni*, *divūni*, etc. (see $ 195) or **karavauni* whose intervocalic *v* would have fallen as happens so frequently, chiefly in the presence of a labial vowel (cf. $ 153); whence *-karauni*, *karoni*, etc. (cf. *karavun*, *karavutan*, *maṃnavun* in the inscription of cikurḍeṃ).

This explanation fits very well with the use of the form, employed to mark the historical or logical succession of two actions (Joshi, $ 620, Navalkar, 346-7).

Verbal Noun and Infinitive

$. 265. The infinitive type of Marathi is the verbal noun in *-ṇeṃ*, which goes back to the Skr. verbal noun in *-anaṃ*. The form of Sanskrit subsists in Simhalese *-ṇu* (Geiger, $ 57), Kashm.—*un*, Sindhi—*nu*, West. Punjabi—*uṇ* (obl. *aṇ*) and Bundeli *-an*. The enlarged form of Marathi is found in the central languages : the dial. of Rajasthan *-ṇo* or *-nū*, Hindi *-nā*, Braj. *-nauṃ*, Panj. *-ṇā* or *-nā* after the cerebral (cf. Beames, III, p. 236 ff., LSI, *Raj*., p. 14; it has also been suggested to take back these forms not to the Skr. verbal noun but to the participle of obligation in *-anīyam*; cf. Sten Konow, JRAS, 1902, p. 418 n.). We have seen that Gujarati and a number of neighbouring speeches on the one hand, and the eastern group on the other, employ a future of the type *-ba-* arisen from the Skr. participle *-tavya-*.

This infinitive is in reality a declinable noun of action, and is construed as such : *tyā cīṃ karṇīṃ cāṃglīṃ āhet* "his acts are good", *malā bāpccī ājñā mānya karṇeṃ prāpt āhe* "I should respectfully obey the order of my father", *mag jeṃ karṇeṃ asel teṃ kar* "then do what is to be done" (lit. "that which is action"). In the nominative it is used to form the nominal sentences expressing obligation : *patr lihīt jāṇeṃ* "keep on writing" and in the dative it expresses intention : *karṇyās* or *karṇyālā* "to do" etc. (cf. Navalkar, $ 643).

In addition to this noun of action and the participles

declined as such, Marathi also possesses an indeclinable infinitive, which signifies intention : *to teṃ karūṃ* (=*karāyās*) *icchito* "he wishes to do it", *tī teṃ karūṃ śakel* "she will be able to do it", *malā yeuṃ de* "give me (the permission) to come", etc. (Navalkar, $ 635, 216). This form has developed, as has been generally recognised, from Skr. *-tum*, Pkt. *-iuṃ* (Pischel, $ 573; re. the loss of *i* in Marathi, see supra, $ 63; regarding the confusion with the Pkt. absolutive in *-ūṇa*, $ 264).

SENTENCE

$ 266. The changes undergone by Marathi words as a result of phonetic alterations or grammatical evolution have not been deep enough for fundamentally transforming the constitution of the sentence. The few observations made below will make it clear that the essential rules of Marathi sentence are almost those of the Sanskrit one. No important innovations are to be found either in the structure of the sentence or in the relationship and arrangement of its elements.

Nominal Sentence and Verbal Sentence

$ 267. A Marathi sentence normally consists of a subject and a verb. Examples are : *udyāṃ pāūs paḍel* "Tomorrow it will rain", *malā ek pustak pāhije* "I need a book", *tūṃ āpleṃ kām kar* "Do your work", *cal, mīṃ tulā kāhīṃ marj dākhvitoṃ* "Come, I will show something strange", etc.

The verb "to be" is not indispensable to the sentence. In poetry it is the most often missing. In current usage it may be missing in the proverbial sentences or in those having an affective value *jetheṃ gāṃv tetheṃ mahārvāḍā* "Where there is a village, there is a quarter of the Mahārs", *tūṃ mūrkh kharā* "you are a true fool." It is generally missing in the interrogative sentences and answers : *tujheṃ nām kāy* "What is your name ?", *mājheṃ nāṃv gopāl* "My name is Gopāl." We can join thereto sentences containing negative *nāhīṃ*, although this word contains precisely the verb "to be" and that *na* exists alone. This is so because the sentiment of the verb is so much lost therein that in the Konkan they say *to ālā nāhīṃ āhe* "he has not come" (Navalkar, p. 272).

However, the verb "to be" can always be expressed and in fact the same is most often the case. Examples are : *Pārīs-śahrāṃt ekandar cāḷīs-var nāṭak gṛheṃ āhet, āditvārīṃ gardī phār aste...sarvā nāṭakgṛhāṃt sarva prkāreṃ śreṣṭ aseṃ jeṃ nāṭakgṛha tyāceṃ nāṃv Aparā. hī imārat phārac sundar āhe* "In the town of Paris, there are in all more than forty theatres. On Sundays they are largely crowded. The best among them, from all points of view, is the Opera. This edifice is extremely beautiful". (*Vilāyat cā pravās*, I, Poona, 1889, p. 185, 187). We have already seen that several of the verbal forms had been composed with the verb "to be" and that in cases where Sanskrit had the pure nominal sentence. The old nominal forms that have subsisted, as for example, third persons of the type *karto* "he does", are in reality, in view of their incorporation in conjugation, forms with the verbal affix zero. In any case, the verb "to be" should not be considered as a pure accessory in the Marathi sentence. In fact it occupies therein the same place as any other verb, that is, generally the last one (cf. Meillet, MSL, XIV p. 22) and it is put in juxtaposition even with the participial tenses already containing it, by conferring on them a nuance of special sense : *mīṃ basloṃ* "I have sat down", *mīṃ basloṃ āheṃ* "I am sitting", *to āplyā mitrāṃs patreṃ lihīt baslā āhe* "He had been sitting writing letters to his friends."

$ 268. Thus without showing an essentially different state of affairs from that of Sanskrit, the Marathi sentence has considerably passed the stage of the Sanskrit of lower epoch. In this language the absence of verb had been normal, not only in general maxims, but also in sentences containing a pronoun, notably an interrogative, relative or demonstrative pronoun and above all in those containing a participle. The verb "to be" in the sense of copula was inserted only in the old type of the nominal sentence, the one lacking all determination (*mama duhkhakāraṇaṃ bahukāraṇaṃ asti* "the cause of my unhappiness is multiple", etc., see J. Bloch, MSL, XIV, p. 82). By adding the adjective in *-ta-*, it would change its meaning as is the case with Marathi (*śāstre kathitam asti* "It is written in the śāstras", *tat tayeti kathitam* "that is what she said", ibid., p. 92).

The state of Marathi is almost near that of the majority of other languages of continental India (see for ex. on Sindhi Trumpp, p. 515, on Hindi Kellogg, $ 856 ff., on Romany Miklosich, XII, p. 27; Kashmiri seems to have been subjected, in regard to its syntax as in its phonetics, to local influences. It will be seen that the order of words therein shows serious innovations and the verb "to be" is also necessary).

It will be noted that in detail, it considerably differs from that of other older Indo-European languages which had preserved traces of the pure nominal sentence (see Meillet, MSL, XIV, p. 15-18; on Latin, Marouzeau, *La phrase á verbe "être"*..., p. 150 ff., the aspect of Gothic is near that of Marathi, but the place of the verb "to be" is less uniform therein, see Meillet, MSL, XV, p. 94, 95, 97).

Concord

$ 269. Like nouns, the adjectives in Marathi are of two types : 1. those that end in a consonant; these are invariable, atleast during the modern epoch (Navalkar, $ 116) and are construed with the substantive with which they constitute a sort of compound. Thus we have in the nominative singular : *lāl āṃbā* (masc.) "red mango", *lāl ciṃc* "red tamarind", *lāl pagoṭeṃ* (neut.) "red turban", in the nom. pl. *lāl pāgotīṃ* "red turbans", in the dative sing. *lāl pāgoṭyās*, etc. , *ati thaṃḍ pāṇyā neṃ sardī hoīl* "with very cold water, it will be very cold"; 2. the adjectives with enlargement in *-ā*, *-ī*, *-eṃ* to which should be joined the demonstrative and relative pronouns, which have been assimilated to nominal declension and the participial tenses of the verb, which are in reality the declined participles. Here it is solely a question of these adjectives with enlargement.

Gender and Number

$ 270. The epithet-adjective is in concord, in gender and number, with the substantive to which it refers. If there be several of them, it is in accord with the nearest, that is to say, the first : *tyālā moṭhā bhāu va bahīn āhe* "He has an elder brother and (an elder) sister", *hyā haveṃtlīṃ* (neut.) *janāvareṃ* (neut.) *va pakṣī* (masc.), *etheṃ āḍhaḷtat* "the native beasts and birds are found there" (Navalkar, $ 516, Joshi, $ 573). Regarding the accord in indirect cases, see infra, $ 272.

$ 272. Rules regarding the concord of the predicate are more complicated. In fact, notwithstanding the persistence in Marathi of old grammatical genders, they depend on the distinction between animate and inanimate beings ($ 180).

When the predicate (adjective or verb) refers to several nouns of different genders, it is in accord with only the last one if it concerns inanimate beings. On the other hand, it is in neuter plural as in the sentences given below : *tyācā bāp āṇi āī moṭhīṃ bhalīṃ ahet* "his father and mother are very good", *Dhākū āṇi Sāḷī hīṃ doghem bekār hoūn ālīṃ* "Dhākū (masc.) and Sālī (fem.) being unemployed have, both, come here" (Navalkar, $ 468, 517, cf. Joshi, $ 574).

A similar distribution is found in Sindhi : If it concerns the animate beings, the predicate is in accord with the nearest noun and is put either in the plural, the gender being variable according to the cases. If it concerns the animate beings, then masculine prevails. It should not be forgotten that there is no neuter in Sindhi (Trumpp, p. 518). In Gujarati the distinction between animate and inanimate beings is absent. But the predicate, related to nouns of different genders is always put in the neuter gender (Tisdall, p. 35, 96). It is to be noted that in Gujarati and Marathi, the neuter plural is used in feminine of respect : Mar. *bāīsāheb ālīṃ astīṃ, paṇ...* "Madame would have come, but...," Guj. *rāṇī āvyāṃ che* "The queen is come" (Navalkar, p. 270, Tisdall, p. 96). There is, undoubtedly, a link between two facts : the neuter termination, designating persons in a less direct manner, is a sign of respect. In a similar, though inverse manner, the neuter is used in humility (Navalkar, $ 484, 2).

The formula of Marathi rule is commonly applied to Jaina Prakrits (Jacobi, *Ausgew. Erz.*, $ 79-80) but it does not seem to go back higher (Speyer, *Ved. u.* Skr. *Synt.*, $ 101).

In Hindi and undoubtedly in the majority of languages that have lost the neuter gender, either there is accord with the nearest noun, which precedes or follows, or the masculine prevails (see for ex. Kellogg, $ 863, 871; Grierson, *Man. Kashm.*, $ 25).

Case

$ 272. In old Marathi the epithet-adjective is, in principle, in accord with all the cases. In the modern language, this is most true about the nominative. There is only one form of oblique that is common to two numbers and three genders, namely, the oblique masc.-neuter singular. This form immediately precedes the substantive, which alone possesses the affix or the characteristic postposition required by the sense. Ex. : *mag mīṃ halkyā lokāṃ śīṃ bolṇār nāhīṃ* "Then I will not talk to petty people", *dusryā divśāṃ* "The day after tomorrow", *āplyā mitrās, āplyā mitrāṃs* "To his friend, to his friends", *yā imārtī lā don koṭ rupyāṃvar kharc jhālā* "More than two crores of rupees have been spent on this edifice" (Navalkar, $ 515).

That the oblique of the adjective be used alone is normal as the oblique of a noun is a declined form of that noun and is an independent word. But it is more difficult to render account of the fact that the oblique masc.-neuter singular is used alone in all the cases. We recognise here traces of a general tendency to simplify the epithet-adjectives, that has been very well noted by Beames, though the reasons of chimerical psychology advanced by him have been justly criticised by Miklosich (Beames, II, p. 240-243, Miklosich, XI, p. 35). The detail of this evolution is quite obscure. This is how it might have taken place. The confusion of the masc.-neuter plural with that of the singular can be conceived of, given the unstable character of nasalisation in the vowels. On the other hand, the application of the termination of the oblique masc.-neuter singular to the feminine can be due to the analogy of the plural, where the three genders normally have only one form of oblique.

The hypotheses possible on this point can not be demonstrated, because other languages do not give any indication that may be put to use. In the western group—Gujarati (leaving aside the affix *-o* of plural), Rajasthani (with certain hesitations in indirect cases other than oblique, see LSI, *Raj.*, p. 7, 22, 37), Panjabi, Sindhi Kashmiri—the accord is observed in all the cases. In the entire eastern group, the adjective is invariable or varies only in the gender (cf. LSI, *East. Hindi*, p. 16, 22, 28, *Bih.*, p. 26, 38, 50, 380), in Simhalese, it is absolutely invariable (see Geiger, $ 43). Hindi and Romany, like Marathi, simplify the declension of the epithet, though in different ways.

Hindi declines the group in this way : *kālā ghoṛā* "black horse", *kālī billī* "black cat" (Kellogg, $ 199):

Sing.	Dir.	*kālā ghoṛā*	*kālī billī*
	Obl.	*kāle ghoṛe*	*kālī billī*
Pl.	Dir.	*kāle ghoṛe*	*kālī billiyāṃ*
	Obl.	*kāle ghoroṃ*	*kalī billiyoṃ*

The various dialects of Romany decline the group, *kalo manuś* "black man", *kalī manuśni* "black woman" in this way (Miklosich, XI, p. 33-5):

Sing.	Dir.	*kalo manuś*	*kali manuśi*
	Obl.	*kale manuśes*	*kalyā manuśñā* (Gk. Rom : *kalim.*)
Pl.	Dir.	*kale manuś*	*kale manuśña*
	Obl.	*kale manuśen*	*kale manuśñen*

If we agree with Miklosich that the forms of the oblique of masculine are due to the dropping of final consonants and take the place of * *kales* * *kalen*, then we are obliged to separate Romany from Marathi and Hindi on the point where an accord could be conceived of in the three languages. Each of them seems to have simplified the declension of the epithet-adjectives in an independent manner.

The Order of Words

$ 273. In classical Sanskrit, the order of words, without being fixed, obeys the rules of sufficiently constant usage. As a matter of habit, the subject opens the sentence and the verb or the predicate terminates the same. In the group of self-determining words, the determinant precedes the determinate (except the apposition, which is, in reality, the predicate of a phrase inserted inside another). However, this order can always be disturbed by momentary reasons. The important word is readily put in the beginning of the sentence, whatever be its nature. Only the enclitic words are fixed and they follow the first word of the sentence or the word whose value they reinforce (Speyer, op. cit., $ 247-50.).

Marathi, which has preserved a less rich inflexion than Sanskrit, but where nothing essential is missing has also kept the same principles regarding the order of words.

$ 274. The usual order is as follows : Subject-complement-adverb-verb; the epithet adjective precedes the noun; the indirect complement precedes the direct one; words designating the circumstances, place, and time are put immediately after the subject and conjunctions are put first in the sentence. In principle there is nothing in the order of words to show the affective value of the sentence : *mājhī tarvār kholīṃt āhe* "My sword is in the sheath" can denote an affirmation, an exclamation, an interrogation and if it follows a sentence containing *jar* (Skr. *yarhi*), it denotes a condition (Navalkar, $ 4 6-7, Joshi, $ 531-6).

The fixity of the order of words is greater in Marathi than in Sanskrit. It is conceivable that the simplification of the epithet-adjective, in opposition to the predicate, constitutes a pair with a greater constancy of its place. Similarly, the indirect complement of the passive verb, expressing the logical subject of action, which had already tended to have the first place in Sanskrit ((Speyer, *l. l.*, $ 248), is installed therein all the more readily, as in this language the sentence with the passive participle is assimilated to the sentence with the active verb. Similarly also the "false prepositions", words fixed in one of their cases and expressing circumstantial or logical relationships, which in Sanskrit had tended to follow the word they determined (Thommen, *Die Wortstelhung im nachved. Altind und im Mittelind,* $ 32) have been fixed at that place in Marathi to the extent of appearing in certain cases as case-terminations.

There is, however, some relative liberty which prevails everywhere except in some rare enclitics employed to emphasize some isolated word, that is *c*, the Mar. word *ci* (Pkt. *ciya*), *hī* (Skr. *hi*), *paṇ* (Skt. *punaḥ*, Pali *pana*, *puna*). Thus we can say *saṃpel koṭhūn* "How would (lit. will) this be finished ?", *pustak mī Harīlā dileṃ* "That book I have given to Hari", *Mumbaīhūn Rāmā kāl sākāklīṃ ālā* 'Ramā came from Bombay yesterday morning", *Pārīs śahrāṃt ekandar* 40 *var nāṭakgṛheṃ āhet*; *āditvārīṃ gardiphār aste* "In Paris, there are in all more than forty theatres. On Sundays the crowd therein is the largest." The neuter interrogative pronoun *kāy* is put at the end of the sentence, when it is used uniquely for denoting the interrogative sense : *āj pāūs paḍel kāy* "Will it rain today ?". But except this use, its place is unrestricted :

to kāy deil, teṃ gheūn de "Bring what he gives you", *kāy heṃ dhairya* "What courage he has ?" (Navalkar, $ 575). Similarly, we say *tūṃ kāṃ ālās, kāṃ tūṃ ālās, tūṃ ālās kāṃ* "Why have you come ?" The negation seems to have even more liberty than in Sanskrit : there its place is before the verb, at a variable distance and it is found after the verb only in certain isolated examples of late period (Thommen, op. cit., $ 19-22). In Marathi, *na* is put ordinarily before the verb, so that, in certain cases, it is agglomerated : *nāthi* Skr. *nāsti*, *navhe* < *na hoy*, *nase* < *na ase*, *nāhīṃ* < *na āhe*; *naye* "This cannot be allowed", *nalage* "This is not necessary" exist only in this form; cf. also *nako* "it should not be" which seems to contain the interrogative pronoun, but has been given certain verbal terminations (Joshi, $ 317, Navalkar, $ 266 ff.). However, *nā* is readily put at the end of the sentence, not only in the poetic language (for ex. *teṇeṃ viśeṣeṃ karmāteṃ tyjāveṃ nā*, *Jñān.*, III, 168 "He should not renounce action", *to karmabandha āṃgīṃ vājail nā*, ibid., III, 175) "The bond of action will not touch his body"), but also actually after the past of habitude or the conditional one : *karī nā*, *astā nā* "He does not do; if he had not been." The final place is so customary that the negation is often put before the termination : second person sing. *karī-nā-s*, *karī-nā-t*, etc. (Joshi, $ 613). This tendency has led in Konkani to the formation of a veritable negative conjugation : *nidnā* "He is not asleep", *nidnānt* "They are not asleep", *nidnātloṃ* "I had not been asleep" (LSI, *Mar.*, p. 171).

$ 275. Except for certain details these rules apply to all the languages of India proper. In Gujarati for example "the usual order is as given below : 1. subject, 2. indirect complement, 3. direct complement 4. predicate. But it can be changed for emphasis" (Tisdall, p. 95). The adjective and the adverb precede the words they determine (ibid., p. 34, 77). The negation *na* generally precedes the verb, but the prohibitive negation *mā* (which is missing in Marathi) is placed afterwards and similarly *nā* when it is used in the same sense (LSI, *Raj.*, p. 343). In the detailed exposition of Kellogg (*Gramm. of the Hindi Lang.*, $ 913-29) can be seen as to how similar has been its use in Hindi.

Of all the Indo-Aryan languages, only Kashmiri has

had a different evolution, which curiously brings it near the languages of central Europe, notably the Germanic. The verb of the principal proposition normally takes the first or second place. A sentence like *sub chuh gāṭulu mahanyuvu* exactly corresponds to the equivalent French sentence "*Il est habile homme*", or the German one "*er ist (ein) geschickter Mann*." In subordinate propositions the verb remains at the end; in Kashmiri as in German : *Yotu--tām zinda roza, tamis kara ādar*, cf. Germ. *so lange ich lebendig bleibe*..."As long I live, I will honour him" (Grierson, *Man. Kashm.*, $ 97-9). But the position of the auxiliary *chuh* does not seem to differ from one sentence to another : cf. *suh chuh prath rĕta aki phiri dawāh karān* "Do you know the doctor who is treating him ?" (Grierson, ibid., Vocab., nos. 1773, 1323; cf. however ibid., nos. 464, 465). It may also be noted that the smallest group of the complement and participle preserve the old order; cf. *kethapoṭhi hĕkān tim kömu karith* "How can they accomplish the work ?" Germ. "*wie konnen sie die Arbeit tun* ?." The same is the case with the word determining the case-relation in an affix, both in Marathi and in Sanskrit : *mūlas andar* "In the root" *mölis sān* "With father" (Grierson, ibid., $ 13). Lastly, the epithet precedes the substantive, whereas the attribute follows the same (ibid., $ 19; cf. Vocab. nos. 462, 465, 467, etc. and the first of the examples cited above). Therefore, it is not some Indo-Aryan language that could have furnished us with the model of the order, substantive-epithet, adopted by Asaṇga, the Buddhist scholar of fifth cent. A.D., in his Sanskrit works (see *Mahāyānasūtrālaṃkāra*, ed. and trnsltd. by S. Lévi, II, *Intr.*, p. 12). It is only from Iranian, that this writer, born in Peshawar, could have come to know of this turn.

Subordination

$ 276. As subordinate propositions, Marathi has only relative propositions or those introduced by a relative adverb (conditional, etc.). The logical subordination is most often marked by the procedure belonging to parataxis.

It consists firstly in the insertion in the sentence of a group depending on the absolutive in *-ūn*, like the Skr. *-tvā* (cf. $ 264): *to asem̄ bolūn gelā* "Having talked in that manner, he went away"; the subject of this second proposition can be different from the principal subject : *bheṭ hoūn varṣa loṭlem̄* "Since our last meeting (lit. the meeting having been) a year has passed."

It also consists in the utilisation of the anaphoric *hem̄* or of the adjective *asem̄* "such a thing, that". These pronouns are normally used to summarise the enumerated substantives, as in the sentence : *Rāmā Kṛṣṇā āṇi Vinū he* (or *ase*) *tethem̄ baslel hote* "R., K. and V., they had been sitting there". The same will be said when only the pronoun is declined and the substantive is left in the absolute nominative : *hattī ghoḍe āṇī bail hyām̄s cārā ghālā* "Give the grass to the elephants, horses and buffaloes". This conforms to the procedure of repeating an entire proposition into neuter with the anaphoric : *Rāmā gelā asem̄ tyāṇem̄ aiklem̄* "He has heard it said that Rām is gone", lit. "Rām is gone; this he has heard"; *mī tujhem̄ kām kārīn asem̄ to mhaṇālā* "He has said that he would do my work", lit. "I will do your work, this he has said"; *tyā mulīcī āī labāḍ navhe...hem̄ tujhyāṇem̄ kaśāvarūn sām̄gavel* "How can you say that the mother of this girl is not a liar ?" (Navalkar, $ 566, Joshi, $ 545, 628 *a*).—There is all the more reason for using the anaphoric with a postposition as in *yā-stav, tyā-mūḷem̄* "because of that."

The preceding two turns are included in the use of the conjunction *mhaṇūn* which is inserted between two propositions : *mhaṇun* for *hem̄ mhaṇūn,* which is also found. It signifies, properly speaking, "having said that" and takes on the sense of "as a consequence of" or even of "that" in the most general sense (Navalkar, $ 357, 4, $ 667-8). This word has lost its etymological sense to this extent that it is now used as an equivalent of the anaphoric, *ām̄bā mhaṇūn phār cām̄glem̄ phaḷ āhe* "The mango is an excellent fruit." It is not without interest that the verbs for "to say" are used in the same way in the Dravidian (see Kittel, *Gram. of the Kannaḍa Lang.*, p. 355, Vinson, *Man. de la langue tamoule*, p. 147). We also find on the other hand the same use in Nepali (Kellogg, *Gram. of the Hindi Lang.*, $ 889). To these turns should be added the use of the absolutive in *-tām̄* and of the infinitives drawn from the participle in *-vā* and in *-lā* and of the verbal one in *-ṇeṃ*, which has been discussed above ($ 262 ff., Navalkar, $ 670).

The liberty of the linking of sentences is such that any sentence can be construed as any noun. Ex. : *mī yeīṃ paryant tyālā vāṭ pāhṇyās sāṃg* "Ask him to wait (lit. look at the road) for me till I do not arrive."

The relative sentence itself preserves some independence. In fact it is construed exactly as a principal sentence. Moreover, the pronoun or the relative adverb may be missing. Lastly, the noun common to two sentences is preferably put in the relative proposition, as it is the first. The anaphoric, on the contrary, is as a rule in the principal proposition, which normally, comes second. The sentence, *jo mulgā mīṃ kāḷ pāhilā toc hā āhe* 'It is the child that I saw yesterday", does not differ from *mulgā mīṃ pāhilā toc āhe* or *mīṃ pāhilā to mulgā āhe* (Joshi, $ 628 *b*, cf. Navalkar, $ 554). The same holds true for *iar pāūs paḍat aslā tar yeuṃ nako* "Do not come if it rains" and *mīṃ lihit nasloṃ tar mātr malā yeūn bheṭ* "Come to see me, only if I am not writing" (lit. having come, see me)" (Navalkar, $ 624).

$ 277. Only during the modern epoch has been formed a sort of subordinate proposition opening, either with *jeṃ* (cf. Skr. *yat*) "that" following the principal one, or with *kīṃ* "that". There is, however, no indirect discourse, *sāhebīṃ...sevakās pusileṃ kīṃ āple pite...yānīṃ* "The Sahib says to his servant, 'Your father..."; *prasann hoūnn bolitā je tujhā vaṃśāṃt* "Satisfied, he said, (In your family..." (cf. Navalkar, p. 204, 205; cf. 298, 357). Nowadays *jeṃ* in this usage is gone out of use but it does not follow necessarily therefrom that *jeṃ* has preceded *kīṃ*. Probably it is this last conjunction that has been the model to the other. Whatever be the case, *kīṃ* in Marathi is probably borrowed from the Hindustani *ki*. Now *ki* in Hindustani itself is extremely recent and is suspected to be a foreign loan. In any case, the recent character of this conjunction in India forcefully recalls the great movement of the extension of Persian *ki* or *kim*. It is known that these conjunctions have also been introduced in Turkish, where normally there is no relative proposition, (see Mirza Kasem Beg, *Gram. der Tūrkish-Tatarischen Spr.*, trnsltd. by Zenker, p. 235-6. This information has been given to me by Gauthiot).

If the turn in question is not the result of a purely autonomous development of Marathi, we would not be surprised to find its equivalents in other Indo-Aryan languages also. Gujarati also makes use of the turn by means of the anaphoric and places the propositions of the relative type first. But the subordinate sentence introduced by *ke* is less authorised therein (see Tisdall, p. 95-6, 99). In Sindhi subordinate sentences, normally, precede the principal one; in any case the relative proposition can be made to follow the same and there are subordinate propositions introduced by *ki*, *jo*, *ta*, but there is no indirect discourse (Trumpp, p. 521, 525-6, 528). The same formulae also apply to Hindi (Kellogg, *l. l.*, $ 883 ff.). In Kashmiri, the relative proposition also precedes the principal one introduced by the demonstrative, but the word *zi* "that" introduces all sorts of subordinate ones (Grierson, *Man. Kashm.*, *Vocab.*, see the word *Yih* (2) and *Zi*).

CONCLUSION

$ 278. From the preceding exposition, it turns out that on no point has Marathi introduced any serious innovations in the linguistic system, it inherited from the Middle-Indian. It is during the most ancient period, that we can attain, that the ancient type of Indo-Iranian has started getting altered in India. Already the Ṛgveda enables us to see the loss of the vowel ṛ, that is to say, of the only sonant which still provided a play of gradations noticeable to the speaking subjects and we see that morphology as also phonetics are seriously changed right from the inscriptions of Aśoka. Marathi has merely reconstructed a new system with the help of the debris preserved by the Middle-Indian and it has done it in the same way as a whole as the remaining modern Indo-Aryan languages, atleast those spoken to the east of the Indus. In fact, Simhalese, Romany and the dialects of the N-W. Himalayas have had, in part, an evolution parallel to the general evolution of Indo-Aryan, but each of them shows special innovations in many respects. Other languages, on the contrary, which could be for this purpose called Prakritic, go back almost all of them to the same common language observed in the various documents of the Middle-Indian and have had an extemely similar evolution. The divergences of detail found in them do not coincide frequently enough to enable us to divide them into clearly separated groups. Thus Marathi, which generally is in agreement with the geographically nearest one, Gujarati, is often different therefrom.

The treatment of the vowels before a geminated consonant is the same in Marathi, Gujarati and in the languages of the centre and of east. It is the opposite of that in Sindhi, Panjabi and Western Hindi. Again with Gujarati, and only with Gujarati, Marathi preserves intact the group nasal+occlusive. In Marathi and in Gujarati, as in the entire western group, the initial and the geminated *v* is preserved and the intervocalic *n* and *l* are cerebral. But the groupings are partially different : Simhalese preserves *v* but also *n* and *l*; on the other hand Oriya, though belonging to the eastern group, has the intervocalic cerebral *l*. In addition Marathi differs from Gujarati in the treatment of *ch*, which is represented by *s* in Marathi and in several isolated dialects, notably in those of the far-east. Similarly several final diphthongs of Prakrit, and as a consequence a certain number of terminations are, for ex., the same in Marathi and Hindi and differ from the corresponding diphthongs and terminations of Gujarati and other Western languages.

In morphology, only Marathi and Gujarati on the continent have preserved the three old genders. Again they alone have extended to the nominative of the demonstratives the stem in *-t* of the oblique cases. The participle in *-la* of Marathi still has its equivalent in Gujarati and also in the speeches of the N-W. and the eastern group. But in the formation of the future, Marathi is different from Gujarati and joins the dialects of Rajasthan. With these dialects, among others, it forms the infinitive in *-ṇ-* and not in *-v-* as in Gujarati and in the eastern speeches. On the other hand it is distinct, not only from Gujarati, but also from the speeches of Rajasthan as regards the method of construing the present. Lastly, as regards the preservation of the terminations *-asi,-anti, -antu,* Marathi has only the eastern speeches as its companions.

$ 279. Therefore, Marathi can not be exclusively put in any one group. But, above all, it has extremely few characteristics which are its own. In phonetics, which is the least original part of this language, the only thing worth mentioning is the special treatment of palatals, according to the timbre of the following vowel. Now this is less of a normal development than the trace of an ancient linguistic substratum. The declension does not differ from that of the related languages except in the choice of affixes or of postpositions. This fundamentally concerns the vocabulary. The formation of possesives *mājhā, tujhā,* and in the verb, of the gerundive in *-ūn*, appear to be the only particularities unique to Marathi. The forms and their use are often more archaic in Marathi than in other languages. But it seems that this is merely a transitory phase. In the formation of an active past tense, in the regularity of the use of the verb meaning "to be", in the simplification of the forms of the epithet-adjective and in the relative fixity of the place of the elements constituting the sentence, can be perceived the action of new tendencies. Largely autonomous, these tendencies are also reinforced by the action of the written language, which borrows ways of expression from other languags, notably from Hindi and English (on English, see Joshi, p. 44). Irrespective of the origin of these tendencies, their action seems clearly to lead Marathi, a language still relatively archaic, to gradually join those of the other Indo-Aryan languages, wherein morphology and syntax have had a more rapid evolution.

APPENDIX

Note on Certain Documents of Old Marathi

$ 280. Rajvade has published in the *Viśvavṛtta* of January, 1907, an inscription found at Cikurḍe in the region of Kolhapur. It carries the date as follows : *bhāva saṃvachare vaiśākhamāse kṛṣṇapakṣe bhaumadive aṣṭamyāṃ tithau.* This corresponds, according to the editor, to the Śaka year 658. Leaving aside the question of the date, there remain certain difficulties which will embarrass us the less as the inscription is not in Marathi, as claimed by Rajvade, but in a strange mixture of correct and incorrect Sanskrit, of whom certain forms have a Marathi aspect or even a Kannada one (at two places is found the termination *-lu* which is characteristic of Kannada). We seem to recognise Marathi in the adjective *magilu* "on the way" (*mārga-*), in the substantives *kuḍo* denoting a measure of capacity (M. *kuḍav*, Skr. *kuḍapa-*), *devul* "temple" (M. *deuḷ*, Skr. *devakula-*), *nāvī* 'barber" (M. *nhāvī*, Skr. *nāpita-*), the present part. *karit* "doing" and the absols. *karavuṇa*, *karavutana* "having done",, *maṃnavunu* "respecting."

But it will be better not to make too much usage of this text, which is full of obscurities, recognised even by an editor, who is as bold as Rajvade.

$ 281. The oldest document of Marathi is the double inscription of Śravaṇa Belgola in Mysore and inscribed in 1118 A. D.

Śrī Cāvuṇḍarājeṃ karaviyaleṃ

"Made on the orders of Śrī Cāvuṇḍarāja."

Śrī Gaṃga rāje suttāle karaviyaleṃ.

"The boundary wall (?) constructed on the order of the king Ganga." These inscriptions have been last edited by Hultzsch in the *Epigraphia Indica*, VII, 109.

$ 282. Later on are found certain fragments of Marathi prose found in the *Mānasollāsa* or *Abhilaṣitārtha-cintāmaṇi* of Bhūlokamalla, written in Śaka 1051. Rajvade has given the two passages in the *Viśvavṛtta* of July, 1907, on p. 8. They are as given below :

jeṇeṃ rasātaḷauṇu matsyarūpeṃ veda aṇiyale manuśivaka vāṇiyale to saṃsārasāyaratarana moha (haṃ) tā rāvo nārāyaṇu (v. 2143).

"The one, Who in the form of Fish, has brought from the Nether world (the deepest of the hells) the Vedas (and) which have been chanted by Manu and Śiva, That One, Who helps cross the ocean of existences, the Vanquisher of bewilderment, He is the King Nārāyaṇa."

The other passage is very obscure :

jo gopijaṇe gāyije (revised reading. R. reads *māyije*) *bahu pari rūpeṃ nirhāṃgo*...(the remaining part can not be understood)...(v. 2162) "Of whom the shepherd-women sing a great deal, but as regards the external aspect who (has) no body."

§ 283. In Śaka 1109 (1186 A. D.) a Sanskrit inscription of Aparāditya, the Śilāhāra, found at Parel, contains an imprecation, whose text and meaning are given below. We have followed herein the edition of Bhagawanlal Indraji (JAS *Bomb*., XII, p. 334).

atha tu jo koṇuhuvi (read *ci* ?) *e śāsan lopi tecyā vedyanāthadevācī bhāl sakuṭuṃbi āpaḍeṃ* l *tehācī māy gāḍhaveṃ jhavije.*

"Anyone who destroys this edict, the lance of the god Vaidyanātha will fall on him and his family, and his mother will be seized by an ass."

§ 284. In the *Epigraphia Indica*, I, p. 343-46, is found an inscription of Śaka 1128, . discovered at Pāṭṇā (or Pāṭaṇ) in Khandesh. This contains a large part in Marathi which Kielhorn has failed to understand. In 1906, Rajvade has tried a new reading of the same and has published it in the *Prabhāt* of Dhulia. In regard to the Marathi part, it differs not only from that of Kielhorn, but even from that of Bhau Daji (JAS *Bomb*., I p. 414 ff.). Here is the Marathi text as given by Rajvade and the translation made following the same :

(22)...*iyāṃ pāṭaṇīṃ jeṃ keṇeṃ ughaṭe tehācā asi āīṃ jo rāulā hoṃtā grāhakapāsīṃ to maḍhā dīnhalā* l *brāhmaṇāṃ jeṃ vikateyāpāsīṃ brahmottara teṃ brāhmaṇīṃ dinhaleṃ* l *grāhā* (23) *kāpāsīṃ dāmācā visovā āsupāṭhī magareṃ dīnhālā* ll *jalādāiyāṃ bailāṃ siddhaveṃ* ll *bāhirilā āsupāṭhī gidhaveṃ grāhakapāsīṃ pāṃca pophalī grāhakapāsīṃ* ll *pahi* (24) *leā ghāṇeā dānācī loṭī maṭhā dīnhālī* ll *jetī ghāṇeṃ vāṃhati tetiyāṃ prati palī palī telā* l *etha jeṃ mavije teṃ maḍhīcena māpeṃ mavāveṃ māpāu maḍhā arddhaṃ* ll *arddhaṃ* (25) *māpahārī* l *tūpaceṃ sūṃka* l *tathā bhūmiḥ* ll *caturāghāṭaviśuddha oṃ-*

dhugrāmu paṣama bāleā kāmatu madhyeṃ vaḍabuṃdhu ll *pukala-vuṃdhu* ll *paṇḍitāṃcā kāmatu* l *cītegrā* (26) *mī cāurā* ll *dhāmojiciā soṃdhiāṃ* ll

"In this town of Patan, (the product of) the tax called *asi* which is levied on the merchandise put out (in the bazar), which is found in the royal palace at the house of the preceptor, is given to the Mutt. The profit obtained by the Brahmins on the merchandise put up for sale is given by the Brahmins to the Mutt. A twentieth part of the sum (received by him) is given by the cavalier Magar ("Crocodile") to the preceptor. (The preceptor) should look after the buffaloes kept for bringing water (to the Mutt). A twentieth part of the tax) on the merchandise coming from outside (is) given to the preceptor by the cavalier Gidhav ("Eagle" ?) The five promises, as set out below, have been made to the preceptor. The outflow of the grain of the first crushing of oil is given to the Mutt. As many times a palī (4 tol) of oil (is given to the Mutt) as there are the number of presses. The oil, that is measured here, has to be measured with the measure of the Mutt. The oil to be poured (is divided) half for the Mutt (according to R. : "in the jar" : *maḍh=māṭh*), half for the checker of measures.

The tax on ghee.

In addition, a plot of land delimited by the (following) four limits : the village of the stream, in the west the earth allotted to Bālā, in the centre the trunk of the Fig tree, the trunk of *pukal*, the land alloted to the Pandits, one cāhūr (120 *bighas*) in the village of the leopard; the spurs of the mountain of Dhamoji."

$ 285. Among later documents, other than literary texts, we have made use here only of the votive inscription of Pandharpur, of Śaka 1195-1199, which is described in the *Gazeteer* of Sholapur (*Gaz. of the Bombay Press*, XX, p. 421-2) and which has been re-edited by Rajvade in the *Granthamālā* of April, 1905. The Marathi part begins as follows :—

(3) *Svasti Śrī saku* 1195 *śrīmukhaṃ saṃvatsare phāgani-puraśrīviṭṭhaladevarāyāsi tisātiti* (?) *phuleṃ dāṃḍe ācaṃdrārka cālāveā nānā bhakti māliāṃ datta paikācā vivaru* l

Rajvade understands it as given below :

"For the king-god Viṭṭhal of Phāganipur...flowers and

canes, for being used as long as the Moon and the Sun, offered by the various groups of devotees; details of objects" (or "details of objects offered by" etc.).

The remaining part of the inscription is too fragmentary to merit the trouble of being inscribed here.

GLOSSARY

aūt n. "instrument; (in Deś) plough; land that can be tilled by two buffaloes". Skr. *āyukta-* ? —$ 142.

aṃk, āṃk, aṃkh m. "number, mark, sign" G. *āṃk, āṃkḍo,* H. *āṃk, āṃkḍā.* S. *aṅgu*; K. *ōkh,* Siṃ. *ak* "mark", *āka* "breast". Pkt. Skr. *aṅka-.* —$ 85.

akrā "eleven". G. *agiār*; S. *ikārahaṃ, yārahaṃ,* Panj. *giārāṃ,* H. *igārah, gyāraha,* E.B. *egār,* K. *kāh,* Siṃ. *ekoḷos, ekoḷaha.* Pkt. Apa. *eggāraha, eāraha,* etc., Amg. *ekkārasa,* P. *ekādasa, ekārasa.* Skr. *ekādaśa.-.* —$ 45, 74, 118, 143, 160, 161, 174, 213, 221.

akāṃt m. "excessive sorrow". Skr. *ākranda-,* probably based on the analogy of Skr. *ākrānta-,* see $ 90.

akhjā, akhitīj, f. "third lunar day of the first fortnight of Vaiśākha". G. *akhātrīj,* H. *akhetij, akhtīj,* K. *achintray.* Skr. *akṣayatṛtīyā* or *akṣatatṛtīyā.* —$ 49.

akhā, ākhā, adj. "entire, in all". G. *ākhalo* "noncastrated bull", *ākhuṃ* "entire". Pkt. *akkhaya-.* Skr. *akṣata-.* "entire". — $ 47, 49, 60, 96.

aṃgṭhā, poet. *aṃguṭhā* m. "thumb". G. *aṃguṭho*; H. *amgūṭhā*; S. *aṅūṭho*; W. Panj. *angūṭh*; Sim. *anguṭa,* Ro. *anguśt.* Skr. *aṅguṣṭha-.* —$ 50, 110.

aṃgaṇ m. *āṃgaṇem* n. "courtyard". G. *āṃgaṇuṃ, āṃgaṇiyuṃ*; S. *aṅaṇu*; H. Panj. E.B. *āṃgan.* Skr. *aṅgana-.*—$ 134.

agyā adj. "of the front". G. *aguvo* "guide"; H. *agvā, agvānā* "one who goes forward", *āge* "in front"; Panj. *agge,* S. *agī, agiāṃ,* B. *āge* "in front", *agyoṃ* "precedent"; cf. Siṃ. *aga* "the first, point", *aghi* "in front"; K. *ogu* "first day of the fortnight" ; Ro. *agor* "point". Pkt. *agga-.* Skr. *agra-.* —$ 49, 62, 63, 98, 154.

aglā aḷā, adj. "anterior, superior". G. *āgluṃ* adj., *āgaḷ,* adv., old G. *āgali* "in front", S. *agaro*; H. *aglā*; E.B. *āgli*; Ro. *angle* "in front". Apa. *aggalau,* derived from Skr. *agra-*;— $ 49, 98.

agaḷ, āgaḷ, āghaḷ m. f. "a bar for a door or window, pit; snood". G. *āgaḷī, āgaḷo*; H. *aggal*; *āgal,* f.; Panj. *aggal*; B. *agaḍ*; Siṃ. *agula.* Pkt. *aggala-.* Skr. *argala-.* — $ 49, 98, 145.

aṃgulī, aṃgḷī, āṃgolī f. "finger"; G. *aṃguḷī, aṃgulī, āṃgḷī*; *āṃglī*; H. *aṃgulī, uṃglī*; S. *aṅuri,* f.; Panj. *uṅgulī*; K. *ongujü,* f. (cf. *oṅgul* m. "measure of a finger"); Siṃ. *āṅgilla.* Pkt. Skr. *aṅguli-* —$ 50, 145.

aṃgocchā, m. "piece of cloth for shoulder, handkerchief". G. *aṅguccho*; S. *aṅgocho*; K. *angöca*; H. *aṃgoch ā,* Skr.

aṅgavastra-.—$ 51, 78, 101.

aghāḍā, *agheḍā*, m. achyranthis aspera". G. *āghāḍo*, *āgheḍo*; H. *aghāḍa*. Deśī. *agghāḍa*-. (*agghāḍammi mauramaurandā*; comm : *mauro tathā maurando apāmārgaḥ*", 224, 12, 14). Skr. *āghāṭa*-. —$ 77, 90, 99, 111.

aṃghūl, *aṃghoḷ* "ablution"; of *aṅga*-+*hoḷṇeṃ*. G. *aṃghoḷ* "both", *aṃghoḷvuṇ* "to bathe". $ 99.

aṃcavṇeṃ "to wash one's mouth after a meal". H. *acvau*. Skr. *ācamana*-. —$ 70, 101, 252.

accher, for *adh-śer* "half a seer". G. *accher*. —$ 164.

aṭṇeṃ "to travel" (poet.). G. *aṭvuṃ*. Pkt. *aṭai* (cf. Deśī. *talaaṃṭai bhramati*, 160, 10). Skr. *aṭati*. —$ 109.

aṭāḷā, *aṭolā* m. "raised platform in a field", *aṭāḷī*, *aṭālī* f. "terrace". G. Panj. *aṭārī*; H. *aṭāl* "heap, grain-reserve", *aṭālā* "heap, pile". Skr. *aṭṭalikā*. —$ 109, 145.

aṭhrā "eighteen". H. *aṭhārah*, Panj. *athārāṃ*, B. *āṭhār*, O. *aṭhar*, G. *aḍhār*, *arāḍ*, S. *aḍahaṃ*, K. *ardah*, Siṃ. *aṭaḷos*. Pkt. *aṭṭhārasa*, Apa. *aṭṭhāraha*. Skr. *aṣṭādaśa*. —$ 221.

aṭhī, f. "kernel". K. *aḍa*, f. pl., Siṃ. *āṭa*. Skr. *asthi*-, *aṣṭhi*-, *aṣṭi*-. —$ 110, 168.

āṃḍ n. "testicle", *aṃḍeṃ* n. "egg'. G. *aṃḍ*, H. Panj. K. *āṃḍ*, O.B. *āṃḍā*, S. *āno* "egg', *anūro* "testicle", Arm. Ro. *anlu* "egg". Skr. *aṇḍa*-. — $ 111.

aḍ- "eight", in. *aḍtīs* "38", *aḍsaṭ* "68". G. *aḍār*, *aḍhār* "18", *aḍsaṭh* "68", H. *aḍtīs*, *aḍsaṭh*. Pkt. *aḍha*-. Skr. *aṣṭa*-, *aṣṭā*-, —$ 89, 112.

aḍ- *āḍ*- in a compound "half., semi-, bad"; *aḍhā* "a coin". G. *āḍ*-, S. *aḍh*- ("and a half"), K. *aḍ*-, Siṃ. *aḍa*. Pkt. (Jaina) *aḍḍha*-. Skr. *ardha*-. —$ 49, 89, 115, 225.

aḍśerī "a weight of two seers and a half." (*aḍīc*+*ser*) to be distinguished from *accher* "half a seer" (*adh* + *śer*). —$ 164.

aḍīc "two and a half"; *aḍceṃ*, *aḍjeṃ* "two times and a half". The forms of other languages do not have a palatal at the end: G. *aḍhī*, *aḍī*, S.H.O. *aḍhāī*, Panj. *ḍhāī*, B. *āḍāī*. In Prakrit only the sonant is found in Ardha Māg. compd. *aḍḍhāijja*- Skr. *ardha*-*tṛtīya*-. It should be noted that Skr. *tṛtīya*-is represented in Pkt. by *taia*,- which explains the modern forms cited above; moreover, there is an Ardha Māg. *tacca*- **tṛtya*- ?), cf. *ducca*—with reference to Skr. *dvitīya*-; we may suppose a form **ticca*-to be the origin of the Marathi word.—$ 30, 63, 89, 101, 115, 225.

aḍaṇ f. "bamboo-frame of fan", *aḍṇī* "tripod". G. *āḍṇi*" the round plate on which Indian bread is made" P. *aṭani*- "frame of bed". Skr. *aṭanī* "curved end of the bow." —$ 111.

aḍulsā m."justicia ganderussa". G. *aḍusī*. Skr. *aṭaruṣa*-. —$ 111, 141, 167.

aṇ—negative prefix, in *aṇvāṇī* "bare-foot" (of *vahāṇ* "sandals"); cf. *anmol* "priceless", *anāṭhāyiṃ* "at a bad place". G. *aṇ*- (very frequent), S. *aṇ*-, Panj. *aṇjān*, H. *anjān* "ignorant", H. *andekhā* "invisible", K. *anpar* (Skr. *apaṭhita-* "not read"); Simhalese like Skr. uses *a-* before a consonant, *aṇ-* before vowel. Pkt. *aṇa-* before consonant. Skr. *a-*, *an-*. —$ 134.

atkārī for tats.—*adhikārī* "authorised person, functionary etc." —$ 164.

aṃtar n. "interior". G. H. *aṃtar*, "interior, intestines," S. *andaru* W. Panj. *āndrā* "intestines", Ro. *andre* "inside". Pkt. Skr. *antara-*. —$. 143.

atāṃ, *attāṃ* " now, at present". cf. G. *atare* "here", *atyār* "this time, now", S. *itāṃ* "there", K. *ati*, *otu* "there". Pkt. *atto*. Skr. *ataḥ*; or Skr. *atra*+ the locative termination ($ 194); or gerundive present of the verb *āh-* "to be" ($ 262) ?—$ 121.

ad- in compd. "half", as in *adkos* "½ kos", *adpāv* "half quarter (of a seer)", *adśer* "½ seer". G. *adh-*, *ad-*, Panj. H. *ad-*, *ād-*; cf. M. *ādhā*. . —$ 115, 164

aṃdhār, *aṃdhārā* m. "darkness". G. *āṃdhḷuṃ* "blind", *aṃdhāruṃ* "darkness", *aṃdheru* "sombre", S. *andho*, *andhero* "blind", *andhāru* "obscurity", W. Panj. *anhā* "blind", *anhārā*, *anherā* "darkness", K. *onᵘ* "blind", H. *andhā* "blind", *andher* m. "darkness", Maith. *ānh*, *ānhar*, Siṃ. *āndura* "obscure". Pkt. *andhaāra-*. Skr. *andhakāra-* "darkness" from *andha-* "blind". —$ 61, 124 258.

ansūd, *anśud*, f. "act of pouring melted butter on rice". cf. H. *an*, S. *an* "grain", K. *an* "meal", Siṃ. *an* "nourishment, meal". Skr. *annaśuddhi-*. — $ 88, 135, 156.

aprā adj. "short (nose, dress)". from Skr. *alpa-* "small", or for *apurā* "incomplete", cf. *purā* "entire". — $ 125.

apūṭ "untouched, unpolluted" (eatable, etc.). Pkt. *apuṭṭha-*. Skr. *aspṛṣṭa-*. — $ 84, 88, 89.

aphaḷṇeṃ "to strike violently" (poet.). Pkt. *apphalia-* "struck, shaken". Skr. *āsphalana-*. — $49, 126.

amū "mute". Skr. *amukha-*. — $ 161.

amūp "immeasurable" (root *a*+*māp*); cf. vulg. *mop* "much". — $ 174.

arsā, *ārsā* m. "mirror". G. *ārsī*, *ārso*, S. *ārisī* f. Skr. *ādarśa-*. — $ 49, 61, 157.

alaṃg f. "long building" (barracks, table etc.)". H. Bih. *alaṃg*, *ālaṃg* "line, trench, town-wall". Per. *alang*. —$ 149.

alitā, *altā*, *alitā* m. "red lacquer paint". G. *alto* m. "lac", H. *altā* m., K. *olutᵘ*. Skr. *alakta-* "lac", probably combined with *ālipta-* "plaster". — $ 50, 121.

alikḍe, *alīkḍe* "from this side"; from *kaḍ* side (Skr. *kaṭi-*); the first part of the word is obscure, cf. m. *alāḍ* "from this side". G. *āle* "near, equal". Deśī. *alīlaṃ nikaṭaṃ bhayam* (28, 10-11). —$ 50.

avakṇeṃ, *avikṇeṃ* "to over-ripen"; from *ava*+*pikṇeṃ* "to ripen". — $ 50, 172.

avatṇeṃ, *āvatṇeṃ*, *avaṃtṇeṃ*, *aumtṇeṃ* "to invite". Siṃ. *amatanavā* "to invite, to wait", *āmatuma* "invitation"; with another preverb, G. *notarvuṃ* "to invite", *notan* "chief invitee", H. *nevatnā*, *nautnā* "to invite", S. *notiru* "invitation". P. *āmanteti*, Pkt. pcpl. *mantida-*. Skr. *āmantrayate*. — $ 49, 71, 152.

avas, *āvas*, *āmūs*, *amos*, *amośā* f. "new moon". G. *amās*, S. *umāsu*, H. *ammās*. Skr. *amāvāsyā*. — $ 49, 78, 152, 157.

avaḷ "pressed, contracted", *avaḷṇeṃ* "to row, to contract". G. *avaḷuṃ* "contrary, obstinate, reversed", S. *avalo* "perverse, difficult, unfavourable", Deśi *avilo paśu kaṭhinaś ca* (24, 13). Skr. **ā-val-*, cf. *āvaraṇa-*. —$ 42, 152.

avlā "myrobolan". G. *āval*, S. *āṃviro*, K. *ōml^a^a*, Panj. H. *āṃvla*, B. *āvlā*. Skr. *āmalaka-*. — $ 60, 145, 152.

avher m. "disrespect". H. *aver* f. Skr. *avahela-*, n.—$142.

aṃsḍī, *āsḍī*, f. "spawn of flies", P. *asāṭikā*. — $ 52, 70.

asṇeṃ "to be, to exist". H. *achnā*, Ro. *ač* "to remain"; this verb is generally defective and is used only in the present and notably in the periphrastic tenses; thus G. *chuṃ*, Jaipuri *chūṃ*, Mevātī *sūṃ*, K. *chus*, Nepalī *chu*, Maith. *chī*, B. *āchi*, O. *achi* "I am"; the root seems to be missing in Sindhi & Panjabi. P. *acchati*, Pkt. *acchai*. IE. **esk-*, cf. archaic future in Latin *escit*, Homeric Greek pretarite éske, éskon, Armenian Subjunctive *isém* "that I be", Tocharian B *sketar*, "is", *skente*. "are" (see S. Lévi and Meillet, M.S.L; XVIII, p. 28). — $ 103, 230, 246, 250.

asval "bear". Deśī. *acchabhallo ṛkṣaḥ* (17, 16). cf. on the one hand Siṃ. *as*, P. *accha-*, Skr. *ṛkṣa-*; on the other M. H. *bhālū*, Deśī. *bhallū ṛkṣaḥ* (218, 2) and sometimes Ro. *balo* "pig". — $ 30, 55, 103, 148.

aseṃ n. "that" anaphoric; for *aiseṃ*; cf. *taisā* "such". — $ 276.

asok, *asog*, *osag* f. "Ashoka tree". G. *āso* (*-pātar*), H. *asog*, *asok*, m. Pkt. *asoa-*, *asoga-*. Skr. *aśoka-*. — $ 98, 156, 167.

ahāṇā, *aṇā* m. "adage, proverb". H. *hannā*. Skr. *ābhāṇaka-*. — $ 52, 62, 159, 161.

ahārṇeṃ "to be indolent following a very big meal"; *āhār* m. "nourishment, meal"; G. B. *āhār*, H. *ahār*, S. *āhāru*. Skr. Pkt. *āhāra-*. — $ 159.

ahāroḷī f. "cake fried on live charcoal"; from *ahār* "live charcoal" and *poḷī* "cake". $ 152.

ahev f. "woman whose husband is alive". H. *ahibāt*, *ahivāt* "condition of a woman whose husband is alive." Skr. *avidhavā*. —$63, 152, 159.

aḷ, *aḷaī aḷī* f. "fruit insects and grains, sort of caterpillar." G. *alāī* "skin irritation", *eḷ* "insect", H. *alī* "a large black bee, scorpion" B. *ali*, Siṃ. *ali* "scorpian". Skr. *alin-* "wasp, scorpion". —$ 145.

altā m. "colour of lac". see *alitā*. $ 50, 145.

aḷambeṃ, *alaṃbheṃ* n. "mushroom". Deśī. *ālaṃbaṃ*

bhūmichhatram yad varṣāsu prarohati (28, 4-5). — $ 49, 145, 149.

aḷṇī "unsalted". H. *alonā*, S. *alūṇa*. Skr. *alavaṇa-*. — $ 51, 149.

alśī f. "flakes". G. *alasī*, *ilsī*, H. *alsī*, S. *elisī*, *alisī*, K. *alish*. Skr. *atasī*. — $ 49, 118.

aḷū m. in the Konkan, *aḷūṃ* n. "Caladium Esculentum", *alkuḍī* "the root of this plant". G. *aḷvī*, H. *alū* potatoe". (cf. Yule Burnell, *Hobson-Jobson*[2], p. 885[1]). Skr. *ālu-* n. — $ 50.

aḷeṃ n. "cavity around a tree". G. *āḷiyo* "a big hole in a wall" H. *ālā* "cavity around a tree" P. *ālaka-*. Skr. *alavāla-* "cavity around a tree". — $ 145 .

ākūḷ "crowded, agitated (by some sentiment)", tatsama. Skr. *ākula-*. — $ 40.

āṃkh m. "axis, axle"; cf. M. *āṃs*. Skr. *akṣa-*. cf. Skr. *akṣi-*, Pkt. *akkhi-*, G. H. *āmkh*, S. *akh*, Panj. *akkh*, K. *achi* f. E.B. *āṃkhi*, Siṃ. *ak* and *äsa* "eye". — $ 69, 96, 104.

ākhāḍ m. "month of *āṣāḍha*", G. *āṣāḍh*, *āśāḍh*, *akhāḍh*, H. *āsāḍh*, *āṣāḍ*, S. *ākhāḍu*, Siṃ. *asaḷa āhāla*. Skr. *āṣāḍha-*. — $ 88, 95.

ākhuḍṇeṃ "to contract, to compress", Pkt. *akkhoḍai* "to unsheathe". Skr. **ā-khuḍ-*, from *khuḍ-* "to break". — $ 96.

āg f. "fire". G. H. *āg*, S. *agi*, K. *ogun*, Panj. *agg*, Maith. *āgi*, B. *āgun*, O. *ṇia*, Siṃ. *aga*, *gina*. P. *gini-*, Pkt. *aggi-*, Skr. *agni-*. m. — $ 29, 41, 69, 98, 188.

āgṭī f. *āgṭeṃ* n., *āgṭhi* f. "fire-place, crucible, whole for fire". Skr. *agniṣṭhikā*, *agniṣṭha-*. — $ 50, 89.

āgśī f. "spark". Skr. *agniśikhā*. — $ 62, 156, 161.

āgas "soon" (better than *àgas*); Skr. *agraśaḥ* —$ 39, 98, 156.

āṃc f. "flame". G. S. H. *āṃc*, Siṃ. *asi* "flash of lightning, splinter". Pkt. *acci-*. Skr. *arci-*. m. *arciṣ-* n. — $ 39, 69, 70, 101.

āj "to day ". G. *āj*, H. *āj*, S. *aju*, Panj. *ajj*, K. *aji*, *āj*, E.B. *āji*, Siṃ. *ada*, Pkt. *ajja*, *ajju*. Skr. *adya-*. — $ 106.

ājā, *ājās* m. "grand-father pat. or mat.)". G. *ājo* "maternal grand-father". H. *ājā* "paternal grand-father". Siṃ. *aya* "individual, person" (used even in case of animals); the word has been borrowed in Dravidian; Kan. *ayya* "master, grand-father, father, school-master", Tam. *ayyan* "Lord" etc. Pkt. *ajja-*, cf. Deśī. *ajjo*, *jino' rhan buddhas' ca* (3, 18) Pali and Inscr. Pkt. *ayya-*, *aya-*. Skr. *ārya-* "noble, venerable". — $ 36, 106.

āṭ f. "rice boiled & mixed with flour." G. S. *āṭo*, H. B. *āṭā*, K. *ôṭu*, Ro. *aro*, *vanro* "flour". This word is found neither in Skr. nor in Middle Indian, but it is Indo-European : zd. *aśa-* "ground", Sogdian *arθ*, "mill", Per. *ārd*, Afghan *ōṛa* "flour", Armenian *atam*, Greek "*'aleo*" "I grind". — $ 109.

āṭkeṃ n. "eighth part". Cf. *āṭh* "eight". — $ 89.

āṭh "eight", G. H. Maith. O. *āṭh*, B. *āṭ*, S. *aṭh*, Panj. *aṭṭh*, K. *öṭh*. In compound, *aṭh-*, *aḍ-*. Pkt. *aṭṭha-*, *aḍha-*. Skr. *aṣṭau-*. — $ 39, 108, 219.

āḍ m. "well". H. S. *āḍ* f. "water- conduit". Deśī. *aḍo kūpaḥ* (4, 29), Pkt. *aḍa-*. Skr. *avaṭa-*, m. "cavity, well". — $ 111.

āḍalī, *āḍī* f. "thrush". H. *āḍ*; cf. S. *āṛī* "wild duck" ?. Skr. *āṭī*, *āti-*. — $ 111.

āṇ f. "oath". G. *āṇ* "order, oath", H. *ān* "order", S. *āṇ* "submission, subjection". (H. Panj. *āgyā*, S. *agyā* "order" are tatsamas), K. *ān* Siṃ. *aṇa* "order". In the beginning of the 10th cent. a Tamil inscription has *āñai*; the modern Tamil form is *āṇai*. (see *Arch. Survey of India*, *Ann. Rep*. 1904-1905, p. 133). P. *aññā*, Pkt. *ajjā*, *āṇā*. Skr. *ājñā*.— $ 106, 135.

āṇṇeṃ "to bring". G. *āṇvuṃ* (cf. *āṇuṃ* "invitation to the young wife to go from the house of her father to that of her husband"), S. *āṇaṇu*, K. *anun*, Ro. *an-*, H. *ānnā*. Skr. *ānayati* -. — $ 134, 282,

āṇi, *aṇkhī* "and", *ān* (poet.) "beside", *n*. (pop.) "and"; *ānsā* adj. (poet.) "other". G. *āṇ*, *ān* "other", *ane* "and", old H. *ani*, *ān*, Siṃ. *anum* *anik* "other", *anikḍā* "day after tomorrow".Besides the Pkt. *aṇṇa-*, correctly derived from Skr. *anya-* "other", Apa. *aṇu* "otherwise" gives evidence for India of another stem **ana-*; cf. probably in Tocharian the opposition of *alyeka* "other" : *alecce* 'a stranger". The radical element is also found in Got. *an-þar*, Lit. *antra-s* "other"; cf. in Latin *alter* with regard to *alius*. —$ 135, 237, 276.

āt f. "father's sister". Deśī. *attā caturarthā*; *mātā jananī*; *piucchā pitṛśvasā*; *śvaśrūḥ śvaśurabhāryā*; *sakhī vayasyā* (24, 8). — $ 39, 41, 121.

āṃt n. "intestines"; *āmt* postposition "inside". G. *aṃtar*, *āmantraḍuṃ* ('intestines"), H. *āṃt*, *āntar*, S. *aṃtar*, m., *aṃtu* m., K. *and*^{a}*r* "intestines", *andar* "inside". P. *anto*. Skr. *antaḥ* "inside", *antram* "intestine" — $ 68, 121, 195, 197.

aṃtharaṇeṃ "to cover", *āṃthar* m. f. "mat of bamboo". G. *āthar* "carpet", *atharavuṃ* "to spread". Skr. *āstar-*.—$ 69.

āthī "there is..." (poet.) pcpl. *āthilā* "been". Siṃ. *äti*, *äta*, Pkt. *atthi*. Skr. *asti*.—$ 147, 69, 122, 230.

ādhā (poet.) adj. "half". S. *adhu*, Panj. *addhā*, W. Panj. *addh*, H. B. *ādhā*, O. *adhā*, Maith. *ādh*, K. *ad*^{i}*hyolu* "half a pice (coin)" H. M. *ādhelā*, Pkt. *addha-*. Skr. *ardha-*. Cf. *aḍ-*, *adh-*, *sāḍe*, *dīḍ*. —$ 49, 89, 115, 164, 225.

āp (in compound), *āpaṇ* "oneself"; *āplā* "ones own". G. *āp*, *āpṇo*, cf. *āte*, *āto*, *pote*; Rajp. *āp*, *āpṇu*, Panj. H. *āp*, *āpan*, *āpas*, B. *āp*, *āpani*, O. *āpe*, *āpaṇ*, Nêp. *āphn*, *aphnu*, S. *pāṇu*, K. *pāna*, Khovār *tán*, Gārvī *tanī* etc. (see Grierson, *Piś. Lang*., p. 76), Ro. *po*, *pes-*, Siṃ. *api*, *āp* "we", *tamā* "ones own". Pkt. *appā* and *attā* (Māhārāshtri has almost always *appā*). Skr. *ātman-*. — $ 18, 47, 69, 125, 165, 205.

āpā "a term of respect towards

an elder or a child" G. *āpo* "father (used by shepherds)." Deśī. *appo pitā* (4, 12). — $ 125.

āṃb f. "type of vineger obtained by covering in the evening a piece of cloth over flowing plants of cicer arietinum." G. *āṃb*, H. *aṃbat*, Siṃ. *āmbul*. Pkt. *amba-*. Skr. *āmla-*. —$ 127.

āmba m. "mango". G. *āmbo* ("mango tree"), H. *ām*, *aṃb*, (poet.) *āmbā* S. *aṃbu*, *āmo*. Panj. *ām*, *āmb*, K. *amb*, B. O. *āmb*, *ām*, Siṃ. *aṃba*. Pkt. *amba-*. Skr. *āmra-*. — $ 60, 127.

ābh. n. (in Konkan) "sky, cloud". G. *ābh*, H. *abhāl*, S. *abhu*, K. *abur*, Siṃ. *aka*. cf. Deśī. *abbhapisāo rāhuḥ* (20. 5); Pkt. *abbha-*, Skr. *abhra-*. — $ 128.

āmhī "us", *āmcā* "ours". G. *ame*, S. Panj. *asīṃ*, W. Panj. *assāṃ*, K. *asi*, Ro. *amen*, Raj. *ham*, *mhe*, H. *ham*, Nep. *hāmi*, B. *āmi*, O. *amhe*, Pkt. *ahme* Skr. *asmad-* (Ved. dat. -loc. *asmé*). $ 39, 75, 138, 194, 210.

ār- in. *kavalār*, *kaulār* "brick-roof.", *dhavalār* poet. "house with a white-washed terrace." Skr. *āgāra-*. — $ 61.

ār m. "bow-constrictor". Skr. *ajagara-*. — $ 41, 65, 143.

ārat, ***ārtī*** f. "lamp used in idol-worship; act of thus using the lamp". G. S. H. *ārtī*, K. *ālath*. Skr. *ārātrikā.-* — $ 39, 52, 121, 143.

āraṃbhṇeṃ "to begin". G. S. H. B. *ārambh*. Siṃ. *araṃba* "beginning", *araba āraṃba* (post-position) "beginning by, relative to", K. *āramba* "beginning". Skr. *āraṃbha-*, *ārambhaṇa-*. — $ 128.

ālā "arrived", past pcpl. of *yeṇeṃ* "to come." Siṃ. *ā* "arrived, present". K. *āv*, from *yinu*. "to come". Pkt. *āa-*. Skr. *āgata-*. One should distinguish *āyā* and Panj. *āeā* from the verb *ānā*, which is for *āvna*; cf. G. S. *āv-*, Ro. *av-*, Skr. *āp-*. — $ 65, 229.

āleṃ n. "ginger". G. *ādu* n., S. *adirak* f. (*ālo* "humid"), H. *ādā* (*ālā* "humid"), K. *ödürü* (*oduru* "humid"), Siṃ. *ada*. Pkt *alla-*. Skr. *ardra-*, *ārdraka-* "humid, ginger". — $ 141.

āṃv f. "dyspepsia". H. *āṃv*, S. *āṃu* f. K. *ômu* "raw", *ām* "intenstinal worm", Siṃ *amu* "raw"; *āmiyāva* "indigestion." Skr. *āma*. "raw", *āmaya-* "dyspepsia, or disease". — $ 152.

āvagṇeṃ "to run riot". cf. H. *bagnā* "to go". Skr. *āvalgate* "to jump". — $ 52, 98, 152.

āṃvas n. "meat of a buffalo killed by tiger and kept for the day after". Siṃ. *äma* "bait". P. *āmisa-*. Skr. *āmiṣa-*. "meat". — $ 42, 156.

āvsā m. "temporary hut made of branches, barrack". G. *avās*, H. *āvās*, Siṃ. *avas*, *avā* "house". Pkt. P. Skr. *āvāsa-*. —$ 52, 152.

āsaṃd f. "physalis flexuosa". H. *asgandh*, *isgandh*, S. *asigandhu*, B. *asān*, Skr. *aśvagandha-* (cf. Pkt. *assa-* from Skr. *aśva-*). — $ 62, 88, 98, 157).

āsupāṭhī "on the horse-back". Skr. *aśvapṛṣṭhe*. —$ 157.

ās, ***āṃs*** m. "axle", G. *āṃs* m. Pkt. *accha-*, *acchi-*. Skr. *akṣa-* m. — $ 69, 104.

ās f. "hope". G. *ās*, H. S. *ās*, *āsā* f. K. *ash*, Skr. *āśā*. — $ 39, 156.

āspās "all around", G. H. K. *āspās*, S. *āsipāsi*, W. Panj. *āsepāse*; Siṃ. *as* "side, corner". Deśī. *āsayaṃ nikaṭam* (28, 10); Pkt. *assa-* and *passa-*, *pāsa-*. Skr. *aśra-* "bank", *pārśva* "side". — $ 39, 198.

āsrā m. "refuge" G. *āsro*, H. *āsrā*, S. *āsar*, *āsiro*, K. *āsara*, Panj. B. Nep. B. O. Ass. *āśrā*. Skr. *āśraya-*. — $ 60, 157.

āsre n. pl. "water-demon". H. *acchar*; Siṃ. *asara* "diety". P. Pkt. *accharā*. Skr. *apsaras-*. — $ 69, 103.

āsū, *āṃsū* n. "tears". G. *āṃju*, *āṃsu*, H. Nep. *āṃsū*, S. *hamj*, Panj. *aṃjhu*, K. *osh,ᵘ* Ro. *asva*, Siṃ. *āsa*. Pkt. *aṃsu-*, P. *assu-*. Skr. *aśru-*. —$ 69, 70, 157.

āhṇeṃ "to be" S. *āṃh-* see H. Avadhī *ah-*, Panj., Raj., Braj., Bundeli, H. *h*(present *hūṃ* etc.); cf. M. H. etc. *nāhiṃ* "is not, no." Etymology uncertain; Skr. *ābhavati* ? — $ 70, 160, 236, 237, 246, 250, 268.

āḷ. m. f. "desire", Siṃ. *ala* "house, desire". Pkt. *ālaa-*. Skr. *ālaya-*. — $ 145.

aḷ f. "path". Siṃ. *äla* "canal". P. Skr. *āli-* "line, path". — $ 145.

āḷas m. "laziness, indolence". G. *āḷas*., H. *ālas*, S. *ārisu*, *alisu*, m. "indolence", *ārisi* "lazy", K. *ālochᵘ* "laziness"; Siṃ. *las* "lazy, slow". Pkt. *ālassa-*. Skr. *ālasya-*. —$ 40, 145, 157.

iṃgaḷ, *iṃgoḷ* m. "char-coal". G. *iṃgāro*. Pkt. *iṅgāra-*. Skr. *ingāra-* (in Harṣa), *aṅgāra-*. —cf. M. *aṃgāra* m. "fire-brand", G. *aṃgāro* (more frequent than *iṃgāro*), S. *aṅaru*, H. *aṃgār*, Siṃ. *aṅguru*, Ro. *angar*. — $ 42, 75, 79, 141.

iṭā, *viṭā* m. "sort of spear"; *iṭī*, *vīṭ* m. "the small stick which is struck in the game of *itīdāṇḍū*". H. *iṭhī*, *īṭī*, S. *iṭī*. Skr. *ṛṣṭi-*.—$ 30, 153.

ītukā (poet.) *itkā* adj. "equally numerous, equally big." G. *eṭlo*, S. *etiro*, H. Panj. *itnā*, K. *yūtᵘ*, B. *eta* O. *ete*, Siṃ. *etakin* cf. M. *kitkā* "how big", H. *kitkā* etc., Ro. *keti*). Pkt. *ittia-*, *ettia*. Skr. *iyat-*, In the opinion of Hemacandra, taken up by Goldschmdit, discussed by Pischel ($ 153), and yet plausible, in view of the rules of contraction of *i*+*a* in Marathi, see $ 63. — $ 75, 206.

ispiṭāl, European *hospital*. — $ 163.

iḷā m. "sickle". *iḷī* f. "pill-hook". Skr. *ilī*. — $ 149.

īṭ, *vīṭ* f. "brick", G. *iṃṭ*; H. *īṭ*, *īṃṭ*. Pkt. *iṭṭā*. Skr. *iṣṭā*. — $ 41, 88, 153, 189.

īs, *isāḍ*, *visāḍ* n. "beam of plough". G. S. *īs* f. "sides of bed-frame".Deśī. *īsaṃ kīlakaḥ* (35, 17); P. *īsā*. Skr. *īṣā*. — $ 44, 153.

ukaṭṇeṃ "to incise". H. *ukaṭnā* "to dig, to uproot"; S. *ukarṇu*, *ukirṇu*, *ukhaṭṇu*. Skr. *utkṛt-*, *utkartana-*. — $ 93.

ukaḍ, *ukḍā*, *ukiḍvā*, *ukuḍvā* adj. "crouching". cf. Siṃ. *ukula* "hip". P. *ukkuṭika-*. Skr. *utkaṭuka-*, *utkuṭaka-* "crouching", and *kaṭa-* "hip". — $ 75, 93.

ukaḍṇeṃ "to boil". Skr. *utkvathati.* — $ 93.

ukaḷṇeṃ "to boil, to boil up". G. *ukaḷvuṃ*, cf. *ukāḷo* "decoction, heat", H. *ukalnā.* Skr. *utkal-* "to release", or. *utkūla-* "over flown (stream of water)". —$ 93.

ukar, *ukīr* m. "a heap of earth"; *ukarḍā*, *ukirḍā*, *ukrīḍ* m. "dunghill". G. *ukarḍo*, *ukayḍo*. Deśī. *ukkuruḍī avakararāśiḥ*, *ukkuruḍo ratnādīnām api rāśiḥ* (46, 10), Pkt. *ukkera-*, *ukkara-*. Skr. *utkara-*, *utkira-*. — $ 75, 93, 143.

ukhaḍṇeṃ "to up-root", *ukhaḷṇeṃ* "to plough the field for the first time; to tear.". G. *ukhaḍvuṃ*, H. *ukhāḍnā.* Pkt. *ukkaḍḍhai.* Skr. *utkarṣati.* —$ 96, 112, 146.

ukhal m. *ukhḷī* f. "mortar". g. *ukhaḷ* n., *ukhlī*; H. *ūkhlī*, *ūkhal* f., S. *ukhirī* f. Pkt. *ukkhala-*. Skr. *udūkhala-*. — $ 96, 118, 145.

ukhāṇā m. "enigma". G. *okhāṇuṃ uhhāṇo ukhāṇuṃ*; S. *okhāṇi* f. "example", *okhāṇaṇu* "to recognise". Skr. *upākhyāna* "a narrative", *upākhyā-* "to narrate, to relate".— $ 52, 96.

ugaṇ f. *ugavaṇ* f. "eruption (of a disease)", *ugavṇeṃ* "to rise (talking of a star)". G. *ugavuṃ* "to climb", H. *ugnā*, S. *ugaṇu* "to push, to grow, to produce oneself". Pkt. *uggama-*, *ugge* "he climbs". Skr. *udgama-*, *udgamana-* — $—98, 153.

ugaḷṇeṃ "to ruminate, to spit, to vomit". S. *ugāraṇu* "to vomit", *ogāraṇu* "to ruminate", W. Panj. *ugālī* "rumination", H. *ugalnā.* Skr. *udgāra.* — $ 140.

uṃc, *uṃcā* adj. "high, on high." G. *uṃco*, S. *ūco* "superior", Panj. *uccā*, H. *ūṃcā*, Ro. *vučo*, Siṃ. *us*, *usa*, *uha*. P. Pkt. Skr. *ucca-*. — $ 69, 101.

ucakṇeṃ "to steal". G. *uṃcakvuṃ*, *ucakvuṃ*. "to raise", G. *uccakko*, W. Panj. *ucakka* "thief"; H. *ucaknā*. Seems to be derived from Skr. Pkt. *ucca* "high". (M. *uṃc*); cf. familiar French "to raise". —$ 94.

ucaṭṇeṃ "to detach", *ucāṭṇeṃ* "to detach oneself, to be disgusted with", *ucāṭ* m. n. "impatience". G. *uccāṭ* "disgust", S. *ucāṭu* "sad", H. *ucaṭnā* "to go away, to be disgusted", *uccāṭ honā* "to be disgusted". Apa. *uccāḍaṇu* "abandonement". Skr. *uccaṭati*, *uccāṭana-*. — $ 101, 109.

ucaṃḍaṇeṃ "to overturn (a vassel full of liquid)". From *ucca*+*andola-*. — $ 51, 145.

ucchāv, *utsav*, *utsāh* m. "festival", H. *ucchāo*, *ucchāhu*; S. *ucchaū*, Siṃ. *usā*. P. *usāha-*. Skr. *utsava-*. — $ 101.

ujavṇeṃ "to be regularly concluded, to succeed". G. *ujavavuṃ*. Skr. *udyāpana-*. — $ 52, 106

ujaḷ adj. "shining", cf. *ujrī* f. (poet.) "brightness". G. *ujḷuṃ*, S. *ujalu*, H. *ujjal*, *ujlā*. Pkt. *ujjala*. Skr. *ujjvala-*. — $ 106, 142.

ujāgar m. "state of wakefulness". G. *ujagaro*; H. *ujāgar* "light". Deśī. *ujjagiram*, *aunnidryam* (49, 3). Skr. *ujjāgara-*. — $ 52, 106.

ujū adj. "straight"; Siṃ. *udu*,

Ro. *uzo* "pure". Pkt. *ujjua-*. Skr. *ṛju-*. — $ 30, 106.

uṭṇeṃ "to rub, to oint". G. *uṭvuṃ*, S. *ubbaṭaṇu*, H. *ubaṭnā* "to oint", Bih. *abṭan* "unguent". Skr. *udvartana-* ? (see Grierson, *Phon.*, p. 27). — $ 51, 64, 114.

uṭhṇeṃ "to get up". G. *uṭhvuṃ*, Panj. H. *uṭhnā*; S. *uṭhaṇu*, K. *woth-* "to get up, to be produced"; B. *uṭhite*; Ro. *uśti*. Pkt. *uṭṭhai*, Skr. *ut+sthā-*. — $ 110.

uḍṇeṃ "to fly"; G. *uḍvuṃ*, S. *uḍāmaṇu*, causative *uḍāiṇu*, W. Panj. *uḍḍ-*, H. *uḍnā*, K. *wuḍ-*, Ro. *uri*. Apa. *uḍḍāṇeṃ* instr., Pkt. *uḍḍei*, *uḍḍāi*. Skr. *uḍḍayate*, *uḍḍīyate*. — $ 51, 111, 119, 230.

uḍīd m. "phaseolus, radiatus". G. *aḍad* m.; H. *urd*, *uṛd* "watch, dolichos pilosus"; S. *uṛdu*, *uṛidu* "cajanus indicus". Deśī. *uḍido māṣadhānyam* (41, 5). — $ 41, 163.

uṇā adj. "missing", G. *uṇu*, S. *ūṇu*, H. *ūn*, *ūnā*, Siṃ. *una* "lack". Skr. *ūna-*. — $ 134.

utaṇṇeṃ "to strip grass from ceiling"; cf. M. *taṇ*. Pkt. *tiṇa-*. Skr. *tṛṇa-*. — $ 121, 232.

utarṇeṃ "to descend, to deposit". G. *utarvuṃ*, S. *utarṇu*, H. *utarnā*; Siṃ. *utaraṇavā*. "to over-flow"'. Pkt. *uttarai*. Skr. *uttarati*, *uttārayati*. — $ 121, 143, 252.

utrān f. "North wind". G. *utarātuṃ*, *utarāduṃ*; H. *uttarāyā*, *uttarāhā*; S. *utaru* "North". Skr. *uttara-*.—One should separate G. *utarān* "Summer solstice". S. *utirāṇu*, from Skr. *uttarāyaṇa-*. — $ 121, 143.

utavṇeṃ "to boil". Skr. *uttapati* (transitive). — $ 152, 230.

utāṇā adj. "outstretch, with face upwards". G. *utān*; H. *uttān*, *utān*, *utānā*. Skr. *uttāna-* "act of stretching oneself". — $ 52, 121.

utāvaḷ f. "haste, impatience". G. H. *utāval*, S. *utāvili* f. "haste", *utāvilu* "hasty". Skr. *uttāpa* "ardour, anxiety". — $ 121.

uthaḷ, *utaḷ* adj. "shallow". G. *uthalvuṃ*, *utaḷuṃ* "to be reversed"; H. *uthalnā* "to overthrow", *uthal* *utthal* "flat", S. *uthilaṇu* "to be overthrown, to over flow", *uthal* f. "inundation". Deśī. *utthaliaṃ gṛham*; *utthaliam unmukhagatam ity anye* (48, 7); Pkt. *utthallai* "to reverse". Skr. *ut-sthala-*. — $ 89.

uṃdar vulg. *undīr* m. "rat". G. *undar*; H. and eastern group *indūr*; Siṃ. *unduru*. P. Skr. *undura-*. — $ 76, 143.

udīm m. "affair". H. *udyam*, *uddam*, *uddim*. Skr. *udyama-* "effort". — $ 74, 138.

udyām, *udaik* "tomorrow", cf. *udeṇeṃ* "to get up". G. *ude* m. "to lift", *udeti* "at sunrise"; H. *uday*, *udae*. Skr. *udaya-*. — $ 57.

udharṇeṃ "to vomit", G. *udharvuṃ*, H. *udhaḍnā* "to be unstitched"; S. *udhārṇu* "to deliver". Skr. *uddharaṇa-*. — $ 124.

udhav, *udav* "get up !, wake up !". G. *udo udo* ! Deśī. *uddhavao uccaḍio... utkṣiptārthāḥ* (48, 2). Skr. *ud+dhav-*, cf. M. *dhāvṇeṃ* "to run"; or should we compare S. *udhṇu* "to grow" and Skr. *ūrdhva-*, Pkt. *uddha-* ? Cf. M. *ubhā-*. — $ 89, 124.

udhalṇeṃ "to throw, to scatter", H. *udhalnā udhaljānā* "to be ruined, to be dissipated". Skr. *uddhūlayati* "to sprinkle with dust or powder." — $ 124, 145.

unmaḷṇeṃ "to up root". Probably a combination of Skr. *unmūlana* and of a tadbhava **umalṇeṃ*, cf. Pkt. *ummūlaṇa-*; Skr. *unmūlana-*. — $ 138.

upakharc m. "petty expenses". A type of tatsamsa, composed of Skr. *upa-* and Per. *xarc*, Ar. harj. —$ 101.

upajṇeṃ "to come from, to be born", G. *upajvuṃ*, S. *upajaṇu* "to produce oneself", H. *upajnā* "to grow up", Siṃ. *upadinavā* "to produce oneself, to grow". pcpl. *upan* "born". Pkt. *uppajjai*. Skr. *utpadyate*. — $ 52, 125, 230.

upaṭṇeṃ "to uproot". G. *upaḍvuṃ*; S. *upaṭṇu*" to draw, to discover"; H. *upaṭnā* "to over flow, to fall, to be ruined, to be abducted," Siṃ. *uparaṇavā*;. Skr. *utpāṭayati*. — $ 125.

upaḍṇeṃ "to fall (tree, nail)." Composed of Pkt. *u-*, Skr. *ut-* and Pkt. *paḍ-*. Skr. *pat-*; cf. M. *paḍṇeṃ* "to fall". — $ 125.

upaṇṇeṃ "to winnow", *upṇeṃ* n. "winnowed grain". G. *upaṇvuṃ*, S. *upaṇanu*. Pkt. *uppaṇaṇa-*. Skr. *utpavana-* ? — $ 125.

uplāṇā adj. "without saddle". From Pkt. *u-*, Skr. *ut* and M. *palāṇ* "saddle", — $ 125.

upāv, upāy m. "means", G. H. *upāv, upāy*, S. *upāū*. Skr. *upāya-*. — $ 57.

upās m. "fast". H. *upās*, Siṃ. *uvasu*. Skr. *upavāsa-*. — $ 61,

upeḍ adj. "elevated (terrain). Deśī. *uppehaḍaṃ ulhasiam*... *udbhaṭārthāḥ* (48, 14). Skr. **utpraidh-*. —$ 125, 161.

uphaṇṇem, uphaṇṇeṃ "to cause eruptions, to ferment". G. *uphān* n., *uphāno* "effervescence"; H. *uppannā* "to boil, to over flow," *uphān* m. ebullition". Skr. *ut- phaṇ-*. —$ 52, 126.

uphalṇeṃ "to beam, (face)"; (fig.) to open one's heart." cf. Deśī. *upphālai kathayati* (49, 5), Pkt. *upphulla-*. Skr. *utphulla-* "in full bloom". — $ 50, 126, 231, 232.

uphāḷṇeṃ "to boil up, to become inflated, to rise (flame);" (*uphāḷ* m. "surplus, ebullition". S. *uphirajaṇu* "to be inflated with wind". Pkt. *upphāla-*. Skr. *utphalati* "to burst, to spread, to jump", *utphāla-* "jump, gallop"; Pkt. *upphāla-*. — $ 126, 145.

uṃbar m. "ficus glomerata", *umbarā* m. "threshold". G. *umro* "threshold", *umarḍo* "fig tree"; H. *ūmri* f. "fig tree"; B. *ḍumur*; O. *ḍumvrī*. Deśī. *ummaro gṛhadehalī* (40, 7; cf. 38, 8), Pkt. *umbara-* M S. D. of Rhins *udumara-*. Vedic *udumbára-*, Skr. *uḍumbara-*. — $ 64, 118, 127, 138, 143,

ubhaḷṇeṃ "to sift". G. *ubheḷvuṃ* "to winnow the wheat", *ubheḷo* m. "husked rice", Deśī. *ubhālaṇaṃ śurpādiuotpavanam* (43, 13). — $ 52.

ubhā adj. "erect, standing" *ubhṇeṃ* "to lift". G. *ubhuṃ*, S. *ubho*, Siṃ. *uḍu*. Pkt, *uḍḍha- uddha-*, *ubbha-*. Skr. *ūrdhva-*. — $ 130.

ubhāra m. (poet.) "rising, diffusion (fragrance). G. *ubhār* "big volume but light weight", *ubhro* "efferves-cence"; H. *ubhār* "inflating"; S. *ubhārṇu*, W. Panj· *ubbharnā* "to get up, to rebound", Panj. H. *ubhārnā* "to lift, to pick up", G *ubhārvuṃ* "to rekindle the fire"; E. B. *ubharaṇ*. Skr. *udbharati*. — $ 52.

umagṇeṃ, *umaṃgṇeṃ* "to be known, to leak (news)" Pkt. *ummagga-*. Skr. *unmagna-* "emerging from water."— $ 138, 231.

umajṇeṃ "to come to mind"- Skr. *unmajjana-*. — $ 138, 252.

umaṭṇeṃ "to become clear, distinct (sound, impression)". G. *umaṭvuṃ*, *umaḍvuṃ* "to appear". Pkt. *ummaṭṭha-*. Skr. *unmṛṣṭa-* "obliterated", cf. for the meaning of causative pcpl. *unmārjita-*. "polished, clean". — $ 89.

umaḍ "jet of water, spurt of blood", *umāḍ* f. disturbance of the sea". G. *umāḍ*, *umāḍo* m. "fire-brand"; H. *umaṇḍnā* "to inflate, to overflow, to abound." Deśī. *ummaṇḍaṃ haṭha udvṛttaṃ ca* (52, 4). —$ 71.

umalṇem "to split, to open out". G. *umalvuṃ* "to be on the point of bringing". Pkt. *ummilla-*. Skr. *unmīlita-*. —$ 50, 138, 231.

umaḷṇeṃ "to wash". Skr. **unmala-*. — $ 138, 145.

umāṇṇeṃ "to compare". Skr. *unmāṇa-*. — $ 138.

umās m. "neausia, fermentation". G. *umas* f. "disgust, swoon". Deśī. *ummacchiaṃ ruṣitam ākulaṃ ca* (57, 7).Skr. *unmathyate* "to be agitated".— $ 40, 103, 138.

ulaṭṇeṃ "to turn, to reverse", *ulaṭ*, *ultī* f. "vomitting". G. *ulṭuṃ* "the contrary, on the contrary", *ulṭī* "vomitting"; S. *ulito* "reverse, strange", *uliṭi* "vomitting". Skr. *ulluṭhati* "to roll" — $ 50, 109.

ulāḷā, *ullāḷa*, *ulhāḷā* m. "leap". G. *ulāḷiyo* "leap", H. *ulahnā* "to surge, to push". Skr. *ullāla-*, *ullalati*. — $ 148.

uleṃḍhāleṃ n. *ulāḍhāl* f. "speculation, adventure". Deśī. *ullehaḍo lampuṭaḥ* (44, 6). — $ 70, 77, 112.

ullū m. "idiot". G. *ullū*; H. *ullū* "owl, idiot". Skr. *ulūka-*. — $ 149.

uver, *uverī* f. "surplus, residue". H. *ubarnā* "to remain over", *ubrā-subrā* "surplus, remain der". Deśī. *uvvariam adhikam anīpsitaṃ niścitaṃ tāpo' gaṇitaṃ ceti pañcārthaṃ* (54, 3). —$ 77, 166.

usteṃ "morning light", Siṃ. *us* f. "sun-ray". Pkt. *usā*. Skr. *usrā* "dawn". — $ 157.

usrāṇ n. "plantation of sugar-cane". Deśī. *ucchuraṇaṃ ucchuaraṇaṃ ca ikṣuvāṭaḥ* (49, 3). — $ 135.

usaḷṇeṃ "to leap, to splash". G. *uchāḷo* "leap, attack"; G. *uchalvuṃ*, S. *uchalaṇu*, Panj. H. *uchalnā* "to leap". Pkt. *ucchalai ūsalai*. Skr. *ucchalati*. — $ 103.

usāṇ n. "spring tide, sudden over flow". Siṃ. *usuvanavā* "to lift", cf. probably S. *osām* f. "wave, bar", H. *usānnā* "to boil". P. *ussāpeti*. Skr. *ucchrāya-*, *ucchrayaṇa-*. — $ 103.

usās m. "to sigh" W. Panj. H.

usās. Apa. *usāsa-*, Pkt. *ussāsa-*. Skr. *ucchvāsa-*. — $ 103, 156.

umśīt n. "repercussions of some particles during eating or drinking" Skr. *utsikta-*, *utkṣipta-* ?. — $ 69, 121.

useṃ n. "pillow", Deśī. *usaam apadhānaṃ śayane mastakottambhanāya yan niveśyate* (56, 8). Ved. Skr. *opaśā-*. One should distinguish G. *osīsuṃ*, H. *usīs*, *osīs* from Pkt. *ūsīsa-*, Skr. *ucchīrṣa-*. — $ 156.

ū, *ūṃ* f. "louse". G. *ju*; H. *jūn*; S. *jūṃā*, *jūṃ* f.; K. *zauv*; Ro. *juv*; Arm. Ro. *dživ*. Deśī. *ūā yūkā* (51, 3), P. *ūkā*. Skr. *yūkā*. — $ 105, 174.

ūṃṭ m. n,. "camel" G. *ūṃṭ* n., S. *uṭhu*, H. *ūṃṭ* W. Panj. *uṭṭh*, K. *wūṭh*, Siṃ. *oṭu-vā*, P. *oṭṭha-*; Pkt. *uṭṭa-*. Skr. *uṣṭra-*. — $ 88, 89.

ūn absolutive termination. —$ 130.

ūn "hot", *ūn*, *ūnh* n., "heat", *unhāḷā*, m. "summer". G. *ūnuṃ*, Siṃ. *uṇu* "hot"; S. *unhāro*, W. Panj. *unhālā* "summer". Pkt. *uṇha-* Skr. *uṣṇa-*, *uṣṇakāla-*. — $ 136.

ūb f. "heat of confinement, animal heat, hot air". G. *ubharo* "effervescence"; H. *ubhā* "heat", *ūbh* m. "heat; indolence caused by heat," *ūbhnā* "to be oppressed by heat"; S. *ubhāro*, *ub* f. "vapour, miasma," *ubāṭaṇu* "to burn", *ubhāraṇu* "to boil". Deśī *uvvā uvvara uvvāha ukkolāś catvāro 'pi dharmārthāḥ*. "This word does not seem to be related to Pkt. *uṃha-*, Skr. *uṣman-*. —$ 127.

uś, *ūṃs* m. "sugar" G. *is*; H. *ūk h*, *īkh*; B. *āku*; O. *ākhu*; Siṃ. *uk*, *ik*, Maldiv. *us*. Pkt. *ucchu-*, Jaina Pkt. *ikkhu-*. Skr. *ikṣu-*. — $ 41, 104, 188.

ek. "one". G. Maith. B. O. *ek*; H. *ek*, *yak*; S. *eku*, *hiku*, *haku*; Panj. *ikk*, W. Panj. *hekk*, *hikk*; K. *ak*; Ro. *yek*; Siṃ. *ek*. P. Pkt. *ekka-*. Skr. *eka-*. — $ 45, 77, 94, 174, 213.

eklā "alone". G. *ekal*, *ekluṃ*; H. *ekal*. Pkt. *ekkhalla*. —$ 45.

ekamīṃ "at one time". From *ek*+*kām* in the locative. —$ 172.

ekuṇīs "nineteen". G. *ogṇīs*; S. *uṇivīh*, *uṇīh*; Panj. *unnī*; W. Panj. *unvī*; H. *unīs*, see H. *agunīs*, *gunīs*; Maith. *unaīs*; B. *unīs*; Siṃ. *ekunvisi*; K. *kunawuh*. Pkt. *eguṇavīṃsa-*, *egūṇavīsa-*, *auṇavīsaṃ*, Skr. *ekonaviṃśati-*.— $ 222.

eḍ f. "pressure of heal" G. Panj. H. B. *eḍi*, *eḍī* "heal." the etymology by Skr. *aṅghri-* "foot" is very doubtful. — $ 77, 161.

eṇeṃ in *eṇeṃkaḍūn*, *eṇeṃkarūn* "by these means", *eṇepramāṇeṃ* "in this way". Instrumental of a stem of demonstrative of *e*-which is missing in Marathi, see $ 203. G. *e*, S. *i*, *hī*, *he*, Panj. *ih*, *eh*, K. *yih*, H. *i* (*h*), *e* (*h*), B.O. *e*, Siṃ. *ē*, f. *ä*, n. *eya*. Pkt. *ea*—. Skr. *eta-*.—The Marathi form is a combination of two pronouns, $ 172.

eth, *etheṃ* adv. "here". S. *iti*, Panj, *itthe*, O. *eṭhā*, Siṃ. *eta*. Pkt. *ettha*. Skr. *atra* according to Hemacandra, which raises a difficulty from the point of view of phonetics; Vedic *itthá* "thus, really", which Pischel brings in, but which does not go well for the meaning . The meaning is a compourd of Skr. *iha*, which is represented by Pkt. inscriptions. (see Fleet *J.R. A.S.*, 1909, p. 1089) and of *-stha-*: the gradation of the dental cerebral (in O. *eṭhā*) is, in fact, a characteristic of this root, see $ 110.— $ 70, 206.

edhvāṃ "now" poet. Pkt. *eddaha-*. Skr. *etāvat-* according to Skr. Grammarians, *īdṛśa-* according to Weber and Pischel; opinions equally difficult to defend. — $ 124, 206.

evhāṃ adv. "now". G. *hev*, cf. *evo* "such". cf. Apa. *eṃvahiṃ*, of obscure origin. — $ 70.

er adj. "other". cf. G. *eruṃ* "there". Pkt. *iara*. Skr. *itara-*. — $ 63,143, 154.

eraṃḍ m. f. "castor-oil plant". G. *eraṇḍo*, , *eraṇkākḍī*; H. *raṇḍi*, *eraṇḍ*, *aṇḍī*. Skr. *eraṇḍa-*. — $ 143.

eṃśīṃ, *aiśīṃ*, in compound *-yaśīṃ* "eighty". G. *eṃśī*, *heṃśī*; S. *asī*; Panj. H. Maith. *assī*; B. *āśī*; O. *aśī*; Siṃ. *asū*, *asūva*; K. *śīth*. Pkt. *asīiṃ*, *asīi*. Skr. *aśīti-*. — $ 58, 77, 154, 166, 223.

eḷā f. pl. "cardamum". H. *elā*, *ilācī* f. sing. Skr. *elā* f. sing. — $ 145.

aikṇeṃ "to listen". Isolated word and of obscure etymology. Should we bring together Pkt. *ahikkhaṇa-*, and Skr. *abhikṣ-* "to look" ? — $57.

aitā pron. "that one, there"; *āytā* adj. "all ready"; old M. *āitī* f. "preparation". G. *āytuṃ* "ready, free"; H. *āyitā*; Siṃ. *ayati*, *ayiti* "depending on, belonging to". Skr. *āyatta-*. — $ 57.

aitvār m. "Sunday". G. *ātvār*, *itvār*; H. *āitvar*; S. *āḍītvār*; W. Panj. *etvār*. Skr. *āditya-vāra-*. —$ 57.

ouṃl, *vauṃḷ* f. "mymusops Elengi". Skr. *vakula-*. — $ 145, 150.

ok f. "vomitting", *okṇeṃ* "to vomit". G. *okvuṃ* H. *oṃknā*, *uknā*; S. *okaṇu*. Deśī. *okkiam uṣitam, vāntam ity anye* (60, 16). — $ 252.

oṃgaḷ "bad, filthy". Skr. *amaṃgala-*. — $ 98, 145.

ogal, *oghaḷ*, *ohaḷ*, *vaghaḷ* m. "stream"; *ogaḷṇeṃ*, *oghaḷṇeṃ* etc. "to seep, to drip". G. *ogaḷvuṃ* "to melt, to trickle". Deśī. *oggālo tathā oālo alpaṃ srotaḥ* (60, 15). *avagal-*. The aspiration comes undoubtedly from the contamination of Skr.*-ghṛ-* "to moisten", or from Skr. *ogha* "current", or lastly from M. *ojhar* (see this word). — $ 78, 86.

oṃcā m. "act of gathering together cloth, bale; knot attaching the clothes to the belt". Skr. *uccaya-* "act of gathering together." — $ 60, 69, 80, 101.

oj. n. "life, vitality". G. *ojvuṃ* "to be strong, to grow big"; S. *oju* m. "height (altitude), force, rapidity." Pkt. *ujja-*; cf. Deśī. *ojjallo balavān* (62, 1) *ujjallā...balātkāraḥ* (41, 2) Skr. *ūrjas-*. — $ 106.

oṃjaḷ, *oṃjhaḷ*, *vaṃjaḷ* m. "the cavity formed by joining the hands side by side". Siṃ. *ädeli*. Skr. *añjali-*. — $ 78.

ojhar "trickling, current, waterfall"; *ojharṇeṃ* "to trickle". Pkt.*avajharei*, *ojhara-*. Skr.*avakṣar*:— $ 86, 107.

ojheṃ "burden". G. *ojho*; H. *bojh* (borrowed in G. and M.). Deśī. *vajjhao tathā vojjhamallo bhāraḥ*. (266, 7); Pkt. *vojjha-*. Skr. *vahya-* influenced by *voḍhum* etc. J. Charpentier admits a prototype *"*voḍhya-*.—$ 78, 107.

oṭh, *oṃṭh* m. "lip". G. *oṭh*, H. *oṃṭh*; O. *oṭh*; Siṃ. *oṭa*; K. *wuṭh*; Ro. *vuśt*. Pkt. *oṭṭha-*, *uṭṭha-* (besides *huṭṭha-*, cf. M. *hoṃṭ*). Skr. *oṣṭha-*. — $ 69, 78, 110, 168.

oḍaṇ, *oḍhaṇ* n. "wrap"; *oḍṇī*, *oḍhṇī* f. "shawl" m. G. *oḍhaṇī*, *oḍhaṇuṃ*; S. *oḍhaṇu* "to cover, (with a cloak etc.)" *oḍhaṇī* "shawl", *oḍhako* "shelter." Deśī. *oḍḍhanaṃ uttarīyam* (62, 7), *ohāḍānī pidhānī* (64, 16). Seems related to skr., *vah*—, cf. infin: *voḍhum* etc. — $ 89, 112.

oṇavṇeṃ, *onavṇeṃ*, *oṇaviṇeṃ*, *onaviṇeṃ* "to bend, to stoop". cf. G. *namavuṃ*; S. *navaṇu*, *naṃvaṃnu*; Panj. *nivaṇā*; H. *navnā*, *binaunā*; B. *nuyāite*; O. *nuṃaībā*. Pkt. pcpl. *oṇavia-*. Skr. *avanam-*. — $ 78, 134, 138.

opṇeṃ "to entrust, to sell". Pkt. *oppei*, *uppei*, pcpl. *oppia-*, *uppia-*; P. *oppita-*. Skr. *arpayati* wherefrom *ṛpy-* ? Or has the word been extracted from M. *soṃpṇeṃ* < *samarpayati* ? — $ 30, 125.

oṃbaḷṇeṃ "to wash lightly, to plunge". G. *ohāḷ* "alluvial deposits, silt brought in by the river". Pkt. *ombālai* (= *plāvayati*, Hemac. IV, 41; cf. Deśīn. 68. 13).— $ 52.

oyrā m. "portion of rice, daily nourishment put aside for being prepared, kitchen, centre of the house". Skr. *abhyavahṛta-*, *abhyavahārya.-* "nourishment". — $ 143, 161.

orapṇeṃ "to uproot, to tear to pieces". G. *rāmp* f. "hoe, plough". Deśī. *oddaṃpia oraṃpia śabdau naṣṭe tathākrānte* (67, 15); cf. *raṃpai raṃphai takṣṇoti* (237, 4). Skr. *raph-*, *ṛph-* "to injure", Ved. *rápas-* "infirmity, disease", *raphitá-* "miserable". — $ 71, 78.

ol f. m. "humidity", *olā* adj. "wet". Pkt. *olla-*, *ulla-*. Skr. *udra-* "aquatic animal", *udrin-* "abounding in water". — $ 80, 141.

oṃvrā m. "kitchen", *ovrī* f. "logings for pilgrims under the portico along a temple wall". G. *orḍo*, *orḍī* "apartment". P. *ovaraka-* "room". Skr. *apavaraka-*. — $ 78, 143, 152.

ovar for *vovar*. — $ 161.

oṃvasṇeṃ "to perform certain rites after a vow (set for women)", *oṃvsā* m. "the said rites". Pkt. *ovavāsa oāsa-*, *ūāsa-*. Skr. *upavasati*, *upavāsa-* "fast".— $ 78, 152, 156.

oṃvāḷṇeṃ "to wave a platter containing offerings around the head of an idol". G. *ovāḷvuṃ*. Skr. *ava+val-*. — $ 52, 78, 145, 152.

ovlā, *oṃvḷā* "impure". Pkt. *omalia*. Skr. *ava+mala-*. —$ 145, 152.

ovī vulg. *oī* f. "a stanza (in Marathi poetry)". Should we compare Deśī. *oviam āropitaṃ ruditaṃ cāṭu muktaṃ hṛtaṃ ceti pañcārtham* (66, 16)? In the *Mānasollāsa* (see. 2052) the word is mentioned and explained: *tathā mahārāṣṭreṣu yoṣidbhir ovī geyā tu kaṇḍaṇe.* — $ 64.

osag for *asog*. Skr. *aśoka-*. — $ 167.

osamg, osaṃgā m. "lap". Skr. *utsanga-*. — $ 80.

osar, osār, usār m. "space left for passage". G. *osarvuṃ* "to go away from"; H. *usārnā* "to lift, to finish". Skr. *apasāra* "exit". — $ 156.

osarṇeṃ "to over flow; to abate (fever); to pass, (rain)." G. *osarvuṃ* "to decline, to hesitate"; S. *avasaru, ausaru* "lack of rain, drought". Skr. *apasar-*. — $ 156.

osrā "verandah". G. *osarī* f., H. *usārā*. Deśī. *osariā alindaḥ* (64, 15). Skr. *apasaraka-*. — $ 78, 156.

osvā m. "shade of trees". Skr. *avacchada-*. — $ 103.

ohaṭ m. "reflex", *ohaṭṇeṃ* "to ebb". G. *oṭ* f. Deśī. *ohaṭṭo apasṛto* (66, 12). Skr. *apahṛta-*? $ — 57, 114.

ohmāy for *vahmāy* "wife's mother". Pkt. *vahumāā-*; Skr. **vadhū mātṛ-*. — $ 64.

ohar m. "a sea-channel". Deśī. *voharaṃ jalasya vahanam* (266, 14). — $ 142.

ohaḷ m. *ohāḷī* f. "streamlet". *vahoḷo vāhaḷī virao trayo'py ete laghujala pravāhavācakāḥ* (250, 5). — $ 142.

oḷ, vaḷ, vaḷī f. "line, conduit". G. *oḷ* f.; H. *bal, bhal* "side, direction, manner"; S. *vari* f. "turn", *varu* m. "curve, turn". Skr. *valī*. — $ 145.

oḷakhṇeṃ "to know". G. *oḷakhvuṃ*. Skr. *upalakṣaṇa-*. — $ 78, 96, 149.

oḷaṃgṇeṃ, oḷaṃghṇeṃ, vaḷaṃgṇeṃ "to be suspended at...". G. *vaḷagvuṃ* "to take hold of"; to hold; to be attached with...", *vaḷagāḷvuṃ* "to be suspended at..."; H. *bihangnā* "to climb at..., to hold on to". Pkt. *valaggai*. Skr. *avalag-*. — $ 86, 145, 149.

oḷaṃbṇeṃ, vaḷaṃdṇeṃ "to be suspended". cf. H. *bilamb* "delay, slowness", *bilambnā*; Siṃ. *olaṃbu* "suspended", *ilaṃbenavā*" "to approach". Skr. *avalamb-*. — $ 145, 149.

authṇeṃ for *ohaṭṇeṃ-* — $ 57.

kaṃkaṇ m. *kaṃkṇī, kaṃgṇī* f. "bracelet". G. *kaṃkaṇ, kaṃgaṇ* (neut.); S. *kaṃgaṇu*, Panj. *kaṃgan*; H. *kaṃkan, kaṃgan*; E.B. *kāṃkan, kāṃgan*; K. *kāṅkam, kaṅgun*. Pkt. Skr. *kaṅkaṇa-*. — $ 82.

kaṃkar m. "pebble". G. H. *kaṃkar*, S. *kakiro*, W. Panj. *kakkar* "frost, ice", Nep. B. Ass. *kāṃkar*. Skr. *karkara-*. — $ 82, 93, 143.

kaṃkvā, kaṃgvā m. "sort of comb". S. *kaṃgo*; H. *kaṃguvā kaṃghā*. Skr. *kaṅkaṭa-*. — $ 55, 82.

kaṃkoḷ m. "capsicum". Skr. *kaṅkola-, kakkola-*. — $ 82.

kac f. "difficulty". Deśī. *kaccaṃ tathā koḍumbaṃ kāryam* (69, 12); Pkt. *kaccā*. Skr. *kṛtyā* "*affair*". — $ 30, 41, 101.

kacrā m. "refuse". G. *kacaro*; S. *kaciro* "remainder of vegitable", *kiciro* "sweepings; H. *kacrā* "chalk, filth". cf. Deśī. *kasso tathā kaccharo paṅkaḥ* (69, 13). Skr. *kaccara-* "dirty". — $ 101, 143.

kaṭ m. "pain, labour". G. *kāṭ* "obstacle", *kāṭhuṃ* "hard, greedy", H. *kaṭh* "pain", K. *kaśt*, *kathyun*[u]. Pkt. *kaṭṭha-*. Skr. *kaṣṭa*. — $ 88.

kaṭār f. "dagger". G. *kaṭār* f., S. *kaṭāro*, H. *kaṭār* m. Deśī. *kaṭṭārī kṣurikā* (70, 7). Skr. *kaṭṭāra-*. — $ 109.

kaṃṭh m. *kāṃṭheṃ* n. "throat". G. H. *kaṃṭh*, S. *kaṃṭhu*, Siṃ. *kaṭa*. Pkt. Skr. *kaṇṭha-*. — $ 88, 110.

kaṭhīṇ, *kaḍhīṇ* "difficult". G. *kaṭhaṇ*, S. *kaṭhanu*, H. *kaṭhan*. Pkt. *kaḍhiṇa-*. Skr. *kaṭhina-*. — $ 40, 110, 134.

kaṃḍ, *kaṃḍū* f. "itching". G. H. *kaṇḍū*. Skr. *kaṇḍū-*. — $ 111.

kaḍ f. "side, belt". G. *kaḍ*, *keḍ*; S. *keṛ* "dike"; H. *kaṭ*, *kaṛ*. Pkt. *kaḍi-*. Skr. *kaṭi-*. — $ 111, 195, 197.

kaḍcī f. "a small *kaḍhaī*" In related languages is found similar word denoting "soup ladle",: G. *kaḍchī*; S. *kaṇchū*, *kaṛchū*; H. *karchī*, *kaṛchī*; cf. Deśī. *kaḍacchū ayodarvī* (71, 10). See the words *kaḍhaī*, *kaḍhṇeṃ*. Skr. *kvath-* "to boil ?" — $ 101.

kaḍtar m. "old basket, fan or worn out mat". Deśī. *kaḍantaraṃ jīrṇaśūrpādyupakaraṇam* (75, 1); cf. *kaḍantariaṃ dāritam* (76, 12). — $ 46, 71, 121.

kaḍap n. "small stack of plants". G. *kaḍap*. Deśī. *kaḍappo nikaraḥ* (73, 15). — $ 46.

kaḍāḍ m. "crakcle". G. *kaḍakaḍ*, S. *kaṛkāṭ*, H. *kaṛākaṛ*, cf. W. Panj. *kaṛak*. Skr. *kaṭakaṭā-*. — $ 62, 111.

kaṃḍārṇeṃ n. "goldsmith's hammer; scissors". Pkt. *kaṃḍārei* "to sculpt"; seems to be a denominative going to a root **kaṇḍ-*, whose doublet with initial *s-* is probably represented by *khaṇḍ-*, *khiṇḍ-*. — $ 52.

kaḍāsana n. "hide or skin used as seat". G. *kaḍāsan*. Skr. *kaṭāsana-*. — $ 52, 111.

keḍī f. *kaḍeṃ* n. "ring." G. *kaḍī*, S. Panj. H. B. *kaṛī*; K. *kor*[u]. Pkt. *kaḍaya-*. Skr. *kaṭaka-*. — $ 46, 111.

kaḍū "bitter". G. *kaḍu*, S. *karo*, H. *kaṛuā karvā*, Siṃ. *kuḷu*. Skr. *kaṭu-*. — $ 111.

kaḍhaī f. "a frying vessel (hemispheric, with a handle)." G. *kaḍhā*; S. *kaṛāhī*, *kaṇāho*; H. *kaḍāhā*, *kaḍhāolī*; B. *kaḍ*, *kaḍāī*; O. *karāī*, *karhāī*, *kaḍheī*, Skr. *kaṭāha-*. — $ 92, 168.

kaḍhṇeṃ "to boil". G. *kaḍhvuṃ*; S. *kaṛhaṇu*; K. *kār-*; Ro. *kirav-* ? Pkt. *kaḍhai*, P. pcpl. *kaṭhita-*. Skr. *kvath-*. — $ 46, 92, 118.

kaṇ m., *kaṇī* f. *kāṇū* n. "grain, particle." G. *kaṇ*, *kaṇī*, *kaṇuṃ*; S. *kaṇo*, *kaṇi*, Panj. *kaṇ*; W. Panj. *kaṇī* "drop"; H. *kan*. Skr. *kaṇa-*. — $134.

kaṇīs n. "ear of corn". G. *kaṇas*. Skr. *kaṇiśa-*. — $ 40, 50.

kaṇer, *kaṇher* f. "oleander". G. *kaṇer* f; H. *kaner* m. Pkt. *kaṇera-*, *kaṇhera*—(probably under the influence of *kaṇha* < (*kṛṣṇa-*), *kaṇavīra-*. Skr. *karavīra-*. — $ 135, 170.

kattī f. "knife". G. *katī* "knife", S. *kātī* "dagger", H. *kātī* "smith's tonges"; Ro. *kat* "scissors"; cf. Kan, Tam. *katti* "knife". Skr. *kartṛkā*, *kartarikā*. — $ 114.

kamp, *kamph* m. "trembling"; *kāmpṇeṃ* "to tremble". G. H.

kamp- kāṃp-, S. Panj. *kamb-*; K. *kōmp-*; Siṃ. *käpavuṃ* "trembling". Skr. *kampa-*. $ 85, 125.

kapūt m. "bad son", G. *kapūt*; S. *kaput*; *kuput*, H. *kapūt*, *kupūt*. Skr. *kuputra-*. — $ 171.

kabrā "grey, variegated". G. *kābar*; S. *kubiro*, cf. *kabari* "jay"; Panj. *kabrā*; H. *kābar*, *kabrā*; Siṃ. *kabara-* "panther". Skr. *karbura-*, *karbūra-*.—$ 48, 50, 127,141.

kamāviṇeṃ "to earn, to acquire". G. *kamāvuṃ* "to earn", *kamāī* "profits"; S. *kamāīṇu*; Panj. *kamāṇā*; H. *kamānā*. cf. Deśī. *kammavai upabhuṅkte* (78, 1). Caus. drawn from. *karma-*, cf. M. *kām*.— $ 152

kamod m. "lotus (nymphiaea esculenta)". H. *kamūd*, *kamod* "drug extracted from Nenuphar"; probably G. *kamod* "scented rice". Skr. *kumuda-*. — $ 171.

kar m. "tax". G. H. *kar*, Siṃ. *kara*, cf. S. *karu* "arm". Skr. *kara-*. — $ 143.

karaṭ, *karavaṭ* m. n. "a bitter fruit". S. *kartu* "unripe musk-melon". cf. M. *kaḍū* "bitter" Skr. *kaṭu-*?— $ 51·

karṭī f. "coconut, skull". Pkt. *karoḍia* "cup". Skr. *karoṭī-*. — $ 51, 109.

karamaṃḍā m. "metal-box". G. *karaṃdo*. Skr. *karaṇḍa-*. — $ 111.

karṇeṃ "to do". Pcpl. *kelā*; caus. *karavṇeṃ* *karaviṇeṃ*, pcpl. n. Sing. *karaviyaleṃ*. H. S. K. Panj. H. etc. *kar-*; Ro. *ker-* (Arm. Ro. *kar-*). Pkt. Skr. *kar-*. — $ 92, 143, 152, 229, 232, 239, 252, 280 281.

kartāṃ, *karitāṃ* "for". — $ 194.

karvat m. "saw". G. *karvat*, H. O. *karot*. Skr. *karapatra-*. — $ 40, 109, 121, 143, 152.,

karūn post position "thanks to". — $ 193.

kalolī, *kulkulī*, *kūlolī* m. "rut of horses". H. *kalol*, *kilol* f. "gambol", Skr. *kallola-*. — $ 76.

kaṃvaṃṭaḷ n. "black magic". Pkt. *kavaṭṭia-*. According to Hema candra, Skr. *kadarthit* —(see. Pischel, $ 246). — $ 69, 114.

kavaṭh, *kavaṃṭh* f. "feronia elephantum". S. *kaviṭu*; H. *kaṭhbel*, *kaith*; O. *kaīṭ*. Pkt. *kavitha-*, *kaviṭṭha-*. Skr. *kapittha-*. — $ 42, 69, 110.

kavḍā m. "cowrie used as coins, cowrie". G. B. *koḍī*, H. *kauṛī*, Siṃ. *kavaḍiya*. Pkt. *kavaḍḍa-*. Skr. *kaparda-*. — $ 46, 115, 152.

kavaḷ m. "mouthful". G. *koḷiyo*, Panj. *kurlī*, H. *kaul*, H. B. *kullī*. Skr. *kavala-*. — $ 40, 46.

kavāḍ n. "door". Panj. H. *kavāḍ*, E.B. *kabāṭ*, see H. *kevār*; Siṃ. *kavuḷuva* "window". P. *kavāṭa-*. Skr. *kapāṭa-*. *kavāṭa-*, — $ 40, 49, 111, 152.

kas. m. "test on the touchstone". G. H. Siṃ. *kas*, S. *kasoṭī*. Pkt. *kasa-*. Skr. *kaṣa-*. — $ 156.

kasṇeṃ "to cause pain". G. *kasvuṃ* "to cause fatigue", H. *kasaknā* "to suffer", *kasak* "curvature". Skr. *kaṣati*. — $ 46, 157.

kaṣṇeṃ "to bind". *kasā* m. "cord, link", *kasu* "leather thong", W. Panj. *kaśk* "saddle-rope", Siṃ. *kas* "whip"; Panj. *kass-*. G.S.H.

kas- "to bind". Pkt. *kasa-*. Skr. *kaśa-*. — $ 156.

kaḷ f. "door-handle; secret contrivance". G. *kaḷ*; S. *kaṛa* f. "barrage", *kala* f. "science, machine"; Panj. *kal* f. Skr. *kalā-*. —$ 41, 145.

kaḷṇeṃ "to be understood, to be sensible; to appear". G. *kaḷvuṃ* "to understand", Panj. *kalnā*, S. *kiṛaṇu* "to learn". Skr. *kalana-*. — $ 46, 145.

kaḷaṃb m. "nauclea cadamba". H. *kadamb*, *kadam*. Pkt. *kalamba-*. Skr. *kadamba-*. — $ 46, 118.

kāḷvā m. "shackle". H. *kalāvā*, Panj. *kalāvā* "embrace". Pkt. *kalāva-*. Skr. *kalāpa-*. — $ 46, 52, 145.

kaśā old M. *kāsayā*, oblique sing. of interrogative pronoun *koṇ*. — $ 204.

kaḷas m. "pinnacle; water-pot". G. *kaḷsī*, S. *kalisu*. Panj. *kals*, H. *kalas*, Bih. *kalsā* Skr. *kalaśa-*. — $ 46, 145.

kaḷho m. "dispute". G. *kaḷo*, S. *kilo*, H. *kalah*. Skr. *kalaha-*. — $ 39, 79, 145.

kaḷī f. "bud". G. *kaḷī*, *kaḷiyo*; S. Panj. H. *kalī*. Skr. *kalikā*. — $ 46, 63, 145.

kāṃ "why ?". G. *kāṃ*, Ro. *ka* "where". Apa. *kahāṃ* (*kutaḥ*). — $ 204, 206.

kāīl "cattle". Rather than with Skr. *kvath-* whose Pkt. and Marathi correspondent *kaḍh-* (cf. s.v. *keḍhṇeṃ*), this word seems to be related to Kan. *kāy-* "to heat", which is also found in other Dravidian dialects; Telugu *kāgu*, *kāyu*, Tulu *kāyi* Tamil and Malayan *kāy*. — $ 92.

kāū m. (childish word), *kāvḷā* m. "crow", G. *kāū*; S. *kāṃ*, *kāṃu*; Panj. *kāṃ*; K. *kāv*; Siṃ. *kā*; H. *kāṃv* "crowing". Pkt. *kāya-*; Deśi. *kāyalo priyaḥ kākaśca* (91, 11). Skr. *kāka-*. — $ 39, 92, 98.

kāṃkḍī f. "cucumber". G. *kākaḍ* n., *kākḍī* f.; S. *kākiḍī-*; Panj. H. *kakḍī kakkaḍī*; E.B. *kākaḍī*; Siṃ. *kākira*; cf. *kakuḷuvā* "crab". Skr. *karkaṭitkā* -.—$ 47, 69, 82, 93, 111.

kākh, *kāṃkh*, *khāṃk* f. "armpit". G. B. O. *kākh*, H. *kāṃkh* (dial. *khākh*), Ro. *kakh*; cf. s.v. M. *kāṃs*. Pkt. (Jaina) *kakkha-*. Skr. *kakṣā*. — $ 69, 92, 95, 96, 104, 168.

kāṃg m. "millet". G. *kāṃg*. Skr. *kaṅgu-*, *kaṅku-*.—Cf. S. *kamgini*, H. *kāṃgau* from Skr. *kaṅgūrī*.- — $ 39, 82.

kāgḍā adj. "wily" seems to be borrowed from H. *kāgḍā* "crow", cf. G. Panj. H. *kāg*, S. *kāṃgu*, Kanarese *kāgĕ*, *kāgi* "crow". — $ 98.

kāṃcyā m. "tuck of the *dhotar*, girdle." Seems to be borrowed from H. *kāchā*; cf. W. Panj. *kāṃch* "tight drawers for games". Skr. *kaccha-*. *kacchaṭikā*. — $ 69, 101.

kāj n. "work". G. Panj. H. *kāj*, S. *kāju*, W. Panj. *kajj* "ceremony". Pkt. *kajja-*. skr. *kārya-*. —$ 106.

kājaḷ n. "lamp-black used as collyrium". G. *kājal*, S. *kajalu*, H. *kājal*, Panj. *kajlā*. Skr. *kajjala-*. — $ 47, 106.

kāṭṇeṃ "to cut". *kaṭṇeṃ* "cut", G. H. E.B. *kāṭ-*, S. K. Siṃ. *kaṭ-*, Panj. *kaṭṭ-*. Pkt. *kaṭṭ-*. Skr. *kart-*. — $ 48, 114.

kāṃṭā m. "thorn". G.H. B.O.

kāṃṭā, S. *kāṃḍī*, Panj. *kaṃḍā*, Ro. *kando*, Siṃ. *kaṭuva*. Pkt. Skr. *kaṇṭaka-*. — $ 109.

kāṭhī f. "trunk, stick". G. Panj *kāṭh*, Siṃ. *kaṭa* "timber"; S. *kāṭhu*, B. H. *kāṭh*, K. *kūṭ*ᵘ, Ro. *kaśt*. Pkt. *kaṭṭha-*. Skr. *kāṣṭha-*. — $ 110.

kāḍhṇeṃ "to draw", G. *kāḍhvuṃ kāhāḍvuṃ*, S. *kāḍhaṇu*, Panj. *kaḍḍhanā*, K. *kaḍun*. H. *kāḍhnā*, B. *kāḍite*, O. *kāḍhibā*; Arn. Ro. *kaś-*, Palestinian Ro. *kśal-*. Pkt. *kaḍḍhai*. Skr. *karṣati*. — $ 112, 231.

kāṇā adj, "blind of one eye". G.S. *kāṇo*, Panj. B. *kāṇā*, H. *kānā*, O. *kāṇā*, Siṃ. *kaṇa*, K. K. *kon*ᵘ, Skr. *kāṇa-*. — $ 46, 134.

kāṃt m. "shavings of food", *kāṃtaṇ* n. "morsel", f. "harmful insect". G. *kātāro* "insect"; S. *kaṭ*, H. *kāṭ* "cut". Skr. *kartana-*, *kṛntana-*. — $ 114.

kātḍeṃ n. "skin or leather". G. *kātḍī*. Pkt. *katti-*, *kitti-*. Skr. *kṛtti-*. — $ 114, 163.

kaṃtṇeṃ, *kātṇeṃ* "to spin, to turn". G. *kāṃtvuṃ*, Panj. *kattṇā*, H. *kātnā*, S.K. Ro. *kat-*; cf. G. *kāṃt* "spindle", H. *kātī* ""woman-spinner". Skr. *kart-*. — $ 114.

kātyā f. pl. "pleiads". Siṃ. *käti*, S. *katīuṃ*; cf. H. *kātik*, Panj. *kattak*, "month of *kartika*". Pkt. *kattia-*. Skr. *kṛttikā*. — $ 30, 114.

kātar, *kātrī* f. "scissors". G. *kātar*, S. *katar*, Panj. *kaṭṭar*, *katī*, H. Panj. *katarnī*, B. *kataran*, O. *katūrā*, Siṃ. *kattura-*; Ro. *kat*. Cf. Deśī. *kaṭṭārī kṣurikā* (70, 7). Skr. *karttarī*, *karttarikā*. —$ 47, 114.

kāṃḍā m. "onion". G. *kāṃdo*, H. *kāṃḍā*. Skr. *kanda-*. —$ 92.

kān m. "ear". G.H. B. O. *kān*, S. *kanu*, Panj. *kann*, K. Ro. *kan*, Siṃ. *kaṇa*. Pkt. *kaṇṇa-*. Skr. *karṇa-*. — $ 92, 185.

kāṇḍā adj. "inhabitant of karnatik"; subst. m. "mode of karnatic music". G. *kānḍī* "Kannarese", G. *kānḍo*, S. *kāṇiro* "musical mode". — $ 47, 92, 111, 135.

kānhū, *kānhobā* m. local name of *Kṛṣṇa*. S. *kānu*, H. Panj. *kānh*; with the meaning of "black". Siṃ. *kiṇu*, K. *kréhonu*. Pkt. *kaṇha-*. Skr. *kṛṣṇa-*. — $ 30, 39, 92, 136.

kāpaḍ n. "cloth". G.B.O. *kāpaḍ*, Panj. *kappaṛ*, H. *kapṛā*, S. *kapaṛu*, K. *kapur*, Siṃ. *kapal-*. P. *kappaṭa-*. Skr. *karpaṭa-*. —$ 40, 47, 92, 111, 125.

kāpṇeṃ "to cut". G. *kāp-*, S. Siṃ. *kap-*, Panj. *kapp-* "to cut"; H. *kāṃp* "slice". P. Pkt. *kapp-*. Skr. *kalp-*. — $ 92, 125, 230.

kāpūr m. "camphour". G. S. Panj. H. B. O. *kapūr*, Siṃ. *kapura*. Pkt. P. *kappura-*. Skr. *karpūra-*. — $ 47, 125.

kapūs m., *kapśī* f. *kap*, *kapās* m. "cotton". G. *kāpus* n., Siṃ. *kapu*; H. B. *kapās*, S. Panj. *kapāh*, K. *kapas* .P. *kappāsa-*. Skr. *karpāsa-*. — $ 47, 85, 92, 125.

kāṃblā m. "sheet". Siṃ. *kaṃbala*; G. *kāblo*, *kāmal*; S. *kamri*; Panj. *kambaḷ*, *kammaḷ*; H. *kambal*, *kammal*; B. *kambal*, *kamlī*, O. *kamal*. P. Pkt. Skr. *kambala-*. — $ 92, 127.

kām n. "work, affair". G.H. *kām*, S. *kamu*, Panj. *kamm*,

K. *kömu*, Arm. Ṙo. *kam*, Siṃ. *kam*, P. Pkt. *kamma*. Skr. *karma*. — $ 92, 138, 252.

kāy n. ' what ?"; *kā* "is it ?" (cf. for the same use H. *kyā*, B. *ki*, etc.). Skr. *kādṛk*-. — $ 204.

kārṇeṃ "because of". S. *kāraṇi*, H. *kāran*; cf. G. Panj. *kāraṇ* "cause"; G. *kāraṇ sar*, *kāran ke* "because of"; K. *kāran* "cause", *kārana*" because of"; Siṃ. *karuṇa* "object, cause". Skr. *kāraṇena*. — $ 46, 197.

kāraṃdā m. *karvaṃd* f. "Corinda"; *karaṃdeṃ* "its fruit". H. *karauṃdā*, *karoṃdā*; probably S. *karno* "tree with scented white flowers". Deśī. *karavandīe a sīhaṇahī*; Comm. *sīhaṇahī karaṃandikā* (286, 7-9). — $ 49, 51, 153.

kāl "yesterday". G. *kāl*, E.B. *kāli*, H. *kal*, S. Panj. *kalh* "yesterday"; K. *kölⁱ-kĕth* "day after tomorrow", Siṃ. *käl* "morning". Pkt. *kalla* "yesterday", P. *kalla*- "morning", Skr. *kalya*-. — $ 148.

kāvaḍ f. "bamboo for transport of loads on the shoulders". G. *kāvaḍ*, S. *kāvāṭhī*, H. *kāṃvar*. Skr. *kamaṭha*-. — $ 49.

kāvrā f. adj. "highly excited (from fear, anger, surprise)." G. H. B. *kāyar* "disgusted, timid, lazy". Skr. *kātara* — $ 143.

kās, *kāṃs* f. "udder, cutting of garments". S. Panj. H. *kacch* m. and f. K. *kac*, Siṃ. *käsa* "arm-pit". Pkt. *kaccha*-. Skr. *kakṣā*. Cf. M. *kākh*. — $ 104.

kās m. "prairie". G. *kās* "lawn", Siṃ. *käsa* "coppice"; cf. G. *kāchiyo* "vegitable-merchant", H. *kāchī* "gardner "?. Pkt. *kaccha* "lawn". Skr. *kakṣa*-, *kaccha*- "herb, prairie, marshland". — $ 141, 103.

kāsav, *kāṃsav* n. m. "tortoise". Panj. H. *kachūā*, H. *kach*, S. *kachaṃuṃ*, *kachūṃ*, B. *kāchīm*, O. *kacim*, Siṃ. *käsup*, *käsba*. Skr. *kacchapa*-, Ved. *kaśyàpa*-. — $ 47, 69, 102, 103, 152, 157.

kāsār, *kāṃsār* m. name of a caste, "vessel- makers of bronze". H. *kāṃsagar*, Nep. *kassar*. Skr. *kāṃsyakāra*-. — $ 143, 157.

kāṃseṃ n. "brass". G. *kāṃsuṃ*, S. *kaṃjho*, Panj. *kāṃsī*, H. *kās* H. B. O. *kāṃsā*. Pkt. *kaṃsa*-, *kāsa*-. Skr. *kāṃsya*-. — $ 157.

kāst "scribe" (name of a caste). G. *kāyat*, H. *kāyath*. Skr. *kāyastha*-.—$61.

kāḷ. m. "time, dead". G. *kāḷ*, S. *kālu*, Panj. H. K. *kāl*, Siṃ. *kala*, P. Pkt. Skr. *kāla*-. — $ 145.

kāḷā adj. "black", G. *kāḷo*, S. *kāro*, Ro. *kālo*, Panj. H. B. *kālā*, O. *kaḷā*, Siṃ. *kaḷu*. Pkt. *kālaa*-, P. *kāḷa*-. Skr. *kāla*-. — $ 46, 145.

kiṃkṇī f. "a little bell", G. *kiṃkiṇī*, H. *kiṃkinī*, Panj. *kiṃgṇī* "ear pendent". Skr. *kiṃkiṇī*. — $ 50.

kiṇ n., *kinā* m., *kiṇeṃ kinheṃ* n. "collosity." H. *kin*. Skr. *kiṇa*-. — $ 134.

kir, *kīr* "certainly". Pkt. *kira*. Skr. *kila*. — $ 41, 142.

kirāṇ m. "ray". G. *kiraṇ kīrṇ*, S. *kirini*, Panj. *kiran kiraṇ*, H. *kiran*. Skr. *kiraṇa*-. — $ 40, 134.

kiristāṃv, dialect of the indigenous Catholics of Thana district, see *L.S.I.*, *Mar.* p. 83. Eur. *Christ.* — $ 162.

kilac, *kilīc* f. "lath". Deśī. *kaliñjaṃ tathā kiliñcaṃ laghudāru* (72, 18). — $ 42, 71, 101, 149.

killī f. "key" G. *kīlī*, H. *killā*, "key". S. *kili*, Panj. *kill*, *kīl*, O. *kilā*, K. *kilu kiju* "nail, peg", Ro. *kilo* "stake". Skr. *kīla*. — $149.

kivaṇ f. "pity". Pkt. *kivaṇa-*, *kiviṇa-*. Skr. *kṛpaṇa-* "miserable"; cf. Skr. *kṛpā* "pity". —$ 30, 134, 152.

kisān m. "peasant". Panj. *kisāṇ*, H. *kisān*; cf. Sim. *kasa* (from skr. *kṛṣaka-*). Skr. *kṛṣāṇa-*.—$ 30, 40, 134.

kisūḷ m. "young shoot". Pkt. *kisala-*. Skr. *kisalaya-*.—$ 79.

kiseṇ, proper n. Panj. *kiṣan*. Skr. *kṛṣṇa*. — $ 30.

kiḷas m. f. *kiḷos* (dialectal) m. "nausia; symptom of disease". P. Skr. *kilāsa-*. "spot of leprosy, fatigue". —$ 79.

kīṃ conj. "that". H. Panj. *ki-* — $ 204, 277.

kīṭ n. "crass". G. *kīṭī* "residue of cotton", *kīṭuṃ* "bottom of sauce-pan", S. *kiṭī* f., H. *kīṭ* m. "refuse"; cf. Sim. *kili* "secretion, rules, urine". Skr. *kiṭṭa-*. — $ 92.

kīḍ f., *kiḍā* m. "worm, insect". G. *kīḍo* "worm" *kiḍī* "ant", S. *kiṛī*, Panj. H. *kiṛā* "worm", Ro. *kiri* "ant". Skr. *kīṭaka-*. — $ 44, 92.

kīṃv f. "lamentation, compassion". Skr. *kṛpā*. In the first sense possibly an expressive word, cf. S. *kīh* f. "cry", cf. Fr. *crier*, Ger. *kreiten*, Gr. ϵκριχον, etc. (see Grammont, *R. L. Rom.*, XLIV, p. 139). — $ 152.

kīl n. "flash". Skr. *kila-* "flame". — $ 145.

kukar m. "dog". G. *kukar*, Panj. *kūkar*, H. *kukar*, *kukur*, B. *kukkur*, Sim. *kukuru*, Skr. *kurkura-*, *kukkura-*. — $ 42, 82, 186.

kuṃkūṃ n. "saffron". G. *kuṃkuṃ*, *kaṃku* (*kuṃkā* "red"), S. *kuṃgū*, Panj. *kuṃggū*, K. *kōng*, H. *kuṃkum*, Sim. *kokuṃ kokum*. Skr. *kuṅkuma-*. — $ 82, 93.

kuṃkotrī f. invitation to a marriage". Skr. *kuṅkuma-* and *pattrikā*. — $ 64, 92.

kukhāvart adj. "(horse) having a ring of hair on the flank". Deśī. *kukkhī kukṣiḥ* (82,15). Skr. *kukṣi-* and Tats. *āvarta*. — $ 96, 104.

kuṃcā m. "brush". G. *kuco*, *kuṃcḍo*; Panj. *kūcā*; H. S. *kūcī*; Palestinian Ro. *kuc* "chin, beard". Pkt. *kucca-* "beard". Skr. *kūrca-*. —$ 101.

kuṃjī f. "key". G. *kuṃcī*; H. Panj. S. *kuṃjī*; K. *kunzü* B. *kūjī*; O. *kuṃjhī*; Sim. *kesi*. Skr. *kuñcikā*. — $ 82, 106.

kuṭṇeṃ "to crush". G. *kuṭvuṃ*, S. *kuṭaṇu*, H. *kūṭnā*, Sim. *koṭanavā*, cf. Ro. *kur-* "to beat". P. *koṭṭeti*. Skr. *kuṭṭana-*. — $ 109.

kuṃṭaṇ, *kuṭīṇ* f. "procuress". G. Panj. *kuṭṇī*, H. *kuṭnī*, O. *kuṭuṇī*, Skr. *kuṭṭanī*, *kuṭṭiṇī*, — $ 69, 109, 134.

kuṭīḷ "perverse". G. *kuṭil*. Panj. *kuṭal*. Skr. *kuṭila-*. — $ 109.

kuṭuṃb n. "family, wife". G. H. *kuṭaṃb*, *kuṭam*; Panj. *kuṭaṃb*, *kuṭumu* "family", *kuḍam* "relationship by marriage alliance"; S. *kuṭimu, kuṭaṃbhu*; cf. H. *kuḍmā* "related". Skr. *kuṭumba-*. — $ 109.

kuṭheṃ "where ?"; cf. *kuṭhne, kuṭhne* "from where ?". B. *kothā*; S. *kathī* "the first element of S. *kithī* Panj. *kithe kithān*, is different. Seems to be N. acc. neut. sing. of Skr. *kvastha* adj. "finding oneself where ?".—$76, 110.

kuṃḍ n. "well, pot". G. H. *kuṇḍ*, S. *kuni*, Panj. *kunāl*, Siṃ. *keṃḍiya*. Skr. *kuṇḍa-*. — $ 111.

kuḍapṇeṃ "to curl over, to crisp". cf. H. *kuḍuk* "ball of string". Skr. *kuṭati* "to be curved". — $ 111.

kuḍav, kuḍo m. "measure of grain". Skr. *kuṭapa, kuḍava-*. — $ 111, 280.

kuṃḍal n. "ear-ring". G. Panj. *kuṃḍal*, S. *kuṃḍhalu, kuniru*, H. B. O. *kuṃḍal*, Siṃ. *koṃḍol*. Skr. *kuṇḍala-*. — $ 170.

kuḍā m. "echites, antidysenteria". Skr. *kuṭaja-*.— $ 60, 111.

kuḍā, kūḍ "false, perfidious". G. *kuḍuṃ*, Panj. *kūṛā*, Siṃ. *kuḷu*; G. *kūḍ*, S. *kūṛu* "falsehood"; Pkt. *kūḍa-*, P. *kūṭa.*- Skr. *kūṭa-*. — $ 92, 111.

kuḍī f. "hut". Siṃ. *kili*; cf. S. *kuṛih* "stable, house", Panj. *kurh* "enclosure for animals", *kurhu* "hut", H. *kūrhī* "house ?" Skr. *kuṭī*. —$ 111.

kutrā m. "dog". G. *kutro*; cf. Panj. H. *kuttā*. To be separated from *kukkura-*; beside both are expressive or childish words, see Sainean, *M.S.L.* Vol. XIV, p. 220 (To the Iranian examples cited there, we can add Sogdian, '*kwt*', Yagnoti *kut* see Gauthiot, *Gramm. Sogdienne*, p. 51). — $ 42.

kudṇeṃ "to jump". G. *kudvuṃ*, S. *kuḍaṇu*, Panj. *kuddaṇā*, H. *kūdnā*, B. *kudan*, O. *kudibā*. cf. Deśī. *kuddaṇo rasakaḥ* (84.5). Skr. *kūrdana-*. — $ 44, 115, 123.

kudāḷ m. "hoe". G. *kodāḷo*, S. *koḍri*, Panj. *kudāl*, H. *kodāl*, B. *kodāl*, Siṃ. *udalu*. Skr. *kuddāla-*. — $ 44, 80, 123, 145.

Kupīṇ f. "piece of cloth covering the sexual parts". G. H. *kopīn*, S. *kopīni*, Panj. *kupīṇ*. Skr. *kaupīna*. — $ 45.

kuṃphal "fruit of *kuṃbhā*". Skr. *kumbhā-phala*. — $ 172.

kubḍā "hunch-back", *kubḍī*; f. "snail", G. *kubḍo*; S. *kubo*. Panj. *kubbā*, K. *kob*ᵘ H. *kubbā*. *kubṛā*. Should be separated on the one hand, Sim. *kuda*, on the other hand, H. O. *kūjā*, B. *kuṃjā*, cf. M. *khujā* "dwarf", with an initial aspirate which recalls M. *khubā* "protuberance, hump, snail" (see these two words later). Skr. *kubhra* "the humped buffalo". — $ 84, 89, 127.

kuṃbh m. "jar". G. Panj. H. *kuṃbh*, S. *kuṃbhu, kuṃbu*, Siṃ. *kuṃba*. Skr. *kuṃbha* -. — $ 128, 138.

kuṃbhār m. "potter". G. *kuṃbhār*, S. *kuṃbharu*, Panj. H. *kumhār*, B. Apa. *kumār*, Siṃ. *kuṃbukaru*. Pkt. *kumbhaāra. kumbhāra*-Skr. *kumbhakara*. — $ 61, 128, 138, 141, 258.

kurhāḍ f. "axe". G. *kuhāḍo*, S. *kuhāṛo*, Panj. *kuhāṛā kulhāṛā*, Bih. *koḍār*, B. *kuhrāḍī*, O. *kuhrāḍī kuṭāḍī*. Pkt. *kuhāḍa-*.

Skr. *kuṭhāra-*. — $ 112, 167, 168.

kurumḍ m. "corundum". S. *kurimḍu* "pumice-stone", Panj. *kurumḍ*. H. *kuramḍ*, Siṃ. *kurumḍu*. Skr. P. *kuruvinda*. — $ 64, 123.

kulā, kullā, kulhā m. "buttock". G. *kulo*, H. *kūlā*. Desī. *kullo grivā* (cf. Panj. *kulhā* "part of buffalo-hump on which the yoke is placed"), *asamarthaś* (cf. M. *kol* "impotent, powerless", Panj. *kūlā* "soft, tender") *chinnapucchaś ceti tryarthaḥ* (92, 5). — $ 148.

kuṃvar m. "small boy", *kuṃvār* f. "young girl". G. *kuṃvar kuṃver*, S. *kuṃyāro*, Panj. *kaṃvar kavār* (*kuār* f. virginity"), W. Panj. *kuṃvār*, H. *kuṃvar kumar*, Siṃ. *kumaruvā*. Pkt. *kumāra-, kumara-*; *kuarī* f. Skr. *kumāra-, kumārī*. —$ 42, 152.

kuvā m. "well". g. *kuvo*, S. *khuhu*, K. *khuh*, Panj. *khūh*, *kūā*. H. *kūāṃ*, Nep. *kuvā*, B. O. *kūā*. Skr. *kūpa*. — $ 64, 92, 152.

kusaḷ f. "sorceress". cf. Panj.H. *kusal* "health", G. *kasḷiyuṃ* "epidemic, cholera". Skr. *kuśala* "prosperous, clever." — $ 142, 145, 156.

kusuṃb m. "dried, seaflower, carthamus tanctorins. ". G. *kasuṃbho*, S. *khuhuṃbo*, Panj. *kusuṃb, kusumbh, kusumh*, H. *kusuṃb, kusumbh, kusum*, Bih. *kosum*. Skr. *kusumbha-*. — $ 127, 138.

kuḷkarṇī m. "treasurer, village record keeper". Composed of *kūḷ* (*kula*) "family", and *kārṇī* (*karaṇika-*) "archivist,". —$ 44.

kūs f. "stomach". S. *kuchiṛi* "hip", Panj. *kucch* f. "corner", *kucchaṛ* "hip, bosom", K. *kòch* "lap", Ro. *koc* "knee", Siṃ. *kus kis*; on the other hand, G. *kukh*, S. *kukki*, Panj. *kukkh*, H. *kokh*, cf. M. *kukhāvart*. Pkt. *kucchī*,. Skr. *kukṣī*. — $ 92, 104.

kūḷ n. "family". G. O. *kuḷ*, S. *kulu*, Panj. *kul* f., W. Panj. *kull*, H. *kul* m. Pkt. *kula-*. — $ 145.

kekat n. "Pandanus odoratissimus"; *kektāḍ* n. "type of palm". G. *ketak*, S. Panj. H. *ketkī*. Skr. *ketaka-*. —$167, 172.

keḍhavat "what a long time". From *kevḍhā* "how big" (see Beames, II, p. 333-334) and *veḷ* "time". — $ 63.

keṇem n. "merchandise". H. *kinnā* "to buy", B. *keṇā* "purchase", K. $K^a n$- "to sell", *kalaśa, kre* "purchase", Ro. *kin-* "to buy". Skr. *krayaṇa-* "purchase"-.—$ 51, 77, 92, 134.

kelā adj. "done". G. *karyo, kīdho, kīto*, Panj. *kītā, kīnā*, H. *kiyā*, Ro. S. *kerdo*, Siṃ. *kaḷa*. Pkt. *kaa-, kaya-*; P. *kaṭa*. Skr. *kṛta-*. — $ 62, 165, 229, 252, 256.

kevḍā m. "pandanus odoratissimus". G. *kevḍo*, S. *keṛo*, Panj. H. *kevṛā*, Siṃ. *kĕ*. Skr. *ketaka-*. — $ 55, 63, 77.

kes, keṃs m. "hair". G. *keś* (plur.), S. *kesu*, Panj. H. *kes, kĕ*; Ro. *keś* "silk". Pkt. *kesa*. Skr. *keśa-*. — $ 70, 77, 156.

keṃsar m., *kesrī* m. "lion". G. *kesrī*, S. *keharī*, Panj. H. *kehar, kehrī* "lion". Skr. *keśara-, kesara-, keśarin-, kesarin-*. — $ 70, 156.

keḷ. f., *keḷem̩* n. "banana". G. *keḷ* f., S. *kelho*, Panj. H. *kelā*, B. *kalā*. Pkt. *kaalī*, *kayalī*. Skr. *kadalī*, *kadala*.— $ 39, 62, 92, 145.

kaik "much". G. *kaim̩k*, H. *kaiek*, *kaek*. Skr. *eka-eka-*. — $ 56.

kaivāḍ n. "ruse, machination". H. *kaitab*, Braj. *kaitau*. Pkt. *kaiva-*. Skr. *kaitava-*. —$ 56.

koil, *koīḷ*, *koyāḷ* f. "cuckoo". G. *koyal*, S. Panj. H. *koil*, O. *koyali*, Sim̩. *kevillī kovullā*. P. Skr. *kokila-*. — $ 64, 145.

koṭ m. "fortress". G. Panj. H. *koṭ*, S. *koṭu*, K. *koṭh*. Pkt. *koṭṭa*-(Deśī. *koṭṭam nagaram*, 87,2). Skr. *koṭṭa-*. — $ 109.

koṭ f. "crore, ten millions". S. *koṭ*, Panj. *koṭ* "much", Sim̩. *keḷa*. Skr. *koṭi-*. — $ 109.

koṭhā m. "shop, store". G. S. *koṭho*, Panj. H. *koṭhā*, K. *kuṭh*ᵘ "room", Sim̩. *koṭuva*, *koṭa*. P. *koṭṭha-* Skr. *koṣṭha*,-*koṣṭhaka-*. — $ 78, 110.

kom̩ḍḷem̩ n. "circle, enclosure". G. Panj. H. *kum̩ḍal*; Sim̩. *kom̩ḍol*, S. *kuniru* "ear-ring". P. Skr. *kuṇḍala-*. — 80, 111.

koḍem̩, *kohḍem̩*, *kuheḍem̩* n. "embarrasment, enigma". G. *koyḍo*, *kohḍo* "enigma", S. *kūṛu* "falsehood", *koṛiko* "trap", Panj. *kūṛā* "falsehood, liar", Sim̩. *kuḷu* "false, disobedient". Deśī. *kūḍo pāśaḥ* (86, 3), Skr. *kūṭa-*. — $ 80, 161.

koḍem n. "earthen plate in which are put oil and the wick of a lamp". G. *koḍiyum*. Deśī- *koḍiam̩ laghuśarāvaḥ* (87, 15). — $ 63.

koḍh. *koḍ* m. n. "leprosy". G. *kohoḍ* *koḍ*, S. *koṛiho*, Panj. H. *koṛh*, Nep. *koṛ*, B. *kuḍh*, O. *kuḍi*. Pkt. *koḍha-*. Skr. *kuṣṭha-*, *koṭha-*; cf. the play of words in *varakoḍhi* "good leper; covered with a foulard (varaka-)" ascribed to Bāṇa by Merutunga (see Ettinghausen, *Harṣa*, p. 126). $— 80, 88, 92, 112.

koṇ (neut. *kāy* obl. *kaśā*) "who?". G. *koṇ*. Panj. *kauṇ*, H. *kaun*, *kon*; Ro. *kon*. Apa. and old M. *kavaṇa-*. Skr. *kaḥ punaḥ* ? — $ 58, 78, 204.

koṇ m. "angle, corner". G. Panj. *koṇ*, H. *kon*; cf. H. *kohnī*, Ro. *kuni* "elbow". P. Skr. *koṇa-*. — $ 78, 134.

kothim̩bīr, vulg. *kothrīb kotrīb* f. "coriander". G. *kothmī kothmīr*, H. *koṭhmīr kothmīr*. Skr. *kustumbarī*. — $ 71, 89, 122, 138, 167.

kon m. "corner; lying in (period when the woman lives in a secluded part of the house)"; *konā konyā* m. "corner, corner-stone". *Deśī konno gṛhakoṇaḥ* (87, 2). — $ 134.

kopṇem̩ "to be angry". G. .S Panj. H. *kop-*, Sim̩. *kō* "anger", *kipenavā* "to be irritated". Pkt. *kuppai*; P. *kuppati*,caus. *kopeti*. Skr. *kupyati* — $ 80.

kopar, *kom̩par* m. "elbow". G. *kopariyum̩*. Pkt. *koppara-*, *kuppara-*. Skr. *kūrpara-*. —$ 69.

komnem̩ "to wither". S. *komāijaṇu*, Panj. *kumāvan*. Deśī. *kummaṇam kuṇṭāram̩ kurumāṇam̩tram api mlānāya rtham* (84, 18). — $ 30.

kom̩ykamal n. "lotus (nymphaea pubescens". S. *kūṇī*, H. *koī komī*; on the other hand G. *kamaḷ*, S. *kam̩valu*, Panj. *kaul*,

H. *kuṃval* "Nile-lily". Skr. *kumudakamala-*. — $ 64, 138, 145, 153.

kor f. "side, direction edge". G. Panj. H. *kor*; S. *koli* "to, near", Panj. *kol* "near, by". Skr. *kora* "articulation (a singer, knee)", *kola-* "side". — $ 78.

kol "incapable, impotent". Deśī. *kullo...asamarthaḥ*. — $ 148.

kolī f. whole for a children's game". G. *kolo* hole in a wall". H. *kol*, K. *kul* "river". Skr. *kulyā*.— $ 80, 148.

kolhā, *kolā* m. "jackal". G. *kohluṃ kolum*; H. *kolhā kolā*; Siṃ. *koṭa*. Pkt. *kuḷha-koḷhua-*; Deśī. *kolhuo...śṛgālaḥ* (93,5) *kulhośṛgālaḥ** (93, 5) *kulho śṛgālaḥ* (82, 16); P. *koṭṭhu*. Skr. *kroṣṭṛ*.—$ 92, 148.

kolhāḷ m. "cry, howling". Skr. *kolāhala-*. — $ 52, 78, 145, 148, 149.

koṃvḷā adj. "young, tender". G. *komaḷ kumḷuṃ*, S. *komalu*, H. *komaḷ*, Panj. *kūlā*, K. *kumol^{u}*, Ro. *kovlo*. Skr. *komala-*. — $ 140, 145.

kos m. league". G. H. *kos*, S. *kohu*, Panj. *koh*, K. *kruh*. Skr. *krośa-*. —$ 92.

kohḷeṃ, *kovhaḷeṃ kohāḷeṃ*, *koholeṃ* n. "gurd". G. *kohḷuṃ*, *koluṃ* H. *koṃhar*, Siṃ. *komaḍu*, *komaṃdu*. Deśī. *kohaḷī*, Pkt. *kūhaṇḍa-*, *kohaṇḍa-*. Skr. *kuṣmāṇḍa-*. —$ 71, 80, 146, 120.

koḷapṇeṃ "to be skinned, tanned"; cf. *kolaṃjṇeṃ* "to burn, to consume", *kolaṃgā koḷsā* "fire brand". G. *koylo kolso*, S. *koilo*, Panj. *kolā*, H. *koyal kolsā* "fire-brand". Deśī *kouā karīṣāgniḥ* (88, 7), *koilā kāṣṭhaṅgārāḥ* (88, 13), P. *koḷāpa-* "dried (tree)"; cf. P. *kuṇḍaka-* "kitchen". Skr. root *kuḍi dāhe*. — $ 146.

koḷaṃbeṃ n. "pot with a large mouth". D. *kolambo tathā kollaro piṭharam* (87, 15); P. *kolamba-*. — $ 145.

kolī m. "fisherman, water-carrier (name of a caste); sort of spider". S. *korī* "weaver; spider", G. *koḷī*, H. *kolī*; pame of a caste, Deśī. *kolio ttantuvāgo jālakāra-kṛmiś ca* (93, 5). Skr. *kaula-*, *kaulika-*. — $ 78, 145.

koleṃ n. "basket containing rice or grain". G. *koḷiyo* "mouthful"; H. *kaulī* "packet of wheat given to a village functionary". Skr. *kavala-*. — $ 145.

koleṃ n. "hump of buffalo". Deśī *kolo grīvā* (87, 1); *kullo grīvā* (92, 5). — $ 80, 145.

kaul n. "tile"; *kaulār* n. "roof of tiles". — $ 143.

khacneṃ "to set (precious stones)". G. *khac* "to press strongly", H. *khacnā* "to be fixed, inserted". Deśī. pr. pcpl. *khaciya-*. Skr. *khacayati*. — $ 48, 95, 101.

khajūr m. "wild dates", *khajurī* f. "date tree". G. *khajur* n. "date", *khajurī* f. "date-tree"; S.Panj. *khajūr* f., H. *khajūr* m. "date, date-tree", Siṃ. *kaduru*. Skr. *khajūra-*. — $ 50, 95, 106.

khaṭaṃg n. "bed". Skr. *khaṭvāṅga*, "club," etymologically "foot of bed"; cf. M. *khāṭ*. — $ 48, 95, 109.

khaḍtar, *khatraḍ* adj. "jarring, importunate". G. *khaḍtal khaḍtal*, H. *khaṛtal*. — $ 167.

khaḍī f. type of steatite used for writing on the board or for white-washing". G. S.

Panj. H. *khaḍī*, O. *khaḍi* "lime". Skr. *khaṭikā*, *khaḍikā*. — $ 95.

khaḍīṇ, *khaḍaṇ* "vicious, difficult (animal)". Deśī. *khaḍḍio maṭṭaḥ*. Skr. *kaṭhina-*. — $ 95.

khaṇṇeṃ "to dig". G. S. *khaṇ-*, H. K. *khan-*, Ro. *xan*, Siṃ. *kaninavā*. Skr. *khan-*.—$ 49, 95, 170, 229.

khaṇṭeṃ n. "instrument for digging holes". H. *khantī*, Bih. *khanti*. Skr. *khanitraka-*. — $ 95.

khapṇeṃ "to work hard, to tire oneself out, to sell oneself". G.S. Panj. H. *khap-*; K. *chap-* "to await the end of rain". Skr. *kṣapita-* "destroyed", *kṣapaṇam* "destruction". — $ 48, 95.

khar adj. "biting, piquant", *kharaḍ* f. "sketch, draft". G. *khar* "uncouth"; G. S. *kharḍo*, H. *kharrā* "draft". Deśī- *kharaḍiaṃ rūkṣaṃ bhagnaṃ ca* (98, 13). Skr. *khara-*. —$ 46, 95, 163.

kharṇeṃ "to suffer from spermatorrheo; to emit semen". G. *kharvuṃ* "to fall", S. *kharaṇu* "to degenerate,", Panj. *kharnā* "to disintegrate", K. *charun* "to go to stool". Skr. *kṣarati*. — $ 46, 75, 95.

khavaṇā . "Digambar Jaina". Skr. *kṣapaṇaka-*. — $ 46, 95, 152.

khavā m. "articulation of shoulder". G. *khabho*, Panj. H. *khavā*. Deśī. *khavao skandhaḥ* (93, 16). cf. Skr. *kaphaṇi-* "elbow," and probably Lat. *scapula*. —$ 45, 95, 152.

khaḷ adj. "vile, naughty". G. *khaḷ khal*, H. *khal*. Pkt. Skr. *khala-*. — $ 95, 145.

khaḷ, f. "paste for cakes". G. *khoḷ* m., S. *kharu* m. f., Panj. *khal* f., H. *khal* m. *khalī* f. "oilcake". Deśī. *khalī tilapiṇḍikā* (95, 11). Skr. *khala-*. — $93, 145.

khāḷ, *khaḷeṃ* n. "area". G. *khaḷī khaḷum*, S. *kharo*, K. *khal*, H. *khallā*. Skr. *khala-*. —$ 95, 145.

khaḷṇeṃ "to slop". G. *khaḷvuṃ*. Pkt. *khalai*. Skr. *skhal-*. — $ 46, 95, 145.

khaḷbaḷṇeṃ "to rhinse, to agitate". G. *khaḷbaḷvuṃ* "to be undecided, in revolution", Panj. *khalbalāuṇā*, H. *khalbalānā* "to boil, to be agitated", Panj. H. *khalbalī* "turmoil" Skr. *skhal-*. — $ 95.

khāī "pit". S. *khāhī* Panj. H. *khāī*, Deśī. *khāiā parikhā* (96, 4). Skr. *khātaka-*. — $ 95.

khāū adj. (in compound) "glutton", f. "pastry". G. *khāū* "destruction"; Panj. H. *khāū*, K. *khāo* "glutton". Skr. *khāduka*. — $ 95.

khāṃk, *khāk* f. arm-pit". H. *khāk*, Ro. *khak*. Metathesis of *kāṃkh*. $ 95, 168.

khāj f. "itching", *khājṇeṃ* "to scratch". S. *khāji*, Panj. H. *khāj*, Ro. *xandz'*. Skr. *kharju-*. —$ 39, 41, 48, 95, 106, 190.

khājeṃ n. "pastry", *paṃckhājeṃ* "five condiments used in sacrifices (whose names begin with *kha*)". G. *khāj*, S. *khāju*, Panj. *khajjā*, H. *khājā* victuals". Skr. *khādya-*. — $ 47, 95, 106.

khāṭ f. "bed". G. *khāṭ*, S. *khat*, Panj. H. *khaṭ khāṭ*. Pkt. *khaṭṭā*. Skr. *khaṭvā*. — $ 48, 95, 109.

khāṃḍ f. "break, piece, sugar",

khāṃḍṇeṃ, *khaṃḍṇeṃ* "to break". G. Panj. H. *khāṃḍ-*, *khaṃḍ-*, Siṃ. *kaḍ-* "to break", G. *khāṃḍ*, Panj. K. H. *khaṃḍ* f. "sugar", S. *khanu*, H. *khaṇā*, K. *khūnḍ*ᵘ f. Siṃ. *kaḍa* "piece", Panj. *khannī* "half", Ro. *xandī* "little". Pkt. Skr. *khaṇḍ-*, *khaṇḍa-*. — $ 30, 68, 75, 95, 111.

khāṃḍā M. "sword". G. Panj. H. B. *khāṃḍ khāṃḍā*, S. *khano*, K. *khaḍak*, Ro. *xando xanro*, Siṃ. *kaḍuva*. In this word is found again the first element of Skr. *khaḍga-*, which in its turn is related to Lat. *clādēs*, *gladius* and Celtic **klad-yo-* (see Vendreyes, *Mel. Saussure*, p. 309-310). The nasal can come from contamination with the family of Skr. *khaṇḍ-* "to break". — $ 95.

khāḍā, *khaḍā* m. "hole". G. *khāḍo*; S. *khaḍ* f., Panj. *khāḍ khaḍ* f., K. *khọḍ* m. Ro. *xar* f. Deśī. *khaḍḍo khāṇiḥ*. Skr. *khaḍ-* "to break". —$ 75, 95, 170.

khāṇ f. "querry. mine". G. *khāṇ*, S. *khāṇi*, H. K. *khān* "mine"; Panj. *khāṇī* "source of birth (egg, sperm, growth)"; Siṃ. *kän* "crowd" Pkt. *khāṇī*. Skr. *khāni-*. — $ 95, 134.

khāṇeṃ "to eat". G. S. Panj. H. B. O. *khā-*, K. *khĕ-*; Maiyā *kha-*, Xower *khō-*, Sīnā *ka-*, Ro. *xa-*, Siṃ. *ka-*. Pkt. *khāi*. Skr. *khādati*. — $ 46, 95, 229, 230, 231.

khāt n. "dung-hill", *khat* n. "wound, sore". Panj. *khāt* m. "hole; dung-heap", H. *khattā* "hole serving for grain storage". Pkt. *khatta-* "hole"; Deśī. *khaṇṇaṃ tathā khattaṃ khātam* (93, 10). Skr. *khātra-*. — $ 95.

khād f. "nourishment"; Old M. *khādilā* "eaten". G. *khādh* n. "provisions", *khādhuṃ* "eaten", Panj. *khādh* f. "nourishment", *khādā* "eaten", S. *khādho* "nourishment; eaten". Deśī. *khaddhaṃ tathā khariaṃ bhuktam* (93, 16). — $ 88, 95, 169, 229.

khād f. "itching". For *khāj*.—$ 106.

khāṃd m. "shoulder" G. *khāṃd khāṃdho*, Panj. *kannhā*, H. *kāṃdhā*, O. B. *kāṃdh*, Siṃ. *kaṃda*; S. *kāṃdho* "hump of buffalo", *khāṃdīyo* "burden carried on shoulder". Pkt. P. *khandha-*. Skr. *skandha-*. — $ 95, 169.

khāpar n. "earthenplate, tile". Panj. *khappar*, H. *khāpar*. Pkt. *khappara-*. Doublet with *s-* prefixed with Skr. *karpara-* (cf. old H. A. *scirbi*, see Uhlenbeck s. v.).— $ 47, 84, 95.

khāṃb m. "pillar". G. H. *khām*, Panj. B. O. *khaṃbhā*. Pkt. *khambha*. Ved. Skr. *skambhà-*. — $ 68, 95, 127.

khār m. "salt, potassium". G. Panj. H. *khār*, S. *khāri*; cf. G. *chār* m-. Panj. H. *chār* f., S. *chāru*, Ro. *čar* "ashes". Pkt. *khāra-*, *chāra-*. Skr. *kṣāra-*. — $ 95, 104.

khāsṇeṃ, *khāṃsṇeṃ* "to cough". G. Panj. H. *khāṃs- khās-*, S. *khaṃgh-*, Ro. *xas-*, Siṃ. *kah-*, cf. *kässa* "to cough"; cf. K. *sās* "cough". Pkt. *khāsia-*. Skr. *kās-*.— $ 48, 84.

khāl f. "barge, leather". G. H. *khāl*, S. K. *khal*, Panj. *khall*; cf. Arṃ. Ro. *xar* "sack".Deśī.

khallā carma (93, 10). — $ 104, 148.

khijṇeṃ "to be vexed, to be irritated". G. S. *khij-*, Panj. H. *khijh-*. P. Pkt. *khijj-*; cf. Deśī. *khijjiam upālaṃbhaḥ*. Skr. *khidyate*. — $ 44, 95, 106.

khiṃḍ f. mountain-lip, hole". G. *khiḍ* "valley, pass", H. *khiṃḍ* "hole, fissure". Related to the family of *khaṇḍ-*, possible contamination with *khid-*. — $ 30, 75, 95.

khīḍkī f. "window, back-door". G. *khaḍkī* "courtyard, street"; S. Panj. H. B. *khiṛkī* "small door, window". Deśī. *khaḍakkī laghudvāram*. — $ 75.

khirṇeṃ "to flow (talking of semen or urine)". H. *khernā*. Pkt. *khirai*. Related to Skr. *kṣar-*. — $ 75, 95, 107.

khirṇī f. "Mimusops kauki". H. *khirnī*. Skr. *kṣiriṇī*. —$ 95.

khīr f. "rice cooked in sweet-milk". G. Panj. H. *khīr* f. cf. S. *khīro*, K. *chir khir* m. "milk", Ro. *khil* "butter, grain", Siṃ. *kira, kiri* "milk". Pkt. *khīrī*. Skr. *kṣīra-* "milk", *kṣīrikā* "sweetmeats prepared with milk". — $ 95.

khīḷ f. "pin, nail". G. *khilo*, S. *kilo kīro*, Panj. *kīl* f. *kīll* m., K. *kyul*u, H. *kīl khīl*. P. Pkt. *khīla-*. Skr. *kīla-*, *khīla-* (Atharvaveda, Taitt. Br.). — $ 84, 145, 149.

khujā, dial. *koṃjā*, *koṃjhā*, adj. "dwarf". H. O. *kūjā*, B. *kujj*, Siṃ. *kuda*. Pkt. *khujja-*, *kujja-*. Skr. *kubja-*. — $ 44, 84, 85, 106.

khuṭṇeṃ khuṭṇeṃ "to be arrested, to be obstructed, to lack"; *khoṭ*. f. "loss, falsehood"; *khuṭṇeṃ*, *khuḍṇeṃ* "to gather, to tear". G. *khuṭvuṃ* "to be finished, to betray", S. *khuṭaṇu* "to mark", Panj. *khuṭṭṇā* "to be finished"; G. Panj. H. *khoṭ* "loss, falsehood", K. *khŏṭ*u "counterfeit"; G. H. *khuṃṭ-* "to gather". Pkt. *khuṭṭai* (*tuḍati*). cf. Skr. *khuṇḍ-khuḍ-* "to break". —$ 68, 95, 107, 109.

khuḍakṇeṃ "to have a cramp", *khuḍā* adj. "affected with cramp". S. H. *khuṛak-khaṛak-* "to crack". Apa. *khuḍukkai* "to cause harm".— $ 94,95.

khaubaḷṇeṃ 'to be agitated". S. *khobhu chobhu*, H. *choh* "agitation, anger". Pkt. *khohai*, *khubbai*. Skr. *kṣubhyati*. —$ 95, 169.

khubā m. "hump, snail". G. *kubḍuṃ*, S. *kubiṛo*, Panj. *kubbā* "hunchback"; S. *kubbu*, Panj. H. B. *kubb*, K. *kaub* "hump",. cf. Skr. *kubhra-* "buffalo".—$ 85,89.

khulṇeṃ "to open (fig. sense)". G. H. K. *khol-*, S. *khul-khol-*, Panj. *khullh-*. Seems related to Skr. *kṣur-khur-* "to cut", *khuḍ-* "to break". — $ 95.

khuḷā adj. "atrophy". G. *khoḍuṃ*, H. *khorā*, Siṃ. *kor* "paralysed". Pkt. *khoḍa-*. Skr. *khoḍa-* a less attented and etymologically less correct form (cf. Latin *scaurus*) than *khora-*. — $ 95, 146.

khūr m. "horse-shoe.". G. Panj. H. *khur*, S. *khuru*, Siṃ. *kuraya*; K. *khōr* "foot", *khūr*u- "heel". P. Skr. *khura-*. — $ 95.

kheṃkaḍ m. "crabbed, crayfish". H. *keṃkḍā*, *kheṃkḍā*; S. *kāṃkiṛo*, B. O. *kāṃkṛā*, Siṃ. *kakuḷuvā*. Skr. *karkaṭa-*. — $ 77, 84.

khedem n. "hamlet". G. *khed* "culture", *khedum* "village", Panj. *kheḍā* "village, ruined village", H. *kheḍā* "cultivated terrain, ruined village", Ro. *kherav* "town". Pkt. *kheḍaya*-. Skr. *kheṭaka*-. — $ 95.

kher khair m. "acacia catechu". G. *kher*, Panj. H. *khair*, Siṃ. *kihiri*. Pkt. *khaira*-. Skr. *khadira*-. — $ 95, 143.

kherij adj. adv. "in addition". Ar. Pers. H. *khārij* "exterior". — $ 77.

khemvā m. "act of rowing". Panj. H. *khevnā* "to row", Panj. *khevā* "a boat-man, cargo", H. *khevā* "passage, price of passage, boat"; K. *khĕv* "cable for towing". Skr. *kṣip-* "to send", cf. *kṣepaṇika-* "boat-man". — $ 77, 95.

khel m. "play", *khelnem* "to play". G. Panj. S.H. B.Ro. *khel-*, G. *khelo-* 'actor", Siṃ. *keli, kiḍa* "play". Pkt. *kīḍā kheḍḍā*, Apa. *khelaṇa-, khellai*. Skr. *khelayati*. — $ 80, 84, 146.

khoḍ n. "paralytic", f. "vice"; *khoḍā* m. "paralysis, cramp". G. *khoḍum*, B. *khoṃḍā*, Siṃ. *khora* "paralytic"; G. *khoḍ* f. "vice", H. *khorī* "vice, wickedness", *khoḍ* "malediction, disease". Pkt. *khoḍa-*: Deśī. *khoḍo...khañjaḥ* (98, 17); Apa. *khoḍi-* (*doṣa-*). Skr. *khoḍa khora-*.

khoḍ n. "tree-trunk, saddlebow", *khoḍī* f. "stake, pillar". G. H. *khoḍ* "piece of wood", H. *khoṛā* "to drive in", S. *khoraṇu* "to drive in (stake)". Deśī. *khoḍo sīmākāṣṭham* (98, 17); *tantukkhoḍī vāyakatantropakarṇam* (159, 9). Skr. *kṣoḍa-* "stake for tying elephants".—$ 95,111.

kholī f. "room". G. *kholī*. Deśī. *khullaṃ kuṭī* (96, 11). — $ 148.

gaṃṭh f. "knot", *gaṃṭhnem* "to be a land". G. H. *gaṃṭh-*, S. *gaṃdh-*, Panj. *gaṃḍh-*, K. *gaṇḍ-*, Ro. *ged-*, B. *gāṃṭ-*, Siṃ. *gäṭ-*. Pkt. *gaṇṭh-*, P. *ganṭh-*. Skr. *granthi-, granth-*. — $ 97, 110. Pkt. *ganṭh*, P. *ganth-*. Skr. *granthi-, granth-* — $ 97, 110.

gaṃḍ m. "cheek, temple" *gāṃḍ*, f. "buttocks". G.H.B. *gaṃḍ*, Siṃ. *gaḍa* "cheek"; G. Panj. H. B. *gāṃḍ*, S. *gāṃḍi* "buttocks". Pkt. Skr. *gaṇḍa-*. — $ 97, 111.

gaḍgaḍnem, gaḍāḍnem "to rumble, to boom (lighning etc.)" Deśī. *gaḍayaḍī* (Var. *gaḍaaḍī*) *vajranirgoṣaḥ*. — $ 62.

gaṇnem "to count". G. *gaṇvum*, Panj. *giṇṇā*, H. *ginnā*, K. *gāṇzar-*, Ro. *gen-*, Siṃ. *gaṇ-*. Pkt. *gaṇei*. Skr. *gaṇayati*. —$ 46, 97, 134.

gadaḷ n. "dirtiness", adj. "dirty". S. *gadāi*; G. *gadlum*, H. *gadlā*. "dirty". The element *gad* seems to go back to **gr̥d-* or **gard-*, cf. Persian *gil* "dirtiness". — $ 97, 123.

gadhḍā m. "donkey". G. *gadhāḍo gadheḍo*, Panj. H. *gadhā*, Gārvi *gadā*, Kalāsa *gardōk*, X ovar *gurdōx*, Maiyā *ghaḍā*, Siṃ. *gadubua-*. Pkt. *gaddaha-*, P. *gaddabha-*. Skr. *gardabha-*. — $ 48, 97, 115, 170.

gaṃdh m. "odour", *gaṃdhā* adj. "stinking". G. Panj. H. *gaṃdh*, Siṃ. *gaṃda*; G. *gaṃdhāvum* "to stink, to putrify", H. *gaṃdhā* 'stinking,' Ro. *khan* "stink". D. *gandhio durgandhaḥ* (99, 16). Skr.

gandha-. — $ 97.
gamūtr n. "urine of cow". Siṃ. *gomu*. for *gomūtr*, tatsama. — $ 45, 74, 171.
garat, *gharat* f. "respectable women", Skr. *gṛhasthā-*. — $ 87, 88, 169.
garodar adj. "pregnant (woman)". S. *garakūṛī*; cf. S. *garo* "heavy". P. Pkt. *garu-*. Skr. *gurūdara-*. — $ 64, 74, 143 171.
garaḷ f. "snake-poison". G. *garal* n., Panj. *garal*. f., H. *garal* m. Skr. *garala-*. — $97, 145.
gartā, *gardā* m. "hole". H. *gart*, *gardoḍā*. Skr. *garta-*. —$ 164.
garhāṇeṃ, *garāṇeṃ* "to complain of, to supplicate". Panj. *gall*, *gālh*, H. *gālī*, S. B. *gāri* "speech, abuse"; cf. S. *garhaṇu* "to inform", K. *gārun* "to inform oneself, to demand", Ro. *khar* "to call" ? Pkt. *garihai*. Skr. *garhaṇa-* "reproach". — $ 97, 143.
gavasṇeṃ "to seek". Panj. *gaveraṇ* "to seek, to steel". Pkt. *gavesai* Skr. *gaveṣayati*.— $ 46, 51, 97, 152, 156.
gavḷī m., *gavḷaṇ* f. "shepherd". S. *gavāru*, Panj. *gavāl*, H. Nep. B. *goāl*. Skr. *gopāla-*. — $ 52, 97, 171.
gahirā, old M. *gahiru* adj. "deep, intense". Panj. *gahirā* "dark", H. *gahrā*. Pkt. *gahīra-*. Skr. *gabhīra-*. — $ 24, 50, 97, 143, 159.
gahūṃ m. "wheat". G. *gahuṃ ghauṃ*, S. *gehuṃ*, E.B. *gôma*, Siṃ. *goyama*, Ro. *giv*. Skr. *godhūma-*. — $ 41, 45, 64, 74, 97, 153, 159, 171.
gaḷṇeṃ "to drip, to fall". G. *gaḷvuṃ*, S. *garaṇu*, Panj. *galṇā*, H. *galnā*, K. *galun*, Siṃ. *galanavā*. Pkt. P. Skr. *gal-*. — $ 97, 140, 145.
gaḷā m. "throat, neck". G. *gaḷuṃ*; S. *garū girū* "neck", *galū* "throat", *galu* "cheek"; Panj. H. *gal*, *galā*; Siṃ. *gala*; cf. Ro. *kurlo* "neck". Pkt. P. Skr. *gala-*. — $ 46, 97, 140, 145.
gāī, *gāy*, f. "cow", *gavlī* "a cow (term of affection)". G. *gāe gāy*, S. *gāṃi gau*, Panj. *gaṃ gao*, H. *gāī gāv*, B. *gāvī*, K. *gāv* (cf. Grierson *Piś. Lāng.* p. 67), Siṃ. *gava go gā*. Pkt. *gāa*, *gaua*. P. *gava-*, *gāvī*. Skr. *gauḥ*.—$ 46, 57, 97.
gāū f. "lullaby,". Ved. Skr. *gātú-*. — $ 57, 97.
gājṇeṃ, *garajṇeṃ* "to thunder, to resound". S. *gāj* "thunder"; G. *gājvuṃ*, Panj. *gajjṇā garajṇā*, H. *gājnā garajnā* "to thunder"; cf. K. *gagarāy* "thunder". Pkt. *gajj-*; cf. Deśī. *gajjaṇa saddo mṛgavāraṇadhvaniḥ*. Skr. *garjana-*. — $ 47, 97, 106.
gāṃjṇeṃ, *gāṃdṇeṃ* "to torment". G. *gāṃjvuṃ* "to subjugate, to intimidate", H. *gāṃjnā* "to agitate, to churn the butter, B. *ganjā-* "to insult". Apa. *gañjidu* (*pīḍitam*); cf. Deśī. *gāgejiaṃ tathā gejjaṃ mathitham* (101, 16) ? Skr. *gañjana-* "contempt", *gada-* "disease". or *gandhayate* "to wound" ?. — $ 106.
gāṃjā m. "dried Hemp". G. *gāṃje* "Hemp flowers", Panj. *gāṃjā* "Hemp for smoking"; S. *gāṃjo*, H. *gāṃjhā* "Hemp, Hemp leaves". Skr. *gañjā*. — $ 97, 106.
gāḍṇeṃ "to bury". G. H. B. *gāḍ-*. Pkt. *gaḍḍa* "hole". Skr.

garta-; or *gāḍha-*? — $ 48, 89, 114.

gāḍī f. "vehicle". G. H. etc. *gāḍī*, K. *göḍī*. Deśī. *gaḍḍī gantrī* (99, 3). — $ 47.

gāḍhav n. "donkey". S. *gaḍahu*, Siṃ. *gaḍumbu*. Pkt. *gaḍḍaha-*. Skr. *gardabha-*. — $ 47, 48, 97, 115, 170, 283, 291.

gāḍhā adj. "heavy, compact". Panj. H. *gāṛhā*, S. *gaharu*. Pkt. Skr. *gāḍha-*. — $ 46, 97, 112.

gāṇ f. "cavity containing water at an elevated place." G. *gāṇ* f. "mine, quarry, store-room", Panj. *gāṇ* m. "small field surrounded by a channel inside another channel to retain water", S. *gāṇ* f. "mine, hole containing water", K. *gān* m. "cave". Skr. *gahana-*. — $ 62, 97.

gāṇeṃ "to sing". G. *gāvuṃ*, S. *gāiṇu*, Panj. *gāuṇā*, H. *gānā*, K. *géwun*, Pasai *gē*, Maiyā *gēla* "to sing", B. *gāun* "song"; Siṃ. *gā* goes back to Skr. *gāya-* or *gāthā*. Pkt. *gāṇa-*. Skr. *gāna-*. — $ 97, 229, 252.

gāt n. "parts of a bad frame". G. H. *gāt*, Siṃ. *gata* "body". Pkt. *gatta-*. Skr. *gātra-*. — $ 97.

gātḍī, *gātāḍī* f. "wooden bar parting animals; barrior before an idol". Deśī. *gattāḍī tathā gāṇi gavādanī*. (99, 10). — $ 47.

gābh m. "embryo". S. *gabhu*, Panj. *gabbh*, H. *gābh*, Siṃ. *gaba*; cf. K. *gabin* "bosom", Ro. *khabni* "pregnant". Pkt. P. *gabbha-*. Skr. *garbha-*. —$ 97, 128.

gābhār m. "sanctuary". Skr. *garbhāgāra-*. — $ 61, 143.

gāl m. "cheek". G. H. *gāl*, Panj. *gallh*, W. Panj. *gālh* "cheek"; S. *galu* "cheek", *galo* "part of throat below the cheecks". Skr. *galla-*. "lower part of the cheeks" (word noticed as *grāmya* by Vāmana, see Regnaud, *Rhèt. Sanskr*, p. 41). — $ 97, 148.

gāṃv, *gāv* m. n. "village". G. *gām*, S. *gāṃu gāmu*, Panj. *girāṃ*, H. *gāṃv*, K. *gām*, Basgali Kalasa *groṃ*, Ro. *gav*, Siṃ. *gama*. Pkt. P. *gāma-*. Skr. *grāma-*. — $ 91, 137, 152.

gāvṭhā m. "villager"; *gāvṭhaṇ* n., *gāvthaḷ* n. "site of a village". Skr. *grāma-* + *stha-*, *sthāna-*, *sthala-*. — $ 110, 122.

gāvḍā "village-functionary". Deśī *gamauḍo*... ... *grāmapradhāna-*(102, 5). Skr. *grāmakūṭa*—.

girhā m. "aquatic demon, eclilipse". S. *girah* "planet, mouthful", Panj. *girāh* "mouthful"; cf. Ro. *gerav* "to hide". Skr. *graha*. — $ 75, 162, 163.

giḷṇeṃ "to swallow". S. *giraṇu*, B. *gilite*, Siṃ. *gilinavā*. Pkt. Skr. *gil-*. — $ 44, 97, 140, 145.

gīdh, *gīd*, *gidhāḍ* m. "vulture". G. *gīd*, S. *gijh*, Panj. *ghiddh*, *gijh*, W. Panj. *girij*, H. *gīdh*, K. *gred*, Siṃ. *gidu* "greedy". Pkt. *giddha-*, P. *gijjha-*. Skr. *gṛdhra-*. — $ 41, 44, 88, 97, 124.

gīm m. "hot season". Siṃ. *gim* "hot", *guma grima* "heat". Pkt. P. *gimha-*. Skr. *grīṣma-*. — $ 97, 138.

gugūḷ m. "bedellium, resin". G. *gugaḷ*, S. *guguru*, Panj. *guggul guggal*, H. *gūgal*. Skr. *guggulu-*. — $ 40, 97.

guch m. "bouquett". G. *guch*, Panj. H. *guchā*. Pkt. Skr. *guccha-*. — $ 101.

guṇ m. "quality"; *guṇṇeṃ* "to multiply; to repeat (a lesson)". G. Panj. H. B. *guṇ*, S. *guṇu*, K. *gôn*; S. Panj. H. *guṇ-* "to multiply, to count". Pkt. *guṇa-* "quality", *guṇ-* "to learn". Skr. *guṇa-*; *guṇana-*. — $ 97.

guṃthṇeṃ, *gutṇeṃ* "to mix up", *gūth* f. "knot", *guttā* m. "contract, monopoly". G. *guṃthvuṃ* "to plaite, to tie", S. *gundhaṇu* "to weave (a mat)", Panj. *gunnhā* (part. *guddhā*) "to braid, to kneed", H. *gundhnā* "to interlace, to kneed", *guthnā* "to tread", Siṃ. *gotanavā* "to attach"; Panj. *gutt* f; K. *gut* m. "plaited hair", G. *gutto*, S. *guto*, H. *guttā* "contract, monopoly". Pkt. part. *guttha-*; Deśī *guttī bandhanam icchā vacanaṃ latā śiromālyaṃceti pañcārthā* (106, 16). cf. Skr. *grantha-*.—$ 30, 97, 110.

guṃphā, *guphā* f. "forest-retreat of a Yogi, craddle, cave," G. S.H. *guphā* f., K. *goph*. Deśī *guṃpho guptiḥ* (102,13). Skr. *guṣp* "to accumulate", *guph-* "to braid" (cf. Ro. *khuv-*), *gup-* "to hide" ?—$ 71, 86, 126.

gurgurṇeṃ, *ghurghurṇeṃ* "to grunt, to growl". G. *gurvuṃ ghurakvuṃ*, S. *guraṇu*, Panj. *guṛguṛāṇṇā*, H. *gurrānā*, *ghurghurānā*. cf. Deśī. *ghugghurī tathā ghurghurī maṇḍūkaḥ* (109, 8); imitative word (other explanation., Pischel *B. B.* III, 237). — $ 76.

gurūṃ n. "cow, buffalo", *gureṃ* n. "cattle", *gurākhyā* "shepherd". Panj. H. *gorū*, Ro. *guruv*. Skr. *go-*+*rūpam*. — $ 66, 97, 172.

gū m. "excrement". G. H. B. Siṃ. *gū*; S. *goho*, Panj. *guhā* "cow-dung", K. *guh* "dung-heap". P. Skr. *gūtha-*. — $ 97, 161.

gūj n. "secret". G. *gūj*, S. *gujho*, Panj. *gujjh*, H. *gujhī* "secret", K. *gūj*[i] "kernel". Pkt. *gujjha-*. Skr. *guhya-*. — $ 88, 97, 107.

gūḷ guḍ m. "raw sugar, molasses". G. *goḷ*, S. *guḍu*, Panj. H. *guṛ-* Pkt. *guḷa-*. Skr. *guḍa-*. — $ 97, 146.

gerū f. "ochre". G. *geru*, S. *geṛū*, Panj. *gerū gerī*, H. *gerū gairū*, B. *gerī*, K. *guruṭ*[u] "brown". Pkt. *geria-*, *geruya-*. Skr. *gairika-*. — $ 77, 97, 143.

gelā adj. "gone". G. *gao*, Panj. *giā*, Maith. *gĕl*, B. *gelo*, H. *gayā*, *-gā* (in future), K. *gauv gayōv*, Ro. *gelo*, Siṃ. *giya*. Pkt. *gaa-*. Skr. *gata-*. —$ 62, 97, 165, 200, 229, 242, 256.

geh n. "house". G. H. B. *geh*, Siṃ. *ge geya*. Pkt. P. Skr. *geha-*. — $ 159.

gokraṇ f. n. "ear of cow, objects having that shape". Skr. *gokarṇa-* — $ 162, 163.

goṭhā m. "cattle-pan", *goṭhī goṣṭh* f. "story". G. *goṭho goṭh* ("confidence"), Panj. *gohth goṣṭ*, H. *goṣṭh*, *goṣṭhī*. Pkt. *goṭṭha-*, *goṭṭhī*. Skr. *goṣṭha-*, *goṣṭhī*. — 78, 97, 110.

goḍ adj. "sugared, soft". G. *goḍī* "softness", Ro. *gudlo* "soft; sugar-sweets". Skr. *gauḍa-*. — $ 78, 97, 116, 146.

goṇ f. "bag". G. B. *guṇ*, S. *gūṇī*, H. *gon*, K. *guna*, Ro. *gono*. Skr. *goṇī*.—$78, 97, 134.

got n. "caste". G. (neut.), Panj. (fem.), H. (mas.) *got*, S. *goṭu*, Siṃ. *got*. Maiyā Sīnā *got* or *goṭ*. Sīnā. *goś* "house". Pkt. P. *gotta-*. Skr. *gotra-*. — $ 78, 97, 121.

gophā m. "ankle, bun". Skr. *gulpha-*. — $ 80, 97.

gorā adj. "white, pale". G. *goruṃ*, S. *goru*, Panj. H. B. *gorā*, Siṃ. *gora*. Skr. *gaura-*. —$ 78, 97, 143.

govaṃḍ m. "trail of cattle". Deśī. *goaṇṭā gocaraṇāḥ* (105, 13).— $ 55, 111.

govar m. "dry cow-dung". G. *gor*, *gobar*, H. B. *gobar*. Deśī. *govaraṃ karīṣaṃ* (105,1). Skr. *govara- gorvara-*. — $ 97.

gosāmī, *gosāvī* m. "ascetic". G. H. *gosāīṃ* Skr. *gosvāmin-*. — $ 97, 138, 152, 153.

goḷā m. "bowl", *goḷī* f. "tablet". G. *goḷ* "round", *goḷī* "tablet"; S. *golu*, *golī*, H. *gol golī*, B. *gol*, *gulī*, K. *gūlⁱ* "ball". Skr. *golaka-*, *guṭikā*. — $ 97, 145, 146.

gair- "extra-, priv ". Ar. *gair* "other". — $ 29.

gyāj f. n. "the string of bells tied to the neck of a buffalo". cf. Siṃ. *giv* "neck". Skr. *grīvā-jyā* ? — $ 97, 106.

ghaḍghaḍṇeṃ "to thunder", *ghaḍghaḍ* "cracking, suddenly". G. *gharakvuṃ* "to grant", S. *gharaknu* (to sound (the bell) H. *gaṛghaṛānā* "to thunder, to crack," *ghaṛaknā* "to grunt, to thunder". Apa. *ghuḍukkai* (*garjati*). — $ 76.

ghaḍṇeṃ "to form, to touch". G. S. Panj. H. *ghaḍ-* "to form, to make", K. *gar-* "to cut, to make", Siṃ. *galvanavā* "to rub". Pkt. *ghaḍaı*. Skr. *ghaṭate*. — $ 46, 99, 111, 253.

ghaḍā "earthen pot". G. *ghaḍuṃ*, Panj. H. *ghaṛā*, K. *gaḍa*, Ro. *khoro*. P. Skr. *ghaṭa-*. — $ 46, 99, 111.

ghaḍī f. "period of 24 minutes". G. S. Panj. H. B. *ghaḍī*. Skr. *ghaṭikā*. — $ 99, 111.

ghaṇ adj. "heavy, dense". G. *ghaṇuṃ*, S. *ghaṇu*, Panj. *ghaṇā*, H. *ghan*, B. *ghan*, Siṃ. *gana*; Pasai *gaṇ*, kalasa *Yona*, Maiyā *Yo* "big". Pkt. *ghaṇa-*. P. Skr. *ghana-*.—$ 99, 134.

ghar n. "house". G. Panj. H. B. *ghar*, S. *gharu*, K. *gar*, Ro. *kher*, Arm. Ro. *khar*, Siṃ. *gara*. Pkt. P. *ghara-*. cf. Skr. *gṛha-*. — $ 99, 143, 194, 197.

ghāgar f. "water-pot". G. Panj. H. *gāgar* f.. Skr. *gargara-*. — $ 84.

ghāṭ m "quay, stair-case". G. Panj. H. B. *ghāṭ*, S. *ghāṭu*, K. *gāṭh*. Skr. *ghaṭṭa-*. — $ 99, 109.

ghāṃṭ f. "bell". G. *ghaṃṭ*, S. *ghaṃṭu*, Panj. H. *ghaṃṭā*, K. *ganṭa*, *gürᵘ*. Skr. *ghaṇṭā*. — $ 99, 109.

ghāṭṇeṃ "to crush", *ghaṭṇeṃ* "to contract". G. *ghaṭvuṃ*, Panj. *ghaṭnā* "to contract, to diminish"; S. *ghāṭu*, Panj. *ghāṭṭā* "loss". Pkt. *ghaṭṭha-*. Skr. *ghṛṣṭa-*. — $ 30, 48, 89, 99, 110, 231.

ghāṇ f. "stink". G. *ghāṇ*, Ro. *khan*; Siṃ. *gahaṇa* "nose". Pkt. P. *ghāṇa-*. Skr. *ghrāṇa-*. — $ 99.

ghām m. "perspiration". G. H. *ghām* "sunlight, heat, perspiration", B. *ghāmite* "to perspire", K. *gam* "sadness, pain", Ro. *kham* "Sun". Pkt. *ghamma*. Skr. *gharma-*. — $ 99, 138.

ghāy, ghāo m. "wound", *ekā-ghāyiṃ* "at one blow". G. *ghā, ghāv*, S.H. *ghāū*, Panj. B. *ghā*. Pkt. *ghāa-*. Skr. *ghāta-* — $ 55, 57, 99.

ghāṣṇeṃ "to rub, to skin". G. *ghās-*, S. *ghāṃch-*, Panj. H.B. *ghas-*, Ro. *khos-*, Siṃ. *gah-*. Pkt. *ghasai*, p. *ghaṃsati*. Skr. *gharṣati*. — $ 99, 231.

ghās m. "grass, hay". G.H.B. *ghās*, Panj. *ghāh*, K. *gāsa*, Ro. *khas*. Skr. *grāsa-*. — $ 99.

ghālṇeṃ "to pour, to throw". G. H. *ghāl-*, Panj. *ghall-*. Apa. *ghallai* (*kṣipati*). cf. Skr. *jigharti* and *galati*. — $ 99, 229.

ghī n. "clarified butter". G., Panj. H. *ghī*, Panj. *gheo*. S. *gihu*. B. *ghi*, S. *ghia*, K. *ghyau*, Siṃ. *gī giya*. Pkt. *ghaa- ghia-*, P. *ghata-*. Skr. *ghṛta-*. —$ 30, 31, 66, 99.

ghumṇeṃ "to resound, to continue, to inflate, to ferment". G. *ghumvuṃ* "to blow"; S. *ghumaṇu*. Panj. *ghummṇā*, H. *ghumnā* "to roll'; cf. O. *ghur-*. Pkt. *ghummai*. Skr. *ghūrṇati*. — $ 99, 138.

ghusalṇeṃ "to churn, to shake". G. Panj. H. *ghus-* "to insert, to enter", Arm. Ro. *khusel* "to wipe, to sweep". Deśī. *ghusalai mathnāti* (109, 13). Skr. *ghṛṣ-*. — $ 30, 99.

gheṇeṃ ghepṇeṃ "to take", *ghaghā cī vidyā* "art of taking", *ghe* (added to nouns of number) "to gather". S. *ginhaṇu*, O. *ghen*, H. *gahnā*, Siṃ. *gannavā* (pcpl. *gattā*, absol. *geṇa*); N. —W. group. *gi-* and Ro. *gelavā*, "to bring"; Panj. *gahā* "act of taking"; K. *hě* "to take?" Pkt. *geṇhai gheppai*, absol. *gahiūṇa, gheūṇa*; Pkt. *geṇhāti*. Skr. *gṛhṇāti, gṛbhāyati, graha-* (Indo-Ira. **ghrabhə-*) —$ 30, 31, 80, 99, 165, 168, 229, 231.

ghoṭ m. "draught", *ghoṭṇeṃ* "to swallow", *ghuṭghuṭ* "by mouthfuls, by one draught". G. *ghoṭ*, Panj. *ghuṭṭ*, H. *ghoṃṭ*; S. *ghuṭakṇu*, H. *ghuṃṭnā ghataknā*, O. *ghuṭanā*, Deśī. *ghuṭṭai pibati* (109, 12), Apa. *ghuṃṭai*, Pkt. *ghoṭṭai*. — $ 76, 80, 109.

ghoḍā m. "horse". G. S. *ghoḍo*, Panj. H. B. *ghoṛā*, K. *gur*ᵘ, Waialā *guṛ*, Gawarbati Pasai *goṛa*, Garwi *gor*, Maiyā *gho*, Ro. *khuro* "colt". Skr. *ghoṭaka-*. — $ 99, 111, 194.

ghov, ghoho m. "husband" Deśī. *gāmaṇī gāmauḍo gāmagoho goho ete catvāro' pigrāmapradhānārthāḥ; goho bhaṭa ity anye* (102, 5).— $ 78, 99.

ghoṃs, ghos m. "bouquett". Skr. *guccha-*. — $ 84.

gholṇeṃ "to shake", G. *gholvuṃ*, Panj. H. *gholnā* "to melt", B. *gholāite* "to mix". Pkt. *ghul-*. Skr. *ghūrṇ-*. — $ 99, 111.

c, old m. *ci*, particle of emphasis (enclitic). Chattisgarhī *c*, G.S. *j*. Pkt. *ccia, ccea*. Skr. *caiva*.

cakvā m. "casarca rutila" (see *Hobson Jobson*, s. v. *Brah miny duck*). G. *cakvo*, S. *cakuo*, P. H. *cakvā*, Siṃ. *sakvā*. Pkt. *cakkāa-*. Skr. *cakravāka-*. —$ 48, 60, 101.-

caṃcarṇeṃ "to stagger, to hesitate", *caṃcal* adj. "trembling". G. *caṃcaḷ*, S. *caṃcalu*, Panj. H. B. *caṃcal* "hesitant" or "active"; Siṃ. *sasal* "agitation, hesitation, eye." cf. Deśī. *caṃcario bhramaraḥ* (113, 6) Skr. *carcarīti*, *cañcala-*. cf. *cañcarin*. "honey-bee". —$ 101.

caḍ, *caḍak*, f. "smack". G. *caḍ*, B. *caḍcaḍī* "cracking", Panj. *caraknā* "to crack". H. *caṛcaṛ* "to crack", Apa. *caḍakka-*. Skr. *caṭacaṭati*. Expressive word; cf. the cited Dravidian forms-. $ 94.

caḍhṇeṃ "to climb". G. *caḍ-caḍh-* S. Panj. H. O. *caḍh-*; Siṃ. *säḍa* "rise". Pkt. *caḍai*. — $ 46, 252.

caṇā m. "grams". G. Panj. *caṇā*, S. *caṇo*, H. B. *canā*, K. *cana*. Skr. *caṇa*. — $ 46, 134.

catrā adj. "clever". Skr. *catura-*. — $ 163.

catkor, *catkar*, *cotkor* m. f. "quarter of a cake, fruit". M. *caut*. m."quarter" +*kor* f. "edge, quarter of a cake". — $ 45, 171.

carṇeṃ "to graze". G. S. Panj. H. B. Kalacha Garvi Ro. *car*. China *cer-*,Maiya *sār*;P.and K. *čār-* "to gather, to peck at". Pkt. P. Skr. *car-*.—$ 49, 143.

carit n. "acts, exploits". H. *carit*, Panj. H. *caritar*, Siṃ. *sirit* "morals". Skr. *caritra-*.— $ 121.

cavṇeṃ "to fall into debauchery, to go mad". G. *cavvuṃ* "to be reborn", Siṃ. *henavā* 'to fall". Pkt. *cavai*. Skr. *cyav-*. — $ 46, 101, 152.

cavdā, *cavvīs*, see *caudā*, *covīs*.

cā adj. used to form adjective of relationship called "genetive." — $ 202.

cāk n. "wheel". G. H. B. *cāk*, S. *caku*, Panj. *cakk*, K. *carakh*, Siṃ. *sak*. Pkt. *cakka-*. Skr. *cakra-*. — $ 48, 93.

cākhṇeṃ "to taste", *cāṭṇeṃ* "to lick". G. S. H. B., *cākh-*, Panj. *cakkh-* "to taste", K. *cah* "to suck"; G. H. *cāṭ*, S. *caṭ-*, Panj. *caṭṭ-*, Ro. *car-* "to lick". Pkt. *cakkhai* "to eat, to taste", *caḍḍai* "to eat". Skr. *caṣ-* "to eat" (not found in the text) cf. Pers. *čāšt* "lunch", *čaś-* "to taste", with reference to *čāś-* "to take", cf. Skr. *caṣṭe cakṣate* "to see, to say". $ 47, 109.

cāṭū m. "wooden ladel, ore". Panj. *caṭṭū* "wooden mortar" We should undoubtedly separate on the one hand G. *cāḍuṃ* "hallow in a spoon, lamp, mouth, (term of contempt), and on the other S. *cāḍī*, Panj. *cāṭṭī*, H. *cāṭī*, Siṃ. *sal sāliya* "earthen pot", Ro. *caro* "plate". Deśī. *caṭṭū dāruhastaḥ* (111, 4.) — $ 47, 109.

cāḍ f. "desire, affection". G. *cāḍ* f. "worry", S. *cāḍi* "desire", Panj. *cāṭ* "predilection". Skr. *cāṭu* m. n. "caress". — $ 111.

cāt m. f. n. "spinning wheel, spindle". G. *cātrī*. Deśī. *catto tarkuḥ* (111, 4). Skr. *cattra-*. — $ 121.

cāṃd m. "moon". G. H. *cāṃd*, S. *caṇḍu*, Panj. *cand*, W. Panj. *can*; Maith. *cāṃd cān*, Ro. *čon*., Siṃ. *saṃda*. Pkt. canda-. Skr. *candra-*. — $ 68, 123.

cāpaṭ, *capḍā* adj. "flat, low". G. *cāpaṭ capaṭ*, H. *capṭā*, S. *capitiṛu* "flat", K. *capaṭhal* "in the form of plank", H.

cāpḍā "plain", b. *capad* "palm", Panj. *cāpaṛ* H. *capṛī* "cow-dung-cake". Skr. *carpaṭa-*. — $ 48, 109, 111, 125.

cāṃpā m. "Magnolia". G. *cāṃpuṃ*, S. *caṃbo*, Panj. *caṃbā caṃpā*, K. *camba*, H. *caṃpā*, Siṃ. *sapu*. Skr. *campaka-*. — $ 68, 71, 125.

cām n. "leather". G. H. B. *cām*, S. *camu*, Panj. *camm*, Arm. Ro. *tsˇam*, Siṃ. *sama*. Pkt. *camma*. Skr. *carma*. — $ 138.

cāmhār m. "leather-worker". G. H. *camār*, S. *camāru*, Panj. *camār camiār*, K. *crôl*[u] *camār*, Siṃ. *sommāru*. Pkt. *cammāraa-*. Skr. *carmakāra-*. — $ 61, 138, 143, 161.

cār, *cyār* "four". G. Panj. H. *cār*, S. B. O. *cāri*, Maith. *cār*[i], China *cār*, K. *cōr* (cf. Grierson, *Piś. Lang.*, p. 37), Ro. *sˇtar*, Arm. Ro. *tsətar*, Siṃ. *hatara*, *hār*. Apa. *cāri*, Pkt. *cattāri*. Skr. *catvāri*. — $ 61, 143, 216.

cār m. "Buchanania latifolia". Deśī. *cāropiyālavṛkṣaḥ* (119, 9). — $ 101.

cālṇeṃ "to go, to advance". G. B. O. *cāl-*, Panj. *call-*, S. H. *cal-*; K. *cal* "to run away", caus. Ro. *ćalav* "to beat, to shake" Siṃ. *sal-* "to shake, to overthrow". Pkt. *callai*. Skr. *calati*. — $ 48, 145, 254.

cāvṇeṃ "to masticate", G. *cāv-*, S. Panj. *cabb-*, H. B. *cāb-*; cf. K. *cop*[u] "bite"? Miklosich wrongly connects Ro. *cam* "cheek" (Skr. *jambha-*). Skr. *carvayati*. — $ 152, 250, 253.

Cāvuṇḍa-, proper noun. — $ 137, 281.

cāḷīs "forty". G. *cāḷīs*, S. *cālīh*, Panj. *cālī*, H. *cālīs*, B. *callīs*, K. *catajih*, Siṃ. *sataliha*, *sāḷis*. Pkt. *cāyālīsaṃ cattāḷīsaṃ*, *cattāḷīsaṃ* P. *cattāḷīsaṃ cattārīsam*. Skr. *catvāriṃśat*. — $ 141, 216. 223.

cikaṇ adj. "sticky". G. *cikoṇuṃ* Panj. *cikkān*, H. *ciknā* "sticky", Ro. *ciken* "grease", cf. M. G. *cīk* "resin", Panj. *cik* "soil", H. *cīk*. "deposit of soot", Ro. *cik* "dung, earth", S. *cīko* "gluttinous", *cikām* "muddy". Skr. *cikkaṇa-*. — $ 93.

cikśā ciksyā f. "suspicion, apprehension". G. *ciksā*. Skr. *cikitsā*. — $ 162, 163.

cike "a little", *cikkar* adj. "little". Deśī. *cikkā alpam vastu tanuddhārā ceti dvyarthā* (119, 9). Kannrese *cikka* "little", *cikke* "spot". —$ 94.

cikhal m. "mud". G. *cikkal*, Panj. *cikkaṛ*, Sim. *sikal*. Deśī. *cikkhallo kardamaḥ* (115, 5). Skr. *cikhalla-*. — $ 101.

ciṇṇeṃ "to construct, to plug". G. *ciṇvuṃ* "fold"; S. *cuṇaṇu*, Panj. *ciṇṇā* "to pile up, to fold", H. *cinnā cunnā* "together, to build", Ro. *cinav-* "to shake". Pkt. *ciṇai*. Skr. *cinoi*. — $ 101, 230.

ciṃtṇeṃ "to think". G. *citvuṃ cintvuṃ*, S. *cītaṇu*, H. *cintnā*. Skr. *cintana-*. — $ 71.

citaḷ m. n. "spotted dear". G. *cītaḷ* "spotted serpent", Panj. *citlā* adj. "spotted", H. *cītal*. Deśī. *cittalaṃ maṇḍītaṃ*, *cittalam ramaṇīyaṃ ity anye* (112, 8). Derived from Skr. *citra-*. — $ 121.

citā cittā m. "leopard". G.

citto, S. *cīto ciṭo*, Panj. *cittā*, H. *citā*; cf. Ro. *cicay* "cat". Skr. *citraka-*. — $ 44, 101, 121.

citārī m. "painter", G. *citāro*, Panj. *citerā*, Siṃ. *sitiyara-*. Skr. *citrakāra-*. — $ 44, 61, 121.

cipṇeṃ cepṇeṃ "to crush". G. *cipvuṃ* "to press, to fold"; Panj. *cippṇā* "to press, to piece"; H. *cepnā* "to paste"; S. *cipaṇu*, B. *cipite* "to crush", K. *cipun* "to hide". Skr. root *cip-* "to crush" (see *Śikṣāmuccaya* ed. Bendall, p. 182, note I), *cipiṭa-* "flattened". It is allowed to think that the vowel of the root rests on an old *ṛ*, cf. on one hand. M. *cupp*, S. *cipu cupu*, H. *cup* etc. "silence", and on the other hand M. *cāpṇeṃ*, H. *cāpnā* etc. "to crush, to print", and M. *cāpaṭ*, Skr. *carpaṭa-* "flat" (see S.V.). — $ 80.

ciraknеṃ "to crack; to have a sudden & scanty stool". Panj. *ciraknā*, H. *ciraknā*; K. *cīr-* "to bring out water by crushing or twisting". cf. Deśī *cirikkā...tanudhārā pratyūṣaś ceti* (119, 10); derived from the root M. *cir-*, G. S. Panj. H. B. *cīr-* "to tear", cf. M. etc. *cīr* "tear", K. *ciran* "hole"; Skr. *cīra-* "strip of cloth, rag", root *ciri hiṃsāyāṃ* ? — $ 50.

circir, circirāṃ, ciriciri adj. "in a drizzle". Deśī. *ciricirā tathā cirimcira jaladhāra* (116, 5). — $ 163.

ciṃvar civar n. "filaments encircling the jack fruit". Skr. *cikura-* "hair". — $ 143.

civaḍṇeṃ "to crush", *civḍā* m. "crushed fruits". H. *cinḍā* "crushed rice". Pkt. *cimiḍha-civiḍha-* Skr. *cipiṭa-*. — $ 44, 152.

cukṭī f. "pinch". S. *cuko* "some drops", H. *cukṭā* "handful". Deśī. *cukko musṭiḥ* (116, 13). — $ 44.

cukṇeṃ "to stray, to mistake". G.S.H.B. *cuk-*, Panj. *cukk-*. Pkt. *cukkai bhraśyati*, see Pischel $ 566 and n. 4; cf. Skr. *cukka vyathane* ? — $ 44, 93, 252.

cukā m. "wild sorrel". S. *cūko*, H. *cūkā* B. *cūk*; G. *cuko*, Panj. *cūkā cukkā* "some vegetable". Skr. *cukra-*. — $ 44, 93.

cuṃc f. "a medicinal plant". Skr. *cuccu-*. — $ 101.

cuḍā m. "bracelet". G. *cūḍo*, S. *cūṛo*, Panj. H. *cūṛā*. Deśī. *cūḍo valayāvalī* (118, 6). cf. *valayabāhū cūḍakākhyaṃ bhujābharaṇaṃ* (255,7). — $ 44.

cuṇī f. "coarse bran having some grit mixed". Panj. H. *cūnī* "dust of precious stones or grain of crushed grains." Deśī. *cuṇio reṇu vicchurita itī tu cūrintaśabdabhavaḥ* (117, 18). Skr. *cūrṇikā-*. — $ 135.

cunā m. "cement". G. *cuno*, *cūno*, Panj. H. *cūnā*, K. *cūna*, Siṃ. *hunu*. Pkt. *cuṇṇa-* Deśī. *cuṇaio cūrṇāhataḥ* (117, 18); *cuṇao......vyatikaraḥ* (119, 14). Skr. *cūrṇa* — $ 44, 135.

cuṃbṇeṃ "to kiss". G. S. *cum-*, Panj. *cumm-*, H. *cūm-*, Ro. *cumb- cum-*; K. *cumun* "to implore, to flatter". Pkt. Skr. *cumb-*. — $ 138.

cuṃbaḷ cuṃbhaḷ n. "a ring (of cloth or grass) to be put

under a load up on the head". H. *cummal cumlī*; Siṃ. *suṃbuḷa* "crown". P. *cumbaṭa-*. — $ 86, 138, 146.

cultā m. "paternal uncle". Pkt. *cullatāya-* "father-in-law". Cf. Skr. *kṣulla*-and-*tāta-*. — $ 60, 101, 141.

cuḷcuḷ f. "impatience". Panj. H. *culcul*. Deśī. *culuculai spandati* (118, 5).

cūḍ f. "torch", cf. Deśī. *cuḍulī ullkā* (117, 4).

cūṇ n. "husks and fragments of grain given as food to cattle", *cūn* n. "scrappings of coconut". Panj. H. *cūn* "bran, flour, dust". Pkt. *cuṇṇa-* Skr. *cūrṇa* — $ 135.

cūl f. "furnace". G. *culo cūl*, S. *culhi*, Panj. *culh*, H. *culhī*. Skr. *cullī*. — $ 148.

celā m. "pupil". G. *celo*, S. *celu*, Panj. *celā*" disciple, slave," *cerā* "disciple, slave", K. *celā*, H.B. *celā*. Deśī. *cillo tathā ceḍo bālaḥ* (114, 15). Panj. *cerā* and Deśī. *ceḍa* go back undoubtedly to Skr. *ceṭa-* "slave"; the Marathi word is related to a Dravidian root, Kanarese *cillaṛa cillu ciṛu* "pettiness", Tamil *śila* "a little" etc. — $ 148.

cevaviṇeṃ cavaviṇeṃ "to wake up, to excite", *ceiṇeṃ ceṇeṃ* "to wake up". G. *cevvuṃ* "to reheat". Pkt. *ceyaṇa-*. Skr. *cetana-*. — $ 55, 77.

cokh adj. "real, pure, beautiful". G. *cokkhuṃ*, Panj. *cokhkhā*, H. *cokh*. Skr. *cokṣa-*. — $ 96.

coclā m. "caress, coquettry". G. *coṃclāṃ* (neu. pl.), Panj. H. *coclā*. Deśī. *cuṃculiam avadhāritaṃ satṛṣṇatā ca* (120, 1); expressive word undoubtedly related to on the one hand to M. *coclā*, G. *cuṃcī*, Panj. *cūcā*, K. *cica*, Ro. *cuci*, Skr. *cūcuka*"bosom", and on the other to Skr. *cañcu-*, M. *coṃc* "beak". — $ 80.

coṃc, *cūṃc*, *ṭoṃc* f. "beak". G. *cāṃc*, *ṭoc*, S. *cūṃji*, Panj. *cuṃj*, K. *comṭ*ᵘ "chin", H. *coṃc*, B.S., *coṃṭ* Siṃ. *hoṭa-*. Pkt. *caṃcū*; Deśī. *cuṃculī cañcuśculukaś ca* (120, 1). Skr. *cañcu-*. — $ 68, 80, 101, 170.

coj m. n. "marble". H. Panj. *coj*. Deśī. *cujjām āścaryam*; *otsaṃyoge*; *iti cojjaṃ ity api* (116, 14). Skr. *codya-*. — $ 80.

cor m. "thief". G. Panj. H.B. Ro. *cor*, K. *cūr*, Siṃ. *horā*. Pkt. *cora*. Skr. *caura-*.—$ 29, 78, 143, 186.

covīs, *cavvīs*, *cyauvīs* "twenty-four". G. *covīs*, S. *covīh*, Panj. *caubī*, K. *côwuh*, H. *caubīs*, B. *cabbīs*. Pkt. *cauvīsa cauvvīsa cauvviha*. Skr. *caturviṃśat*.- — $ 59, 216.

coḷṇeṃ "to rub, to friction" G. *coḷvuṃ*. cf. Skr. *cūrṇa*. ?— $ 141.

cauk m. "tower, building, quadriangular space". G. *cok*, Panj. H.B. *cauk*, K. *cokh*. Deśī. *caukkam catvaram* (111, 11). Skr. *catuṣka-*. — $ 56, 93.

cauth f. "the fourth day of the moon". G. Panj. H. *cauth*, S. *cothi*; K. *coṭh* "a quarternary fever". Skr. *caturthī*. — $ 56, 108, 114, 216.

cauthā adj. "fourth". G. *cothuṃ*, S. *cotho*, Panj. H. *cauthā*, B. *cauṭhā*, O. *cauth*. Pkt. *cauttha-cottha-*. Skr. *caturtha-*. — $ 29, 56, 108, 114, 216, 226.

caudā cavdā "fourteen", *caudas*

cāvdas f. "fourteenth day of the month". G.B.O. *caud.* S. *coḍahaṃ*, Panj. *caudām*, W. Panj. *coḍā*, H. *caudah*, K. *côdāh*, Sim. *tudus* "fourteen"; G. *caudaś*, Panj. *caudas* "fourteenth day". Pkt. *cauddasa*, *coddasa* (texts), *côddaha* (Gramm.), Apa. *cauddaha-*. Skr. *caturdaśa-*, *caturdaśī*. — $ 56, 57, 115, 123, 156, 216, 221,

chabilā adj. "beautiful, gracious". G. *chabilo*, Panj. H. *chabīlā*. cf. Deśī. *chāillo pradīpaḥ...surūpaś ceti* (124, 18). Skr. *chavi-*. — $ 101.

chāvaḍ n. "term of affection for a child"; *chāvā* m. "young elephant". G. *chorum* "child", Panj. H. *chaunā* "baby animal", Panj. *chohār* "child", H. *chāvā* "young elephant", B. *chā chāṃ* "baby-animal", *chāval chālā* "child", Ro. *cāvo* "child, son", cf. G. *chokro*, S. *chokṛo*, Panj. H. B. *chokṛā*, K. *chūkur* "child", Arm. Ro. *coki* "daughter", Pkt. *chāva-*, P. *chāpa-*. Skr. *śāva-*. — $ 101.

chāvṇī chāvnī f. "shelter, camp, ceiling". G. Panj. H. *chāvṇī chāvnī*, S. *chāṃviṇī*; cf. S. *chaiṇu* "roof", G. H. *chā-* Panj. *chāu-* "to cover". Skr. *chādana-*. — $ 101.

jaklā "vulg. for *sakal* "all". Skr. *sakala-*. — $ 90.

jag n. "world", G.H. *jag*, S. *jagu*, Panj. *jagg*, Siṃ. *diya*. Pkt. *jaaṃ*, Apa. *jagu*. Skr. *jagat*. — $ 98.

jaṭ f. "matted hair of ascetics", *jaḍ* f. "root". G. H. *jaṭā*, Panj. *jaṭ* "matted hair, hanging roots of the Bunyan tree", G. Panj. H. B. *jaṛ*, S. *joṛha* "root", Ro. *jar* "hair". Skr. *jaṭā-*. — $ 105, 109

jaḍ adj. "cold, apathetic, heavy". G. H. *jaḍ*, S. *jaṛu*. Skr. *jaḍa-*. — $ 105.

jaḍṇeṃ "to combine, to set". G. S. Panj. H. B. *jaḍ-jaṛ*. Deśī. *jaḍiaṃ khacitam* (116, 12). Skr. *jaṭ jhaṭ saṃghāte*; cf. Kannada *jaḍi* "to crush, to set", Tamil *śaḍei-* "to nail"; Kannada *jaḍḍa*, Telugu *jaḍḍe* "union", etc. — $ 46, 109, 111.

jaṇ m. f. n. "person, individual". G. *jaṇ*, S. *jaṇū*, Panj. H. B. *jan*, Ro. *jeno*, Siṃ. *dana*. Pkt. *jaṇa-*. Skr. *jana-*. — $ 105, 134.

jar, *jarī*, *jarīṃ* "if". Skr. *yarhi-*. — $ 38, 39, 105, 143, 274.

jar m. "fever". S. *jara* f. "heat of a hearth", H. *jar* "fever". Pkt. *jara-*. Pkt. *jvara-*. — $ 105, 143.

jarḍī, *jaraṃḍī* "old, infirm, woman". Deśī. *jaraṃḍo vrddhaḥ*; *jaraḍo ity anye* (126, 7). Skr. *jara-*, *jaraṭha-* — $ 105.

jav m. "barley". G.S.H. *jav*, *jau*, Ro. *jov*, cf. *Iabadion* name of Java according to Ptolemy. Skr. *yava-*. — $ 105, 129, 152.

javaḷ "near". *javḷūn* "close to". Ara. Per. *jiwār* proximity.- — $ 149.

jamv joṃ "at the moment when", *jauṃ* "until". G. *jav* "when", Panj. *jau* "like", H. *jab* "when", Siṃ. *yav* "until", cf. Ro. *ji* "until" ?. Apa. *jāu jāuṃ* Skr. *yāvat*, To be distinguished from G. Panj. H. *jo* "if", S. *jo* "because", Skr. *yataḥ-*. — $ 105, 206.

jas n. "success". S. *jasu*, G. Panj. H. *jas*, Siṃ. *yasa* "honour, glory". Pkt. *jasa*, Skr. *yaśaḥ*. — $ 105.

jaḷ n. "water", G. *jaḷ*, S. *jaru*, Panj. H. *jal*. Pkt. Skr. *jala-*. — $ 39, 41, 105, 145.

jaḷṇeṃ n. "to burn", *jāḷ* m. "flame", *jāḷṇeṃ* act. "to burn". G. Panj. H. B. *jal-*, S *jar-*, O. *jval-*, K. *zāl-*, Siṃ. *dal-*; and G. *baḷ-*, S. *bar-*, H. Panj. *bal-*. Pkt. *jalai*, *jālā*. Skr. *jvalati*, *jvālā*, *jvālayati*. — $ 105, 145.

jaḷū f. "leech". G. *jaḷo*, S. *jaru* Panj. *jalam* P. *jalogī-*. Skr. *jalaukā-*. — $ 46, 64, 105, 145.

jāī. f. "Jasmine". *jāiphaḷ* n. "nut-mag". G. *jāī* S. *jā*, H. *jāhī*, Siṃ. *dā*; G. *jāyphaḷ*, S. *jāfur*, Panj. *jāfal*. H. *jaephal*, Siṃ. *dāpala*. Pkt. *jāi-*. Skr. jāti — $ 46, 105, 145.

jāū f. "wife of husband's brother". Skr. *yātṛ-*. — $ 46, 105.

jāgṇeṃ "to wake up". G. S. Panj. H. B. *jāg*, Ro. *jang*, K. *zāg-* "to be attentive". Pkt. *jaggai*. Skr. *jāgarti*, part. *jāgrat-*. — $ 105, 230.

jāṃg, *jāṃgh* f. "thigh". G. S. Panj. *jaṃgh*, H.B. *jāṃgh*, Nep. *jāṅ*, Ro. *caṅg* "leg", Siṃ. *daṃga* "calf". Pkt. Skr. *jaṅghā-*. — $ 88, 105.

jāṇṇeṃ "to know", *jāṇau jaṇo jāṇū* "as if". G. S. Panj. O. *jāṇ-*, H. B. *jān-*, K. *zān-*, Ro. *jan-*, Siṃ. *dan-* "to know, to reflect (in this latter sense, comes undoubtedly Skr. *dhyāna-*, P. *jhāna-*); G. Panj. *jāṇe*, S. *jaṇu*, H. *jāno jane*, K. *zan* "as if". Pkt. *jāṇai*; Apa. *jaṇu jaṇi* (*iva*). Skr. *jānāti*. — $ 46, 60, 105, 134, 230.

jāṇeṃ "to go". Ro. G. *ja-*, Panj. H. B. *jā-*, O. *ji-*, Russian Ro. *yā-*, K. *yi-* ? (Grierson, *Piś. Lang*. p. 119), Siṃ. *ya-*. Pkt. *jāi*. Skr. *yāti* . — $ 46, 105, 229, 230, 232, 261.

jānavsā jānivsā m. "stay of one of the betrothed in the other's house", H. *janvās*. "place where the boy is received for a marriage". Skr. *janya-* and *vāsā-*. — $ 52, 74, 105, 135, 172.

jānveṃ, *jānū*, *jānhavī*, *jānhaveṃ*, n. "sacred thread". G. *janoī* f. S. *janyo*, Panj. H. *janeu*. Pkt. *jaṇṇa- ovavia-*. Skr. *yajñopavīta*. — $ 63, 105, 135, 136, 153.

jāp, *jāb* "response, speech". Per. *jawāb*, probably contaminated with the following word. — $ 99.

jāpṇeṃ, *jāṃpṇeṃ* "to say, to speak". Siṃ. *dap-*. Pkt. *jampai*, P. *jappati*. Skr. *jalpati*. — $ 47, 105.

jāṃb, *jāṃbh*, *jāṃbūl*, *jāṃbhūḷ*, m. "rose-apple tree". G.H. B. *jām*, S. Ass. *jāmu*, Siṃ. *daṃba*; S. *jāmūn*, Panj. H. *jāmun*, Siṃ. *diṃbuḷ*. Skr. *jambu-*, *jambula-*. — $ 39, 85, 86, 105.

jābāḍ, *jābhāḍ* '*jāmbhāḍ* n. "cheek". Skr. *jambha* and M. *hāḍ* (Skr. *asthi-*). — $ 89, 105, 128.

jāvaī, *jāṃvāī* m. "son-in-law". G. *jaṃāī*, S. *jāṭo*, Panj. *jamāī javāī*, H. *jaṃvāī*, Ro. *jamutro*, Palestinian Ro. *jatro*. Skr. *jāmātṛ-*. — $ 46, 105.

jāḷ f. "bush". *jāḷī* f. *jāḷeṃ* n. "net". G. *jāḷuṃ* "net", *jāruṃ* "spider-web", S.

jāru Panj. H. *jāl*, K. *zāl*, Siṃ. *dāla*. Skr. *jāla-*. — $ 46, 105, 145.

jiṃkṇeṃ "to vanquish". S. *jīt.-*, K. *zēn-*. Skr. *ji.-* — $ 70.

jiṇeṃ "to live"; n. "life". G. Panj. *jīv* S. *ji-*, H. *jī-*, B. *ji-* K. *zuv-*, Ro. *jiv-*. Pkt. *jiai*, *jīanta-*. Skr. *jīvati*. — $ 44, 63, 105.

jirṇeṃ "to be absorbed, to be digested", G. *jīravvuṃ* "to digest", Panj. *jīrṇā jīurṇā* "to grow old, to absorb, to infiltrate", Siṃ. *diıaṇavā* to grow old, to decompose", Siṃ. *diriṇi* "old woman", K. *zirin* "old man", H. *jīrnī* "oldage, digestion". Pkt. *jīıai*. Skr. *jīryati*. — $ 44, 105.

jireṃ jirīṃ jirūṃ n. "cumin-seed", G. *jīrum*, S. *jīrū*, Panj. *jīrī jīrā*, H. *jīrā.*, Siṃ. *duru*. Skr. *jīraka.-* — $ 105.

jī, particle of respect, consent; used with the names of non-Brahmins. G. Panj. H. *jī*, S. *jīu*, *jī*. Skr. *jīva* "long live!", — $ 105.

jībh. f. "tongue". G. Panj. H. *jībh*, S. *jibha*, Kalacha china *jib*, K. *zèv* (Iranian ? see Grierson, *Piś. Lang.*, p. 78), Ro. *cib jib*. Pkt. *jibbhā* (Jaina) and *jīhā*. Skr. *jihvā-*. — $ 105, 128.

jīv m. "life". G. H. *jīv*, S. Panj. *jīu*, K. *zuv*, cf. Siṃ. *divi* (*jīvita-*). Pkt. *jīva- jīa-*. Skr. *jīva-*. — $ 105.

jīvā f. "bow-string". H. *jīvā*, *jyā*; Siṃ. *diya-*. Skr. *jyā-*. — $ 44.

juī f. "Jasminum auriculatum". G. *jūī*, *juī*, H. *jūhī*. Skr. *yūthikā*. — $ 44, 64, 105.

jujṇeṃ, *jumjṇeṃ*, *jumjhṇeṃ*, *jhujṇeṃ* "combat". G. *jhujhujh-*, Panj. *jūj- jūjh-*, H. *jūjh-*, K. *yod-*, Arm. Ro. *juj* "battle". Pkt. *jujjhai jhujjhai*. Skr. *yudhyate*. — $ 69, 84, 107, 168, 169, 230.

junā adj. "old". G. *junuṃ*, S. *jhuno*, H. *jūn jaun*, Siṃ. *duṇu*. Pkt. *jiṇṇa- juṇṇa-*. Skr. *jīrṇa-* Vedic *jūrṇà-* — $ 44, 105, 135.

juṃpṇeṃ "to yoke together, to join, to arrange". G. *juṃpvuṃ*. Pkt. *juppai*. Skr. root *yup-* (*ekīkarṇe samīkaraṇe*). — $ 105.

juṃvaḷ, *jūḷ* n. "group of twins, pair". Panj. *jūlā* "yoke", Siṃ. *yuvala* "pair". Pkt. *juvala-*. Skr. *yugala* — $ 64, 105.

juvā m. "game of dice". G. *juvuṃ*, S. *juvā*, Panj. H. B. *jūā*, Siṃ. *duva dū*. Pkt. *jūa-*. Skr. *dyūta-*. — $ 44, 55, 105.

juvārī, *juārī* f. "sorghum". G. *juvār*, S. *juāri*, H. *juvārī*. Deśī. *joṇaliā jovārī*, *dhānyam*; *jovārī śabdo'pi deśya eva* (130, 10). — $ 64.

jūṃ, *juṃv* n. "yoke". H. *jū*; Siṃ. *yu* "period of two months". Pkt. *jua-*. Skr. *yuga-*. —$ 64, 105.

jūg n. "age of the world". S. *jugu*, H. *jug*. Skr. *yuga-*. — $ 98, 105.

je "particle of respect, invocation" for example *je rājā*. G. *je*. Skr. imperative. *jaya*. — $ 105.

je f. archaic for *jī* fem. of *jo* "who". — $ 203.

je, *jeṃ* "that" (neut. and conjunction). G. *je*, W. Panj. *je*, S. Panj. *jo*. Nom. Acc. neut. of *jo* "who", cf. Skr.

yat, pronoun and conjunction. — $ 206, 277.

jeṭhvaḍ f. *jeṣṭh*, *jyeṣṭh* m. "month of *Jyaiṣṭha*. G. Panj. H. *jeṭh*, S. *jeṭhu*, K. *zeṭh*. Skr. *jyaiṣṭha*-. — $ 105, 110.

jeṭhā m. "the first and the strongest colour from saffron". *jeṭhī* m. "wrestler". G. H. *jeṭh* "elder", S. *jeṭhu*, Panj. *jeṭh* "husband's elder brother". B. *jeṭh* "father's elder brother". Panj. *jeṭṭhā*, H. *jeṭhā* "elder, superior, excellent." H. *jeṭhī* "champion of wrestling, wrestler", K. *zyuṭh*ᵘ "elder", Siṃ. *deṭu* "the better". Pkt. *jeṭṭha*-. Skr. *jyeṣṭha*-. — $ 105, 110.

jetī, *jetulā* adj. "in asmuch as". G. *jetlo*. S. *jetiro jetaro*, Panj. *jilī jitlā jitnā*, K. *yūl*ᵘ H. *jitnā*, B. *jata*, O. *jete*. Pkt. *jettia*-, remade on *ettia*- (Skr. *iyat*-, see s. v. M. *itukā*). ... $ 206.

jevṇeṃ "to make a meal, to eat". G. *jamvuṃ*. Panj. *jeuṇā*, H. *jeonā jemnā*, B. *jeman* "meal". Skr. root *jim*-, *jemana*-. — $ 152.

jai, *jaiṃ* "if, when". G. S. Panj. *je* "if". Pkt. *jai*. Skr. *yadi*-. — $ 206.

jo relative pron. "who". G. O. *je*, S. Panj. H. *jo*, B. *je jini*, K. *yih*; Siṃ. *yam*-, rel. particle. Pkt. *jo*. Skr. *ya*-. — $ 58, 105, 203.

jogā adj. "suitable, worthy". G. *jog*, S. *jogu*, Panj. *jog joggā*, H. *jog jogā*, K. *yōgy* Pkt. *jogga*-. Skr. *yogya*-. — $ 78, 98, 105.

joḍ m. f. "pair, junction", *joḍṇeṃ juṭṇeṃ* "to join". G, Panj. H. *joḍ*, S. *joṛu*; G. S. Panj. H. *joḍ*-. Pkt. *joḍ*-. Skr. *juṭ*- *juḍ* (*bandhane*)-. — $ 109, 111, 114, 230.

jot n. "yoke". G. Panj. *jotar* "harness", S. *joṭo* "cord", H.B.O. *jot*, Ro. *juto*, Siṃ. *yota*. Skr. *yoktra*-. —$ 29, 78, 105, 121.

joṃdhḷā m. "sorghum". cf. undoubtedly Deśī. *joṇṇaliaṃ jovārī*; *dhānyam* (130, 10). — $ 136.

jopāvṇeṃ "to watch over". The first element is found again in G. *jovuṃ*, Panj. *johṇā*, H. *jovnā johnā* "to look". Deśī. *joaṇaṃ locanam* (130, 9), Apa. *joedi* "to see". Skr. *dyotana*-. — $ 105.

jov f. "lightning", *jauḷ* n. "storm". Deśī. *joī vidyut* (130, 3). Skr. *dyota*-, *jyotis*-. — $ 55, 56, 105.

jośī, see M. *joisī* m. "astronomer, astrologer"; *joskī* f. *jospaṇā* m. "profession of astrologer". G. *jośī dosī*, S. *josī*, Panj. *josī*, *joṣī*, H. *joṣī*, K. *zichi*. Skr. *jyotiṣika*-. — $ 38, 50, 78, 105, 156.

jauṃ "until". See *jaṃv*.

jhaṭakṇeṃ "to shake", *jhaṭkā* m. "sudden blow". G.S.H. *jhaṭak*-, Panj. *jhaṭak jhaṛāk*. cf. Skr. *ujjhaṭita* "lost".- — $ 107.

jhaṭpaṭ "speed". G. *jhaṭāpaṭ* "haste"; S. *jhaṭpaṭi*, H. *jhaṭpaṭ* "quick". Cf. *jhaḍṇeṃ*, *jhaḍap*.

jhaḍ f. "continous rain". G. S. Panj. H. *jhaḍī*, B. *jhaḍ* "tempest". Deśī. *jhaḍī nirantaravṛṣṭiḥ* (131, 11), and *jhāḍajhaḍīsu vaḍappam* (VII, 84) and the comm. *vaḍappaṃ latāgahanaṃ nirantaravṛṣṭiśca* (268, 1).

Kannada *jaḍi jidi*, Telugu *jhaḍi* "rain, trouble; (adj.) continuous."—$ 107.

jhaḍṇeṃ "to whither". Pkt. *jhaḍai*. Skr. *śad-* ?. — $ 46.

jhaḍṇeṃ "to be active" *jhaḍap* f. "bond", *jhaḍpaḍ* f. "violent agitation". G. *jhaḍap* "jump, rapidity", S. *jhaṛap* "blow" H. *jhaḍap* "heat" Deśī. *jaaḍai tvarate* (128, 3); Apa. *jhaḍappaḍahiṃ* (*vegaiḥ*) — $ 107.

jhaṇi, jhaṇeṃ "by chance, even if". See *jāṇū*. — $ 84.

jhapjhap "suddenly, quick", G. Panj. H.B. *jhapjhap*, Panj. *jhapp* "alive", H. *jhap jhapaṭ* "jump, elan", G. *jhaṃplāvavuṃ* "to rush". Skr. *jhampa-*. "jump" (cf. *kṣap-* ?). — $ 107.

jharṇeṃ "to flow, to drip". G.S. H. B. *jhar-*. Pkt. *jharai*. Skr. *kṣarati*. — $ 75, 107.

jhavṇeṃ jhaṃvṇeṃ "to gush out, to spurt out". Panj. *jahiṇā*; S. *jahāṇī* "price of prostitution", *jāhū* "debauched". Skr. *yabhati*. — $ 46, 107, 168, 232, 283.

jhaḷ. f. "Sun-stroke"; *jhalak* f. "lightning", *jhaḷakṇeṃ* "to shine". G.S. Panj. H. *jhalak-*. Deśī. *jhaḷā mṛgatṛṣṇā* (131, 11); Apa. *jhalakkia-* (*dagdha-*). Skr. *jval-* ?. — $ 107.

jhāṃkaṇ n. "cover". See *ḍhāṃkaṇ*.

jhāṃkar n. "thick bush". G. *jhāṃkharuṃ* H. *jhāṃkar*, Panj. *jhaṃgaṛ*. Deśī *jhaṅkharo śuṣkataruḥ* (131, 17). — $ 107, 169.

jhāṃj, jhāṃjrī f. "cymbals, castanets". G. H. *jāṃjh jhāṃj*, G. *jhāṃjrī*, S. *jhaṃjhu*. Panj. *jhāṃj* "sound of a musical instrument". Skr. *jamjhā* "sound of high wind", *jharjharī* 'a drum or a flute". — $ 69, 169.

jhāṃṭ m. "the hair of the pubis," f. "hanging mat". G. *jhamṭuṃ*, S. *jhāṃṭa*, Panj. *jhāmṭh jhāmṭ*, H. *jhāṃṭ*. Deśī. *jhaṃṭī laghūrdhvakeśāḥ* (131, 11). — $ 107.

jhāḍ n. "tree, bush". G. *jhāḍ*, S. *jhāṛu*, "tree"; Panj. H.B. *jhāṛ* "bush". Skr. of lexicon. *jhāṭa-* Cf. *jāḍ-*. — $ 84.

jhālar f. "fringe", G. S. Panj. H. B. *jhālar*, Skr. of lexicon *jhallarī*. — $ 47, 148.

jhālā, old M. *jālā* pcpl. "been". Skr. *jāta-*. — $ 84, 161, 202 229, 261.

jhijṇeṃ "to wear out, to become weak". S. *jhijṇu*. Apa. *jhijj-*. Skr. *kṣīyate*. — $ 107.

jhiṇā adj. "worn out". G. *jhīṇuṃ* "skin, small"; S. *jhīṇo*, Panj. *jhiṇī*, H. *jhīnā* "weak". Pkt. *jhīṇa-*. Skr. *kṣīṇa-*. — $ 107.

jhujṇeṃ, jhujhṇeṃ, jhuṃjṇeṃ "to combat". Panj. *jhūjṇā, jhūjhṇā*. Old M. *jujṇeṃ*.

jhūṭ. f. "lie". G. *juṭhuṃ*, Panj. *jhūṭh*, H. *jhūṭ*. Deśī. *jhuṭṭhaṃ alīkam* (133, 13). — $ 107.

jheṃ particle of emphasis, used as *jo* see *jeṃ, jo*. — $ 84.

jheṃḍā m. "flag, banner". S. *jhaṃdo*, Panj. H. *jhaṃḍā*. Pkt. *jhaa-*. Skr. *dhvaja-* m. — $ 68, 107, 130.

jheṃḍūṃ parkia biglandulosa (the birds look like balls of red velvet, clot of blood vomitted upon the bite of certain serpents)" Deśī. *jheṇḍuo kandukaḥ* (134, 4). — $ 107.

jhoṃṭ f. "loose tress". G. *jhuḍo* "tress of false hair", S. *jhuṭu* "lock of hair (on the top of the head".Deśī. *jhuṃṭaṇaṃ pravāhaḥ* (133, 14). — $ 107.

jhoḍṇeṃ "to crush". Panj. *jhauṛ* "attack", H. *jhauṛnā*. cf. Deśī. *jhoḍio vyādhaḥ* (134, 10)? Skr. *kṣud-*. — $ 107.

jhoṃpḍī f. "hut". H. *jhompṛā*. Apa. *jhuṃpaḍā* (*kuṭīraka-*). — $ 107.

jhoṃpṇeṃ "to sleep". rare; besides are found representatives of Skr. *svap-*. G. *suvuṃ*, S. *sumahṇu* (part. *suto*); Panj. *sauṇā*, H. *sonā*, B. *sau*, K. *śông-*, Ro. *sov-*, Siṃ. *hov-*. Kannaḍa *jompu jōmu* "drunkenness, stupour." *jômpa* "asleep" — $ 84.

jhoḷī f. "bag of a mendicant". Panj. *jholī*. Deśī. *jholiāi jhalajhaḷiā* (III, 56); Comm: *jholikā śabdo yadi saṃskṛte na rūḍhas tadāyam api deśyaḥ* (133, 1); cf. *jhāulaṃ karpāsaphalam* (133, 8). Skr. *jhavlika-*. — $ 107, 145.

ṭaṃk m. "chisel of a sculptor", "*ṭāṃk* m." the nib of a pen, a metal plate with an image of God impressed, silver rupee, *ṭāṃkā* m. "sewing", *ṭāṃkī* f. *ṭāṃkeṃ* n. "cistern". G. *ṭako ṭaṃk* "rupee, silver", *ṭāmkṇuṃ* "chisel", *ṭāṃkvuṃ* "to sew", *ṭāṃkī* "cisterne" S. *ṭāṃkū* "sewing"; Panj. *ṭāṃkṇā* "to sew"; H. *ṭāṃkā* "needle, cisterne", *ṭāṃkī* "chisel", *ṭāṃkṇā* "to sew"; B. *ṭaṃko* "showel, knives, chisel, lag, coin", *ṭāṃkite*" "to sew". Deśī. *ṭaṃko khaḍgaś chinnaṃ khātam jaṅghā khanitraṃ bhittis taṭaṃ ceti saptārthaḥ* (137, 12). — $ 119.

ṭaḷṇeṃ "to pass, to flow, to miss". G. *ṭaḷ-*, S. *ṭir-*, Panj. H. B. O. *ṭal-*. — $ 119.

ṭār m. "bad horse". Deśī. *ṭāro adhamaturaṅgaḥ* (136, 11). Vedic Skr. *tắru-*, "rapid, speed" ? — $ 119.

ṭāḷī f. "hand-clapping". G. *ṭaḷī*, S. *ṭāṛa*, Panj. *tālī*. Skr. *tālikā* f. — $ 119, 145.

ṭāḷū f. "roof of mouth". G. *tālu*, *tāḷvuṃ*, S. *tārūṃ*, Panj. H. *tālū*, K. *tāl*. Skr. *tālu-* n. m. — $ 119, 145.

ṭāḷeṃ n. "face, shoe-sole". G. *taḷiyuṃ*, Panj. *ṭalā*, H. *tālā*. Skr. *tala-* n. — $ 119, 145.

ṭikṇeṃ "to live, to stay, to endure'„ G. *ṭak-*, S. Panj. H. B. *ṭik-*. — $ 119.

ṭikā, *tikkā* m. "circular mark put on the fore-head", G. *ṭīko tikko*, S. *ṭiko*, Panj. *ṭikkā*, H. *ṭīkā*, B. O. *ṭikā*. Deśī. *ṭippī tathā ṭikkaṃ tilakam* (136, 16). — $ 119·

ṭirṭir f. "sudden flash" adv. "in a flash". cf. Pkt. *ṭiriṭillai bhrāmyati* cited in the comm. of the *Deśīṇāmamālā*, 137, 1. — $ 119.

ṭilā m. "coloured mark on the fore-head indicating the sect". G. *ṭilo*, Panj. til. Skr. *tilaka-* m. — $ 119, 145.

ṭip n. "drop, tear", G. *ṭīpuṃ*, S. *ṭipo*, Panj. *ṭipp*. H. *ṭīpnā* 'to cause to drip", *ṭapkā* "continuous dripping". Skr. root *tip* "to drop". — $ 119.

ṭekaḍ, *ṭekāḍ* n. "height, hill'. G. *ṭekrī*, H. *ṭekar*, Panj. H. *ṭekrā*. — $ 119.

ṭoḷ m. "locust". Deśī. *ṭolo*

śalabhaḥ (137, 7). — $ 119.

ṭhak, ṭhag m. "pick-pocket". G. H. *ṭhag*, Panj. *ṭhag, ṭhagg*; K. *ṭhag* "to pick the pocket". Pkt. *thag-*. Skr. *sthag* "to hide" — $ 110.

ṭhākṇeṃ "to hold on". Apa. *thakkei* (*tiṣṭhati*). — $ 94, 110.

ṭhāḍā adj. "straight". Panj. *ṭhāḍhā*, H. B. *ṭhāḍ*, Siṃ. *taḍa* "hard", K. *thoḍ*ᵘ "high". Pkt. *ṭhaḍḍha-*, P. *thaddha-*. Skr. *stabdha-*. — $ 47, 110, 169.

ṭhāṇ n. "stable, place". *ṭhāṇeṃ* n. "post". G. *thāṇ thāṇuṃ*, S. *ṭhāṇu*, Panj. *thān thānā ṭhāṇā*, H· *ṭhān*, B. *thānā*, Siṃ. *tan ṭāna*, Ro. *than*. Pkt. *ṭhāṇa-*, *thāṇa.-*. Skr. *sthāna-* n. — $ 110.

ṭhāy m "place". Panj. *thahi*, H. *thāī*. Deśī. *ṭhaio utkṣiptaḥ*; *ṭhaio avakāśa ity anye* (137, 17). Skr. *sthā-*. — $ 110.

ṭhār adv. "entirely, suddenly"; *ṭharṇeṃ* "to be fixed, to continue". G. *ṭhār*, S. *ṭharṭhap* "at the moment", Panj. *ṭhar* "cold, frozen". Cf. Deśī. *ṭhariaṃ*...... *ūrdhvasthitaṃ* (238, 6)? Skr. *sthāvara-*. — $ 110.

ṭhāv m. "bottom, place". H. *ṭhāv* m. f. "place". Apa. *ṭhāu*. Skr. *sthāman-* n.? cf. under M. *thā-*. — $ 110, 152.

ṭhī f. "woman". K. *tsiy* (cf. Grierson, *Piś. Lang.*, p. 79), H. *tiriyā*, B. *tiri*. Skr. *strī* f. — $ 110, 174.

ṭhuṃṭhaṇ 'trunk, amputed member". G. *ṭhuṃṭhuṃ* "trunk, one armed person to break off a piece", S. *ṭhuṭhu*", "leaf-less, dry" Panj. *ṭhoṭh* "stupid", H. *ṭhūṃṭh* "trunk" leafless branch, amputed arm". Deśī, *ṭuṃṭo chinnakaraḥ* (137, 2. cf. Skr. *prastumpati* (*gauḥ*).see. *gaṇapāṭha* 140). — $ 110.

ṭhulī, thulī f. "coarse flour". S. *thulhāī*, Panj. *ṭholh* "bulk, corpulence", Ro. *thulo* "big, coarse", Arm. Ro. *thulav* "curdled milk", Siṃ. *tul* "big". Pkt. *thulla-*. Skr. *sthūla-*. — $ 110, 122.

ṭheṇeṃ "to stand erect", *ṭhepṇeṃ* "to lean against", *ṭhevṛeṃ* 'to put, to keep". Panj. *the* "place", *thenī* "deposit", *thevā* "set stone", *thī the* imp. of verb "to be", H. *thā* adj. "been", Maith. *thik-* "to be", K. *thav- thāv-* "to hold", Arm. Ro. *thenav* "place". Pkt. *uṭ- ṭhei*, *ṭhia-* beside *ṭhāi*. Skr. *sthita-*. *sthā-* (*tiṣṭhati*). — $ 45, 77, 110, 230.

ṭhomb m. stake". G. *ṭhomb*, *thāmlo*, S. *thambhu*, Panj. *thamm*, H. *thaṃb*, Siṃ. *ṭāmba*. Pkt. *ṭhambha-*. Skr. *stambha-* m. — $ 79, 110.

ḍaṃkh f. "bite" *ḍaṃkhṇeṃ* "to bite, to prick" G. *ḍaṃkh*, S. *ḍaṃgu*, *ḍaṃgaṇu*, Panj. *ḍaṃg*, *ḍaṃk*, *ḍaṃggṇā*, H. *ḍaṃk*, O. *ḍaṃkibā* Pkt. part. *ḍakka-*, cf. Pkt. Deśī; *ḍhaṃkuṇa-*, *ḍheṃkuṇa-* "bug". Skr. *daṃś-*. —$ 119.

ḍabbā m. "a little box". Panj. H. *ḍabbā*, Bih. *ḍābā*, *dābā*. Skr. *darvī* f. — $ 119, 127, 152. Cf. M. *ḍav*.

ḍaṃbh, daṃbh., m. "hypocrisy"; *ḍaṃbhī*, *daṃbhī* adj. "hypocrite". K. *ḍāmb, dambī*. Deśī. *ḍaṃbhio dyūtakaraḥ* (139, 4). Skr.*dambha-*,*dambhin-*.—$119.

ḍar m. "fear", *ḍarṇeṃ* "to be afraid of", G. Panj. H.B.K. *ḍar*, S. *ḍaru*, Ro. *ḍar* "fear"; G.S. Panj. H.B. *ḍar-* "to be afraid of". Pkt. *ḍara- ḍarai*, P. *ḍaro*. Skr. *dīryate*, *ḍarati*. — $ 119.

ḍav m. "hollowed cocoanut used as vessel". H. *ḍavā ḍovā* "laddle", Siṃ. *dāvi*. Skr. *darvī* f. — $ 119, 127, 152. Cf. M. *ḍoī* and *ḍabbā*

ḍasṇeṃ "to bite", *ḍāṃs* m. "mosquito, bite". G. *ḍaṃs*, Panj. *ḍas* "bite", H. *ḍasnā* 'to bite". Pkt. *ḍasai*. Skr. *daṃśa-*. — $ 120, 253.

ḍākhiṇ f. "south-wind". S. *ḍākhiṇo*, Panj. *dāhnā*, H. *dāhinā*, B. *ḍāin*, O. *ḍāhan*, K. *dachyun*ᵘ, "right"; K. *dakhin* "south", Siṃ. *dakuṇa* "straight, meridional". Pkt. *dakkhiṇa-*, *dāhiṇa-*. Skr. *dakṣiṇa-*. — $ 47, 52, 96, 119.

ḍāṃg m. n. "wild and mountainous region around Nāsik"; *ḍāṃgī*, *ḍāṃgyā* m. ' customs officer". H. *dāṃg* "summit", B. *ḍāṃg* "dry earth, high land", G. *ḍāgḷī* "head, brain", K. *ḍeng*ᵘ "observation post in a field", *drag* "eminence", *drang* "custom-post". Deśī. *ḍaggalo bhavanopari bhūmitalam* (169, 3). Skr. *draṅga-*. "military and custom posts in mountain passes". Cf. M. *ḍoṃgar*.

ḍāgṇeṃ "to burn" G.H. *ḍāgh* "funeral procession", S. *ḍāghu* "funeral pyre", K. *dāg* "burn"; S. *ḍāgṇu*, Panj. *ḍāgṇā*, H. *ḍāghnā* "to set on fire". Pkt. *dāgha-*. Cf. Skr. *dagdha-*. — $ 49.

ḍājṇeṃ "to be hct". G. *ḍājhvuṃ* "to be burnt", S. *ḍajhṇu* "to be burnt with envy", *ḍājho* "burning desire", Panj. *dājh* "thirst in fever", K. *dazun* "to burn". Pkt. *dajjhai*. Skr. *dahyate-*. — $ 47, 49, 89, 230.

ḍāl f. n. "sort of basket". G. *ḍāluṃ*, S. *ḍālī*, Panj. *ḍall*, H. *ḍāl*, *ḍallā*, B *ḍālā ḍālī*. Deśī. *ḍallaṃ piṭikā* (138, 16). — $ 119.

ḍāvā adj. "left". G. *ḍābuṃ ḍābhuṃ*, S. *ḍāiu*. H. (dial.) *ḍāvā*; where this word is used, the word for "right" does not go back to Skr. *dakṣina-*. Deśī *ḍavvo tathā ḍāvo vāmakaraḥ* (138, 9). — $ 47.

ḍāh, *ḍāho* m. "burn". G. Panj. K. *ḍāh* 'burn", S. *ḍāh* affliction", H. *ḍāh* "rage". Pkt. *ḍāha-*. Skr. *dāha*. m. — $ 119.

ḍāhaḷ m. "tree—loppings", *ḍāhḷā* "plant, branch with leaves". G. *ḍāḷ*, S. *ḍāru*, Panj. H. B. *ḍāl* "branch"; Deśī. *ḍālī śākhā* (139, 10). Skr. *dala-*n? — $ 161.

ḍāḷ m. "pile", G. *ḍalo*, Panj. *ḍalā ḍalā*, H. *ḍāllā*. Deśī. *ḍalo loṣṭaḥ* (138, 16). — $ 119.

ḍiṃb m. "son". H. *ḍimb* "newborn", B. *ḍimb* "egg, small animal". Pkt. Skr. *ḍimbha-* m. — $ 119.

ḍulṇeṃ "to balance, to roll". G. H. *ḍol*, S *ḍol- ḍoṛ-*, K. *dul-*. Skr. *dolayati*. — $ 119.

ḍoī, *ḍoy*, *ḍokī* f. "head". G. *ḍok* f. "neck", *ḍokuṃ* n. "head", *ḍoī* "laddle", *ḍoko* 'penis, nothing at all"; S. Panj. *ḍoī* "laddle"; H. *ḍoī* "laddle, oar, head", *ḍovā ḍavā ḍohrā* "laddle", Maith. *ḍoī*, Ro. *roy* "spoon"; K. *ḍêka* "fore-head". Deśī. *ḍoo dāruhastaḥ* (140, 9). — $ 64, 94, 119. Cf. M. *ḍav*.

ḍoṃgar m. "mountain". G. *ḍuṃgar*, S. *ḍoṃgaru*, H. *ḍoṃgar*. Deśī. *ḍuṃgaro śailaḥ* (140, 8). —119. Related to M. *ḍāṃg*?

ḍoṇ, *ḍoṇi* f. "boat, ship". H. *ḍoṇī*, Siṃ. *deṇa*. Pkt. P. *doṇi-*. Skr. *droṇī* f. "vat". — $ 119, 123.

ḍoṃb m. (name of caste) undertaker's mute". G. *ḍumu*, Panj. *ḍomṛā* "roaming musician (caste"), H. B. *ḍom* "under taker's mute, basket-worker", K. *ḍūmb* "night-watchman"; Ro. *rom*, Arm. Ro. *lom*, Palestenian Ro. *dom* "gypsie, man". Deśī. *ḍumbo śvapacaḥ* (140, 8). — $ 119.

ḍohḷa, *ḍohāḷā* m. "desire of pregnant woman", Siṃ. *doḷa*. Pkt. *dohaḷa*. Skr. *dohada-* m. — $ 79, 118.

ḍoḷā m. "eye". G. *ḍaḷo*. Skr. *dola-* m. "agitation". — $ 78, 119, 145.

ḍoḷī f. "swinging litter, *dooly*". S. Panj. H. *ḍolī*, K. *ḍuli*. Deśī. *ḍolā śibikā*; *andolanavācakas tu dolāśabdabhavaḥ* (140, 9). Skr. *dolā* f. —$ 119.

ḍhakā, *dhakā* m. "shock, blow". G. *ḍhak- dhak-*, S. *dhiko*, Panj. *dhakkā* K. *daka*, H. *ḍhakkā dhakkā*, B. *ḍhak*, O. *dhakā-*. — $ 94, 119.

ḍhāṃkṇeṃ, *jhāṃkṇeṃ*, "to cover", *dhāṃkaṇ*, *jhāṃkaṇ* n. "to lid"; G. *dhāṃkvuṃ*, S. *ḍhakṇū*, Panj *dhakṇā*, H. *ḍhaknā ḍhāmknā*, B. *ḍhakite* "to cover". Pkt. *ḍhakkai*: Deśī. *ḍhaṃkaṇī pidhānikā* (141, 12). —$ 94, 119.

ḍhāmḍhulṇeṃ ḍhumḍhālṇeṃ "to search carefully". G.H. *ḍhuṃḍh-*, S. *ḍhūṃḍh-*, Panj. *ḍhumdh- ḍhumḍ-*. Deśī. *ḍhaṃḍhallai bhramati ḍhaṃḍholai gagaveṣayati* (142, 2). — $ 119.

ḍhālā m. "branch". see *ḍāhḷā*.

ḍhilā adj. "loose, slack". G. *dhīluṃ*, S. *ḍhilo ḍhiro*, Panj. *ḍhillā*, H. *ḍhīlā*, B.O. *ḍhil*, Siṃ. *ihil lihil līl*; K. *ḍīl ḍal* "softness". Pkt. *ḍhilla-*; cf. Deśī *ḍhello nirdhanaḥ* (142, 11). — $ 119.

ḍhusṇeṃ "to rush in head down". Panj. *dhūsṇā*, H. *dhasnā* S. *dhūsu* "violent hurry". Pkt, *ḍhusai* (*bhramati*). —$ 119.

ḍheṃk f. "bellowing". G. *dhikṇu* "to bellow". Deśī. *ḍhikkai vṛṣabho garjati* (142, 7). — $ 119.

ḍhekā m. the curved piece of wood which passes over the head of the *lāṭ* (roller of oil mill) *ḍhekī* f. an apparatus with a lever for pounding lime, rice etc."; Deśī. *ḍheṃkā harṣaḥ kūpatulāceti dvyarthā* (143, 3). — $ 119.

ḍhekūṇ, *ḍheṃkūṇ* m. "bug". Desī. *ḍhaṃkuṇo tathā ḍheṃkuṇo matkuṇaḥ* (141, 12). —$ 77, 119.

ḍher f. "pile". Panj *ḍher*, K. *der*, "pile". Deśī. *daharī aliñjaram* (138, 16). — $ 112.

-ṇer. . in the names of the Deccan towns (*Amalnner*, *Amner*, *Atner*, *Badnera*, *Dhanera*, *Jamner*, *Koner*, *Parner*, *Pimpalner*, *Sangamner*, *Saoner*, *Shivner*) and of Rajasthan (*Bahaner*, *Bikaner*, *Bhatnair*, *Buner*, *Raner*, *Sanganer*, *Sankhnera*, *Susner*); the exceptions in Maratha country are very rare: *Sinnār* near

Nasik; *Junnar* seems to be a recent form : Thus as Mr. F. W. Thomas has kindly indicated to me, *Juner* is found 14 times in the *Storia do Mogor* of N. Manucci (W. Irvin, Transl., index), similarly *Janneere* for the year 1621 in *The English Factories in India* (Ed. W. Forster, Oxford, 1906, p. 315) and *Juneere* in the portion of same collection concerning the year 1636 (p. 281). Similarly several *Ner*, *Neri*, *Nereṃ* are found in Maratha country. In Gujarat, a form like *Champaner* is less usual : cf. *Girnar*, *Nar Nara* : in Bengal *Mohnar* and *Mohner*, *Dinara* (beside *Dinanagar*, *Dinapur*). Cf. still in Rajasthan *Bijnaur*, *Bijnor*. Siṃ. *nuvaru* "town'. Pkt. *ṇaarā*. Skr. *nagara*. -n. — $ 62.

taṭtaṭ adv. "sound of cracking, (sparks crust etc.)," *taṭtaḍṇeṃ* "to be cracking, to spit, to be ready to crack." G. *taḍtaḍ*, Panj *taṛtrāṭ*, H. *taṛnā* "cracking", G. *taḍakvuṃ*, Panj. *taṛtaṛavṇā*, H. *taṛaknā* "to crack", K. *traṭ* "sound of thunder". Skr. *traṭat* adv. —One should certainly separate Panj. *taṛnā* "to be drawn, tense, tight", Ro. *trd* "to draw", cf. Pkt. *taḍ* for Skr. *tan-*. — $ 146, 163.

taṃṭā m. "dispute". G. *ṭaṃṭo*, *taṃṭo*, S. *ṭaṃṭu*, Panj. *ṭaṃṭā*, H. *ṭaṃṭā taṃṭā*. cf. Desi. *taṃṭaṃ pṛṣṭaṃ* (157, 4) ? — $ 119.

taḍ f. "edge, bank". G. Panj. H. *taṭ* m. Beng. *taṛ*. Pkt. *taḍa-*. Skr. *taṭa-*, *taṭī-*. — $ 121.

taḍphaḍ f. "shake tussle", *taḍaphaḍṇeṃ* "to shake violently". S. *taṛphaṇu*, B. *taṛpāite*, G. Panj H. *taṛphaṛ-*. Apa. *taḍapphaḍai* (*uttāmyati*, *ākulībhavati*, *capalāyate*). — $ 146.

taṇ n. "grass". G. *taṇkhaḷuṃ* "straw", Panj *tiṇ*, H. *tinkā*, Siṃ *taṇa*. Pkt. *taṇa-*, *tiṇa-*. Skr. *tṛṇa-* n. —$ 30, 31, 121, 134.

taṇārā m. "stack of straw of rice etc. ". Skr. *tṛṇa-* + *ākara* m. — $ 52, 61.

taṃt, *tāṃt* f. *taṃtū* m. "thread, fiber, cord of musical instrument". G. *taṃt taṃtu*, S. *taṃdu*, Panj. *taṃd*, H. *taṃt tāṃt taṃtu*, Siṃ. *tata tatu*. cf. Deśī. *taṇtukkhoḍī vāyakatantropakaraṇam* (159, 9). Skr. *tantu.-* m — $ 39, 68, 121.

tattā adj. "low, infamous", *tattāmāl* m. "the best part, cream, quintessence". Panj. *tatt*, H. *tat* "element, essence." Apa. *tattu-*. Skr. *tattva-*. n. — $ 121, 129.

tan f. n. *tanu* f. "body". G. *tan*, Panj. *taṇ*, G.S.H.B. *tanu*, Siṃ. *tunu*. Pkt. *taṇu-*. Skr. *taṇu-*. f. — $ 39, 121.

tar, *tarhīṃ*, *tarīṃ* "then". Skr. *tarhi*. — $ 38, 39, 70, 121, 143.

tarṇeṃ "to float, to swim, to pass". G.S. Panj. K.H. Panj. *tar-*. Pkt. Skr. *tar-*. — $ 46, 121, 252.

tarṇā adj. "young". G. *taruṇ*, Panj. *tarn*, H. *tarun*, Ro. *terno*, Siṃ. *turuṇu-*. Pkt. Skr. *taruṇa-*. — $ 46, 50, 121, 134.

tarvaḍ, *taroḍ* "cassia auriculata". H. *tarvar*, Deśī. *tara-*

vaṭṭo prapunāṭaḥ, taḍavaḍā āulivṛkṣaḥ (158, 11). — $ 46.

taras, taraṃs m. n. "hyena." G. *taras,* W. Panj. *tarkh,* Siṃ. *tarasa.* Pkt. *taraccha-.* Skr. *tarakṣa-* m. — $ 46, 69, 104, 121.

tarasgāṃḍyā m. "chicken-hearted", *tarās* m. "annoyance, vexation". S. *tarsu,* H. *taras,* Panj. *tarāh, tarās,* Siṃ. *tāti* "fear", W. Panj. *tars* "pity"; Ro. *traš* "to fear". Apa-; causative *tarāsai,* Pkt. *tasai.* Skr. *tras-.* — $ 162.

taraḷṇeṃ, tarāḷṇeṃ "to be a vagabond". Pkt. *tarala-.* Skr. *tarala-.* — $ 121, 145.

taṃv "till then". S. *toṃ* "since", *toṃyāṃ* "until"; K. *tām tāñ* "till; in some way"; G. *tāv,* H. *tauṃ toṃ* "thus, then". Apa. *tāṃva, tāuṃ.* Skr. *tāvat-.* — $ 121, 198.

tav, taṃv, tavā f. "dizziness".H. *taṃvālā;* Ro. *tam* "blind". Pkt. *tamo, tamaṃ.* Skr. *tamas-, tāmyati.* — $ 121, 152.

tavā m. "iron plate for baking *chapatis*". G. *tavo,* Panj. H. *tavā,* K. *tāo;* cf. Siṃ. *tava* "asceticism". Pkt. *tavao;* cf. Deśī. *tamo ṣokaḥ* (157, 6), *tamaṇaṃ cullī* (157, 11). Skr. *tāpake-* m. — $ 46, 121, 137.

tahān, tānh f. "thirst", Siṃ. *taṇa,* Panj. *tāṃgh* "desire". Pkt. *taṇhā.* Skr. *tṛṣṇā*—besides are found either tatsamas as K. *trèśnā* or representatives of Skr. *tṛṣā* : S. *ṭih,* Panj. *tihā,* H. *tis,* K. *trĕś,* Ro. *truś* or of Skr. *tarṣa*—: G. *taras,* S. *tiras,* H. *tirkhā-* — $ 30, 31, 52, 121, 136.

taḷ m. "bottom, soil". G. S. *taḷ,* S. *taru,* Panj. H.B. *tal,* Siṃ. *tala;* K. *tal, tal*[1], Ro. *tele* "below, in", Skr. *tala-* n. — $ 121.

taḷṇeṃ "to fry", G. *taḷvum,* S. *taṛṇu,* Panj. *talṇā,* H. *talnā.* cf. Deśi. *talimo..bhrāṣṭraḥ* (164, 11). — $ 46.

taḷapṇeṃ "to shine; to be branded". Panj. *tappṇā tarappṇā,* H. *taṛapnā* "to leap". cf. M. *tāḍṇem.* — $ 146.

talāv m. *taḷeṃ* n. "pond". G. *taḷāv,* S. Panj. *talāu,* H. *talāo talāb tarāv,* Siṃ. *taḷā.* Pkt. *talāa-.* Skr. *taḍāga-* n. — $ 46, 55, 121, 146.

tāk n. "butter-milk". G. *tāk,* Siṃ. *tāk.* Pkt. *takka-.* Skr. *takra-* n. — $ 93, 121.

tāṭ, tāṭī, f. "hedge". G. *tāṭī,* S. *ṭaṭī,* Panj. *ṭaṭṭī,* H. *taṭṭā ṭaṭṭā ṭāṭī.* Deśi. *taṭṭi vṛtiḥ* (157, 5). — $ 48, 119.

tāṭh adj. "stiff". S. *ṭāṭu,* H.B. *ṭāṭ;* Skr. *tṛṣṭa-.* — $ 30, 110, 119.

tāḍ, tāl m. "palm tree". G. Panj. H.B. *tāṛ,* S. *tāṛī.* O. *tāḷ,* H.B. *tāl.* Siṃ. *tal.* Skr. *tāla* —m. — $ 121.

tāḍṇem "to strike, to punish". G. *tāḍ-,* Panj. H.B. *tāṛ-,* Siṃ. *taḷ-.* Pkt. Skr. *tāḍ-.* — $ 76, 111, 121, 146.

tāṇ "tension", *tāṇṇeṃ* "to strech", G. *tān tāṇvuṃ,* S. *tāṇṇu ṭāṇṇu,* Panj. *tāṇ tāṇṇā,* H. *tān ṭan tānnā,* O. *ṭanibā.* Pkt. *tāṇa-.* Skr. *tāna-.* m. — $ 121, 134.

tāṃt f. "thread". See *taṃt. tātāvṇeṃ* "to be tired, impatient". Siṃ. *täta* "fatigue"; S. *tati* "heat"; G. *tātuṃ,* Panj. *tattā,* H. *tāt,* B. *tātā.* K. *tòt,* Ro. *tato* "hot". Pkt. *tatta-.*

Skr. *tapta*-. — $ 47, 121.

tāp m. "fever", *tāpṇeṃ* "to warm oneself, to shine", *tapṇeṃ* "to shine, to get irritated". G. Panj. H.B. *tāp*, S. *tapu* f., K. *tap* "fever", *tāp* "heat of Sun", Ro. *thab* (*tab*) "hot"; G. *tap*- "to burn", *tāp*- "to warm oneself", S. *tap*-, Panj. *tāp*-*ṭāp*-, W. Panj. *tap*-, H. *tap*, B. *tāp*-. Skr. *tāpa*- m. , *tapyate*. — $ 47, 48, 121, 230.

tāpā m. "float". G. *tāpo tāphā*, H. *ṭāpā*; cf. Panj. *ṭāppū* "island", Middle Indian pl. tr'appaga Periplus. — $ 121, 125.

tāṃb f. "rust", *tāṃbeṃ* n. "copper", G. *taṃbuṃ*, S *ṭāmo*,. Panj *tāmbā tāmrā*, K. *trām*, H. *tām tāmbā*, B. *tāmā*, Siṃ. *tamba*, "copper". Pkt. *tamba*-. Skr. *tāṃra*- n. — $ 121, 127.

tārā m. "star". G. *tāro*, S. *tāru*, Panj. H.B. *tārā*, K. *tāruk*, Siṃ. *taru turu*. Pkt. Skr. *tārā* f. — $ 121, 143.

tāl m. "pool (of liquid)". Panj H. *tāl* "pond". Deśī. *tallaṃ palvalam* (164, 7). Skr. *talla*- (*grāmya* word according to Vāmana, see Regnaud, *Rhét. Sanskrit.*, p. 141). The relation of *talla*- with *taḍāga*- is inverse of that between M. *tāḍ* and Skr. *tāla*-; old M. *talā*, *tāḍ*

tāv m. "act of heating metals to red". *tāvṇeṃ* "to heat, to beat". G.H. *tāv* S. *tāu*; Panj. *tā*, *tāu*; G. *tāvuṃ*, S. *tāiṇu*, Panj. *tāuṇā*, H. *tāvnā*, B. *tāvāite*, K. *tāvum tovarun*, Ro. *thav*- (*tav*-) "copper", Pkt. *tāva*-. Skr. *tāpa*-, *tāpayati*-. — $ 46, 121, 152, 230.

tā ṇeṃ "to chip, to cut with adz". G. *tāchvuṃ*, S. *tachaṇu*, Panj. *tacchṇā*, W. Panj. *tachaṇr*, K. *tachun*. Pkt. *tacchai*. Skr. *takśṇoti*. — $ 47, 104, 121.

tāḷīs (in compound) "forty". G. S. Panj. H. B. *tālis*, K. -*tōjih*. Pkt. *cattālisaṃ*. Skr. *catvāriṃśat*-. — $ 223.

tāḷū f. "palate", S. *tārūṃ*, Panj. H. B. *tālū*- Skr. *tālu*-. n. — $ 46, 121, 145.

ti- (in compound) "three". G. Panj. H. Siṃ. *ti*-, S. *ṭi*-, K. *trĕ tĕ*-. Pkt. P. *ti*-. Skr. *tri*-. — $ 121, 215.

tiḍeṃ n. "a buttock", Deśī. (*Pāiya lacchī*) *tiya*-. Skr. *trika*-. n. — $ 63, 121.

titkā, *titlā* adj. "as much". S. *te tiru*, H. *titnā*, K. *tyūt*ᵘ-. Pkt. *tettia*-, *tettula*-. — $ 206.

titar m. "francolin partridge". G. H. *tītar*, S. *titiru*, Panj. B. *tittar*; cf. Siṃ. *tit* "spot", *titmuvā* "spotted deer". Pkt. Skr. *tittira*- m. — $ 42. 44, 121, 143.

tirkā adj. "oblique", *tirsā* adj. "squint (eye)". G. *tiracchuṃ tirkas*, Panj. H. *tirchā* "oblique"; S. *tirku* "reflection of light"; Siṃ. *tirisanā* "animal" (cf. Skr. *tiryag-yoni*-). Pkr. *tiriccha*-. Skr. *tiryak*-; *tiryagīkṣa*- or *tiryagakṣi* ? — $ 143.

tivaṇ f. "a tripartite leaf". S. *ṭipāṇu* "indigofera with tripple leaf" Skr. *triparṇa*- m. — $ 44, 152.

tisrā adj. "third". H. *tisrā*, Panj. *tisrāt f.* "third person, arbitrator; third time", S. *ṭihara* "third time". — $ 226.

tisaḷ m. f. "zanthoxylon Rhetsa (thorny tree"). Ro. *truśul* "cross". Skr. *triśūla-* n ? — $ 145, 156.

tīkh adj. "biting". G. *tīkhūṃ*, Panj. *tikkhā*, H. *tīkhā*; Siṃ. *tik* "burning sun-ray", *tiyuṇa* "biting", Ro. *tikno* "small" ?. Pkt. *tikkha-*, P. *tikhiṇa-*. Skr. *tīkṣṇa-*. — $ 96, 121.

tīj f. "third lunar day", G. S. Panj. H. *tīj*; G. *tījo*, S. *ṭījo*, Panj. *tījā* "third"; cf. M. *akhitīj*, Pkt. *tiijja-*; Apa. *taijjī*. Skr. *tṛtīyā* f. — $ 30, 63, 106, 215, 226.

tīn "three". G. *traṇ taṇ triṇ tīn*, Panj. *tiṃn tinn*, H. *tīn*, Maith. *tin*[1], B. *tin tīn*, O. *tini*, Siṃ. *tun tuṇa*, Ro. *trin*; on the other hand S. *ṭi*, K. *trih tréh*. Pkt. *tiṇṇi*. Skr. *trīṇi-*. — $ 29, 121, 215.

tīr n. "shore". G. H. B. *tīr*, S. *tīru*, Siṃ. *tera*; Panj. *tiṛ* f. "ford". Pkt. Skr. *tīra-* n. — $ 121, 143.

tīs "thirty". G. H. Maith. *tīs*, S. *ṭīh*, Panj. *tīh*, K. *trah*, Siṃ. *tisa tiha*. Pkt. *tīsaṃ tīsā*. Skr. *triṃśat*. — $ 223.

tīḷ m. "sisamum". G. Panj. H. B. *til*, S. *tiru*, Siṃ. *tala*. Skr. *tila-*. m. — $ 41, 121, 145.

tuṭṇeṃ "to break". G. *tuṭ-*, S. *ṭuṭ-*, Panj. *ṭuṭṭ*, H. *ṭūṭ-tuṭ-*. Pkt. *tuṭṭai*. Skr. *truṭyati-*. — $ 76, 80, 109, 111, 121, 230.

tuṃd adj. "corpulent". Panj. H. B. *tuṃd*; cf. Panj. *tunnī* "navel". Deśī. *tundaṃ udaram* (162, 7). Skr. *tunda-*. — $ 80.

tumbḍi f. "begging bowl made of a goord". G. *tuṃbḍī*, G. *tumbī*, S. *tuṃī*, Panj. *tūṃbaṛ tomrī torī*, H. *tomrā tuṃbṛā* "goord". Deśī. *tumbī alābū* (162, 8). Skr. *tumba-* m. — $ 121, 127.

ṭurūt adv. "quick". G. H. *turat*, S. *turtu*, Panj. *turt*, Panj. H. *turaṃt*; Siṃ. *turu* "bird" ? Pkt. *turia-*. Skr. *tvaritam*. — $ 130.

tuśī adj. "of a yellowish red". Deśī. *tucchaṃ avaśuṣkam* (162, 7). — $ 103.

tusār m. "drizzle". Panj. *tukkār*, H. *tusār* "coldness"; Siṃ. *tusara* "dew, fog". Pkt. *tusāra-*. Skr. *tuṣāra-* m. — $ 44, 121, 156.

tuḷ f. "balance", *tuḷaī* f. "beam, sort of a balance", *tuḷṇeṃ* "to weigh". S. *tulu* m. "Balane, (constellation)", *toro* "weight", *torṇu* and *talṇu* "to weigh"; Panj. *tulāī* "weighing"; Panj. H. *tulnā*; K. *tulun* "to raise, to take up"; Siṃ. *talan* "beam". Skr. *tulā* f., *tula yati*. — $ 44, 121, 145.

tuḷas, *tuḷśī* f. "basilisk". G. S. Panj. H. B. *tulsī*, Siṃ. *talā*. Deśī. *tulasī surasalatā* (162, 8). Skr. *tulasī* f. — $ 44, 145.

tuṃ "thou". *tujhā* "thine"; *tuhmī* "you". G. *tuṃ tame*, S. *tūṃ tāuihiṃ*, Panj. *tūṃ tusīn*, H. *tūṃ tum*, B. *tūṃ tumi*, Ro. *tu tumen*, Siṃ. *tō topi*, K. *c^ah tôh^i*. Pkt. *tumaṃ tujjhaṃ, tumhe*. Skr. *tvam*, Pkt. *tumaṃ tujjhaṃ, tuṃhe*. Skr. *tvam, tubhyam, yuṣma-*. — $ 39, 54, 64, 70, 107, 208, 210.

tūp n. "clarified butter". G. *tūp* Deśī *tuppo..mrakśitaḥ snigdhaḥ kutupaś ceti* (165, 1). — $ 284.

tūr f. "profession of weaver". Panj. B. *tur*, S. *turi*. Skr. *turī* f. — $ 39, 41.

tūs n. m. "ball of rice, wheat etc". Panj. *toh tuhā*, S. *tuhu*, K. *toh*, H. *tus*, Siṃ. *toho*. Skr. *tuṣa-* m. — $ 156.

teṃ post-position "to". — $ 299.

ter "name of a town". Skr. *Tagara-*. — $ 62.

terā "thirteen". G. O. ter, S. *terahaṃ*, Panj. *terāṃ*, H. *terah*, B. *tero*, Siṃ. *teḷesa*, K. *truwah*. Pkt. , *terasa- teraha-*. Skr. *trayodaśa-*. $ 11 8, 143, 221.

tel n. "oil". G. Panj. H. B. Arm. Ro. *tel*, S. *telu* K. *tīl*, Siṃ. *tela*. Pkt. *tella-*, *tela-*. Skr. *taila-*. n. — $ 29, 77, 121.

tevṇeṃ "toshine, to burn". Siṃ. *teda* "gleam". Pkt. *tea-*, *teavai* (pradīpyate). Skr. *tejas-* n. — $ 55, 63, 121.

tevṇeṃ "to dissolve, to ooze". Panj. *ṭemṇā* "to soak", Siṃ. *tem* "to wet". Ro. *tindo* "wet". cf. Deśī. *timiṇaṃ ārdradāru* (161, 4). Cf. Skr. *timita-*. — $ 152.

taiṃ "them". G. *tav*, S. *ta* "then", Ro. *te* "when", Pkt. *taīa*. Skr. *tadā* (K. Ro. *ta* "and" = Skr. *tathā*). — $ 56.

taisā, *tasā* adj. "such". G. *tasuṃ*; Panj H. *taisā*; cf. Ro. *aso*. Pkt. *tādisa-*. Apa. *taisa-*. Skr. *tādṛśa-*. — $ 30, 31, 57, 58, 143, 156.

toṭā m. "loss,". G. S. *ṭoṭo*, G. *toṭo*, Panj. *ṭoṭṭā*, H. *ṭoṭā*, B. *ṭoṭā*. adj. Apa. *tuṭṭau*. Skr. *truṭita-*. — $ 80, 119.

toṃḍ m. "mouth". G. B. *ṭuṃḍ*, Siṃ. *tuḍa* "mouth (of dog etc.), *tola* "lip". Pkt. *toṃḍa*; Deśī. *tuṃḍaṃ āsyam* (162, 7). Skr. *tuṇḍa-* n. — $ 68, 80, 121.

toḍṇeṃ "to break", G. S. Panj. H. B. *toṛ-*. Pkt. *toḍai*. Skr. *troṭayati*. — $ 76, 80, 109, 111, 230.

toḍī f. "name of a rāg". G. S. H. *toṛī*. Skr. *troṭakī* f. —;$ 80, 109, 111.

toṃdel adj. "corpulent". H. *tomdail toṃdīl*. Pkt. *tundilla-*. Skr. *tundila-*. — $ 80.

tol m. "weight". S. *toro tora*, G. Panj. H. *tol*; S. *tor*, K. *tōl-* "to weigh". Siṃ. *tul* "similar". Pkt. *tulla-*. Skr. *tulya-*. — $ 78, 148.

thakṇeṃ, *thākṇeṃ* "to be tired, embarrassed". G. B. *thāk*, S. K. H. *thak-*, Panj. *thakk-*. Pkt. *thakkai* "to stop". — $ 48, 110, 122.

thaṃḍ adj. "cold". G. *ṭaḍhuṃ thaṃḍuṃ*, Panj. *thaṃḍā ṭhaṃḍhā*, H. *ṭhaṃḍā-*. — $ 119.

thanā m. *thān* n. "breast". G. *thān*, S. *thaṇu*, Panj. *thaṇ*, K. *tan*, H.B.O. *than*, Siṃ. *tana*. Pkt. *thaṇa-*. Skr. *stana-* m. — $ 122.

tharār adv. "trembling". *tharakṇeṃ thartharṇeṃ* "to tremble". G. *tharakvuṃ tharthar-vuṃ*, S. *ṭhaṛkaṇu*, *tharthilu* "disorder", Panj. *ṭharakṇā thartharāuṇa*, H. *thartharnā thalthalna*, B. *thurthurite*, *tharthar* "shock". Pkt. *thara-tharai*; Deśī. *tharahariaṃ kampitaṃ* (166, 13). Skr. *tharatharāyate*. — $ 122, 158.

tharū m. "handle". Panj. *tharī*; Deśī. *tharū tsaruḥ* (165, 10). Skr. *tsaru-* m. — $ 46, 122. Cf. M. *sarū*.

thavā m. "troop, crowd". Pkt. *thavaa-*. Skr. *stabaka-* m. — $ 46, 122, 152.

thaḷ n. "plantation, spot". G. O. *thaḷ*, B. H. *thal*, Panj. *thal*; S. *tharu* "desert" ?. Pkt. *thala-*. Skr. *sthala-* n. — $ 122, 145.

thā f. "bottom, base". S. *thāhu*, Panj. H. *thāh*, B. *thā*. Pkt. *thāha-*; Deśī. *ṭhāṇaṃ sthānam*; *uṇḍaṃ gambhīrajalam*; *pṛthu vistīrṇaṃ*;; *tatra traye'pi thāha ṣabdaḥ*; *thāho dīrgha ity anye* (168, 5); cf. *thaho nilayaḥ* (165, 10), and see Pischel $ 88. Skr. *sthāgha*. (Lüders Brūchstūcke Fragm. I Recto 1. 3 : *sthāghaṃ labhate* "establishes oneself; it need not be corrected in *sthānaṃ*; cf. *stāgho gādhaḥ*, Hem. *Uṇādi-* 109). — $ 41, 61, 122, 161, 169.

thāṃg m. "exact place or bottom". G. *thāg*, H. *thāṃg*. Deśī. *thaggho gādhaḥ* (165, 10). — $ 122, 169. Cf. the preceding one.

thāpṇeṃ "to establish, to fix". G. S. Panj. H. *thāp-*. Apa-*thappi* (*sthāpya-*). Skr. *sthāpayati*. — $ 122.

thāṃbṇeṃ , *thāmṇeṃ* "to stop", H. *thāmnā*, B. *thāman* "appeasement"; Siṃ. *tabanavā* "to place"; S. *thambhaṇu*, Panj. *thammhṇā* "to support". *stambhate*, *stabhyate*. — $ 79, 122, 127. 169, 230.

thār m. "residence, support, constancy", *thārṇeṃ* "to stop, to rest", *thāvarṇeṃ* "to stop; to rise again; to restore, to detain.", G.H. *thāvar ṭhārā*, Siṃ. *tavura* "fixed"; S. *thāra* "calm"; Panj. *ṭhaur* "residence"; G. Panj. *ṭhār-* "to co-agulate, to congeal". S. *ṭhar-* "to become cold, to be calm"; H. *ṭhār* "determination, co-agulation"; O. *seṭhāre* "there". Pkt. *thāvara-*; Deśī. *thāro ghanaḥ* (166, 13). Skr. *sthāvara-* adj. — $ 61, 110, 122.

thāḷā m. "metal plate". G. *thāḷo*, S. *thālu thālhu*, Panj. H. *thāl*, Siṃ. *tali*. Pkt. *thāla-*. Skr. *sthāla-* n. — $ 46, 122, 145.

thīr adj. "calm, serious". G. Panj. H. *thir*, S. *thiru*, Siṃ. *tara tira*; H. *ṭhir* "difficult". Pkt. *thira-*. Skr. *sthira-*. — $ 122.

theṃ post position, "to ". — $ 199.

theṃb them m. "drop". G. *uthevo*; Siṃ. *tem* "humidity". Cf. Deśī. *thevo binduḥ* (167, 9); *thippai*. Skr. *stimyati*. — $ 84, Pkt. 122.

ther adj. "decrepit". S. *theru thairu* "goat, skin", Siṃ. *tera* "priest". Deśī. *thero brahmā* (167, 10). Pkt. *thera-*. Skr. *sthavira-*. — $ 58, 122.

thoṃṭ n. "trunk". S. *ṭhumṭhu*, H. *ṭhūṃṭ*, B. *ṭhoṃt*, O. *thoṃṭ*. — $ 119, 122.

thoḍā adj. "a little". G. *thoḍuṃ*, S. *thoro*, Panj. H. *thoṛā*; cf. sim. *ṭika* "little, small"? Pkt. *thoa-*. Skr. *stoka-*. — $ 64, 122.

thor adj. "big". G. *thor*, Ro. *thulo*; S. *tholhī*, Panj. *tholh* f. "bulk". Pkt. *thora-*. Skr. *sthūrá- sthūla*. — $ 80, 122, 140.

daṃḍ dāṃḍ m. "baton". G. *daṃḍ*, *dāmḍo*. S. *ḍaṃḍ*; Panj. *dannā*, *ḍann* "punishment". h. *daṃḍ*, *dāṃḍ*, *dannā*; K. *dan* "handle", *dōna* "pestle"; Ro. *ran*; Siṃ. *daḍa* "punishment, fine". Pkt. Skr. *daṇḍa* — $ 111, 123.

daṃt, *dāṃt* m. "tooth, elephant-tooth". G. H. *dāṃt*, S. *ḍaṃdu*, Panj. *ḍaṃd daṃd*, K. Ro. *dand* Siṃ. *data*. Pkt.

Skr. *danta.* -m. — $ 123, 135.
daṃd n. "discard". Pkt. *dandā-.* Skr. *dvandva-* n. — $ 130, 135.
dabḍā m. "leather-pot". See. *ḍabbā, ḍav.*
daṃb, daṃbhī "hyprocite, hypocrisy". see *daṃb, daṃbhī.*
daravḍā, daroḍā m. "attack". (by a band of thieves). G. *daroḍo.* Deśī. *daḍavaḍo dhāṭī* (169, 17). —$ 78, 170.
daṃv n. "dew, humidity". Deśī. *dayaṃ jalam* (169, 1). $ 123.
devaḍṇeṃ, deuḍṇeṃ "to run". S. *doṛ-,* Panj. H. *dauṛ-,* K. *dōr-.* Skr. *dravati.* — $ 57, 78, 123.
das, dahā "ten". G. H. Maith. B. O. *das,* S. *ḍaha ḍāh,* Panj. *das dah,* K. *dah* (cf. Grierson, *Piś. Lang.*, p. 37), Ro. *deś,* Arm. Ro. *las,* Siṃ. *dasa daha.* Pkt. *dasa-, daha-.* Skr. *daśa-.* — $ 39, 156, 160, 220.
dasrā m. "tenth day of the bright fort-night of Āśvina". G. *dasrā daserā,* K. *dasʹĕhār,* H. *dasahrā.* Skr. *daśaharā* f. — $ 52, 220.
dahīṃ n. "curd". G. *dahīṃ,* Panj. *dahīṃ* f., H. *dahī,* B. *daī,* Siṃ. *dī.* Pkt. *dahi-.* Skr. *dadhi-* n. — $ 46, 123, 159.
daḷ n. "army; leaf". G. O. *daḷ,* S. *dalu,* Panj K. *ḍal dal,* Siṃ. *dala.* Skr. *dala-* n. — $ 123, 145.
daḷṇeṃ "to crush". G. H. *dal-.* Skr. *dalana-* n. — $ 123, 145.
daḷvai daḷvī m. "general". Skr. *dalapati-* m. — $ 152.
dākhaviṇeṃ "to show". G. *dākhvuṃ;* Siṃ. *dakhinavā* "to see". Pkt. *dakhavai;* P. *dakkhati.* Cf. Skr. Aor. *adrākṣīt,* root. *darś-.* — $ 30, 123.
dāṭ adj. "thick". G. *dāṭ* "dense"; S. *ḍaṭo,* Panj. *ḍaṭṭā* "heavy, fat"; K. *droṭᵘ* "strong", *droṭhᵘ* "hardened". Deśī. *saṃdaṭṭayaṃ saṃlagnam; kapratyayābhāve saṃdaṭṭaṃ ity api, saṃdaṭṭaṃ saṃghaṭṭa ity anye* (280, 2). — $ 109, 119.
dāḍh f. "molar tooth, cheek". G. *dāḍh,* S. *ḍāṛhi,* Panj. *dāhaṛ dāṛh,* H. *ḍāṛh,* B. *ḍāṛ,* Siṃ. *daḷa.* Pkt. *dāḍhā,* P. *dāṭhā.* Skr. *daṃṣṭrā* f. — $ 76, 112, 119.
dāḍhā adj. "courageous, strong". Panj. *ḍuḍḍhā* B. *daḍ,* K. *dorᵘ,* Siṃ. *daḷa* "fat", *dāḍi* "hard". Pkt. *daḍḍha-.* Skr. *dṛḍha-.* — $ 30, 31, 111.
dāḍhī f. "beard". G. *dāḍhī,* S. Panj. *ḍaṛhī.* H. *ḍaṛhī,* K. *dör,* Siṃ. *däli.* Skr. *daṃṣṭrikā dāḍhikā* f. — $ 112, 119.
dāṇīṃ "now". Siṃ. *dān.* Pkt. *dāṇi, dāṇiṃ.* Skr. *idānīṃ.* — $ 134, 174.
dād f. "dartre", *dādar* n. "herpes", G. *dādar,* S. *ḍaḍaru,* Panj. *dadd ḍadhar,* B. *dadru,* Siṃ. *dada.* Skr. *dadrū-* f. — $ 119, 123.
dābṇeṃ "to press, to oppress". G. H. B. O. *dāb-,* S. K. *dab-,* Panj. *dabb* "pressure", Ro. *dab* "blow". — $ 127.
dābh m. "sacred grass Poa-cynosuroides." G. *ḍābh dabh,* S. *dabhu,* Panj. *dabbh,* H. *dābh,* K. *darb.* Pkt. *dabbha-.* Skr. *darbha-* m. —$ 178.
dār n. "door". S. *daru,* K. *dar dār,* Siṃ. *dora.* Pkt. *dāra-.* Skr. *dvāra-* n. — $ 130.
dāv m. "forest, forest on fire". G. H. *dāv,* B. *dāb,* Siṃ. *dava.* P. Skr. *dāva-.* — $ 152.
dāvaṇ f. "cord". G. *dāmaṇī,* S. *ḍāvaṇu,* Panj. *dauṃ dāuṃ*

ḍāuṃ, H. *dāman dāvan*. Skr. *dāmanī* f. — $ 39, 46, 152.

dāvṇeṃ "to show". cf. probably H. *dāo* "strategem, feint". Pkt. *dāvai*. — $ 30, 152.

dās m. "slave". G. Panj. K. H. B. *dās*, S. *dāsu*, Siṃ. *das*, Greek Ro. *das* "Bulgarian". Pkt. Skr. *dāsa-* m. — $ 123, 156.

dāhṇeṃ, *dahāṇeṃ* "to burn" (act. neut.). G.S. Panj. *dah-*, H. *dāh- ḍāh-*, O. *dāh-*; K. *daz-* (neu. ; part. *dod*[u] = Skr. *dagdha-*) ; Siṃ. *dahan* "fire" ; Geiger puts aside Siṃ. *dav-* "to burn". Pkt. *ḍah- dah-*. Skr. *dahati*. —$ 49, 52, 54, 123.

divā m. "lamp". G. *divo*, S. *ḍīathu*, Panj. *dīā*, H. *diyā divā*, Siṃ. *divu*. Pkt. *dīva-*. Skr. *dīpa-* m. — $ 61, 123, 152, 172.

disṇeṃ "to appear, to look". Siṃ. G.H.Q. *dis-*, S. *ḍis*, Panj. *ḍiss- diss-*; K. *ḍēś-* "to see". Pkt. *dīsai*. Skr. *dṛśyate*. — 30, 157, 230.

dī m. "day". G. *dī*, S. *dīo*. Pkt. *diaha-* ; Deśī. *dio divasaḥ* (171, 7). Skr. *divasa-* m. — $ 63, 160.

diṭh f. "sight". S. *ḍīṭhi*, H. *dīṭh*, K. *drēṃth*, Siṃ. *diṭu* "view" ; cf. G. *dīṭhuṃ*, S. *ḍiṭhu* "seen". Pkt. *diṭṭhi-*. Skr. *dṛṣṭi-* f. — $ 30, 110.

dīḍ, *ḍīḍh* adj. "one and a half, and a half". G. *doḍh*, S. *ḍeḍhu*, Panj. *ḍeḍh ḍiḍh*, *ḍeuḍh*, *ḍūḍh*, H. *ḍeḍh*, Maith. *ḍeoṛhā*, B. *ḍeḍ*, O. *deḍh*, K. *ḍôḍ*. Pkt. *divaḍḍha-*. Skr. *dvi-* + *ardha-*. — $ 63, 88, 89, 115, 214, 225.

dīr m. "brother-in-law". see *der*.

dīs m. "day". G. *dīs dahāḍo*, S. *dīṃhuṃ*, Panj. *deh diṃh*, K. *doh*, Ro. *dives*, Siṃ. *davasa*. *diasa- divasa-*. Skr. *divasa-* m. — $ 63, 156, 160.

dukām n. "double-work". Skr. *dvi-*, *karma-*. — $ 172.

dukal, *dukāḷ* m. "famine". G. *dukāḷ*, H. *dukāl*. Skr. *duśkāla-* m. — $ 44, 78, 89, 93.

dūjā adj. "second, other". G. *bījo*, S. *bījo bīo*, K. *biya*; Panj. *dūjjā*, H. *dūjā*. *dujā*. Pkt. *duia- ducca- biia- biijja-*. cf. Skr. *dvitīya-*. — $ 106, 130, 214, 225.

duṇā adj. "double". S. *ḍuṇu*, Panj. *dūṇā*, H. *dunā dūnā*, B. *duṇā*, Siṃ. *diyuṇu*, Pkt. *diuṇa- duuṇa-*. Skr. *dviguṇa-*. — $ 63, 130, 214.

dudhī; *dudhīṇ* f. "gourd". G. *dudhī*. Deśī. *dudhiṇī* . . *tumbī* (177, 2). — $ 40.

dubḷā adj. "weak". G. *dubal*, S. *ḍubiro ḍoblo*, Panj. H. *dublā* "weak", Siṃ. *duṃbuḷ* "old man". Skr. *durbala-*. — $ 127, 145.

dubhṇeṃ "to yield milk (cow)". S. Panj. *ḍubh-*. Pkt. *dubbhai*. Skr. *duhyate*. — $ 123, 230.

dusrā adj. "second". H. *dusrā*. — $ 226.

duhī, *duī* f. "disagreement". S. *ḍuhil*, Panj. *duhelī* "difficult"; Panj. H. *duhāī* "complaint", Pkt. *duha-* (according to Pkt. *suha-*, from Skr. *sukha-*) ; Deśī. *duhaṃ asukham* (172, 9), cf. *dūhālo*. . *durbhaga-* (172, 16). Skr. *duḥkha-* n. and adj. — $ 159, 161.

dūdh n. "milk". G. H. *dūdh*, S. *ḍodhu*, Panj. *duddh dūdh*, B. O. *dudh*, K. *dôd*, Ro. *thud'*, Arm. Ro. *luth*, Siṃ. *dudu*. Pkt. *duddha-*. Skr. *dugdha-* n.

— $ 123, 124.
dūr adj. "far off". G. Panj. K. H. B. *dūr*, S. *ḍūr dūr*, Ro. *dur*. Siṃ. *duru*, Pkt. Skr. *dūra-*. — $ 123, 143.
deuḷ H. "temple". See *deval*.
dekhṇeṃ "to see". G. H. B. O. *dekh-*, S. *ḍekh-*, Panj. *dekh- ḍekh-*, Ro. *dikh-*, Arm. Ro. *lekh-* ; Pkt. *dekkhai*. Skr. *dṛś-*. — $ 30, 252, 253.
dej n. "money given at marriages by the bridegroom to the father of the bride". G. *dej* ; S. *deju* "dowry" ; H. *dāejā dejā dahez*, K. *dāj* "dowry" seem to result from the contamination of the same word with Pers-*jahez*. Pkt. *dejja-*. Skr. *deya-*. — $ 106.
deṇeṃ "to give". Siṃ. G. H. B. *de-*, S. *ḍe- ḍia-*, Panj. *de-*, *dev-*, K. *di-*, Ro. *dā-*. Pkt. *dei*. Skr. *da- dāti*. — $ 62, 136, 183, 229, 231, 252.
denlen m. "commercial dealings". Panj. *ḍeṇ deṇ*, K. *dēn*, H. *den*, B. *denā* "debt"; M.*dinnalā*, Siṃ. *dunnā*, Ro. *dino* "given". Pkt. *diṇṇa-*. —$ 80, 229, 231.
der, *dīr* m. "husband's younger brother", G. *devar diyar*, S. *ḍeru*, Panj. *deur*, K. *dryuy*^{u}, O. *deyur*. Pkt. *diarā-*, *devara-*. Skr. *devara-* m. — $ 63, 123, 143, 153.
der f. "delay". G. H. B. *der*, S. *deri*, Panj. *ḍer der*. Pkt. *dīhara-*. Per. *der* "long". — $ 167.
dev m. "god". G. *dev*, S. Panj. *deu*, H. *deo*, B. O. de (name of a family), K. *div*. Pkt. Skr. *deva-* m. —$ 77, 152, 177, 186.
devaḷ deuḷ n. "temple". S. *devalī*, Panj. *devālā*, H. *deval*, B. *deul*; Ro. *devēl* "god, sky", Arm. Ro. *leval* "god". Pkt. *devaula-*, *deula-*. Skr. *devakula-* n. — $ 59, 77, 145, 152, 280.
des m. "country". S. *ḍesu desu*, Panj. H. *des*, K. *dīś*, Arm. Ro. *leśi leśvav* "village", Siṃ. *desa*. Pkt. *desa-*. Skr. *deśa-* m. —$ 25, 77, 156.
deh m. "body". G. B. *deh*, S. *ḍehi dehi*, Panj. H. *deh* f. Pkt. *deha-* m. n. — $ 77, 159.
dain m. "distress." H. *dain* K. *dīn*. Pkt. *dainna-*. Skr. *dainya-* n. — $ 56.
doṇ f. "trough". G. *doṇī dohṇī*, B. *dunī*; Siṃ. *deṇa* "boat"; Panj. *dūṇ* valley", K. *dran* f. "marsh-land". ?
P. *doṇi*. Skr. *droṇī* f. — $ 120, 123, 134. cf. M. *ḍon* "boat".
don "*two*". Konkani *doni*, Maith. *dun*^{u}; Panj. *ḍo do*, H. *do*; Avadhi *doi dūi* , Maith. O. B. Ro. *dui*; K. *z*^{a}*h*, Obl. *dôn*; Siṃ. de-; G. *be*, S. *ba*. Pkt. *doṇṇi*, *beṇṇi* pl. neut. of *do duve*, *be*; Apa. *dui*, *bi*, instr. *dohiṃ*, Skr. *dvau*. — $ 130, 193, 214.
dor m. "rope". G. *dor*, S. *ḍori*, Panj. H. *ḍor*, K. *dūr*^{u}, Ro. *dori* (all feminine). Deśī. *davaro tantuḥ* (169, 15), *dāro tathā doro kaṭisūtram* (170, 17). — $ 153.
dohṇeṃ, *duhṇeṃ* "to milk". Panj. *ḍoh-*, S. *duh-*, H. B. *doh-*, K. *dôy-*, Siṃ. *dòv-*. Skr. *dohati*. —$ 123, 159.
dvāvā. pcpl. of obligation of *deṇeṃ*. — $ 52, 152, 154.
dhaj n. f., *dhajā* f. "banner". G. S. Panj. *dhaj* f., Panj. *dhajā* f., H. *dhajā* m., Siṃ. *dada*, K. *dôz*. Skr. *dhvaja-* m. — $ 130.

dhaṭ, dhaṭṭ adj. "courageous". Panj. *ḍhaṭṭh, ḍhaṭṭā* "heavy" (it seems that there has, here, been a contamination of meaning with Skr. *dṛḍha-*, see M. *dāḍhā* as also M. *dāṭ*). Pkt. *dhaṭṭha-*. Skr. *dhṛṣṭa-*. — $ 30, 169.

dhaṇ f. "riches, luck". G. Panj. *dhaṇ*, S. *dhanu*, H. *ḍhan*, K. *dana*, B. *dhan* (all masc.). Pkt. *dhaṇa-*. Skr. *dhana-* n. — $ 124, 134.

dhaṇī f. "desire, satiety. Deśī. *dhaṇī bhāryā* (cf. *dhaṇiā priyā*, 178, 3) *paryāptir*.. (179, 15). — $ 134.

dharṇeṃ "to hold". G. S. Panj. H. B. *dhar-*, K. Siṃ. *dar-*, Arm. Ro. *thar-*. Pkt. *dharai*. Cf. Skr. *dhārayati*.— $ 46, 124, 143.

dhavlār n. "house with white-washed terrace". Panj. *dhaular* "palace". Skr .*dhavala+āgāra-*. — $ 61, 163.

dhavaḷ adj. "white". G. *dhoḷuṃ*, S. *dhauro*, Panj. H. *dhaulā*, B. O. *dholā*. Skr. *dhavala-*. — $ 165.

dhāḍ f. "assault". G. S. H. *dhāṛ*. Skr. *dhāṭī* f. — $ 111.

dhān n. "grain, rice". G. H. B. *dhān*, Panj. *dhāṇ*, K. *dāñé*, Siṃ. *dan*. Pkt. *dhaṇṇa-*. Skr. *dhānya-* n. — $ 135.

dhāṃgaṃḍ, dhāmā m. term of abuse for the Mādhyandina of Yajurvedī. S. *dhāma* f. Panj. *dhāmmā dhāmāṃh* "festival"; H. *dhāmīyāṃ*, name of a sect; cf. Siṃ. *dam* "religion", *dāmitu* "good". Skr. *dharmya-*. — $ 138.

dhāvṇeṃ dhāṃvṇeṃ "to run", *dhāv* f. "race". G. *dhāvuṃ*, Panj. *dhāuṇā*, H. *dhāvnā dhānā*, K. *davun*, Ro. *thav-*, Pkt. *dhāvai, dhāi*. Skr. *dhāvati*.- — $ 152.

dhāsaḷṇeṃ, dhaṃsaḷṇeṃ "to give way, to tumble in". Panj. H. *dhas-*; G. *dhas-*, *dhass-* "to push". Skr. *dhvaṃs-*. — $ 130.

dhīṭ adj. "courageous". G. *dhīṭ*, S. *diṛhī*, Panj. H. *dhīṭh*. Pkt. *dhiṭṭha-*. Skr. *dhṛṣṭa-*. — $ 30, 169.

dhīr m. "patience, firmness". G. S. Panj. *dhīr* f., H. *dhīr* m., K. *dīrī dörī*, Siṃ. *diri*. Skr. *dhairya-* n. — $ 143.

dhuī f. "fog". cf. S. *dūṃhāṃ*, Panj. *dhūṃ*, Panj. H. O. *dhuāṃ*, B. *dhuyāṃ*, K. *d^ah*, Siṃ. *dum* "smoke"; Ro. *thuv* "tobacco". Skr. *dhūmikā* f. — $ 64, 153.

dhukdhukṇeṃ "pulpitate". S. *dhakidhaki* "pulpitation" Panj *dhukdhukā*, B. *dhukdhukni* "anxiety". Pkt. *dhukkā-dhukkai*. — $ 164.

dhuṇeṃ, dhuvṇeṃ "to wash"; *dhuvaṇ* n. "water in which wheat has been washed". G. Panj. H. *dho-*, S. *dhua-*, B. *dhoṃ- dhu-*, Siṃ. *dov-*, Ro., *thov-*; K. *ḍuw-* "to sweep"? Pkt. *dhuai*. Skr. *dhunoti*.- — $ 64, 172, 229, 230.

dhutārā m. "imposter". G. *dhūtāruṃ*; cf. S. *dhut ḍhuṭo*, Panj. *ḍhuṭā*, H. *dhuttā*, Siṃ. *dut*. Pkt. *dhutta-*. Skr. *dhūrta-kāra-*. — $ 44, 114, 119.

dhūn f. "vibrant sound, humming". Panj. *dhuṇ dhun*, H. *dhunī*, Siṃ. *dani*, Pkt. *dhuṇi-*. Skr. *dhvani-*. m. — $ 76, 130.

dhūp m. "incense", *dhupāṃgrā* m. "a live coal brought to enkindle orant incense". Panj. H. *dhūp*, K. *dūph*. Skr. *dhūpa, aṅgāra-* n. — $ 44.

dhūv f. "daughter". Siṃ. *dū*

duva, Basgali Waialā *jū*, Gawarbati *zū*, Gārwī *dūī*; G. Panj. H. *dhī dhīyā*, S. *dhiu dhiya*, B. *jhī*, O. *jhia* Maiyā *dhī*, Sīna *dī*. Pkt. *dhūā dhiā*. Skr. *duhitṛ-* f. — $ 64, 124.

na nā n. negation; in compound : *nage naye nalage* "not wanted, not proper," *nahve* "is not", *nasṇeṃ* "not to exist"; *nāhīṃ* "not"; *nako* "no, dont"; *numajṇeṃ* "not to understand", *ḥeṇṇeṃ noḷakhṇeṃ* "not to know", *nedṇeṃ* "not to give" etc. G. etc. *na n*. Pkt. P. Skr. *na*. — $ 51, 57, 70, 135, 237, 267, 274.

naī nahī f. "river". S. *nāṃīṃ*, Panj. *nai*, Cambi *nei*, Siṃ. *nī*. Pkt. *ṇaī*. Skr. *nadī* f. — $ 46, 57, 135, 161.

nakṭā adj. "nose-cut, camus". G. *nakṭuṃ* and *nākkaṭṭum*, H. *nakṭā*. By syllabic superposition, from *nāk+kāṭ-*.—$ 48, 172.

nakh m. n. "nail". G. H. B. *nakh* m., Panj. *nakh* f., tadbhava is also found in H. *nah*, Panj. *nahuṃ nahi* m., Ro. *nai* "nail", G. *nahiyuṃ* "skin near the nail". Pkt. *ṇakkha-* (cf. Deśī. 143, 10). Skr. *nakha-* m. n. — $ 48, 96.

naṭhārā adj. "useless, bad". G. *naṭhāruṃ*; Pkt. *ṇaṭṭha-*. Skr. *naṣṭa-*. —$ 48, see also M. *nāṭ*.

naḍṇeṃ "to go with difficulty, to be embarrased". G. *naḍvuṃ* "to obstruct, to prevent". Pkt. *naḍai*, *naḍijjai*; Deśī. *ṇaḍio vañcitaḥ* (cf. M. *ṇāḍṇeṃ* "to steal, to strip"); *khedilā iti anye* (143, 12). Skr. *naṭ-*, cf. *unnaṭ-*. —$ 111, 135.

nath f. "nose—ring; medicine given through the nose." G. S. B. *nath*, G. B. *nāth*, W. Panj. *natth*. Deśī. *ṇatthā nāsārajjuh* (143, 5). Skr. *nastaka-* m. *nastā* f. — $ 48, 122.

nantar "after". cf. Siṃ. *not*, Pkt. *ṇanta-* "infinite" (Skr. *ananta-*). Skr. *anantaram*. — $ 174.

naroṭī f. "skull, hallowed half of cocoanut, cow yielding little milk". cf. Deśī. *nāroṭṭo bilam* (145, 10). — $ 48.

navrā naurā m. "a bridegroom, a young boy arrived at the age of marriage, husband". Skr. *nava- varaka-* m. — $ 46, 57, 172.

navas m. "wish". Deśī. *naṃsiaṃ upayācitakam*; *navasiaṃ ity anye* (145, 3). cf. Skr. *namasyati* "to pay homage", *namaḥ* n. "homage", meaning influenced by Iranian. Per. *namāz*, Balouchi *ṇamās navāś* "prayer". — $ 152.

nav nau "9". G. H. Maith. *nau*, Panj. *nauṃ*, S. *naṃuṃ*, B. *nay*, K. *nav nau*, Siṃ. *nava nama*. Pkt. Skr. *nava-*. — $ 152, 219.

navvad "90". G. *ṇevuṃ*, S. *nave*, Panj. H. *nave*, Maith. B. *nabbai*, O. *nabe*, K. *namat*; Siṃ. *anū* (under the influence of *asū* "80"). Pkt. *nauī*,- *ṇavai*. Skr. *navati-*. — $ 223.

navā adj. "new". G. *navuṃ*, S. *naṃiuṃ*, Panj *navāṃ*, H. *navā*, B. *naī*, Siṃ. *nava*, K. *nov*^{u}, Ro. *nevo*. Pkt. Skr. *nava-*. — $ 46, 152.

nahāṇ nhān n."ablution" *nāhṇeṃ* "to take a bath", G. *nāhṇu* "bridegroom bath"; Panj. *nhāuṇā*, H. *nhānā*, Ro. *nand*, *nay*, Siṃ. *nānavā* "to take a bath"; K. *śrān* is an adapted tatsama. Pkt. *ṇhāṇa-*. Skr. *snāna-* n. — $ 52, 136.

naḷ naḷā m. *naḷi* f. "tube, lotus stalk, Tibia." G. *naḷ*, S. *naṛu*, Panj. H. B. *nal*. Skr. *naḍa-*. *nala-* m. *nalikā* f.—$ 145.

nāū, *nāhu*, *nhāvī*, *nāhāvī* old M. *nāvī*, m. "barber". G. S. Panj. H. B. *nāī*, K. *nāyid*, H. B. also *nāū*. Pkt. Māg. Śaur. *ṇāvida-*, Mah. *ṇhāvia-*. Skr. *nāpita-* m. — $ 46, 57, 62, 136, 152, 280.

nāk n. "nose". G. H. B. *nāk*, S. *naku*, Panj *nakk*, Ro. *nakh*, Arm. Ro. *lank* (of **nank*). Pkt. *nakka-*; cf. Deśī. *nakko ghrāṇaṃ mūkaś ca* (135, 5). Skr. *nas-*, *nās-* enlarged into **naska-*; the old form is represented only by Siṃ. *nahaya*. — $ 48, 94,

nāk. affixed by courtesy to the names of Mahārs and Parvārīs as Rāmnāk. Skr. *nāyaka-* m. — $ 61.

nāgar, *nāgor*, *nāṃgar*, *naṃgor*, m. "plough". H. *nāṃgar nāṃgal laṃgar*, B. *nāṃgal*, Siṃ. *nagala nagula*; S. *laṅgaru*, G. Panj K. *laṅgar* "anchor", Ro. *nanari* "comb". Pkt. *naṅgala- laṅgala-*. Skr. *laṅgala-lāṅgala-* n. — $ 98, 142, 170.

nāṃgḷī f. "liana". Skr. *laṅgalikā* f. — $ 98, 142, 145, 146, 170.

nāgvā, *nāgā* adj. "naked". G. *nāguṃ*, S. *naṃgo*, Panj H. *naṃgā*, O. *naṃglā*, K. *nanga*, Ro. *nango*; Arm. Ro. *ngalel* "to make naked"; H. B. *nāgā* "mendicant", Siṃ. *nagā naṅgā* "little sister", term of affection. Pkt. *nagga-*. Skr. *nagna*. — $ 47, 55, 98.

nāṃgḍā nāṃgoḍā m. "tail of scorpion". G. *laṃgur laṃgul*, Siṃ. *nagal naguṭa* "tail". Pkt. *naṃgola- naṃgūla-*. Skr. *lāṅgūla-* n. ?— $. 146, 170.

nācṇeṃ "to dance". G. H. B. *nāc-*, S. K. *nac-*, Panj *nacc-*. Pkt. *naccai*. Skr. *nṛtyati*. — $ 47, 101, 230.

nāṭ adj. "bankrupt", *nāṭā nāṭhā* "vile, mischievous". Panj. *nāṭā*, H. *naṭh* "destroyed". *nāṭ nāṭ* "vicious, vile", Siṃ. *naṭa* "destroyed". —Cf. M. *nāthārā*. Pkt. *ṇaṭṭha-*. Skr. *naṣṭa-*. — $ 47, 48, 88.

nāḍ f. "artery, tube". G. Panj. H. *nāḍ*, S. *nāṛi*. Skr. *nāḍī* f. — $ 111, 146.

nāṇeṃ n. "coin". G. *nāṇuṃ*, S. *nāṇu*. Skr. *nāṇaka-* n. — $ 46.

nātū m. grand son". H. B. O. *nātī*, Siṃ. *natu*. Pkt. *nattua- nattia-*. Skr. *naptṛ-* m. — $ 47, 121.

nāteṃ n. "relationship". G. *nātuṃ*, G. S. *nāto*, Panj *nāttā*, H. *nātā*; cf. Siṃ. *nā* (P. *ñāti-*). Skr. *jñātitva-* n. — $ 130, 135, 172.

nāthi "is not; not". G. *nathī*, Siṃ. *näti* Arm. Ro. *nath*. Pkt. *ṇatthi*. Skr. *nāsti*.— $ 122, 135.

nāṃd f. "jar with a big mouth". S. *nādī*, Panj *nāṃd* m., H. *naṃd* f. Deśī. *ṇaṃdaṃ ikśunipīḍanakāṇḍaṃ kuṇḍākhyo bhāṇḍaviṣeśaś ceti dvyartham* (154, 17).

nāṃdṇeṃ "to reside; to continue thrivingly; to come together." H. *nāndnā* "to live in peace, to reside", Siṃ. *nadan* "joy"; G. *naṃdvuṃ* "to break" (for a sacred object). Skr. *nandana-*. — $

123, 135.

nānā m. "term of respect for some person". Panj. *nānnā*, S. *nāno*, H. B. *ṅānā* "maternal grandfather". Deśī. *naṇṇo.. jyeśṭho bhrātā* (155, 5). — $ 135.

nār f. "woman", G. Panj. H. *nār nārī*, S. *nāri*, B. *nārī*; Siṃ. *narā* m. Pkt. *nārio* n. pl. Skr. *nārī* f. — $ 39.

nāreḷ nāraḷ m. "coco nut". G. *nāriyaḷ*, S. *narelu nāiru*, Panj. *narel naler*, H. *nāriyal*, Siṃ. *neraḷu*. Pkt. *ṇāriela-*, *ṇāliara-*. Skr. *nārikela-* m. — $ 42, 46, 63, 145.

nāv, *nau*, *naukā* f. "boat". G. *nāu* neut., S. *nāukā* Panj. H. *nāo*, K. *nāv*, B. *nā*, Siṃ. *nāva*. Pkt. *nāvā*. Skr. *nau-*, *nāvā* a pax f. — $ 135, 152.

nāṃv nāv n. "name". G. *nām*, S. *nāṃuṃ*, Panj. *nāuṃ*, H. *nāṃv*, K. *nāv*, Ro. *nav*, Siṃ. *nama*. Pkt. *nāma-*, Apa. *ṇāuṃ*. Skr. *nāmaṇ-*. n. — $ 39, 152.

nās m. "ruin, loss", *nāsṇeṃ* "to corrupt, to be corrupted". G. B. *nāś*, Panj. *nās* f. S. *nāsu*, H. *nās* m.; Siṃ. *nahanavā* to desdestroy"; H. *nāsnā* "to perish, to disappear, to run away"; similaly G. *nāsvuṃ* "to run away, to fly away". Panj. *nasāuṇā* "to chase". Ro. *nasˇ--* (Arm. *nas-*) "to save oneself, to go away". Pkt. *ṇāsaṇa-*, *ṇassai*. Skr. *nāśa-* m. *nāśana-* n; *naśyati*. — $ 46, 156.

nāh, *nāth* m. "master ". H. *nāh*; but every where *nāth* is not usual. Pkt. *ṇāha-*. Skr. *nātha-* m. — $ 24.

nāḷ n. "lotus stalk, umbilical cord". G. *nāḷ*, Panj. H. B. *nāl*. Skr. *nāla-* n. — $ 145, 146.

nikhorḍā adj. "miserable, abandoned". H. *nikhorā nikhoṛā*. Deśī. *ṇikhuriaṃ aḍṛḍham* (152,3). Skr. *nikhuryapá-* "protector of the affiliated". ('á pax, see Taitt. *saṃh.* tr. Keith p. 595, n. 7). — $ 80.

nikāmī adj. "useless". S. *nikamo*, Panj. *nikammā* H. *nikāṃ nikāṃī*, Siṃ. *nikam*. Skr. *niśkarman-*. — $ 44, 89, 138.

nikāl m. "passage, exit". G. *nikaḷvuṃ*, S. *nikiraṇu*, Panj. *nikkalṇā*, H. *nikalnā*, Ro. *nikalnik-* "to get out". Apa. part. *nikkaliu*. Skr. *niṣkālya* "having chased", *niṣkālana-* n. "conduit (for animals)". — $ 89, 141.

nical adj. "motionless". Panj. *nicall*, H. *niclā* Sim. *nisal*. Pkt. *ṇiccala-*. Skr. *niścala-*. — $ 101, 145.

niciṃt adj. "free from anxiety". G. Panj. H. *nicint*. Apa. *ṇiccintai*. Skr. *niścinta-*. — $ 71, 101.

nijharṇeṃ "to drip, to ooze". H. *nijjhar* "cascade, spring of water". Pkt. *ṇijjharai*, Skr. **niṣkṣarati*. — $ 30, 107.

nijhūr adj. "decrepit (man), poor (soil)". Deśī. *ṇijjharaṃ jīrṇaṃ*; *ṇijjhūraṃ ity anye* (146, 11). — $ 30.

niṭhūr adj. "hard, cruel". H. B. *niṭhur*; S. *niṭaru* "obstinate". ? Pkt. *ṇiṭṭhura-*. Skr. *niṣṭhura -*. — $ 40, 110.

niḍhaḷ niḍhāḷ nīḍāḷ n. "forehead". S. *nirāṛu nirṛu*, H. *lilāṛ*, Siṃ. *naḷala*. Pkt. *nalāḍa-nilāḍa- niḍāla-* cf. Deśī. *neḍālī paṭṭavāsitā śirobhuṣaṇa bhedaḥ* (153, 18); P. *nalāṭa-*. Skr. *lalāṭā-*, *niṭāla-*, *niṭala-*, *niṭila-*, n. — $ 86, 167, 170, 171.

niṃdṇeṃ "to weed out (a corti-field) G. *nīṃdvuṃ*, K. *nindā*. Deśī. *niṃdiṇī*.........*kuṭṛnod-dharaṇam* (150, 4).

nipajṇeṃ "to derive from, to become". G. S. *nipaj-* ; cf. Siṃ. *nipan niput* "birth". Pkt. *nippajjai* Skr. *niṣpa-dyate*. — $ 106, 230.

nipṭ "absolutely, very much". G. Panj. H. B. *nipṭ*. Deśī. *ṇipaṭṭho adhikaḥ* (148, 10).

niphal adj. "sterile". Pkt. *ṇiphala-*. Skr. *niṣphala-*. — $ 126, 145.

nimb m. "azadirachta indica" (see *Hobson-Jobson* S. V. *neem*). S. *nimu* f. Panj. *nimm*, H. *nīm*. Pkt. Skr. *nimba-* m. — $ 68.

nibhagṇeṃ "to be cracked (a vessel). Pkt. **nibbhagga-*, cf. Deśī. *ṇibbhuggo bhagnaḥ* (149, 1) from Skr. *nirbhagna-*. — $ 128.

nibhṇeṃ "to surmount, to endure, to succeed". G. *nibh-vuṃ* "to endure", Panj. *nibhāuṇā nibāhuṇā* "to accomplish, H. *nibhnā* "to succeed, to endure" caus. *nibahnā* "to practice to survey", K. *nibāv-* "to direct, to pastime". Skr. *nirvāhaṇa*. The etymology proposed in $ 128 fits in much less with the meaning or the word in various languages. But it shows that the Marathi word is borrowed as also the Gujarati one; Cf. for example M. *cāvṇeṃ* and — $ 152, 2-.

nirakhṇeṃ nirekhṇeṃ "to contemplate". G. Panj. H. *nirakh-* H. also...*nirekh-*. Pkt. *ṇirikk-haṇa-*. Skr. *nirīkṣate*. — $ 50.

nirutā nirutᵊṃ adv. "certainly" (poet.). Deśī. *ṇiruttaṃ niś-citam* (148, 3). Skr. *nirukta-*. — $ 50, 121.

nirū adj. "pure". G. *niruṃ*, S. *niru*; Panj. H. *nirā* undoubtedly by suffix-substitution ; Siṃ. *nirō* "healthy" represents Skr. *nīroga-*. Skr. *niruja-*. — $ 64.

nivaṭṇeṃ "to destroy, to kill" (poet.). H. *nibatnā* "to be consumed", Panj. *nibiraṇu* "to finish", B. *nibaḍite* "to finish", Siṃ. *navat-* "to end". Pkt. *ṇivattai*. Skr. *nivartayati*. — $ 114, 152.

nivaṭṇeṃ nivaḍṇeṃ "to become visible, to look full (fruits), to come out". G. *nivaḍvuṃ* Panj. *nibbaḍnā*, H. *nibaṭnā* "to be produced," *nibaḍnā* "to be determined", cf. Siṃ. *nivat* "origin, birth" (skr. *nivṛtti-*) Pkt. *ṇivvaḍai*. Skr. *nirvartayati-* — $ 52, 109, 111. Cf. M. *vāṭṇeṃ*.

nivṇeṃ "to cool, to decrease"; Siṃ. *nimanavā nivenava* "to cool oneself, to be extinguished". Pkt. *ṇivvāi*. Skr. *nirvāti*. — $ 52, 152. Cf. the following word.

nivāṇeṃ n. "destruction, ruin". cf. Deśī. *ṇivvāṇaṃ duḥkhakatha naṃ* (149, 8). Skr. *nirvāṇa-* n. — $ 52.

nisaṭṇeṃ "to slip from, to go away from". Skr. *nisṛṣṭa-*. — $ 30, 89, 231.

nisaṇ niśīṇ f. "ladder". H. *nisenī nasenī nisainī nasainī*, Siṃ. *nisini* Pkt. *ṇisaṇiā nisseṇī*. Skr. *niśreṇī* f. — $ 42, 44, 52, 157.

nisṇā m. "whetstone". Siṃ.

nihunugā, whetstone; *nihunu* "act of whetting". Skr. *niśāna-* n. — $ 52, 156.

nīm m. "regular offering to a demon", *nem niyam* m. "rule, observance" G. *nīm nem*, meanings distributed as in M.; S. *nemu*, H. *nīm*, Panj. *nem*, K. *nēm* "rule", S. *nemī* "regular". Tats., Skr. *niyama-* m. — $ 75.

nīḍ n. m. "nest". H. B. *nīḍ*. Tatsama, Skr. *nīḍa-* m. n. — $ 108.

nīd f. "sleep". G. *niṃdrā nidār*, K. *nendᵃr*, H. *nīd nīṃd*, Siṃ. *nidi nidu*, Ro. *lindr*. P. Pkt. *niddā*. Skr. *nidrā* f. — $ 123.

neṭī prep. adv. "near, beside". G. S. H. Panj. *neḍe*. Skr. *nikaṭe*. — $ 63, 109.

neṇeṃ "to lift, to conduct". Panj. *neṇā*; K. *ni-*, Arm. Ro. *nenel* "to carry"; cf. G. *neṇ*, S. *neṇu*, H. *nain*, Siṃ. *nuvana* "eye". Pkt. *naaṇa-*. Skr. *nayati*, *nayana-* n. $ 62.

nev, name of a locality of Khandesh, Pkt. *ṇaara-*. Skr. *nagara-*. — $ 62 see under M. *ṇer*.

nesṇeṃ "to put on (a dress)." Skr. *nivasana-* n., *nivaste*. — $ 63.

nyāv, old M. *nyāvo* m. "justice". S. H. *niāu*, G. B. K. *nyāy*, Siṃ. *niyāva niyāya*. Pkt. *ṇāa-*, P. *ñāya-*. Skr. *nyāya-* m. — $ 57.

pakhāl f. "leather bag for water". G. Panj. H. *pakhāl*. Skr. *payaḥ-*. *khalla-* m. Cf. under M. *khāl*. — $ 148.

paṃcāvann "55". G. H. *paṃcāvan*, B. *paṃcānn*, cf. Maith. *pacpan* with reference to S. *paṃjoṃjāh*, Panj. *pacvaṃj*, K. *pöncavanzāh*. Deśī. *pañcāvaṇṇā tathā paṇavaṇṇā pancādhikapañcāśat* (191, 7). — $ 223.

paṃchī m. "bird". Panj. H. *paṃchī*; but G. *paṃkhī*, S. *pākhī*, B. *pākhī*, Siṃ. *pak*. Pkt. *pacchi-pakkhi-*. Skr. *pakṣin-* m. Borrowed; the usual word in Marathi is *pākhrūṃ*. — $ 101.

paṭhār n. "plateau, elevated plain, bottom", cf M. *pāthar*. Skr *prastāra-* m. — $ 48, 110, 122, 125.

paḍ- prefix. G. H. etc. *paḍ-*, Siṃ. *piḷi-*. Pkt. *paḍi-*. Skr. *prati-*. — $ — $ 39, 111, 125, 170.

paḍkay f. "practise among farmers of lending men or cattle on mutual assistane basis." Deśī. *peḍikkao pratikriyā* (188.9); cf. P. *katikā* "convention". Skr. *pratikrti*. — $ 30, 57, 154.

paḍkhar adj. "blunt". Deśī. *paḍikkhāro kṣūraḥ* (190, 12). Skr. *prati+kṣāra-* ? — $ 42.

paḍṇeṃ "to fall". G. *paḍvuṃ*, H. *paḍnā*, B. *paḍite*, Ro. per-, Arm. Ro. *par-*; with reference to S. *pavaṇuj*, Panj. *paiṇā pauṇā*; K. *pě-*, caus. *pāv-*. Pkt. *paḍai*. Skr. *patati*. — $ 46, 48, 79, 118, 125, 232, 251, 253.

paḍsāḍ m. "echo". Skr. *pratiśabda-* m. — $ 49, 123. Cf. M. *sāḍ*.

paḍaḷ n. film over the eye; swarm of the bees (poet.)". G. *paḍal*. Pkt. *paḍala-*. Skr. *paṭala-*n. — $ 111, 145.

paḍos "near". *paḍosā* m. "neighbourhood", *paḍośī* m. "neighbour". G. S. Panj. H. *paḍosī*, B. *paḍsī*, O. *paḍisā*. Skr. *prativāsa-*, *prati-*

vāsin- m. — $ 49, 50, 78.

paḍhṇeṃ "to read". G. *paḍhvuṃ*, S. *paḍahṇu*, Panj. *paḍhṇā*, H. *paḍhnā*, B. *paḍite*, Ass. *parh-*, O. *paḍhibā*, K. *parun*. Pkt. *paḍhai*. Skr. *paṭhati*. — $ 46, 112, 230, 252.

paṇ "but, also". old M. *paṇi*. G. *paṇ*, S. *puṇi piṇi*, H. *phun phin pun puni*, B. *pani*, Nêp. *pani*, Siṃ. *pana puna*. Pkt. *puṇa*, *puṇo*, *uṇa* (end.), P. *pāna*, *punā*. Skr. *punaḥ*. — $ 39, 41, 274.

paṇat f. "great grand daughtre", *paṇtū* m. "great grand son". H. *panātī* f. Epigraphic Pkt. *pranatika-*, *paṇatika-* (Aśoka). Skr. *pranaptṛ-* m. — $ 46, 121, 125.

pant=prefix of honour added to proper name". Skr. *paṇḍita-*. — $ 162. See M. *pāṃḍyā*.

paṃth pāṃth m. "path", G. S. Panj. H. *paṃth*, S. Panj also *paṃdh*, B. *panthā* Arm. Ro. *panth*., Pkt. *pantha-*. Skr. *panthan-* m. — $ 122.

pathvar m. "betrothed for the first time." By syllabic super.position of Skr. *prathama*. *vara-*. — $ 172.

pathārī f. "mattress, carpet". G. *pathārī*, S. *patharu*, H. *patthar*, Siṃ. *patara* "expanded object". Deśī. *pathārī nikaraḥ prastaraśca* (206, 15). Skr. *prastāra* m. — $ 48, 84, 110, 122, 125.

paṃdhrā "fifteen". G. *paṃdar*, S. *paṃdhrāṃ*, *paṃdrahaṃ*, Panj. *pāṃdrāṃ*, H. *paṃdrah*, B. *poner*, K. *pandah*; Siṃ. *pasaḷosa*. Pkt. *paṇṇorasa-*, Apa. *paṇṇaraha-*. Skr. *pañca daśa-*. — $ 118, 124, 143, 164, 221.

pannās "fifty". G. H. *pacâs*, Panj S. *pañjāh*, B. *pañcās*, O. *pacāś*, K. *pancāḥ*, Siṃ. *paṇas*. Pkt. *paṇṇasaṃ pannasā*, Skr. *pañcāśat-*. — $ 217, 223.

paraṇṇeṃ "to marry". G. *paraṇvuṃ*, S. *parṇaṇu*, Panj *parṇāhu* "marriage", H. *parnā*. Skr. *pariṇayati*. — $ 49, 50, 51, 134.

parvat m. "commerce, business", *paratṇeṃ*, *parvatṇeṃ* to turn, to change". Pkt. *pariyatta-*. Skr. *parivarta-* m. — $ 49, 51, 114.

parvāṃ parvhāṃ "day after tomorrow, day befor yesterday". G. *parāṃ* "at a distance"; S. *parimhaṃ*, Panj. *parsoṃ*, H. *parsoṃ parhauṃ*, *paroṃ*. Skr. *paraśvaḥ* "day after tomorrow". — $ 152, 157.

paral, *pareḷ* m. "earthen pot". Deśī. *pariali sthālam*; *bhojanabhāṇḍaṃ iti yāvat* (185, 6). — $ 42, 63.

parasṇeṃ, *pariyesaṇeṃ*, *parisṇeṃ* "to hear, to listen". Skr. *paryeṣ.-* "to search". — $ 49, 51, 63, 143, 253.

parāyā, *parāvā* adj. "stranger, of another"; G. *parāyuṃ*; S. *parāyo*,*parāo*,*parāī*; H. *parāyā*, Skr. *parāgata-*. — $ 54, 55.

parīṭ m. "washer-man". S. *parīṭu*. Deśī. *pariaṭṭo rajakaḥ* (186, 18). — $ 63.

parīs m. "the philosopher's stone", Cf. *paras parīs*. "than" (...in comparison). cf. Skr. *parikṣā* f. "test". — $ 42, 49.

paryaṃt "upto". Skr. *paryanta-* m. — $ 68.

palaṃg m. "bed". G. Panj. H. B. *palaṃg*, S. *palaṃgu*, Siṃ. *palaṃga*. Pkt. *pallaṅka-*. Skr.

paryaṅka- m. — $ 48, 82, 141. Cf. M. *pālak*.

palāṭān, paleṭaṇ n. "tour, perigrination." Pkt. *pariaṭṭai*; Deśī. *allaṭṭapallaṭṭaṃ pārśva parivartanam* (23, 6) Skr. *paryaṭana-* n. — $ 48, 51, 77, 109, 141.

palāṇ, pālāṇ n. "saddle". G. O. *palāṇ*, S. *palaṇu*. Panj. *palāṇ*, H. B. *pālāṇ*. Pkt. *pallāṇa-*. Skr. *paryāṇa-* n.— $ 48, 125, 141,

pavḷeṃ povḷeṃ n. coral". G. *parvāḷuṃ*, Siṃ. *pavaḷa*. Pkt. *pavala-*. Skr. *pravāḍa-, prabāla-* m. n. — $ 70, 79, 125.

paṃvāḍā povāḍā m. "a historic ballad". G. *pavāḍo*, H. *poāḍā*; S. *pavāḍo* "noise, tumult" (*-ḍā*, *-ḍo* is a suffix). Skr. *pravāda-* m. — $ 61, 70, 79, 125.

pasar m. "expansion", *pasarṇeṃ* "to spread", G. Panj. H. B. *pasar*, S. *pasār-*. Pkt. *pasarai*. Skr. *prasara-* m., *prasarati*. — $ 52, 65, 125.

paṃsaṣṭ "65", *pastīs* "35". — $ 252.

pasāy m. "favour". Skr. *prasāda-* m. — $ 164.

pastāv m. "regret". G. *pastāvuṃ*, S. *pachutāo*, H. *pachtāo*, B. *pastān*, Siṃ. *pasutāv*; cf. G. O. *pache*, H. *pāche*, Siṃ. *pas*, S. *poe puāṃ* "after". Śaur. Pkt. *pacchādāva-*; cf. Pkt. *pacchā*. Skr. *paśchāttāpa-* m. — $ 103, 152.

pahār, pār m. "interval of three hours". G. *por*, Panj. *pahir*, H. *pahar, pahirā*, B. *pahar*. Skr. *prahara-* m. — $ 40, 125, 161.

pahilā adj. "first". G. *pehluṃ*, Panj. O. B. *pahilā* H. *pahlā pailā*; — S. *paharyo*, Ass. *poṅa*, Siṃ. *paḷamu*. Apa. *pahila-*; Pkt. *paḍhama-* (cf. the Siṃhalese form). Skr. *prathama-*. — $ 46, 125, 226, 256.

paḷṇeṃ "to flee", G. *paḷvuṃ*, B. *palāitē*; Siṃ. imper. *pala*. Pkr. *palāi*, Skr. *palāyate*. — $ 46, 52, 145.

paḷas m. "butea frondosa". S. *palāsu*, Panj. *palāh*, Siṃ. *palas*. Skr. *palāśa-* n. — $ 42, 46, 145.

paḷheṃ, paḷeṃ n. "cotton tree". G. *pel* "spun cotton". Deśī. *palahī karpāsaḥ* (182, 7), *phalahī karpāsaḥ* (210, 15). — $ 46, 169.

pāṃ "expletive particle". Apa. *pāu*. Skr. *prāyaḥ*. — $ 60, 125.

pāīk, m. "messenger, peon". Panj. H. *paik*, B. *pāīk*. Pkt. *pāikka-*. Per. *paig*, Pehlvi *paik*; to separate from Skr. *padāti-* "foot-soldier", *padika-* "pedestrian".

pāūṇ adj. (in compound,) "less by one quarter". G. *poṇo*, S. *pauṇo*, Panj. *pauṇā* H. *paune*, B. O. *paune*, K. *dūn*ᵘ. Skr. *padona-*. — $ 46, 57, 225.

pāūs m. "rain" G. H. *pāvas*. Pkt. *pāusa*, pali *pāvusa-*. Skr. *prāvṛṣa-* m. "rainy season". — $ 30, 46, 125, 253.

pāṃkḷi, pākḷi, pākōlī f. "flower-petal". G. *pāṃkhḍī*, H. *pakh* (*u*) *ḍī*. Pkt. *pamha-*, *pamhala* has a different treatment.....cf. Skr. *pakṣman-* n. — $ 47, 69, 79, 89.

pākh, pāṃkh m. "wing, side of roof, half of a lunar month" G. H. B. *pākh*, Panj. H. *pakh*, S. *pakhu paṃgho paṃgu*, O. *pakṣa* (pronounced *pakhô*); K. *paccha-*, Siṃ. *pak* "part",

Ro. *phak pak*. Pkt. *pakkha-*. Skr. *pakṣa-* m. — $ 96.

pākhar f. caparison", G. Panj. H. *pākhar*, S. *pākhiṛu* "saddle for camel." Deśī. *pakkharā turagasannāhaḥ* (184, 10). Skr. *upaskara-* m. — $ 40, 47, 125, 174.

pākhrūṃ n. "bird". Skr. **pakṣi-rūpa-*. — $ 47, 50, 66, 96.

pākhaḷṇeṃ "to scour an idol". G. *pakhālvuṃ*, Panj. *pakhalṇā pakharṇā*, H. *pakhālnā*. Skr. *prakṣālayati*.- —$ 125, 145.

pāṃg, pāṃglā, pāṃgu "paralytic, bowlegged". G. *pāṃgaluṃ*, Panj. *pāṃgulā*, H. *paṃgu paṃgā paṃglā*, S. *paṃgo* "weak", B. *paṃgrī*, Ro. *pango* (? see Miklosich, S. V. *phag*. Pkt. Skr. *paṅgu-*. — $ 39, 68, 98.

pāṃc "five". H. G. B. O. K. *pāṃc*, S. Panj. *paṃj*, Ro. *panc*, Siṃ. *pas*. Pkt. *paṃca-*. Skr. *pañca-*. — $ 39, 101, 217.

pāj f. "mountain-pass". G. *paj* f. "quay, bridge". Deśī. *pajjā adhirohiṇi..mārga-vācakaḥ tu padyāṣabdabhavaḥ* (181, 5, 6). Skr. *padyā* f. — $ 106.

pāṃjrā m. "cage", G. *pāṃjruṃ*, H.B. K. *paṃjar*. Skr. *pañjara-* n. — $ 75, 106; Cf. M. *piṃjar*.

pājharṇeṃ "to drip". Pkt. *pajjharai*. Skr. *prakṣarati*. — $ 125.

Pāṭaṇ name of a town. Skr. *paṭṭaṇa-* n. — $ 194, 284.

pāṭ. m. "stool", *pāṭā* m. "slab, plank". G. *paṭo*, "strip of cloth, belt", G. Panj. *pāṭ*, "plank, bench", S. *pāṭi* f. "plateau", H. *pāṭ* "slab, stool, B. *pāṭā* "plank", *pāṭī* "plateau", Siṃ. *paṭa* "joint, silk," *paṭi* "belt", K. *pūṭü* "plank", *poṭ*ᵘ "silk", Ro. *phar* "silk". Skr. *paṭṭa-* m. (cf. *pattra-*). — $ 109.

pāṭīl, pāṭel, old M. *pāṭaiḷu*, m. "chief of village". G. *Paṭel*, S. *paṭelu*. Skr. *paṭṭalika- paṭṭa-kila-* m. — $ 38.

pāṭh m. "back", G. *pīṭh pūṭh*, S. *puṭhi*, Panj. *piṭṭhi puṭṭh*, H. B. *pīṭh*, O. *piṭhi*, Siṃ. *piṭa*, Asian Ro. *pušto* (see Miklosich S. V. *phiko*); K. *pušt* "back of chair" *peṭhi* "on, in," *peṭha* "from below, since". Pkt. *paṭṭha-*, *piṭṭha-*, *puṭṭha-*. Skr. *pṛṣṭha-* n. — $ 30, 31, 110, 197.

pāṭhaviṇeṃ "to send". G. *pāṭhā-vavuṃ*, S. *paṭhaṇu*, P. *paṭhānā*, B. *pāṭhaite*, O. *paṭhāibā*. Pkt. *patthāvai*. Skr. *prasthā-payati* (cf. Siṃ. *paṭan* "beginning", from Skr. *prasthāna-*). — $ 47, 48, 110, 125.

pāḍṇeṃ "to cause to fall". G. *pāḍvuṃ*, H. *pāḍnā*, B. *pāḍite* "to spread". Pkt. *pāḍei*. Skr. *pātayati*. — $ 48.

pāḍśī. f. "sterile cow". Deśī *paḍicchiā ciraprasūtā mahiṣī* (186, 4). — $ 49.

pāḍā m. "calf". G. *pāḍuṃ*, S. *pāḍo*, H. *pāḍā*. Deśī. *paḍoo balaḥ* (184, 3); *paḍḍi pra-thama prasūtā* (181, 3). — $ 47.

pāḍvā m. "first day of the fort-night, first day of the year". G. *paḍvo*, H. *parivā*, *paḍvā*, B. *parab*. Pkt. *pāḍivaā*. Skr. *prātipada-* adj. — $ 60, 152.

pāṃḍyā m. "proper name of Brahmin". H. *pāṇḍe* "Savant, school-master," *pāṃḍā* "tem-ple-priest". Skr. *paṇḍita-* m.

—$ 65, 111, 154.
pāṃḍhar f. "white soil, inhabited land" G. H. B. *pāṃḍur* "pale", H. *pāṃḍrī* "whitish soil", Siṃ. *paṃdara* "white, yellow". Skr. *pāṇḍara-* adj. — $ 86.
pāṇī n. "water". G. S. *pāṇī*. Panj. *paṇi*, H. B. *pānī*, K. *pôñ*ᵘ, Ro. *pani*, Siṃ. *pän*. Pkt. *pāṇia-*. Skr. *pānīya-* n. — $ 46, 66, 134, 152.
pāt m. "leaf". G. *pattuṃ pātruṃ*, Panj. *patt*, H. *pattā pātā*, B. *pāt*, Siṃ. *pat*, Ro. *patr*. Pkt. *patta-* Skr. *pattra-* n. — $ 121.
pāṃt f. "line, row". G. H. *pāṃt*, S. *paṃgati*, Siṃ. *pet*. Pkt. *paṃti-*. Skr. *paṅkti-* f. — $ 121.
pātaḷ adj. "thin, weak". G. *pātḷuṃ*, S. *patiru*, Panj. H. *patlā*, B. *pātal*, *pātlā*. Deśī. *pattalaṃ kṛśam* (186, 3); derived from *pattra-*. $ 47. —
pāthar f. "flat and smooth stone". G. *pathro*, S. *patharu*, Panj. *patthar* H. B. *pāthar*, K. *pathur* "soil", *pathar* "on the earth", Siṃ. *patara* "dispersion". Deśī. *pathārī nikaraḥ prastaraśca* (206, 15). Skr. *prastara-* m. — $ 48, 52, 84, 110. 122, 125
pāḍṇeṃ "to break wind". G. H. B. *pād-*, S. Siṃ. *paḍ-*. Skr. *pardate*. — $ 47, 115, 123.
pān n. "leaf". G. H. *pān*, S. *panu*, K. Siṃ. *pan*, B. O. *pān*. Skr. *parṇa-*. — $ 39, 135.
pānhā m. "descent of milk into the udder". G. *pāno*; B. *pānāite* ("to put a calf to his mother's udder so that she yields milk"). Deśī. *paṇho stanadhārā* (182, 1). Skr. *prasnava-* m. — $ 60, 125, 136.
pāpṇi f. "eye-lid". The *rapprochement* with Skr. *pakṣman-* n. is doubtful. Cf. however Pkt. *ruppa-*. of Skr. *rukma-*; and for the absence of aspiration, cf. M. *pākḷī-* — $ 89.
pāphūḍṇeṃ "to form into crusts". Pkt. *papphoḍaï*. Skr. *prasphuṭati*. — $ 125, 126.
pāy m. "foot; quarter (rare)". Undoubtedly borrowed from Hindi. See the word *pāv*. — $ 57.
pāyrī f. "foot-step". G. *pāyrī*, S. *pairo*, H. *pair*, *pairā*, Siṃ. *piyavara* "foot-print". Skr. **pādākāra-*. Cf. — $ 52, 62.
pār m. "end, limit"; adv. "on the other side". G. Panj. H. B. *pār*; S. *pāru* "limit", *pāri* "on the other side". Skr. *pāra-* n; *pāre*. — $ 39.
pārakhṇeṃ "to examine, to verify". G. *pārakhvuṃ*, S. *parkhaṇu*, Panj. *parakhṇā*, H. *parakhnā*, B. *parkh*. Skr. *parīkṣate*. — $ 49.
pārkā, *pārkhā* adj. "other, stranger." G. *pārkuṃ*, with reference to Panj. *parāī*. Pkt. *pārakka-*. cf. Skr. *pārakīya-*. — $ 86, 93.
pārad f. "hunting". G. *parad*. Pkt. *pāraddhi-*, cf. Deśi. *pāraddhaṃ..ākheṭakaḥ* (209, 7). all semi- tatsama : Skr. *pāparddhi-* f. — $ 46, 88.
pāravḍā, m. "1/4 of a village". S. *pāṛo*, H. B. *pāḍā*. Pkt. *pāāra- pārāa-*, *pāra-*. Skr. *prākāra-* m. — $ 46, 61.
pārvā m. "blue-pigeon". G. H. *parevo*, S. *parelo*, Siṃ. *paraviya*. Pkt. *pārāvaa-*. Skr. *pārāvata-* m. — $ 46, 52, 152.
pāras parīs m. "philosopher's stone". S. *pārasu*; G. Panj.

H. *pārab*, B. *paras parespākhar* "philosopher's stone, touchstone." If Skr. *parīkṣā* is at the base of this word, then the change of gender in Marathi and Sindhi remain unexplained; it seems that there has been somewhere a confusion with the skr. *sparśa* (G.H.B. *paras* to "*touch*") cf. *sparśa maṇi* dictionary word philosopher's stone,
S. V. the word *parasṇem* — $ 42, 49.

pārā m. "mercury". G. S. *pāro*, Panj. H.B. *pārā*. Skr. *pārāta*, *pārāda*- m. — $ 46, 60.

pārusṇem "to become stale", *pāravsā* adj. "stale", *pārosā* adj. "who has not accomplished his daily ablutions". G. *pāroṭh* "rotten", Panj. *parossā* "part kept for late invitee", S. *pāruthu* "stale". Skr. *paryuṣita*-, *paryuṣṭa*-. —$ 49, 50, 51, 63, 65.

pālak, *pālakh* m. "cradle", *palkhī*, *palkī* f. "seat". S. *pāliki*, Panj. H. *pālki*—, Siṃ. *paḷak*. Pkt. *pallaṅka*-. Skr. *paryaṅka*- m. — $ 82, 86, 141. Cf. m. *palaṃg*.

pālaṭ m. "turn, vicissitude"; *pālaṭṇeṃ* "to turn, to change"; *pālṭhā*, adj. "over-turned, returned". Panj. H. *palṭā* "overturned"; G. *palaṭvuṃ* *pālaṭvu ṃ*, S. *palaṭṇu*, H. *palaṭnā*, B. *pālaṭite* "to overturn". Deśī. *pallattho pallaṭṭo paryasta iti paryasta-śabda bhavam* (186, 8); *pallaṭṭai palhatthai parysyati* (192.11). Skr. *paryasta*-. — $ 48, 88, 110, 122, 141, 148.

pālā, *pālav* m. "bud." G. *pālo*, *palāv*; Siṃ. *paḷu* "bone, articulation." Skr. *pallava*- m. n. — $ 47, 48, 60, 148, 152.

pāv m. "a quarter". G. *pāv*, S. Panj. H. *pāo*, B. *poā*, Siṃ. *pā*, Arm. Ro. *pav*; on the other hand M. G. *pāy*, H. O. *pāe*, *pā*, K. *pūr*[u]. Siṃ. *paya*. Pkt. *pāa*.. Skr. *pāda*- m. — $ — $ 55, 125, 225.

pāvṇā m. "mariner". cf. B. *pānsī* "boat". cf. Pkt. *paviuṃ* inf. Skr. **plāvanaka*-. —$ 49, 125, 152.

pāvṇeṃ "to wait" (part. *pātla*, *pāvlā*). G. *pāmvuṃ*, S. *pāiṇu*, Panj. *pāuṇā*, H. *pānā*, *pāunā* B. *pāite*, O. *pāiba*, Siṃ. *päminenavā*, K. *prāvun*. Pkt. *pāvai*. Skr. *prāp*-. — $ 46, 125, 152, 229, 230, 237, 256.

pās, *pāśīṃ* "near". G. *pāsuṃ* "side, shore", S. *pāsu* "side", Panj. *pās*, *pāh*, H. B. *pās* "near", Siṃ. *pas*, *pasa*, "side, proximity.", Ro. *paś* "half", *pas'o* "near", probably K. *pāsa* "page of a book". Skr. *pārśva*- n. — $ 84, 157, 194, 195.

pāsoḷi phāṣlī f. "coast". S. *pāsirī*, H. *paslī pasulī*; Panj. *pāslā* "on the side" adj. P. *phāsulikā*. derived from Skr. *pārśva*-. — $ 69, 84, 157.

pāhṇeṃ "to see, to look", *pāhije* "is necessary, it should be." S. *pahaṇu* "to consider, to deliberate", with reference to *pasṇu* "to see, to look". To be separated from Pkt. *pās*-, Skr. *paśyati*. From Skr. *spṛh*- "to desire, to seek" ? — $ 52, 160, 232, 237.

pāhuṇā, *pāhoṇā* m. "guest". G. *paṇo*, Panj. *pāhuṇā*, H. *pāhunā* "guest, son-in-law". Skr. *prāghūrṇa*- *prāghuṇa*- m. — $ 125, 159.

pāḷ f. "the outer and curving edge of the auricle, parapet, objects scattered in a circle around other objects". G. *pāḷ* "edge, curb stone of a well", S. *pālu* "layers of", straw used for rippening the fruits."Panj. *pāl* "series", H. *pāl* "dyke", Siṃ. *pela* "line, text," K. *palⁱyār* "palisade Pkt. P. Skr. *pāli-* f. — $ 145.

pālṇeṃ"to nourish, to bring up". G. *pāḷvuṃ*, S. *pālaṇu*, H. *pālnā*, B. *pālite*, Siṃ. *palna*. Pkt. *pāḷ- pāl-*. Skr. *pālayati*. — $ 46, 145.

pikā adj. "ripe". Isolated with reference to H. *pakkā* (borrowed every where), K. *pap*. "to ripen"; Ro. *pek.-* "to cook" is ambiguous. Pkt. *pikka-* beside *pakka-*. Skr. *pakva-*. — $ 75, 93.

piṃjar n., *piṃjrā* m. "cage, thorax". S. *piñiro*, Panj. *piṃjrī*, H. B. *piṃjar*, O. *piṃjirā*. Skr. *piñjara-*. — $ 75. Cf. M. *pāṃjar*.

piṭṇeṃ "to beat, to crush". G. S. Panj. H. B. O. *piṭ-*. Pkt. *piṭṭha-*. Skr. *piṣṭa-*. — $ 89, 231. Cf. M. *pīṭh*.

piṃḍ m. "ball", *piṃḍī* f. "tablet". G. *piṃḍlo* "ball of chalk or of wheat flour", W. Panj. *pinn-* "to bake", S. *pina* "alms" *pinu* "packet". H. *peḍ piṃḍī*, B. *piṃḍ*, Siṃ. *piḍa* "small quantity, small ball". Skr. *pinḍa-* m. — $ 111.

pīḍheṃ m. "stool, support". G. *pīḍhiyuṃ* "supporting the floor planks"; S. *pīṛhī*, Panj. *pihṛā*, Siṃ. *piḷa* "throne", K. *pīū-* "stool". Pkt. *pīḍha-*. Skr. *pīṭha-* n. — $ 80, 112.

piṇeṃ "to drink". G. Panj. H. *pī-*, S. B. Ro. *pi-*, Siṃ. *bo* (part. *bīvā*), Caus. *pova-* (part. *pevvā*), Pkt. *piai*, *piei*. Skr. *pibati*. — $ 63, 229, 230, 231, 252.

piṃpḷī f. "long pepper". G. *pipar* f., S. *pipirī*, H. *piplī*, B. *pipūl piṃpūl pippalī*. Skr. *pippalī* f. — $ 140.

piṃpaḷ m. "ficus riligiosa". G. *pipaḷo*, *pipaḷ*, S. *pipiru*, Panj. B. *pippal*, O. *pimpal*. Skr. *pippala-* m. — $ 69, 125, 145.

piṃpaḷṇer name of town. Skr. *pippalanagara-*. — $ 62. See also *ṇer*, *ner*.

pilūṃ pillūṃ n. "small animal". G. *pilõ* "bud", H. *pilū*, *pillā* "pup." B. *pil*, Siṃ. *pilavā*. P. *pillaka-* (cf. Tam. *piḷḷei* "son" ?) — $ 149.

pivḷā adj. "yellow". G. *pīḷuṃ*, S. *pīlo*; Panj. H. *pīlā*; H. *piyūḍī pevḍī* "yellow chalk, yellow colour". Deśī. *pīvalaṃ pītam iti tu pītaśabdabhavam* (200, 13). Skr. *pītala-*. — $ 44, 145.

pisṇeṃ "to crush". G. *pis-pīs-*, S. *pīh-*, Panj. *pīh- pīs-*, H. *pīs-*, B. *piṣ-*, K. *pih-*, Ro. *pis-*. Pkt. *pīsai*. Skr. *pinaṣṭi*. — $ 44.

pisā adj. "mad", *piseṃ* n. "madness", *pisāleṃ* n. "madness". Pkt. *pisāa-*, *pisalla-*. Skr. *piśāca-* m. — $ 52, 60, 61, 156.

piyo pihū m. "lover". G. *piyuṃ*, Panj. S. *piyu*, Panj. *piā*, H. *piyā*, Siṃ. *piya*; cf. Ro. *piryav-* "to debauch, to prostitute oneself." Pkt. *pia-*. Skr. *priya-*. — $ 39, 125, 161.

piḷṇeṃ "to crush". Panj. *pelṇā*, H. *pelnā*; Siṃ. *paḷenavā* "to be tortured", *piḷa* "pain". Pkt. *pīlaṇa- pīḍaṇa-*. Skr. *pīḍ-*. — $ 44, 146. Cf. M. *pīḍṇeṃ*.

pī f. *piyahā pihā* m. "spleen". H. *pīlhā pilhā*, B. *pila*, O. *pilhāī*. Skr. *plīhan-* m., *plīhā* f. (lexicon). — $ 64, 154, 161.

pīṭh n. "flour". G. Panj. *pīṭh* f., H. *pīṭhā* "cake of rice-powder", Siṃ. *piṭi*. Pkt. P. *piṭṭha-*. Skr. *piṣṭa-*. — $ 41, 110.

pīḍṇeṃ "to torment". G. *pīḍvuṃ*, S. *pīḍṇu*, Panj. *piḍhnā*, H. *peḍnā*, B. *pīḍite*. Skr. *pīḍ-*. Cf. M. *piḷṇeṃ*. — $ 44, 111, 146.

pīs m. "plume", G. *pīṃch*. Pkt. Skr. *piccha* n. — $ 103.

puḍā m. "packet". G. S. *puḍo*, H. *puḍā*. Deśī. *pudaiaṃ puṃḍaiaṃ pinḍīkṛtam* (201, 15), cf. *abhiṇṇapuḍo riktaputaḥ* (21, 1). Skr. *puṭa-* m. n. — $ 111.

putḷā m. "statue of man", *putḷī* f. "doll". G. *putḷī putḷuṃ*, S. *putili*, Panj. H. *putḷī*, B. *putul*. Skr. *putraka-* m. *putrikā* f. — $ 44.

punav m. "sterculia foetida, *poon*-tree". Panj. *pūnnā*. Pkt. *puṇṇāa-*, *puṇṇāma-*. Skr. *puṃnāga-* m. — $ 44, 55, 135.

punav f. "day of ful moon". cf. Siṃ. *puṇu* "full". Skr. *pūrṇimā* f. — $ 39, 42, 44, 135.

purā, adj. "full". G. *puro*, S. S. *pūro*, Panj. H. B. O. *pūrā*, Siṃ. *piri*, K. *pur*ᵘ. Skr. *pūrita-pūra-* (Buddhist). — $ 44.

pulā m. "small bundle of grass, of hey". G. H. *pulā*, Panj. *pūlā*. Pkt. *pollaa-*. Skr. *pūla-* m. — $ 44.

puvā m. "cake", H. *pūā*, *pū*, Siṃ. *puva*, *pū*. Skr. *pūpa-apūpa-* m. — $ 44, 64, 125, 174.

pusṇeṃ "to sweep" G. H. *puṃch-*, Panj. *pūṃjh-*, B. *puṃch- poṃch-*, Siṃ. *pis- pih-*. Deśī. *puṃchai puṃsāi pusai* : *mārśṭi* (201, 11). Skr. *proñch-*, *poñch-* (Buddhist). — $ 44, 71, 103, 125.

pusṇeṃ "to ask". G. S. H. B. Ro. *puch-*, Panj. *pucch-*. Pkt. *pucchai* Skr. *pṛcchati*. — $ 31, 71, 103, 230, 253.

puḷaṇ n. "plain, sandy-shore". Skr. *pulina-* m. n. — $ 42, 134, 145.

pū m. "pus", S. *pūnī* f., B. *pūyā pūṃj*. Skr. *pūya-* m. n. — $ 64.

pūt m. "son", *potī-* f. "daughter". G. Panj. *pūt*, S. *puṭu*, H. B. *put*, O. *pua*, Siṃ. *pit*, *put* "son"; K. *pūt*ᵘ "chicken". Pkt. *putta-*. Skr. *putra-* m. — $ 29, 121.

pūl "bridge". G. *pūl*, Panj. H. *pul.*, S. *puli* f. Per. *pul*. — $ 41, 149.

pūs m. "month of *Pauṣ*." G. *pos*, *poṣ*, S. *pohu*, Panj. *poh*, H. *pus*, O. *pūṣ*, Skr. *puṣya-* m. — $ 157.

pekṣāṃ "in comparison with". Skr. *apekṣā* f. —$ 125, 174.

pekhṇeṃ pekṇeṃ "to wait". G. *pekhvuṃ* "to see, to observe", Panj. *pekhṇā* "to observe", H. *pekhnā* "to desire" Siṃ. *pekaṇiya* "navel" ("the visible one"). Pkt. *pekkhai-*. Skr. *prekṣate* — $ 30, 77, 89, 96, 125, 230.

pej f. "rice gruel"; *pejiṃ* n. "milk". S. H. *pej* f. Pkt. *pejja-*. Skr. *peya-*, *peyya-* (Buddhist). — $ 77, 106, 125.

peṭī f. "box, basket, belt". G. S. Panj. H. *peṭī*, B. *peṭiyā*, *peḍā* "travel basket", Siṃ. *peli*, Pkt. *peḍā*. Skr. *piṭaka-* n., *peṭī* f. — $ 109.

pemṭh f. "town, market". H. *pemṭh paimṭh*. Skr. *pratiṣṭhā* f. — $ 125.

pemḍ m. "mud sticking to shoes", f. "the refuse of seeds or nuts from which the oil has been expressed"; *pemḍhī* "packet". G. *pemḍo* "small ball of clay", H. *peḍ pemḍ* "ball, bowl." Pkt. *peṇḍa-*; cf. Deśī. *pemḍabālam pemḍaliyam*. . . .*piṇḍīkṛtam* (201, 15). Skr. *piṇḍa-* m. — $ 77, 86.

peḍhī f. "seat, throne". G. *peḍhī*. Pkt. *peḍha-*. Skr. *pīṭha-* n. — $ 80.

per m. "spreading paddy on the flour for being husked by the bullocks; *perṇem* "to sow". Cf. Deśī. *payaro ṣarah*. . *pradara śabda bhava-* (186, 8). Skr. *pradara-* m. — $ 62.

pelṇem "to push". H. *pelnā*. Pkt. *pellai, pellana-*. Skr. *preryate*. — $ 41, 230, 231.

pesṇem "to send a demon to some body". Skr. *preṣayati*. — $ 77, 125.

pehraṇ peraṇ n. "shirt of a child". G. *paheraṇ*, S. *pahirāṇu*. Deśī. *parihaṇam paridhānam* (189, 3). Skr. *paridhāṇa-* n. or rather Per. *pērāhan* (Mod. *pīrāhan*). The family of Skr. *paridhā-* is also found in M. *pehrāv* "dress", G. *pahervum*, S. *paharaṇu* (caus. *parahāiṇu*), Panj. *pahinhā* (caus. *pahirāuṇā*), H. *pahinnā*, K. *pair-* "to dress". — $ 80, 167.

pai- prefix common to certain number of words. Skr. *prati-*. — $ 29, 125, 170.

paiṃ "certainly, generally". G. Panj. H. *pai* "but". Apa. *prāiva*. Skr. *prāyeṇa*. — $ 57, 125.

paikṇem paikhṇem "to wait". Skr. *pratīkṣate*. Or contamination of *pekhṇem* "to wait" and *aikṇem* "to hear, to listen" ? — $ 56, 89.

paij f. "bet, promise". S. *paij* m. "standing of firm, credit", Panj. H. *paīj* "vow, promise"; Ro. *prinjan-* "to know, to recognise". Skr. *pratijñā* f. — $ 56, 106, 135.

Paiṭhaṇ name of a town Deśī. *paiṭṭhāṇam nagaram* (192, 3). Skr. *pratiṣṭhāna-* n. — $ 42, 56.

paiṭhā m. "name of a tree". H. *paiṭh*, B. *paiṭhā* "ladder, stair-case", Siṃ. *piviṭu* "entrance"; G. *peṭhuṃ* (pcpl. of *pesvuṃ*) "entered"; cf. G. *pesvuṃ*, S. *pehṇu*, H. *paiṭhnā*. .*paisnā*, Arm. Ro. *pesel* "to enter". Deśī. *paiṭṭho jñātaraso viralammārgaṣceti tryarthaḥ* (216. 3). Skr. *praviṣṭa-*. For the fall of *v.-* cf. *baisṇem* (Skr. *upasviś-*). — $ 56, 125.

paiṇ f. "convention, wet". Skr. *pratijñā*. Cf. *paij*.- — $ 56, 106, 135.

pail "opposite", *pailā* "who is on the other side" (poet.). G. *pelum*; H. *pailār* adv. "of the other side". Derived from Pkt. *pai-* with the Pkt. Suffix *-illa* (cf. $ 256). — $ 56.

pais m. "place, space". Siṃ. *piyes*. Pkt. *paesa-*. Skr. *pradeśa-* m. — $ 56, 125, 156.

paisāv adj. "spread". m. "release". Skr. *prati srāva-* m. — $ 152, 157.

poṃkh n. "end of a line, of a row". Skr. *puṅkha-* m. ? — $ 80.

pokhar n. "pond". Panj. H. *pokhar*, B. *pūkūr*, O. *pokhuri*; Siṃ. *pokura* "lotus". P. Pkt. *pokkhara-*. Skr. *puṣkara-* n. — $ 80, 89, 96.

poṭ n. "stomach". G. S. B. Panj. H. *peṭ* "stomach", H. *pūṭlī* "anus", *pūṭ* "bone of buffaloe-tale". Deśī. *poṭṭam udaram* (204, 5). Skr. *puṣṭa-* adj. "fat". — $ 80, 63.

poṭlā m., *poṭli* f. "objects tied in a piece of cloth". G. *poṭ*, *poṭlo*, S. *poṭri*, Panj. H. *poṭ*, *poṭlī*, B. *puṃṭalī*. Deśī. *kuṃṭi poṭṭalaṃ*; *vastranibaddhaṃ dravyam* (82, 16). — $ 145.

pot m. f. "pearl of glass or gold, precious stone." G. Panj. *pot* f., S. *pūti* f. H. *pot* m., B. *pot*. Deśī. *pottī kācaḥ* (204, 5).

pothī f. "book". G. *pothī*, S. *pothī*, *pothu*, Panj. H. *pothī*, *pothā*, B. *puthī*, Siṃ. *pota*, K. *puthi*. Pkt. *pottha-*, *potthiā*, P. *potthaka-*. Skr. *pustaka-* n. — $ 80, 122, 125, 252.

pophaḷ f. "areca-tree". G. *phophaḷ* n. Pkt. *popphala-*. Skr. *pūgaphala-* n. — $ 64, 126, 145.

pol n. "a hollow grain". G. *poluṃ*, S. *poro*, Panj. *pol*, H. *polā* "hollow". Pkt. *polla-* (*rikta-*; cf. Meyer *Hindu Tales*, p. 129, n. 5). Skr. *pūlya-* (a"pax; Whitney, *Atharvaveda transl.*, p. 765, translated as shrivelled grain"). — $ 84.

pohaṃcṇeṃ "to arrive, to obtain". G. *pocvuṃ*, S. *pahucṇu*, Panj. *pahuṃcṇā*, H. *pahuṃcnā*, B. *paṃhucan*, O. *pahuṃcihā* Etymology unknown; cf. M. *pāhuṇā*, Skr. *prāghūrṇa-* ? — $ 252.

pohā m. "troop". Pkt. *pūha-*. Skr. **apyūha-*, wrongly quoted without observation — $ 125, is an arbitary restitution of Pischel ($ 286).

pohā m. "pressed rice". Skr. *pṛthuka-* m. n. $ 30, 159.

poḷ m. "ox dedicated to gods". Pkt. *poala-*, cf. Deśī. *poālo vṛṣabhaḥ* (204, 17). Skr. *potalika-* (derived from *pota*:- cf. Siṃ. *po*, H. *pūā* "the young of cattle"). — $ 64, 145.

poḷ pauḷ f. "low wall of loosely thrown-up stones." G. *poḷ* f. "street", H. *pol*, *paul*, *paur*, m. "door, court-yard," Himalayan dialects *proḷ*. Skr. *pratoli-* f. — $ 56, 59, 125, 145.

poḷṇeṃ "to burn", *poḷī* f. "sort of fried cake". G. *poḷī*, Pan.j *polī pollī* S. *porī*, B. *puli*, "fried cake", B. *poḍāite*, *puḍite* "to burn", Deśī. *paulai pacati* (192, 11). — $ 152.

pyār adj. "dear". G. *pyāruṃ*, S. *pyāro*, Panj. *piārā*, H. *pyār*. Skr. *priyakāra-*. — $ 63, 154.

pyās f. "thirst". G. S. Panj. H. B. *piyās*. Pkt. *pivāsa- piāsa-* (adj.). Skr. *pipāsā* f. — $ 63, 125, 154, 156.

pragaṭ, adj. "well known". G. H. *pragaṭ*, S. *praghaṭu*, Panj. H. *pargaṭ*; But Siṃ. *pahala*. Skr. *prakaṭa-*. — $ 98.

pramāṇeṃ "in the manner of". Skr. *pramāṇa-*. — $ 193.

phaṭ f. "chasm", *phaṭakṇeṃ* "to leap, to separate, to sift grain husk" G. Panj. H. *phaṭak-*, S. *phaḍak-*, K. *phyār-*. Skr. *sphaṭ-*. — $ 48, 84, Old

M. *phāṭṇeṃ*.

phaḍā f. "hood of serpent, end of branch of leaf of datetree." H. *phaḍa* "end of branch, ear of maize", B. *phadki* "twig". Deśī. *phaḍaṃ sarpasya sarvaṣarīraṃ phaṇaśca* (212, 13). Skr. *phaṭā* f. — $ 111.

phaṇ m. "hood of cobra". G. *phaṇā*, *phaṇī*, *pheṇ*, S. *phaṇi* f. Panj. *phaṇ* f., H. B. O. *phaṇā*, Siṃ. *paṇa*. Skr. *phaṇa-* m. — $ 134.

phaṇas, *paṇas* m. "jack fruit tree". G. *phaṇas*, H. *panas*, *phanas*, B. *paṇas*. Pkt. *paṇasa-* *phaṇasa-*. Skr. *panasa-* m. — $ 84.

phattar m. "stone" (figurative use). H. *phattar*. —see M. *patthar*. — $ 168.

pharas m. "battle-axe". G. *pharsī* *pharśī*, H. *pharsā*, B. *pharsā*, *phalsā*. Pkt. *parasu*, Pkt. P. *pharasu-*. Skr. *paraśu-* m. — $ 84.

pharā m. "shoulder-blade". Panj. *phar*. Deśī. *pharao phalakaḥ* (210, 15). Skr. *phalaka-* n. m. — $ 125, 142.

phaḷ m. "fruit". G. Panj. H. B. K. *phal*, S. *pharu phalu*, Siṃ. *pala*. Skr. *phala-* n. — $ 126.

phaḷā m. "plank". S. *pharuhō*, H. *phaḍī*, Siṃ. *paliha*, Ro. *phal*. Pkt. *phalaga-*. Skr. *phalaka-* n. m. — $ 46, 126, 142, 145.

phaḷār, *pharāḷ* m. "light meal (of fruit etc.)." G. *phaḷār*, *pharāḷ*, H. *phalār*, *phalyār*, B. *phalār*. Skr. *phalāhāra-* m. — $ 126, 145, 161, 167.

phāg m. "the verses in honour of Kṛṣṇa recited in the month of Holi." G. *phāg*, *phāgvo* "present received in Holī", *phāgan* "the month of Phalguna"; S. *phāgu* "name of month, amusements in the month of Holi, showering of red powder"; Panj. *phāg* "Holi" *phaggū* name of month. H. *phāg*, B. *phāgū* "red powder". Deśī. *phaggū vasantotsavaḥ* (210, 15). Skr. *phalgu-*, *phalguna-*. $ 38, 39, 126.

phāṭṇeṃ "to get torn". G. S. Panj. H. B. K. *phaṭ-* *phaṭ-* *phaḍ-*, Ro. *phar-*, Siṃ. *paḷ-*. Skr. *sphaṭati-* — $ 48, 126, 146.

phāḍṇeṃ "to worry". see M. *phāḷṇeṃ*.

phāṃḍṇeṃ "to jump, to leap (about an animal)." H. B. *phāṃd* Skr. *spand* $ 126.

phānūs, *phāṇas* m. n. "lantern". G. *phānas*, S. *fānosu*, *fanūsū*, Panj. H. *fānūs*. Ar. Pers. *faṇūs*. — $ 42, 46, 134.

phār adj. "numerous", adv. "very", G. *phār* adv. Pkt. *phāra-*. Skr. *sphāra-*. — $ 126.

phāvḍā m. "wooden hoe". H. *phāoṛā*, *phauṛā* "mattock, spade", Bih. *phaurā*, B. *phāoḍā* "shovel for ashes". Skr. *sphyá-* n. ? — $ 126.

phāṃs m. "net, snare". G. *phāṃso*, S. *phāsī*, *phāsiṇī* "snare, trap", *phāsaṇu*, "to get bogged to be caught", B. Panj. *phāsnā*, Siṃ. *pasa*. Pkt. *phaṃs-*. Skr. *pāśa-* m. — $ 84.

phāsā m. "dice". G. *pāso*, Panj. H. *pāsā*. Skr. *pāśaka-* m. — $ 84, 156.

phāḷ m. "ploughshare" S. *phāru*, Panj. *phālā*, H. B. *phāl*, Skr. *phāla-* m. — $ — $ 126, 145.

phāḷṇeṃ "to tear" *phāḷā* m.

"torn of piece, rent". G. *phāḷvavuṃ* "to share", *phāḷo* "part"; G. S. H. B. *phāḍ-* "to tear"; O. *phālā-phālā* "torn". Skr. *sphaṭati*. — $ 126, 146.

phiṭṇeṃ "to get loose". G. S. *phiṭ-*. Pkt. *phiṭṭai-* — $ 80, 126,, 230 cf. M. *pheḍṇeṃ*.

phirṇeṃ "to turn", G. *pherphar-*, S. H. B. K. Ro. *phir-* "to turn, to circulate". Etymology unknown.

phulel "perfumed sesamum oil". From M. *phūl* "flower" and tel "oil". — $ 44.

phukaṭ phukā adv. 'free", G. *phok* "hallow, vain", S. *phokaṭu* "without reason, free", Panj. *phok phog* "scraps" *phokā* "vain, insipid", H. *phokaṭ* "good for nothing, free", B. *phukār* "free space, opening". Deśī. *phukkā mithyā* (211; 10).

phuṭṇeṃ "to break", *phoḍṇeṃ* "to burst,". G. *phuṭvuṃ phoḍvuṃ*, S. *phuṭṇu* and *phoḍaṇu* "to crack, to burst"; H. *phūṭnā phoḍnā*, B. *phuṭite* "to burst", *pholan* "swelling". Pkt. *phuṭṭai, phuḍai*. Skr. *sphuṭayati* — $ 126.

phurṇeṃ "to have convulsions". G. *phurvuṃ*, Pan. *phurṇā*, S. *phuraṇu* "to rob, to steal", Siṃ. *pupura* "spark". Pkt. *phuranta-*, *phurphuranta-* "trembling". Skr. *sphurati* — $ 126.

phel m. "pod, empty shell". Deśī. *phello daridraḥ* (211, 17).

phūl m. "flower". G. H. B. *phūl*, S. *phulu*, Pan. *phull*, Siṃ. *pil*, *pul*. P. Skr. *phulla-* adj. — $ 126, 148.

pheḍṇeṃ active form of *phiṭṇeṃ* "to demolish, to loosen". G. *pheḍvuṃ*, B. *phelite* "to throw", *phelāite*. Ap. *pheḍai*. — $ 80, 126.

pheṇ m., *pheṇī* f. "foam". H. *phen*, *phenā* m. S. *pheṇu* m. *pheṇi*., B. *phen*, *pheṇi* "sugar cane juice". Skr. *phena-* m. — $ 126, 134.

phoḍ m. "pestule, hole". H. B. *phoḍā*, Siṃ. *pola*. P. *phoṭā-*. Skr. *sphoṭā-* m. — $ 111, 126.

phoḍṇī f. "oil or ghee fried with mustard grain to make a sauce". G. *phoḍṇī*. Deśī. *phoḍiayaṃ rājikā, dhūmitam* (213, 1).

phoḍṇeṃ "to burst". G. *phoḍvuṃ*, S. *phoṛaṇu* "to crack" *phori* f. "fissure, rent", H. *phoḍnā*, B. *pholan* "swelling", *pholāite* "to irritate". Skr. *sphoṭati*. — $ 126. Cf. M. *phuṭṇeṃ*.

bak baglā m. "heron". G. *bak*, *bag*, *baglo*, S. *bagu*, *bagulo*, Pan. H. *baglā*, *bagulā*, *buglā*. Pkt. *bakka-*. Skr. *baka-* m. — $ 98, 127, 165.

bakrā, m. "he-goat". G. *bakro*, S. *bakiro*, Pan. *bakkarā*, H. B. O. *bakrā*, K. *bakar*, Ro. *bakro*. Skr. *barkara-* m. — $ 93, 127, 163.

band m. "link, dam". Panj. *band-*. — $ 88.

baḍbaḍṇeṃ, *vaṭvaṭṇeṃ* "to chatter, to gossip, " G. S. Pan. H. *baḍ baḍ-*. Pkt. *vaḍavāḍai*, Deśī. *baḍabaḍai vilapati* (214, 12). — $ 150, 252.

barū m. "reed", G. S. Pan. H. *barū*. Deśī. *baruaṃ ikṣusadṛśatṛṇaṃ;....atra barua-bala-vaṭṭi-śabdau dantoṣṭhyādī kaścin nibaddhau* (214, 3-5). — $ 46, 150.

barā adj. "good", *bareṃ* (in Konkan, *boreṃ*) "well". Skr. *vara-* ? — $ 79.

bahirā adj. "deaf". G. *behero bero*, H. *bahirā bahrā*, B. *baherā*, O. *bahirā*, Siṃ. *bihiri*, *bihirā*. Skr. *badhira-*. — $ 50, 128, 159.

bahīṇ f. "sister" (Konkani : *boiṇ*). G. *behen ben*, S. *bheṇu*, Panj. *bainh*, *bhaiṇ*, B. *bahin*, *bahnī*, B. *bain*, O. *bhauṇī*, K. *beñe*, Siṃ. *bihini*, *buhun* "elder sister" Ro. *phen*. Pkt. *bahini*. Skr. *bhaginī* f. — $ 46, 79, 134, 167.

baḷ f. "offering, sacrifice". G. *baḷī*, Panj. *balī*, S. B. *bali*, H. K. *bal*, Siṃ. *bili billa*. Skr. *bali-* m. — $ 145.

baḷ n. "force". G. *baḷ* n., S. *balu*, Panj. H. B. K. *bal*, Siṃ. *bala*. Pkt. Skr. *bala-* n. — $ 145.

baḷī adj. "strong". G. *baḷī*, S. Panj. H. B. *balī*. Deśī. *balio pīnaḥ* (213, 3). Skr. *balin-*.

bāj m. "fear". Pkt. *bajjai*, Deśī. *vajjai trasyati* (251, 6). — $ 150.

bāṃdhṇeṃ "to tie". G. *baṃdhāvuṃ* "to be tied", S. *baṃdhaṇu*, H. *bāndhnā*, Panj. *bannhṇā*, B. O. *bāmdh*, Siṃ. *bandinavā* (pcpl. *bāda*), Arm. Ro. *banthel*. Pkt. Skr. *bandh-*. — $ 124, 230.

bāp m. "father". G. Panj. H. B. Arm. Ro. *bāp*, S. *bābū*. Pkt. *bappa-*, Apa. *bappīkī*, Deśī. *bappo subhaṭaḥ, pitety anye* (213, 3). — $ 150.

bāpuḍā adj. "poor, pitiable". G. *bāpḍuṃ*, H. *bāpḍā*, *bāprā*. Apa. *bappuḍā* (=*varākāḥ*). — $ 165.

bābar f. "dishevelled hair". G. *bābrī* "combings", H. *bābar* "grass for rope-making", Panj. H. *bābriyāṃ* "long and ill kept hair". Deśī. *babbarī keśa racanā* (213, 15). Skr. *barbara-*. — $ 47, 127.

bābhūḷ f. "accacia arabica". G. *bāvaḷ*, S. *baburu*, Panj. H. *babūl*, H. *babūr bābul*. Skr. *vāvūla-*, *varvūra-* (lex.). — $ 86.

bāmbhurḍā (used pejoratively), *bāmaṇ* m. "Brahmin". G. H. B. *bāmaṇ*, S. *bāṃbhaṇu*, Panj. *bāmhaṇ*, Siṃ. *baṃba*, Pkt. *bambhaṇa-*, *bambaṇa-*. Skr. *brāhmaṇa* m. — $ 127, 128, 138.

bāyko f. "woman", old M. instr. *bāyakeṃ*. G. H. *bāī*, K. *bāy*. Etymology unknown. — $ 64, 193.

bārā "twelve". G. O. *bār*, S. *bārahaṃ*, Panj. *bārāṃ*, H. *bārah bārā bāro*, Siṃ. *bara daḷasa doḷaha*, K. *bāh*. Pkt. *bārasa*, *bāraha duvālasa*. Skr. *dvādaśa-*. — $ 118, 143, 214, 221.

bārī f. "window". S. *bārī*, G. *bārī*, *baruṃ* ("door"), K. Arm. Ro. *bar*. Skr. *dvāra-* n. "door". — $ 130.

bāvḍī f. "large well with open sky, *bowry*". G. *vāo vāīṃ*, S. *vāī*, H. *bāvdī bāvlī bāvrī bāīṃ*, Siṃ. *voeva* (old Siṃ. *vaviya*, Maldiv. *wen*). Skr. *vāpī*, *vāpikā* f. — $ 150.

bāvan "fifty two". G. H. *bāvan*, Panj. *bavaṃjā*, S. *bāvaṃjāh*, B. *bāyan*, O. *bāan*, K. *dowanzāh*. Pkt. *bāvaṇṇaṃ*. Skr. *dvāpañcāśat-*. — $ 223.

bāvīs bevīs "twenty-two". G. *bāvīs*, S. *bāvīh*, Panj. *bāī*, H. Maith *bāīs*, B. O. *bāīś*. Pkt.

bāvīsaṃ, Apa. *bāisa*. Skr. *dvāviṃśati-*. — $ 214.

bāhṇeṃ "to call, to cry". Skr. *bṛṃhati* "to talk (meaning given in Dhatup.)" — $ 30, 52, 160.

bāhattar "72". G. *bāḥoter*, S. *bāhatari*, Panj. *bahattar*, H. B. *bāhattar*, Maith. *bahattari*, K. *dusatat*. Pkt. *bāvattariṃ*. Skr. *dvāsaptati-*. — $ 160, 223.

bāhī f. "arm". S. *bāṃhān*, Panj. H. *bāṃh*, Siṃ. *bā*, K. *bāū* (*bāhi* "bracelet"), Ro. *bay*. Buddhist. Pkt. *bāhā*. Skr. *bāhu-* m. — $ 70, 159.

bāhulā bāvlā (dial. *bāholā*) m. "idol, doll, statue". G. *bāvaluṃ*. Deśī. *bāullī pañcālikā*; *atra bapphāula- bāullī śabdau keśāṃcid dantyoṣṭhyādī* (214, 13). — $ 46, 50, 57, 150, 161.

bāher "outside"; *bāhirilā* (inscription of 1206), adj. "from outside". G. *bahār*, *bāher*, S. *bāhari*, *bāharu*, H. *bāhīr*, Panj. H. *bāhar*, B. *bāhir*, Siṃ. *bāpāra*. P. Pkt. *bāhira-*. Skr. *bahiḥ*. — $ 46, 80, 159.

bāḷ n. "child", adj. "young". G. Panj. H. B. K. *bāl*, S. *bāru*, *bālu*, Siṃ. *bal*, Ro. *balo* "pig" ? P. Pkt. Skr. *bāla-* m. and adj. — $ 145.

bijlī f. "lightning". G. *vijlī*, Panj. H. B. *bijlī*, O. *bijulī*, Siṃ. *viduliya*. Pkt. *vijjuliā*. Skr. *vidyut-* f. Hindi loan. — $ 150.

biṭī f. "excretion, ordur". Siṃ. *beṭṭa*; K. *boṭh*ᵘ "cow-dung used as fuel". To be probably separated from the family of H. *bīṭh*, Skr. *viṣṭhā*; cf. M. *viṭāl*. — $ 150.

biṃd m. *biṃdeṃ* n. "drop of sperm, sperm". G. S. H. B. *biṃdu*; H. K. *biṃd*, Siṃ. *biṃda-* "drop". Pkt. Skr. *bindu-* m. — $ 76, 166.

bīṃ n., *bī* f. "seed." G. *bī bīj*, S. *bīhaṇu*, Panj. *bīṃ*, H. *bīhan*, *bīj*, *biyā*, B. *bīj*, *bīc*, O. *bīhan*, K. *byôl*ᵘ. Skr. *bīja-* n. — $ 41, 127, 150, 191.

bī "also, moreover". G. S. *bī*, Panj. H. *bī bhī*, Ro. *vi*. Pkt. *pi*, *vi*. Skr. *api*.— $ 127.

bīj f. "second day of the month". G. S. *bīyā*; G. S. *bijo*, Panj. *biā* "second", K. *biya* "other". Pkt. *biijja-* with reference to *bīa-*. Skr. *dvitīya-* adj. — $ 130, 214, 226.

bīḷ n. "hole (of serpent, rat etc.)". S. *biru*, H. B. *bil*, Siṃ. *bala*. P. Pkt. Skr. *bila-* n. — $ 145, 150.

bujṇeṃ "to frighten". Deśī. *vojjhāraṃ atītaṃ bhītaṃ. ca*; *vojjai trasyati* (271, 8). — $ 86, 150.

bhujhṇeṃ "to understand". G. Ass. *buj-*, S. H. B. O. *bujh-* Panj. *bujjh-*, K. *bōz-*. Pkt. *bujjhai*. Skr. *budhyate* — $ 44, 85, 107, 127, 230.

buḍṇeṃ "to drown". G. S. B. *buḍ-*, H. *būḍ-*, K. *bôḍ-*; Ro. *bol-* "to plunge". Pkt. *buḍḍai*. — $ 150.

buṃd m. "drop". G. Panj. H. *buṃd*, S. *buṃḍo*, *bund*. Skr. *bindu-* m. — $ 39, 76, 166, 188.

budh f. "reason". S. *budhi*, Panj. *buddh*, H. *budh*, K. *bôd*, cf. Siṃ. *budu* "the Buddha." Skr. *buddhi-* f.— $ 124.

be "two" Hindi formula of multiplication (*be ek be*, *be trik sahā*) or in compound (*bevīs* "22", *becāḷis* "42"). G. *be ben*, S. *bā*, Siṃ. *de*. Pkt. *be*. Skr. *dve*. — $ 77, 130, 214.

beḍā m. "raft". G. *beḍo*," S. *beṛī*, Panj. H. *beḍā*, Ro. *bero*. Deśī. *beḍo nauḥ* (216, 6). — $ 150.

bel m. "aegle marmelos". G. *bīlī*, H. *bel*, Siṃ. *bela*, K. *bĕl bil*. Pkt. *bella-*. Skr. *bilva-* m. — $ 77, 80, 127, 148.

beḷkeṃ n. " fork of a tree or furcated post". H. K. *bel* "shovel". Deśī. *belī sthūṇā* (216, 6). — $ 150.

baisṇeṃ, basṇeṃ "to sit". G. *besvuṃ*, S. *bihaṇu*, Panj. *besnā*, H. *baisnā*, K. *bĕhun*, Ro. *bes'-*, Arm. Ro. *ves-*. Skr. *upaviśati*. — $ 46, 56, 127, 174, 230, 232.

bokaḍ m. "goat". G. *bokḍo*, Panj. *bok*, H. *bokrā*; S. *boka* f. "cry of a goat". Deśī, *bokkaḍo chāgaḥ* (216, 13). Skr. *bukka-* m. — $ 80, 127.

boṃḍ n. "bud, teat". Deśī. *boṃḍaṃ cūcukaṃ* (216, 12). Dravidian ? cf. Kannarese *buḍḍe* "swelling". protuberence", Telugu. *boḍḍu* "prominent navel". — $ 70.

bor f. "jujube tree". G. *bor* n., Panj. H. *ber*, S. *beru*, *berī*, B. *bair*, K. *bray*. Pkt. *bora-*, *borī*. Skr. *badara-* m. *badarī* f. — $ 55.

bolṇeṃ "to talk". G. S. Panj. H. B. K. *bol-*. Pkt. *bollai*; cf. Buddhist. Skr. *bahubollaka*. "chatter box". — $ 252.

bhaṃgṇeṃ "to break, to destroy". G. Panj. *bhaṃg* "break", S. *bhāṃgo* "dry twigs", *bhaṃgo* "interruption", Panj. *bhāṃggā* "damage", B. *bhāṃgite* "to break, to be broken", Ro. *phag-* (*bang-*) "to break". Skr. *bhaṅga-* m., cf. *bhanakti*, *bhañjayati*. — $ 230.

bhaṭakṇeṃ "to stray". G. S. Panj. H. *bhaṭak-*; Siṃ. *baṭa* "sunken, disappeared (sun). Pkt. *bhaṭṭha-*. Skr. *bhraṣṭa-*. — $ 48, 89, 169.

bhaṭṭā m. "vessel containing fire", *bhaṭṭī* f. "oven, forge." G. *bhaṭṭhī*, Panj. *bhaṭṭh*, H. *bhaṭṭhā bhaṭṭhī*, *bhaṭī* "fire, furnace", B. *bhāṭī* "furnace of distillery". Skr. *bhrāṣṭra-* m. — $ 169.

bhalā adj. "good". G. *bhaluṃ*, S. *bhalo*, Panj. H. *bhalā*, H. *bhāl*; Panj. H. *bhaddā* "imbecile", Siṃ. *bada-kaḷa* "lucky". Skr. *bhalla-* (indicated as "villager" by Vāmana, see Regnaud, *Rhét. Skr.*) *bhadra-*. — $ 48, 141.

bhar, *bhār*, m. "weight, burden," *bharṇeṃ* "to carry". G. *bharvuṃ bhār*, S. *bhar* preposition "on"; H. *bhār* m., *bharnā* "to support", Siṃ. *bara* "weight; heavy", K. *bôr*ᵘ, Ro. *pharo* "heavy". P. Pkt. Skr. *bhāra-*, *bhara-* m. — $ 128.

bhaṃvaī f. "eye-brow". G. *bhavuṃ*, H. *bhauṃ*, Panj. *bhauṃh*, B. *bhomā*, Siṃ. *bāma*, K. *bum*, Ro. *phov*. P. *bhamuka-*, Pkt. *bhumaa bhamuhā*. Skr. *bhrū-* f. — $ 128.

bhāī bhāū m. "brother". S. Panj. *bhāū*; G. Panj. S. (in compound) H. B. *bhāī*, K. *bôy*ᵘ, Siṃ. *baē bā*; the geographical distribution according to the general rules of Marathi phonetics, see $ 31, show that *bhāī* is borrowed; another group is that of Arm. Ro. *phal*, Euro. *phral*, see $ 18. Pkt. *bhāyā*; cf. Deśī. *bhāo jyeṣṭha-bhaginīpatiḥ*.. (216, 5); P. *bhātika-bhātā*. Skr. *bhrātṛ-* m. — $ 128.

bhāj f. "wife". K. *bōriyā*, Siṃ. *bāri*. Pkt. *bhajjā*. Skr. *bhāryā*. f. — $ 106.

bhāgṇeṃ "to get tired, to give way". G. H. B. Ass. *bhāg-* "to escape", O. *bhāṃg*. Skr. *bhagna-*. — $ 230.

bhājṇeṃ "to roast, to grill". G. *bhajyuṃ* "fried cake"; S. H. *bhāj-*, B. *bhaj-*, K. *baz-*, Siṃ. *bad-* "to roast". P. *bhajjati*. Skr. *bhṛjjati*. — $ 47, 106, 128.

bhāṃjṇeṃ "to share". G. H. *bhāṃj-*; Panj. *bhāṃjīṃ* "part". Pkt. *bhañjai*. Skr. *bhañjayati*. — $ 106, 230.

bhāḍ f. "money obtained by prostitution of women". G. S. H. *bhāḍ*, Panj. B. *bhāḍā* "rent"; Siṃ. *bala* "salary". Skr. *bhāṭi-* f. — $ 111.

bhāṃḍ m. "buffoon, (name of caste)". G. Panj. H. B. *bhāṃḍ*, S. *bhaṃḍu*, K. *bāṇḍ*. *bhaṃḍo* ...*māgadho* (221, 16). Skr. *bhaṇḍa-* m. — $ 111.

bhāṃḍ n. "pot". G. *bhaṃḍuṃ*, S. *bhāṃḍo*; Panj. H. *bhāṃḍā*, H. B. *bhāṃḍ*; Siṃ. *baḍr* "stomach" K. *bāra* "pot, flank". Pkt. *bhaṇḍa-*. Skr. *bhāṇḍa-* n. — $ 68, 111, 159.

bhāṃḍaṇ n. "dispute", *bhāṃḍṇeṃ* "to quarrel", *bhāṃḍ* "quarreler". G. *bhāṃḍvuṃ* "to abuse, to querrel", *bhāṃḍaṇ* "quarrel", S. *bhāṃḍaṇu* "to shout", H. *bhāṃḍnā-* "to criticise, to abuse, to slender". Deśī. *bhaṃḍaṇaṃ kalahaḥ* (218, 15). — $ 111.

bhāṃḍār n. "treasure". G. Panj. *bhaṃḍār*, S. *bhāṃḍāru*, H. *bhāṃḍār*, B. *bhāṇḍār*. Pkt. *bhāṇḍāra-*. Skr. *bhāṇḍāgāra-*. n. — $ 61, 111, 143.

bhāt m. "boiled rice". G. H. B. O. *bhāt*, S. *bhatu*, Panj. *bhatt*, K. *bata*, Siṃ. *bāt*. Pkt. *bhatta-*. Skr. *bhakta-*. — $ 121, 128.

bhādarṇeṃ "to shave". cf. Panj. *bhaddan* "tonsure", *bhaddan karvāuṇā* "to get oneself shave (in morning, etc.)" Skr. *bhadrākaraṇa-* n. (Cf. M. *bhalā* and following). — $ 47, 61, 123.

bhādvā m. name of a month. G. *bhādaravo* W. Panj. *bhad-dhro*, *bhadruṃ*, *bhaduṃ*, H. *bhādvā*, Panj. H. *bhādoṃ*, K. *bādarapēth*. Skr. *bhādra-pada-* m. — $ 47, 60, 123, 152.

bhāmbhal adj. "forgetful, scatterbrained." S. *bhaṃ-bhulijaṇu* "to be busy, to be proud". Deśī. *bhaṃbhalo mūrkho* (222, 3). Skr. *bharbh-* (*hiṃsāyāṃ*). — $ 69, 128.

bhāl f. "lance". G. *bhāluṃ*, G. S. *bhālo*, Panj. *bhālā*, H. *bhāl*, K. *bāla*. Skr. *bhalla-* m. *bhallī* f. — $ 48, 283.

bhāv m. "nature". H. B. *bhāv*, *bhāo*; K. *bāv*, Siṃ. *bava*. Skr. *bhāva-* m. — $ 142.

bhāvjaī f. "brother's wife". G. *bhojāī*, S. *bhājāī*; Panj. *bharjāī*, W. Panj. *bhijāī*, H. B. O. *bhāuj*, H. *bhaujī*,

bhaujāī. Deśī. *bhāujjā bhrātṛjāyā* (216, 11). Skr. *bhrātṛjāyā* f. — $ 61.
bhāvaṇeṃ (poet.) "to consider, to examine, to desire". G. *bhāvavuṃ* "to desire, to please", S. *bhāṃiṇu*, Panj. *bhāuṇā* "preference", H. *bhāvnā*, *bhaonā* m. "reflection", B. *bhābite*, K. *bāwun* "to explain, to say". Skr. *bhāvana-* n. — $ 152.
bhālū f. "bear, female of jackal living alone". H. O. *bhālū* m., Bhojp. *bhāul*, B. *bhālūk*, "bear"; Siṃ. *ballā baḷu* "dog". Deśī. *bhallū ṛkṣaḥ* (218, 2). Skr. *bhalluka-*, *bhallūka-* m.; cf. *acchabhalla-*, M. *asval*. — $ 148.
bhāḷ n. "fore-head". G. *bhāl*, H. B. *bhāl*, K. *bāl*. Skr. *bhāla-*. — $ 145. The true word is *māthā*.
bhiṃgrūṭī f. "cricket". Siṃ. *biṃga*, *biṃgu* "honey-bee, wasp." Deśī. *bhiṃgārī cīri, maśaka ity anye* (220, 6). P. Pkt. *bhiṅga-*. Skr. *bhṛṅga-* m. — $ 30, 52.
bhijṇeṃ "to get wet". G. *bhijvuṇ bhiṃjvuṃ*, S. *bhijaṇu*, Panj. *bhijjṇā*, H. *bhījnā*, B. *bhijite*. Pkt. *bhījai*. Skr. *abhyañjana-* n. — $ 71, 75, 106, 128.
bhiṇeṃ bihiṇeṃ bheṇeṃ "to fear". G. *bihavuṃ bivuṃ*, Arm. Ro. *biel*. Pkt. *bīhei bihei*, Deśī. *bīhai* (215, 8). Skr. *bibheti*. — $ 128, 229, 230.
bhiṃt bhīṃt f. "wall". G. *bhīṃt* f., S. *bhiti*, H. *bhīt*, B. *bhit*, Siṃ. *bita*, *bitu*. Pkt. Skr. *bhitti-* f. — $ 69, 190.
bhitar (poet.) "in side". G. *bhitar*, H. B. *bhītar*. Pkt. *abhintara-*. Skr. *abhyantara-*. — $ 44, 71, 75, 121, 128, 174.
bhinṇeṃ bhiṃdṇeṃ "to penetrate". Siṃ. *biṃdinavā* "to break", K. *bĕnnun bĕnun* "to get broken", *bĕn*ᵉ *run* "to break". Skr. *bhind-*, *bhinna-*. — $ 229.
bhiseṃ n. "lotus stalk". H. *bhis* m. "lotus root (edible)", Siṃ. *bisi* "straw mattress". Pkt. P. *bhisa-*. Skr. *bisa-* n. — $ 84.
bhīṃs f. "long and coarse animal hair." Siṃ. *bisī* "straw-mat for wiping feet, seat. (of an ascetic)." Pkt. *bhisī*. Skr. *bṛsī* f. — $ 84.
bhīk f. "alms". G. H. *bhīkh*, S. *bīkha*, Panj. *bhīkkh*, H. B. *bhīk*, K. *bīkh bĕcha*, Siṃ. *bik*. Pkt. *bhikkhā*. Skr. *bhīkṣā* f. — $ 88, 169.
bhuī bhuīṃ f. "earth". G. *bhoṃ bhoṃy*, S. *bhuṃī bhūṃ*, Panj. *bhuṃ*, H. *bhūīṃ bhūmīṃ bhūṃ*, B. *bhū bhūṃī*, Siṃ. *bima*, K. *bum*, Ro. *phuv*. Hemacandra also notes the nasal. Deśī. *bhūmipisāo tālaḥ* (221, 3). P. Pkt. Skr. *bhūmi-* f. — $ 64, 71, 153.
bhukṇeṃ "to bark". G. *bhoṃkvuṃ*, *bhukvuṃ*, S. *bhauṃkaṇu*, H. *bhoṃknā*, *bhūknā*, *bhoknā*, K. *bakun*; Ro. *phukav-* "to say, to denounce." ? Pkt. *bhukkai*; cf. Deśī. *bhukkaṇo śvā* (222, 3). — $ 44, 80, 84.
bhulṇeṃ "to forget, to be mistaken". G. S. H. B. *bhul-*, Panj. *bhull-*, K. *bul-*. Pkt. *bhullai*. — $ 252.
bhūk f. "hunger". *bhukṇeṃ* "to be hungry". G. S. *bhukh*,

Panj. *bhukkh*, H. *bhūkh*, H. B. *bhūk*, Ro. *bokh*; K. *bukha*, Arm. Ro. *bukhav* "famished". Deśī. *bhukkhā kṣut* (220, 13). Skr. *bubhukṣā* f. — $ 88, 89, 128, 169.

bhūṃs "ball of grain". G. *bhuṃsuṃ*, H. *bhus*, *bhūṃs*, *bhūṃsā*, B. *bhūsī*, K. *bos*[u]; Ro. *phus* "straw". Skr. *busa-* n. — $ 34.

bheṃ n. "fear". G. O. *bhe*, S. *bhai*, *bhau*, Panj. *bhai*, H. *bhai*, *bhae*, B. *bhay bhī*, Siṃ. *baya*, *-bā*, K. *bay*. Skr. *bhaya-* n. — $ 62, 128.

bheṃjūḍ bheṃjhūḍ, adj. "fearful". Deśī. *bheḍo bhejjo bhejjalao trayo*'. *pyete bhīrūvācakāḥ* (221, 4) Skr. *bheya*? — $ 106.

bheḍ. adj. (poet.) "fearful, coward, timid" — see the preceding.

bher f. "jujube". H. B. *ber*. Skr. *badara-* m. — $ 84, see M. *bor*.

bhetṇeṃ "to divide in lengthwise", *bhet* n. f. "slice". S. *bhetu* "difference or secret". Panj. *bhet* "secret". Skr. inf. *bhettuṃ*. — $ 230.

bher f. "kettle-drum". (musical instrument). G. H. *bher*, *bherī*, S. *bheri*, Siṃ. *beraya*. Skr. *bherī* f. — $ 128.

bhoj m. "birch". G. Panj. H. *bhoj*, S. *bhoja-*, K. *burza*. The form Deśī. *bhauṃ* (220, 13) does not seem to be attested. Skr. *bhūrja-* m. — $ 80, 116.

bhorpī, *bhorūp* m. "charlaton". H. *bahrūp*. Skr. *bahurūpa-*. — $ 128.

bhoṃvaḍṇeṃ "to whirl (round)". H. *bhauṃriyānā*. Pkt. Deśī. *bhammaḍai bhamāḍai bhamaḍai* (219, 4). Skr. *bhramati*. — $ 79, 128.

bhoṃvṇeṃ "to turn". G. *bhramvuṃ bhamvuṃ*, S. *bhaṃvaṇu*, Panj. *bharamnā bhauṃnā*, H. *bhāmnā*, *bhaonā*, K. *bramun*; Siṃ. *bamaṇa* "tower, circle". Pkt. *bhamai*. Skr. *bhramati-*. — $ 79, 128, 152.

bhoṃvar m. "black bee" *bhoṃr* adj. "black". S. *bhauṃru*, Panj. H. *bhaṃvar*, *bhauṃrā*, B. *bhomār*, S. *bhaṃar*, Siṃ. *baṃbarā*ˇ, Pkt. P. *bhamara*—. Skr. *bhramara-* m. — $ 79, 128, 152, 153.

bhoṃvrā m. "lock of hair". S. Panj. H. *bhauṃrī*, Siṃ. *baṃburukes*. Skr. *bhramaraka-* m. n. — $ 128.

bhorḍī f. "type of heron". Deśī. *bhoruḍo bhāruṇḍapakṣī* (221, 10).

bhoṃs, *bhoṃśāūs* m. "sugarcane", *bhoṃs* m. "type of reed". Deśī. *bhamāso ikṣusadṛśatṛṇaṃ*; *bhamaso itī Dhanapālaḥ* (218, 13). — $ 79, 155.

mau (mono syllabic and dissyllabic) adj. "to stretch". G. *mau*. Pkt. *maua-miu-*; cf. Deśī. *māilī*, *māuccho*, neut. *māukkaṃ* (228, 18). Skr. *mṛdu-*.—$ 30, 31, 46,56,138.

mag "then, after, immediately;" *magilu* adj. "on the way". G. *mag* "path", adv. "towards". Deśī. *magā paścāt* (3, 8), *maggo paścāt* (222, 9). Skr. *mārga-*. Old M. *māg*.. — $ 280.

maṃgaḷ n. "favourable fortune", *maṃgaḷvār* m. "Tuesday". G. *maṃgaḷ* "Mars, Tuesday", S. *maṃgalu*, Panj. *maṃggal*, H. B. *maṃgal*, Siṃ. *magula*. Pkt. Skr. *maṅgala-*. — $ 98, 145.

maccā adj. "medium". For *madh-cā*. — $ 101, 164.

macṇeṃ "to swell, to climb". G. S. H. *mac-*. Pkt. *maccai* beside *majjai*. Skr. *mādyati*. — $ 48, 90.

maṃjirī f. "compound, flower, castanets". G. *maṃjarī* "bouquet", *maṃjirā* pl. masc. "cymbals"; H. *maṃjarī* "boquet, bud, flower, pearl", *maṃjīr* m. "ornament for the feet, bracelet". *maṃjirā* m. „cymbals." B. *maṃjīr* m. "bracelet for feet", *maṃjarī* f. "bud, bouquet" etc. Pkt. Skr. *mañjarī* f. — $ 75, 166.

maṭgā adj. "too small", *māṭkulā* "small'. G. *māṭhuṃ* "incomplete, bad", S. *maṭho*, B. *māṭ* "bad". Deśī. *maṭṭo śṛṅgavihīnaḥ*; *maṭṭo tathā marālo alasaḥ* (222, 14). Seems to be related to the root of *mṛṇāti* "to crush"; cf. Skr. *muṭati* "to crush", m. *muṭkaḷeṃ* "a ball of paste", *muṭakṇeṃ* "to pat"; for the enlargement in *-t-* of the root i.e. *mer-*, cf. Lat. *mortārium* (see Walde², p. 464) — $ 48, 109.

maṭhā m. "churned curd". G. *maṭho*, *maṭṭho*; S. *maṭho* "beaten and spiced curd"; Panj. H. *maṭhā*; B. *māṭhā*. Skr. *mastu-* n. — $ 48, 110.

maḍ m. "hateful person, pest, nuisance", *maḍeṃ* n. "corpse". G. *maḍuṃ*, B. *maḍā*, Siṃ. *maḷa*. Deśī. *maḍo kaṇṭho mṛtaśca* (233, 9); *maḍavojjhā śibikā* (226, 5); *maḍiyā samāhatā* (223, 9), Skr. *mṛta-*. — $ 30, 31, 108, 115.

maṃḍ m. "rice gruel, scum of a boiling or fermenting infusion", *māṃḍā* m. "cake". Panj. *mann* "cake", *māṃḍ* "rice-water", H. *māṃḍ* "rice gruel, paste", *māṃḍā* "cake"; B. *maṇḍ*, Siṃ. *maḍa*, Ro. *manro* "bread". Pkt. *maṇḍa-*. Skr. *maṇḍa-*, *maṇḍakam*. — $ 111.

maṇḍal n. "circle", *māṃḍaḷ* f. "ring". Panj. B. O. *maṃḍal*, S. *maṇḍalu*, K. *maṇḍūjᵘ*, Siṃ. *maḍulla* (pl. *maḍulu*), *māḍillā* "serpent". Skr. *maṇḍala-*. — $ 111.

maḍhṇeṃ "to cover, to furnish". G. S. H. *maḍh-*, B. *māḍ-* "to crush", Panj. *maḍh* "cover (of leather, of gold-leaf)." Pkt. *maḍhai*. Skr. *maṭhati* is a late form; it is undoubtedly a contamination of Skr. *mardati* (Pkt. *maḍḍai*, represented by Siṃ. *maḍ-* "to press, to rub), and of Skr. *mṛṣṭa-* : Whatever is said in the text should be corrected accordingly. $ 46, 112, 231.

maḍhī f. "ascetic's hut", old M. *maḍh*, *maḍhā*, G. *maḍhī* "hut", S. *maḍhu* "residence", *maḍhī* "residence of an ascetic", Panj. *maḍh* "funeral monument", H. *maḍhī*, *maḍhā* "temporary building", K. *-mar*. Skr. *maṭha-* m. n. — $ 112, 183, 193, 198.

maḍhū adj. "(fruit)." Contamination of Skr. *mṛdu-* and *madhu-*. — $ 46, 118.

maṇ m. "measure of capacity and of weight". G. S. Panj. *maṇ*, H. *man*. Per. Ar. *man*. "weight". see Hobson-Johnson S. V. *maund*. — $ 134.

maṇi, *maṇī* m. "pearl, precious

stone", *manyar*, *mãṇer*, *manerī* "jeweller", name of caste, G. *maṇi* n., S. *maṇi* f., Panj. *maṇī* f., H. *man*, *maṇ* m., *maṇi*, *maṇī* m. f. Siṃ. *miṇa*, *māṇa*. Skr. *maṇi-* m. — $ 62, 134, 154.

mathṇeṃ *maṃthṇeṃ* "to churn, to shake". G. *mathvuṃ*, S. *mathaṇu*, Panj. *mandhṇā* *maddhṇā*, H. *mathnā* *māhnā*, B. *mathite*, K. *mathun*. Skr. *mathati*, *manthati*. — $ 71, 122.

maṃd adj. "slow, stupid". G. Panj. H. B. *maṃd*, S. *maṃdo* "slow", K. *mand* "lazy", Siṃ. *mada* "petty, weak" (M. Panj. H. *māṃdā*, S. *māṃdo* "exhausted, side" is a Persian loan). Pkt. Skr. *manda-*. — $ 123.

madhbhāg m. "middle part"; *madhīṃ*, *madheṃ*, *madhyeṃ* "in the middle, in". G. *madhrāt* "midnight", *madhbhāg* "middle parts", H. *madh*, *maddh*, *madhi*, B. *madhya* (pron. *moddh*). Skr. *madhya-*. — $ 124, 197.

manāviṇeṃ "to reconcile, to persuade". G. *manāvavuṃ*, S. *manāīṇu*, Panj. *manāvṇā*, H. *manānā*, B. *mānāite*. Pkt. *manāvai*. Causative of *mānṇeṃ*. — $ 48.

maft *muft*, adv. "gratis". G. *maft*, *muflas*, S. *muftu*, Panj. H. *muft*, Ass. *muftis*. Per. *muft*. — $ 74.

markaḷ, *margaḷ*, *marāḷ* adj. "one who keeps obstinately lying pretending exhaustion"; *maragal*, *maraḷ* f. "exhaustion to make one fall down". B. H. *marāl*. Deśī. *marālo alasaḥ* (222, 13). Pkt. derivative of root *mar-*.

marṇeṃ "to die". G. S. Panj. H. K. *mar-*, Siṃ. *mär-*, Ro. *mer-*. Pkt. *marai*. Skr. *marati*. — $ 46, 48, 229.

marvā m. "origanum majorana". Panj. *marūā*, H. *māruā* *marvā*. Skr. *maruvaka-* m. — $ 152.

marāṭhā m. "Maratha". G. *marāṭhā*. Pkt. *marahaṭṭa-*, epigraphical Pkt. *mahāraṭhi-*, P. *mahāraṭṭha-*. Skr. *mahārāṣṭra-*. — $ 52, 62, 161, 167.

marāḷ m. "duck with red legs and bill". G. *marāḷ*, H. B. *marāl*. Deśī. *marālo haṃsa iti Śātavāhanaḥ* (222, 14). Skr. *marāla-* m. — $ 145.

malaī f. "noise and blows (in a dispute)". cf. Panj. etc. *mall* "wrestler", Siṃ. *mal* "barbarian". Skr. *malla-*. — $ 141.

malhār f. name of a melody (rāg). G. Panj. *malhār* m., S. *malāru*, H. *malār* *mallār* *malhār*. Skr. *mallārī* f. — $ 148.

maśī f. "soot". G. *masī* *mes meṃs*, S. *masu* f. "ink", Panj. *mas* *massu* "ink", H. *masī* *maṣī*, Siṃ. *mäsidā* "black substance used as medicine." Pkt. *masi-*. Skr. *maṣi-* f.

masīd, *maśīd* f. "mosque". G. H. *masīd*, S. *masīti*, Panj. H. *masīt*, B. *masid*. Ar. *masjid*. — $ 162.

mhasaṇ, *masaṇ* n. "crematorium". G. *masāṇ*, S. *masāṇu*, Panj. *masāṇ*, H. *masān*, B. *maśān*, O. *maśāṇ*; Siṃ. *sōna*, *sohona*, *bōn*. Pkt. *masāṇa-susāṇa-*. Skr. *śmaśāna-* n. — $ 42, 46, 156, 157.

mahā-, mhā- "big". cf. for example Siṃ. *maha-mā-*. Skr. *mahā-*.— $ 168.

mahāg, mhāg adj. "dear, costly". G. *moṃghuṃ, moghuṃ*, S. *mahaṃgo*, H. *mahaṃg* (*ā*), Panj. *mahiṃgā*. Skr. *mahārgha-*. — $ 46, 69, 79, 88, 168.

mahāt, mahāvat, māūt, m. "Mahout". G. *mahāvat, mahāt*, Panj. H. *mahaut*. Skr. *mahāmātra-*; remade on the model of *rāūt*, Skr. *rājaputra-*, According to Thomas Bloch, *Z.D.M.G.*, 1908, p. 372. — $ 121, 138, 152, 168.

mahāḷ m. "funeral rites of the second fortnight of Bhādrapada". cf. H. *mahāṛī* "palace, sanctuary", and probably Siṃ. *mahal* "residence, palace" (if it is not the Arabic word everywhere). Skr. *mahālaya-* m. — $ 46, 145.

mahinā m. "month, monthly payment". G. S. *mahino*, Panj. H. *mahīnā*. Per. *mahīn*. — $ 50.

maḷ m. "filth", *maḷīṇ* "dirty". G. *maḷ*, S. *maru*, Panj. H. B. *mal*, Ro. *mel*; Siṃ. *mala* "excretion" *malina* "dirty". Pkt. *maḷa-*; cf. Deśī. *malo svedaḥ* (222, 9). Skr. *mala-* n. m. — $ 46, 145.

maḷṇeṃ "to beat out wheat, to press, to trample". G. Panj. *maḷ-*, S.H.B.O. *mal-*; Ro. *malav-*. Pkt. *malaī*. Cf. Skr. *mardana-* ? (see Pischel, $ 244, 294). — $ 145.

maḷā m. "orchard, flat and rich terrain". cf. Siṃ. *maḷuva* "court-yard of the house" (Geiger links it with P. *mālaka*). Deśī. *malao giryekadeśa upavanaṃ ca* (234, 4). — $ 145.

maḷī f. "part of field, piece of land". Deśī. *maliaṃ laghukṣetraṃ kuṇḍaṃ ceti dvyartham* (234, 4). — $ 145.

māī f. "mother". G. *mā, māī*, S. *māī, māu*, Panj. *māū*, H. *mā, mài, māū*, B. *mā* (*māī* = "breast"), Siṃ. *mav, mā*. Pkt. *māā* (gen. pl. *māīṇaṃ*). Skr. *mātṛ-* f. — $ 283.

mākaḍ m. n. "monkey". G. *mākḍuṃ* "monkey", S. *makoṛa* "big ant", Panj. *makkaṛ* "locust, spider", W. Panj. *mākoṛā* "big ant", H. *mākḍā*, B. *mākaḍ* "spider", Siṃ. *makul* "monkey, spider". Pkt. *makkaḍa-*. Skr. *markaṭa-* m. — $ 93, 111.

mākhṇeṃ "to rub, to oil", *mākhaṇ* n. "unguent." G. *mākhaṇ* n. "butter", S. *makhaṇu* "to oil, to apply butter", Panj. *makkhan*, H. *mākhan makkhan*, B. *mākhaṇ* "butter" *mākhite* "to oil, to rub", Siṃ. *makanavā* "to uproot, to disturb", Ro. *makh-*. Pkt. *makkhei*, P. *makkheti*. Skr. *mrakṣayati, mrakṣaṇa-* n. — $ 47, 96, 230.

māg m. "path, track, trace". G. *māg*, S. *māgu* "place, residence", H. *māṃg, mag*, Panj. *magg*, Siṃ. *maga*. Pkt. *magga-*. Skr. *mārga-* m. — $ 69, 98, 197, Cf. M. *mag*.

māṃg m., name of caste. G. *māṃg* m. "a design in soot on a piece of brass representating a family of scavengers and which is worshipped. Pkt. *māyaṅga-*. Skr. *mātaṅga-* m. — $ 61.

māgṇeṃ "to demand". G.

māgvuṃ, S. *manaṇu*, Panj. *maṃggṇā*, H. *māṃgnā*, B. *māgite*, *māngite*, O. *māgan*, Siṃ. *mägun* "view, perception". K. *mangun*, Ro. *mang-*. Pkt. *maggai*. Skr. *mārgayati*. — $ 47, 98, 229, 230.

māgeṃ "In time past, behind, after". Instr. of *māg* "path". Cf. Deśī. *magā paścāt* (3, 8), *maggo paścāt* (222, 9). Skr. *mārga-*. — $ 197.

māgauteṃ māgutā adv. "again". — $ 59.

māc m. "frame (of bed etc.), foundation", *māṃcī* f. "frame for potters", *mācī* f. "palisade, platform". G. *mācī* f. "high stool", *mācḍo* "wooden frame", *māco* "series of squares drawn on a wooden plank for the game of *sogṭā*", S. *maṃjī* "high stool, frame", *māṃjaṇu* "frame, support", Panj. *maṃjā* "frame for cot"; H. *mācī* "high stool", *mācā* "platform", Bih. *maciyā* "chair", *māṃc macān* "scaffolding, platform"; Siṃ. *mässa* "platform, hut of watchman in the rice field." Skr. *mañca-* m. — $ 71, 101.

māj m. "rut, pride", *mājṇeṃ* "to be drunk", *mājīrā* m. "madness". H. *māṃj*, *mājā*, *maṃjhā* "scum of the water of first showers of rain," Siṃ. *mada* "rice-wine". Pkt. *majja-*. Skr. *madya-* n. — $ 106, 193.

māj m. "belt", *mājīṃ māji* "among". S. *maṃjnī*, Panj. *maṃjh*, H. *mājh*, *māṃjh*, B. *majhāmājhīṃ*, *mājh*; O. *majhi*, Siṃ. *mäda* "middle", K. *manz* "middle, in", Arm. Ro. *mandz* "middle, height", Eur. Ro. *maskare* "in the middle". Pkt. *majjha-*. Skr. *madhya-*. — $ 69, 72, 88, 89, 107, 197.

māṃjṇeṃ "to oil. to wipe". G. *māṃjvuṃ*, S. *mājaṇu* "to polish by rubbing", Panj. *māṃjṇā*, H. *maṃjnā*, B. *mājite*, O. *mājībā*, Siṃ. *madinavā* "to rub, to sharpen", *maṭa* "polished, brilliant". Pkt. *majjai*. Skr. *marjati*. — $ 47, 69, 106, 231.

māṃjar, *mājar* m. "cat". G. *māṃjar*, H. *maṃjār*, *maṃjāḍ*, Siṃ. *mädira*. Pkt. *majjāra-*, *maṃjăra-*. Skr. *mārjāra-* m. — $47, 69, 70, 106.

mājhā adj. "mine"; *majlā*, *malā* "to me, personal pronoun". oblique case G. *maj muj*, Panj. H. *mujh*; as against S. *mūṃ moṃ*, Bih. B. O. *mo-* etc. Pkt. *majjhaṃ* "of me". Skr. *mahyam*. — $ 107, 183, 208, 210.

mājhārīṃ "inside of". G. *mojār*, S. *maṃjhāru*, H. *majhāre* (adv.); B. *mājhār* "the middle", cf. Panj. *majherū* "spindle of a spinning wheel" Deśī. *majjha āraṃ madhyam* (225, 17). Skr. *madhya-*. — $ 89, 107.

māṭhṇeṃ "to polish". G. *maṭhārvuṃ maṭhervuṃ*, Panj. *māṭhaṇ* "to plane (wood)", H. *maṭṭhā* "softened by rubbing, wear and tear", *māṃḍnā* "to rub, to crush", Siṃ. *maṭa* "polished, brilliant", *madinavā* "to polish". Pkt. *maṭṭha-*, P. *maṭṭha-*, *maṭṭa-*. Skr. *mṛṣṭā-*. — $ 30, 31, 48, 89, 110, 231.

māṃḍṇeṃ "to dispose, to arrange". G. *maṃḍvuṃ*, S.

maṃḍaṇu, H. *maṃḍnā*, B. *maṃḍaṇ* "cover" (of metallic planks, copper etc.)", Siṃ. *maḍa* "decoration". Skr. *maṇḍana-* n. — $ 68.

māṃḍav m. "tent for festivals, consecreted peristyle", *māṃḍvī* f. "light canopy over an idol". G. *māṃḍavī*, S. *maṃḍapu*, H. *maṃḍuā*, *maṃḍavā*, Siṃ. *maḍuvä* "hut". Pkt. *maṇḍava-*. Skr. *maṇḍapa-* m. n. — $ 111, 152.

māḍī f. "storey of a one storey home, loft with planks". S. Panj. *māṛī* "upper story". Deśī. *māḍiaṃ gṛhaṃ* (228, 12). Cf. S. V. *māḷā*. — $ 46, 146.

māṇūs, *māṇas* m. "man". G. Panj. *māṇas*, S. *māṇhū*, H. *mānūs*, *mānus* *mānas*, Siṃ. *minisā* "man", *minī* "corpse", Arm. Ro. *manus*, Eur. *manuś*. Skr. *mānuṣa-*, *mānuṣya-*. — $ 40, 46, 50, 134.

mātī f. "earth". G. Panj. *māṭī* *miṭṭī*, H. Aussi—*maṭṭī*, S. *miṭī*, Siṃ. *mäṭi*, K. *mẽcū*. Pkt. *maṭṭiā*, P. *mattikā*. Skr. *mṛttikā* f. — $ 30, 31, 47, 114.

māthaṇ *māthṇī* "earthen pot with large mouth for churning". G. *mathanī*, H. *manthanī*. Cf. M. *mathṇeṃ*. — $ 71, 122.

māthā m. "fore-head, head". G. *māthuṃ*, S. *matho*, Panj. *matthā*, H. B. *māthā*, O. *mathā*, Siṃ. *mat*. Pkt. *mattha*" Skr. *mastaka-* m. n. — $ 47, 48, 122.

māṃdṇeṃ "to smear" "the usual word is *mājṇeṃ*", says Molesworth; is the former a doublet of the latter (see under *māṃjṇeṃ*) ? But cf. Siṃ. *ma ḍinavā* "to rub, to press", and Pkt. *maḍḍai*, *sammadda-*, P. *maddati*, Skr. *mardate*. — $ 47.

māṃdūsf. "box, chest" (poet.) Siṃ. *mados*. Pkt. P. *mañjūsā*. Skr. *mañjūṣā* f. — $ 106.

mān f. "neck". Ro. *men*, Skr. *manyā* f. (du. and. plur.). — $ 135.

mānṇeṃ "to obey, to believe, to agree". G. H. B. K. *mān-*, Panj. *man-*. Pkt. *maṇṇai*. Skr. *manyate* . — $ 47, 48, 135, 230.

mānbhāv m. name of a religious sect. Skr. *mahānubhāva-*. — $ 152, 161.

māpṇeṃ "to measure", *māp* n. "measure". G. S. Panj. H. B. *māp-*; cf. K. *mẽn-*, Siṃ. *man-* (Skr. *māna-*) "to measure", *mavan-* (*māpaya-*) "to fabricate". Tatsama, of Skr. *māpayati*. On the fate of the root *mā-* in Prākrit, see Pischel, $ 487. — $ 193, Cf. M. *māvṇeṃ*.

māmā m. "maternal uncle". G. S. *māmo*, H. *mām*, Panj. B. *māmā*, S. *māmu*. Cf. Deśī. *mammī mallāṇī māmā trayo'py amī mātulanī vācakāḥ*; *māmī* —*śabdo'pi* (which is used as a Prākrit form in the verses of Hemacandra) *deśyaḥ*, *paryāyabhaṅgyā* *tūpāttaḥ* (222, 15). Cf. M. *māvḷā*.

mārṇeṃ "to strike, to kill". G. S. Panj. H. B. K. *mār-*, Siṃ. Ro. *mar-*. Pkt. *mārei*, *māraṇa-*. Skr. *mārayati*, *māraṇa-* n. — $ 48, 251.

māv f. "fraud, sorcery", Siṃ. *mā*, *mā*. Skr. *māyā* f.—$ 55.

māvṇeṃ "to hold in a receptacle". G. *māvuṃ*, S. *māiṇu* *māṃijaṇu*, H. *mānā*. Pkt.

mīai. Skr. *mīti* for the meaning; *mīpīyīti* for the form.; cf. *māpṇeṃ*, where the meaning of the word has also been altered. — $ 51, 55, 232.

māvḷā m. "maternal uncle", *mavlaṇ* f. "wife of maternal uncle, for the sister". H. *māvlī* "mother"; Siṃ. *mayil* "maternal uncle, father-in-law". Deśī. *māaliā mātṛṣvasā* (229, 11); Pkt. *māulaga-*. Skr. *mātulaka-* m. *mātulānī* f. $ 42, 48, 57, 145.

māvśī f. "maternal aunt", *māūsā* m. "husband of maternal aunt". G. S. Panj. B. *māsī* (G. *mās* m., S. *māsaṛu* m.), H. *mausī*, *māsī*. Pkt. *māussiā*, *māucchā*. Skr. *mātṛsvasṛkā* f. — $ 57, 63, 102, 157.

mās m. "month". G. H. B. *mās*, S. W. Panj. *māṃh*, Siṃ. *mas*, Ro. *masek*. Skr. *māsa-* m. — $ 156.

māṃs mās n. "meat". G. *māṃs*, S. *mā(ṃ) su māhu*, Panj. *mās*, H. *mā(ṃ)s*, K. *māz*, Siṃ. Ro. *mas*. Pkt. *maṃsa-*. Skr. *māṃsa-* n. — $ 71, 156.

māsā m. "fish", *māsḷī* f., "fish" (collective, diminu tive) G. *māchalī*, H. *macch*, *machalī*, Panj. *macch*, S. *māchu*, *machaḍī*, B. O. *māch*, Eur. Ro. *maco*, Arm. *manthsav*, Siṃ.*mas*. Pkt. *maccha-*, *maścalī*. Skr. *matsya-* m. — $ 103.

māśī f. "fly". G. *mākh*, S. *makhi*, H. *mākhī*, *māchī*, *māṃkhī*, *māṃchī*, Panj. *makkhī*, B. *māchī*, K. *machi*, Siṃ. *mässā*, *mäkkä*, Ro. *makhi*. Pkt. *macchiā makkhiā*. Skr. *makṣikā* f. — $ 46.

māhār, *māherghar* m. "maternal house of wife". Skr. *mātṛgṛha-* n. — $ 159.

māhī māhō m. name of a month. G. *māho*, Panj. *māh*. Skr. *māgha-* m. — $ 39, 46, 78, 159.

māḷ f. "flower garland, corolla". G. *māḷ*, S. *mālā* f., H. *māl*, B. *mālā*, Siṃ. *mala* "flower". Skr. *mālā* f. — $ 145.

māḷ m. "platean, stage", *māḷā* "loft, scaffolding". G. *māḷ* "stage of a house", *māḷo* "stage, house, rest". Deśī. *mālo....mañcaḥ* (234, 146). — $ 46, 146. Cf. M. *māḍī*.

micakṇeṃ "to wink (eye), to press (lips)". G. *mīcvuṃ*, Panj. *mīcṇā*, H. *micnā*. Pkt. *miṃcaṇa-* (= *cakṣuḥsthagana-*, see *Desīnāmamālā* 122, 12). —Cf. the family of Latin *Micāre*, Ballouchi *mičaē-* "twinkling of an eye", Ger. *micken*; on the other hand Kannarese *miṃcū* "give off a flash", *miṭakisu* "to wink", Telugu *miki-* "to wink", *miṃcū* "splinter". — $ 71, 94.

miṭṇeṃ "to close (lips, eyes)." G. *miṭ* "endurance; meeting of glances"; S. *miṭṇu* "to close the eyes, to dissimulate". Pkt. *miṭṭha-*. Skr. *mṛṣṭa-*, *mṛṣṭi-*, from *mṛś-*. But. cf. also Kannarese *miṭakisu* "to wink", and the preceeding word.

miṭṇeṃ "to wipe of; to disappear". G. S. Panj. B. O. *miṭ-*; H. *miṭh-*. Pkt. *maṭṭa-*. Skr. *mṛṣṭa-*, from *mṛj-*. — $ 30, 31, 231.

miṭhā adj. "sweet, sugared". G. *miṭhḍuṃ*, *mīṭhuṃ*, S. *mīṭhu* "sweetness" *miṭho* "sweet", H. *mīṭhā*, *miṭh*, B.

miṭh, K. *myūṭh*ᵘ "sweet, exquisite", Ro. *miśto* "good". Skr. *miṣṭa-*. — $ 110.

mirī f. "black pepper". G. *marī*, n. ; *mirī*, *miraī*, Panj. *miric*, *mirc*; H. *maric*, *mirī*, *mirc*; Siṃ. *miris*. Pkt. *miriya-*. Skr. *marica-* m. — $ 75, 166.

misṇeṃ "to mix"; *missī* f. "power for blacking the teeth". G. S. H. *misī*; Panj. H. *misā*, Siṃ. *musu muhu* "mixed". Pkt. *missa-*, *mīsa-*. Skr. *miśra- miśrita-*. — $ 157.

misaḷ adj. "mixed", f. "mixture". B. *miśāl* "mixture", *masālā* "ingradients". Deśī. *misāliaṃ miśritam iti tu miśraśabdabhavam* (230, 5); Pkt. *mīsa-*, *missa-*. Skr. *miśra-*. — $ 145, 157.

miḷṇeṃ "to mingle, to mix", part. *millā*, *minlā*. G. *meḷavavuṃ*, S. *milaṇu*, Panj. H. *milnā*, *melnā*, B. *milite*, *milāite*. Pkt. *melavai*. Skr. *milati*. — $ 145, 229.

mī, *mīṃ* "I, me". Pkt. *mai*, *me*. Skr. *mayi*. — $ 208.

mīs n. "pretext, imposture". H. *mis*. Skr. *miṣa-* n. To be separated from H. B. *michā*, Siṃ. *misa* "false", from Skr. *mithyā*.— $ 156.

mukṭā, *mugūṭ* m. "crest". S. *moḍu*. Skr. *mukuṭa-*. — $ 98.

mukṇeṃ "to loose". G. *mukvuṃ* "to leave, to untie", S. *muku* part. of *muṃjaṇu* "to send", Panj. *mukkṇā* "to fall, to be lost", Ro. *muk-* "to leave"; Siṃ. *muk* "demon (spirit released from the body)" cf. Siṃ. *mud-*, K. *mucar* "to release". Pkt. *mukka-*. Skr. *muñcati*, *mukta-*. — $ 94, 231, 252.

mukā adj. "dumb, silent". G. *muṃguṃ*, H. B. *mūk*, Siṃ. *muk*. Pkt. *mukha-*, *mūa-*; the second form doesn't seem to have any representative, despite Deśī. *mūallo mūalo mūkaḥ* (231, 16). Skr. *mūka-*. — $ 94.

mukh n. "mouth, face"; *mukhīṃ* "on the tip of a tongue, by heart", *mukheṃ* "under the pretext of ". Skr. *mukha-* n. The usual word is *toṃḍ*; almost all the languages have a *tadbhava* of *mukha-*, cf. M. *mohaḷ*. — $ 96.

muṃgūs, *maṃgūs*, *muṃgas* m. "mongoose". H. *muṃgūs maṃgūs*. Deśī. *maṃgūso muggusū muggaso trayo'py ete nakulavācakāḥ* (224, 15). Original form : Telugu *maṅgīsu*, *muṅgīsu*, Mais G. *noḷiyo*, S. *noriaṛu*, H. *neolā neval* etc., from Skr. *nakula-*. — $ 74.

muṃḍ n., *muṃḍī muṃḍhī* f. "head". G. Panj. H. B. *muṃḍ muṃḍī* (H. *muḍṃḍāsā* "turban"), S. *muṃḍhī*. Pkt. *muṃḍha-*. Skr. *mūrdhan-* m. — $ 85, 89.

muṃḍṇeṃ "to shave", *muṃḍā muṃḍhā* adj. "bald, shave, decapitated". G. *muṃḍvuṃ*, S. *muṃḍaṇu*, Panj. *munnā*, H. *muṃḍnā* "to shave"; H. *muṃḍū* "monk". *muṃḍo* "widow"; Siṃ. *maḍu* "bald", fem. *miḍi* "shave"; K. *mônḍ* "widow"; Ro. *mur-* "to shave". Pkt. Skr. *muṇḍa-*. — $ 85, 111.

mudī f. "ring". S. *muṃḍī* "ring", *muḍā*, *mudrā* "ear-ring", Siṃ. *muduva*, *mudda*. Pkt. *mudda-* Skr. *mudrikā* f. — $ 44, 123.

musaḷ n. "pestle". G. *musḷuṃ*, S. *muhurī muhuliru*, Panj. *mohlā*, H. *mūsal*, Bih. *mūsar*, Siṃ. *mohol mōl*. Pkt. *mūsala-musala-*. Skr. *musala-* m. n. — $ 145.

mūg m. "phaseolus mungo". S. *muṅu*, Panj. *mugg*, H. Bih. *mūṃg*, O.B. *mug*, Siṃ. *muṅ*. Pkt. *mugga-*. Skr. *mudga-* m. — $ 69.

mūṭh f. "fist, handle". G. *muṭṭhī*, S. *muṭhi*, Panj. *muṭth*, H. *mūṭh*, H. B. *muṭhā*, Siṃ. *miṭa*, K. *moth* "fist", *moṭh* "handle, full hand". P. Pkt. *muṭṭhi-*. Skr. *muṣṭi-* m. f. — $ 110.

mūt n. m. "urine", *mutṇeṃ* "to make water". G. *mutarvuṃ*, *mūtra*, *mūtar*; S. *muṭaṇu muṭu*; Panj. *mutāī mutālā* "who wishes to make water"; H. B. *mūt*, Siṃ. *mū*; Arm. Ro. *murrel*, *murel* "to make water"; Eur. Arm. *muter*, *mutt* "urine". Pkt. *mutta-*. *mūtra-* n. — $ 121.

mūs f. (dial. *mos*) "crucible". G. H. *mūs*, B. *mūṣī*, Siṃ. *musā*. Skr. *mūṣa-* m. — $ 80.

mūḷ n. "root"; *mūḷeṃ* "by, because of". G. *mūḷ* n., S. *mūlu*, Panj. H. B. K. *mūl*, Siṃ. *mul*, *mula*. Pkt. P. Skr. *mūla-* n. — $ 145, 193, 197, 276.

meḍ, *meḍh*, *meḍhī* f. *meḍhā* m. "post, poll pillar", B. *mei*, *medhi*; *meḍ* "bamboo framework around an idol"; Bih. *meṃh* "stake, post" (see *Bih. Peas. Life* $ 889). Pkt. *meḍhī*. Skr. *methi-* m. — $ 88, 118.

meṃḍūkmukh m. "head of frog" (monk on a horse). G. H. *meṃḍak*, Siṃ. *māḍiyā* "frog", cf. Scandinavian Ro. *marokka* "frog". Skr. *maṇḍūka-* m. — $ 77.

meṃḍhā m. "ram, hook". G. *meṃḍho bheḍ*; Panj. *meḍā*; H. *meṃḍhā*, *bheṃḍā*; B. O. *meḍā*, *meḍhā*, *bhelā*, Ass. *mer*, Siṃ. *māḍa*. P. Pkt. *meṇḍa-*. Skr. *meḍhra-menḍha-* m. — $ 112.

meṇ menā m. "sheath." Per. *myān*, — $ 63, 134.

mer f. "limit, bank". G. *mer*, H. *maḍī*, *meṃḍ*, Siṃ. *māra*. Deśī. *majjā tathā merā maryādā* (223, 3). — $ 77, 143, 166.

melā adj. "dead". Isolated; G. *muo muelo*, Panj. *moā*, H. *muā*, K. *mūdᵘ*, Siṃ. *maḷa*, Eur. Ro. *murdal*, Arm. Ro. *mul-*. Pkt. *maa-*, *mua-*, *maḍa-*. Skr. *mṛta*. — $ 30, 31, 62, 229.

mehtar mehetar mhetar m. "sweeper", G. *mehtar*, *metar*, B. *mehtar*, B. *metar*. Per. *mihtar*. — $ 80, 168.

mehuḍā m. "cloud", (poet.). G. *meh mehulo*, S. *mīṃhu*, Panj. H. *meṃh*, Siṃ. *mė*. Pkt. *meha-*. Skr. *megha-* m. — $ 39, 51, 77, 159.

mehuṇā mevṇā m. "wife's brother, sister's husband", *mehuṇī* f. "cousin sister", *mehuṇ* n. "couple of newly weds". Siṃ. *mevun* "pair, couple". Deśī. *mehuṇiā patnyā bhaginī mātulātmajā ca*, *mehuṇao pitṛṣvasṛsuta iti*.. (231, 5). Skr. *Maithuna-* "in the act of mating, married," The Evolution of meaning is same in Dravidian. Kannarese *madyuna* "husband, relation, brother-in-law", Tam. *maittunan maccinan* "brother-in-law". — $ 55, 77, 159, 161.

meḷ m. "accord, group" *meḷā*

m. "assembly, fair" (poet. *meḷāvā*). G. *meḷ*, *meḷo* "fair, assembly", S. *melu* "friendship, company" *melo* "fair", Panj. H. B. *mel*, *melā*, K. *mĕl*, Siṃ. *mela*. P. Pkt. Skr. *mela*. — $ 145.

maiṃd adj. "heavy, lazy, stupid". B. *maind* "monkey". Skr. *manda-*. — $ 58.

mail adj. "dirty". G. *meluṃ*, S. *mail* f., *mailu* m. "dirt' *mero* "dirty", Panj. H. *mailā*. Pkt. *maila-*. Skr. *malina-* doesn't go well for the form; even in Marathi, the dental *-l-* betrays the word is borrowed. Cf. M. *maḷ*.

mokaḷ f. "loosely lying objects, liquidation (of debt), liberty", *mokḷā* adj. "free", *mokaḷṇeṃ mokalṇeṃ* "to free". G. *mokḷuṇ* "free", S. *mokal* "permission" *mokalṇu* "to send", Panj. *muklāvā* "conducting the wife to her house", Panj. H. *moklā* "loose, vast", K. *mŏkal-* "to be freed, to be terminated", *mŏkolᵘ* "unoccupied". cf. Apa. *mokkalaḍa* "liberal". Cf. under M. *mukṇeṃ*. — $ 94, 145.

mogaṛ m. "millet". G. *mogar*, *madgal*, *magdal*, S. *muṅiro*, H. B. *mūgrā*, *mogrā*, *mugdar*, Panj. O. *mugdar*, B. *mugur*, *mugdar*, Siṃ. *muguru*. P. Pkt. *moggara-* *muggara-*. Skr. *mudgara-* M. — $ 80, 98.

mocā m. "slipper". G. S. Panj. H. *mocī* "cobbler, shoemaker", S. *mocaṛu* m. "shoe (used to denote a blow given with slipper"), B. *mucī* "cobbler", Deśī. *mocaṃ ardhājaṅghī* (232, 11). Pehlvī *močak* (Persian *mōze*).— $ 80.

moṭ f. "packet", *mūṭh* m., "bullock's pack saddle", *muḍī* f. "packet of grains". G.*moṭiyuṃ* "bag of grains", S. *moṛi*"small packet", *mūṛo* "ball", Panj. *moṭṭā*"fat", H. *moṭ(h)*f. *moṭā*, B. *moṭ*, *moṭā*, Siṃ. *miṭiya* "packet, bad"; K. *mŏṭᵘ* "fat, heavy". Skr. *moṭa-* m. n.— $ 80, 109.

modṇeṃ "to break, to change". G. S. H. B. *moḍ-*. Pkt. *modei*. Skr. *moṭati*.—$ 111.

motīṃ n. "pearl". G. S. Panj. H. *mōtī*, B. O. *mŏti*, Siṃ. *mutu*, K. *mŏkhta*. Skr. *mauktika*-n.—$ 78.

moth f. "cyperus rotundus". G. S. *moth*, Panj. H. *mothā*, B.O. Ass. *muthā*. Pkt. *motthā*. Skr. *mustā* f.—$ 80.

mop adj "very much (vulgar form for *amop*). Skr. *māp-*. —$ 174.

mor m. "peacock". G. Panj. H. *mor*, S. *moru*, Siṃ. *miyuru*. Pkt. *mora-*. Skr. *mayūra*-m. $ 56.

morāṃbā, *murabbā* m. "jam". Arabic *murabbā*.—$ 80

mol n. "price" G. H. B. *mol*, S. *mulhu*, Panj. *mull*, O. *mūl*, Siṃ. *mila*, K. *mŏl*, Ro. *mol* "worthy". Pkt. *molla-*, *mulla-*. Skr. *mūlya-*, *maulya-* n. —$ 78, 80, 143.

moh moho m. "fascination, bewilderment". G. H. B. *moh*, Panj. S. *mohu*, Siṃ. *mō*; K. *muhun* "betray, deceive". Pkt. Skr. *moha-* m. $ 39, 78, 159, 168, 193, 252.

moh moho n. m. "nest, honey comb of bees". H. *mau* "honey", Siṃ. *mī* "mead", cf. Ro. *mol* "wine". Skr. *madhu-* n. — $ 188.

moh, mohā, mhomv m. "bassia latifolia", G. *mahuḍuṃ*, Panj. H. *mahūā, mahvā*, Siṃ. *mihiṅgu, mīgaha*. Skr. *madhuka-* — $ 55, 59, 159, 188, 190.

mohar f. "the front-side, vanguard", *mohrā* adj. "having a bent for"; *mohre* "in front", cf. *samor* "opposite". G. *mor* "in front", *mohḍūṃ* n. "face"; Panj. *mohar*, H. *mohrā* "advanced guard"; S. *moru* "principal, capital", *muharu mohri* "front, origin", *mahuru* "face, prow, " cf. for the form in Skr. *mukhara-* "talkative".—$ 64,79, 161. see the following.

mohaḷ mohḷeṃ n. "muzzle for the calf". Siṃ. *muhul muhuna* "visage". Pkt. *muhulla-*, Deśī. *muhalaṃ mukhaṃ* (230, 12). Skr. *mukha-* n. The simple one, with the meaning of "visage", has been preserved in G. *moṃh*, S. *muhuṃ*, Panj. *mūṃh mūhuṃ*. H. *muṃh*, Siṃ. *muva*, Eur. Ro. *muy*, Asiatic Ro. *moh*, Arm. Ro. *mus*. — $ 64, 145, 161.

moḷī f. "faggot". Skr. *mulikā* f. — $ 80, 145.

mhaṇṇeṃ (part. *ṃhaṭlā*) "to say", *mhaṇije* "that is to say", *mhaṇūn* "this being said." Isolated word, for which phonetics forbids all linking up with G. *bhaṇvuṃ* "to recite, to read, to study" H. *bhannā*, Siṃ. *baṇinavā*, Eur. Ro. *phen-*, Arm. Ro. *phan-*, "to talk", which correctly represent Pkt. P. Skr. *bhaṇ-*. — $ 79, 229, 232, 252, 253, 276.

mhātārā m. "old". Pkt. Skr. *mahattara-*. — $ 168.

mhais f. *mhaisā* m. "buffalo". G. *bheṃs*; S. *meṃhi, maṃjh*; Panj. *maiṃh meṃh, majjh*; H. Bih. *bhaiṃs, bhaiṃsā*; B. *bhaiṃs*, O. *bhayeṣ*, Siṃ. *miyu mivu mī*. Pkt. *mahisa-*. Skr. *mahiṣī* f., *mahiṣa-* m. — $ 46, 56, 70, 156, 168.

yek, yeṇeṃ, yer for *ek, eṇeṃ, er*. — $ 174.

yeṇeṃ eṇeṃ "to come, to arrive", part. of obligation *yāvā*. K. *yinu* (defective) "to come" ? cf. Grierson, *Piś. Lang.*, p. 66. Skr. *eti*. — $ 24, 29, 77, 154, 174, 229, 230, 253.

raṃg m. "colour, beauty, appearance". G. Panj. H. B. K. *raṃg*, S. *raṃgu*, Siṃ. *raṃga*. P. Skr. *raṅga-* m. — $ 98, 143.

raḍṇeṃ "to weep". G. *raḍvuṃ*, S. *raḍṇu* "to cry", H. *raṭnā* "to exclaim", B. *raṭāite* "to talk". Apa. *raḍaṃtaü*. Skr. *raṭati*. — $ 46, 111.

ratī f. "seed of abrus precatorius, used as a measure of weight". G. S. *ratī*, Panj. H. B. *rattī, ratī*. Skr. *raktikā* f. — $ 48, 121, 143.

ravī f. "churn". Deśī. *ravao manthānaḥ* (237, 4).

ras m. "juice, taste", *rasā* m. "sauce". G. H. Bih. B. *ras*, S. *rasu*, Panj. *ras rasā* "juice", *rahā* "soup", Siṃ. *rāharā* "taste, alcoholic drink". Pkt. Skr. *rasa-* m. — $ 156.

rasāl, rasāḷ adj. "juicy". G. *rasāl rasāḷ.*, H. B. *rasāl*. Pkt. *rasāla* "juicy". Skr. *rasāla-* m. "sugar-cane, sweet-meats." — $ 46, 145.

rassā m. "cord", *rassī* f.

"thread". G. *rasī*, *raso*, *rās* f., S. *rasi* "towing cable", Panj. *rassā rassī*, H. *rās* "rein" *rassī* "cord", B. *rasā rasī*, Ass. *raśi*, K. *raz*, Siṃ. *räs* "ray of light". Pkt. *rassi-*. Skr. *raśmi-* m. — $ 157.

rahaṃvar (poet.) "excellent chariot, car". Skr. *ratha-* m. *rathavara-*, *rathānāṃvara-* ?). Isolated word; undoubtedly the simple word has been driven out by the Per. *rah* "route"; It is found in Siṃ. *riya* "vehicle". — $ 46, 59.

rahas n. "secret, mystery". H. *rahas*; B. *rahas* "in private". Pkt. *rahassa-*. Skr. *rahasya-* n. — $ 46, 157, 159.

rahāṭ m. "machine for drawing water, " G. H. *reṃṭ*, S. *araṭu*, Panj. *raṭṭ raṭ*, H. *rahaṭ arhaṭ*. Pkt. *rahaṭṭa-*. Skr. *araghaṭṭa-* m. — $ 40, 46, 159, 174.

rahāṇeṃ rāhṇeṃ "to stay, to abide". G. *rahevuṃ*, S. *rahaṇu*, Panj. *rahiṇā*, H. *rahnā*, B. *rahite*, K. *rōzun*. Jaina Pkt. *rahae* "stayed", cf. Deśī. *rāho..nirantaraḥ* (142, 2). — $ 52.

rāī f. "mustard". G. S. Panj. H. B. *rāī*. Skr. *rājikā* f. — $ 46, 57.

rāuḷ n. "palace, temple". H. *rāul*, *rāval* "warrior-prince", *rāur raūl* "royal palace". Pkt. *rāula-*. Skr. *rājakula-* n. — $ 46, 57, 59, 61, 145.

rāo, *rāvo*, *rāy* m. "king". G. S. Panj. H. *rāo rāy* or *rāī*, B. Ro. *rāy*, K. *rāza*, Siṃ. *rada*. Pkt. *rāā rāa-*. Skr. *rājan-* m. — $ 38, 39, 55, 193, 198, 282.

rākh f. "ashes", *rākhī* f. "cotton-string tied round the wrist". G. Panj. H. *rākh* f., S. *rakhyā* "preservation, bracelet or necklace (amulet)". Skr. *rakṣā* f. $ 96, 104.

rākhṇeṃ "to guard". G. B. *rākh-*, S. H. O. Ro. *rakh-*, Siṃ. *rak-*, K. *rach-*. Pkt. *rakkhai*. Skr. *rakṣati*. — $ 47, 96.

rākhismukh f. n. "the South", *rākhesmohrā* "towards the south". G. Panj. H. *rākhas*, S. *rākhasu*, *rākhāsu*, Bih. *rākas*, Siṃ. *rakus* "demon". P. Pkt. *rakkhasa-*. Skr. *rākṣasa-* m. — $ 96.

rāṃjaṇ m. "water-pot". Deśī. *raṃjaṇo ghaṭah*; *raṃjaṇaṃ kuṇḍam iti kecit* (237, 3).

rājā m. "prince". Tatsama; cf. *rāo*, *rāut*, *rāuḷ*. — $ 100, 155.

rāṃḍ, f. "widow". H. G. O. B. *rāṃḍ*, S. *ran*, *raṇḍī*; Panj. *rann* "woman, wife". Skr. *raṇḍā* f. — $ 111.

rāṇī f. "queen". S. Panj. H. *rāṇī*, S. *rāṇo* "king". Skr. *rājñī* f. — $ 47, 135.

rāt f. "night". G. Panj. H. K. *rāt*, S. B. O. *rāti*, Ro. *rāt*; Siṃ. *rā rāya*. Pkt. *ratti-*, *rāī*. Skr. *rātri* f. $ 121, 190.

rātā adj. "red", *rāt* m. "blood-shot state of eyes". H. *rātā*, G. *rātuṃ*, S. *rato*, Panj. *rattā*, Siṃ. *rat* "red; blood", K., Ro. "blood". Pkt. *ratta-*. Skr. *rakta-*. — $ 47, 48, 121.

rāṃdhṇeṃ "to cook" (*rāndhatem ghar* n. "kitchen" etc.). G. *rāndhvuṃ*, S. *rāndhaṇu*, H. *rāndhnā*, B. *rāndhite*, K. *ranun*, Arm. Ro. *əranthel*; Siṃ. *riddanavā* "to destroy". Skr. *rāndhyati*. — $ 135.

rāṇ rān n. "forest, bush, desert". G. *rān*, S. *riṇu rañ riñ*, Panj. H. *raṃj*, H. *ran*, Siṃ. *raṇa ran*. Pkt. *araṇṇa- raṇṇa-*. Skr.

araṇya- n. — $ 72, 135, 174.

rāpṇeṃ rāṃpṇeṃ "to blacken through exposure to air, to lose colour". Pkt. *rāvei* (*rāñjayati* Hemacandra, IV, 49; cf. *rāviaṃ rañjitam, Deśīnāmamālā* 238, 1). is the causative, whose passive, in the Sanskrit stage would have had been the form **rāpya-*.

rāṃpā m. "scraper", *rāṃpī* f. "instrument of carrier". G. *rāṃp* f. S. *raṃbu*, Panj. *raṃbā*, G. H. Bih. *rāṃpī*. Pkt. *raṃpai raṃphai* (*takṣṇoti*; see *Deśīnāma-* 237, 4), *rampa- rumpa-* "shaving". — $ 82.

rāb m. "goings and comings", *rābṇeṃ* "to frequent, to live, to work". Deśī. *rambhai gacchati* (237, 4). — $ 47.

Rām, Rāmā, Rāmū (proper n.). Skr. *Rāma-*. — $ 39, 276.

rās f. "sign of zodiac, heap". G. Panj. H. *rās*, S. *rāsi* "sign of zodiac, property", Siṃ. *rās* "troup, ensemble", P. Pkt. *rāsi-*. Skr. *rāśī* f. — $ 156.

Rāhī name of woman, common among the Kunbis. Skr. *Rādhā* f. — $ 46, 159.

rāḷ f. "resin". G. S. *rāḷ*, Panj. H. B. *rāl*. Skr. *rāla-*, *rāli-* m. — $ 145.

rikāmā adj. "empty, vain", *rikāmṭī* f. "leisure". S. *rīkamu* "useless". Deśī. *rikkaṃ stokam* (238, 8); Pkt. *ritta-*, *rikka-*. Skr. *rikta-karma-*. — $ 44, 138, 172.

righṇeṃ "to enter". Pkt. *riggai*, Deśī. *riggo praveśaḥ* (238, 2). Obscure link with the group: G. *righvuṃ*, B. *riṃghan*, Skr. *riṅkh-*, *riṅg-* "to creep":

riṭhā m. *riṃṭhī* f. "sapindus detergens". G. *rīṭh*, Panj. *reṭhā*, H. *rīṭhā*, B. *riṭhā*, Siṃ. *riṭi*. Pkt. *ariṭṭha-*. Skr. *ariṣṭaka-* m. — $ 44, 110, 174.

ritā adj. "empty". Panj. *rītī*, H. *rītā*, Siṃ. *rit*. Pkt. *ritta-*. Skr. *rikta-*. — $ 44, 121.

rīṇ n. "debt". Panj. H. *rin*. Pkt. *riṇa-*. Skr. *ṛṇa-* n. — $ 30, 134.

rīs, rīṃs m. "bear". G. *rīṃch*, S. *ricchu*, Panj. *ricch*, H. *rīch*, Ro. *ric* (fem. *ricini*); but K. *ich*. Pkt. *riccha-*, *rikkha-*. Skr. *ṛkṣa-* m. — $ 30, 69, 104.

rīs f. "offence, aversion". G. *rīs*, Panj. H. *ris*, S. *rīs* "rivalry". Skr. *riṣ-* f. *risyati*. — $ 156.

ruī f. "calotropis gigantea." Deśī. *rūvī arkadrumaḥ* (239, 10). — $ 44, 64.

rukhā adj. "dry, hard". S. *rukhu*, Panj. *rukkhā*, H. *rūkhā*; Siṃ. *ruk* "torment, disease". Pkt. *rukkha-lukkha-lūha-* (H. *ruhai* "roughness", see Huber, *B. E. F. E. O.*, VI p. 9, n. 2; Pischel, $ 257). Skr. *rūkṣa-*. — $ 96.

rucṇeṃ "to be delicious to the palate; to please". G. S. Panj. H. B. *ruc-*; Siṃ. *risi* "desirous, desire", *russanavā* "to be pleasant to ", K. *rūc* "preference". Pkt. *ruccai* skr. *rucyate*. — $ 101.

rujṇeṃ, rujhṇeṃ, rudhṇeṃ "to bud". Pkt. *ruh-*. Skr. *rohati*, absol.—*ruhya*; cf. Ved. *ròdhati* and *rodhana-*. — $ 89, 107, 230, 231.

rudhṇeṃ, rudhavṇeṃ, ruṃdhṇeṃ "to be obstructed", *rodhṇeṃ* "to obstruct". G. *ruṃdhvuṃ*, S. part. *rudho* from the verb *ruṃbhaṇu*, H. *rodhnā*, *rūndhnā*, passive *rujhnā*, B. *rodhite*. Skr. *ruddha-*. — $ 230, 231.

rumeā, *rumdh*, *rumdhā* adj. "wide". Deśī. *rundo vipulo* (241, 6). Skr. (Lex.) *rundra* "abundant."

rupem n. "silver". G. *rūpam*, S. *rupu*, Panj. *ruppā*, H. *rūp*, B. *rūpā*, K. *rŏp*, Ro. *rup*; only Sim. has *ridī*, from Skr. *rajata-*. Skr. *rūpya-* n. — $ 125.

rusnem "to feel offended". G. Panj. S. B. *rus-* (Panj. *roh* "anger"), H. *rūs-ros-*, Ro. *rus*ˇ—. Pkt. *rūsai*. Skr. *ruṣyati*. — $ 156.

rūm neuter suffix has the sense of diminutive or pejorative, being added in particular to the names of animals, as *gurūm*, *pākhrūm*, *vāsrūm* (see these words; cf. Navalkar, p. 68; Joshi, p. 290), *hatrūm* "elephant" (in contempt), etc. The isolated tadbhava is not known in India (but Sim. *rua*, *rū*). The usage in Marathi goes back to Prakrit (see Jacobi, *Erzählungen*, index, and Mayer, *Hindu Tales*, p. 127, n. 6; for example *dāsarūva-* "slave", *ḍikkaruvā-* (M. *lekrūm*) "child") "infant". and already in Pali (*gorūpa-* "buffalo" in the *Milinda pañho*). Skr. *rūpa-* n. — $ 39.

rū m. *ruī* f. "carded cotton". G. *rū* n., S. *raī*, Panj. *rūm*, *rūīm*, H. *rūī*, Bih. *rū rūī*. Deśī. *rūam tūlam* (239, 10).

rūkh m. "tree". G. H. *rūkh*, Panj. *rukkh*, Sim. *rik ruk*, Ro. *ruk* Pkt. *rukkha-*. Skr. *vṛkṣa-*, Ved. *rukṣa-* m. — $ 96.

regh f. "line". G. H. *rekh*, S. *reghī* "traits of mischief", Sim. *le*. Skr. *rekhā-* f. — $ 99.

rumjnem "to respect, to fear". Deśī. *revayam praṇāmaḥ* (239, 11) is made on the causative of the word, whose Marathi form is made with the suffix *-ya-*, but this word is unknown.

reṇem n. "excrements of young, black calves". S. *reṇī* "irrigation", B. *rīṇ* "exudation", Sim. *reṇavā* "to filter". Deśī *reṇī paṅkaḥ* (239. 10). Skr. *rīyate* " to flow", cf. *raya-* m. "current"; Geiger compares for the meaning with Persian *rītan*.

revṇem "to fill up". G. *revvuṃ* "to cement". Deśī. *ahiremai pūrayati* (23, 2). — $ 152.

romcnem "to push in, to penetrate". Pkt. *romcai-* = *pinaṣṭi*. cf. Skr. *roṭate* "to strike against". Cf. the following. — $ 101.

roṭ m. "paste of cooked flour", *roṭā*, *roṭī* "bread". G. *roṭlī* "small cake", *roṭī*, S. *roṭu*, *roīlu*, Panj. H. *roṭ*, *roṭā*, *roṭī*, B. *ruṭī*. Deśī. *roṭṭam taṇḍulapiṣṭam* (240, 5); Jaina Pkt. *roṭṭaga-* Cf. preceding one. — $ 164.

rov, *roh* m. "germinated seed". B. *roā* "planted" (rice of cold weather). Skr. *roha-* "growth" — $ 55, 159.

rovamth, *rohamt*, *ravamth*, *romth*, *romt* m. "rumination, mastication of betel". H. *romth*. Skr. *romantha-* m. — $ 88, 152.

rovnem "to plant". G. *ropvuṃ*, B. *ruite*. Skr. *ropayati*. — $ 55, 152.

rohī f., *rohem* n. "antelope". Skr. *rohi-* m.— The same

animal is called in G.S. Panj. H. *rojh*, cf. Deśī. *īsao rojj hākhyo mṛgaḥ* (35, 17). — $ 159.

rohī f. "carp". H. *rohū*, *ruī*, *rohī*, B. *ruī*, Siṃ. *rehemas*, *rēmas*. Skr. *rohita-*. — $ 140, 159.

lakḍā, *lākaḍ*, *lakūḍ*, m. "wood, baton". G. *lākḍī* "baton", *lākaḍ* "wooden"; S. *lākuḍyo* "wooden"; Panj. *lakkaḍ*, H. *lakḍā*, B. *laguḍ* "baton", *lagī* "hook of bamboo", *lagā* "pole", *lagaḍ* f. "metal-bar". Deśī. *lakkuḍo lakuṭaḥ* (243, 1); P. *laguḷa-*. Skr. *lakuṭa-*, *laguḍa-*, m. — $ 40, 49, 50, 94.

lakārī m. "varnisher, maker of lac-bangles". From *lākh* "lac" + *kār-*. — $ 48, 172.

laṃg adj. "weakened by fast or disease". *laṃgḍā* "paralysed". G. *laṃgaḍ*, S. *laṅu*, Panj. H. *laṃgā laṃgḍā*, K. *longᵘ*; Ro. *lang* "lame". Skr. *laṅga-*. — $ 98.

laṃghṇeṃ "to grow thin (due to fasting, due to fasting); to transgress" S. *laṃghaṇu* "to jump over; fasting"; Panj. *laṃghaṇ*, H. *laṃghan* "fasting", B. *laṃghite* "to pass, to transgress". Pkt. Skr. *laṅgh-*. — $ 99.

laṭ laṭṭh m. "mace". G. *lāṭhī*, *lāṭ* f., *laṭh* m., S. *laṭhi*, Panj. *laṭṭhī*, H. *lāṭh*, B. O. *lāṭhī*, *laḍī*; Siṃ. *laṭu* "name of a creeper"; Ro. *laxti* "kick of foot; to fight"? Pkt. *laṭṭhi-laṭṭha-* — $ 48, 88, 148, 188.

lavaṃg f. "clove". G. *lavaṃg* n., S. *lauṃgu*, Panj. *lauṃg*, H. *lavaṃg lauṃg*, *loṃg*, B. O. *laṃga* (*loṅgo*). Skr. *lavaṅga* m. n. — $ 46, 152.

lavḍā m. "penis". S. *lauṛu*, H. *lauḍā* "penis"; Panj. *laukī*, H. *lāvū*, B. *lāu* Siṃ. *labba* (pl. *labu*) "gourd". Pkt. *lāū*. Skr. *alābu-* m. n. — $ 48, 57, 152, 174.

lavṇeṃ (vulgar doublet of *navṇeṃ*) "to sleep, to bend". Skr. *namati*. — $ 170.

lavā lāṃv m. "partridge". Panj. *lavā*, H. *lāvā*, B. *lab*. Skr. *lāba- lāvaka-* m. — $ 152.

las f. "mucus, pus". S. *laso* "united, brilliant"; S. Panj. *las* f. H. *las*, *lassā* m. "viscosity". Deśī. *lasuaṃ tailaṃ* (242, 11). Skr. *laśa-* "resin". m. — $ 141, 156.

lasaṇ n. f. *lasūṇ* m. f. "garlic". G. Panj. *lasaṇ*, H. *lasun*, *lasan*, B. *laṣūn*; Siṃ. *lūna* "onion". Pkt. *lasuṇa-*. Skr. *laśuna-* n. m. — $ 40, 42, 46, 148, 156.

lahar f. "wave, convulsion". G. *leher*, *ler* f., S. *lahariʼ*, Panj. *lahir*, H. *lahar*, B. *laharī*. Skr. *lahari-* f. — $ 46, 159.

lahān adj. "small". Pkt. *laṇha-* for **lhaṇha-*, Skr. *ślakṣaṇa-* (see Wackernagel, p. 255). Cf. M. *sahān*. — $ 52, 136.

lahulahān adj. "small and pretty". Panj. *lahuḍā* "young", K. *lŏtᵘ*, Siṃ. *luhu* "slight, small". Pkt. *lahu-*. Skr. *laghu-*. — $ 46, 148, 159, Cf. M. *haḷū* and the preceding word.

lā, post position "for". — $ 180, 195, 197, 200.

lākh f. "red colour, shellac, sealing-wax". G. S. Panj. *lākh*, H. *lākh lāh* m., B. *lāhā*, *lā*, Siṃ. *lā*, K. *lācch*. Skr. *lākṣā* f. — $ 48, 96, 172.

lākh m. "hundred thousand". G. Panj. H. *lākh*, S. Panj.

lakh, B. *lāk*, K. *lach*; Siṃ. *lak* "sign". Pkt. *lakkha-*. Skr. *lakṣa-* m. — $ 96, 224.

lākhṇeṃ "to have as an aim". (an object)". G. S. Panj. H. B. *lakh-* "to observe, to understand", Deśī. *ahilaṃkhai ahilaṃghai kāṅkṣati* (23, 3). Skr. *lakṣayati*. — $ 96.

lāgṇeṃ "to touch, to hit, to agree, to happen". G. *lāgvuṃ*, S. *lagṇu*, Panj. *laggṇā*, H. *lagnā* (dial. *lāgnā*), B. *lāgite*, K. *lāgun* active, *lagun* neut., Siṃ. *laginavā*, "to rest, to reside". Pkt. *laggai*. Skr. *lagna-* or *lagya-*. — $ 47, 98, 231.

lāgīṃ "near, towards". G. *lāgu* "near", S. *lāge* "because of", Panj. *lagge*, H., old B. *lāgī*, Siṃ. *laṃga* "near, in relation with" P. Pkt. *lagga-*. Skr. *lagna-*. — $ 98, 197, 200.

lāṃc f. "bribe". G. S. H. (dial.) *lāṃc*; Siṃ. *lasa*. Pkt. P. *lañca-*. Skr. *lañcā* f. — $ 101.

lāj f. "shame". G. O. B. *lāj*, S. *laj*, Panj. *lajj*, Siṃ. *lada*, Ro. *laj*. Pkt. Skr. *lajjā* f. — $ 106, 148.

lāṭ interj. "well done, bravo !". Panj. *laṭī* "mistress". Deśī. *laṭṭho anyāsakto manoharaḥ priyaṃvādaś cetī tryarthaḥ* (245, 16); Pkt. *laṭṭha-*. —To separate from S. *lāḍlo*, H. *lāḍā* "dear", S. *lāḍa*, Panj. *lāḍā* "betrothed (boy)", Panj. *lāḍ* "love", H. *lāḍhiyā* "one who cajoles," which are more directly related to the family of M. *lāḍu* "a sweet-meat", Panj. H. *laḍḍū*, Siṃ. *laḍu* etc., Pkt. Skr. *laḍḍu-*. Skr. *laṣita-* (**laṣṭa-*). — $ 88.

lāḍ f. "muck-pit". S. *liḍi*, B. *lāḍī laḍḍī* "dung, droppings". Skr. (Divyāv.) *laḍḍī* f. — $ 111.

lāḍṇeṃ "to load, to freight (out)". G. *lādvum lādhvuṃ*, S. *laḍṇu*, Panj. *laddṇā*, H. *lāḍnā lādnā*, K. *ladun*, Ro. *ladav-*. Skr. *lardayati*. — 47, 115, 123.

lāḍhṇeṃ "to increase, to accrue as profits". G. *lāḍhvuṃ* "to grow, to be found", S. *ladhu ladhi* "find, profit', Panj. *laddhṇā* "to be found", to seek", old H. *laddhiyā* (Mod. *liyā*) "taken", Siṃ. *lada* "attained, terminated". Pkt. *laddha-*. Skr. *labdha-*. — $ 47, 49, 124, 231.

lāṃb adj. "long, far". G. *laṃbuṃ*, S. *laṃbu*, Panj. *lammā*, H. *lāṃb*; S. Panj. *lām* f. "length". Skr. *lamba-*. — $ 127.

lābhṇeṃ "to be acquired, to be profitable", *lābh* m. "profit". G. *lābhvuṃ* "to acquire, to find", S. *labhaṇu* "to be obtained, acquired"; Siṃ. *labanavā* "to receive"; K. *labun* "to take, to find". Pkt. *labbhai*. Skr. *labhyate*. — $ 49, 128, 230, 231, 252.

lāṃv f. "ogress, hateful woman". Deśī. *lāmā ḍākinī* (243, 14). Doublet of Skr. *rāmā* ? — $ 141, 152.

lāvṇeṃ "to place upon, to send". G. *lāvvuṃ* "to bring, to shut", Panj. *lāuṇā* "to apply, to fix, to put, to seek", H. *lāvnā lānā* "to bring, to purchase, to make", Siṃ. *lanavā* (part. *lāvā*) "to place upon", K. *lāy-* "to strike". Skr. *lāgayati* with a meaning not attested in Sanskrit, but normally corresponding to *lagati*. — $ 55, 200, 242.

lāhṇeṃ "to acquire, to take, to present oneself", *lāṇī lāhṇī* f. "reading", *lāho* m. "profit." G. *lahaṇ* n. "profit", probably *lahevuṃ* "to listen attentively", S. *lahaṇu* "to obtain", S. *lāho*, Panj. *lāh*, "profit", H. *lāosāo* "profit, advantage", *lahnā* "to obtain, to find, to grow, to do well", subst. "profit, gain", Siṃ. *labanavā* "to receive, to obtain". Pkt. *lahaī*, P. *labhati*. Skr. *labhate*, *lābham*. — $ 39, 49, 159, 161, 186, 230, 231, 252.

lāḷ f. "saliva". G. *lāḷ*, H. *lāl lālā*, *lār*, *rāl*. Skr. *lālā* f. — $ 145.

likṇeṃ "to hide, to be hidden". S. *likṇu*, *lukṇu*; H. *luknā*, Panj. *lukaṇ*, B. *lukite*. Deśī. *likkai lhikkai nilīyate* (244, 7); Pkt. also *lukkai*. — $ 594.

limpṇeṃ "to plaster". G. *lipvuṃ*, S. *limbaṇu*, Panj. *limmṇā*, H. *līpnā*, *lepnā* (passive *lipnā*). Skr. *limpati*. — $ 70, 125, 138.

limb m. "azadirachta indica". G. *limḍo*, S. *limu*. Pkt. *limba-*. Skr. *nimba-* m. — $ 127, 138, 148, 170. Cf. under M. *nimb*.

līkh f. "louse, slow". G. S. Panj. H. *līkh*, B. *līkhā*, Siṃ. *likkā*, Ro. *likh*, Skr. *likṣā līkṣā* f. — $ 96.

luksān, *luskān* n. f. "loss, damage", adj. "weak, tired". H. *luqsān*. Arab. *nuqṣān*. — $ 167, 170.

luṭṇeṃ "to rob", *lūṭ* f. "robbery". G. *luṃṭ- luṭ-*, S. H. B. *luṭ-*, Panj. *luṭṭ-*, K. *lūr-*, Ro. *lur-* (*lurdo* "soldier"). Skr. *luṇṭati*. — $ 109.

lulā adj. "withered, weak". G. *lūluṃ*, S. *lūlo*, Panj. H. *lūlā*. Pkt. *lua-*, plus. the suffix *-alla-*. Skr. *lūta-* (*ápax* = *vichinna-*), *lūna-*. — $ 64.

lek, *lekrūṃ* n. "child". Deśī. *liṃko tathā līvo bālaḥ* (244, 3); Jaina Pkt. *ḍikkarūva-ḍekkarūva-*. — $ 148, Cf. M. *rūṃ*.

lekh m. "writing, document". G. Panj. *lekh*, G. *lekhuṃ* "account". To distinguish from S. H. B. *lekh* f. "line" tatsama from Skr. *lekhā*, whose tadbhava is found in G. *līh*, Siṃ. *lé* "line". Skr. *lekhya-*. — $ 96. Cf. M. *lehṇeṃ*.

leṭṇeṃ "to be lying". G.S. Panj. H. *leṭ-*. root *lī-*. — $ 80.

leṃḍ m. "dung", *leṃḍūk* n. "heap of excrements". S. *leṇḍu leḍuṇo*, H. *leṃḍ*, *leṃḍī*. Deśī. *leḍukko lampaṭo loṣṭaśca* (246, 11), *lehuḍo leḍhukko leḍuo trayo'py ete loṣṭa vācakāḥ* (245, 3), *lehaḍo..lampaṭaḥ* (245, 8). Skr. *lemḍa-* n. — $ 111.

leṇeṃ "to place, to apply, to dress oneself in". G. *levuṃ*, H. *lenā*, B. *leite*, Arm. Ro. *liel* "to take", S. *letī* "reception", Deśī. *laiaṃ parihitam*; *laiaṃ aṅge pinaddham ity anye* (242, 10) : Apa : *lehi* imper. , *levi* beside *lai* absol. Alteration from Skr. *lā-* (cf. Euro. Ro. *la-* "to take") on the model of Pkt. *dei*; cf. M. *leṇḍeṇ*, *levdev* "exchanges". — $ 77, 200, 229, 252.

lehṇeṃ lihṇeṃ "to write". Siṃ.

liyanavā; but G. *lakh-*, S. Panj. H. B. *likh-*, K. *likh-*. Pkt. *lihai*. Skr. *likhati*. Cf. M. *lekh-* $ — 80.

loṃ, loṃv, laṃv f. "hair of the body, fleece." G. *ruṃuṃ*, S. Panj. *lūṃ*, Panj. H. *roāṃ*, B. *roṃā*, H. Siṃ. *lom*. Skr. *loman-*, *roman-* n. — $ 78, 140, 153.

lok "people", tatsama ; same form everywhere; is also found H. *log*. Skr. *loka-* m. — $ 45, 197.

lokhaṃḍ n. "iron", *lohār* m. "black-smith", G. H. *lokhaṃḍ*, S. *lohu*, Panj. H. *lohā*, B. *loh*, Siṃ. *loho lō*, G. *loḍhuṃ* "iron"; G. Panj. H. B. *lohār*, S. *luharu luhāru*, Siṃ. *lovaru* "black-smith; cf. Ro. *lovo* "silver (coins)." Pkt. Skr. *loha-*, Skr. *lohakāra-* m. Cf. of Skr. *lohita-*, Panj. *lohī*, Ro. *lolo* "red", Panj. *lohū* "blood". For the second part of the word, see M. *khāṃḍ*.— $ 78, 143, 148, 159, 161, 169.

loṭṇeṃ "to roll". G. Panj. H. B. *loṭ*—; S. *loṭiko*, "sparse, errant". Pkt. *lôṭṭai*. Skr. *luṭyati*.— $ 109.

loṇ f. "a plant growing in salty marshland, salinity of soil". G. *lūṇ* n., S. *lūṇu*, Panj. *lūṇ*, H. *nŏṇ*, *nūṇ*, *lūṇ*, *loṇ*, B. *nūn* (*lonā*, "salted"), O. *nūṇ*, Siṃ. *luṇu*, K. *nūn*, Ro. *lon* "salt" (the Marathi word denoting "salt" is *mīṭh*). Pkt *loṇa*—Skr. *lavaṇa*-m.— $ 78, 134.

loṇī n. "butter" H. *lūnī*, *lōnī*, B. *lanī*, *nanī* Arm. Ro. *nol*, Ro. Per. *nul*. Skr. *navanīta-* n.— $ 66, 78, 134, 148, 170.

loṃbṇeṃ "to be suspended". S. *lamṇu* "to be suspended, to soar", H. *lumnā* "to hang, to be low (clouds)" Skr. *lambate*.—$ 79.

loṃbaṭ, *loṃbaḍ* f. ("heap of coconuts, etc.)" *loṃbaṇ* f. "cluster, bunch". G. *lūm* f. "bunch", B *lūm* "tail". Deśī. *lumbī stabako latā ca* (246, 7). Skr. *lamba-*. — $ 79.

loho m. "tenderness" (used in relig. language and in proverbs). Siṃ. *loba* "desire". Skr. *lobha-* m. — $ 39, 78, 79, 159, 186.

loḷ m. "instability", *loḷṇeṃ* "to roll", *loḷā* m. "clapper of a bell, uvula". G. *loḷo* "tongue", S. *rolu*, *rolāku*, *rolo* "vagabond" *rulaṇu*, "to roam", Panj. *lull* "penis", H. *lol* "trembling, agitated", *lolā* m. "ear-rings, penis", *lolnā* "to shake", B. *lol* "hanging, unstable", *lol dāite* "to hang", Siṃ. *lela* "unstable, moving", *lelavannā* "to go here and there, to shake". P. Pkt. *lol-*. Skr. *lolati*, *lola-*. — $ 80, 145.

vauṃl, *vaghal*, *vaṃjal*, *vaṇavṇeṃ*, *vapṇeṃ*, *vasvā*, *vaḷ*, *vaḷaṃgṇeṃ*, see *oṃuḷ*, *oghaḷ*, etc. — $ 78.

vakhār f. "warehouse, depot". G. S. *vakhār*, H. B. *bākhār* cf. Deśī. *vakkhārayaṃ ratigṛhaṃ*, *antaḥpuram ity anye* (252, 13). Skr. *avaskara-* m. "dung heap". ? — $ 151, 152.

vagar (common form : *bagar*) "except, without". G. *vagar*, Panj. *vagār*, B. *begar*. Arab.-Per. *bighair*, *baghair*. — $ 150.

vaṭ f. "loss or waste in washing raw silk" Deśī. *vaṭṭiṃaṃ atiriktam* (248, 9).

vaṭṇeṃ "to roll cotton to force out its seeds". G. *vāṭvuṃ*, S. *vaṭṇu*,, H. *baṭnā*, B. *bāṭite*, cf. G. *vāṭṇo* "pestle". Skr. *ἄpax vaṭyante* "are crushed". — $ 48, 78, 114, 151.

vaṭhāṇ n. "room, apartment". S. *vāthānu* f. "enclosure for cattle, place, residence"; Panj. *vaṭan*, K. *vatan* "country, residence"; H. *bathān* "hut in the jungle (for cattle-breeders)", *baṭhān* "pasture". Skr. *upasthāna*- or *avasthāna*- n. — $ 48, 110, 151, 152, 174.

vaḍ m. "Banyan tree, ficus Indica". G. *vaḍ*, S. *baṛu*, Panj. *vaḍ* and *baḍ* H. B. *baḍ*. Pkt. *vaḍa*-. Skr. *vaṭa*-m. — $ 151.

vaḍhṇeṃ oḍhṇeṃ "to draw, to stretch". G. *oḍvuṃ*. Pkt. *vaḍḍhai* (=*kaḍḍhai* H c. IV, 187). — $ 78.

vaṇ m. n. "scar". Siṃ. *vaṇa* "wound, abcess". Pkt. *vaṇa*-. Skr. *vraṇa*-m. — $ 134, 151.

vaṇ, -*vaṇī* (in comp.) "water". From M. *pāṇī*. — $ 152.

vaṇaj f. "journey for trade", *vaṇjār* m. "troop of *brinjaries*, travelling merchants, dealing in grains and salt". G. *vaṇaj* m., S. *vaṇij* m., Panj. *banj* m., K. *banj* m. "trade"; G. *vaṇjar* f. "caravan"; S. *vaṇijaro*, Panj. *vaṇjārā* "trader", H. *banjārā*, name of caste, "seeds man", Skr. *vāṇijyā* f. *vāṇijya*- n. — $ 42, 48, 106.

vaṇvā m. "forest-fire". Deśī. *vaṇavo davāgniḥ* (249, 10). Skr. *vanavāta*- m. — $ 46.

vaṭīṃ "by the side of, because of, in the name of". G. *vaṭī* "by the side of, in place of, on behalf of", *vaṭe* "by means of"; S. *vaṭi* "near, in exchange for, with", *vaṭūn* "close to, of"; Siṃ. *vat* K. *buth*ᵘ "face". P. *vatta*-. Skr. *vaktra*- n.—To separate from Panj. *vāt* "news", H. *bāt* "talk, thing", K. *bāth* "discourse", from Skr. *vārtā* f. — $ 48, 78, 151.

vaṃth m. "part of patrimony". S. *vathu*, Siṃ. *vat* "thing, money, history". Pkt. *vatthu*-. Skr. *vastu*- n. ?— $ 122, 151.

vamṇeṃ "to vomit". H. *bamnā*; B. *vāṃit* "vomiting". Skr. *vamati*-. — $ 138.

var "betrothed (man), husband". G. Panj. *var*; S. *varaītī* "married woman (whose husband is alive)", *varaṇu*, "to marry"; H. B. *bar* "betrothed (man)", Skr. *vara*- m. — $ 151.

varaī "a gold coin" (pagoda). cf. Siṃ. *varā* "wild boar". Skr. *varāha*- m. — $ 46, 57, 161.

var, *varī* post position "on, until", *vartā* adj. "above", *varlā*, *varīl* "superior, exterior". G. *par*, S. *pari*, H. *upar*, *par*(*i*), B. O. *pare*- "on". Skr. *upari*. — $ 151, 152, 166, 174, 197.

varaṃḍ f. *varaṃḍā* m. *varaṃḍī* f. "parapet, low edging wall". Deśī. *varaṃdo prākāraḥ kapotapālī ceti dyarthaḥ* (268, 11). The concordance of meaning is to be noted; on the other hand, Panj. *barāṃḍā*, H. *barāṃḍā*, B. *bārāṃḍā*, K. *brānd* denote a portico with columns (a platform —at the entry of a house), as

Fr. *véranda*. This is, without doubt, another word, see for example *Hobson Jobson*, S. V. *Verandah*, or Dalgado, *Influencia do vocabulário português*.. S. V. *Varanda*. In any case the Marathi word is anterior to all contact with any Roman language. — $ 48.

varasṇeṃ "to rain". G. *varasvuṃ*, *varas* "rain"; S. *varsāru* "season of rains", *varsaṇu* and *vasaṇu* "to rain", *varhu* "year", *vas* "rain, greenery". Panj. *varhṇā* "to rain", *varah varhā* "year"; H. B. *baras-bars-*; K. *wuhur*ᵃ "of the age of..years"; Ro. *berś*. (Asiatic *bers vers*) "year"; Siṃ. *vas* "rain" *vasbah-* "to rain", Pkt. *varisa-*, P. *vassa-*. Skr. *varṣa-* m., *varṣati*. —$ 157.

varāt, *vārtī* f. "cord, cable". G. *varot* n.; G. S. *varat* H. *barat* f., Skr. *varatrā* f. — $ 46, 121.

varāt f. "marriage procession". G. Panj. *varāt*, H. *barāt*, Bih. *barāyit*. Skr. *varayātrā* f. — $ 61, 121.

vasṇeṃ "to reside". G. *vāsvuṃ*, S. *vihaṇu* (no doubt coming from—**vah-* contaminated by **vih-* "to sit", see under M. *basṇeṃ*), Panj. *vassṇā*, H. *basnā*; Siṃ. *vasanavā*. Pkt. *vasai*. Skr. *vasati*. — $ 46, 156.

vasne "in the opinion of, according to, on behalf of". S. *vasu-* "to be able to", *vasi* "docile", K. *vaś* "in the power of"; Ro. *vaś* "because of", Siṃ. *vasin visin* "thanks to". Pkt. *vasa-*. Skr. *vaśa-* m. — $ 156, 193.

vasvā osvā m. "shade". G. *occhino* "protection against heat, protection" *occhāyo* "shade". Skr. *avacchada-* m. — $ 78, 152.

vahāṇ vāhāṇ f. "sandal". Panj. *pāhaṇ*, O. *panāī*, Siṃ. *vahan*. Pkt. *uvāṇaha-*, *pāhaṇa-*, *vāhaṇa-*; P. *upāhana*. Skr. *upānah-* f. — $ 40, 52, 159, 167, 174.

vahilā adj. (poet.) "separated, distinct; quickly; certainly". G. *vahelum*, S. *vahalu*. Pkt. *vahilla-*, root *vah-*.. — $ 50.

vahū f. "daughter-in-law" ; *vahūmai vomāi* "mother-in-law" G. *vahu*, S. *vahū*, Panj. *bohū*, H. *bahū*, B. *bau*, O. *bahu*. Deśī. *vahuvvā kaniṣṭhaśvaśruḥ* (250, 12), Pkt. *vahū*. Skr. *vadhū-* f. — $ 46, 78, 159, 161.

vahvar, *vavar*, *ovar* n. "married couple". G. *vahuvar*. Skr. *vadhūvara-* n. — $ 78, 161, 163.

vaḷṇeṃ "to turn, to plait", *vaḷ* m. "tumour, rolling". G. *valavuṃ*, S. *varaṇu*, Panj. *valṇā*, H. *balnā*, K. *valun*. Skr. *valayati*.—$46, 52, 78, 145.

vaḷeṃ n. "ring". S. *varu*, Panj. *vālā*, H. *balā*, O. *bali*, K. *vöjü*, Siṃ. *valā*. Pkt. *valaa-*. Skr. *valaya-* m. n. — $ 46, 77, 145.

vāṃk m. n. "curve,", f. "brass-ornament", *vāṃkā* adj. "curved". G. *vāṃku*, S. *viṃgo*, Panj. *vaṃgg*, H. *bāṃk*, B. *bāṃkā*, Siṃ. *vak*. Pkt. *vaṃka-*, P. *vakka-*. Skr. *vakra-* (cf. (Ved. *vaṅku-*)— — $ 92.

vāṃkaḍ f. "continuous rain", *vāṃkḍī* f. "hard winter". Deśī. *vaddalaṃ tathā vakka-*

ḍaṃ durdinam; *vakkaḍaṃ nirantara vṛṣṭir ity eke* (248, 16). Derived from Skr. *vakra-*, as the preceding one; cf. also M. *vāṃkḍā* adj. "hostile".

vāk vākh m. "filamentous integuments of certain plants, used for cordage"; *vākh vākhal vākaḷ* f. "quilt made of pieces, rags". G. *vākh vāk*, Siṃ. *vak*; H. *bakal* B. *bāklā* "bark". Skr. *valka-* m. n. — $ 85.

vākhāṇ f. "panegyric". G. *vakhāṇ* n., Panj. S. *vakhān*. f., H. *bakhān*; B. *bākhān* "abuse", K. *vakhunᵘ* "lesson, subject of study". Pkt. *vakkhāṇa-*. Skr. *vyākhyāna-* n. — $ 47, 48, 96, 151.

vāṃg m. "spot on the skin, pustule, numbness, dull pain (due to a contusion)". S. *viṃg* f. "defect, vice"; K. *vongᵘ* "crippled", Siṃ. *vaṃgi* "twisted, hunch-back". Skr. *vyaṅga-*. — $ 151.

vāṃgī f. "aubergine". Panj. *vaṃgā*, B. *baṃg*. Deśī. *vaṃgaṃ vṛntākaṃ* (246, 13). —Several names of aubergine have an evident, though difficult to define, relationship with this word. Thus G. *veṃgaṇ*, S. *vāṅanu*, Panj. *baiṃgaṇ*, H. Bih. *baingan*, B. *beṃgan*, and *bāgun*, which recall, besides Persian *badinjān*. Cf. also in Dravidian, Kannada *badani* (and Tamil *valudalei*, Malay. *valudini* ?)

vāguḷ f. "act of chewing". G *vāgoḷvuṃ*, Deśī. *vaggolāi romanthayati* (254, 4). — $ 47.

vāgh m. "tiger". G. *vagh*, S. *vāgh*, *bāgh*, Panj. H. B. *bāgh* Pkt. *vaggha-*. Skr. *vyāghra-* m. — $ 99, 151.

vācṇeṃ "to read". G. *vāṃcvuṃ*, S. *vācaṇu*, Panj. *vācṇā*, H. *bācnā*, B. *bācāite* "to explain". Tatsama, Skr. *vācayati*. — $ 101.

vāṃcūn "excepting" (gerundive of *vāṃcṇeṃ* "to escape". Skr. *vāñcayati*. — $ 197.

vājṇeṃ "to emit a sound, to resound". G. *vājvuṃ*, S. *vāju* "musical instrument", *vajaṇu* "to resound", Panj. *vajnā*, H. *bājnā*, B. *bājite*. Skr. *vādya-*. — $ 47, 106, 232.

vāṃjho vāṃjā adj. "sterile", *vaṃj vāṃjh* f. "sterile woman". G. S. *vāmjh*, H. *bāṃjh* B. *bāṃjhā*, Siṃ. *vaṃda*; K. *banjar* "desert". Skr. *vandhya-*. — $ 88, 107.

vāṭ f. "path". G. S. Panj. *vāṭ*, H. B. *bāṭ*, Siṃ. *vat*, K. *vāt*. Deśī. *vaṭṭā panthāḥ* (247, 8); Pkt. *vaṭṭā* Skr. *vartman-* n. — $ 39, 114, 197.

vāṃṭṇeṃ "to share". G. *vāṃṭvuṃ*, Panj. *vaṃḍan*, S. *vāṭṇu*, H. *bāṃṭnā*, B. *bāṃṭite*; Bih. *bāṃṭ* "share-cropping". Skr. *vaṇṭati*. — $ 68, 109.

vāṭṇeṃ "to seem or appear unto" (cf. *nivaṭṇeṃ*). B. *baṭe* "yes", O. *aṭai aṭe* "he is"; B. *baṭi* Bih. *bāṭīṃ* "I am"; Siṃ. *vaṭinavā* "to merit", *vāṭenavā* "to fall"; K. *vātun* "to arrive, to come, to happen". Pkt. *vaṭṭai*. Skr. *vartate*. — $ 47, 114, 163.

vāṭlā adj. "around", *vāṭvā* m. "round bag" (of banker and jeweller). G. *vāṭ* f. *vāṭo* "iron-band of a wheel", H. *batvā*, "round bag", Siṃ. *vaṭa* "circle, belt, circular" *vāṭa* "hedge". P. Pkt. *vaṭṭa-*

vaṭṭi-. Skr. *vṛtta-*. — $ 47, 114.

vāṭī f. "metal-bowl". G. S. *vāṭī*, Bih. *bāṭī*, *baṭṭā*. Pkt. *vaṭṭiya-*. — $ 114.

vāḍ (poet.) "big". G. *vaḍuṃ*, S. *vaḍo*, Panj. *vaḍḍā*, H. B. *baḍā*, Siṃ. *vāḍi*, K. *boḍu*, Ro. *baro*. Deśī. *vaḍḍo mahān* (246, 13). Skr. *vaḍra-*. — $ 111.

vāḍā m. "quarter", *vāḍī* f. "enclosure, hamlet" *-vāḍeṃ* n. in comp. in proper names, *āitvāḍeṃ*, *vilvavāḍeṃ* etc. G. *vāḍī*, *vāḍo*, S. *vāḍī* "vegetable-field", *vāḍ* f. "enclosure", *vāḍo* "enclosure for cattle", Panj. *vāḍā* "enclosure". H. *bāḍ*, *bār* f. *bāḍā*, B. *bāḍī*, beside B. *bāṭī*, Siṃ. *vāṭa* "hedge". Deśī. *vāḍī*..*vṛti-* (251, 16),. Skr. *vāṭa-* m. — $ 46, 51, 111.

vāḍhṇeṃ "to grow". G. *vaḍhvuṃ*, H. *baḍhānā* (cf. *buḍhā* "old man"), B. *bāḍite*, Siṃ. *vaḍinavā*, K. *bāḍun*, Ro. *phuro* "old man"; with a dental, S. *vadhṇu*, Panj. *vadhṇā* and *vadhan* beside *vaḍhan*. Pkt. *vaḍḍhai*. Skr. *vardhate*. — $ 48, 115.

vāḍhāyā m. "carpenter". H. B. O. *baḍhaī*, Siṃ. *vaḍuvā*; cf. G. *vāḍhvuṃ*, Panj. *vaḍdhṇā*, S. *vaḍhaṇu*, "to cut"; G. *vaḍh*, S. *vaḍhu*, Siṃ. *vaḍ*, "cutting, cut". Pkt. *vaḍḍhaia-*. Skr. *vardhaka-* m., *vardhayati*. — $ 47, 115.

vāṇ n. "pious donation of fruits, cakes, clothes, etc." H. *bāyan*, *bainā*. Deśī. *vāyaṇaṃ bhojyopāyanam* (257, 3). Skr. *vāyana-* n. — $ 61.

vāṇ vān, m. "colour", *vāṇī* "according to, like". G. *vān* S. *vanaku* m., *vanik* f., H. *bān* "quality", *bānā* "aspect, colour", Siṃ. *vaṇa* "colour", *van* "similar to". Pkt. *vaṇṇa-*. Skr. *varṇa-* m. — $ 135.

vaṇṇeṃ vāṇiṇeṃ (poet.) "to do an eulogy of". Siṃ. *vaṇanavā* "to praise, to say", K. *vanun* "to talk"; on the other hand H. *bannā* "to be decorated, to be made, made", B. *banāite* "to make"; Cf. Panj. *vannovannī* "of different types," *vankī vannaggī* "specimen, mark". Pkt. *vaṇṇiuṃ*., inf., P. *vaṇṇeti*. Skr. *varṇayati*. — $ 51, 135.

vāṇī m. "merchant". G. *vāṇiyo*, *vāṇiu*, H. *baniyā*, B. *bāṇiyā*; Siṃ. *veṇaṃda*; cf. K. *vān* "shop". Pkt. *vāṇia-*. Skr. *vāṇija-* n. — $ 46, 48, 61, 63.

vāt f. "wick of lamp". G. *vāṭ*, S. *vaṭi*, Panj. H. *battī*, H. B. *bāti*, O. *bati*, Siṃ. *vāṭiya*. Pkt. *vaṭṭi-*, *vatti-*, P. *vaṭṭikā*. Skr. *vartikā* f. — $ 114.

vāṃdar and *vānar* m. n. "monkey". G. *vāndar*, S. *vānaru*, Panj. H. B. *bāndar*, *bānar*, Siṃ. *vaṃdura*. K. *vādur*. Skr. *vānara-* m. —The insertion is old; but in Marathi the word has the air of being a loan; see under *mākaḍ*. — $ 123, 136, 164.

vādaḷ m. f. n. "bad weather". G. *vādaḷ* S. *badalu*, Panj. *baddal*, H.B.O. *bādal*. Deśī. *vaddalaṃ tathā vakkaḍaṃ durdinam*; *vakkaḍam nirantara vṛṣṭir ity eke* (248, 16); P. *vaddaṭikā*. Skr. *varadalikā* f. — $ 47, 115, 123, 145.

vādī vādhī f. "leather thing". G. *vādhar* f. S. *vaḍhi*, *vaddhrī*, Siṃ. *vada*. Pkt. *vaddha-*. Skr.

vardhra- m. n. — $ 47.

vāp m. "sowing", f. "field of young wheat"; *vāphṇeṃ* "to sow", *vāphā* m. "plantation". G. *vāpho*, Siṃ. *vap*; K. *vapun* beside *vavun* "to sow". Pkt. *vappa-* (*see Deśīnāmamālā* 267, 14; cf. *vappiṇo* 268, 7, *vappīḍiaṃ* 253, 15). Skr. *vapra-* m. n. Cf. G. *vavvuṃ*, H. *bonā*, K. *vavun*, Siṃ. *vavanavā* "to sow, to plant", from Skr. *vapayati*; M. *vāvar* "field, meadow", from **vāpakāra-*, or Semi-tatsama of *vapra-*. — $ 86, 89.

vāph bāph bhāph f. "steam". G. *vāph*, G. S. H. *bāph*; Siṃ. *bapa* "tears". Pkt. P. *bappha-bappa-*. Skr. *vāṣpa-* m. — $ 84, 89, 126.

vām adj. "left". G. *vām*, Panj. *bāiāṃ*, H. *bāwāṇ*, *bāyāṃ*, B. O. *bāṃ*, Siṃ. *vam* "left", *vami* "woman". Skr. *vāma-*. Tatsama. The indigenous word is *ḍāvā*. — $ 138,

vār m. "day, time, times (in comp.)". G. Panj. *vār*, S. *vāru*, H. B. K. *bār*, Siṃ. *var*, Ro. *var*. Skr. *vāra-* m.

vārṇeṃ "to cry". G. *vhār vār* f. "complaint, appeal for aid, " is probably to be separated, cf. S. *vāhuru* "protector", Panj. *vāhar* "protection". Pkt. Part. *vāharia-*. Skr. *vyāhārati* — $ 46, 151, 161.

vārā m. "wind; air". G. *vāyaro*, H. B. *bayār*; S. *vārāiṇu* "to ventilate" Deśī. *vāyāro śiśira-vātaḥ*(256, 14). Derived from Skr. *vāta*-m.—$ 46, 61, 193.

vārīk (dial.) "barber" H. *bārī* "caste, whose occupation is of selling torches (and who also works as barber)".Deśī. *vacchīutto tathā vārio nāpitaḥ* (253, 10). Skr. **vāpakārin-* (cf. *kṛtavāpa-*, *vāpana-*). — $ 46.

vārū m. "war-horse" (poet., popul.). G. *vārī* m. "horse". Skr. *vāru-* m. — $ 46.

vāv m. "wind, air". G. *vā*, *vāī*, S. Panj. *vāu*, H. *bāv*, *bāī*, B. *bāo*, *bāī*, O. *bāô*, K. *vāv*, Siṃ. *vā*, Ro. *balval valval*, Palestenian Ro. *wai*. Pkt. *vāa-*. Skr. *vāta-* m. — $ 55, 61.

vāṃv f. n. *vovā* m. "fathom". G. *vām* f. m., H. *bām* m., *byānū*, B. *vāṃū*, Siṃ. *baṃbaya*, *vāma*. Skr. *vyāma-* ,. m. — $ 78, 138, 151, 152.

vāvar m. "activity, domestic work". G. *vavarvuṃ*, *vāparvuṃ* "to use, to occupy, to employ, to live," *vorvuṃ* "to buy, to gather, to beg," S. *vapāru* "business, trade," *vapirī* "trader;" H. *bepar*, *byopār*, *bepārī*, K. *vévahār*. Pkt. *vāvāra-*. Skr. *vyāpāra-* m. — $ 46, 151, 152.

vāvsāv, *vivsā*, *vevsā* m. "business, traffic." Pkt. *vavasāa-*. Skr. *vyavasāya-* m. — $ 75, 151, 156.

vās m. "odour, stench". G. *vās* f., S. *vāsu*, H. B. *bās*. Skr. *vāsa-* m. — $ 156.

vās m. "habitation", *vasṇeṃ* "to inhabit". G. Panj. *vās*, S. *vāso*, H. B. *bās*, Siṃ. *vas*; G. *vāsvuṃ*, Panj. *vassṇā vāsnā*, H. *basnā*. Skr. *vāsa-* m., *vasati*. — $ 156.

vāṃsā vāsā m. "pole, beam-"; *vasebīṃ* n. "grain of bamboo" (cf. under M. *bīṃ*). G. *vāṃs vaṃsḍo*, S. *vaṃsu*, Panj. *vaṃjh*, H. B. *bāṃs*, Siṃ.

vas. Skr. *vaṃśa-* m. — $ 71, 156.

vāsrūṃ vāṃsrūṃ n. "calf". G. *vachrūṃ vach*, S. *vachi*, Panj. *vach* f., H. *bachā*, B. *baccā bāchā* "child" *bāchur* "calf", K. *voch*ᵘ, Siṃ. *vasu vassā*. Pkt. *vaccha*, Skr. *vatsa-* m., *vatsarūpa-* m. cf. M. *-rūṃ-*. — $ 47, 66, 69.

vāhṇeṃ "colour", *vāhaṇ*ᵘ f. "current", G. *vahevuṃ* "colour, to flow out, to be deceived", *vāhvuṃ* "to deceive", *vahāṇ* "boat", Panj. *vahiṇā* "to flow", H. *bahnā* "to flow, to float", B. *bāhite* "to row" *bahite* "to flow out", Siṃ. *vahana* "raft". Pkt. *vahaṇa-*. Skr. *vahati*, *vāhana-* n.—$ 52.

vāhḷī f. "brook". G. *vehḍo vahḍo*, S. *vāhuru* "canal, arm of river", Siṃ. *vahala*. Deśī. *vaholo vāhalī virao trayo'pi laghujalapravāhavācakāḥ* (250, 5). — $ 78.

vāḷā m. "andropogon muricatum *khaskhas*". G. *vāḷo*, S. *vāro*, B. *bālā*; cf. Panj. K. *vāl*, Siṃ. *vala*, Ro. *bal*, "hair". Skr. *vāla-* m.— $ 46, 145.

vāḷū f. "sand", G. *vāḷu veḷu* f. S. *vārī*, H. *bālvā*, *bālū*, B. *bālī*, O. *bāli*, Siṃ. *vāli*. Pkt. *vāluā*. Skr. *vālukā* f. — $ 46, 145.

vikṇeṃ "to sell, to sell oneself". G. *vecvuṃ*, S. *vikiṇṇu*, Panj. *vecṇā* "to sell" *vikṇā* "to be on sale", H. *becnā biknā*, B. *becite bikāite*, Siṃ. *bikuṇavā*, Arm. Ro. *vignel*, Eur. Ro. *biknavā*; the simple word, wherever it exists, signifies "to buy" as in Sanskrit : H. *kinnā*, Ro. *kinavā*, Bg. *kenā*; K. *k*ᵃ*run* "to sell" is an exception, but "to buy" is expressed by *hè-* "to take", as in Marathi *gheṇeṃ*, the word *keṇeṃ* having taken on a special meaning (see these words). Pkt. *vikiṇai vikkei* ; cf. Deśī. *vikkeṇuaṃ vikṛeyaṃ* (261, 15). Skr. *vikrīṇīte*, *vikraya-* m. — $ 51, 71.

vikh. *vīkh* n. "poison". G. Panj. *vikh*, S. *vikhu*, *vihu*, (*visiharu* "poisonous"),Panj. *veh*, W. Panj. *viss*, H. *bis*, H. B. *bikh*, K. *vēh*, Siṃ. *visa vaha*. Pkt. *visa-*. Skr. *viṣa-* n. Loan-word. — $ 95.

vikharṇeṃ, *vikhurṇeṃ* "to spread in disorder". G. *vikhervuṃ* "to spread, to disperse", *vikharvuṃ* "to be spread", S. *vikhirāiṇu*, "to separate, to divide" *vikhiru* "part, separation", Panj. *vikhrāuṇā* "to spread", H. *bikharnā*, *bikhernā*, Pkt. *vikkhirai*, *vikkirai*. Skr. *vikirati* **viṣkirati*, cf. *viṣkira-*. — $ 50, 89, 96, 107.

vighaḍṇeṃ "to demolish". G. *bagaḍvuṃ*, S. *bigiṛaṇu*, Panj. *vigaḍṇā*, H. *bighaḍnā* "to be spoiled", B. *bigaḍite*. Skr. *vighaṭayati*. — $ 99.

viṃcṇī f. "small hole in a metal-vase . (ascribed to scorpion-bite)". Deśī. *viṃciṇiaṃ pāṭitaṃ dhārā ca* (270, 8). — $ 43, 50, 101. Cf. the following.

viṃcū m. "scorpion". G. *viṃchī*, *vīchu*, *vīchī*, S. *vichūṃ*, H. *bichu*, *bichuā*, B. *bichā*. Pkt. *viṃchia- vicchua-*, P. *vicchika-*. Skr. *vṛścika-* , m. — $ 30, 69, 101.

vijṇā vijnā m. "fan". G. *viṃjṇo*, S. *viñiṇu*, H. *bijnā benā*, Siṃ. *vidini*. cf. Pkt. *vīaṇa-*. Skr. *vījana-* n. Tatsama. The Sanskrit form *vyañjana-*, wrong cited in the text ($ 71, 76, 106), is, however, attested by the lexicons and confirmed by Sindhi and Gujarati words.

vijū vīj f. "lightning". S. *viju* f. Panj. *bijj vij* , H. *bijjāg*, Siṃ. *vidu*. Pkt. *vijju-* Skr. *vidyut-*. f. — $ 39, 106, 150, 190.

vijhaṇ n. "extinction", *vijhṇeṃ* "to be extinguished, to expire". S. *viñāiṇu* "to destroy", H. *bujhnā* "to get extinguished (light), to be satisfied (thirst)", Siṃ. *vidavanavā* "to destroy". Pkt. *vijhāvai*, Skr. *vikṣiṇāti*. — $ 107.

viṭā visāḍ, vīṭ; see *iṭā, isāḍ, īt*. — $ 153.

viṭāḷ m. "impurity". G. *vaṭāḷ*, S. *viṭārṇu*, B. *viṭāl*. Apa. *viṭṭāla-*, Pkt. part. *viṭṭāliya-*. of the family of M. *vīṭ* "disgust", *viṭṇeṃ* "to make dirty", Skr. *viṣṭhā* f. "excrement", which term is preserved in S. *viṭhi*, Panj. *viṭṭh*, H. *bīṭh*; cf. also M. *biṭī*. — $ 109, 150.

viṭhū viṭhobā viṭṭhal m., god of Pandharpur, to whom are dedicated the poems of Nāmdev and Tukārām (cf. Molesworth, p. XXV, XXVII); he is identified with *Kṛṣṇa*. The name goes back to a stem in—*a*—: *viṭho-bā* and *viṭhū* are explained as *Kānho-bā* and *kānhū* (see under this word). The correspondence with Skr. *Viṣṇu* is admitted very early : To the name of the country P. *Veṭhadīpa-* corresponds on an inscription *Viṣṇudvīpa-* ; similarly a Kannarese *Biṭṭa* is called *Viṣṇuvardhana* (see the notes of Vogel, Sten Konow, Fleet, Grierson, in *J.R.A.S.*, 1907, p. 1049-1051; 1908, p. 164). But there is no phonetic relationship between *Veṭha-*, *Viṭṭha-* and *Viṣṇu-*; The idea of a loan in Marathi from an eastern speech, proposed in $ 110, is to be rejected, the Bengali pronunciation *Biṣṭu* being quite modern and much later than the assimilation *ṣṭ* *ṭṭh* of Middle-Indian. Moreover, the cult of *Viṭhobā* is local and modern. The normal representative of *Viṣṇu-* in Marathi is *Vinū* n. Pr., the expected form ($ 136; see example given on p. 272, 1.4); cf. Siṃ. *veṇu ven*.

viḍī f. "cigarette; roll of betel leaf". H. *bīḍī*. Skr. *vīṭikā* f. — $ 111.

viṇṇeṃ "to weave". G. *vaṇvuṃ*, Panj. *vuṇṇā*, H. *binnā*, Siṃ. *viyanavā* (part. *vivvā*; *viyannā* "weaver"), K. *wonun*. P. *vīyati*. Skr. *vayati*, *vayana-*. whose nasal has been incorporated in the root.

viṇeṃ, viṇ, vinā "without". G. *viṇ, vinā*, S. *binu, binā*, H. *bin, binā*, B. *biṇā*, Siṃ. *vinā*. Skr. *vinā*. — $ 183.

viṇeṃ "to beget". G. *viāvuṃ*, W. Panj. *viāvaṇr*, S. *vyāū* "child" *viāṭū* "prolific", H. *byānā*, B. *biyani* "bearing", Siṃ. *vadanavā*. Cf. Pkt. *jāai jāi, jaṇia-*. Skr. *vijanana-*, *vijāyate*. — $ 63, 229.

vithar m. "dispersion, ruin", adj. "deviated, irregular",

S. *vithīro* "separated", H. *bithārnā*, K. *vatharāvun* "to extend" *vatharun*[u] "bed", Siṃ. *vātireṇavā* "to spread oneself, to overflow", *vatura* "flood", *vitara* "breadth". cf. Pkt. *vittharai*. Skr. *vistara- vistāra-* m. — $ 122.

viṃdrūṃ viṃdhrūṃ n. "hole". Skr. *vidra-* n., poorly attested and M. *-rūṃ* ? Cf. G. *viṃdhuṃ* "hole", S. *viṃdh* "perforation of pearls", H. *bedh bīṃdh* "hole", which are related to the following word. — $ 89, 123.

viṃdhṇeṃ "to pierce, to perforate". G. *viṃdhvuṃ*, S. *viṃdhṇu*, Panj. *vinnhṇā*, H. *beṃdhnā bedhnā*, B. *biṃdhite*. Pkt. *viṃdhai* beside *vehai* (cf. Panj. *veh*; H. *beh* "hole") Skr. *vidhyati*. — $ 82, 124, 230.

vinaviṇeṃ "to supplicate, to implore". G. *vinavavuṃ*, H. *binaunā* "to revere, to to venerate". Pkt. *viṇṇavei*. Skr. *vijñāpayati*. — $ 135, 152.

vinātī vinantī f. "request". G. *vinati*, *vinanti*, S. *vīnati*, H. *binatī*, B. *binati*. Skr. *vijñapti-* f. — $ 70.

vipārā adj. "contrary, perverse, idiot, child who comes with feet first". G. B. *biparīt*. Skr. *viparyaya-*, *viparīta-*. — $ 65, 143.

virṇeṃ "to melt, to become threadbare". G. *varvuṃ* "to be tired out", Siṃ. *virīyanavā* "to melt, to flow out", with reference to *vilin* "liquid", Ro. *bil-* "to melt". Pkt. *virāi*, cf. Ved. Skr. *niriṇīte* with reference to *vilīyate*. — $ 142.

virhā m. "stream, brook". H. *barhā*. Deśī. *vaholo vāhalī virao trayo'py ete laghujalapravāhavācakāḥ* (250, 5). Related. to the preceding word; the aspiration, does it come from the words, cited by Hemacandra at the same time, and which belong to the family of M. *vāhṇeṃ*, *vhāḷ* ?

vivaḷṇeṃ "to grunt, to sigh". Deśī. *vimaliaṃ matsarabhaṇitaṃ śabdaṃ ceti dvyartham* (270, 3). — $ 137, 152. Curious coincidence of meaning with *viḷavṇeṃ* (*vilapana-*) : Is it an old metathesis ?

vivāh m. "marriage", *vyāhī* m. "related by the marriage of children". G. *vivāh*, S. *vihāṃīu*, Panj. *viāh*, H. *bīvāh byāh*, Siṃ. *vivā*. Skr. *vivāha-* m. — $ 63, 159.

visarṇeṃ "to forget". G. *visarvuṃ*, S. *visāraṇu*, Panj. *visārnā*, H. *bisarnā*, Ro. *bistrāva*. Pkt. *vīsarai*, Skr. *vismarati*. — $ 157, 252.

visavṇeṃ visāvṇeṃ "to stop", "to rest", G. *visāmo* "rest", S. *visāmṇu*, Panj. *visamṇā*, to be extinguished". Pkt. *visamm-*, *vissam-*. Skr. *viśrāmyati-*. — $ 49, 52, 152, 157.

visaḷṇeṃ visulṇeṃ "to wash". G. *vichaḷvuṃ*. Skr. part. *vikṣālita-*. — $ 79, 104, 145 .

vihū "tactical formation". Pkt. *vūha-*. Skr. *vyūha-* m. — $ $ 151.

viḷavṇeṃ "to groan, to sigh". Panj. *vilapṇā*, H. *biḷāpnā*, *billānā*. Skr. *vilapati*. — $ 145, 149, 152. Cf. *vivaḷṇeṃ*.

vīt vīth f. "palm". G. *veṃt*, H. *bītā bittā*, Siṃ.

viyat. Alberuni gives the form *biyatt(u)*; Pkt. *vihatthi-*. Skr. *vitasti-* f. Cf. K. *vyēth*, W. Panj. *vehat* "the river *Vitastā*." — $ 63, 88, 122.

vīr virī f. "force". H. *bīrj*. m., Siṃ. *vera* "force". P. Pkt. *vīria- vīrya-*. Skr. *vīrya-* n. — $ 143.

vīs "twenty". G. *vīs*, S. Panj. *vīh*, H. *bīs*, B. *bis*, Siṃ. *visi vissa*, K. *vuh*, Ro. *bis biś*. Pkt *vīsaṃ*. Skr. *viṃśati-*. whose nasal is unique in all I.E. languages (except in Auss. : *insāi*, see Brugmann, *Grundriss*[2]. II, 2, p. 31 n.). — $ 150, 153, 223.

vīḷ f. "ebb and tide". G. *vīl vīḷ*, S. *vīri*. Deśī. *vīlī taraṅgaḥ* (263, 9)

vecṇeṃ "to spend" "to be separated from G. Panj. *vec-*, H. B. *bec-* "to sell", see under M. *vikṇeṃ* Apa. *veccai* (*prayacchati*). Skr. *vyayati*. — $ 151.

vejīt adj. "vanquished". Skr. *vijita-*. Tatsama with dissimilation. — $ 171.

veṭh f. "forced labour, burden". G. *veṭh*; Siṃ. *vīṭ* "price. pay". Pkt. *viṭṭhi-*, *veṭṭhi-*. Skr, *viṣṭi-* f. — $ 77, 80.

veḍheṇeṃ "to surround", *veḍh* n. f. "ring, circle". G. *vīṭvuṃ* (*veḍh* "ring"), S. *veḍhaṇu*, H. *beḍhnā*, B. *beḍite*, Siṃ. *veḷanavā*. P. *veṭhati*, Pkt. *veḍhai*; Deśī. *veṃḍhia-* for Pkt. *veḍhia-* (264, 11, 13). Skr. *veṣṭayati*.- — $ 112.

veṇ f. "pain". Pkt. *viaṇā*, *veyaṇā*. Skr. *vedanā* f. — $ 63.

vet m. "rush (plant)". Panj. H. B. *bet*, Siṃ. *veta*. Pkt. *vetta-*. Skr. *vetra* m. n. — $ 77, 121.

veṃḍhḷā adj."stupid, disordered, improper". *veiddho ūrdhvīkṛto visaṃsthula āviddhaḥśithilatāṃ gataśceti caturarthaḥ* (271, 1). — $ 63.

verīṃ "dial. postposition. "until, towards" (time and space). G. *vere* "(to marry) with". Skr. *upari*, which normally gives *var*, *varī*. — $ 142, 166.

vel m. f. "creeper". G. Panj. *vel*, Panj. also *valh*, S. *vali*, H. *bel*, Siṃ. *vāl*. Deśī. *vellā vallī* (270, 13). Pkt. *velli-*. Skr. *vallī* f. — $ 148, 166.

velhāḷ m. "dear", f. "mistress". Deśī. *vellahalo komalo vilāsī* ca (271, 7). — $ 148.

vevsā. *vevsāy vevsāv* m. "business". — See S. V. *vāvsāv*.

veve exclamation of terror. S. Panj. *ve*. Pkt. Deśī. *vevve* (*bhaya vāraṇa viṣādāmantraṇārtheṣu*, 270, 14.)

vesvā f. "adulteress, debauched woman". Panj. *vesvā* m., H. *besvā* f. Siṃ. *ves-* (in comp.). Pkt. *vesā*. Skr. *veśyā* f. — $ 77, 157.

vehḷā vheḷā m. "myrobolon". H. *baheḍā*; K. *bulela* (Persian *balīl*, Arabic *balīlij*) is to be separated. Skr. *vibhītikā- vibhīdaka-* m. $ 80, 118, 171

veḷ f. "sea-shore". S. Panj. *ver*, H. *ber* beside Panj. H. *velā*, K. *velā*, "time"; Siṃ. *vel* "river-bank". Skr. *velā* f. — $ 39, 142, 145, 153, 154, 194.

vevhār n. "business, profession". S. *vavahār* "business"; Panj. *beorā*, H. *byorā*, K. *vēvahār*, Siṃ. *vahara* "custom". Skr. *vyavahāra-*

m. semi tatsama; cf. M. *vāvar* from *vyāpār-*. —$ 158.

veḷū m. "bamboo". Isolated; cf. under M. *vāṃsā*. P. Pkt. *veḷu-*. Skr. *veṇu-* m. — $ 147.

vai, vaī, vahī, vay f. "closure, palisade". Pkt. *vai*, cf. Deśī. *vattī tathā vaivelā dvāv etau sīmavācakau* (247, 9) Skr. *vṛti-* f. — $ 57, 154, 161.

vair n. "enmity". S. *veru*. Pkt. Skr. *vaira-* n. — $ 57.

vhaṇse, vhaṇje, hoṇse hoṇje, vainseṃ vanseṃ n. and fem. pl. "husband's sister", M. *vahinī* "wife of my elder brother", Panj. *vannīṃ* "woman, wife" gives the first member of the compound; for the second cf. Pkt.—*ssiā* (Skr. *svasṛkā* f.) whose normal representative in Marathi is *śī*, for example in *māvśī* "aunt". — $ 63.

vhāḷ m. f. "streamlet". Siṃ. *vahala* beside *vahana*. *Deśī vaholo vāhalā virao trayo'pi laghujala pravāhavācakāḥ* (250, 5). Cf. M. *virhā*.

—*s, si* post position. — $ 197, 198.

—*s* suffix of nouns of relationship, as *ājās* "grandfather", *ājīs* "grand mother", *ātes* "aunt", *bāpūs* "father", *bhāūs* "father", *sāsūs* "mother in-law". Similarly *lāṃs*, see S. V. Skr. *śrī-* f. — $ 38, 157.

saī, say f. "female friend, female companion". G. *saī, saīyar* f., S. *sahī* m. S. Panj H. *sahelī*, Siṃ. *saha* "friend". Pkt. *sahī*. Skr. *sakhī* f. — $ 46, 57, 156, 161.

saī, say f. "recollection". Siṃ. *sihiya sihi*. P. *sati-*. Skr. *smṛti* f. — $ 57, 156.

sak n. m. "group of 6: on a die, 6 multiiplied by ...etc." Panj. *chakkā* K. *śaka*. Pkt. *chakka-*. Skr. *ṣaṭka-* n. — $ 48, 93, 156.

sakṇeṃ "to be able to". G. *śakvuṃ*, S. *saghṇu*, Panj. *sakkṇā*, H. *saknā*, K. *hĕkun*, Ro. *śay-* ? Siṃ. *sàki hāki* "capable". Pkt. *sakkei, sakkai*. Skr. *śaknoti śakyate*. — $ 48, 93, 156. 230.

sakār m. "acceptance of a credit note", G. *sakār*, S. *sakāraṇu*, "to accept, to do honour to", H. *sakārā*. Pkt. *sakkāra-*. Skr. *satkāra-* m. — $ 156.

sagā adj. "own, relation". S. *sago*, H. *sagā*, Panj. *sagg*, Siṃ. *siya, siyau*. Skr. *svaka-*. — $ 98, 157.

sagḷā adj. "all, each". G. *saghḷum*, Panj. *sagal, sagrā*, H. *sagar, sagrā, sagal, saglā*, Siṃ. *siyala, siyalla* "totality". Pkt. *saala-*, Apa. *sagala-*. Skr. *sakala*— $ 98, 156.

saṃgeṃ "with, in company of". G. H. O. *saṃge*, Panj. H. *saṃg*, Panj. *sagg*; Panj. *sane*, H. *san*, K. *sān* (*sang* "company"), S- *saṅī* "in consideration of" (*saṅu* "parent by marriage). Skr. *saṃgata-*. — $ 98, 156, 193.

saṃcarṇeṃ "to penetrate, to possess, (demon)". G. Panj. H. *saṃcar-*. Apa. absol. *saṃcāri*. Skr. *saṃcarati-* — $ $ 49, 101, 156.

saṭ saṭh f. "sixth day of the fort-night"; *saṭ saṭh saṭhī* deity of the sixth day after birth (Durgā); the cult which is rendered to Durgā". G. *chaṭh*, S. *chaṭhi* Panj. H. *chaṭh chaṭ* "sixth day"; G.

chaṭṭhī, S. H. *chaṭhī* "cult rendered to Durgā"; H. *chaṭhā*, *chaṭā* "sixth". Skr. *ṣaṣṭhi-* f. — $ 88, 110, 218. Cf. *sāṭh* "sixty".

saḍṇeṃ "to rot". G. S. Panj. H. B. *saḍ-*. Skr. *śaṭati-* — $ 46, 111, 156.

saḍhaḷ adj. "liberal, prodigal". Pkt. *siḍhila-*, P. *sithilo-*. Skr. *śithila-*. Cf. M. *ḍhilā*. — $ 30, 31, 42, 112, 156.

saṇ m. "festival, vocation". G. *khaṇ* f. Panj. *khiṇ* m., *chin* f. "moment", S. *khuṇu* "interval, respite"; H. *chan*, *chin*, *khaṇ*, *khiṇ* "instant, certain day of the moon-lit fortnight"; Bg. *e-khan*, *ta-khan* "then"; K. *vuñ-kén* "at that time"; Siṃ. *sāna*, *sana*, "moment, festival", *saṃda* "whilst", *keṇehi* "at that very moment". Deśī. *chaṇo utsavaḥ* (120, 8); Pkt. *chaṇa-*, *khaṇa-*, P. *chaṇa-*festival", *khaṇa-* "moment". Skr. *kṣaṇa-* m. — $ 104, 134.

saṇ m "hemp of Bengal". G. Panj. *saṇ*, S. *siṇu* "name of a species of herb", H. *san*. Skr. *śaṇa-* m. — $ 134, 156.

sat n. "essence, force, virtue", G. S. H. *sat*, Panj. *sati* m. "essence", Siṃ. *sata* "creature". Pkt. *satta-*. Skr. *sattva-* n. — $ 130, 156.

saṃt m. "saint, devotee". G. Panj. H. *saṃt*; S. *saṃtu*. Pkt. *santa-*. Skr. *san-*, or *śānta-* ? Mr. Meyer informs me that if the *Zend* word *spəntō* had a parellel in India, it could not have had any othcr form. One could then more simply think of the European word "saint", Italian, Portug. *santo*. — $ 121, 156.

saṃt adj. "soft, calm (breeze, flame, temperament)." Panj. *saṃt* f., Siṃ. *set* "tranquility", cf. Siṃ. *sati* "end, annihilation". P. Pkt. *santa-* (*santi-*). Skr. *śānta-* (*śānti-* f.). — $ 121, 156.

sattar "seventy". G. *sitter*, S. *satari*, Panj. H. B. *sattar*, O. *sattori*, Maith. *sattari*; Siṃ. *sättā* (*va*), K. *satāth*. Pkt. *sattari*; P. *sattali*, *sattari*. Skr. *saptati-* f. — $ 118, 121, 143, 160, 219, 223.

satrā "seventeen". G. O. *satar*, Panj. *satārāṃ*, S. *satrahaṃ*, H. *sattrah*, B. *sater*, Maith. *satrah*; Siṃ. *sataḷos*, K. *sadah*. Pkt. *sattarasa-*. Skr. *saptadaśa*. — $ 118, 121, 143, 221.

saṃdhevīṃ "in doubt"; for *saṃdehīṃ*, G. *sandhe* "doubt", S. *sandehu*, Panj. H. *sandeh*. Skr. *saṃdeha-* m. — $ 55, 124.

saṃpat f. "richness, prosperity". G. H. *saṃpat*, Siṃ. *sapat* *sāpat*. Pkt. Skr. *sampatti-* f. — $ 121, 156.

sapan m. "dream". Tatsama, Skr. *svapna-* m. Cf. the words for "to sleep" cited under M. *jhoṃpṇeṃ*. — $ 162.

saphāṃśī (coin, medal) provided with a hook for hanging the same". From *sa*+*phāṃs* (Skr. *pāśa-*), see under the word. The compound with *sa-* remains alive. — $ 84.

śambhar "hundred". Skr. *śatam*+*bhar*—or *bhār*— ? — $ 224. Cf. *śeṃ*.

samajṇeṃ "to understand". G. *samaj-*, S. Panj. *samajh-*, H. *samujh-* (cf. H. *mujh* from Skr. *mahyam*); cf. Panj. *sohaj* f. "intelligence, view, ostentation". Skr. *samādhyāyati* ? In this case, the beginning of the word would be treated as tatsama; several Prakrit words as representing Sr. *sammanyate sammantrayati* would have behaved in this manner. — $ 89, 107, 252.

sar m. "necklace, garland". S. *sar* f. Deśī. *sarā mālā* (272, 12). — $ 156.

samor "opposite". G. *sāmuṃ samhoṃ*, Panj. *sauheṃ* "opposite"; Siṃ. *hamuva* "opposite". Skr. *sammukha-*. — $ 64, 138, 161. Cf. M. *mohar*.

sarḍā sarḍhā m. "chamelèon, lizard". G. *sarḍo*, W. Panj. *saḍḍur*, H. *saraṭ*. Deśī. *saraḍa* (276, 1), Skr. *saraṭa-* m. — $ 111.

sarṇeṃ "to advance, to do well". G. S. Panj. H. *sar-*; K. *hᵃr-* "to grow" ? Pkt. *sarai*, Skr. *sarati*. — $ 46, 156.

sarvā m. "heavy shower". G. *saravā* m. pl. Deśī. *sarivāo tathā sīharao āsāraḥ* (276, 9). — $ 46, 50.

saraḷ "straight, honest". G. *saraḷ*, S. *saraḷo*, Panj. H. *saral*. Pkt. Skr. *sarala-*. — $ 145.

sarm, *śarm* n. "shame". G. *sarm*, *śarm*, S. *śaramu*, Panj. *śarm*, H. *sarm*, *śarm*. Persian *śarm*. — $ 155.

sarsā adj. "similar, contiguous", *sarśīṃ* "with". G. *sarsuṃ* "against, with", H. *saras* "similar, according to", Panj. *sarīh* "in the presence of", Siṃ. *sari* "resemblance, with", cf. Ro. *sar* "like, why", S. *sārū* "according to" (or shou.d they be linked with the family of Skr. *sar-*, cf. *anusāreṇa* ? In any case, the long *ā* presents no difficulty, cf. M. *sārkhā* parellel to *sarsā*). Pkt. *sarisa-* (cf. Deśī. *sarisāhulo* 175, 5). If Śaur. Pkt. *tādisa-*, from Skr. *tādṛśa-* (M. *taisā*) is to be separated from Pkt. P. *tārisa* = Gr. *tēlixos*, which is far from being sure, it should be admitted that the confusion is very old, because are found on the model or *tārisa-* : *etārisa- -yārisa-* in Aśoka and in Pali (by the side of *īdisa- kīdisa-*), then *erisa- sarisa ahmārisa-* in the anthology of *Hāla* and following the equation of Skr. *sadṛśa-* : *sadṛkṣa-*. Pkt. *sariccha- sāriccha-* in the same collection; see all the Pkt. forms in Pischel — $ 245. — $ 143.

sarā m. "liquor of palm-juice, spirituous liquor". S. H. *saro*. contamination of Skr. *surā* f. and *sāra-* m. n. ? — $ 74.

sarū m. "sleeve, handle (axe, etc.)" — G. *charo*, *charī* "knife". Siṃ. *saru* "sleeve of sword". Pkt. *charu-*. Skr. *tsaru-* m. Cf. m. *tharū*. — $ 46, 103.

sal f. piercing, acute pain", *sal* m. n. "splinter". G. *saḷak* f., *salko* m., Panj. *sall* "piercing pain", H. *sal* "thorn, embarrassment, Siṃ. *sala* "porcupinequill". Skr. *śalya-* m. n. — $ 148.

salag adj. "continuous". G. H. *salag*. Skr. *saṃlagna-*. — $ 71, 98, 148, 156.

sav f. "the North". Skr. *savya-* "left". — $ 152, 156.

sāv f. "taste, pleasure". S. *sah* "love", Panj. *sah* "rut". Ved.

Skr. *sapati* "to look for, love", *śapa-* m. "penis" ? — $ 156.

savaṃg "cheap". G. *soṃghuṃ*, S. *sahāṃgo*. Skr. *samargha-*. — $ 46, 69, 88, 152.

savaḍ "in face of", *savḍyāṃ* "opposite". Deśī. *savaḍaṃmuho abhimukhaḥ* (281, 7) — $ 46.

savat f. "rival". H *savat*, *saut*; Panj. *saut* "fertile" (*saputrā*) is to be separated. Pkt. *savattī*. Skr. *sapatnī* f. — $ 40, 46, 121, 152, 156.

savā adj. "and a quarter". G. S. Panj. H. B. *savā*, Maith. *savaiyā*, O. *sauyāī*. Skr. *sapāda-*. — $ 46, 60, 61, 152, 156.

savāśā m. "Brahman tribe, member of this tribe". G. *savāso*, H. *savāsan*. Deśī. *savāso brāhmaṇaḥ* (273, 17) shows the antiquity of this form. Skr. *sapāda- śataka-*. — $ 155, 156, 224.

saveṃ "in company, with". Prob. Skr. *sahitam*. — $ 198, Cf. M. *śiṃ*.

saveṃ- c "immediately, spontaneously"; *save* (*sāṃj-cā*) "at the moment (of twilight)". G. H. *samo*, Panj. H. Siṃ. *samā* "time". Skr. *samaya-* m. (*samayena*, *samaye*).— $ 46, 58, 152, 156, 193.

saṃvthaḷ n. "flat terrain". Skr. *sama-sthala-*. — $ 46, 122, 152, 156.

saver "exactly at". G. *saverā saveḷā*, S. *savere savele savero* (adj. and adv..) "early", H. *saver savel*, H. *saverā* "dawn"; the presence in these languages of S. Panj. *ver*, H. *ber* "time" by the side of Panj. H. *velā* "time", which Marathi has only *veḷ*, in the sense of "river-bank", leads us to regard M. *saver* as loan. — $ 142.

sasā m. "hare". G. *saso*, Panj. H. *sasā*, Siṃ. *sāvā hāvā sā hā*, Ro. *śośoy*. Skr. *śaśa-* m. — $ 46, 156.

saṃsār m. "world, human life". G. H. *saṃsār*, S. *saṃsāru*, Siṃ. *sasara*. Pkt. Skr. *saṃsāra-* m. — $ 156.

sahā, *sāy*, *saī* f. "cream". Deśī. *sāho.. dadhisaraḥ..dadhi saro dadhna upari sāraṃ* (291, 15). — $ 46, 52, 161.

sahā "six", *sahāvā* "sixth". G. *cha*, S. *cha(h)*, Panj. *che*, H. *cha*, *che*, B. *chay*, O. *chôh*, Maith. *chau*, Siṃ. *sa*, *saya*, *ha*, *haya*, K. *śih*, Ro. *śo*, *śov*. Pkt. *cha-*, Apa. *chaha*. Skr. *ṣat* (Indo-Iranian, **ksˇaksˇ*).—$ 39, 41, 104, 156, 218, 226.

saḷ "irritating, tormenting conduct". G. S. *chaḷ*, Panj. H. *chal*, Siṃ. *saḷa sala* "ruse". Skr. *chala-* n. 103, 145.

sāī m., term of respect, origininally "master". G. *sāṃī* "fakir"; S. *sāṃīṃ*, Panj. H. *sāīṃ*, B. o. *sāīm*, Siṃ. *sāmi*, *himi*, *himinā*. Pkt. *sāmi-*. Skr. *svāmin-* m. — $ 153, 157.

śāī f. "ink". G. *śāī*, Panj. *siāhī*, H. *sāhī*, *syāhī*. Persian. *syahī*. — $ 155.

sāk f. "person sent on a search, guard; credit, reputation." S. Panj. *sākhī*, K. *sōkśī* "witness", H. *sākh*. "credit, evidence". Skr. *sākṣin-* — $ 156.

sāṃkaḷ sākaḷ sāṃkhaḷ f. "chain". G. *sāṃkal*, S. *saṃghar*, Panj. *saṃggal*, H. *sāṃkal sāṃkar sikaḍ*, B. *sikhal*, K. *hönkal*, Siṃ. *sākilla hökilla*.

Pkt. *saṃkhalā siṃkhalā*. Skr. *śṛṅkhalā* f. — $ 30, 31, 71, 89, 96, 156.

sāṃkaḍ n. "difficulty". G. *sāṃkaḍuṃ* S. *saṃkaṭu* "vexation, misfortune", *saṃgaṭu* "interruption", K. *sakhtᵃh* "hard", Siṃ. *sakuḷu*,, *sākuḷu*, "hard, compact". Pkt. *saṅkaḍa-*. Skr. *saṃkaṭa-* n. — $ 82, 93, 111.

sākhar, *sākar* f. "sugar". G. *sākar* f. Panj. H. *sakkar*, Siṃ. *hakuru* "palm-sugar". Pkt. *sakkara-*, *sākcharin* (Per. Erythrian Sea), P. *sakkharā*. Skr. *śarkarā* f. — $ 47, 89, 93.

sāṃkhṇeṃ "to get congeal, to co-agulate". Panj. *saṃghṇā* adj. "thick, close". Deśī. *saṃkhāi saṃstyāyate* (276, 2). — $ 89.

sāṃkū m. "bridge". H. *sāṃkhū*. Skr. *śaṅku-* m. — $ 156.

sāṃgaḍ m. f. "raft made of two boats tied together". G. *saṃghāḍo* "tower", Siṃ. *saṃgala* "pair", *haṃgulu* "raft"; — Cf. Tamil *śaṅgaḍam*, Tulu *jangala* "raft". Deśī. *saṃghāḍī yugalam* (174, 12); in Limurike *saggarai*, name of raft according to Periplus of Erythrian Sea. ; cf. P. *nāvāsaṃghāṭa-*. Skr. *saṃghaṭa-*, *saṃghāṭa-*. — $ 89.

sāṃgaḍṇeṃ "to hold, to attach", *sāṃguḷṇeṃ* "to get congealed to be co-agulated". Deśī. *saṃgalai saṃghaṭate* (280, 13). — $ 79, 89, 146.

sāṃgṇeṃ "to say". Pkt. *saṃghāi sāhai*, Mss. of Dutr. de Rhiṇs *śajhati*. Skr. *śaṃsati*. A word without a parellel in any other modern language, but which seems to be old; for the change of internal *s*, which is already present in the Pkt. forms, see $ 160; the guttural articulation, which goes back to the same period, is due to the nasalisation of the preceding vowel, cf. Pkt. *siṃgha-* from Skr. *siṃha-*. — $ 89, 156, 229, 239, 253.

sāc, *saṃcā* adj. "true". G. *sāc* n. "truth", *sāsuṃ* "true". *sāce* "truly", S. *sacu*, *saco*, Panj. *sacc*, *sāṃcā*, H. *sac*, *sāṃc*, B. O. *sācā*; Siṃ. *sasa* "truth", Ro. *caco*. Pkt. *sacca-*. Skr. *satya-*. — $ 69, 101, 156.

sāṃc m. "place, countenance", *sāṃcā* m. "mould", *sāṃcṇeṃ* "to accumulate". G. *sāṃcvuṃ* "to gather", *sāṃco* "machine; mould"; S. *sāṃcaṇu* "to supervise", H. *samcnā* "to accumulate", Panj. H. *sāṃcā* "mould, matrix" K. *sancĕt* "accumulation". Pkt. *saṃcinai*. Skr. *saṃcaya-* m. — $ 60, 101, 230.

sāṃj sāṃjh f. "evening". G. *sāṃj*, S. *sāṃjhī saṃjho*, Panj. H.B.O. *samjh*, H. *saṃj*, Siṃ. *sāṃdī saṃda*. Pkt. *saṃjhā*. Skr. *sandhyā* f. — $ 88, 107, 156.

sājṇeṃ "to decorate, to suit". G. *sajvuṃ*, S. *sijilāiṇu*, Panj. *sājṇā*, H. *sājnā*, Siṃ. *sādenavā*. Pkt. *sajjei*. Skr. *sajjayati*. — $ 47, 106, 156.

sāṃjeṃ n. "vow, promise". Else where the word has the sense of "sign, signal"; G. *sān*, H. *sān sain*, Siṃ. *san*. Pkt. *saṇṇā*. Skr. *saṃjñā* f. — $ 106, 135.

sāṭh "sixty". G. H. *sāṭh*, S. S. *saṭhi*, Panj. *saṭṭh*, B. *sāiṭh*,

O. *sāṭhie*, K. *śaith*, *śeṭh*, Siṃ. *hāṭa säṭa*. Pkt. *saṭṭhi-*. Skr. *ṣaṣṭi-* f. — $ 110, 218, 223.

sāṃṭhṇeṃ "to accumulate". H. *sāṃṭhnā*; Siṃ. *saṭahan* "sign, form". Pkt. *saṃṭhāṇa-*. Skr. *saṃsthāna-*, *saṃsthāpayati*. — $ 89, 110.

sāṭhīṃ, *sāṭīṃ* "in view of, for". G. *sāṭe* "in exchange, for", *sāṭhī* "because, why, how", S. *saṭo* "exchange", *saṭhaito* "at an advantageous moment", *saṭhāiṇu*, Siṃ. *ṭa* "for". Skr. *sārtha-*. — $ 89, 114, 197, 198. See *sāth*.

sāṃḍṇeṃ "to spread, to throw down". G. *chaṃḍvuṃ*, S. *chaṃḍṇu*, Panj. *chaḍḍhṇā chaṃḍṇā*, H. *chāṃḍnā*, B. *chādite*, K. *chaḍun*, Siṃ. *heḷanavā*, Ro. *cat-* "to vomit". Pkt. *chaḍḍei*, *chaḍḍai*. Skr. *chardayati*. — $ 47, 69, 70, 103, 115, 230.

sāṃḍ m. "free bull". G. H. *sāṃḍ*, S. *sānu*, Panj. *sānh*. Skr. *ṣaṇḍa-* m. — $ 111, 156.

sāḍī f. *sāḍā* m. "woman's dress". G. H. *sāḍī*, S. Panj. *sāḍhī*, Siṃ. *saḷuva*, *haluva-*. Pkt. *sāḷaka-*. Skr. *śāṭa-* m. — $ 156.

sāḍe n. "a half" (from three onwards). G. *sāḍā*, S. *sāḍhā*, Panj. H. *sāḍhe* (Panj. *sāḍ* f. "half"), B. *sāḍe*. Pkt. *saaḍḍha-*. Skr. *sārdha-*. — $ 46, 89, 115, 156, 225.

sāḍhū m. "husband of wive's sister". G. *sāḍū*, S. *saṃḍhū*, Panj. *sāḍhū saṃḍhū*, H. *sāḍhū*, *sāḍū*. Skr. *śyālivoḍhṛ-* m. — $ 89, 112, 157, 164.

sāṇ f. "place for the palanquin of Holīdevi". G. *chāvaṃ*, S. *chāṃviṇī* "camp", H. *chānā* "to cover", Panj. *chann*, H. *chān* "straw-roof", *chāvnī* "cantonement, ceiling", Siṃ. *hivanavā* "to cover, to shelter." Pkt. *chāaṇa-*. Skr. *chādayati*, *chādana-* m. — $ 61.

sāṇ sahāṇ f. "mill-stone". Panj. *sāṇ*, Siṃ. *saṇa-haṇa-*, Ro. *asan*. Deśī. *chāṇa-* (124, 14). Skr. *śāṇa-* m. —$ 52, 156, 161.

sāt "seven". G. H. Bih. *sāt*, S. *sat*, Panj. *satt*, B. O. *sāto*, Siṃ. *sat*, *hat*, K. *saᵛth* Palest. Ro. *ḥōṭ*. Pkt. *satta*. Skr. *sapta*. — $ 121, 156, 219.

sātvaṇ n. *sātvīṇ* m. f. n. "echites scholaris", plant which has seven leaves and one stalk, cf. Siṃ. *satpät*, *satdala*. Pkt. *sattavaṇṇa-*. Skr. *saptaparṇa-* m. n. — $ 47, 121, 135, 152.

sātā sāṃtā adj. "being". Panj. *saṃdā*, S. *haṃdo*, K. *sondᵘ hondᵘ* (used to form the adjective of belonging). Pkt. *santa-*. Skr. *sant-*. — $ 71, 156, 202.

sātū, *sattū* m. "barley, flour of parched barley". G. *sātu* m., Panj. *sattū*, H. *sātū*, *sattū*, "flour of parched wheat". Skr. *saktu-* m. — $ 47, 121, 156.

sāth f. "company, companion", *sāthī sātī* m., "companion". G. Panj. H. *sāth sāthī*, S. *sāthu sāthī*, K. *söthī*, cf. Siṃ. *satvā* "merchant". Pkt. *sattha-*. Skr. *sārtha-*. — $ 114, 156. Cf. m. *sāṭīṃ*.

sād m. f. "appeal, cry". G. H. *sād*, Panj. *sadd*, S. *saḍo*, K. Siṃ. *sada*. Pkt. *sadda-*. Skr. *śabda-* m. — $ 123, 156.

śādaḷṇeṃ "to be humid". Pkt. *saddala-*. Skr. *śādvala-*. — $ 47, 130, 145, 156.

sāṃdh, *sāṃd* f. "joint, fissure". G. *sāṃdh* f. "joint, cleft", *sāṃdhavuṃ* "to join", S. *saṃdhu* m. "joint", *saṃdhi* f. "hole made by thieves", *seṃdhī*, *seṃdho* "friendship"; Panj. *sannh*, H. *seṃdh* "hole made by thieves", B. O. *siṃdh*; Siṃ. *sanda* "articulation", *haṇḍiya* "joint". Pkt. *saṃdhai*. Skr. *saṃdhi*- m. — $ 88, 124, 156.

sāp m. "serpent". G. B. O. *sāp*, S. *sapu*, Panj. *sapp*, H. *sāṃp*, Siṃ. *sapu*, *hapu*, Ro. *sap*. P. Pkt. *sappa*-. Skr. *sarpa*- m. — $ 69, 125, 156.

sāṃpaḍṇeṃ "to fall in, to find oneself at, to encounter." G. *sāṃpaḍvuṃ* "to find, to discover"; K. *sömbar*- "to gather, to collect" ?. Deśī. *saṃpaḍiaṃ labdham* (277, 15). Skr. *saṃpatati* "to encounter" ? Cf. M. *paḍṇeṃ*.

saṃpṇeṃ "now", *sāṃpecā* adj. "actual, of to day". Pkt. *sampayaṃ* Skr. *sāmpratam*. — $ 62, 71, 156.

sāṃbar m. n. "cervies Elaphas". G. *sābar*, S. *sāṃbaru*, *sāṃvaru*, H. *sābar*, *sāmbar*. Skr. *śambara*- m. — $ 127.

sābūṇ, *sābaṇ* m. "soap". *sābu*, Panj. *sabūṇ saban*, H. *sābūn*, K. *sāban*. Ar. Per. *ṣābūn*. — $ 42, 134.

sāmāśī adj. "of six months"; *sāmaśeṃ*, *sāmāseṃ* n. "commemorative rite performed after six months from death". *sahā+mās* (*māsa*-). — $ 138, 161.

sāy sǎvā, *sāg* m. "teak wood". G. H. *sāg* m., S. *sāgu*. Skr. *śāka*- m. — $ 98, 156.

old M. *sāyar* m. "ocean". Siṃ. *sayuru*. Skr. *sāgara*- m. — $ 46, 54, 156, 282.

sār n. "essence, juice; fruits-syrup". G. Panj. H. K. *sār*, S. *sāru*, Siṃ. *sara* "substance, cream, etc." Skr. *sāra*- m. n. — $ 156.

sārā adj. "all, entire"; part. of *sārṇeṃ* "to activate, to terminate". G. *sāruṃ*, S. *sāro*, Panj. B. *sārā*, K. *sāru-y* "all, complete" (Panj. *sārā* also "each"), with reference to H. Panj. *sārnā*, B. *sārite* "terminate, to repair". This is not exactly similar to Skr. *sarva*-, Pkt. *savva*-, P. *sabba*-: G. *savi*, S. *sabhu*, Panj. *sabh habb*, H. *sab*, Siṃ. *sav hav*, Arm. Ro. *sav*, Eur. Ro. *savoro saro* "all". Nevertheless one could attach M. *sārā* to the large group of which Skr. *sarva*- is one of the representative and particularly, despite the difference of meaning to Lat. *sōlus*, Got. *sēls* "good, apt"; cf. Walde, in the article on *salvus*.

sārkhā sārikhā adj. "similar, equal". G. *sarkhuṃ*, S. *sarkho*, H. *sarīkhā sārkhā sārkā*; Pkt. *sārikkha*-. — $ 143, Cf. M. *sarsā*.

sārī f. "thrush, *turdus salica*". H. *sār*, Siṃ. *säla*, *häla*. Pkt. *sariī*. Skr. *sārikā* f. — $ 46, 140.

sāl f. "bark, skin", G. *chāl* f. "skin, peel, bark, cover", S. *chil* (*u*), Panj. *chall* f. "bark, husk", H. *chāl* f. *chālā* m. "skin, bark", K. *chal* "morsel". Deśī. *challī tvak* (120, 8). — $ 104, 148.

sāv, *saū*, m. "banker, respectable man". G. *sāhu*, *sāu*, S. *sāhū*, Panj. *sāū*, H. *sāhū* "respectable, banker", *sāū* "docile, innocent", K. *sôvu* "rich". Pkt. *sāhu-*. Skr. *sādhu-*. — $ 46, 55, 156, 161.

sāṃv f. "muscle". Different treatment in Pkt. *ṇhāru-ṇhāu-*, P. *nahāra-* and Siṃ. *naharaya-*. Skr. *snāyu-* f. n. — $ 157.

sāṃvar f. "bombax heptaphyllum". G. *sāmar*, Panj. *saṃbhal*. Deśī. *sāmarī śālmalī* (282, 2). Cf. under *śeṃvrī*. — $ 46, 77, 142, 152.

Old M. *sāvaṃtu* m. Panj. *savāṃdrī* "neighbour". Skr. *sāmanta-* m. — $ 38, 46, 121, 152, 156.

sāvlī f. "shadow" *sāvaṭ* f. "shady-spot". The original word **sāv-* of whom only derivatives found in Marathi is found in G. *chāṃī*, S. *chāṃ*, *chāṃv*, Panj. H. *chāṃ*, Siṃ. *sē* (is used in compounds for forming adverb : *suva- sē* "happily", *ese* "thus"). Skr. *chāyā* f. — $ 46, 90, 103.

sāvaḷ n. f. "big branch of palm-tree" *sāvḷī* f. "small or medium size branch of cocoanut & palm-tree" Deśī. *sāhuḷī....śākhā* (292, 1). Probably derived from Skr. *śākhā* f. — $ 46, 55.

sāṃvlā adj. "of clear complexion; purple". Only meaning. G. *śamḷu*, S. *sāṃvilo sāṃviro*, Panj. H. *sāvlā* "sombre"; cf. Panj. *sāvā* "green, grey", Siṃ. *sam* "black". Skr. *śyāmala-* (*śyāma-*). — $ 46, 152, 157.

sāvā sāṃvā m. "millet". Skr. *śyāmāka-* m. — $ 152, 157.

sāsrā m. "father-in-law". G. *sasro* "in compound" *sāsar-*), S. *sahuro*, Panj. *sahurā sauhrā*, H. B. O. *sasar*, Ro. *sasro sasˇtro*, cf. Siṃ. *hūrā* "brother-in-law". Skr. *śvaśura-* m. — $ 50, 157.

sāsū f. "mother-in-law". G. *sāsu*, S. *sasu*, Panj. *sassu sass*, H. B. O. *sās*, Siṃ. *suhul*, Greek Ro. *sasūy*. P. Pkt. *sassū*. Skr. *śvaśrū-* f. — $ 47, 50, 157.

sāhṇeṃ "to suffer, to endure". G. S. Panj. H. K. *sah-*. Pkt. Skr. *sah-*. — $ 52, 156, 159.

sāhan san adj. "small, thin". S. *saṇho*, Siṃ. *sumga*, Ro. *sano*. Pkt. *saṇha-*. Skr. *ślakṣaṇa-*. — $ 136, 157.

sāḷ f. "unhusked rice". G. *śāḷiyuṃ*, *śāḷ*, H. *sālī*, Siṃ. *hāl*, *äl* "standing paddy". P. Pkt. *sāli-* Skr. *śāli-* m. — $ 145, 156.

sāḷ f. "school, workshop". G. *śāḷ*, Panj. *sālā* f. H. B. O. *sāl*, Maith. *sār*, K. *hāl* "covered market, house", Siṃ. *sal hal* "market-place". Pkt. *sālā*. Skr. *śālā* f. — $ 145, 156.

sāḷā m· "brother-in-law". G. *sāḷo*, S. *sālo*, Panj. H. B. *sālā*, Ro. *salo*. Skr. *śyāla-* m. — $ 46, 145, 157.

sāḷī f. "porcupine". Panj. *sallā* "tatoo", G. *saliyo*, Siṃ. *sala*, "porcupine-quill". Skr. *śalya-*, *śallaka* are not the direct prototypes, as is shown by the cerebral *ḷ* — $ 156.

śikṇeṃ śikhṇeṃ "to learn". G. *śikhvuṃ*, S. *sikhṇu*, Panj. *sikkhṇā*, H. *sikhṇā*, K. *hěchun*, Ro. *sik-*; Siṃ. *hik* "study". Pkt. *sikkhai*. Skr. *śikṣati*. — $89, 96, 156, 252, 254.

śikeṃ n. "chord for hanging

objects". G. *śiṃkuṃ* m. Skr. *śikya-* n. — $ 93, 156.

śiṃg śiṃg n. "corn". G. *śiṃg*, S. *siṅu*, Panj. *siṃgg*, H, *sīṃg*, K. *hĕng*, Siṃ. *siṃgu sigu aṃga*, Ro. *s'ing*. Pkt. *siṃga-*. Skr. *śṛṅga-* n. — $ 30, 31, 156.

śiṃgā m. "young horse, colt". Deśī. *siṃgao taruṇaḥ* (284, 15).

siṃcṇeṃ "to water, to sprinkle", G. *siṃcvuṃ* Panj. *siṃjnā*, H. *sīcnā sīṃcnā* Skr. *siñcati* — $ 101.

śiṅgāḍā m. "trapa bispinosa". G. *śiṃgoḍuṃ*, Panj. H. *siṃgāḍā siṃghāḍā*. Pkt. *siṃghāḍaga-*. Skr. *śṛṅgāṭaka-* m.

śijṇeṃ śijhṇeṃ "in the process of being cooked, to be agitated". G. S. H. *sijh-*, Panj. *sijjh-*; Siṃ. *id-* "to mature". Pkt. *sijjhai*. Skr. *sidhyate*. — $ 89, 156.

śiṃd f. "wild date-tree". Deśī. *sindī tathā sindolī kharjurī* (284, 3).

śiṃdal śinnaḷ śinaḷ adj. "licentious". G. Panj. H. *chinā̆l*. Deśī. *chiṇṇo tathā chiṇṇālo jāraḥ;....chiṇṇā chiṇṇālī strīṣy api* (121, 12). Skr. *chinna-*. Cf. the following for the dental, cf. M. *śeṃdṇeṃ*. — $ 103, 123, 136, 145.

śinā adj. "separate, distinct". G. S. *chin-*, Panj. *chinn-*, H. *chīn-*, K. *chĕn-*, Ro. *cin-*, "to cleave, to uproot"; Siṃ. part. *sun*. Skr. *chinna-*. — $ 135.

śiṃpī m. "tailor" (name of caste). Siṃ. *sipa* "art, work of art", *sipi* "artiste". Pkt. *sippino* gen. Skr. *śilpin- śilpika-* m. — $ 125, 156.

śiṃgā m. "*holi* or the month of holi". Deśī. *atra sugimhao phālgunotsava iti sugrīṣmaka śabdabhavaḥ; dṛśyate cāyaṃ saṃskṛte; yad Bhāmahaḥ; sugrīṣmako na dṛṣṭa iti* (287, 17). Skr. *sugrīṣma-* m. — $ 138, 167.

śiras m. "mimosa". Panj. *siris*, *sirīṃh*, H. *siris*, *siras*, *sirsā*. Pkt. *sirīsa-*. Skr. *śirīṣa-* m. — $ 42, 156.

śivṇeṃ "to touch". G. H. *chū-*, S. Panj. *chuh-*, B. *chuṃ-*. Pkt. *chivasi chihai*. P. Skr. *chupati*. — $ 253.

śivṇeṃ "to sew". G. *sivvuṃ*, S. *sibaṇu*, Panj. *sīṃṇā* (caus. *sivāuṇā*), H. *sīnā*, B. *siāite*, K. *suvun*, Ro. *sivāva*. cf. Deśī. *sivvī tathā sivviṇī sūcī* (284, 3). Skr. *sīvyati* — $ 152, 156.

śivrā m. "light sprinkling". Deśī. *sarivāo* (cf. M. *sarvā* "heavy shower") *tathā sīharao āsāraḥ* (276, 9). Or. from Skr. *kṣip*? — $ 55.

śiṃsav m. "rose-wood, dalbergia sisoo". G. *sisam*, Panj. *sissū sīsam*; H. *sīso*. Skr. *śiṃśapa* f. — $ 152, 156.

śiseṃ siseṃ n. "lead". G. *sīsuṃ* n., S. *śihu*, H. *sīs*, *sīsā*. Skr. *sīsa-* n. — $ 156.

śilā adj. "settled, cold" G. *śiluṃ*, H. Panj. *sīlā*, S. *siyu*, Ro. *śilalo*, for ex. Siṃ. *hila hāl*. Skr. *śītala-*.— $ 63, 145, 156.

śīṃ post position "with". See words cited on p. 199. Skr. *sahita*. — $ 65, 66, 156, 183, 193, 198.

śiṃk f. "sneezing". G. H. *chīṃk*, S. *chik*, Panj. *chikk*, Ro. *cik*, cf. K. *chīh*. Deśī. *chikkaṃ spṛṣṭaṃ kṣutaṃ ca*

(125, 4); cf. Pkt. part. *chīyamāṇa-*. Skr. *chikkā* f. — $ 93, 103.

śīṭ f. "bird-dropping". Panj. *siṭṭ* "act of throwing, of lifting", H. *sīṭh* "ordure, spittle of beatle", Siṃ. *hātiya* "sort, character". Pkt. *siṭṭhi-*. Skr. *sṛṣṭi-* f. To be separated from Panj. *seṭh* "residue of sugar-cane", H. *sīṭh* "residue of indigo", from *śiṣṭa-*. — $ 30, 31, 88, 156.

śīṇ m. "lassitude", *śiṇṇeṃ* "weary". Siṃ. *sun* "annihilation" ? rather undoubtedly, as *sun* "cut", from *chinna-*, old M. *śinā*; Cf. Siṃ. *huṇu* "cement" from *cūrṇa-*, old M. *cunā*. Skr. *śīrṇa-*. — $ 135, 156.

śīt n. "grain of boiled rice, rice offering. H. *sīth*. Skr. *siktha-* m. n. — $ 88, 156.

śīt n. "bow-string". Deśī. *sitthā lālā jīvā ca* (292, 6). — $ 88.

śīr śir n. "head". G. Panj. H. *sir*, S. *siru* m., Ro. *séro*. Pkt. *sira-*. Skr. *śiras-* n. — $ 156.

śīl n. "breach, place of the river where a barrage is desired to be conststructed." Panj. *chill* "skin, bark" (cf. *chall*); Panj. *chillṇā*, H. *chīlṇā* "to peel a fruit, to decorticate". Deśī. *chillaṃ chidraṃ kuṭī ca* (124, 18). — $ 141.

śīv G. "bank, limit". G. *śīm*. "end", *seḍo seḍho* "limit", Panj. *sīṃ sīm*, *sīṃa*, H. *sīṃv*, Siṃ. *siṃ*, *hima*, *ima*. Pkt. Skr. *sīma* f. $ 156. To be separated from *śev* m., see S. V.

śīs m. "head". G. *śīś*, S. *sīsu*, Panj. H. *sīs*, Siṃ. *sis his*, Arm. Ro. *sis*. Pkt. *sissa-*, *sīsa-*. Skr. *śirṣa-* n. — $ 156.

śis n. "unripe fruit of cucurbitaceous". Deśī. *kecic chichayaṃ śalāṭu phalam āhuḥ* (125, 5). Skr. *śīrṣa-* n. ? — $ 156.

śīl f. "stone (chiefly flat stone for washing and ironing)". Panj. *sil*, S. *sir* f. and K. *sirü* "brick". Panj. H. *sil*, B. O. *śil*, Siṃ. *sal*, *sala*, *sel*, *sela*, *hela hāl*, "mountain, rock". P. Pkt. *silā*. Skr. *śilā* f. — $ 156.

śīḷ n. "nature, disposition, good nature". G. *śīḷ*, S. *sīlum*, *sīru*, Panj. H. *sil*, Siṃ. *sil*. P. Pkt. *sīla-*. Skr. *śīla-* n. — $ 145, 156.

suī sū f. "needle". G. *soy*, S. Panj. H. Maith. *sūī*, Siṃ. *hiṃdu idi-* ? Ro. *suv*. Pkt. *sūī*. Skr. *sūcī* f. — $ 44, 64, 156.

suā, *suvā* m. "parrot". G. *śuḍo*, H. Panj. *sūā*, Siṃ. *suva*. Skr. *śuka-* m. — $ 55, 156.

suār m. "cook". H. *suārā*, Siṃ. *suvaru*. Skr. *sūpakāra-* m. — $ 44, 61, 64, 156, 258.

sukā sukhā adj. "dry". G. *sūkuṃ*, S. *suko*, Panj. *sukkā*, H. *sukhā sukā*, K. *hökh*ᵘ, Ro. *śuko*, Siṃ. *siku*. Pkt. *sukkha-sukka-*. Skr. *śuṣka-*. — $ 44, 89, 93, 156, 231.

suṃgṇeṃ "to smell, to snif". G. *suṃghvuṃ*, Panj. *suṃghṇa*, H. *sūṃghnā*, *sūṃgnā*, Ro. *sˇung-*. Deśī. *suṃghiaṃ ghrātaṃ* (287, 1). Skr. (Dhātup.) *śiṅghati*). — $ 89.

sugī f. "maturity, perfection

abundance of seasm." Deśī. *suggaṃ ātmakuśalam nirvighnam*.... (292, 16). Made on the model of Pkt. *dugga-*, from Skr. *durga-*. — $ 44, 98, 156.

sugūm sugam adj. "easy". Skr. *sugama-*. — $ 76.

suṭṇeṃ "to relax, to become undone". G. *chuṭuvuṃ*, S. *chuṭaṇu*, Panj. *chuṭṭṇā*, H. *chuṭnā*. Pkt. *chuṭṭa-*, part. of *choḍei*. root. *chuṭ-* (*chedane*) — $ 103.

suḍāvaṇeṃ "to dash.". Pkt. *chūḍha-*. Skr. *kṣubdha-*. — $ 231.

suṇeṃ n. "dog". H. *sūnā*, K. *hūn*ᵘ. Pkt. *śuṇaha-*, *suṇaa-*; P. *sunakka-*. Skr. *śunaka-* m. — $ 156.

sutār m. "carpenter." Skr. *sūtradhāra-* m. — $ 156.

suṃdṇeṃ "to crush". G. *chuṃdvuṃ*. Pkt. *chuṃdai*. Skr. *kṣodati kṣuṇatti*. — $ 104, 230.

sudā sudhā "correct, good". G. *sūdhuṃ*, S. *sudhi*, Panj. *suddhā*, H. *sudh*, Siṃ. *sudu hudu*, K. *sŏd*; Ro. *śul-av-* "to clean". Skr. *śuddha-*. — $ 89, 156.

sunā adj. "empty". G. *sūnuṃ*, S. *sun* f. "insensibility, torpor", *suño*, Siṃ. *sun, hun*. P. Pkt. *sunna- suṇṇa-*, P. *suñña-*. Skr. *śūnya-*. — $ 44, 135, 156.

suṃb n. m. "twists of the fibrous integuments of coca-nut." Panj. *subb* "twisted tobacco"; Ro. *selo* "chord" is to be kept aside. Pkt. *subba-*. Skr. *śulba-*. n. — $ 127, 156.

suraṃg m. "mine". H. Bih. *suraṃg*, B. *suḍang*, S. *siriṅgha-* Skr. *suruṅgā suraṅgā* — $ 156.

sūraṇ m. "edible root, arum campanulatum." G. *sūraṇ* n., S. *sūraṇu*, H. *suran, soran*. Deśī. *suraṇo kandaḥ* (288,9). Skr. *sūraṇa-* n. — $ 156.

surā m. "knife". G. *charo*, G. S. H. *churī*, Panj. H. *churā*, B. *chorā*, Ro. *curi*; K. *khūr*ᵘ "razor", isolated, contradicts the doctrine explained in — $ 104, Pkt. *chura-*. Skr. *kṣura-* m. — $ 104.

susar f. "alligator". S. *sesāru*, Panj. *sinsār*, W. Panj. *sisār*, H. *sūsmār, sūs*. Pkt. *susumāra-suṃsumāra-*. Skr. *śiṃśumāra-* m. — $ 156, 166.

sūk m. "Venus". Panj. *sūk*, H. *suk*. Skr. *śukra-* m. — $ $ 93, 156.

sūṃṭh f. "ginger". H. G. *suṃṭh*, *śuṃṭh* S. *suṃḍhi*, Panj. *suṃḍh*, H. *soṃṭh*, B. O. *śuṃṭh*, K. *śoṃṭ*. Skr. *śuṇṭhi-* f. — $ 110, 156.

sūt m. "yarn". G. *sutar*, S. *suṭu*, Panj. H. B. O. *sūt*, Siṃ. *suta*. Pkt. *sutta-*. Skr. *sūtra-* n. — $ 121, 156, 187.

sūṇ f. "daughter-in-law". H. *sūnū* (has undoubtedly taken the final of the more frequently used *bahū* Skr. *vadhū-*), but S. *nuhuṃ nuhaṃ* Panj. *nhūṃ*. Pkt. *suṇhā* beside *ṇhusā susā*. Skr. *snuṣā* — $ 136, 137.

sūp n. "winnowing basket". H. *sūp*, G. *supḍuṃ*, S. *supu*. Skr. *śūrpa* n.— $ 125, 156.

sūr m. "note of music". G. H. *sūr*, S. *suru*, Panj. *sur*, K. *sôr* "breath". Skr. *svara* m. — $ 76, 157.

sūr f. "spirituous liquor". Skr. *surā* f. — 156.

sūḷ m. "hook". G. *sūḷ*, *śūḷ*, Panj. H. *sūl*, Siṃ. *sul*, *hula*, *ul*; K. *holᵘ* "hooked (wire etc.)". P. Pkt. *sūla*. Skr. *śūla* m. n. — $ 145. 156.

śeṃ, "hundred". G. *śo, seṃ*, S. *sau*, Panj. H. *sau, sai*, B. *śaye*, O. *śae*, Maith. *sai*. Siṃ. *siya*, K. *hat*, Ro. *śel*. Pkt. *saa saya-*. Skr. *śata-*. n. $ 39, 62, 66, 155, 156, 224.

śegaṭ, *cegvā* m. "moringa pterygosperma". Skr. *śigru-* m. — $ 39, 156.

śej. f. "bed". G. *śej*, *sajj*, S. Panj. H. *sej*, H. O. *sajyā*, Siṃ. *āṃda* ?. Pkt. *sejjā*. Skr. *śayyā* f. — $ 77, 106, 156, 166.

śejī f. "woman-neighbour", *śejhār cejār* m. "neighbourhood". Deśī. *saijjho prativeśmikaḥ*; *saijjhiaṃ tu prātiveśyaṃ* (175, 11).

śeṭ śeṭh śeṭhi śeṭī m. title of respect given to bankers & merchants. G. *śeṭh*. S. *seṭhi*, Panj. H. *seṭh*, Siṃ. *hiṭu*. Pkt. *seṭṭhi-*; Deśī. *seṭṭhī grāmeśaḥ* (288, 17). Skr. *śreṣṭhin-* m. K. *seṭhāh* "much", Siṃ. *seṭu* "noble" go back to Skr. *śreṣṭha-*, — $ 77, 89, 110, 157.

śeṃḍā m. "head, end", *śeṃḍī* f. "wick, crest". Deśī. *chiṃḍaṃ cūḍā....cheṃḍaṃ ity api* (124, 19), *cheṃḍā śikhā....* (126, 1). Skr. *śikhaṇḍa-* m. $ 63, 111, 156, 161.

śeṇ. n. "cow-dung". S. *cheṇu*, *cheṇo*. Skr. *chagaṇa-* m. n. $ 103.

śeṇvai śeṇvī śeṇai, name of a group of Brahmins, See M. *senavai*. m. "general". cf. Pkt. *vāṇaravai-*. Skr. *senāpati-* m. Cf. m. *dalvī* (*dalapati-*) see under this word; *surve* (*surapati-*). — $ 58, 77, 152, 156, 193.

śet n. "shield". S. *kheti*, Panj. H. B. O. *khet*, K. *khītⁱ*, Siṃ. *ketu*; on the other hand G. *kheḍ*, S. *kheṭu*, H. *kheḍā*, See also in M. *kheḍeṃ*. Pkt. *chetta- khetta-*. Skr. *kṣetra-* n. — $ 77, 104, 194.

śeṃḍṇeṃ "to make small incisions". Siṃ. *sindinavā* "to uproot". Pkt. *chindai*. Skr. *chinatti*. Cf. m. *śinā, śiṃḍaḷ*.. — $ 80, 103, 230.

śeṃdūr m. "minium", *śendrā* adj. "colour of minium". S. *sindhuru*, H. *sendūr*, Bih. *senur*, Ass. *sendur sindur*. Pkt. *sindūra-*, *sendūra*.. Skr. *sindūra-* m. — $ 80, 156.

śep śeṃp m. "tail". Pkt. *cheppa-*, Pkt. Deśī. (125, 4; cf. 122, 8) *chippa-*. Skr. *śepa-* m. — $ 102.

śeṃbā m. *śeṃb śem* f. "mucus flowing from the nose of horse". H. *seṃbhā*, Siṃ. *sem*, *sema*. Pkt. *siṃbha-*, *seṃbha-*, P. *silesuma- semha-*. Skr. *śleṣman-* m. — $ 88, 127, 157.

śera m. "end, extremity". Panj. H. *sihrā* "diadem, crown, "; K. *hyorᵘ*, "at the top, above". Pkt. *sihara-*. Skr. *śikhara-* m. n. — $ 63, 156, 161.

śev m. g. "cut in a palm tree to make the juice flow." H. *chev, cheo*, S. *chehu*. Pkt. *chea-*. Skr. *cheda-* m. — $ 55, 63, 77, 103.

śev m. "bank, extremity", *śevaṭ* m. n. "end". G. *śevaṭ chevaṭ* "end", *chek* f. "end", adv. "entirely, very"; S. *chehu*; see H. *chee* "at the end", H. *sevaṭ* "extremity, conclusion" should be a loan. Deśī.

cheo anto (125, 14). This word, as also the preceding one should be distinguished from M. *śiv*.

śemvtī f. "rosa glandulifera, salvia indica." G. *sevtī*, Panj. H. *seotī*. D. *sīmantayaṃ sīmante bhūṣaṇabhedaḥ* (286, 8). Skr. *sīmantikā* f. — $ 71, 121, 152, 156.

śemvrī f. "bombax". G. *simḷo*, Panj. *simbaḷ*, H. *semal*, *simbal*, B. O. *śimul*, Siṃ. *iṃbul*. Pkt. *simbalī*. Skr. *śālmalī* — $ 77, 142, Cf. M. *sāṃvār*.

śelḍūṃ n. *śeḷī* f. "she-goat, billy-goat". H. *chelā*, *cherā*. Deśī. *chelao chāgaḥ*; *kapratyayābhāve chelo ity api* (123, 10); Pkt. *chāla-*. Skr. *chagala-* M. — $ 62, 103, 145.

sair adv. "freely, without restriction". Pkt. *saira-*, cf. Deśī. *sairavasaho dharmāya tyakto vṛṣabhaḥ* (282, 9). Skr. *svaira-*. — $ 57, 157.

somḍ f. "trunk of elephant". G. *suṃd*, *suṃḍh*, S. *sūṃḍhi*, Panj. B. *suṃḍ*, H. *sūṃḍ*, Siṃ. *soṃḍa*, *hoṃḍaya*. P. *soṇḍā*. Skr. *śuṇḍā* f.—$ 80, 111, 156.

soḍṇeṃ "to loosen, to release". G. S. H. *choḍ-*, Panj. *chuḍ-*, Ro. *cor-* "to pour". Pkt. *choḍei*. Skr. *choṭayati*. — $ 103.

soneṃ "gold" n., *son-vaṇī* "gold-water" (medicine), *sonā* adj. "gilded" (appellation of a child). G. *sonuṃ*, S. *sonu*, Panj. H. *sonā*, B. *soṇā*, O. *sunā*, Siṃ. *suvan*, K. *sôn*, Ro. *sovna-* *sorna-*. Skr. *suvarṇa-* n. — $ 78, 156.

soṃpṇeṃ, *sopṇeṃ* "to entrust". G. *soṃpvuṃ*, H. *saumpnā*. Pkt. *samoppia-* part.. Skr. *samarpayati*. — $ 125, 153, 156.

solṇeṃ "to peel". G. H. *chol-*, Ro. *col-*. Pkt. *chollai* "to rub". Cf. m. *colṇeṃ*? — $ 103.

soyrā m. "a relation by alliance, friend". Skr. *sahodara-*, *sodara-* ? — $ 54, 156.

soṃval, *somal* adj. "fragile, tender". Siṃ. *sivumāli* "tender". Deśī. *somālaṃ sukumāram*; *somallaṃ saukumāryam*; *etau śabdabhavau* (290, 3); Pkt. *suumāra-*. Skr. *sukumāra-*, contaminated with *sukomala-*; the *o* causes a difficulty in any case. see $ 64. — $ 138, 140, 145, 152, 156.

sos m. "envy, violent desire". G. *sos* "acute thirst, desire, S. *sosu* "anxiety"; Panj. *sos* "dry". Skr. *śoṣa-* m. — $ 78, 156.

soḷā "sixteen". G. *soḷ*, S. *soraṃhaṃ* Panj. *solāṃ*, H. Maith. *solah*, B. *sol*, O. *sohaḷ*, Siṃ. *soḷasa*, K. *śurāh*. Pkt. *soḷasa*, Apa. *soḷaha soḷā*. Skr. *ṣoḍaśa*. — $ 78, 146, 156, 221.

stav, *tav* postpos. "because of, for". See — $ 198. Cf. $ 276.

hakārṇeṃ "to call", *hakkār* m. "cry, appeal". G. *hākārvuṃ hākalvuṃ*, H. *haṃkārnā hakārnā*, B. *hāṃkite*; Panj. *hāk hakkal* "call", G. *hakār*. "a cry of animal." Pkt. *hakkārai*. Cf. Skr. *hakkayati*. — $ 93.

hagṇem "to discharge excrement, to throw". G. *hagvuṃ*, *hāṃgaṇu*, Panj. *haggṇā*, H. *hagnā*. Cf. Skr. *hadati*. — $ 252.

hajār "1000". Persian *hazār* borrowed almost everywhere in India. See — $ 224.

haṭ hāṭ m. "market, bazar". G. *hāṭ* f. n., S. *haṭu*, Panj. *haṭṭ hāṭ* f., H. B. *haṭ haṭṭ* f., K. *aṭh* m. Pkt. Skr. *haṭṭa-* m. — $ 48.

haḍakṇeṃ "to strike (for crushing)" *haḍasṇeṃ* "to draw violently". G. *haḍselvuṃ* "to push violently". Skr. root *haṭh-*, *haṭha-* m. — $ 46, 169.

haḍḍā m., *haḍḍeṃ* n. "shackle, embarrassment." B. *haḍi*. Buddh. Skr. *haḍi-* — $ 46, 111.

haṃḍī f. "pot". S. H. *haṃḍī*, G. Panj. H. O. *hāṃḍī*, B. *hāṃḍi*. Huen-Tsang *utakia hanch'a*, i. e. **udaka-hāṇḍa-*, the *Waihand* (see Stein *Rājat*. II, 338). Skr. *haṇḍikā*, *hāḍikā* f., Cf. *bhāṇḍa-* m. — $ 159.

haṇṇeṃ "to strike". G. *haṇvuṃ*, S. *haṇṇu*, H. *hannā*. Pkt. *haṇai*. Skr. *hanti*, *hanana-* n. — $ 46, 159, 229.

haṃbarṇeṃ "to low", *haṃbarḍā* m. "lowing". Skr. *hambhā* f. — $ 89, 138, 169.

haraṇ m. n. "antelope". G. *haraṇ* n., S. *harṇu*, Panj. *harn*, H. *harin*, *hariṇ*, *haran*, *hiran*, B. *hariṇ*. Skr. *hariṇa-* m. — $ 42, 46, 159.

harṇeṃ hārṇeṃ, "to carry off, to uproot, to lose". G. S. Panj. H. B. Siṃ. K. (meaning of "to grow") *har-*. Pkt. Skr. *har-*. — $ 46, 49.

haryāḷ m. f., "small green serpent". G. *harvuṃ haruṃ hariyaluṃ* "green", S. *hariyāli hariyāī hariyāṇi* "greenery" *hariyo* "green, fresh", Panj. *harā hariā* "green, fresh; parrot" *hariālā* "verdant", H. *hariyā harīlā* "verdant", H. *hariyal* "green pigeon", B. *halidā* "turtle-dove". Pkt. *hariāla-haliāra-*. Skr. *haritāla-* "green pigeon", n. "orpiment"; *harita-* "green". — $ 46, 63, 75, 141, 145.

hasṇeṃ haṃsṇeṃ "to laugh, to ridicule". G. *has-*, S. *hās-*, Panj. *hass-*, H. *has- haṃs-*, H. *hās- hāṃs-*, Siṃ. *has-*, K. Eur. Ro. *as-*, Arm. Ro. *xas-*. Pkt. *hāsa-*, *hasai.*, Skr. *haṃs-*. — $ 46, 71, 156.

haḷad f. "Indian saffron, termeric. G. *haḷad*, *haḷdar*, Panj. *haḷdhī haladar*, H. B. O. *haldī*, B. *halud*, Siṃ. *haladu*; Cf. K. *ledor*ᵘ "yellow". Pkt. *haliddā*, *haladdā*. Skr. *haridrā*. — $ 42, 46, 52, 75, 123, 141.

haḷ m. "plough". G. *haḷ*, S. *haru*, Panj. *hal*, H. *har hal hāl*, K. *ala*. Skr. *haḷa-* m. n. — $ 145.

haḷhāḷ f. "anxiety". G. *haḷmaḷ* "agitated". Deśī. *halahalaṃ tumulaḥ kautukaṃ ca* (299, 10). Cf. under M. *hāḷṇeṃ*. — $ 48.

haḷīs m. n. *haḷas* m. f. "beam of plough". S. *hala* f; H. *halas*, *haris* f. Skr. *haleṣā*, *haḷīṣā* f. — $ 40, 145.

haḷū halkā adj. "light". G. *haḷu haḷve*, H. *halū*, "lightly"; G. *halkuṃ*, S. *halko*, Panj. B. H. *halkā* "light". Pkt. *halua-*. Skr. *laghu-*. —$ 46, 145, 167. Cf. M. *lahulahān*.

hā adj. "he, him". Deśī. *aha asau* (4, 19). Cf. for the initial G. *ahe* (*ahiyāṃ* "here").
The relationship with S.

hū, H. *wuh*, Ro. *ov* is not fool proof. Should be distinguished in any case. H. Panj. K. *yih*, arm. Ro. *hev*, and for example G. *ahe*, from Pkt. *ehu*, Skr. *eṣa*. The aspiration recalls that of P. *h-evaṃ*, Asoka *h-edisa-*. — $ 58, 160, 203, 276.

hāṃkṇeṃ, *hākṇeṃ*, *hakṇeṃ* "to drive". G. H. B. *hāṃk-*, Panj. *hakk-*. Pkt. *hakkai* "to push-back'. — $ 48, 69.

hāṭṇeṃ "to break, to chop". Pkt. *parihaṭṭai*. — $ 47.

hāḍ n. "bone". G. H. *hāḍ*, S. *haḍu*, Panj. B. *hāḍ haḍḍ*, K. *aḍijü*, Siṃ. *āta*, Palestinian Ro. *ḥar*. Deśī. *haḍḍam asthi* (193, 13). Pkt. *aṭṭhi-*. Skr. *asthi-* n. "bone", *aṣṭi-* f. "kernel". — $ 110, 112, 168, 188.

hāṇ f. "loss, damage". G. Panj. *hāṇ*, S. *hāṇi*, H. *hāni hān*, K. *hönī-*. f. Skr. *hāni-* f. — $ 134.

hāt m. "hand, arm". G. H. *hāth*, S. *hathu*, Panj. *hatth hāth*, Nep. Bih. B. O. *hāt*, Siṃ. *ata at*, K. *atha*, Arm. Ro. *hath ath*, Palestinian Ro. *hàst*, Eur. Ro. *vast*. Pkt. *hattha-*. Skr. *hasta--* m. — $ 88, 122, 169.

hattī m. "elephant", *hattīṇ* f. G. S. Panj. H. *hāthī*, H. B. O. *hātī*, K. *hostu*, Siṃ. *ātā* m. *ātini* f., Pkt. *hatthī*. Skr. *hastin-* m. *hastinī* f. — $ 40, 122, 169.

hāḷṇeṃ "to move, to stir", *hal-halṇeṃ halhāḷṇeṃ* "to stir, to tremble from over excitement". G. *hālvūṃ* to move". S. *halṇu* "to go", Panj. *hallṇā*, H. *hālnā* "to shake"; G. *halphalvuṃ* "to stir", S. *halhali* "instablity", Panj. *hall halhalāṭ* "shaking"; H. "*halphal*" haste, confusion K. *al*ᵃ*rāvun* "to shake". Deśī *halliaṃ calitam* (194, 16); *hallapphaliaṃ śīghrārtham* (293, 13) Cf. m, *haḷhāḷ*. — $ 47.

hiṃg m. "assa foetida". G. Panj. *hiṃg*, S. *hiṅu*, H. *hīṃg*, *hīṃgū*, B. *hiṃ*. Skr. *hiṅgu-* m. — $ 39.

hiṃgūḷ m. "vermillion". G. *hiṃgḷo*, S. *himgulū*, H. *hiṃgul*, B. *hiṃgūl*, Siṃ. *iṃgul*. P. Skr. *hiṅgula-* m. n. — $ 40, 50.

hiṃḍuḷā hiṃdoḷā m. "craddle". G. *hindoḷo*, S. *hindoro*, H. *hindulā*, B. *hemdlā*, Sim. *idolu*. Skr. *hindola-* m. $ 145.

hiyyā m. "courage ardour", old M. *hiyeṃ* n. "heart". G. *haiyuṃ*, S. *hiṃāṃu*, Panj. *hāṃ hiyāṃ*, *hiyūṃ*, H. B. O. *hiyā*, Ro. *yilo*; Siṃ. *la* (Pkt. **haḍaa*). Pkt. *hiaa-*. Skr. *hṛdaya-* n. — $ 30, 31.

hirḍā m. "green myrobolan". S. *harīr harīṛ*, Panj. *haraḍ harīḍ*, H. *harrā*, *har*, *haṛrai*, *harlā*, *harḍā*. Skr. *harītakī* f. — $ 75, 141.

hiḷagṇeṃ "to be suspended at, to hang". H. *hilagnā*. Skr. *abhilagna-*. —$ 149, 159, 174.

hiṃv n. "cold, cold fever". Panj. *hiuṃ* f. "snow"; elsewhere the tatsama : G. B. *him*, H. *hīm hīmā*. Skr. n *hima*. — $ 152.

hiṃsṇeṃ hisṇeṃ "neigh". S. *hiṃkṇu*, H. *hīṃsnā*, Panj. *hīṃgnā* "to bray" *hiṃknā* "to neigh". Deśī. *hikkiaṃ tathā hīsamaṇaṃ heṣāravaḥ* (297,

7). Skr. *heṣate* Cf. M. *hesṇeṃ*. — $ 70, 80.

hukūm m. "order". Panj. *hukam* etc. Arabic *hukm*. — $ 76, 102.

heṭ adv. "below". G. Panj. H. *heṭh*, S. *heṭhi*, B. *heṃṭ*, Siṃ. *yaṭa*. Pkt. *heṭṭhā*. Buddh. Skr. *heṣṭā heṣṭhā*; Skr. *adhastāt*. — $ 39, 88, 110.

heṃsṇeṃ "to neigh". Pkt. *hesia-*. Skr. *heṣate*. $ 70, 80, Cf. M. *hiṃsṇeṃ*.

heḷā adv. "easily". G. *helāmāṃ* "easily", *helī* "instead." Deśī. *helā vegaḥ* (298, 9); Pkt. instr. *helāa*. Skr. *helayā*. — $ 61, 193.

heḷṇeṃ "to look down upon". Bg. *helite*. Sk . *helana-* n.— $ 142, 145.

hoṭ hoṃṭ m. "lip". G. *hoṭh*, S. *hūṃṭhu*, Panj. H. *hoṃṭh*, B. *ṭhoṃṭ*. Pkt. *huṭṭha-*. Skr. *oṣṭha-* m. — $ 168, 170. see under the word M. *oṭh*.

hoḍ f. "bet, stake". G. S. H. *hoḍ*. Deśī. *huḍḍā paṇaḥ* (298, 3).

hoṇeṃ "to be"; *hoūn*, *hūn* "of". G. *hovuṃ*, S. *huaṇu hūṇu*, Panj. *hoṇā*, H. *honā*, B. *hoite*, S. *hoibā*, Siṃ. *venavā*, part. *vū*, for example Ro. *uv-*: on the other hand K. *bôwun*. Pkt. *hoi*, *huvai*, *havai*. Skt. *bhavati*. The radical *ho* is already found indirectly in the Vedic period through *bodhi*. "I may" see Wackernagel $ 108, p. 128. —$ 71, 159, 195, 197, 202, 229, 230, 232, 237.